D0515620

BOOK 1

Math Matters

Authors

FRANK EBOS, Senior Author
Faculty of Education
University of Toronto

PAUL ZOLIS
Head of Mathematics
Woburn Collegiate, Scarborough, Ontario

Reviewer Consultants

LESLIE H. DUKOWSKI
D.W. Poppy Secondary School,
Langley, British Columbia

JOHN F. HOPKINS
Stephen Leacock Collegiate Institute
Scarborough, Ontario

WILLIAM KORYTOWSKI
Sisler High School,
Winnipeg, Manitoba

REG PHILIP
Mathematics Consultant
Durham Board of Education, Oshawa, Ontario

SID RACHLIN
Assistant Professor, Mathematics Education,
University of Calgary

NELSON CANADA LIMITED

Contents

7. Applying Skills with Rate

8. Working with Per Cent

9. Applications and Skills with Geometry

10. Extending Your Skills: Geometry

11. Working with Data: Graphs and Applications

12. Introduction to Algebra

13. Solving Equations and Problems

The metric usage in this text has been reviewed by the Metric Screening Office of the Canadian General Standards Board.

Metric Commission Canada has granted permission for use of the National Symbol for Metric Conversion.

© NELSON CANADA LIMITED 1981

All rights reserved. It is unlawful to reproduce any portion of this book, by any means, without the written permission of the publisher.

ISBN – 0-17-601501-9

Printed and bound in Canada.
14 15   432

Technical Art: Frank Zsigo
Book Design: Frank Zsigo
Cover Design: Robert McPhail

Cdn. Cataloguing in Publication Data

Ebos, Frank, 1939-
Math Matters, book 1

For use in grades 9-10
Includes index.
ISBN 0-17-601501-9
1. Mathematics – 1961 –
I. Zolis, Paul.

II. Title.

QA39.2.E26   510   C81-094981-4

PHOTO CREDITS

Atmospheric Environmental Services, Canada – 90; Air Canada – 221; Australian High Commission, Ottawa – 222; The Billiards and Snooker Control Council – 10; The Bubble Shop, Inc. – 96; George Brown College – 140, 142; Canadian Football League – 16; City of Calgary, Public Information Dept. – 42; Canadian Pacific – 51; Chisholm Fleming and Associates – 62; Continental Can Company of Canada – 67, 83; CP Air – 78, 82; Canadian Water Polo Association, Game Plan – 173; C.I.L. – 192, 196; Canadian Amateur Swimming Assoc. – Ont. – 235; Charlton Press – 258, 260; Bob Cunningham Photography – 285; CBS Records Ltd. – 351; Dairy Products Advertising – 93; De Havilland Aircraft – 178; D.C. Comics Inc. – 192; Ebos, Frank – 278, 290, 327, 336, 337, 340, 392; Ebos, Rose Mary – 287, 297, 321, 323; Patrick Gallagher – 2, 24, 25, 28, 39, 56, 57, 58, 60, 62, 63, 64, 65, 66, 67, 76, 84, 85, 87, 94, 107, 139, 202, 229, 254, 260, 392; General Motors – 12; Goodyear Tire Co. – 82; Health and Welfare Canada – 78,.85; Honda – 80, 222; Inco Metals Co. – 247; Interfoto MTI – 96; Interprovincial Lottery Corp. – 103; Jellco Packaging Ltd. – 100; Edward Kurtz Enterprises, Ltd. – 285; Miller Services – 10, 73, 81, 86, 90, 94, 127, 207, 210, 225, 236, 243, 244, 248, 252, 260, 270, 274, 275, 277, 280, 282, 284, 297, 307, 327, 350, 355, 379, 420, 425; Mitsubishi Canada Ltd. – 100; National Air Photo Library – 207; Lyn Nelson – 129; Jack Nemchin – 125, 157, 168, 251; National Film Board – 149, 187; New Brunswick Dept. of Tourism – 208; Olympic House – 17; Ontario Ministry of Industry and Tourism – 1, 171, 186, 199; Ontario Ministry of Agriculture – 372; Ontario Ministry of Transportation and Communications – 25, 54, 230; Ontario Ministry of Housing – 63; Ontario Ministry of the Environment – 100; Ontario Sportscene Magazine – 120; Ontario Ministry of Highways – 286; John Patrick Photographers Ltd. – 210; Pit Machinery Co., Ltd. – 285; Road Development Co. – 100; Sail Canada Committee – 73; South African Consulate, Toronto – 178; Studio Canada – 186; Sheridan Nurseries Ltd. – 285; Rob Stocks – 252, 261, 264, 275, 283, 352; Toronto Stock Exchange – 1, 130; Telesat Canada – 1; Toronto Blue Jays Baseball Club – 50; Tywood Industries Ltd. – 288; United States Travel Service – 12, 149; United States Dept. of the Interior, National Park Service – 42; Frank Vetere's Restaurants – 13, 103; Winnipeg Mint – 323; Winnipeg International Airport – 8; Wardair – 112, 224; Winnipeg Blue Bombers Football Club – 123; Wer Canada Ltd. – 288.

The authors wish to express their thanks to Sheila Bassett, John Reber, Rob McPhail, Andrew Clowes and Peter McBride for their invaluable contribution.

The authors gratefully acknowledge the advice and assistance of George Adams, David Coules, Rose Mary Ebos, John Flanagan, Blair Lyttle, Dave Johnson, Albert Jones, Todd Kirby, Paul Macallum, Ralph Peter, Warner Pirak, Tony Pontes, Barry Scully and Woody Sparrow.

Essential Skills With Numbers

operations with whole and decimal numbers, skills with substitution, exponents, applications and problem-solving

Introduction

Numbers are used in many ways to show information.

How many people?

How fast?

How far to go?

Numbers are used to solve problems.

Numbers and their properties are important in your life. In this chapter you will learn skills with whole numbers and decimal fractions, and use them to solve problems.

1.1 Whole Numbers Around Us

You will often use whole numbers
in your everyday activities.

Indoor Soccer
Attendance Figures Soar
to 2346

To do calculations, you need to understand place value. The place
value of whole numbers is shown below. With the digits 0, 1, 2, 3, 4,
5, 6, 7, 8, and 9 you are able to write any number.

Whole Numbers	hundred thousands	ten thousands	thousands	hundreds	tens	ones
486				4	8	6
2 345			2	3	4	5
12 483		1	2	4	8	3
346 891	3	4	6	8	9	1

The place value of the digit
3 is *hundred thousands*.
There are 3 *hundred thousands*.

The place value of the
digit 6 is *thousands*.
There are 6 *thousands*.

The place value of the digit 9 is *tens*.
There are 9 *tens*.

To add or subtract, you line up the same place values.

Example 1

(a) Find the sum of 483, 2963, and 48.

(b) How much greater is 4165 than 2984?

Solution

(a) Find the sum.

$$\begin{array}{r} 483 \\ 2963 \\ +\ 48 \\ \hline 3494 \end{array}$$

Line up the same place values.

The sum is → 3494

(b) Find the difference.

$$\begin{array}{r} 4165 \\ -\ 2984 \\ \hline 1181 \end{array}$$

Line up the same place values.

The difference is → 1181

To check whether your answer to a problem is reasonable you must
learn to *round off* numbers.

Round off to the nearest ten.
43 is rounded off to 40   Examine the *ones* digit.
45 is rounded off to 50   • If it is 5 or more, round to the next 10.
49 is rounded off to 50   • If it is less than 5, round to the lower 10.

Round off to the nearest hundred.   *Round off to the nearest thousand.*
236 is rounded off to 200   Examine the *tens*   4358 is rounded off to 4000   Examine the *hundreds*
250 is rounded off to 300   digit. What is   4596 is rounded off to 5000   digit. What is the
296 is rounded off to 300   the rule?   4900 is rounded off to 5000   rule?

To check an answer, you can always redo the calculation.
However, to quickly check if an answer is reasonable, use rounding
skills as shown in the next example.

Example 2

Calculate

a) 48×316 (b) $3570 \div 42$

Check whether your answer is reasonable.

Solution

(a) $48 \times 316 = 15\ 168$ Calculation

$$
\begin{array}{r}
316 \\
\times\ 48 \\
\hline
2528 \\
12640 \\
\hline
15168
\end{array}
$$

Check (mentally)
48 is about 50
316 is about 300
$50 \times 300 = 15\ 000$
The answer is
reasonable.

(b) $\dfrac{3570}{42} = 85$ Calculation

$$
\begin{array}{r}
85 \\
42\overline{)3570} \\
336\ \ \\
\hline
210 \\
210 \\
\hline
0
\end{array}
$$

Check (mentally)
3570 is about 3600
42 is about 40

$\dfrac{3600}{40} = 90$

The answer is
reasonable.

Try These

1 What is the place value of each
   underlined digit?
   (a) 4876   (b) 321   (c) 4897
   (d) 9980   (e) 4813   (f) 12 816
   (g) 36 481   (h) 2891   (i) 6489

2 Round off each number to the nearest 10.
   (a) 483   (b) 2629   (c) 325
   (d) 1352   (e) 3862   (f) 348

3 Round off each number to the nearest 100.
   (a) 4638   (b) 9215   (c) 7361
   (d) 2951   (e) 3849   (f) 2351

4 Round off each number to the nearest 1000.
   (a) 13 416   (b) 12 517   (c) 23 476
   (d) 46 903   (e) 28 500   (f) 17 055

5 Round off each of the following.
   (a) 483 to the nearest 10.
   (b) 483 to the nearest 100.
   (c) 3491 to the nearest 100.
   (d) 3491 to the nearest 1000.
   (e) 13 485 to the nearest 10.
   (f) 13 485 to the nearest 100.
   (g) 13 485 to the nearest 1000.

Written Exercises

1 Perform the operations shown.

(a)
```
   3816
 + 2815
```

(b)
```
   4961
 - 3192
```

A

(c)
```
   4613
 +  289
```

(d)
```
   3261
 - 1999
```

(e)
```
    4 863
 + 10 123
```

(f)
```
  10 123
 - 4 863
```

2 Add the following numbers.

(a) 38, 46, 783, 2816

(b) 416, 32, 4819, 283

(c) 12 481, 9632, 148, 4891

(d) 3643, 483, 9613, 10 481

3 Calculate.

(a) 486 + 3891   (b) 2861 + 3841

(c) 3862 − 2196   (d) 9631 − 2893

4 Do not multiply. Three numbers are given as the answer for the product 43 × 59. Which one is reasonable?

A 253   B 2537   C 25 370

5 For each product, which answer, A, B, or C is reasonable? *Do not multiply* the product.

	A	B	C
(a) 27 × 32	1864	8640	864
(b) 45 × 69	3105	6105	31 050
(c) 87 × 91	797	7917	17 917
(d) 23 × 456	105	1035	10 488
(e) 18 × 253	455	45 540	4554

6 Do not divide. Three numbers are given as the answer to 2080 ÷ 32. Which one is reasonable?

A 25   B 65   C 650

7 For each question, which answer, A, B, or C is reasonable? *Do not divide.*

	A	B	C
(a) 3698 ÷ 86	23	43	430
(b) 931 ÷ 19	19	29	49
(c) 2850 ÷ 75	38	78	380
(d) 2829 ÷ 69	21	41	71

8 Find each product.

(a) 28 × 36   (b) 28 × 365

(c) 36 × 296   (d) 93 × 480

Did you check your answers
by rounding off?

9 Find each quotient.

(a) 943 ÷ 23   (b) 2666 ÷ 62

(c) 4189 ÷ 71   (d) 7826 ÷ 86

(e) What do you notice about the remainders above?

10 For each of the following,
 • what is the quotient?
 • what is the remainder?

(a) $\dfrac{869}{31}$ (b) $\dfrac{1766}{49}$ (c) $\dfrac{4899}{96}$

(d) $\dfrac{7726}{78}$ (e) $\dfrac{8175}{95}$ (f) $\dfrac{7014}{73}$

B

11 The attendance at a football game was 39 594. If you were a sports reporter how would you report this number if you rounded it off to the nearest hundred?

12 The Star Phoenix has a circulation of 68 655. On the front page of each paper, this number is rounded off to the nearest hundred. What number is used?

13 An album, just released, sold 3025 copies. How would you round this number off for an advertisement?

14 The amounts of energy in the following servings of foods are shown.

Food	Energy
15 mL cream	203 kJ
1 ice cream bar	598 kJ
250 mL glass of chocolate milk	804 kJ
250 mL glass of skim milk	376 kJ
125 mL rice pudding	617 kJ
250 mL glass goat milk	737 kJ
125 g yoghurt (fruit)	632 kJ
1 raw egg	328 kJ

(a) Which serving has the greatest amount of energy?

(b) Which serving has the least amount of energy?

(c) Round off the amounts of energy to the nearest 10 kJ.

The number of newspapers sold per day is called the circulation. The circulations of various newspapers are shown below.

The daily circulation of various newspapers has increased.

Newspapers	Circulation
Calgary Herald	127 248
Edmonton Journal	172 908
Halifax Chronicle-Herald	71 807
Hamilton Spectator	145 308
London Free Press	131 482
Montreal Gazette	194 409
Saskatoon Star-Phoenix	53 477
Vancouver Sun	249 712
Winnipeg Free Press	141 890

15 (a) Which newspaper has the greatest circulation?

(b) Which two newspapers together have the greatest circulation?

16 (a) Which newspaper has the least circulation?

(b) Which two newspapers together have the least circulation?

17 Round off the circulations of the following newspapers to the nearest hundred.

(a) Edmonton Journal

(b) Winnipeg Free Press

18 Round off the circulations of the following newspapers to the nearest thousand.

(a) Halifax Chronicle-Herald

(b) Hamilton Spectator

(c) Montreal Gazette   (d) Vancouver Sun

C   The masses of various animals at the Philadelphia Zoo are shown.

Animal	Mass (kg)
tiger	988 kg
lion	1080 kg
elephant (African)	29 462 kg
hippopotamus	17 305 kg
rhinoceros	8242 kg
Alaskan brown bear	4136 kg
Canadian moose	4092 kg
Arctic wolf	55 kg
whale	26 030 kg
polar bear	4051 kg
giraffe	3975 kg

19 (a) Which animal is the heaviest?

(b) Which animal is the lightest?

20 Round off each mass to the nearest 100 kg.

21 Round off the mass of each of the following animals to the nearest 10 kg.

(a) Arctic wolf   (b) tiger

(c) lion   (d) giraffe

22 Round off the mass of each of the following animals to the nearest 1000 kg.

(a) elephant   (b) hippopotamus

Calculator Tip

Before you do any calculations with a calculator, always push ⌷ first in order to clear the calculator.

Add 368 + 4961.

Enter	Calculator Display
⌷	0
368	368
⊞	368.00000
4961	4961
⊟	5329.0000

1.2 Organizing Your Work: Solving Problems

One of the main reasons for learning skills with numbers is to be able to solve problems. There are two important questions you must answer before solving a problem:

    I What information am I given?

    II What information am I asked to find?

The following *Steps For Solving Problems* are suggested to help you organize your work while solving any problem. Compare the steps of the solution to Steps A, B, C, D, and E.

Example 1

A professional athlete earned $67 536. If 36 games were played, how much was earned for each game?

	Steps for Solving Problems
Step A	Do you understand the problem?
	I What information am I given?
	II What information am I asked to find?
Step B	Decide on a method. (What operation do you use?)
Step C	Find the answer.
Step D	Check your answer in the original problem.
Step E	Write a final statement to answer the question.

Solution

Amount earned $67 536. ←—— Step A
Number of games played 36.
Amount earned each game —— Step B
is given by
    $67 536 \div 36 = 1876 ←—— Step C

     Step D

       36 games
       $1876 each game
       Total earned
       $36 \times $1876 = $67 536$
              checks

The athlete earned $1876 per game.
                    Step E

To solve some problems you need to remember the meaning of important words. The word "average" in Example 2 is such a word.

Example 2

A radio station plays a different number of records during each week in June.

    Week 1 301   Week 3 314
    Week 2 293   Week 4 496

Find the average number of records per week in June.

Solution

Total number of records played is 1404.
Number of weeks in June is 4.
Find the average.

$$\frac{\text{Number of records}}{\text{Number of weeks}} = \frac{1404}{4}$$

$$= 351$$

                  301
                  293
                  314
                + 496
                1404

The average number of records played is 351 records.

Be sure to check your work.

Try These

For each question, decide
- what information is given.
- what information you are asked to find.
- which operation is used to solve the problem.

1 Willie Mays of the Giants hit 660 career home runs and Hans Wagner hit 101 home runs. How many more home runs did Mays hit than Wagner?

2 Eight students receive $48 in deposits on bottles found at the beach. How much should each receive?

3 A V8 Ford needs 8 sparkplugs at a cost of $2 each. What is the total cost of the spark plugs?

At the Trans Canada take-out stand, 2 buses pulled in and placed the following orders.

4 How many hamburgers in all?

5 How many more hamburgers than fishburgers?

6 How many soft drinks in all?

7 How many more milkshakes than soft drinks?

Bus 28
14 Hamburgers
13 Fries
12 Cokes
13 Milkshakes

Bus 29
25 Fishburgers
13 Hamburgers
12 Milkshakes
12 Orange Drinks

Written Exercises

A 1 How many people in all in attendance?

Attendance
4861 adults
963 students
425 children

2 The number of times that a hit record was played at Station CRQS is shown. How often, on the average, was it played each month?

Station CRQS	
Jan.	313
Feb.	486
Mar.	392

3 Television was actually thought of in 1884. The year that it became television as you know it was 1947. How many years passed from 1884 to 1947?

4 Canada has 675 740 km of paved roads and 170 813 km of gravel roads. What is the total length of roads in Canada?

5 Your heart beats about 75 times/min. How many times does it beat in 1 a? (365 d = 1 a)

6 Bev Johnson raises worms for bait. One year she raised 23 167 worms. The next year her business increased so she raised 15 154 more worms. How many did she raise that second year?

B

7 On election night across Canada it was reported that out of the 1545 polling stations that were closed, 698 had counted their votes and 150 stations were still counting. How many stations had not even started to count?

8 The "midnight sun" creates unusual conditions in lands that lie north of the Arctic Circle. In northern Finland, for example, in midsummer, there is constant daylight for 1752 h! How many consecutive days is this?

9 Canada's population in 1871 was 3 689 257 and by 1971 had grown to 21 568 311. What was the increase in Canada's population during the hundred years?

10 A human breathes faster awake than asleep. A sleeping person breathes an average of 15 times per minute.

(a) How many breaths would you take during a 7-h sleep?

(b) How many breaths would you take in 1 a while sleeping if you sleep 7 h/d? (1 a = 365 d)

11 In the 1976 Olympics, Bruce Jenner won the Decathalon with 8618 points. Kratscher of West Germany had 8411 points and Avilov of the U.S.S.R. had 8369 points. What were the total points scored?

12 The longest river in the world, the Nile river in Africa, is 6690 km long. The Amazon river in South America is 6280 km in length. What is the difference in length between these two rivers?

13 Kesper Auto Limited carries sparkplugs in boxes of 10. Currently they have 24 boxes of plugs in stock. How many 6-cylinder cars could they service?

14 Newfoundland consists of Labrador, which is 180 521 km² in area, and an island which is 69 374 km² in area. What is the total area of Newfoundland?

15 A ski resort has just purchased a new chairlift. It takes 12 min to ride to the top of the hill and 4 min to ski down the hill. If you skied continuously for a 8-h day, how many times did you ski down the hill?

16 An N.H.L. player plays in 5 games. In each of the 5 games he plays for a different amount of time.

Game 1 34 min
Game 2 28 min
Game 3 48 min
Game 4 40 min
Game 5 35 min

What is the average number of minutes per game he played?

17 The numbers of hours per month of bright sunshine for Moncton are shown.

| Jan. | 103 h | Mar. | 135 h | May | 212 h |
| Feb. | 120 h | April | 168 h | June | 226 h |

(a) What is the total number of hours of sunshine from January to June?

(b) The yearly total for Moncton is 1918 h. How many hours of sunshine are yet to come?

C

18 The monthly amounts of bright sunshine available last year at Winnipeg International Airport are given below.

Jan.	112 h	May	246 h	Sept.	183 h
Feb.	139 h	June	259 h	Oct.	158 h
Mar.	176 h	July	331 h	Nov.	81 h
April	209 h	Aug.	276 h	Dec.	86 h

(a) What was the total sunshine available for the year?

(b) What was the average monthly sunshine?

(c) For which month was the amount of sunshine nearest the average in (b)?

Applications: World Distances

The chart below shows the shortest distances between several cities. The distance between Paris and Port Said is 3178 km. This is 3000 km to the nearest thousand kilometres.

	Berlin	Bombay	Darwin	Los Angeles	Mexico City	Paris	Peking	Port Said	Quebec	Rome	Tokyo	Wellington
Berlin, Germany		6 292	12 932	9 305	9 715	872	7 350	2 811	5 766	1 181	8 912	18 129
Bombay, India	6 292		7 247	14 003	15 646	7 015	4 770	4 279	11 862	6 185	6 740	12 355
Darwin, Australia	12 932	7 247		12 609	14 614	13 800	5 999	11 521	15 649	13 180	5 419	5 327
Los Angeles, U.S.A.	9 305	14 003	12 609		2 482	9 014	10 058	12 115	4 150	10 180	8 803	10 805
Mexico City, Mexico	9 715	15 646	14 614	2 482		9 183	12 445	12 345	3 949	10 224	11 321	11 103
Paris, France	872	7 015	13 800	9 014	9 183		8 209	3 178	5 206	1 098	9 709	18 975
Peking, China	7 350	4 770	5 999	10 058	12 445	8 209		7 377	10 337	8 122	2 103	10 779
Port Said, Egypt	2 811	4 279	11 521	12 115	12 345	3 178	7 377		8 449	2 119	9 402	16 494
Quebec, Canada	5 766	11 862	15 649	4 150	3 949	5 206	10 337	8 449		6 345	10 327	14 851
Rome, Italy	1 181	6 185	13 180	10 180	10 224	1 098	8 122	2 119	6 345		9 855	18 546
Tokyo, Japan	8 912	6 740	5 419	8 803	11 321	9 709	2 103	9 402	10 327	9 855		9 270
Wellington, New Zealand	18 129	12 355	5 327	10 805	11 103	18 975	10 779	16 494	14 851	18 546	9 270	

19 How far is it from Peking, China to
(a) Bombay?   (b) Quebec?
(c) Tokyo?   (d) Los Angeles?

20 Round your answers in Question 19 to the nearest 100 km.

21 How far is it from Rome to
(a) Paris?   (b) Peking?
(c) Port Said?   (d) Wellington?

22 Round your answers in Question 21 to the nearest 1000 km.

23 Which trip is longer?

A Darwin to Los Angeles
B Mexico City to Wellington

24 How much farther is Wellington from Quebec than from Tokyo?

25 If you are halfway between Peking and Berlin, how far have you gone?

26 You are in Paris and fly first to Rome and then to Berlin. How far do you fly in all?

27 Which trip is longer?

A Port Said to Quebec to Rome
B Tokyo to Peking to Wellington

28 An aircraft flies 18 round trips each week between Paris and Rome. What is the total distance flown?

29 You travel from Mexico City to Tokyo via Los Angeles. How many more kilometres do you still need to go if you have already gone 4500 km?

1.3 What's the Order?

When you play any game you must follow certain rules. For example,

5.—A ball is not considered to be *Ball Properly* spotted unless it has been placed by *Spotted.* hand on its prescribed spot.

6.—All strokes must be made with the *A Fair Stroke.* tip of the cue. The ball must be struck and not pushed. The ball must not be struck more than once in the same stroke either before or after contact with another ball. At the moment of striking, one of the player's feet must touch the floor. A ball or balls must not be forced off the table.

Similarly, to do mathematics there are certain rules you must follow. While evaluating the expression $21 + 3 \times 4$, two people obtained the following answers. What rules did each follow?

Solution A	Solution B
$21 + 3 \times 4$	$21 + 3 \times 4$
$= 21 + 12$	$= 24 \times 4$
$= 33$	$= 96$

So that the same answer is obtained, regardless of who does the arithmetic, certain rules have been written for the order of operations performed when $+$, $-$, $\times$, or $\div$ occur in one problem.

> Order of Operations
> - Do all calculations in brackets ( ) first.
> - If more than 1 pair of parentheses occur, do the calculation in the innermost pair first. Then multiply or divide in the order they appear, left to right.
> - Finally add or subtract in the order they appear, left to right.

Example 1
Find the value of
$$30 - 8 \div 2 + 6 \times 3.$$

Solution
$$30 - 8 \div 2 + 6 \times 3$$
$$= 30 - 4 + 18$$
$$= 26 + 18$$
$$= 44$$

Do division and multiplication in the order they appear.

If brackets or parentheses occur then do the calculations inside the brackets first.

Example 2
Simplify
$$↑ \quad 32 + 64 \div (16 - 8) \times 2.$$

Means: Find the value of the expression.

Solution

Do the operations in parentheses first.

$$32 + 64 \div (16 - 8) \times 2$$
$$= 32 + 64 \div 8 \times 2$$
$$= 32 + 8 \times 2$$
$$= 32 + 16$$
$$= 48$$

Then do the operations of $\times$, $\div$ as they occur.

With practice some of these steps may be done mentally.

Example 3

Simplify
$$64 - \{10 \times (7 - 3) + 9\}.$$

Give reasons for each in the solution.

Solution

$$64 - \{10 \times (7 - 3) + 9\} \quad \text{Why?}$$
$$= 64 - \{10 \times 4 + 9\} \quad \text{Why?}$$
$$= 64 - \{40 + 9\} \quad \text{Why?}$$
$$= 64 - 49$$
$$= 15$$

Try These

1. Find the value of each expression.
   - (a) $8 + 4 \div 2$
   - (b) $8 \div 4 + 2$
   - (c) $16 - 2 \div 2$
   - (d) $16 \div 2 - 2$

2. Simplify.
   - (a) $2 + 3 \times 2$
   - (b) $8 \div 4 - 2$
   - (c) $6 \times 3 \div 2$
   - (d) $6 + 4 - 3$

3. Find the value of each of the following.
   - (a) $3(8 + 2)$
   - (b) $3(8 - 2)$
   - (c) $12 - (2 + 2)$
   - (d) $12 - (2 - 2)$

4. Simplify.
   - (a) $\dfrac{4 + 6}{2}$
   - (b) $\dfrac{10 - 2}{4}$
   - (c) $\dfrac{8 \times 4}{2}$
   - (d) $\dfrac{18 - 2}{4}$
   - (e) $\dfrac{4 - 4}{4}$
   - (f) $\dfrac{4 + 4}{4}$

5. Use only one of the operations $+$, $-$, $\times$, or $\div$ to make each of the following true.
   - (a) $8 \bullet 4 \bullet 2 = 1$
   - (b) $12 \bullet 9 \bullet 3 = 0$
   - (c) $6 \bullet 2 \bullet 4 = 12$
   - (d) $2 \bullet 3 \bullet 4 = 24$

Written Exercises

A 1. Calculate. Watch the order of operations.
   - (a) $6 \times 4 - 2$
   - (b) $8 - 2 \times 3$
   - (c) $8 \times 3 \div 6$
   - (d) $(9 + 1) \div 5$
   - (e) $24 \div (3 + 5)$
   - (f) $16 - 4 + 2$
   - (g) $(30 + 9) \div 3$
   - (h) $26 - 2 \times 5$
   - (i) $4 \times (5 + 1)$
   - (j) $(10 + 4 \times 2 - 1) \times 0$

2. (a) Calculate.
   A $36 \div (6 \div 6)$ B $(36 \div 6) \div 6$
   (b) Why are the answers for A and B different?

3. (a) Calculate.
   A $7 \times (3 \times 2)$ B $(7 \times 3) \times 2$
   (b) Why are the answers for A and B the same?

4. These two expressions mean the same thing.
   $\dfrac{12 + 14}{2}$ fraction form $(12 + 14) \div 2$ uses brackets.
   Calculate.
   - (a) $\dfrac{10 + 15}{5}$
   - (b) $\dfrac{40 - 8}{4}$
   - (c) $\dfrac{140 - 10}{2}$
   - (d) $\dfrac{86}{49 - 6}$
   - (e) $\dfrac{20 - 11}{10 - 7}$
   - (f) $\dfrac{16 + 8}{16 - 8}$
   - (g) $\dfrac{14 + 24 \div 6}{3 \times 3}$
   - (h) $\dfrac{30 \div 6 - 3}{5 \times 5 - 23}$

B 5. Find the value of each of the following.
   - (a) $66 - 18 \div 3 - 5$
   - (b) $36 + 27 \div 3 - 3 \times 2$
   - (c) $52 \div 4 - 8 \times 3 + 33$
   - (d) $480 \div [(12 - 4) \times 3] + 25 \div 5$
   - (e) $[36 - 2 \times 9 + 8 - 3 \times 2] \div 4 + 15$

6 Simplify.

(a) $56 - \{12 \times (6 - 4) + 17\}$

(b) $24 + 16 \div 4 \times 16 - 4$

(c) $15 + \dfrac{64 + 2}{3} - 16$

(d) $18 + 6 \div 3 - 3 + 2 \times 5$

7 Find the value of $[15 \times 2 + (9 \div 3)] + 3 \times 20$.

8 Simplify the expression
$9[28 \div (7 + 2)] - [3 \times (2 + 3)]$.

9 Perform the following operations.

(a) Add 678 and 314. Then subtract 254 from the sum.

(b) Subtract 196 from 1520. Then multiply the difference by 2.

(c) Multiply 315 by 4. Then multiply the product by 2.

(d) Divide 846 by 2. Then multiply the quotient by 4.

10 In a contest you are to answer the skill-testing question:

Solve the expression $(6 + 6) + 12 \div 6 - 4$.

If Samuel's answer is 10 and Jamie's is 18 which person has won the car?

11 Find the answer to the skill-testing question for an exciting vacation.

Skill-Testing Question

$10 + 2(12 - 8) \times \dfrac{1}{2} \times 8 \div 2$

12 Will you win a new compact Omega car? Answer the skill-testing question.

The Omega Skill-Testing Question

$64 - 72 \div (8 \times 3) + 5 \times 7$

The operations $+$, $-$, $\times$, and $\div$ may be used in place of ⊘ to make the following true.

$6 ⊘ 3 ⊘ 8 = 16$ becomes $6 \div 3 \times 8 = 16$

13 For each of the following, replace ⊘ by $+$, $-$, $\times$, or $\div$ to obtain the answer. Use brackets as necessary.

(a) $8 ⊘ 2 \times 5 = 20$

(b) $9 + 3 ⊘ 4 = 21$

(c) $10 ⊘ 6 \div 3 = 12$

(d) $15 ⊘ 5 + 7 = 10$

(e) $25 ⊘ 3 ⊘ 2 = 5$

(f) $18 ⊘ 6 ⊘ 3 = 1$

(g) $10 ⊘ 9 ⊘ 50 = 40$

(h) $10 ⊘ 9 ⊘ 0 = 0$

(i) $42 ⊘ 3 ⊘ 4 = 10$

(j) $42 ⊘ 3 ⊘ 4 = 6$

C

14 Insert brackets and operation signs $+$, $-$, $\times$, $\div$ to make each of the following true.

(a) $7 ? 3 ? 1 = 9$

(b) $8 ? 3 ? 6 = 4$

(c) $9 ? 6 ? 4 = 50$

(d) $12 ? 3 ? 4 = 1$

(e) $10 ? 5 ? 5 = 10$

(f) $12 ? 3 ? 4 = 16$

(g) $28 ? 4 ? 7 = 49$

(h) $6 ? 4 ? 3 ? 5 = 40$

1.4 Variables and Substitution

Every day you see examples of symbols that give information.

In mathematics, symbols also convey information.

+ tells you to add numbers
− tells you to subtract numbers
× tells you to multiply numbers
÷ tells you to divide numbers

To learn how other symbols are used, begin with this example.

Michael has a part-time job. He makes pizza bases and earns $4/h.

This symbol means $4 per hour.

You can use a table to write his earnings.

Length of time worked (h)	Earnings received ($)
1	$4 × 1 = $4
2	$4 × 2 = $8
3	$4 × 3 = $12
4	$4 × 4 = $16
5	$4 × 5 = $20

Money made per hour.   Number of hours worked.   Total amount of money made.

The following expression represents the amount of money earned when Michael works for n hours. The expression shows generally what Michael earns.

$$\$4 \times n$$

Money made per hour by Michael.   Number of hours worked by Michael.

The symbol n is called a **place holder** or **variable**. It stands for a number. In the above chart n stands for any of the following numbers.

$n = 1$ or $n = 2$ or $n = 3$ or $n = 4$ or $n = 5$

You may also write $\$4 \times n$ as $\$4n$.   The operation of multiplication is understood here.

To solve problems in everyday situations, you will often use the skills of substitution.

Example 1

Find the value of $8n - 3$,
if $n = 4$.

$8n - 3$ is called
a **variable expression**.

Solution

Write the original
expression first.

$8n - 3$
$= 8(4) - 3$ ← Use brackets.
$= 32 - 3$
$= 29$

substitute the
value of the variable.

Example 2

Calculate the value of $2x + 5y$.
Use $x = 2$ and $y = 3$.

Other symbols may be
used as variables.

Solution

$2x + 5y$ ← Write the expression.
$= 2(2) + 5(3)$ ← Substitute.
$= 4 + 15$ ← Do the calculations.
$= 19$

Example 3

If $\blacksquare = 9$, find the value of
$(\blacksquare - 5) \times 4$.

Solution

$(\blacksquare - 5) \times 4$
$= (9 - 5) \times 4$
$= 4 \times 4$
$= 16$

Example 4

The number of dollars earned per week is
given by the variable expression, $28n + 5$.
Find the amount earned in 6 weeks.

Solution

$28n + 5$
$= 28(6) + 5$
$= 168 + 5$
$= 173$

Find the amount of
dollars for 6 weeks.
Use $n = 6$.

The amount earned in 6 weeks is $173.

Make a final statement to
answer the question.

Try These

1 Evaluate each expression for $n = 3$.
   (a) $2 + n$ (b) $2n$

2 Evaluate each expression for $p = 4$.
   (a) $5p$ (b) $5p - 3$

3 Find the value of each expression.
   (a) $6r$, $r = 5$
   (b) $6r + 1$, $r = 6$ (c) $6r - 3$, $r = 7$

4 If $n = 3$, find each expression.
   (a) $4n - 2$ (b) $4n + 2$

5 Calculate.
   (a) $n + n$, if $n = 2$
   (b) $m + n$, if $m = 3$, $n = 2$
   (c) $2p - q$, if $p = 5$, $q = 3$
   (d) $p - 2q$, if $p = 8$, $q = 2$

14

Written Exercises

A 1 Evaluate each expression if the value of s is 2.

   (a) $3s$ (b) $3s - 2$

   (c) $3s \div 3$ (d) $3s \times 2$

2 Find the value of $6w$ if w is replaced by 9.

3 (a) The value of m is 8. Find the value of $4m$.

   (b) The value of p is 4. Find the value of $7p$.

4 (a) Replace y by 12 in the expression $y + 19$.

   (b) What is the value of the expression?

5 If m is replaced by 5, find the value of the expressions.

   (a) $3 \times m + 14$ (b) $3m + 6$

6 Evaluate each expression.

   (a) Replace a by 6. What is the value of $a + 3 \times 8$?

   (b) Replace w by 4. What is the value of $w - 2 + 6$?

   (c) Replace m by 9. What is the value of $m + 17 - 2$?

   (d) Replace z by 28. What is the value of $35 + z - 7$?

7 $k = 3$ is often written to mean "replace k by 3".

   (a) Find the value of $3k + 5$ if $k = 2$.

   (b) Find the value of $7 + 2a$ if $a = 6$.

   (c) Find the value of $16 - w + 6$ if $w = 5$.

8 Find the value of $4a + 15$ for each of the following.

   (a) $a = 3$ (b) $a = 0$

   (c) $a = 6$ (d) $a = 10$

9 Evaluate.

   (a) $4a + 7$ for $a = 3$.

   (b) $7 + 6m$ for $m = 4$.

   (c) $p + 30 - 16$ for $p = 24$

   (d) $2m - 4$ for $m = 10$.

B

10 Evaluate each expression.

   (a) $\square + 9$ if $\square = 8$

   (b) $(3 \times \square) + 7$ if $\square = 4$

   (c) $(\square \div 3) + (\square \times 2)$ if $\square = 9$

   (d) $2\square + 15$ if $\square = 15$

   (e) $9 \times \square - 4\square$ if $\square = 6$

   (f) $(\square + 8) \times 4 - \square$ if $\square = 1$

11 Find the value of each expression for the values of the variable.

   (a) $3p + m$, $p = 4, m = 12$

   (b) $14q - 2p$, $q = 3, p = 5$

   (c) $12k + 20t$, $k = 3, t = 4$

12 If $x = 3t + 2q$, find the value of x for each of the following.

   (a) $t = 2, q = 3$ (b) $t = 6, q = 0$

   (c) $t = 0, q = 8$ (d) $t = 12, q = 14$

13 Find the value of each of the following expressions if $a = 5$, $x = 2$, $y = 1$.

   (a) $3a$ (b) $a - 5$ (c) $8a - 2$

   (d) $4a + 10$ (e) $4(a - 2)$

   (f) $8x + 3y$ (g) $6 + 9x$

   (h) $6 + 9(2x - y)$ (i) $3a + 8x - 14y$

C

14 Evaluate each expression using the values shown.

   (a) $10m - 2$, $m = 1, 2, 3$

   (b) $12m - 4$, $m = 1, 2, 3$

   (c) $8m + 3$, $m = 2, 4, 6$

Applications: Team Standings in Sports

Teams in sports play hard so that they may be the first in the standings.

The number of points P, a team has is given by

$P = 2\overset{\downarrow}{w} + t$

w is the number of games won.

t is the number of games tied.

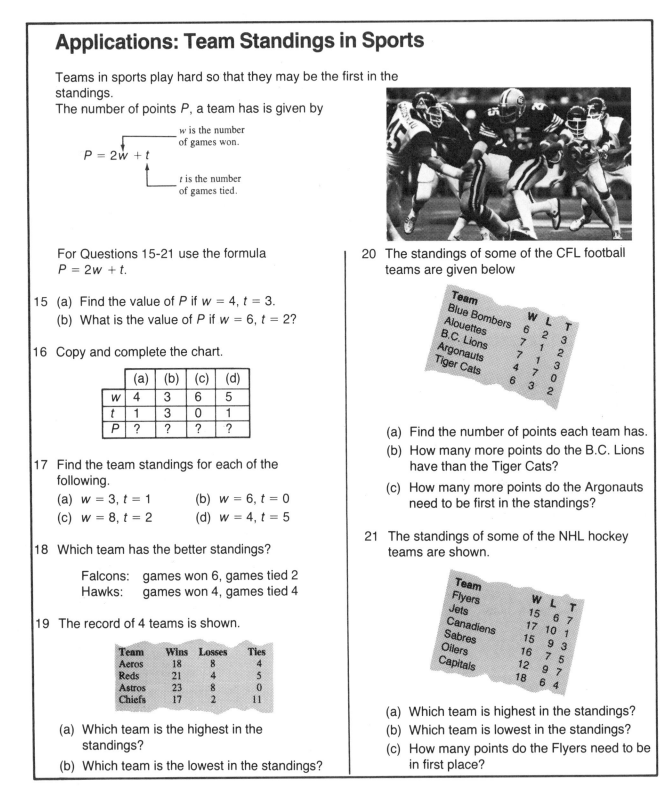

For Questions 15-21 use the formula $P = 2w + t$.

15 (a) Find the value of P if $w = 4$, $t = 3$.
   (b) What is the value of P if $w = 6$, $t = 2$?

16 Copy and complete the chart.

	(a)	(b)	(c)	(d)
w	4	3	6	5
t	1	3	0	1
P	?	?	?	?

17 Find the team standings for each of the following.
   (a) $w = 3$, $t = 1$ (b) $w = 6$, $t = 0$
   (c) $w = 8$, $t = 2$ (d) $w = 4$, $t = 5$

18 Which team has the better standings?

   Falcons: games won 6, games tied 2
   Hawks: games won 4, games tied 4

19 The record of 4 teams is shown.

Team	Wins	Losses	Ties
Aeros	18	8	4
Reds	21	4	5
Astros	23	8	0
Chiefs	17	2	11

   (a) Which team is the highest in the standings?
   (b) Which team is the lowest in the standings?

20 The standings of some of the CFL football teams are given below

Team	W	L	T
Blue Bombers	6	2	3
Alouettes	7	1	2
B.C. Lions	7	1	3
Argonauts	4	7	0
Tiger Cats	6	3	2

   (a) Find the number of points each team has.
   (b) How many more points do the B.C. Lions have than the Tiger Cats?
   (c) How many more points do the Argonauts need to be first in the standings?

21 The standings of some of the NHL hockey teams are shown.

Team	W	L	T
Flyers	15	6	7
Jets	17	10	1
Canadiens	15	9	3
Sabres	16	7	5
Oilers	12	9	7
Capitals	18	6	4

   (a) Which team is highest in the standings?
   (b) Which team is lowest in the standings?
   (c) How many points do the Flyers need to be in first place?

16

1.5 Decimal Fractions

In days gone by, sports event times were recorded in whole numbers of seconds.

As sports records improved, times were recorded in tenths of a second so that records could be more accurately compared.

100-m race won by Percy Williams in 10.8 s in the 1928 Olympics.

To record the time for a race, decimal fractions, accurate to hundredths of a second, are often used.

The skills you have learned for whole numbers extend to the study of decimal fractions.

To write any number, only the digits
    0, 1, 2, 3, 4, 5, 6, 7, 8, 9
are needed. A decimal point is used as a reference point.

Decimal Fraction	hundreds	tens	ones	tenths	hundredths	thousandths
28.3		2	8	3		
386.4	3	8	6	4		
6.45			6	4	5	
8.239			8	2	3	9

The place value of the digit 2 is *tenths*. There are 2 *tenths*.

The place value of the digit 9 is *thousandths*. There are 9 *thousandths*.

Example 1

In the Olympics, the finishing time of any contestant in track and field is important. If you were a judge looking at the finishing times of two runners, who would you say had won the race?

    Beatty 15.343 s   Erikson 15.342 s

Solution

To compare the numbers, you compare the digits.

three thousandths   *two thousandths*
15.343   15.342
└────────── the same ──────────┘

Since 3 > 2
then 15.343 > 15.342.
Thus Erikson won the race.

To check whether the answer to a problem is reasonable, round off the numbers.

Rounded off to the nearest tenth
0.83 is rounded off to 0.8
0.85 is rounded off to 0.9
0.89 is rounded off to 0.9

Examine the hundredths digit. If it is 5 or more, round off to the next tenth as shown. If it is less than 5, round off to the lower 10 as shown.

Rounded off to the nearest hundredth
0.464 is rounded off to 0.46
0.465 is rounded off to 0.47
0.469 is rounded off to 0.47

Examine the thousandths digit. What is the rule?

Rounded off to the nearest thousandth
0.4263 is rounded off to 0.426
0.4265 is rounded off to 0.427
0.4269 is rounded off to 0.427

Examine the ten thousandths digit. What is the rule?

Example 2

Round off 1.362 to

(a) the nearest tenth.
(b) the nearest hundredth.

Solution

(a) 1.362 ← Round off to the nearest tenth. Hundredths digit is more than 5. Thus 1.362 rounds off to 1.4.

(b) 1.362 ← Round off to the nearest hundredth. Thousandths digit is less than 5. Thus 1.362 rounds off to 1.36.

In rounding off decimal numbers, these statements mean the same.

- Round off to the nearest tenth.
  Round off to 1 decimal place.

- Round off to the nearest hundredth.
  Round off to 2 decimal places.

And so on.

In working with decimals remember how the words relate.

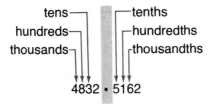

tens — ┐   ┌ tenths
hundreds — ┐ ┌ hundredths
thousands — ┐ ┌ thousandths
4832 • 5162

Try These

1 What is the place value of each underlined digit?

(a) 486.<u>2</u>   (b) 38.9<u>4</u>   (c) 48<u>9</u>.3
(d) 0.28<u>9</u>6   (e) 1.<u>3</u>41   (f) <u>2</u>0.96
(g) 38.9<u>1</u>5   (h) 4.<u>9</u>6   (i) 9.211<u>3</u>
(j) <u>4</u>89.69   (k) 38.94<u>5</u>   (l) 1.<u>9</u>632

2 What is the place value of the digit 5 in each of the following?

(a) 48.5   (b) 385.9   (c) 496.35
(d) 3.6150   (e) 5.132   (f) 69.865
(g) 4.8965   (h) 24.353   (i) 4.5132

3 Round off each number to the nearest tenth (to 1 decimal place).

(a) 48.19   (b) 48.32   (c) 48.45
(d) 63.25   (e) 63.52   (f) 63.59

4 Round off each number to the nearest hundredth (to 2 decimal places).

(a) 8.135   (b) 8.139   (c) 8.193
(d) 0.238   (e) 0.235   (f) 0.232

5 Round off each number to the nearest thousandth (to 3 decimal places).

(a) 4.1362   (b) 4.1326   (c) 4.1329
(d) 0.0013   (e) 0.0015   (f) 0.0019

Written Exercises

A 1 Which number of each pair is the greater, A or B?

	A	B
(a)	129.63	129.36
(b)	48.961	48.909
(c)	8.813	8.831
(d)	0.0135	0.0203
(e)	0.413	0.399
(f)	28.381	28.318

2 Round each number as indicated.

(a) 4.6838 to the nearest tenth
(b) 5.9328 to the nearest hundredth
(c) 0.1368 to the nearest thousandth
(d) 2.4849 to 1 decimal place
(e) 3.8915 to the nearest tenth
(f) 4.6219 to the nearest thousandth
(g) 9.9215 to 2 decimal places
(h) 8.7654 to the nearest tenth

3 For each pair of odometer readings, which indicates the greater distance travelled?

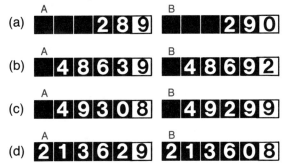

4 For each race, which person had the better time?

(a) men's 200-m race: Eddie Tolan 21.2 s, Livio Berruti 20.5 s
(b) men's 400-m race: Eric Liddell 47.6 s, Ottis Davis 44.9 s
(c) women's 400-m race: Monika Zehrt 51.08 s, Irena Szewinska 49.29 s
(d) women's 100-m hurdles: Annelie Ehrhardt 12.59 s, Johanna Schaller 12.77 s

5 Arrange each set of numbers from least to greatest.
   (a) 0.1, 1.0, 11.0, 1.01, 1.11, 1.011
   (b) 0.22, 22.2, 0.232, 2.22, 22.0, 2.2
   (c) 1.23, 0.123, 1.123, 123.0, 12.3, 123.1

6 Arrange each set of numbers from greatest to least.
   (a) 45.6, 56.4, 0.465, 5.064, 6.54
   (b) 12.2, 12.01, 12.23, 12.1, 12.96, 12.11
   (c) 0.0086, 0.013, 0.150, 0.039, 0.0099, 0.015

B 7 At Mt. Peaks ski resort, 0.98 m of snow fell. At Wood Trails resort, just across the valley, 0.897 m of snow fell. Which resort had more snow?

8 The thickness of a coat of paint is 0.1 mm. The width of a pin head is 1 mm. Which is the smaller measure?

9 In an election, candidate Trevor obtained 0.042 of the votes and candidate Collins received 0.089 of the votes. Which candidate received more votes?

10 For each rally, these cars participated. Arrange the readings from least to greatest.

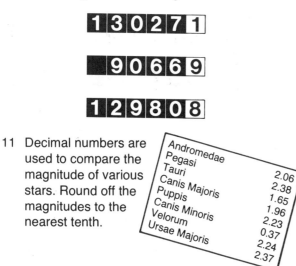

11 Decimal numbers are used to compare the magnitude of various stars. Round off the magnitudes to the nearest tenth.

Andromedae	
Pegasi	
Tauri	2.06
Canis Majoris	2.38
Puppis	1.65
Canis Minoris	1.96
Velorum	2.23
Ursae Majoris	0.37
	2.24
	2.37

12 The points awarded for the springboard diving contest are listed. Round off the points to 1 decimal place.

Springboard Diving	
Pete Desjardins	
Michael Gallitzen	
Richard Degener	185.04
Bruce Harlan	161.38
David Browning	161.57
Robert Clothworthy	163.64
	205.29
	159.56

13 Patricia went to Nassau on her holidays and stayed 6 full days. During this period of time Nassau had the following number of hours of sunshine.

Day 1	4.69 h	Day 2	8.72 h
Day 3	8.27 h	Day 4	4.96 h
Day 5	1.36 h	Day 6	3.16 h

↖ A bad day!

   (a) Which day had the most sunshine?
   (b) Which was the dullest day?
   (c) Arrange the amounts of sunshine from greatest to least.

C 14 The precipitation in January is shown for 10 cities.

St. John's	
Charlottetown	
Sydney	145.0 mm
Fredericton	110.7 mm
Val D'or	137.2 mm
Kapuskasing	90.7 mm
The Pas	57.2 mm
Regina	53.3 mm
Medicine Hat	18.5 mm
Prince George	18.3 mm
	22.6 mm
	59.2 mm

   (a) Which city had the least precipitation?
   (b) Which city had the most precipitation?
   (c) Arrange the amounts of precipitation from least to greatest.

15 Contestants were asked to make the largest and smallest decimal fractions using each of the digits 1, 2, 3, 4 once. Could you win this contest?

1.6 Addition and Subtraction: Decimal Numbers and Solving Problems

What you learn in one part of mathematics often extends other skills.
- To add whole numbers, you lined up the ones, tens, hundreds, and so on and then added each column.
- To add decimal fractions, you line up the tenths, hundredths and so on and then add each column.

How are these the same?

Addition

692	69.2
417	41.7
2583	258.3
+ 16	+ 1.6
3708	370.8

How are they different?

Subtraction

6953	69.53
− 3697	− 36.97
3256	32.56

Example 1

(a) Find the sum of 28.6, 3.89, 136.2.

(b) How much greater is 486.23 than 319.96?

Solution

(a) Find the sum.

	28.6
	3.89
	136.2
The sum is	168.69

Line up corresponding place values.

(b) Find the difference.

	486.23
	− 319.96
The difference is	166.27

Line up corresponding place values.

Example 2

George received a guitar for Christmas. He then bought the following:

Case $69.98   Stool $29.98

Music Stand $14.48

The sales tax was $7.84.

(a) What was the total cost (including tax)?

(b) How much money will he have left from $140.00?

Solution

(a) Cost of the items given in the problem.

	$69.98
	29.98
	14.48
	7.84
Sum	122.28

The total cost is $122.28.

(b)

Amount of money	$140.00
Cost of items	122.28
Difference	17.72

Thus, he will have $17.72 left.

Written Exercises

A 1 Find each sum.

(a)
0.6
0.5
+ 0.9

(b)
7.4
3.2
+ 5.8

(c)
6.84
0.25
+ 9.01

(d)
0.7
35.68
+ 7.5

(e)
19.03
6.7
9.54
+ 3.11

(f)
942.32
705.31
415.44
+ 986.33

2 Subtract each of the following.

(a)
6.9
− 4.1

(b)
30.8
− 5.4

(c)
6.8
− 4.1

(d)
16.45
− 12.10

(e)
96.04
− 6.32

(f)
85.32
− 8.15

3. Add each of the following.

(a) 6.94, 48.77, 65.2, 148.4
(b) 356.5, 3496.8, 524.617
(c) 9.64, 0.551, 86.8, 77.04
(d) 6.66, 66.66, 666.6, 66.666
(e) 6.489, 14.8, 39.774, 54.3

4 Calculate.

(a) 7.08 + 15.04 + 39.841
(b) 96 + 48.4 + 520 + 0.19
(c) 1600.9 − 652.8
(d) 16 419.8 − 12 416.7
(e) 1642.5 + 1699.7 − 2844.4

5 Add 6948 to the sum of 569.34 and 562.947.

6 Subtract 84.924 from 97.21

7 Find the sum of the following numbers.
  69.71, 16.7, 491.52, 8994

8 Subtract 69.521 from the sum of 124.69 and 7.25.

9 Add the sum of 6942 and 599.7 to the sum of 516.6 and 3741.5.

10 Find the following values.

(a) $6.29 + $16.29 + $4.28
(b) $469.28 − $123.39
(c) $1.69 + $28.28 + $36.45
(d) $1456.69 − $1297.70
(e) $1.48 + $3.69 − $2.10
(f) $21.69 + $36.42 − $48.25

11 Find the missing amounts for these sales receipts.

(a)
$17.98
4.06
7.52
ST
TX 1.56
T

(b)
$69.50
16.51
9.95
ST $95.96
TX 7.58
T

(c)
$ 6.59
3.04
13.55
1.98
ST 25.16
TX
T 26.92

(d)
$15.09
3.52
1.98
7.55
16.20
0.79
ST
TX
T 48.72

12 Two odometer readings — before and after — are given for each car. How far has each car travelled?

(a)  1362   4983

(b) 11629   12818

(c) 125679   134563

13 For each car, the reading before and after the trip is shown. What distance was travelled?

Before   After

(a) 152396   163918

(b) 267843   286932

(c) 904327   934516

Solve each problem. Refer to the *Steps For Solving Problems* to help you plan your work.

> *Steps For Solving Problems*
> Step A   Understand the problem.
>   I What am I given?
>   II What am I asked to find?
> Step B   Decide on a method.
> Step C   Find the answer.
> Step D   Check your answer.
> Step E   Write a final statement.

B 14 The tallest mammal in the world was a giraffe, with a record height of 6.02 m. How much taller was the giraffe than a man with an average height of 1.87 m?

15 Jupiter has a diameter of 141 966.4 km. Mercury has a diameter of 4849.6 km. What is the difference between the two?

16 Satellite Alouette 1 takes 105.4 min to circle the earth. Alouette 2 takes 121.4 min to circle the earth. What is the difference in time, rounded off to the nearest minute?

17 A chemist has 0.626 L of hydrochloric acid (HCL) in one flask, 0.98 L in another flask, and 1.26 L in a third flask. How many litres of HCL are there in all?

18 A camp counsellor was in charge of buying hamburgers for the group. Twenty three wanted hamburgers with cheese and 47 wanted them without cheese. How much will the counsellor have to spend?

With cheese $1.65

Plain $1.45

19 (a) For each gymnastic event, the scores are shown. Find the total points awarded to each competitor.

	Elizabeth Pinkston	Patricia McCormick	Aileen Riggin
Floor Exercises	8.3	8.7	9.1
High Bar	9.1	8.9	8.6
Beam Balance	8.3	9.1	8.7
Parallel Bars	9.3	8.7	9.3

(b) Who had the greatest point total?

20 An apartment building was being overhauled. It needed 240 fluorescent lights at $6.98 each. How much will the lights cost in total to the nearest $10?

C 21 The precipitation for each month in Estevan Point, B.C., is given.

Jan.	385.3 mm	April	232.7 mm
Feb.	318.0 mm	May	120.4 mm
Mar.	292.1 mm	June	97.0 mm

(a) What was the total precipitation for January to June?

(b) The total precipitation for 1 a averages 3027.99 mm. How much more precipitation is due to fall for the year?

22 Gary works at a local restaurant after school. One week his gross pay was $34.55 and he paid $8.75 in taxes. What was his take-home pay?

Applications: Consumer Buying

As a consumer, you need to make decisions about money.

► What is the total cost?
► How much am I saving?
► Do I have enough money?
► Is it the best value?

Often information is given about the product so that you can decide if it is a good deal.

Solve each of the following problems.

23 The regular price of the hairsetter is $33.58. How much is saved by buying it now?

Special
$26.88

24 The regular price of the typewriter is $139.95. How much is saved if you buy it on sale?

Special
$99.89

25 Sarah bought an album for $7.95 at A & B records. When she was at another record store, she saw the same album for $6.49. How much cheaper was the album at the second store?

26 Robert paid $54.85 for each of four new radial tires. After 1 month, a crack developed on one tire and he returned it for replacement. If the tire company gave him a refund of $35.95 for the tire, how much more would he need to buy a new tire?

27 Karen made a series of long distance telephone calls last month. Her telephone bill showed the following charges: $1.98, $2.57, $1.83, $3.45. The bill was incorrectly totalled at $10.24. What was the amount of the overcharge?

28 Mark saved $20 to go to the Canucks hockey game. His return fare cost $6.35, ticket $8.00, a program at $2.50, and food cost $1.55. How much did he have left?

29 It costs $9.94 for 2 pairs of shorts. Dan bought 4 pairs of shorts and the total sales tax was $1.39. How much change will Dan get from $25.00?

30 Amanda wants to buy 5 blouses. Each blouse costs $17.89 and the total sales tax is $6.25. How much will Amanda spend altogether?

31 Use the information given in the advertisement.

LARGE CANS
DOG FOOD
CASE 24
8.99

(a) Find the cost of 20 tins of dog food.
(b) The sales tax is 55¢ on your purchase. What is the total cost?

1.7 Multiplication and Division: Decimal Numbers and Solving Problems

In many everyday situations, you need to know how to multiply or divide decimal numbers.

Skills with whole numbers are extended in developing skills in decimal numbers.

How are these the same? How are they different?

Multiplication		Division	
67	6.7	194	1.94
× 23	× 2.3	36)6984	36)69.84
201	201	36	36
1340	1340	338	338
1541	15.41	324	324
		144	144
		144	144
		0	0

Example 1

Find the product of each of the following.

(a) 6.3 × 9.2   (b) 16.4 × 0.98

Solution

How do you place the decimal point in the answer?

(a)
```
    6.3    1 decimal place
 × 9.2     1 decimal place
   126
  5670
 57.96     2 decimal places
```

(b)
```
    16.4   1 decimal place
 × 0.98    2 decimal places
   1312
  14760
 16.072   3 decimal places
```

25

Example 2

Calculate.

(a) 23.76 ÷ 24

(b) $\dfrac{11.178}{2.3}$

Solution

(a) $\dfrac{23.76}{24} = 0.99$

$$\begin{array}{r} 0.99 \\ 24\overline{)23.76} \\ \underline{216} \\ 216 \\ \underline{216} \\ 0 \end{array}$$

Step 1	Step 2
To divide by a decimal rewrite the expression to make the denominator a whole number.	Then perform the division.

(b) Step 1

You may think of the step as

$$\dfrac{11.178}{2.3} = \dfrac{111.78}{23}$$

$$\dfrac{11.178 \times 10}{2.3 \times 10} = \dfrac{111.78}{23}$$

Step 2

$$\begin{array}{r} 4.86 \\ 23\overline{)111.78} \\ \underline{92} \\ 197 \\ \underline{184} \\ 138 \\ \underline{138} \\ 0 \end{array}$$

Try These

1 For each product, use an estimate to decide which answer, A or B, is correct.

Product	A	B
(a) 4.6 × 30	138	13.8
(b) 42 × 5.8	24.36	243.6
(c) 1.9 × 2.8	5.32	53.20

2 For each quotient, use an estimate to decide which answer, A or B, is correct.

Quotient	A	B
(a) 17.28 ÷ 4.8	36	3.6
(b) 39.2 ÷ 14	2.8	0.28
(c) 56.7 ÷ 6.3	90	9

3 Find each product.

(a) 10 × 1.3 (b) 10 × 2.6
(c) 10 × 8.5 (d) 100 × 0.31
(e) 100 × 0.45 (f) 100 × 0.86
(g) 1000 × 4.62 (h) 1000 × 5.63
(i) 1000 × 8.52

4 Find each quotient.

(a) $\dfrac{12.3}{10}$ (b) $\dfrac{1.36}{10}$ (c) $\dfrac{45.3}{10}$ (d) $\dfrac{12.4}{100}$

(e) $\dfrac{48.96}{100}$ (f) $\dfrac{483.6}{1000}$ (g) $\dfrac{98.36}{1000}$ (h) $\dfrac{489}{1000}$

Written Exercises

A 1 Find each product.

(a) 10 × 48.3 (b) 4.96 × 100
(c) 100 × 41.96 (d) 1000 × 2.963
(e) 41.298 × 10 (f) 6.961 × 100
(g) 100 × 0.03 (h) 1000 × 0.345

2 For each product, the digits are given in the calculator display. Place the decimal point correctly.

Product	Digits in the answer
(a) 0.4 × 0.7	280000
(b) 0.3 × 0.74	222000
(c) 0.7 × 19.2	134400

3 For each product, decide which is the correct answer, A or B.

		A	B
(a)	4×3.68	14.72	147.2
(b)	5.1×38	19.38	193.8
(c)	4.6×3.8	174.8	17.48
(d)	3.36×4.2	14.112	141.12

4 Find each product.
   (a) 8×6.8 (b) 4×7.2 (c) 6×9.6
   (d) 3.2×5 (e) 4.8×4 (f) 3×6.9

5 Find each product. Round off your answer to the nearest tenth.
   (a) 1.6×3.8 (b) 4.7×3.9
   (c) 56.42×0.9 (d) 18×0.47

6 Find each product. Round off your answer to 2 decimal places.
   (a) 6.7×9.25 (b) 8.41×0.34
   (c) 8.604×5.96 (d) 0.907×8.52

7 For each quotient, the digits are given in the calculator display. Place the decimal point correctly.

	Quotient	Digits
(a)	$577.7 \div 5.3$	10900
(b)	$524.8 \div 4.1$	12800
(c)	$10.08 \div 2.8$	36000
(d)	$7.68 \div 1.6$	48000
(e)	$5.778 \div 3.21$	18000

8 Estimate which answer is correct, A or B.

		A	B
(a)	$29.16 \div 12$	24.3	2.43
(b)	$54.30 \div 15$	3.62	36.2
(c)	$63.18 \div 1.3$	4.86	48.6
(d)	$10.07 \div 2.65$	3.8	38

9 Find each quotient.
   (a) $\dfrac{206.18}{13}$ (b) $\dfrac{16.94}{22}$ (c) $\dfrac{94.56}{6}$
   (d) $\dfrac{1.44}{12}$ (e) $\dfrac{655.2}{104}$ (f) $\dfrac{40.64}{16}$

10 Divide. Round off your answers to 1 decimal place.
   (a) $\dfrac{348.52}{27.6}$ (b) $\dfrac{8.492}{1.4}$ (c) $\dfrac{2046.9}{10.8}$
   (d) $0.5964 \div 0.29$ (e) $5.691 \div 12.42$

11 Divide. Round off your answers to the nearest hundredth.
   (a) $\dfrac{45.15}{5.7}$ (b) $\dfrac{96.38}{2.8}$ (c) $\dfrac{2186.3}{24.1}$
   (d) $9.041 \div 3.5$ (e) $3652.3 \div 41.8$

12 Calculate. Round off your answer as shown.
   (a) 52.47×6.2 to the nearest tenth
   (b) $484.27 \div 8.14$ to 2 decimal places
   (c) $4.799 \div 2.658$ to the nearest thousandth
   (d) 654.2×348.7 to 1 decimal place
   (e) 174.8×16.3 to the nearest hundredth
   (f) $86.42 \div 26.17$ to the nearest hundredth

B 13 Each time a piece of wire is passed across a laser beam, 0.004 mm are cut off. If it is passed over the beam 15 times, how much will be cut off altogether?

14 A class of 35 students went to lunch at Hardy's. The total bill was $61.25. How much did each student pay?

15 Tickets for a rock concert cost $9.95 each. The attendance at the concert was 989. How much ticket money was collected?

16 Find the cost per person for each of the following to 2 decimal places.

MENU A	MENU B
DINNER FOR FOUR 16.75	DINNER FOR SIX 28.50
4 Egg Rolls	6 Egg Rolls
Breaded Jumbo Shrimps	Fried Won Ton
Sweet and Sour Chicken	Breaded Jumbo Shrimps
Beef Vegetable and	Beef Chow Mein
Almond	Chicken Soo Guy
Chicken Chow Mein	Honey Garlic Spareribs
Barbecued Pork Fried Rice	Moo Goo Guy Pan
Fortune Cookies	Beef Vegetable and
	Almond
	Barbecued Pork Fried Rice
	Fortune Cookies

17 A prescription calls for 2.5-mg doses 5 times each day. How many milligrams of the drug will a patient take in 1 week?

18 Carol bought a package of 3 small lipsticks on sale for $2.44 and the total sales tax was $0.17. How much was one lipstick including sales tax? (Round off to the nearest cent.)

19 A brick costs 31¢. Find the cost of
   (a) 485 bricks for a barbecue pit.
   (b) 1100 bricks for a cabana.

20 Use the photograph. What is the cost per litre of the gas?

21 Use the Special Suggestions menu.

```
              SPECIAL SUGGESTIONS

Breaded Dry Spareribs ..................... $2.45
Deep Fry Spareribs .......................... 3.80
Honey Garlic Spareribs ...................... 3.95
Honey Garlic Chicken Wings ................. 3.45
Garlic Spareribs with Black Bean Sauce ........ 3.80
Garlic Chicken Wings with Black Bean Sauce ... 3.45
Beef with Chinese Green ..................... 3.75
Beef with Mushroom ......................... 3.75
Beef with Green Peppers ..................... 3.75
Beef with Tomatoes .......................... 3.75
Chicken Soo Guy ............................ 3.80
Breaded Chicken with Tomatoes .............. 4.00
Breaded Jumbo Shrimp with Sliced Lemon ...... 4.30
Shrimp with Green Pepper with Garlic .......... 4.30
Shrimp with Tomatoes ........................ 4.30
Bar B.Q. Pork with Bean Sprout .............. 3.15
Bar B.Q. Pork with Chinese Green ............ 3.75
Moo Goo Guy Kew ........................... 4.50
```

Find the cost of

(a) 4 orders of breaded dry spareribs.

(b) 3 orders of honey garlic chicken wings.

(c) 8 orders of beef with mushrooms.

22 Use the menu in Question 21. Find the cost of
   (a) 4 orders of deep fry spareribs and 3 orders of beef with green peppers.
   (b) 6 orders of chicken soo guy and 3 orders of moo goo guy kew.

23 An aquarium fishdealer must buy a number of fish for his store. He needs 6 mollies at $0.79 each, 7 guppies at $0.59 each, 12 swordtails at $1.89 per pair, and 14 platies at $1.69 per pair. What will be the total cost?

24 Read the newspaper clipping.
   (a) Find the sum of the lengths.
   (b) Find the average length.
   (c) Which fish is closest to the average?

Great Bass Derby
Finally the Derby has ended and these record fish lengths were pulled out.

Category A 45.9 cm
Category B 43.7 cm
Category C 40.5 cm
Category D 39.8 cm
Category E 37.9 cm

C
25 Janice made the following tips as a part-time waitress for the week.

Monday $2.85   Thursday $12.75
Tuesday $9.75   Friday $16.50
Wednesday $3.95   Saturday $17.35

(a) Find the total of her tips for the week.

(b) Her total pay (basic wage + tips) was $170.65. What is her basic wage?

Calculator Tip

When you compute with decimals on the calculator you often need to round off the final answer. Find $46.83 \div 12.71$.

Enter	Calculator Display
C	0
46.83	46.83
÷	46.830000
12.71	12.71
=	3.6845003

Final answer is 3.7 to 1 decimal place.
Final answer is 3.68 to 2 decimal places.

Applications: Pizza Prices

Probably everyone has ordered a pizza. But did you know how much mathematics is involved in ordering a pizza? For example, would you believe, with the ingredients available, you could order millions of *different* pizzas!

INGREDIENTS

PEPPERONI
MUSHROOMS
BACON
TOMATOES

GREEN OLIVES
GREEN PEPPERS
ONIONS
SALAMI

ANCHOVIES
HOT PEPPERS
PINEAPPLE
HAM

Basic Prices	small	med.	large	extra large
BASIC TOMATO SAUCE and CHEESE	3.00	4.00	5.00	6.75
Any ONE INGREDIENT	3.75	4.75	5.75	7.75
Any TWO INGREDIENTS	4.25	5.25	6.25	8.50
Any THREE INGREDIENTS	4.75	5.75	6.75	9.25
Each ADDITIONAL INGREDIENT	0.25	0.50	0.75	1.00

26 What is the cost for each pizza?
   (a) small with pepperoni and bacon
   (b) medium with olives, bacon and tomato
   (c) extra large with salami, mushrooms and hot peppers

27 What would be the cost per person of each of the following pizzas?
   (a) 3 people ordered a medium with one ingredient.
   (b) 5 people ordered an extra large with two ingredients.
   (c) 8 people ordered two mediums each with 2 ingredients.

28 Calculate the cost of pizza for each person for each of the following orders.

   (a) A party of 15 orders
      3 extra large with onions, pepperoni, mushrooms
      4 medium with mushrooms, bacon, tomato, and hot peppers

   (b) A class of 28 orders
      4 extra large pizzas with pepperoni, bacon, olives, and ham
      2 extra large pizzas with peppers and bacon
      4 medium pizzas with salami, hot peppers, pepperoni

29 After school, Jean, Harriet and Joe ordered a large pizza with green olives, pepperoni, and mushrooms. What is each person's cost?

Many pizza places have a special of the house. But, beware! The value may in some cases be misleading. Use the prices for a Mini Special to solve Questions 31 to 33.

Mini Special	small	med.	large	extra large
PEPPERONI, MUSHROOMS, GREEN PEPPERS, & BACON	5.25	6.25	7.25	9.95

30 (a) How much does a small pizza cost with pepperoni, mushrooms, green peppers, and bacon?
   (b) What is the cost of a small Mini Special?
   (c) Which is the better buy, (a) or (b)?

31 (a) How much does a medium pizza cost with pepperoni, mushrooms, green peppers, and bacon?
   (b) What is the cost of a medium Mini Special?
   (c) Which is the better buy, (a) or (b)?

32 (a) How much does an extra large pizza cost with pepperoni, mushrooms, green peppers, and bacon?
   (b) What is the cost of an extra large Mini Special?
   (c) Which is the better buy, (a) or (b)?

1.8 Working With Exponents

In order to make the study of mathematics easier, it is necessary to invent compact ways of writing mathematics. The following equation has affected each of you in one way or another.

$$E = mc^2$$

This equation has been written in a compact form using an **exponent**.

A TYPICAL ATOM

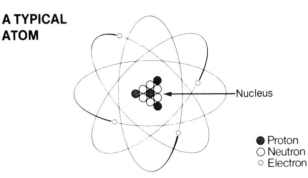

Nucleus

● Proton
○ Neutron
○ Electron

You may write sums in a more compact way by using the operation of multiplication.

Sum	Product	
2 + 2 + 2 + 2	4 × 2	means add 4 twos
5 + 5 + 5	3 × 5	means add 3 fives
10 + 10 + 10 + 10 + 10	5 × 10	means add 5 tens

Similarly, a shorter way has been invented of writing a product of factors that are the same.

Factors	Short method	
2 × 2 × 2 × 2	2^4	means multiply 4 factors of 2
5 × 5 × 5	5^3	means multiply 3 factors of 5
10 × 10 × 10 × 10 × 10	10^5	means multiply 5 factors of 10

In order to develop skills with exponents, you have to know the names of these parts.

4 is called the exponent
It tells you to multiply 4 factors of 2.

2^4 2^4 is called the exponent form.

2 is called the **base**. It tells you what factors are multiplied.

2^4 is called a **power**.

Read:
2 to the exponent 4 or the fourth power of 2.

Some powers are read in other special ways.

3^2 — 3 squared

2^3

2 cubed

Example 1

What is the value of ▨?

(a) $5^3 = 5 \times ▨ \times 5$
(b) $7^▨ = 7 \times 7 \times 7 \times 7 \times 7$

Solution

(a) Since 5^3 means
$5 \times 5 \times 5$,
then ▨ = 5.

(b) $7^▨ = 7 \times 7 \times 7 \times 7 \times 7$
Since $7 \times 7 \times 7 \times 7 \times 7$
means 7^5, then ▨ = 5.

To calculate the value of 2^3, remember what each number means.

$2^3 = 2 \times 2 \times 2$ ——— The exponent 3 tells you
how many 2's to multiply.
$= 8$

Thus, the value of 2^3 is 8.

The base of a power may be numbers other than a whole number.
For example, $(0.3)^2$ is a power. The value of $(0.3)^2$ is found by
writing,

$(0.3)^2 = (0.3)(0.3) = 0.09.$
Thus $(0.3)^2 = 0.09.$

Example 2

Find the value of each power.

(a) 3^4 (b) 5^2 (c) 7^3 (d) 10^4

Solution

(a) 3^4 means $3 \times 3 \times 3 \times 3 = 81$
(b) 5^2 means $5 \times 5 = 25$
(c) 7^3 means $7 \times 7 \times 7 = 343$
(d) 10^4 means $10 \times 10 \times 10 \times 10 = 10\ 000$

To calculate expressions containing exponents, evaluate the
powers before doing the rest of the calculations, as shown in
Example 3. Why?

Example 3

Calculate.

(a) $5^2 - 3^2$ (b) $3^2 \times 3^2$
(c) $2(1^5 + 4^2)$ (d) $(8^2 - 5 \times 4) \div 2$

Solution

(a) $5^2 - 3^2$ ◄— Evaluate the   (b) $3^2 \times 3^2$
$= 25 - 9$ powers first, $= 9 \times 9$
$= 16$ then subtract. $= 81$

Do the calculations in
the parentheses first.

(c) $2(1^5 + 4^2)$ (d) $(8^2 - 5 \times 4) \div 2$
$= 2(1 + 16)$ $= (64 - 20) \div 2$
$= 2(17) = 34$ $= 44 \div 2 = 22$

Remember, 8^2
means $8 \times 8 = 64$.

Try These

1 What is the base and exponent of each power?

(a) 2^3 (b) 5^6 (c) 7^4 (d) 10^5

(e) 4^2 (f) 3^4 (g) $\left(\dfrac{1}{2}\right)^2$ (h) 1^6

2 Use exponents to write each of the following in a compact form.

(a) $5 \times 5 \times 5$ (b) $3 \times 3 \times 3 \times 3$

(c) $2 \times 2 \times 2 \times 2 \times 2$ (d) 10×10

(e) $6 \times 6 \times 6 \times 6$

(f) $10 \times 10 \times 10 \times 10$

3 What is the value of ▨?

(a) $3^2 = ▨ \times 3$ (b) $2^▨ = 2 \times 2 \times 2$

(c) $6 \times 6 \times 6 = ▨^3$ (d) $5^▨ = 5 \times 5$

4 Find each value.

(a) 2^2 (b) 3^2 (c) 3^3 (d) 4^2

(e) 5^2 (f) 2^5 (g) 4^3 (h) $\left(\dfrac{1}{2}\right)^2$

5 What is the value of each of the following?

(a) 1^2 (b) 1^3 (c) 1^4

(d) 10^2 (e) 10^3 (f) 10^4

Written Exercises

A 1 Write the base and exponent of each power.

(a) 3^2 (b) 2^3 (c) 10^2 (d) 2^{10}

(e) $\left(\dfrac{1}{2}\right)^3$ (f) 2^6 (g) 6^2 (h) 3^5

2 Use exponents to write each of the following in a compact form.

(a) $3 \times 3 \times 3$

(b) $2 \times 2 \times 2 \times 2 \times 2 \times 2$

(c) $6 \times 6 \times 6 \times 6$

(d) $10 \times 10 \times 10 \times 10 \times 10$

3 What value do each of the following have?

(a) 2^3 (b) 3^5 (c) 4^4 (d) 1^4

(e) 10^3 (f) 5^3 (g) 2^5 (h) 10^5

4 (a) What is the value of the fourth power of 2?

(b) Find the third power of $\frac{1}{4}$.

(c) Find the second power of 15.

(d) Evaluate the third power of 7.

5 Find the value of ▨.

(a) $4^3 = 4 \times 4 \times ▨$

(b) $▨^3 = \dfrac{1}{5} \times \dfrac{1}{5} \times \dfrac{1}{5}$

(c) $2^▨ = 2 \times 2 \times 2 \times 2$

(d) $9^3 = ▨ \times 9 \times 9$

(e) $▨^3 = 7 \times 7 \times 7$

(f) $6^▨ = 6 \times 6 \times 6 \times 6 \times 6$

(g) $▨^2 = 10 \times 10$

(h) $10^▨ = 10 \times 10 \times 10 \times 10$

6 Find the value of each power.

(a) 2^2 (b) 2^4 (c) $\left(\dfrac{1}{3}\right)^3$ (d) $(0.5)^2$

(e) 6^2 (f) 3^3 (g) 3^4 (h) 7^2

(i) 1^{10} (j) $\left(\dfrac{1}{5}\right)^2$ (k) 10^2 (l) 10^3

7 Copy and complete the chart below.

	Power	Meaning	Base	Exponent	Value
(a)	2^3	$2 \times 2 \times 2$	2	3	?
(b)	3^5	?	?	?	?
(c)	?	?	3	?	27
(d)	10^4	?	?	?	?
(e)	?	6×6	?	?	?
(f)	?	?	9	2	?
(g)	?	?	3	?	81

B 8 Use $<$, $>$ or $=$ in place of ◉ to make each of the following true. The first one has been done for you.

(a) 3^2 ◉ 2^2

$$3^2 = 3 \times 3 \quad 2^2 = 2 \times 2$$
$$= 9 \qquad\qquad = 4$$
$$\text{Since } 9 > 4 \text{ then } 3^2 > 2^2.$$

(b) 2^2 ◉ 3^2 (c) 2^4 ◉ 2^5 (d) 1^6 ◉ 2^3

(e) 3^2 ◉ 2^3 (f) 1^{15} ◉ 15^1 (g) 8^3 ◉ 6^3

(h) 10^4 ◉ 4^{10} (i) 9^2 ◉ 7^3 (j) 6^4 ◉ 4^6

9 Find the value of each of the following.

(a) $3^2 + 3^2$ (b) $2^3 + 2^2$

(c) $3^3 - 3^2$ (d) $2^3 - 2^2$

(e) $(3^2 + 4) \times 2$ (f) $(3^2 + 7) - 2$

(g) $(8^2 - 5) - 7$ (h) $9^2 - (6^2 + 6^2)$

(i) $10^3 - (10^2 + 2)$ (j) $15^2 + (3^2 - 2)$

10 Use $<$, $>$ or $=$ in place of ◉ to make each of the following true.

(a) $4^2 + 2$ ◉ 4^3

(b) 6^2 ◉ $6 \times (2^3)$

(c) 4^3 ◉ $4^3 - 10$

(d) 10^4 ◉ $10 + 10 + 10 + 10$

(e) $7^2 + 1$ ◉ $6^2 + 14$

(f) $10^3 - 10^2$ ◉ $3^2 \times 100$

11 Match equal values in Columns I and II.

Column I	Column II
(a) $10^2 - 5^2$	A 300×2
(b) $10^3 - 10^2$	B $10^2 + 13$
(c) $7^2 + 1^4$	C $8^2 - 4^2 + 2$
(d) $5^3 - 2^3$	D $9^2 + 6^2$
(e) $8^2 + 7^2$	E $10^2 \times 9$
(f) 6×10^2	F $9^2 - 6$

12 (a) Find the sum of 2^3 and 3^2.
   (b) By how much does 5^2 exceed 4^2?
   (c) Find the product of 3^2 and 2^5.
   (d) Find the quotient if 8^2 is divided by 2^3.

13 (a) Calculate the squares of 0.3 and 0.03.
   (b) How are your answers in (a) alike?
   (c) How are your answers in (a) different?

14 (a) Write the cube of 0.2 and 0.02.
   (b) How are your answers in (a) alike?
   (c) How do your answers in (a) differ?

15 Which of A, B, or C is $(0.4)^3$ equal to?
   A 0.064   B 0.0064   C 0.000 64

16 Calculate.
   (a) $(0.1)^2$ (b) $(0.1)^3$ (c) $(0.1)^4$
   (d) $(0.2)^2$ (e) $(0.2)^3$ (f) $(0.2)^4$
   (g) $(0.5)^2$ (h) $(0.3)^3$ (i) $(0.1)^5$
   (j) $(0.01)^2$ (k) $(0.02)^2$ (l) $(0.03)^2$

17 Find the value of each of the following.
   (a) 3^2 (b) $(0.3)^2$ (c) $(0.03)^2$
   (d) 300^2 (e) $(1.3)^2$ (f) $(0.13)^2$
   (g) 13^2 (h) 130^2 (i) 3^3
   (j) $(0.03)^3$ (k) 30^3 (l) 300^3

C 18 Find each of the following.
   (a) The second power of 0.5.
   (b) The fourth power of 0.2.
   (c) The fifth power of 0.1.

Order of Operations: Exponents

In much of the work you do in measurement, skills with exponents
are needed. If an expression contains exponents, do the
calculations with exponents first, as shown.

$$2 \times 3^2 \qquad\qquad 7 + 2 \times 3^2$$
$$= 2 \times 9 \qquad\qquad = 7 + 2 \times 9$$
$$= 18 \qquad\qquad\quad = 7 + 18$$
$$\qquad\qquad\qquad\qquad = 25$$

If an expression also contains brackets, then simplify the
calculations in the brackets first. Compare these examples.

$$3 \times 2^3 \qquad (3 \times 2)^3 \qquad (3 \times 2)^3 - 4$$
$$= 3 \times 8 \qquad = (6)^3 \qquad = 6^3 - 4$$
$$= 24 \qquad\quad = 216 \qquad = 216 - 4$$
$$\qquad\qquad\qquad\qquad\qquad = 212$$

19 Simplify each of the following.
   (a) $2^4 + 4$ (b) $2^4 \div 4$
   (c) $2^4 - 4$ (d) $2^4 \times 4$

20 Simplify each of the following.
   (a) 4×3^2 (b) $(4 \times 3)^2$
   (c) 5×2^3 (d) $(5 \times 2)^3$

21 Simplify each of the following.

   Remember the order of operations.

   (a) $3^2 + 2$ (b) $5 + 6^2$ (c) $2^3 - 4$
   (d) $3^4 - 3^2$ (e) $9^2 \times 2$ (f) $6^2 \div 2^2$
   (g) $3^3 \div 3^2$ (h) $81 - 7^2$ (i) $10 \div 2 - 2^2$

22 Simplify each expression.
   (a) $4 \times 5 + 9^2$ (b) $21 - 6^2 \div 3$
   (c) $18 \div 3^2 + 20$ (d) $4 \times 6 \div 2^3$
   (e) $60 - 4^2 \div 2^2$ (f) $9 + 4^3 \div 2^4$
   (g) $5 \times 4^2 - 3^3$ (h) $7 \times (5 - 3)^2 \div 2^2$
   (i) $2 \times 4^2 - 7$ (j) $3 \times 5 + (3 + 5)^2$
   (k) $3^4 \div 9 + (7 \times 3)$ (l) $15^2 \div 25$

23 (a) Simplify.
        A $5 \times 3^2 - 6^2$ B $(5 \times 3)^2 - 6^2$
   (b) Why do the answers differ?

24 Simplify.
   (a) $2 \times 3^2 - 2^3$ (b) $(2 \times 3)^2 - 2^3$
   (c) $2 \times (3^2 - 2^3)$ (d) $2 \times (3^2 - 2)^3$

   Why do the answers differ?

25 Copy each of the following. Insert parentheses
   to make each of the following correct.
   (a) $3 \times 3 - 1^2 = 12$ (b) $3 \times 2^2 - 4 = 32$
   (c) $3 \times 2^2 - 4 = 0$ (d) $2 \times 5^2 - 1 = 99$

26 Calculate each of the following.
   (a) $\dfrac{3^2 + 4^2}{5^2}$ (b) $\dfrac{5^2 - 4^2}{3^2}$ (c) $\dfrac{5^2 - 3^2}{4^2}$
   (d) $\dfrac{12^2 + 5^2}{13^2}$ (e) $\dfrac{13^2 - 12^2}{5^2}$ (f) $\dfrac{13^2 - 5^2}{12^2}$

27 For the following magic square

   • find the magic number.

   • find the missing values A, B, . . . , E.

$2^3 - 2^2$	A	B
$1^2 + 2^2 + 3^2$	C	D
$5^2 - 2 \times 6 - 1$	E	$6^2 - 5 \times 4$

1.9 Problem Solving: Is My Answer Reasonable?

Often you want to obtain an approximate cost. For example, Lesley ordered 30 prints of a negative and John ordered 40 prints of a negative.

A negative is used to make a photograph print.

Lesley was charged $17.40 and John was charged $26.20. If the cost of one print is 58¢, were Lesley and John charged the correct amounts?

To obtain the approximate cost round off 58¢ to the nearest 10¢, i.e. 60¢.

Lesley: 30 photos made

Amount charged	$17.40
Approximate cost	30 × 60¢ = $18.00

This tells us the actual cost of $17.40 is reasonable.

John: 40 photos made

Amount charged	$26.20
Approximate cost	40 × 60¢ = $24.00

Check
Correct Cost 40 × 58¢ = $23.20

This tells us the actual cost of $26.20 needs to be checked.

The above skill of finding approximate answers helps you to check quickly whether an answer is reasonable.

Example 1
Without multiplying, decide which is the answer to 4.79 × 6.98.

  A 0.334 342   B 3.343 42
  C 0.033 434 2   D 33.4342

Solution
Round each number in the problem to the nearest whole number.
    4.79 is rounded to 5.
    6.98 is rounded to 7.
The approximate answer is 5 × 7 = 35.
The correct answer is D. 4.79 × 6.98 = 33.4342

Example 2
Calculate each product. Then round off and estimate each product to check your answer.
(a) 69 × 31   (b) 13.9 × 8.4

Solution
(a) 69 × 31 = 2139
Round to the nearest 10.
    70 × 30 = 2100

The estimated answer tells you that 2139 is a reasonable answer.

(b) 13.9 × 8.4 = 116.76
Round to the nearest 1.
    14 × 8 = 112

The estimated answer of 112 tells you that 116.76 is a reasonable answer. The products 11.676, 1167.6, would not be reasonable.

Example 3

The cost of 1 ticket is $2.25.

Which of the following is incorrect?

(a) 9 tickets
Total cost $20.25

(b) 28 tickets
Total cost $73.00

Solution

(a) Approximate cost
10 × $2.00 = $20.00

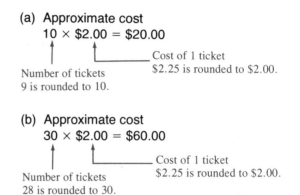

Number of tickets
9 is rounded to 10.

Cost of 1 ticket
$2.25 is rounded to $2.00.

(b) Approximate cost
30 × $2.00 = $60.00

Number of tickets
28 is rounded to 30.

Cost of 1 ticket
$2.25 is rounded to $2.00.

The price of $73.00 is definitely incorrect.

Try These

1 Round off each of the following.
   (a) 38   (to the nearest ten)
   (b) 386   (to the nearest hundred)
   (c) 42   (to the nearest ten)
   (d) 536   (to the nearest hundred)
   (e) 4931 (to the nearest thousand)

2 Estimate each of the following.
   (a) 41 × 39   (b) 83 ÷ 39   (c) 58 × 23
   (d) 119 ÷ 22 (e) 128 × 42 (f) 469 ÷ 96
   (g) 408 ÷ 76 (h) 69 × 319 (i) 73 ÷ 6.9

3 Round off
   (a) 0.19   (to the nearest tenth).
   (b) 0.283   (to the nearest tenth).
   (c) 0.0068 (to the nearest hundredth).
   (d) 0.148   (to the nearest tenth).
   (e) 0.0292 (to the nearest hundredth).

4 Estimate each cost.
   (a) 12 records at $4.99 each.
   (b) 11 tickets at $2.25 each.
   (c) 29 pocketbooks at $3.95 each.

Written Exercises

A 1 Find each product. Check your answer by
rounding off.

   (a) 12 × 1.2   (b) 19 × 3.9   (c) 18.2 × 16
   (d) 23.9 × 2.3 (e) 0.9 × 4.6 (f) 0.09 × 4.6

2 Calculate. Round off your answers to 2 decimal
places. Check your answers by estimation.
   (a) 43 ÷ 1.9   (b) 123 ÷ 4.2 (c) 43.2 ÷ 9.3
   (d) 131 ÷ 9.6 (e) 64.8 ÷ 8.3 (f) 438 ÷ 23.2

3 Estimate each of the following. (Do not multiply
the numbers shown.)
   (a) 63 × 91   (b) 459 × 19
   (c) 6997 × 51   (d) 79.8 × 4.2

4 Estimate each of the following. (Do not divide
the number shown.)
   (a) 72 ÷ 11   (b) 697 ÷ 68
   (c) 3007 ÷ 49   (d) 39.8 ÷ 7.9

5 For each of the following, three answers are given: A, B, and C. Estimate which answer is correct.

		A	B	C
(a)	16 × 47	752	7522	75 222
(b)	512 × 58	2969	29 696	296 966
(c)	39 × 489	1907	190 711	19 071
(d)	591 × 3452	20 401	204 013	2 040 132
(e)	61 × 56 × 49	16 738	167 384	1 673 844
(f)	79 × 42 × 98	325 164	32 516	3 251 644

6 Calculate. Round off your answers to 2 decimal places. Then check if your answer is reasonable by estimation.
(a) 4.89 × 62.41   (b) 79.2 ÷ 4.1
(c) 0.2 × 58.95   (d) 103 × 6.97
(e) 1980.2 ÷ 5.45   (f) 4.97 × 5.96
(g) 698.961 ÷ 3.522   (h) 6.3 × 7.9 × 7.8
(i) 45.4 × 59.7 × 39.1 (j) 79.6 × 33.1 ÷ 6.2

B 7 Find each cost. Check your answer by rounding off.
(a) 20 × $1.86   (b) 23 × $1.19
(c) 49 × $1.99   (d) 63 × $19.50
(e) 123 × $2.10   (f) 412 × $3.69

8 Calculate each cost.
(a) 12 tickets at $1.99. (b) 28 tickets at $1.10.
(c) 39 tickets at $3.25. (d) 119 tickets at $4.99.

9 Estimate the cost of each group going to the movie. Then find the answer.

THE FORMULA
Starts Friday
Marlon Brando
recommended as
ADULT ENTERTAINMENT
$3.75

(a) Rifle Club, 25 persons
(b) Wrench Club, 28 persons
(c) Basketball Team, 18 persons
(d) Junior Football Team, 32 persons

10 Estimate each bill. Then calculate the cost.
(a) 4 fries, 4 milkshakes
(b) 6 hamburgers, 6 milkshakes   99¢
(c) 5 hamburgers, 2 fries,
     5 milkshakes
(d) 8 hot dogs, 5 milkshakes,
     3 fries
(e) 4 hot dogs, 4 hamburgers,
     8 milkshakes

$1.25

$1.45

60¢

Answer each of the following. (Did you estimate the answer?)

11 Joanne swims 12.8 km each day. How far does she swim in 30 d?

12 There are 2.8 g of protein in a tablespoon of peanut butter. How many grams in 40 tablespoons?

13 Sam's Record store sells special L.P.'s at $4.99. What is the cost of 12 records?

14 Teenagers watch about 3.8 h/d of television. How many hours of television per week do they watch?

C
15 The equipment manager purchased the following equipment for next season.

        22 helmets $19.60 each
        15 pants $28.40 each
        28 sticks $12.20 each

(a) Calculate the approximate cost.
(b) Calculate the exact cost.
(c) How close are your answers in (a) and (b)?

Skills To Practise: A Chapter Review

1.1 (a) Round off

    A 362   to the nearest 10.
    B 362   to the nearest 100.
    C 5381   to the nearest 100.
    D 5381   to the nearest 1000.
    E 29 694 to the nearest 10.
    F 29 694 to the nearest 100.
    G 29 694 to the nearest 1000.

  (b) For each of the following, which answer, I, II, or III, is reasonable?

	I	II	III
A 16×83	138	1328	13 218
B $2976 \div 62$	28	48	483
C 43×361	155	1552	15 523
D $13 524 \div 28$	483	843	4813

1.2 Find each total.

  (a) 3829 adults
      469 students
      363 children
      ▨▨▨▨ people

  (b) 12 636 adults
      9 132 students
      4 136 children
      ▨▨▨▨ people

1.3 Simplify.

  (a) $9 + 6 \div 3 - 5 + 4$
  (b) $64 - 80 \div (48 \div 3) - 8$
  (c) $\dfrac{58 - 4}{3 \times 6}$
  (d) $\dfrac{22 - 42 \div 7}{64 \div 4}$

1.4 Evaluate each expression.

  (a) $6a + 3$, for $a = 4$.
  (b) $3k - 2$, for $k = 8$.
  (c) $12p - 3q$, for $p = 3$, $q = 2$.

1.5 (a) Round off

    A 3.692   to the nearest tenth.
    B 14.9361 to the nearest hundredth.
    C 9.8793 to the nearest thousandth.
    D 14.854 to the nearest tenth.
    E 3.9651 to the nearest hundredth.

  (b) Arrange the numbers from least to greatest.
    3.45 0.543 3.54 0.5043 3.054

1.6 (a) Find the sum of 48.3, 23.6, and 143.2.
  (b) Calculate $369.2 + 433.9 - 268.5$.
  (c) Find the total dollar amount.
    $46.31 + $29.36 - 13.69.

1.7 (a) Calculate.
    A 0.4×6.93 B 12.1×6.9 C $30.24 \div 4.8$
  (b) Calculate. Round off each answer to the nearest tenth.
    A 4.6×3.82 B $\dfrac{128}{17}$ C $\dfrac{12.35}{1.2}$

1.8 (a) Find the value of each of the following.
    A $2^3 + 2^4$ B $3^3 - 2^2$
    C 3.92×100 D 4.86×10^2
    E $4.92 \div 100$ F $3.42 \div 10^2$

  (b) Simplify.
    A $3 \times 8 + 2^2$ B $4^3 + 3 \times 2^3$
    C $(5 \times 2)^2 - 3$ D $5 \times 2^2 - 3$

1.9 (a) Find each cost. Check whether your answer is reasonable.
    A $12 \times 1.69 B $18 \times 3.75
    C $23 \times 4.25 D $29 \times 0.99
    E $36 \times 4.99 F $62 \times 4.12

  (b) Calculate. Check whether your answer is reasonable.
    A 12×29.5 B 53×12.2
    C 1.5×6.8 D 9.3×9.1
    E 39×1.36 F 18×2.96
    G 1.2×3.68 H 4.5×5.96

  (c) Calculate. Check whether your answer is reasonable. Round off your answer to 1 decimal place.
    A $143 \div 12$ B $396 \div 29$
    C $49.6 \div 4$ D $123.1 \div 28$
    E $12.6 \div 0.8$ F $26.9 \div 0.65$
    G $4.63 \div 0.3$ H $9.86 \div 4.3$

Problems To Practise: A Chapter Review

1.1 Round off the mass of each animal to the nearest 100 kg.
   (a) Alaskan brown bear, 4136 kg
   (b) polar bear, 4051 kg
   (c) giraffe, 3975 kg
   (d) rhinoceros, 8242 kg

1.2 In a local election, 14 962 people were eligible to vote. Only 12 495 people actually voted.
   (a) How many people did *not* vote?
   (b) Perry received 8492 votes and the rest of the votes went to Susan. How many votes did Susan get?
   (c) By the next election the number of eligible voters increased by 5180. How many eligible votes were there for that election?

1.3 To win a new stereo system, answer the skill-testing question.

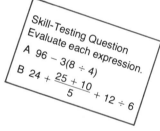

Skill-Testing Question
Evaluate each expression.
A $96 - 3(8 \div 4)$
B $24 + \dfrac{25 + 10}{5} + 12 \div 6$

1.4 The amount of money collected, A, in dollars, for the concert is given by

$$A = 4a + 3s.$$

   number of adults   number of students

   Find A for the following.
   (a) $a = 126$, $s = 43$ (b) $a = 1239$, $s = 4863$

1.5 On a holiday weekend in Vancouver, the following amounts of bright sun were recorded.

   Friday 4.21 h
   Saturday 4.63 h
   Sunday 4.43 h

   Arrange the amounts from least to greatest.

1.6 Three students went out record buying. They each returned with the same album but at different prices. The three prices of the album were $4.98, $5.67, and $4.63.
   (a) How much in total did the students pay for the records?
   (b) What is the difference between the highest and lowest price?

1.7 (a) Larry is in charge of buying tennis balls for the tennis team. He bought 25 balls at 69¢ each. What was the total cost?
   (b) If an astronaut has a planned space trip of 64.4 h and has to stretch his muscles every 8.05 h to keep his circulation going, how many stretching periods will he have?

1.8 (a) By how much does $3^2 + 2^2$ exceed $3^2 - 2^2$?
   (b) What is the sum of $2^2 - 2$, $3^2 - 3$, $4^2 - 4$?
   (c) Replace ⬤ by >, < or = to make each of the following true.
      A $5^2 - 4^2$ ⬤ $(5 - 4)(5 + 4)$
      B $12^2 + 5^2$ ⬤ $(12 - 5)(12 + 5)$

1.9 Estimate the cost of each purchase.
   (a) 6 8-tracks and
       2 cassettes
   (b) 4 cassettes and
       3 L.P. records
   (c) 3 45 r/min records and
       5 L.P. records
   (d) one of each

$6.89

$7.52

$5.49

$1.42

Chapter Checkup: A Practice Test

1.1 (a) Round off
- A 466   to the nearest 10.
- B 961   to the nearest 100.
- C 2383   to the nearest 10.
- D 19 432 to the nearest 1000.

(b) The Gazette has a circulation of 78 439. On the front page they rounded off this number to the nearest hundred. What number did they use?

1.2 The attendances at a football stadium over the last 4 games were as follows:

Game 1   42 850
Game 2   29 755
Game 3   58 605
Game 4   32 894

(a) Find the average attendance.
(b) Which game is closest to this average?

1.3 Simplify.
(a) $3 + 6 \div 2$
(b) $4 + 9 \div 3 - 2 + 5$
(c) $\dfrac{3(10 - 6) \div 2}{36 \div 6}$

1.4 (a) Find the value of each expression.
- A $3 + 2k$, for $k = 6$
- B $12m - 3p$ for $m = 3$, $p = 2$.

(b) What is the value of $2p + 3q - 123$ if $p = 24$ and $q = 36$?

1.5 (a) Arrange the numbers from greatest to least.
4.93   0.493   4.093   4.0039   3.4009   4.1

(b) Round the points awarded in the 10-m dive to the nearest tenth.

Jeneer   183.08
Bolton   169.93
Sanguine   178.39
Jerome   183.19

1.6 (a) Calculate.
- A $198.3 + 28.1 - 36.9$
- B $469.28 + 16.3 - 10.36$

(b) Solve.
Tim received a $10 food certificate for Hungry Burgers on his birthday. He and four friends spent the following amounts: $1.75, $1.90, $2.20, $1.85, and $1.60. If he left a $0.50 tip, how much of the certificate was unspent?

1.7 (a) Calculate. Round off your answer to the nearest tenth.
- A 12×4.36 B $312 \div 8$ C $69.3 \div 4.5$

(b) Jean is paid $4.65/h to work at the car wash. If she works 4 h, 6 h, 3 h, and 2 h, how much is she paid in all?

(c) In a walkathon of 26.6 km there is a rest station every 3.385 km. How many rest stations are there in this walkathon?

1.8 (a) Find the value of each of the following.
- A $3^3 - 2^3 - 1^3$ B $5^2 - 4^2 - 3^2$

(b) Find the product of $3^2 - 3$ and $2^3 - 2^2$.

(c) Find each missing value.
- A $6.9 \div \blacksquare = 0.069$
- B $4.89 \times \blacksquare = 48.9$
- C $\blacksquare \times 10^3 = 46.32$
- D $16.86 = \blacksquare \div 10^2$

1.9 (a) Calculate each of the following and check whether your answer is reasonable. Round off your answers to 1 decimal place.
- A 43×12.1 B $16.9 \div 3.2$
- C $42 \times \$1.79$ D 1.8×3.6
- E $122 \div 0.8$ F 2.9×3.59

(b) Solve. Check whether your answer is reasonable.
- A There are 4.9 g of protein in a cookie. How many grams are in a box of 48 cookies?
- B The following equipment is purchased for the Badminton Club.
  8 rackets at $6.19 per racket
  24 birds at 3 birds for $2.89
  Calculate the approximate cost.

Consumer Tip: Working With Metric

The metric system is a convenient method of measurement because, like the decimal system, it is based on tens. To use the metric system, you need to know

▶ the base units shown in the chart.

Base Units		
Quantity	Unit	Symbol
Length	metre	m
Volume	litre	L
Mass	gram	g

▶ the prefixes shown in the chart.

Prefix	Meaning
kilo	1000
hecto	100
deca	10
deci	0.1
centi	0.01
milli	0.001

The common units for measuring distance are

kilometre	metre	centimetre	millimetre
1 km = 1000 m	m	1 cm = 0.01 m 100 cm = 1 m	1 mm = 0.001 m 1000 mm = 1 m

The common units for measuring mass are

kilogram	gram	milligram
1 kg = 1000 g	g	1 mg = 0.001 g 1000 mg = 1 g

The common units for measuring volume are

kilolitre	litre	millilitre
1 kL = 1000 L	L	1 mL = 0.001 L 1000 mL = 1 L

Written Exercises

1. Write each measure in metres.
   (a) 4 km
   (b) 165 cm
   (c) 23 mm
   (d) 0.36 km
   (e) 16.2 cm
   (f) 169 mm

2. Write each measure in grams.
   (a) 6 kg
   (b) 128 mg
   (c) 4.6 kg
   (d) 1685 mg
   (e) 0.95 kg
   (f) 4 mg

3. Write each measure in litres.
   (a) 3 kL
   (b) 1126 mL
   (c) 6.3 kL
   (d) 486 mL
   (e) 363 mL
   (f) 0.5 kL

4. Find the missing values.
   (a) 1.2 m = ▯ cm
   (b) ▯ mL = 4.2 L
   (c) 128 g = ▯ kg
   (d) ▯ cm = 1.68 m
   (e) 4.1 km = ▯ m
   (f) ▯ mg = 3.6 g
   (g) 1.6 kL = ▯ L
   (h) ▯ mL = 6.8 L
   (i) 196 cm = ▯ mm
   (j) ▯ g = 19.1 kg
   (k) 169 m = ▯ km
   (l) ▯ L = 1936 mL

Applications and Skills: Measurement

measurement, perimeter, area, volume, surface area, applications and problem-solving

Introduction

Problems involving measurement arise in many different situations.

You might want to measure the width of the canyon. How long would the bridge be?

To construct this city, measurement was used to answer questions about,

How long?   How wide?   How much?
How much time?   How heavy?

and so on. Do you know what city it is?

2.1 Skills With Perimeter

Before you install a fence, you have to know how much fencing you need. To calculate the amount of fence needed, measure the distance, called the **perimeter**.

Top view of property

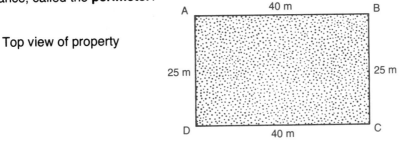

The perimeter of a property is the distance around the property. In the diagram above, this is given by

40 m + 25 m + 40 m + 25 m = 130 m

Example 1

The cost of fencing is $8.92/m. Calculate the cost of the fence required for the above property.

Solution

Perimeter of property is 130 m.
  1 m of fence costs $8.92
  130 m of fence costs
  130 × $8.92 = $1159.60.
Thus, the cost of the fence for the property is $1159.60

If you were really fencing the property, you would also need to get a price for the fence posts.

Example 2

Calculate the perimeter for each of the following.

(a) (b)

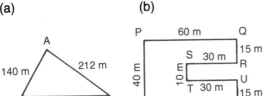

Solution

(a) The perimeter is the distance around.
   Distance around △ABC is
   140 m + 212 m + 246 m = 598 m.
   The perimeter is 598 m. *Be sure to make a final statement.*

(b) The perimeter is the distance around.
   Distance around shape PQRSTUVW is
   60 m + 15 m + 30 m+10 m + 30 m
   + 15 m + 60 m + 40 m = 260 m.
   The perimeter is 260 m.

A diagram may be used to help calculate the amount of fence needed around a pool.

Example 3

(a) Find the perimeter of the pool area ABCD.
(b) Calculate the cost of enclosing the pool if fencing costs $5.25/m.

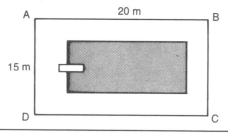

Solution

(a) Distance around the pool is
20 m + 15 m + 20 m + 15 m = 70 m
Perimeter of pool area is 70 m.

(b) 1 m of fencing costs $5.25.
70 m of fencing cost 70 × 5.25 = $367.50.
Cost of enclosing the pool with fencing is $367.50.

Try These

What is the perimeter of each figure? The length of 1 side of each square represents 1 m.

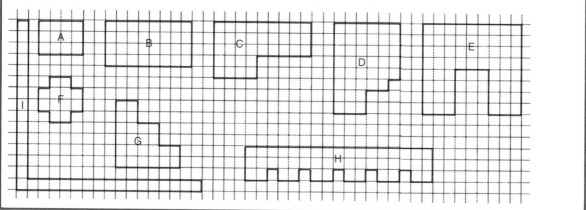

Written Exercises

A 1 Calculate the perimeter of each figure.

2 Which figure has the greatest perimeter?

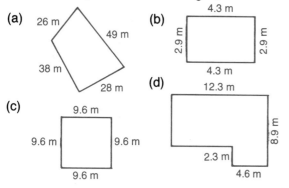

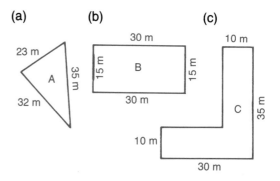

3 The perimeter of each figure is shown. Find the measure of the missing side.

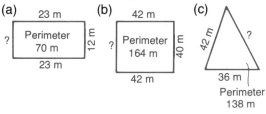

(a) 23 m · Perimeter 70 m · ? · 12 m · 23 m

(b) 42 m · Perimeter 164 m · ? · 42 m

(c) 42 m · ? · 40 m · 36 m · Perimeter 138 m

4 For each figure,
  • find the missing sides.
  • find the perimeter.

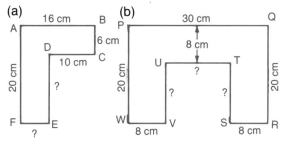

(a) 16 cm · A · B · D · 6 cm · C · 10 cm · 20 cm · ? · F · ? · E

(b) P · 30 cm · Q · 8 cm · U · T · 20 cm · ? · ? · ? · W · 8 cm · V · S · 8 cm · R · 20 cm

B 5 Find each missing side, then calculate the perimeter. All sides are measured in centimetres.

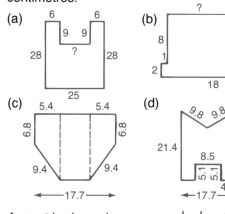

(a) 6 · 6 · 9 · 9 · 28 · ? · 28 · 25

(b) ? · 8 · 8 · 1 · 6 · 2 · 18 · 2

(c) 5.4 · 5.4 · 6.8 · 6.8 · 9.4 · 9.4 · ←17.7→

(d) 9.8 · 9.8 · 21.4 · 21.4 · 8.5 · 5.1 · 5.1 · 4.6 · ←17.7→

6 A court is shown in the diagram.
  (a) Calculate the perimeter.
  (b) What is the cost of placing a railing around the court if railing costs $6.29/m?

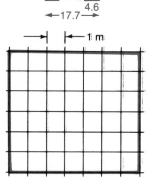

|← 1 m

7. The path walked in a golf game is shown on the diagram.
  (a) Calculate the distance.
  (b) How long will it take you to walk the course if you walk at a rate of 5 km/h?

  Each unit represents 100 m.

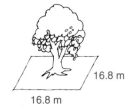

8 Find the perimeter of a rectangular swimming pool if it is 12.4 m long and 5.6 m wide.

9 Find the perimeter of a square courtyard if each side measures 16.8 m.

16.8 m · 16.8 m

10 A rectangular Japanese garden is 27.4 m by 43.5 m.
  (a) Calculate the perimeter.
  (b) Calculate the cost of placing a low decorative fence around it if fencing costs $2.69/m.

C 11 The perimeter of a square is 141 m. Find the length of one side of the square.

12 The amount of fencing needed for a square vegetable garden is 17.6 m. Find the length of one side of the square garden.

13 A triangular rose garden has two sides that measure 4.84 m each. The perimeter measures 14.56 m. Calculate the measure of the remaining side.

14 The side of a rectangle measures 17.1 m. The perimeter is 45.9 m. Calculate the measures of the other 3 sides.

Applications: Maps And Perimeter

The distance between 3 cities can be measured.

Charlottetown to Sydney	4.8 cm
Sydney to New Glasgow	4.1 cm
New Glasgow to Charlottetown	1.8 cm
Total	10.7 cm

The total distance
on the map is 10.7 cm.

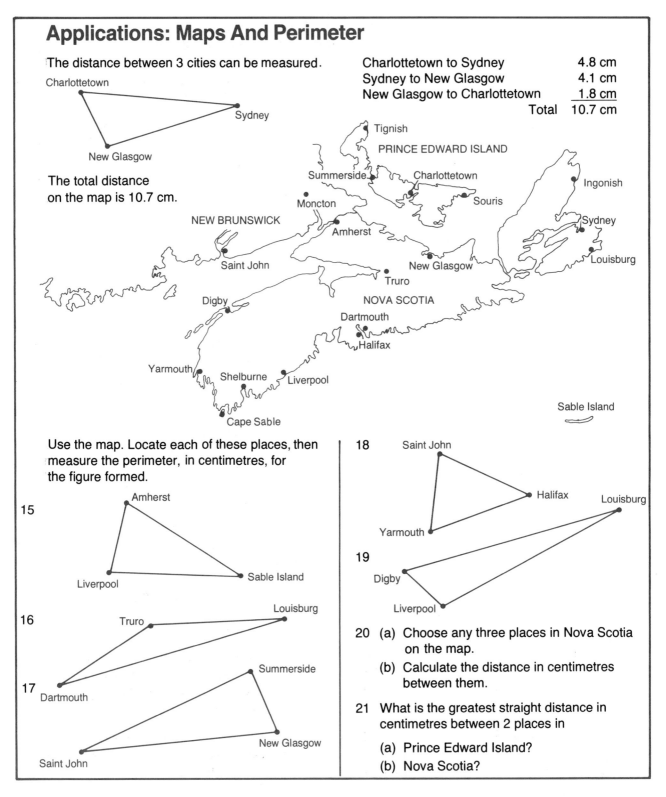

Use the map. Locate each of these places, then measure the perimeter, in centimetres, for the figure formed.

15

16

17

18

19

20 (a) Choose any three places in Nova Scotia on the map.

(b) Calculate the distance in centimetres between them.

21 What is the greatest straight distance in centimetres between 2 places in

(a) Prince Edward Island?

(b) Nova Scotia?

2.2 Working With Area

For each of the following, you need to know how to calculate area.
- cutting the grass
- tiling a floor
- wallpapering a room
- playing sports

The area, A, of the rectangular shape can be calculated by using the formula

$$A = l \times w$$

area   length   width

$$A = 6 \times 4$$
$$= 24$$

cm² means
square centimetres

The area is 24 cm².

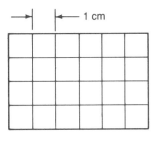
1 cm

Example 1

The dimensions of a field on a sod farm are shown.

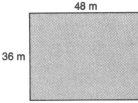
48 m
36 m

(a) Calculate the area of the field.

(b) If the cost of ploughing the field is 7.5¢/m², calculate the total cost of ploughing the field.

Solution

(a) Area of the field is given by
$$A = l \times w$$
$$A = 48 \times 36$$
$$= 1728$$
The area is 1728 m².

m² means
square metres

(b) 1 m² costs 7.5¢
1728 m² cost 1728 × 7.5¢ = $129.60
Thus, the total cost is $129.60.

Remember to make a final statement when answering a problem.

Example 2

The dimensions of a square stamp are shown.

2.4 cm
2.4 cm

PRODUTIVIDADE

PORTUGAL 1.00

(a) Calculate the area of a stamp to 1 decimal place.

(b) The total area of stamps used to mail a parcel is about 105 cm². About how many stamps were used?

Solution

(a) The area of the stamp is given by
$$A = l \times w.$$
$$A = 2.4 \times 2.4$$
$$= 5.76$$
The area of 1 stamp is 5.8 cm².

(b) Area of sheet is 105 cm².
Area of 1 stamp is 5.8 cm².

$$\text{Number of stamps} = \frac{105}{5.8}$$

area of sheet
area of 1 stamp

$$= 18.1$$
to 1 decimal place

The number of stamps used is about 18.

Remember, always to check whether your answer is reasonable.

Try These

1 Calculate the area of each of the following.

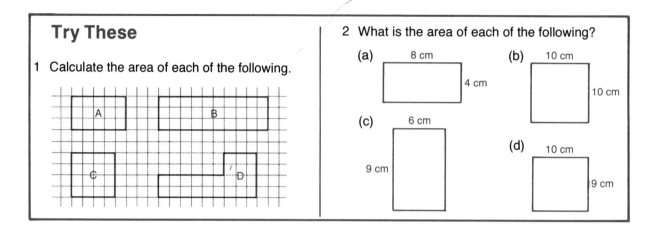

2 What is the area of each of the following?

(a)
8 cm
4 cm

(b)
10 cm
10 cm

(c)
6 cm
9 cm

(d)
10 cm
9 cm

Written Exercises

A 1 Calculate the area of each of the following.

(a)
30 cm
12 cm

(b)
24 cm
24 cm

(c)
40 m
32 m

2 Find the area of each piece of land. Round off your answer to the nearest square metre (m²).

(a)
47.5 m
87.5 m

(b)
69.2 m
16.5 m

(c)
22.3 m
22.3 m

3 The dimensions of each stamp are shown. Calculate the area of each stamp.

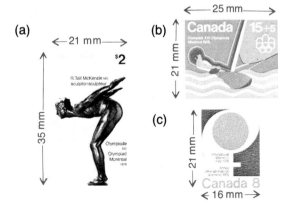

(a)
←21 mm→
$2
R. Tait McKenzie MD
sculptor/sculpteur
35 mm
Olympisde
XXI
Olympiad
Montreal
1976

(b)
←25 mm→
Canada 15+5
Olympiad XXI Olympics
Montreal 1976
21 mm

(c)
21 mm
International
Women's
Year 1975
Année
internationale
de la femme 1975
Canada 8
←16 mm→

4 The length and width of rectangular pieces of land are given in the chart. Calculate each area to 1 decimal place.

	length	width
A	7.9 m	4.2 m
B	3.54 km	8.96 km
C	16.7 m	24.9 m
D	341.4 m	148.7 m

← Check whether your answer is reasonable.

Express your answers in Questions 5 to 10 to 1 decimal place.

B 5 Calculate the area of a rectangular floor with sides 5.3 m by 4.6 m.

6 Rose's square yard has sides 8.5 m. Calculate its area.

7 The dimension of a rectangular ice rink are 10.8 m by 24.5 m.
(a) Find the area of the rink to the nearest tenth of a square metre.
(b) Calculate the cost of making ice at $7.95/m².

8 Jim bought a component stereo. The base of each of the two speakers is 40 cm long and 35 cm wide. His amplifier measures 93 cm long and 48 cm wide. What total area do the three pieces cover?

48

C 9 Three equal rectangular areas are to be painted on an airfield strip. The length of each is to be 27.8 m and the width 9.7 m. What total area must be painted?

10 A frozen rectangular lake, 115 m wide and 145 m long is to be used for skating. If half of this lake will be used for pleasure and the other half for hockey, how big will each area be?

Extending Your Work: Area

This figure is made from these rectangles.

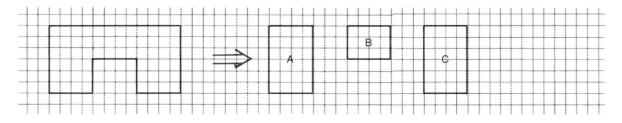

To calculate the area of the whole figure, you calculate the area of parts A, B, and C and then add the 3 areas.

11 Calculate the area of each shape.

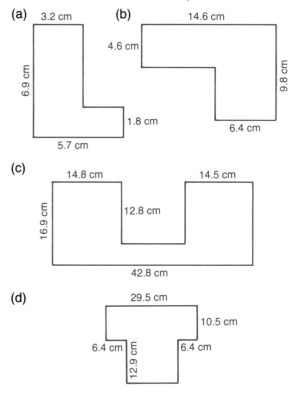

(a)
3.2 cm
6.9 cm
5.7 cm

(b)
14.6 cm
4.6 cm
1.8 cm
6.4 cm
9.8 cm

(c)
14.8 cm
16.9 cm
12.8 cm
14.5 cm
42.8 cm

(d)
29.5 cm
10.5 cm
6.4 cm
12.9 cm
6.4 cm

12 The first floor outline of Jennifer's house is shown.

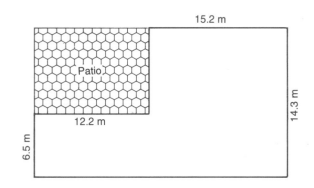

15.2 m
Patio
12.2 m
6.5 m
14.3 m

(a) Calculate the area of the first floor.
(b) Plywood sheets are used for the base of the floor. If plywood costs 8.25/m², calculate the total cost of covering the first floor.

Applications: Baseball Strike Zone

In American League baseball, a pitcher must throw the ball over home plate and between the batter's armpits and knees as shown. The shaded area ABCD is called the **strike zone**. For the baseball player, you may calculate the strike zone.

Distance BC is 78 cm.
Distance DC is 30 cm.
Use $A = l \times w$
$= 78 \times 30$
$= 2340$

The baseball strike zone area is 2340 cm².

For Questions 13-16 assume the width of the home plate is 30 cm.

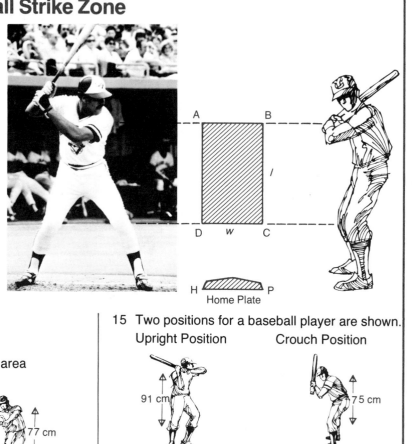

Home Plate

13 Calculate the baseball strike zone area for each player.

(a)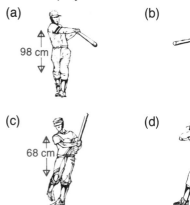
98 cm

(b) 77 cm

(c) 68 cm

(d) 85 cm

14 The dimensions of the strike zone are shown for each player. Calculate its area.

	Player	Dimensions	
		l	*w*
(a)	Joe Stenko	69 cm	30 cm
(b)	Abe Hoffman	82 cm	30 cm
(c)	George Mako	93 cm	30 cm
(d)	Brett Stevens	87 cm	30 cm
(e)	Norm Greg	72 cm	30 cm

15 Two positions for a baseball player are shown.

Upright Position   Crouch Position

91 cm   75 cm

By how much does the area of the strike zone decrease if the above player crouches?

16 Calculate by how much the area of the strike zone decreases if each player crouches as shown.

(a) 84 cm   72 cm

(b)
96 cm   68 cm

2.3 Skills With Volume

All objects occupy space. In the situation pictured below, you need to know how much space is occupied.

These containers are used to ship cargo by boat and then by truck. The manufacturer needs to know the amount of space each one takes up.

The amount of space an object occupies is called its **volume**.

To find the volume of the solids in the above photograph, you need to be able to find the volume of shapes called **rectangular solids** or **prisms**.

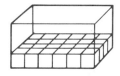

To find a method of computing the volume of this shape, first find how many cubic centimetres are in one layer.

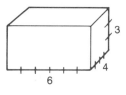

Then find how many cubes are in 3 layers. (Think of the container as being filled with cubes.)

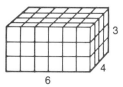

$$\text{Volume} = \overbrace{6 \times 4}^{\text{cubes in 1 layer}} \times \overset{\text{3 layers}}{3} \text{ cubic centimetres}$$

length width height

$$= \underline{72 \text{ cubic centimetres}}$$

You write 72 cm³.

Other examples provide a method of
calculating the volume of any rectangular solid.
Volume = length × width × height

$$V = l \times w \times h$$

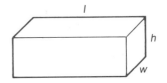

Example

Find the volume of the bin.

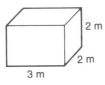

2 m
2 m
3 m

Solution

length = 3 m, width = 2 m, height = 2 m

Volume = length × width × height   Record the
= 3 × 2 × 2   information
= 12   you know.

The volume of this bin is 12 m³.

Make a final statement to answer the question.

You may also combine your earlier skills with computation to solve
some problems about volume.

This relationship is often used to relate litres in terms of cubic
centimetres.

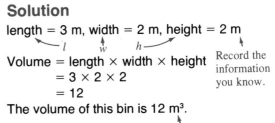

10 cm
10 cm
10 cm

1 L is the volume of
a box which measures
10 cm by 10 cm by 10 cm.

Thus,
1 L = 1000 cm³ or 1 mL = 1 cm³.

You will use this relationship to
answer problems.

Try These

1 What is the volume of each box? What
pattern do you see?

(a)   (b)   (c)

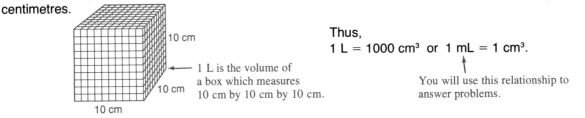

1 cm

(d)   (e)   (f)

2 What is the volume of this box?

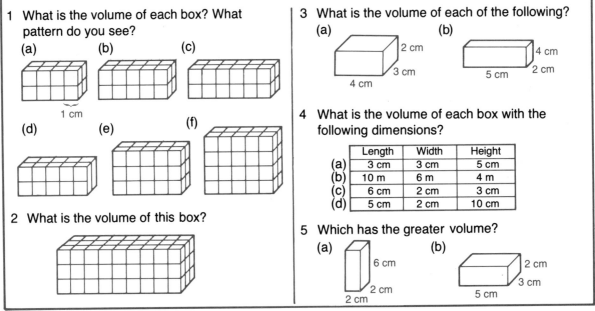

3 What is the volume of each of the following?

(a)   (b)

2 cm
3 cm
4 cm

4 cm
2 cm
5 cm

4 What is the volume of each box with the
following dimensions?

	Length	Width	Height
(a)	3 cm	3 cm	5 cm
(b)	10 m	6 m	4 m
(c)	6 cm	2 cm	3 cm
(d)	5 cm	2 cm	10 cm

5 Which has the greater volume?

(a)   (b)

6 cm
2 cm
2 cm

2 cm
3 cm
5 cm

52

Written Exercises

In the following questions, round off your answers when necessary to 1 decimal place.

A 1 Calculate the volume of each rectangular solid.

(a)

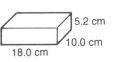
6 cm, 3 cm, 2 cm

(b)

10 cm, 8 cm, 4 cm

2 Find the volume of each box.

(a)

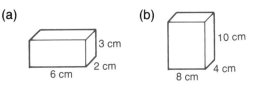
5.2 cm, 10.0 cm, 18.0 cm

(b)

10.5 cm, 6.4 cm, 6.4 cm

3 Calculate the volume for each rectangular solid.

(a)

2.2 m, 3.6 m, 5.4 m

(b)

6.0 m, 4.5 m, 4.6 m

4 Which has the greater volume, A or B?

(a)

A: 16 cm, 14 cm, 21 cm

B: 28 cm, 12 cm, 15 cm

(b)

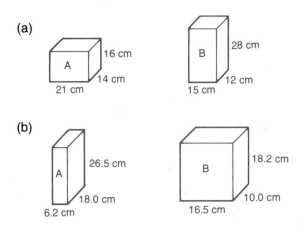

A: 26.5 cm, 18.0 cm, 6.2 cm

B: 18.2 cm, 10.0 cm, 16.5 cm

5 The measurements of various common items are shown. Find the volume of each box.

(a) (b)

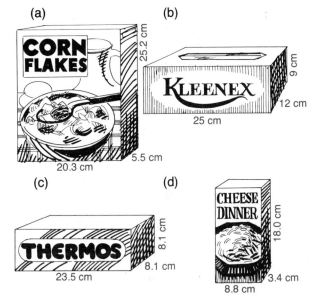

CORN FLAKES — 25.2 cm, 20.3 cm, 5.5 cm

KLEENEX — 9 cm, 12 cm, 25 cm

(c) (d)

THERMOS — 8.1 cm, 8.1 cm, 23.5 cm

CHEESE DINNER — 18.0 cm, 3.4 cm, 8.8 cm

6 The length, width, and height of some box sizes are given. Calculate the volume of each box.

	Length	Width	Height
(a)	6 cm	10 cm	15 cm
(b)	6 cm	8 cm	20 cm
(c)	10 cm	10 cm	8 cm
(d)	30 cm	25 cm	10 cm

7 The length, width, and height are given for rectangular solids. Calculate each volume.

	Length	Width	Height
(a)	2.5 m	5.38 m	9.25 m
(b)	5.6 m	3.84 m	10.2 m
(c)	8.7 m	6.41 m	14.8 m
(d)	1.9 m	9.25 m	18.7 m
(e)	10.4 m	8.50 m	6.32 m

8 Calculate each volume. Check whether your answer is reasonable.

(a) 93 cm by 51 cm by 20 cm

(b) 85 cm by 69 cm by 28 cm

(c) 24.6 cm by 16.1 cm by 9.8 cm

(d) 45.8 cm by 30.2 cm by 24.1 cm

B 9 How many cubic metres of sand will the truck hold?

10 The base of a rectangular feed bin measures 10.8 m by 3.9 m. The depth of the bin is 1.7 m. Calculate how much the bin will hold (to 1 decimal place).

11 A rectangular bin has dimensions 2 m by 3 m by 4 m and contains salt and sand. After a snowfall, 20 m³ are used on the roads. How much sand and salt is left?

12 A bale of hay is 1.5 m long, 0.8 m wide, and 1.4 m high. How much hay is there?

13 Each container contains 4.5 m³ of rubbish.

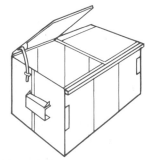

There are 10 containers at an apartment site. If the truck has a closed trailer with dimensions 4.5 m by 2.5 m by 2 m, how many trips will it take to haul away the rubbish?

14 An aquarium is 180 cm by 150 cm by 70 cm.
   (a) What is its volume?
   (b) How many litres of water will it hold?
   (c) A goldfish requires about 1000 cm³ of space to survive. How many goldfish can this aquarium hold?

15 Before an ice surface is safe an area of 75.1 m long and 74.8 m wide must be frozen to a depth of 18 cm. How much water is frozen?

16 A speaker has dimensions 30 cm by 90 cm and 20 cm deep. What is its volume?

17 The measurements for two similar boxes of facial tissues are shown below.
   (a)   (b)

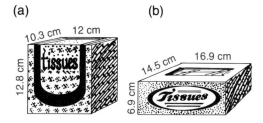

Which box can contain more? By how much?

18 Find the volume of water in each tank.
   (a)   (b)

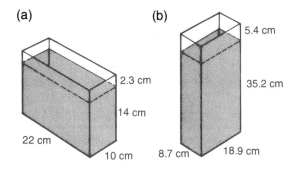

C 19 An aquarium is 42.8 cm long, 19.5 cm wide, and 15.2 cm deep.
   (a) Calculate how many litres of water the tank will hold when full.
   (b) The tank above is filled so that the water is 4.7 cm from the top. Calculate how much water is in the tank.

Extending Your Work

20 To calculate the volume of this solid, you may think of 2 rectangular solids.

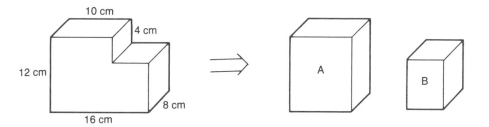

(a) Calculate the volume of rectangular solid A.

(b) Calculate the volume of rectangular solid B.

(c) What is the volume of the original shape?

21 Calculate the volume of each solid.

(a) (b)

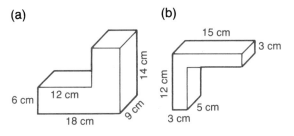

22 Calculate the volume of each solid to 1 decimal place.

(a) (b)

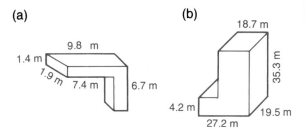

23 Calculate the volume of bronze needed to construct the solid base for a sculpture.

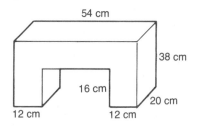

24 Calculate the volume of the apartment complex. A courtyard is in the middle.

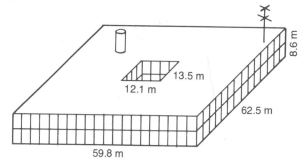

Applications: Business And Volume

In business, the amount of space used is very important. For example, in the warehouse, the amount of space available for storage is important.

25 The dimensions of each carton in the above photograph are 0.5 m by 0.3 m and 1.5 m high. There are 43 cartons altogether. What is the total volume of the stock?

26 The truck has the shown dimensions. Calculate the volume available for storage.

27 Calculate the volume of each of the following.

(a)
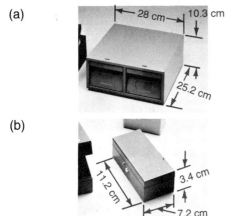

(b)

28 The container on a water cooler is rectangular in shape with measurements 58 cm × 34 cm × 34 cm.

(a) What volume of water does it hold?

(b) Each person in the office consumes 0.5 L/d. How many persons will the container service?

29 The baskets on each level of the mail cart are shown.

(a) Calculate the volume of each basket.

(b) The space available on the mail cart is more than your answer in (a). Explain.

30 An expanding file has a maximum width of 10 cm. The dimensions of each side are 38 cm by 23 cm. What is the maximum volume?

2.4 Understanding Surface Area

Manufacturers must be able to calculate how much cardboard or paper is needed to construct boxes. The size and shape of a box depends on how the box will be used. For example:

To find the surface area of a box, you may unfold it.

Certain faces of the box are the same shape and size. For the above box
there are 2 faces like A.
there are 2 faces like B.
there are 2 faces like C.

You call this shape the **net** of the box.

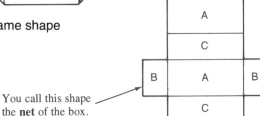

The **surface area** of the box, is the total area of all the faces (or sides) of the box (2 of A, 2 of B, 2 of C).

Example

Calculate the surface area of the box.

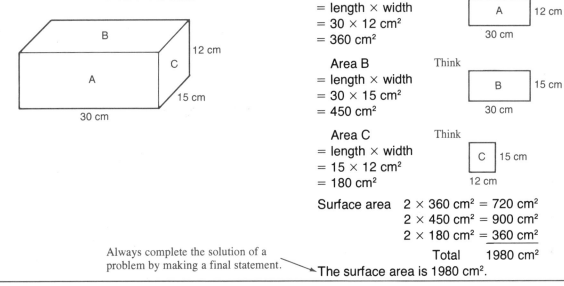

Solution

Area A
= length × width
= 30 × 12 cm²
= 360 cm²

Think

| A | 12 cm |
30 cm

Area B
= length × width
= 30 × 15 cm²
= 450 cm²

Think

| B | 15 cm |
30 cm

Area C
= length × width
= 15 × 12 cm²
= 180 cm²

Think

| C | 15 cm |
12 cm

Surface area   2 × 360 cm² = 720 cm²
2 × 450 cm² = 900 cm²
2 × 180 cm² = 360 cm²
Total   1980 cm²

Always complete the solution of a problem by making a final statement.
The surface area is 1980 cm².

Try These

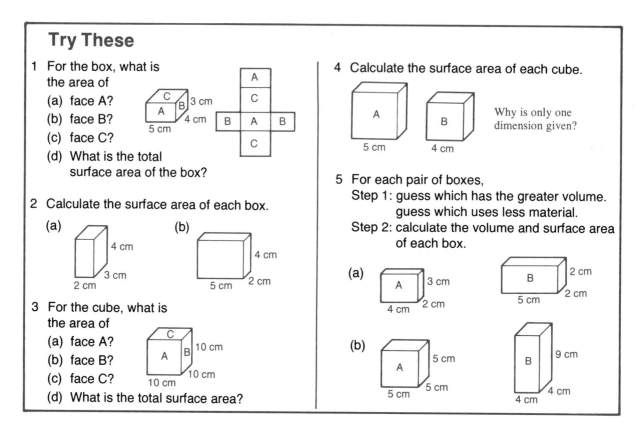

1 For the box, what is the area of
   (a) face A?
   (b) face B?
   (c) face C?
   (d) What is the total surface area of the box?

2 Calculate the surface area of each box.
   (a)
   4 cm
   3 cm
   2 cm
   (b)
   4 cm
   5 cm
   2 cm

3 For the cube, what is the area of
   (a) face A?
   (b) face B?
   (c) face C?
   (d) What is the total surface area?

   10 cm
   10 cm
   10 cm

4 Calculate the surface area of each cube.
   A
   5 cm
   B
   4 cm
   Why is only one dimension given?

5 For each pair of boxes,
   Step 1: guess which has the greater volume.
             guess which uses less material.
   Step 2: calculate the volume and surface area of each box.
   (a)
   A
   3 cm
   4 cm
   2 cm
   B
   2 cm
   5 cm
   2 cm
   (b)
   A
   5 cm
   5 cm
   5 cm
   B
   9 cm
   4 cm
   4 cm

Written Exercises

For each of the following questions, round off your answers when necessary to 1 decimal place. Draw a net of the various solids to aid your work in calculating the surface area.

A 1 Calculate the surface area of each of the following.
   (a)
   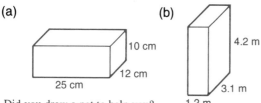
   10 cm
   12 cm
   25 cm
   Did you draw a net to help you?
   (b)
   4.2 m
   3.1 m
   1.2 m

2 Find the surface area of the cube.

   30 cm

B 3 (a) Calculate the surface area of the box.
      (b) What is the volume of the box?

   1.2 m
   0.8 m
   0.5 m

4 Calculate the surface area of each container.

   50 cm
   12 cm
   33 cm
   38 cm
   45 cm
   16 cm

5 To understand the steps in solving a problem, it is often helpful to draw a diagram. A box and its net are shown.

(a) Calculate the area of the ends of the box.

(b) Calculate the surface area of the box.

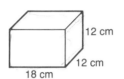

6 (a) Draw the net of the box shown.

(b) Calculate the surface area.

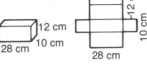

7 Draw the net for each rectangular solid, then calculate its surface area.

(a)   (b)   (c)

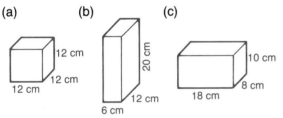

8 The dimensions of a box are

18.5 cm by 12.2 cm by 10.0 cm.
| | |
length   width   height or depth

(a) Calculate the surface area of the box.

(b) Calculate the volume of the box.

9 (a) Which box has the greater surface area?

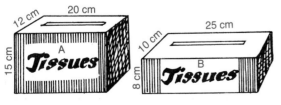

(b) Which box holds more?

10 (a) Calculate the amount of glass needed to construct the aquarium.

(b) What is the volume of the aquarium?

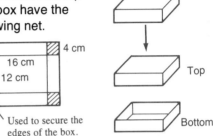

11 The bottom and top of a box have the following net.

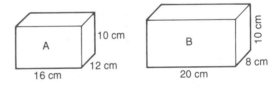

Used to secure the edges of the box.

(a) Calculate the amount of paper used to make the box.

(b) What is the volume of the box?

(c) How much paper is used to secure the sides of the box?

12 (a) Estimate which box holds more.

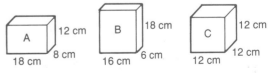

(b) Calculate the volume of each box. Compare your answer with your estimate in (a).

(c) Which box uses more material?

C

13 (a) Calculate the volume of each box. What do you notice?

(b) Calculate the surface area of each box.

(c) Which box uses the least amount of material?

59

Applications: Consumer Packaging

In order to make it easier to stack an irregular shaped item on a shelf, the manufacturer often packages the item in a rectangular box. Often an item such as a radio is first packed in a styrofoam jacket for protection and then the radio and styrofoam jacket are packed in a rectangular box.

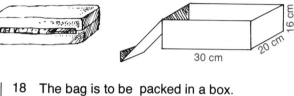

15 (a) Calculate the volume of the radio above.

(b) Calculate the volume of the box above.

(c) By how much do the answers in (a) and (b) differ? Why is this so?

16 Use the photograph at right.

(a) What are the dimensions of the box required to ship the hamper.

(b) What is the surface area of the box?

17 A box is used to ship the rocking chair.

(a) What are the dimensions of the required box?

(b) What is the surface area of the box?

18 The bag is to be packed in a box.

(a) What are the dimensions of the box?

(b) What is the total surface area of the box?

19 (a) Which box appears to have the greater volume?

(b) Calculate the volume of each box.

(c) Which box uses less material?

(d) Box A uses less material than box B, but contains more. Why would a manufacturer do this?

2.5 Problem Solving: Using Clue Words

When you are solving a problem, you must first answer two important questions.

> I What information am I given?
> II What information am I asked to find?

When you are deciding which method to use to solve the problem, you must look for important clue words in the problem to help you. For example, what are the *important* clue words in the following problem, which would help you solve the problem?

Problem

For fire protection, a sprinkler system is to be placed on the apartment floor. Calculate the amount of piping used in the diagram.

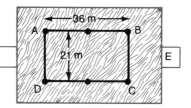

Clue Words

"Calculate" means you need to decide which operation to use. "Amount of pipe" in the problem suggests that you calculate the *distance around* the figure ABCD. In calculating the distance around, you are *actually* calculating the perimeter of ABCD. However, the problem did not say "find the perimeter". Thus you must correctly *interpret* the *clue word* to decide which skill and which operation is needed to find the answer to the problem.

Use the *Steps For Solving Problems* below to organize your work.

Steps For Solving Problems.	
Step A	Understand the problem.
Step B	Decide on a method.
Step C	Find the answer.
Step D	Check your answer.
Step E	Make a final statement.

Think
I What am I given?
II What am I asked to find?
Are there any clue words?
Which skills do I need?
Is my answer reasonable?
Have I used the correct units?

Try These

1 What operation is suggested by each clue word?

   (a) total   (b) add   (c) increase
   (d) difference   (e) share   (f) amount
   (g) decrease   (h) exceed   (i) in all
   (j) half-full   (k) more than   (l) perimeter
   (m) area   (n) volume   (o) average

2 Which of the following, perimeter (*P*), area (*A*), or volume (*V*), is suggested by each of the following?

   (a) wallpaper needed   (b) distance around
   (c) amount of water   (d) tiles for a floor
   (e) how much fencing   (f) soil in a trench
   (g) tank of oil   (h) amount of cereal
   (i) sugar in box   (j) gift wrapping paper

Written Exercises

For each of the following problems,
- ▶ look for clue words to help you decide which skills you need to use to solve the problem.
- ▶ then, organize your work. (Refer to the *Steps For Solving Problems*, page 61).

A 1 A new park is 88 m × 72 m. Sod costs $1.10/m². Calculate the total cost of sodding the park.

2 A square swimming pool has sides that measure 10 m. If the pool is 1.2 m deep, how much water is required to fill the pool?

3 A rectangular field is 150 m by 120 m.
   (a) Find the area.
   (b) How much fencing is needed to enclose the field?

B 4 To place the pipe underground a rectangular trench is dug. The dimensions of the trench are 1.9 m by 1.9 m, and 150 m long.

   (a) How much soil is removed?
   (b) A truck can transport 9.2 m³ of soil at one time. How many truck loads will be required?

5 A cubical tank for storing syrup has sides measuring 1.2 m. What volume of syrup is in the tank if the tank is half full?

6 Jean has two cartons. One has dimensions 20 cm by 15 cm by 12 cm. The other has dimensions 15 cm by 12 cm by 10 cm.
   (a) The contents of the smaller carton are poured into the larger carton. How much space is still available in the larger carton?
   (b) How many times could the contents of the smaller carton be poured into the larger carton?

7 A sugar box is shown.

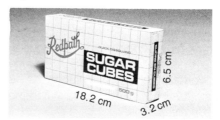

   (a) Find the volume of the sugar box.
   (b) If a sugar cube is 1.5 cm by 1.5 cm by 1.5 cm, find how many sugar cubes there are in the box.
   (c) What assumption do you make in finding your answer in (b)?

8 A floor is 8.2 m × 7.4 m. It costs $10 to tile 0.6 m² of the floor. How much will it cost to tile this floor?

9 A mirror is in the shape as shown in the diagram.

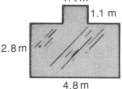

   (a) Calculate the amount of moulding needed to be placed around the edge of the mirror.
   (b) Calculate the area of the mirror.

10 A tape recorder measures 20 cm by 25 cm by 12 cm. Manufacturers place a 2-cm thick piece of insulation around the tape recorder for shipping. Find the volume of the smallest carton that can be used to ship the tape recorder.

11 A mine shaft has dimensions 4.2 m by 3.1 m and is 2 km deep. What is the volume of the shaft?

12 A sidewalk of uniform width around a parking lot is shown in the diagram.

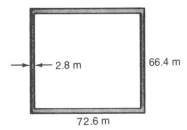

2.8 m   66.4 m

72.6 m

How much does it cost to install cobblestone on the walk if it costs $3.80/m²?

13 The measurements of the sides of the solar panel on the roof of a house are shown.

0.69 m

6.1 m

(a) What is the area of each section of the solar panel?
(b) Calculate the total area of the solar panel?

14 How much paint is needed to give 2 coats of paint to the walls of a room with dimensions 5.2 m by 3.8 m and 2.5 m high if paint covers 7.5 m²/L?

15 The container of a dump truck has dimensions 4.5 m by 2 m by 2 m. How many trips would it need to haul 90 m³ of backfill?

C16 (a) What are the dimensions of a box used to ship the stacking tables shown?

83 cm

28 cm   64 cm

(b) The box in (a) is covered with wrapping paper. How much paper is needed?

Use the farm plan to answer the following questions.

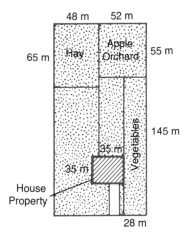

48 m   52 m

65 m   Hay   Apple Orchard   55 m

145 m

35 m

35 m

Vegetables

House Property

28 m

17 Calculate the area of the apple orchard.

18 The cost of fertilizing a vegetable garden is 63¢/m². Calculate the total cost.

19 A fence is placed around the property of the house.
(a) How much fence is needed?
(b) What is the total cost if fencing, supplied and installed, costs $9.80/m?

20 Each apple tree requires 25 m² of space.

   (a) Calculate the number of apple trees in the orchard.

   (b) On the average, each tree provides 300 kg of apples. What is the total amount obtained?

Skylights come in the following sizes. The dimensions are shown.

Overall Wood Frame, width × height

9	550 × 700 mm	4	1140 × 1180 mm
6	550 × 980 mm	7	1340 × 980 mm
1	780 × 980 mm	3	940 × 1600 mm
5	700 × 1180 mm	8	1340 × 1400 mm
2	780 × 1400 mm		

21 Calculate the area of each skylight.

   (a) 1   (b) 4   (c) 6

22 Which of the following pairs of skylights provides more light?

   (a) 3 or 8   (b) 1 or 5   (c) 2 or 5

23 (a) Estimate which skylight has the greater area,
      4, 3 or 7.

   (b) Calculate which skylight has the greater area.

   (c) How do your answers in (a) and (b) compare?

24 The haulage part of the transport truck is shown.

Calculate the volume of the haulage part of the truck.

25 The delivery cost for short trips is $9.65/m³. How much will it cost to transport each container?

   (a)   (b)

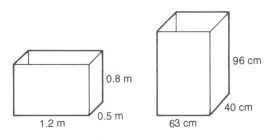

26 (a) The transport truck in Question 24 is packed full. How much money will be earned for a short haul?

   (b) The expenses for the trip and costs of operating the truck are $183.50. How much profit is made?

Skills To Practise: A Chapter Review

2.1 The sides of a triangle measure 27.3 cm, 42.5 cm, and 38.9 cm. Find the perimeter.

2.2 Calculate the area of each of the following.

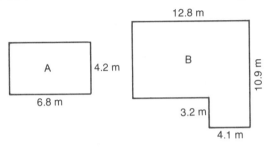

2.3 Calculate the volume.

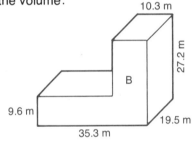

2.4 Calculate the surface area of each of the following rectangular solids.

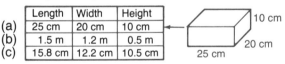

	Length	Width	Height
(a)	25 cm	20 cm	10 cm
(b)	1.5 m	1.2 m	0.5 m
(c)	15.8 cm	12.2 cm	10.5 cm

2.5 (a) What operation is suggested by each clue word?

    A quotient   B exceed
    C share   D total

(b) Which of perimeter, (*P*), area (*A*) or volume (*V*) is suggested by each of the following?

    A fence around a field   B filling a gas tank
    C amount of grass to cut   D painting a fence

Problems To Practise: A Chapter Review

2.1 (a) The perimeter of a square is 160 cm. What is the measure of each side?

(b) The amount of fence used to enclose a triangular garden is 32.4 m. If two of the sides measure 16 m and 9.8 m, find the length of the missing side.

2.2 Refer to the Applications on page 50.

(a) At bat, Jerome crouches and lowers his shoulders by 12 cm. By how much does the area of the strike zone decrease?

(b) If Samantha crouches at bat, she lowers her shoulders by 8.5 cm. By how much does the area of her strike zone decrease?

2.3 A top view of the Manadrino home is shown. Asphalt is poured on a driveway to a depth of about 6 cm.

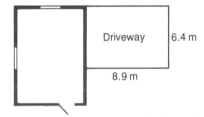

(a) Calculate the amount of asphalt required for the driveway.

(b) Calculate the cost of pouring and paving it if it costs $49.98/m³.

2.4 Calculate the amount of cardboard needed to construct the box and its top.

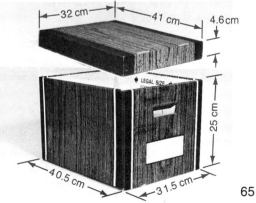

65

Chapter Checkup: A Practice Test

2.1 (a) What is the perimeter of each of the following?

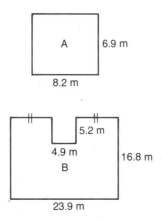

A   6.9 m

8.2 m

5.2 m

4.9 m

B   16.8 m

23.9 m

(b) A rectangular parking lot has one side that measures 82 m. The total amount of fencing around the parking lot is 294 m. Find the lengths of the missing sides.

2.2 The floor plan of a cottage is given. Calculate the area of each room.

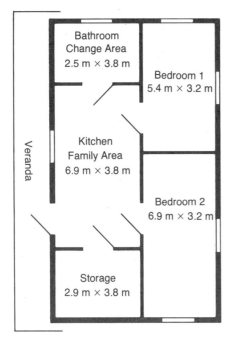

Bathroom Change Area
2.5 m × 3.8 m

Bedroom 1
5.4 m × 3.2 m

Kitchen Family Area
6.9 m × 3.8 m

Bedroom 2
6.9 m × 3.2 m

Veranda

Storage
2.9 m × 3.8 m

2.3 A dump truck has a rectangular trailer with dimensions 4 m by 2 m by 2 m. Half of it is filled with rubbish. How many cubic metres is this?

2.4 The box for chocolates is constructed as shown.

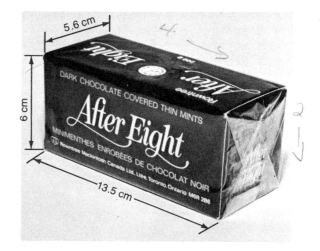

5.6 cm

6 cm

13.5 cm

(a) Draw a net of the box.
(b) How much cardboard is used?
(c) What is the volume of the box?

2.5 (a) What operation(s) is suggested by each clue word?

A total   B increase

C distribute   D more than

(b) Note the clue words in the following problem and solve the problem.

Each team needs 120 m² of space to practise. How many teams can practise on a rectangular field that measures 60 m by 200 m?

3 Applying Skills With Measurement: Circles

working with triangles, parallelograms, prisms, circles, cylinders,
applications and problem-solving

Introduction

The manufacturer is concerned
with how much material is
needed
- to construct a can.
- to make the label for the can.

The food processor is interested
in how much the can holds.

The consumer is concerned with
how much the can holds and
how much it costs.

Every manufacturer and consumer is, at times, concerned with
- area
- volume
- both area and volume

For example, it is important to the manufacturer of sporting goods,
to know how much material is needed to make the items below.

3.1 Area: Triangles and Parallelograms

You often need to be able to calculate the areas of triangular shapes in order to determine how much material to use. The patterns you obtained in your earlier work will help you calculate the areas of these figures.

rectangle

$A = l \times w$

parallelogram

$A = b \times h$

To calculate the area of a parallelogram, you need to know
• the measure of a side (called the base)
• the measure of the height (with respect to the chosen side above).

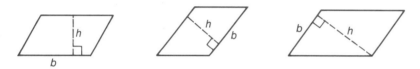

Example 1
Calculate the area of each parallelogram.

(a)

16 cm

21 cm

(b)

16 cm

24 cm

Solution
Use the relationship
Area = base × height

(a) base 21 cm,
   height 16 cm
   Area = 21 × 16
        = 336
   The area is
   336 cm².

(b) base 24 cm,
   height 16 cm
   Area = 24 × 16
        = 384
   The area is
   384 cm².

Area of a Triangle

To calculate the area of a triangle, use the information:
   area of the triangle is half of the area of the related parallelogram.

Area of Parallelogram

Area of Triangle = $\frac{1}{2}$ the area of parallelogram

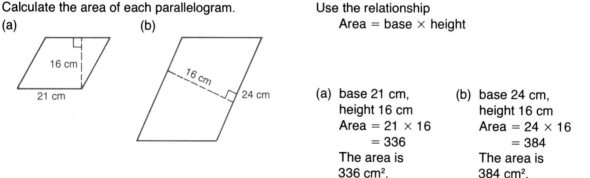

$A = bh$

$A = \frac{1}{2}bh$

To calculate the area of a triangle, you again need to know
- the measure of a side (called the base).
- the measure of the height (with respect to the chosen side above).

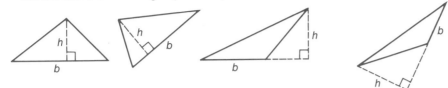

Example 2
Find the area of each triangle.

(a)

(b)

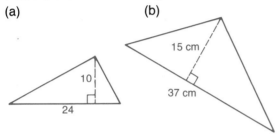

15 cm

37 cm

Solution

(a) $A = \dfrac{1}{2}bh$ $b = 24, h = 10$

$\quad = \dfrac{1}{2}(24)(10)$

$\quad = 120$

The area is 120 square units.

(b) $A = \dfrac{1}{2}bh$ base, b, 37 cm
   height, h, 15 cm

$\quad = \dfrac{1}{2}(37)(15)$

$\quad = (18.5)(15)$

$\quad = 277.5$

The area is 277.5 cm².

Try These

1 Calculate the area of each parallelogram.

(a)   (b) 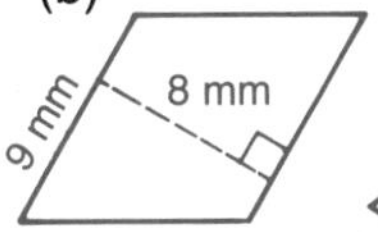   (c)

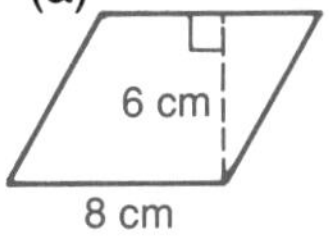

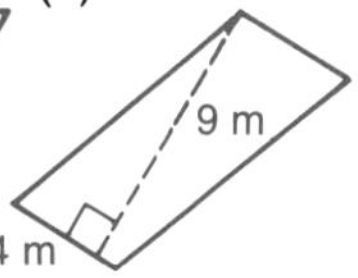

6 cm

8 cm

9 mm   8 mm

9 m

4 m

2 Calculate the area of each triangle.

(a)   (b) 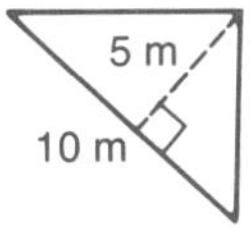   (c)

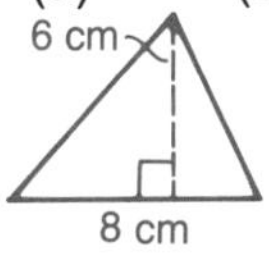

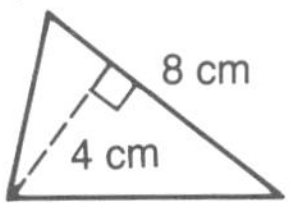

6 cm

8 cm

5 m

10 m

8 cm

4 cm

(d) 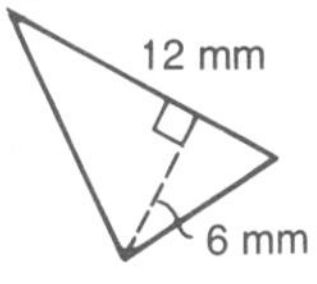   (e) 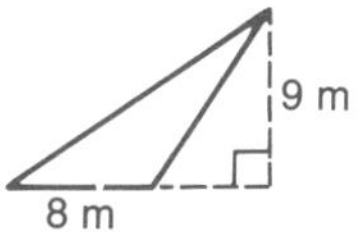   (f)

12 mm

6 mm

9 m

8 m

20 cm

9 cm

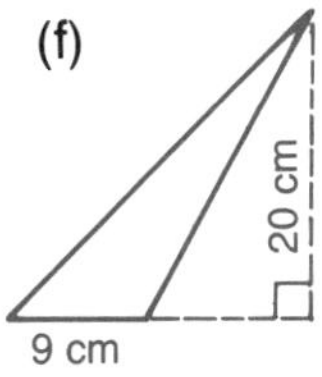

3 What is the area of each figure?

	Figure	Base	Height
(a)	triangle	10 m	9 m
(b)	parallelogram	30 cm	10 cm
(c)	triangle	20 mm	30 mm
(d)	parallelogram	20 m	30 m

4 The base of a parallelogram is 8 m. The height is 9 m. Calculate its area.

5 The height of a triangular shape is 40 cm. The base is 60 cm. Calculate its area.

Written Exercises

Round off answers to 1 decimal place unless indicated otherwise.

A 1 Calculate the area of each parallelogram. Remember $A = bh$.

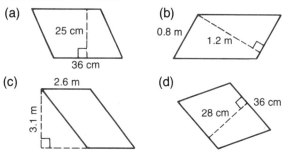

(a) 25 cm, 36 cm

(b) 0.8 m, 1.2 m

(c) 2.6 m, 3.1 m

(d) 28 cm, 36 cm

2 Calculate the area of each parallelogram. Each square represents 1 square unit of area.

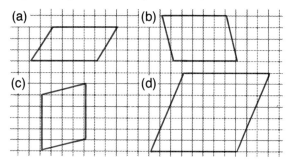

(a)   (b)   (c)   (d)

3 The formula for area, A, of a parallelogram is given by $A = bh$.
Find the area of each of the following parallelograms.

(a) $b = 10, h = 6$ (b) $b = 14, h = 10$
(c) $b = 20, h = 20$ (d) $b = 25, h = 20$
(e) $b = 32, h = 12$ (f) $b = 60, h = 40$

4 Calculate the area of each triangle.

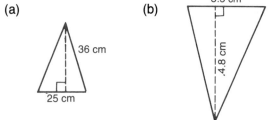

(a) 36 cm, 25 cm

(b) 3.5 cm, 4.8 cm

5 Find the area of each of the following triangles.

(a)   (b)   (c)   (d)   (e)   (f)

6 The formula for the area, A, of a triangle is given by $A = \frac{1}{2} bh$.
Find the area of each of the following triangles.

(a) $b = 14, h = 8$ (b) $b = 20, h = 10$
(c) $b = 25, h = 20$ (d) $b = 28, h = 12$
(e) $b = 34, h = 20$ (f) $b = 50, h = 25$

B 7 Find the area of each of the following.
(a) parallelogram: base 12 cm, height 8.5 cm
(b) rectangle: length 14 cm, width 7.2 cm
(c) triangle: base 1.8 m, height 5.5 m
(d) square: sides 2.5 m
(e) triangle: base 4.5 m, height 3.6 m

8 The height of a parallelogram measures 18 cm and the base is 26 cm. Calculate its area.

9 The base of a triangle is 19 cm. The height is 32 cm. Calculate the area.

10 The base of a parallelogram is 15.4 cm and the height is 7.8 cm. Calculate the area.

11 The altitude of a triangle measures 23.7 cm and the base is 38.4 cm. Calculate the area.

12 The measures of the altitude and base of a triangle are 17.92 m and 11.58 m respectively. Calculate the area to the nearest hundredth.

13 (a) A parallelogram has a base that measures 19 cm and a height of 10 cm. Calculate its area.
   (b) Calculate the area of a rectangle whose sides measure 10 cm and 19 cm.
   (c) Draw a diagram to illustrate the answers in (a) and (b).

14 (a) Calculate the area of the stamp.
   (b) What is the total area of a sheet containing 100 stamps?

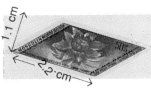

15 Calculate the area of each stamp.
   (a)   (b)

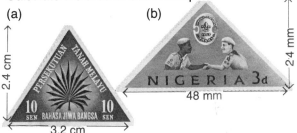

16 Calculate the area of the tail.

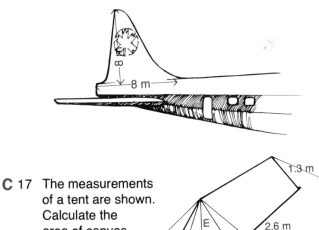

C 17 The measurements of a tent are shown. Calculate the area of canvas needed for the ends of the tent.

To Find the Area of Figures

To calculate the area of figure A, you need to calculate the areas of figures B and C.

4.5 cm

A

4.5 cm

8.9 cm

⟹

4.5 cm

B

4.5 cm

4.5 cm

C

4.5 cm

4.4 cm

8.9 cm − 4.5 cm = 4.4 cm

18 Use the data above. Calculate the area of
   (a) figure B   (b) figure C   (c) figure A

19 Calculate the area of each shaded region.
   (a) 25 cm, 6 cm, 16 cm
   (b) 12 cm, 4 cm 4 cm, 3 cm, 3 cm, 2 cm 16 cm 2 cm, 8 cm

20 Calculate the area of each shaded region.
   (a) 8 cm, 18 cm
   (b) 4.6 m, 5.8 m
   (c) 16.4 m, 3.8 m

21 Calculate the amount of aluminum siding used to cover the side of the house.

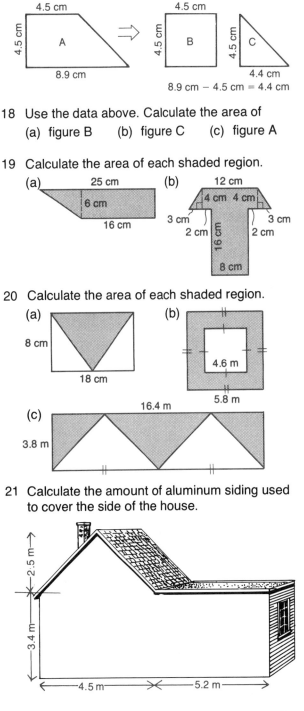

2.5 m, 3.4 m, 4.5 m, 5.2 m

71

22 Cedar wood is used to cover an A-frame cottage.
   (a) Calculate the area of each end.
   (b) Calculate the total area to be covered.

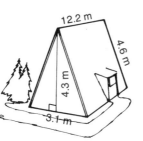

23 The container is made from the net shown.
   (a) Calculate the area of each triangular piece.
   (b) Calculate the total area.

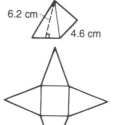

6.2 cm
4.6 cm

24 Calculate the area of the following.

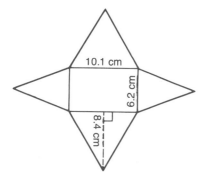

10.1 cm
6.2 cm
8.4 cm

25
   The box lid shown, is constructed from the net shown.
   (a) Calculate the total area of the triangular pieces.
   (b) Calculate the total amount of material used to make a box lid.

4 cm
16 cm
22 cm

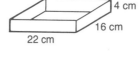

These shapes are used to glue the corners.

Measuring and Area

26 (a) What measurements are needed to calculate the area of this triangle?

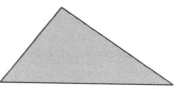

   (b) Make suitable measurements for the triangle and calculate its area.

27 (a) What measurements are needed to calculate the area of this parallelogram?

   (b) Make suitable measurements for the parallelogram and calculate the area.

28 For each figure,
   • make suitable measurements.
   • calculate the shaded area.
   (a)   (b)

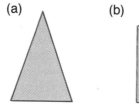

29 For each figure
   • make suitable measurements.
   • calculate the shaded area.
   (a)   (b)

Applications: Sailing

Most modern sailboats are called sloops. They have 2 basic sails, the jib and the mainsail. The leading edge of a sail is called the luff. The trailing edge is called the leech. The area of a sail may be calculated from the measures of the luff and the leech.

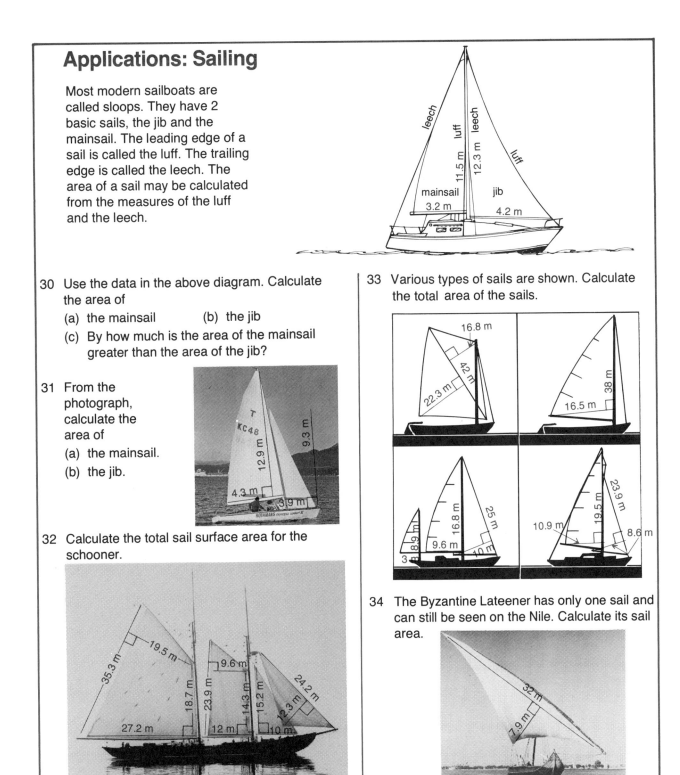

30 Use the data in the above diagram. Calculate the area of
  (a) the mainsail   (b) the jib
  (c) By how much is the area of the mainsail greater than the area of the jib?

31 From the photograph, calculate the area of
  (a) the mainsail.
  (b) the jib.

32 Calculate the total sail surface area for the schooner.

33 Various types of sails are shown. Calculate the total area of the sails.

34 The Byzantine Lateener has only one sail and can still be seen on the Nile. Calculate its sail area.

73

3.2 Working With Prisms

Something you learn in one topic in mathematics may help you to develop skills in other topics.
The *principle* involved in calculating the volume of figure I may be used to show how to calculate the volume of figure II.

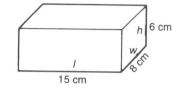

To calculate the volume of water in the tank (rectangular solid, or prism) you may use the formula

$$V = l \times w \times h$$
$$= 15 \times 8 \times 6$$
$$= 720$$

The volume of water is 720 cm³.
The volume can be calculated using another method. The base of the tank has an area, *B*, given by

$$B = l \times w$$

You may now calculate the volume of the rectangular solid as shown.

$$V = B \times h$$

You may use the above method to calculate the area of a triangular prism.

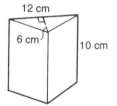

$$\text{Area of triangular base, } B = \frac{1}{2} \times 12 \times 6 \text{ cm}^2$$
$$= 36 \text{ cm}^2$$

Use
$$V = B \times h$$
$$= 36 \times 10$$
$$= 360$$

The volume of the triangular prism is 360 cm³.

Example

A trench for a pipe is dug with dimensions as shown in the diagram. Calculate the volume of earth removed.

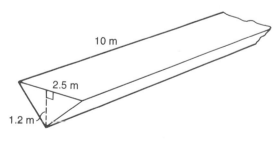

Solution

The trench is a triangular prism.
I Calculate area, *B*, of one end of prism.

$$B = \frac{1}{2} \times b \times h \qquad b = 2.5, h = 1.2$$
$$= \frac{1}{2} \times 2.5 \times 1.2$$
$$= 1.5$$

Area of end (base) of trench is 1.5 m².

II Calculate volume, *V*, of the prism.
$$V = B \times h \qquad A = 1.5, h = 10$$
$$= 1.5 \times 10$$
$$= 15$$

The volume of earth removed is 15 m³.

When calculating volume, the dimensions must be in the same units. To calculate the amount of earth removed from this trench, write 1.2 km as 1200 m.

$V = B \times h$ $B = 1.5, h = 1200$
$ = 1.5 \times 1200$
$ = 1800$

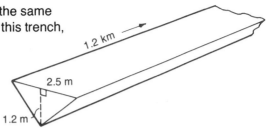

The volume is 1800 m³.

To calculate the volume of any of these prisms,
- calculate the area, B,
- then find the volume, $V = B \times h$.

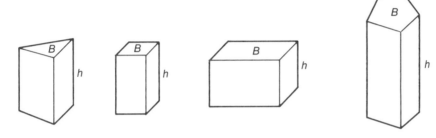

Try These

1 (a) What is the area of the base of each figure?
   (b) Calculate each volume.

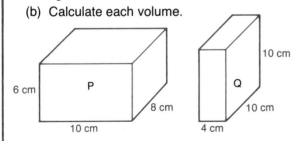

2 Calculate the volume of each prism.
      B, represents area of the base.
      h, represents the height of the prism.

	B, Area	h, height
(a)	6 m²	4 m
(b)	8 cm²	6 cm
(c)	10 m²	12 m

3 (a) What is the area of the base of each shape?
   (b) Calculate each volume.

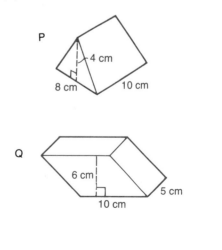

Written Exercises

Round off answers to 1 decimal place unless indicated otherwise.

A 1 (a) Calculate the area of the base of each solid.

(b) What is the volume of each solid?

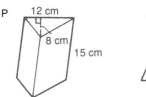

P 12 cm
8 cm
15 cm

Q
6 cm
9 cm
12 cm

2 Calculate the volume of each prism.

(a)

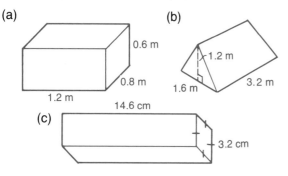

0.6 m
0.8 m
1.2 m

(b)
1.2 m
1.6 m
3.2 m

14.6 cm

(c)
3.2 cm

B 3 The area of the base of a prism is 84 cm². The height is 24 cm. Calculate the volume.

4 The area of the base of a prism is 37.3 m². The altitude is 8.2 m. Calculate the volume.

5 The base area of a prism is 49.2 cm². Its height is 16.8 cm. Calculate its volume.

6 (a) The area of the base of a prism is 128.5 cm². The height is 2.5 cm. Calculate its volume.

(b) The area of the base of a prism is 36.2 cm². Its height is 7.5 m. Calculate its volume.

7 The dimensions of a classroom floor are 12.6 m by 7.9 m. The room is 4.3 m high.

(a) Calculate the volume of air in the classroom.

(b) There are 30 students in this classroom. Calculate how much air per person is available.

8 (a) Calculate the volume of the wedge of cheese.

(b) A box has 12 wedges. Calculate the total mass if cheese has a mass of 6.8 g/cm³.

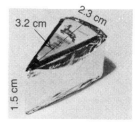

3.2 cm
2.3 cm
1.5 cm

9 Calculate the volume of air in the tent.

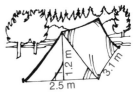

1.2 m
3.1 m
2.5 m

10 The cost of heating the air in a room measuring 3.2 m × 4.8 m × 2.9 m is 1.5¢/m³. What is the cost of heating the room?

11 The basement of a house is to be constructed with dimensions 10 m by 5 m by 2 m. A dumptruck can haul 25 m³ of dirt each trip. How many trips must the dump truck make to remove all the dirt?

12 A bar of gold is shown. The ends are square-shaped. Calculate the volume of gold in the bar.

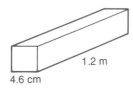

1.2 m
4.6 cm

13 (a) To calculate the volume, V, of this prism, first calculate the area, B, of the base.

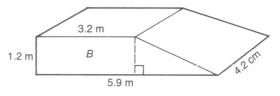

3.2 m
1.2 m
B
5.9 m
4.2 cm

(b) How much concrete is needed to construct the ramp?

76

14 (a) Calculate the area, B, of the end of the shape.
   (b) Calculate its volume.

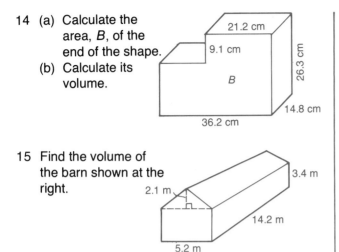

21.2 cm
9.1 cm
B
26.3 cm
14.8 cm
36.2 cm

15 Find the volume of the barn shown at the right.

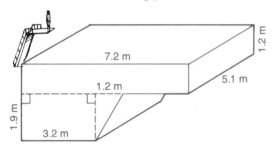

3.4 m
2.1 m
14.2 m
5.2 m

16 The sideview of a swimming pool is shown.

7.2 m
1.2 m
5.1 m
1.2 m
1.9 m
3.2 m

Calculate the volume of water in the pool, if the surface of the water is 0.3 m below the top edge of the pool.

17 The tunnel through a hill has the following shape. The tunnel is 120 m long. Calculate the volume of the tunnel.

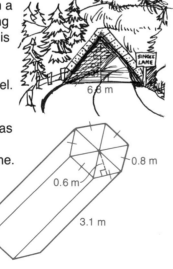

SINGLE LANE
6.8 m

C 18 A concrete pillar has the shape shown. Calculate its volume.

0.8 m
0.6 m
3.1 m

Surface Area of Prisms

Previously you calculated the surface area of a rectangular solid by calculating the area of each face.

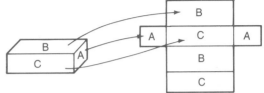

B
A
C
B
A
C
A
B
C

Similarly, to calculate the surface area of any prism, you calculate the area of each face of the prism.

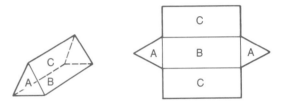

C
A
B
A
B
C
A
C

19 Find the surface area of each of the following prisms.

(a)
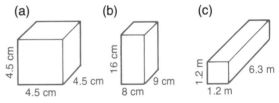
4.5 cm
4.5 cm
4.5 cm

(b)
16 cm
9 cm
8 cm

(c)
1.2 m
6.3 m
1.2 m

20 Find the amount of paint required to paint a room (4 walls and ceiling) measuring 4.2 m long, 5.4 m wide, and 2.6 m high. One litre of paint covers about 14 m².

21 A cheese box is in the shape of a triangular prism. Calculate its surface area.

6.2 cm
CHEESE
3.2 cm
6.8 cm
7.5 cm

77

3.3 Applications with Circumference

When working with circles, you often need to know about distances.

How long is 1 lap?

How far does the jet go for 1 turn of the tire?

The parts of a circle are given special names. The perimeter of a circle is given a special name, the **circumference**.

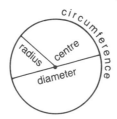

To find a relationship between the circumference and its diameter, a chart is completed.

Object	Circumference, C	Diameter, d	$C \div d$ or $\frac{C}{d}$ (to 3 decimal places)
waste paper basket	88 cm	28 cm	3.143
wheel	220 cm	70 cm	3.157
dish	69 cm	22 cm	3.136
roll of tape	25 cm	8 cm	3.125

From the chart, the value of
    circumference ÷ diameter
is about the same in every case. The reason the values differ somewhat is because measurement is not exact.

$C \div d$ or $\frac{C}{d}$ has the same value.

Write $C \div d = \pi$ or $\frac{C}{d} = \pi$.

To calculate the circumference of a circle, the formula used is
    $C = \pi \times d$.
The approximate value, $\pi \doteq 3.14$, is used. Thus the formula is
    $C \doteq 3.14 \times d$.

Example 1

The diameter of a tire is 70 cm. Calculate the circumference to the nearest centimetre. Use $\pi \doteq 3.14$.

Solution

Use the formula

$$\text{circumference} = \pi \times \text{diameter}$$
$$\text{or} \quad C = \pi \times d$$

Use $\pi \doteq 3.14$, $d = 70$

$$C \doteq 3.14 \times 70$$
$$\doteq 219.8$$

The circumference is 220 cm (to the nearest centimetre).

For any circle, the diameter is related to its corresponding radius.

$$\text{diameter} = 2 \times \text{radius}$$
$$d = 2 \times r$$

To calculate the circumference, either formula may be used.

$$C = \pi d \quad \text{or} \quad C = 2\pi r.$$

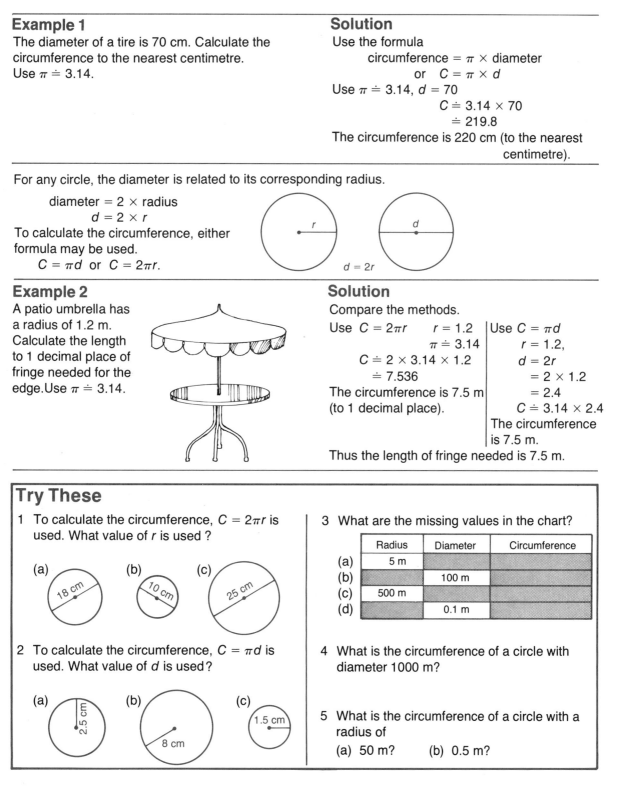

$d = 2r$

Example 2

A patio umbrella has a radius of 1.2 m. Calculate the length to 1 decimal place of fringe needed for the edge. Use $\pi \doteq 3.14$.

Solution

Compare the methods.

Use $C = 2\pi r$ $r = 1.2$
                    $\pi \doteq 3.14$

$$C \doteq 2 \times 3.14 \times 1.2$$
$$\doteq 7.536$$

The circumference is 7.5 m (to 1 decimal place).

Use $C = \pi d$
$r = 1.2$,
$d = 2r$
   $= 2 \times 1.2$
   $= 2.4$
$C \doteq 3.14 \times 2.4$
The circumference is 7.5 m.

Thus the length of fringe needed is 7.5 m.

Try These

1 To calculate the circumference, $C = 2\pi r$ is used. What value of r is used?

(a) 18 cm   (b) 10 cm   (c) 25 cm

2 To calculate the circumference, $C = \pi d$ is used. What value of d is used?

(a) 2.5 cm   (b) 8 cm   (c) 1.5 cm

3 What are the missing values in the chart?

	Radius	Diameter	Circumference
(a)	5 m		
(b)		100 m	
(c)	500 m		
(d)		0.1 m	

4 What is the circumference of a circle with diameter 1000 m?

5 What is the circumference of a circle with a radius of
(a) 50 m?   (b) 0.5 m?

Written Exercises

Round off your answers to 1 decimal place unless indicated
otherwise. Use $\pi \doteq 3.14$.

A 1 Calculate the circumference of each circle.

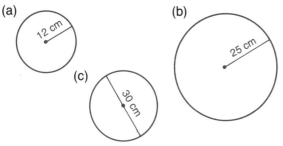

(a) 12 cm (b) 25 cm (c) 30 cm

2 The strip of crust around the edge of a pizza is
not eaten. Calculate the length of crust left for
each pizza.

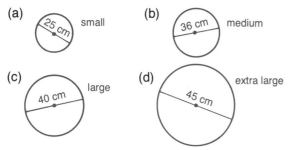

(a) 25 cm small (b) 36 cm medium (c) 40 cm large (d) 45 cm extra large

3 Calculate the circumference of the wheel.

35.2 cm

4 The diameter of a circle is 14.8 cm. Calculate
its circumference.

5 Find the circumference of a circle with diameter
23.6 cm.

6 The radius of a circle is 32.8 cm. Calculate the
circumference.

7 Calculate the circumference of the circle with
diameter

(a) 18 cm. (b) 5.4 cm. (c) 12.5 cm.

8 Calculate the circumference of the circle with
radius

(a) 12 cm. (b) 5.8 cm. (c) 12.2 cm.

9 Copy and complete the table.

	Radius (r)	Diameter (d)	Circumference (C)
(a)	50 cm	?	?
(b)	180 cm	?	?
(c)	?	6.6 m	?
(d)	?	36.2 m	?

B 10 The diameter of the face-off circle in hockey is
6 m. Calculate its circumference.

11 A circular rope barrier is to surround the
reviewing stand. Calculate the length
of rope needed.

16.8 m

12 A satellite travels
226 km above the
earth's surface.
Calculate the
distance travelled in
1 orbit. The radius of
the earth is 6400 km.

13 One of the most famous clocks in the world is Big Ben in London, England. If the diameter of its face is about 7.1 m, find its circumference.

14 A redwood tree has grown to a diameter of 8.1 m. Calculate its circumference.

15 A circular lampshade has a diameter of 28 cm. Calculate the length of fringe needed.

16 In 1893, George Ferris constructed the first ferris wheel at the midway in Chicago. The diameter of the wheel was 76 m. Calculate the circumference.

17 The world's largest solar furnace is a circular mirror with a diameter of 46 m. Calculate its circumference.

18 The diameters of various records are shown. Calculate the distance travelled by the needle if placed at the outside edge of the record for 1 single turn of the record.

	Record	Diameter
(a)	$33\frac{1}{3}$ r/min	30.1 cm
(b)	45 r/min	17.4 cm
(c)	78 r/min	25.1 cm

19 Find the size (circumference) of an engagement ring if the diameter of the ring is 1.8 cm.

20 A Montezuma Cypress (a tree) in Mexico had a diameter of 14.6 m. Calculate the circumference of the tree.

21 The diameter of Earth is about 12 800 km.
   (a) Calculate the distance around the equator.
   (b) The diameter of Mars is about 6800 km. How much further will you walk "once around" Earth than around Mars?

22 The diameter of a car tire is 70.4 cm. How many turns will the wheel have to make to travel 1 km?

A circular path is shown. Runner A runs on the outside track. Runner B runs on the inside track.

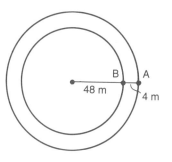

23 Calculate the distance run by
   (a) runner A.   (b) runner B.

24 If the two runners start at the same place, how much further will runner A have run than runner B after
   (a) 5 laps?   (b) 10 laps?   (c) 100 laps?

C 25 The school field at Fayeteville has the dimensions shown. Calculate the length of one lap of the track.

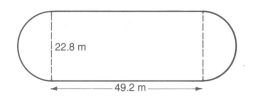

Applications: Wheels

Without wheels what would you do?

26 The tire of a jet has a diameter of 2.4 m.
  (a) Calculate the circumference of the tire.
  (b) The runway is 648 m long. Calculate the number of turns the tire will make during take-off.

27 The radius of the front wheels of a racing car is 42.3 cm and of the rear wheels is 47.9 cm.
  (a) Calculate the distance travelled by the car for 1 turn of the rear wheels.
  (b) If the front wheels have turned 100 times, how many times have the rear wheels turned?

28 Calculate the circumference of
  (a) the large wheel.   (b) the small wheel.

  (c) How many times will each tire turn in travelling 1 km?

29 The world's largest tire has a diameter of 3.8 m.
  (a) Calculate the distance travelled for 1 turn of the tire.
  (b) How many turns will the tire make in travelling 1 km?

30 The diameter of an ordinary car tire is about 70 cm. How many times will a car tire have to turn to travel the same distance as 1 turn of the tire in Question 29?

31 The tire of an earth mover has a diameter of 2.4 m. Calculate the circumference of the tire.

3.4 Area of the Circle

It's often important to know how to calculate
the area of a circle.

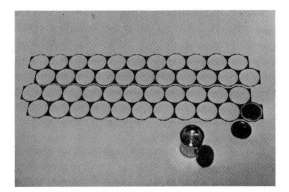

For example, a manufacturer cuts can tops
from rectangular pieces of sheet metal.
How much material is not used?

If you know the radius, r, of the can top, you can calculate the
amount of scrap by first calculating the area, A, of the can tops.
$A = \pi \times r \times r$ or $A = \pi r^2$

Example 1

Calculate the area of each circle to the nearest
square centimetre. Use $\pi \doteq 3.14$.

(a)

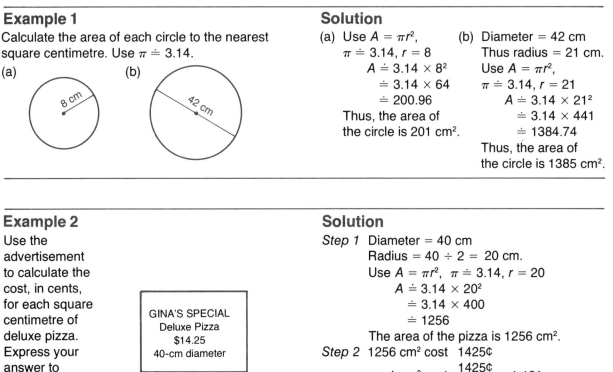

8 cm

(b)

42 cm

Solution

(a) Use $A = \pi r^2$,
$\pi \doteq 3.14$, $r = 8$
$A \doteq 3.14 \times 8^2$
$\doteq 3.14 \times 64$
$\doteq 200.96$
Thus, the area of
the circle is 201 cm².

(b) Diameter = 42 cm
Thus radius = 21 cm.
Use $A = \pi r^2$,
$\pi \doteq 3.14$, $r = 21$
$A \doteq 3.14 \times 21^2$
$\doteq 3.14 \times 441$
$\doteq 1384.74$
Thus, the area of
the circle is 1385 cm².

Example 2

Use the
advertisement
to calculate the
cost, in cents,
for each square
centimetre of
deluxe pizza.
Express your
answer to
2 decimal
places.
$\pi \doteq 3.14$.

> GINA'S SPECIAL
> Deluxe Pizza
> $14.25
> 40-cm diameter

Solution

Step 1 Diameter = 40 cm
Radius = $40 \div 2 = 20$ cm.
Use $A = \pi r^2$, $\pi \doteq 3.14$, $r = 20$
$A \doteq 3.14 \times 20^2$
$\doteq 3.14 \times 400$
$\doteq 1256$
The area of the pizza is 1256 cm².
Step 2 1256 cm² cost 1425¢
1 cm² costs $\dfrac{1425¢}{1256}$ or 1.13¢

The cost is 1.13¢ for each square
centimetre of pizza.

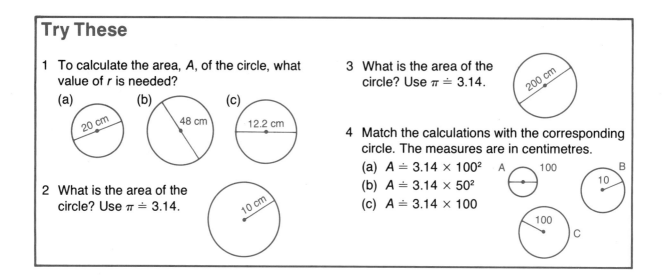

Try These

1 To calculate the area, A, of the circle, what value of r is needed?
(a) 20 cm (b) 48 cm (c) 12.2 cm

2 What is the area of the circle? Use $\pi \doteq 3.14$.
10 cm

3 What is the area of the circle? Use $\pi \doteq 3.14$.
200 cm

4 Match the calculations with the corresponding circle. The measures are in centimetres.
(a) $A \doteq 3.14 \times 100^2$
(b) $A \doteq 3.14 \times 50^2$
(c) $A \doteq 3.14 \times 100$

A 100   B 10   C 100

Written Exercises

Express each answer to 1 decimal place unless otherwise indicated. Use $\pi \doteq 3.14$.

A 1 Calculate the area of each circle.
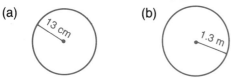
(a) 13 cm   (b) 1.3 m

2 Calculate the area of each circle with radius
(a) 12 m.   (b) 36 cm.   (c) 9.8 cm.

3 Calculate the area of each circle with diameter
(a) 16 m.   (b) 30 cm.   (c) 4.6 cm.

4 By how much does area A exceed area B?
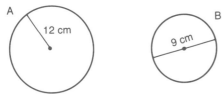
A 12 cm   B 9 cm

5 Calculate the area of a circle with diameter 26.2 cm.

6 What is the area of a circle with diameter 9.5 m?

7 The radius of a quarter circle is 1.3 cm. Calculate its area.

8 The diameter of a circular disc is 12.6 cm. Calculate the area of the disc.

9 Calculate the area of a circular garden with radius 2.6 m.

B 10 A patrol aircraft can observe a distance of 12.1 km in all directions.

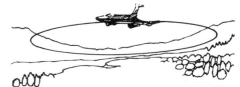

Calculate the area of coverage by the plane.

11 Calculate the area of the top of the can.

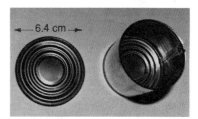

6.4 cm

84

12 Calculate the area of the top of the pie.

38 cm

13 In Olympic events, the diameter of the circle used in the shot put is 2.1 m. Calculate the area of this circle.

14 The lid of a circular can has a diameter of 26 cm. Calculate the area of the lid.

15 A circular garden has radius 4.2 m. Calculate its area.

16 Throwing the discus is one of the Olympic events.

(a) The discus is circular with a radius of about 11 cm. Calculate its area.

(b) The discus is thrown by the competitor from a circle with diameter about 2.8 m. Calculate the area of this circle.

17 The free throw area in basketball is a semicircle as shown.

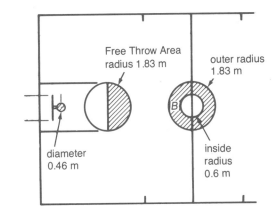

Free Throw Area
radius 1.83 m

outer radius
1.83 m

B

diameter
0.46 m

inside
radius
0.6 m

(a) Calculate the area of the throw area.

(b) Calculate area B.

(c) Calculate the area of the basketball hoop.

For Questions 18 to 26, use the pizza prices.

	Small 25 cm	Medium 35 cm	Large 40 cm	Ex Large 45 cm
BASIC TOMATO SAUCE AND CHEESE	$3.00	$5.00	$5.75	$7.25
One Choice	3.30	5.50	6.25	7.90
Two Choice	3.60	6.00	6.75	8.55
Three Choices	3.90	6.50	7.25	9.20
Four Choices	4.20	7.00	7.75	9.85
Extra or Double Choice	0.30	0.50	0.55	0.65
Double Cheese & Shrimps each Count as two Choices	0.60	1.00	1.10	1.30
Pep. Mush, Gr. Pepper, Onions	4.00	6.50	7.25	9.20
Pep. Mush. Gr. Pepper, Onions, Olives, Ham, Bacon	4.50	7.75	8.50	11.15

MINI PIZZA WITH PEPPERONI $1.50
(pick-up only)

18 Calculate the area of
(a) a small pizza.   (b) a large pizza.

19 Two people share a medium pizza. How much pizza will each person eat?

20 Twelve people share 2 extra-large pizzas. How much pizza will each person eat?

21 (a) Calculate the cost of a small pizza with 3 choices.
    (b) Calculate the cost per square centimetre of the pizza in (a).

22 What is the cost per square centimetre of a large pizza with 3 choices?

23 Calculate the cost per square centimetre of each of the following pizzas?
    (a) small with 2 choices
    (b) medium with 2 choices
    (c) large with 2 choices
    (d) Which of (a), (b), or (c), is the best buy?

24 How much greater in size is a large pizza than a small pizza?

25 (a) Calculate the area of 2 small pizzas.
    (b) Calculate the area of 1 large pizza.
    (c) Which has the greater area, (a) or (b)?

26 Which is the better buy?
    A 2 small pizzas (2 choices)
    B 1 large pizza (2 choices)

27 (a) Which has the greater area: a square with sides 8 cm or a circle with diameter 9 cm?

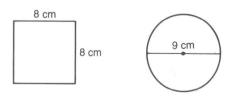

    (b) What is the difference in their area to the nearest hundredth?

C 28 Calculate the area of each shaded region.

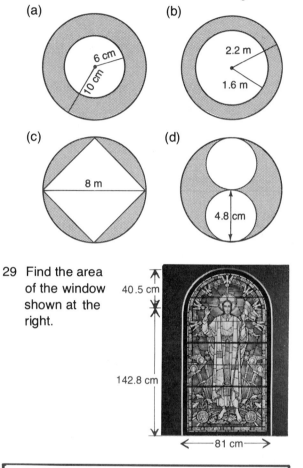

29 Find the area of the window shown at the right.

40.5 cm

142.8 cm

← 81 cm →

Calculator Tip

Some calculators have a key which provides the value of π. If they do not, use $\pi \doteq 3.1415926$ to the required number of decimal places.

Find the area of a circular garden with radius 1.25 m. (Use $A = \pi r^2$.)

Enter	Calculator Display
C	0
1.25	1.25
×	1.2500000
1.25	1.25
×	1.5625000
π	3.1415926
=	4.9087384

Write Area is 4.91 m²

3.5 Cylinders and Their Applications

Shapes such as these occur frequently in the supermarket. They are called **cylinders**. Each end of a cylinder has the same shape and size.

To find the volume of a cylinder, you may use the following principle.

$V = B \times h$

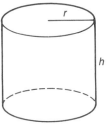

The area of the base of the cylinder, B, is given by

$B = \pi r^2$

Thus, to calculate the volume, you use

$V = B \times h$
$= (\pi r^2) \times h$ or $V = \pi r^2 h$

Example 1

Find the volume of a cylinder with height 36 cm and diameter of the base 16 cm. Use $\pi \doteq 3.14$. Express your answer to 1 decimal place.

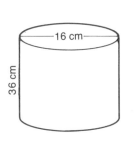

16 cm

36 cm

Solution

Use $V = \pi r^2 h$ h, height $= 36$ cm
d, diameter $= 16$ cm
r, radius $= 8$ cm

Substitute the values.

$V \doteq 3.14 \times (8)^2 \times 36$
$\doteq 3.14 \times 64 \times 36$
$\doteq 7234.56$ (to 2 decimal places)

Thus, the volume of the cylinder is 7234.6 cm³ (to 1 decimal place).

The volume of a container is often given in millilitres. Use the relationship 1 cm³ = 1 mL in Example 2.

Example 2

Find the volume of the can to the nearest millilitre. Use $\pi \doteq 3.14$.

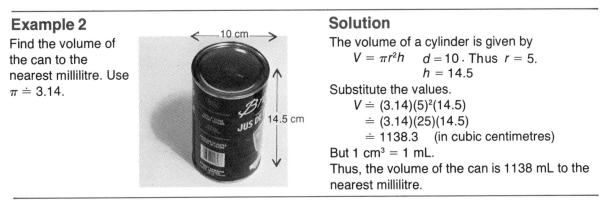

10 cm

14.5 cm

Solution

The volume of a cylinder is given by

$V = \pi r^2 h$ $d = 10$. Thus $r = 5$.
$h = 14.5$

Substitute the values.

$V \doteq (3.14)(5)^2(14.5)$
$\doteq (3.14)(25)(14.5)$
$\doteq 1138.3$ (in cubic centimetres)

But 1 cm³ = 1 mL.

Thus, the volume of the can is 1138 mL to the nearest millilitre.

Try These

1 What are the measures of the radius and the height of each of the following cylinders?

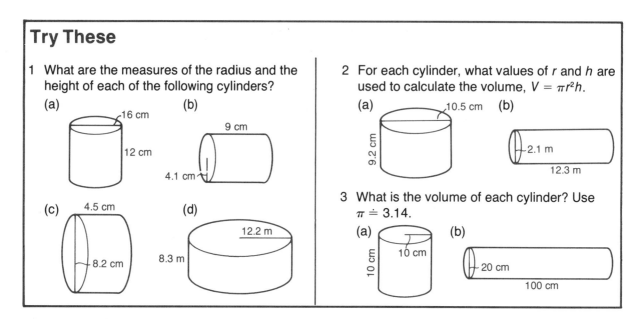

(a)
16 cm
12 cm

(b)
9 cm
4.1 cm

(c)
4.5 cm
8.2 cm

(d)
12.2 m
8.3 m

2 For each cylinder, what values of r and h are used to calculate the volume, $V = \pi r^2 h$.

(a)
10.5 cm
9.2 cm

(b)
2.1 m
12.3 m

3 What is the volume of each cylinder? Use $\pi \doteq 3.14$.

(a)
10 cm
10 cm

(b)
20 cm
100 cm

Written Exercises

Round off each answer to 1 decimal place, unless otherwise indicated.
Use $\pi \doteq 3.14$ throughout.

A 1 For each cylinder, the area of the base is given. Find the volume.

(a)
14 cm
area 78 cm²

(b)
area 140 cm²
10 cm

2 Find the volume of each of the following cylinders.

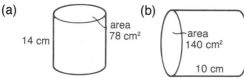

(a)
6 m
4 m

(b)
4.5 m
3.5 m

(c)
12.2 cm
16.8 cm

3 The measures are given for cylinders. Copy and complete the table.

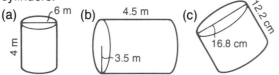

	Diameter of base (d)	Radius of cylinder (r)	Height (h)	Volume (V)
(a)	6 cm	?	8 cm	?
(b)	18 cm	?	23 cm	?
(c)	?	6.9 cm	4.2 cm	?
(d)	?	2.5 m	4.8 m	?

4 The height of a can is 25.4 cm. Its radius is 12.9 cm. Find its volume.

5 The diameter of a cylinder is 24 cm. The height is 16 cm. Calculate its volume.

6 An oil drum is 94 cm high. The radius of the base is 35 cm. What is its volume?

B 7 A cylindrical storage tank with a radius of 3.4 m and a height of 7.3 m is filled with wheat.
   (a) Find the volume of wheat in the tank.
   (b) Find the mass of wheat in the tank if wheat has a mass of 120 kg/m³.

8 A juice can has a height of 9 cm. The diameter of the base is 10.6 cm.
   (a) How many millilitres of juice will the can hold? (Remember 1 cm³ = 1 mL.)
   (b) If you increase the diameter by 2 cm, by how much is the volume increased?

9 A car engine has 8 cylinders each with a diameter of 7.2 cm and a height of 8.4 cm. The capacity of the engine is the total volume of the cylinders. Calculate the engine capacity.

10 Estimate which can holds more, A or B. Then calculate to check your estimate.
  A   radius 5.3 cm, height 13.7 cm
  B   diameter 10.2 cm, height 13.8 cm

11 A water pipe has an inner radius of 14.6 cm and an outer radius of 18.2 cm.
  (a) Find the number of litres of water it can hold if its length is 6 m.
  (b) Find the mass of this pipe (without the water) if the piping has a mass of 10 g/cm³.

12 The dimensions of 3 cans are shown below.

  (a) Estimate which can you think holds the most.
  (b) Calculate the volume of each can. Was your estimate in (a) correct?

C 13 Ginger drinks 5 glasses of milk a day. The dimensions of the glass are shown.

  (a) Calculate the volume of milk she drinks each day.
  (b) Calculate the number of litres of milk she drinks in a year.

Surface Area of Cylinders

The surface area of the cylinder below is shown.

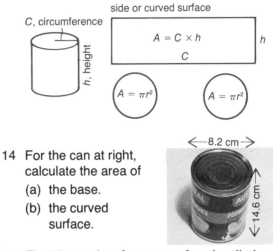

14 For the can at right, calculate the area of
  (a) the base.
  (b) the curved surface.

15 Find the total surface area of each cylinder.

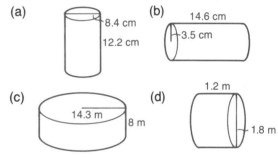

16 The height of a tuna can is 6.2 cm. The diameter is 6.6 cm. Calculate the total surface area.

17 The diameter of a can of tomatoes is 9.4 cm and the height is 16.2 cm. Calculate the total surface area.

18 A tin is 12.5 cm high and has a diameter of 8 cm. Calculate the area of the label that needs to be used.

19 The outside of an oil drum is to be painted with 2 coats of underwater paint. The diameter of the drum is 0.6 m and has a height of 1.2 m.
  (a) Calculate the surface area.
  (b) There are 8 drums. How many litres of paint are needed if 1 L covers 6.5 m²?

Applications: Thunderstorms and Tornados

Thunderstorms and tornados are two of Nature's most destructive phenomena. After a tornado the average loss to property is about $24 300 000.

The average duration of a tornado is less than 30 s. A thunderstorm lasts an average of 2 h.

The disturbance created by a thunderstorm is approximately cylindrical in shape.

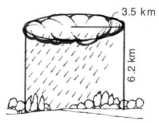

3.5 km

6.2 km

20 Calculate the volume of the disturbance shown by the above thunderstorm.

21 The smallest thunderstorm on record measured 2.7 km in diameter and its cloud formation had a height of 8.4 km. Calculate the total volume of the disturbance in the atmosphere.

22 The largest thunderstorm on record measured 43.9 km in diameter. It had a height of 20.3 km. Calculate the total volume in the atmosphere which this storm occupied.

23 A tornado is a narrow funnel-shaped cloud which extends downwards from cumulonimbus clouds. Calculate the area of destruction of a tornado that destroys a tract of land 8 km wide and 6.9 km long.

24 Specially equipped aircraft and ground crews record data about thunderstorms.

These measurements were taken of 2 thunderstorms.

Storm A		Storm B	
diameter	9.6 km	diameter	8.5 km
height	5.9 km	height	6.3 km

Which storm, A or B, occupied the greater space?

25 A tornado in the state of Massachusetts covered a path 0.256 km wide and 27.5 km long. Calculate the area of destruction.

26 A small tornado covered a tract of land 0.04 km wide and 7.8 km long. Calculate the area that was destroyed.

3.6 Working With Other Surface Areas

Your earlier skills can be used to calculate the surface area of the pyramid.

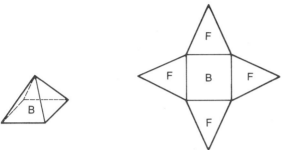

- Calculate the area of the triangular face, *F*.
- Calculate the area of the base, *B*.

To calculate the surface area of this spherical tank, you use the formula

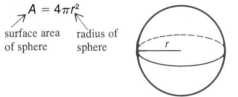

$$A = 4\pi r^2$$

surface area of sphere   radius of sphere

The amount of canvas needed for the conical tent is calculated in two steps: the area of the curved surface plus the area of the base.

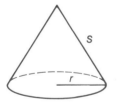

Step 1: Area of curved surface.

$$A = \pi rs \longleftarrow s \text{ is called the slant height as shown in the diagram.}$$

area of curved surface   radius of the base of the cone

Step 2: Area of the base of the cone.
Use your earlier work to calculate the area of a circle.

$$A = \pi r^2$$

area of base   radius of the base of the cone

Example

Calculate the surface area of each of the following to the nearest square centimetre.

(a) 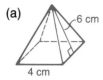 6 cm

4 cm

(b) 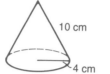 10 cm

4 cm

(c) 8 cm

Solution

(a) The shape is a pyramid. The area of a triangular face is given by

$$A = \frac{1}{2}bh \quad b = 4, h = 6$$

$$= \frac{1}{2}(4)(6) = 12$$

Total area of triangular faces is 4×12 cm² or 48 cm².

Area of square base

$$A = s^2 \quad s = 4$$

$$= (4)^2 = 16$$

Area of base is 16 cm².

Sum of areas	triangles	48 cm²
	base	16 cm²
	total	64 cm²

Surface area of pyramid is 64 cm².

(b) The shape is a cone.
Area of base of cone is

$$A = \pi r^2 \quad \pi \doteq 3.14, r = 4$$

$$A \doteq 3.14(4)^2$$

$$\doteq 50.24$$

Area of curved surface

$$A = \pi rs \quad \pi \doteq 3.14$$

$$r = 4, s = 10$$

$$A \doteq 3.14(4)(10)$$

$$\doteq 125.6$$

Sum of areas	125.6 cm²
	50.24 cm²
	175.84 cm²

Surface area of cone is 176 cm² (to the nearest square centimetre).

(c) The shape is a sphere.
Surface area of sphere is

$$A = 4\pi r^2 \quad \pi \doteq 3.14,$$

$$r = 8$$

$$A \doteq 4(3.14)8^2$$

$$\doteq 4(3.14)(64)$$

$$\doteq 803.84$$

The surface area of sphere is 804 cm² (to the nearest square centimetre).

Written Exercises

Round off answers to 1 decimal place unless otherwise indicated. Use $\pi \doteq 3.14$.

A 1 Find the surface area of each sphere.

(a) 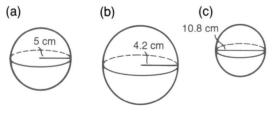 5 cm

(b) 4.2 cm

(c) 10.8 cm

2 Calculate the surface area of the sphere with diameter

(a) 16 cm.   (b) 58 cm.   (c) 9.6 cm.

3 (a) Calculate the area of the base.

(b) Calculate the area of the curved surface.

 16 cm

6 cm

4 Find the surface area of each of the following cones.

(a) 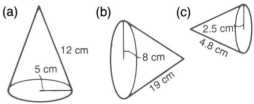 12 cm

5 cm

(b) 8 cm

19 cm

(c) 2.5 cm

4.8 cm

92

5 (a) For the pyramid
(square based),
calculate the area of
each triangular
face.
(b) Calculate the area
of the base.
(c) What is the surface
area of the
pyramid?

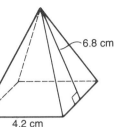

6.8 cm

4.2 cm

6 Find the total surface area of each pyramid
(square based).

(a)
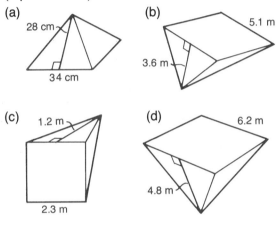
28 cm
34 cm

(b)
5.1 m
3.6 m

(c)
1.2 m

2.3 m

(d)
6.2 m
4.8 m

B

7 The slant height of a cone is 16.2 cm.
Calculate the
surface area of
the cone if the
radius is 7.9 cm.

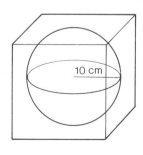

8 The diameter of the earth is 12 800 km.
(a) Calculate the surface area of the earth.
(b) What assumption do you make in obtaining
your answer in (a)?

9 Calculate the surface area of each planet.
(a) Venus, radius 6050 km.
(b) Mars, diameter 6800 km.

10 A major league baseball is in the shape of a
sphere and has a radius of 3.8 cm. Find the
surface area of the ball.

11 Plastic tree
ornaments are made
from sheets of
plastic. Calculate
how many ornaments
can be made from a
sheet of plastic
60 cm by 80 cm.
(There is no wastage.)

4 cm

12 A building is in the
shape of a square
based pyramid.
Plywood is used to
construct the sides.
Calculate the surface
area of the sides.

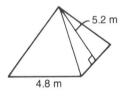

5.2 m

4.8 m

13 The radius of a sphere is 15.2 cm. By how
much does the surface area of the sphere
increase if the radius increases by 2 cm?

14 Which has more surface area?
A two spheres each with radius 5 cm
B one sphere with radius 10 cm

C 15 The diagram shows a
sphere inside a cube
with edges 20 cm in
length.
(a) Calculate the
surface area of
the cube.
(b) Calculate the
surface area of
the sphere.
(c) Which solid has the greater surface area?
By how much?

10 cm

3.7 Volumes of Spheres, Cones and Pyramids

To calculate how much peel there is on an orange, you need to be able to calculate the volume of a sphere.

Sphere

To calculate volume use the formula.

$$V = \frac{4}{3}\pi r^3$$

To calculate the volume of the flask in a hospital room, you need to be able to calculate the volume of a cone.

Cone

To calculate volume use the formula.

$$V = \frac{1}{3}\pi r^2 h$$

How is this formula related to the volume of a cylinder?

To calculate how much a truck can carry, you need to be able to calculate the volume of a square-based pyramid.

Pyramid

To calculate volume use the formula.

$$V = \frac{1}{3} \times l \times w \times h$$

How is this formula related to the volume of a prism?

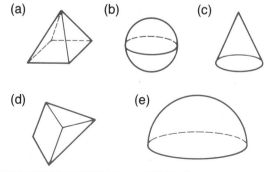

Try These

1 For which shape is each of the following formula used to calculate the volume?

(a) $V = \frac{1}{3}\pi r^2 h$ (b) $V = \frac{1}{3}lwh$ (c) $V = \frac{4}{3}\pi r^3$

2 For which shapes can the following be used to calculate the volume?

$$\text{Volume} = \frac{1}{3} \times \text{area of base} \times \text{height}$$

3 What formula is used to calculate the volume of
(a) a square-based pyramid?
(b) a cone?   (c) a sphere?

4 Which formula will you use to calculate the volume of each shape?

(a)   (b)   (c)

(d)   (e)

Written Exercises

Round off your answers to 1 decimal place unless otherwise indicated. Use $\pi \doteq 3.14$.

A 1 (a) Record the formula used to calculate the volume of a sphere.

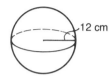
12 cm

  (b) Calculate the volume of the sphere.

2 Find the volume of each sphere.

  (a)

15 cm

  (b)

4.8 cm

3 Find the volume of each sphere with radius
  (a) 8 cm.   (b) 25 cm.   (c) 6.8 cm.

4 Find the volume of each sphere with diameter
  (a) 18 cm.   (b) 9.2 m.   (c) 13.6 mm.

5 (a) Record the formula used to calculate the volume of a cone.

6.2 cm
1.8 cm

  (b) Calculate the volume of the cone.

6 (a) Record the formula used to calculate the volume of a pyramid.

1.5 m
3.6 m
2.2 m

  (b) Calculate the volume of the pyramid.

7 Find the volume of each pyramid or cone

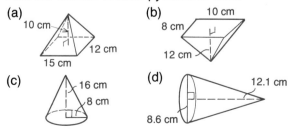

  (a)
  10 cm
  12 cm
  15 cm

  (b) 10 cm
  8 cm
  12 cm

  (c) 16 cm
  8 cm

  (d) 12.1 cm
  8.6 cm

8 Find the volume of a cone 3.8 m in diameter and 5.1 m high.

9 Find the volume of a pyramid, 10.2 m high, with a rectangular base measuring 7 m by 3 m.

10 A baseball has a radius of 3.6 cm. What is its volume?

B 11 Calculate the volume of a cone-shaped funnel with radius 150 mm and height 220 mm.

12 A billiard ball has a diameter of 5.3 cm. Calculate the mass of 9 balls made of ivory if ivory has a mass of 2 g/cm³.

13 A tent is in the form of a pyramid with base 2 m wide, 3 m long and 2.4 m high. Find the volume of this tent.

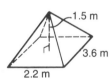
2.4 m
2 m
3 m

14 Phosphate is stored in a conical pile. Calculate the volume of the pile, if the height is 7.8 m and its radius is 16.2 m.

15 The thickness of a grapefruit peel is 0.5 cm. If the diameter of an unpeeled grapefruit is 12.8 cm, how much of the grapefruit is peel?

C 16 How much more does a hemispherical tank (half of a sphere) hold than a conical tank?

2.1 m
2.1 m
2.1 m

Applications: Sports and Cross-Sectional Area

The large waterbag has a diameter of 8.4 m. You may calculate its cross-sectional area to 1 decimal place.

$A = \pi r^2 \quad \pi \doteq 3.14, r = 4.2$
$\doteq 3.14(4.2)^2$
$\doteq 3.14(17.64)$
$\doteq 55.39$ (to 2 decimal places)

The cross-sectional area, to 1 decimal place, is 55.4 m².

17 A soccer ball for international competition has a diameter of 22.3 cm.
   (a) Calculate the circumference of the regulation soccer ball.
   (b) Calculate its cross-sectional area.

18 A volleyball for international competition has a diameter of 21.8 cm.
   (a) What is the circumference of a regulation volleyball?
   (b) Calculate its cross-sectional area.

19 (a) A basketball for international competition has an official diameter of 24.2 cm. What is the circumference of a regulation basketball?
   (b) The basketball hoop is 45 cm in diameter. What is the circumference of the regulation hoop?
   (c) How much area is not used when the ball passes through the hoop?

20 (a) An international tennis ball has a diameter of 6.8 cm. Calculate the circumference of one tennis ball.
   (b) A North American hardball has a diameter of 7.4 cm. Calculate the circumference of the official baseball used in the National and American Leagues.
   (c) Which ball has the greater cross-sectional area and by how much is it greater?

21 The diameter of the ball in the photo is 224 cm. Calculate its cross-sectional area.

22 (a) A regulation softball or fastball has a diameter of 9.7 cm. What is its cross-sectional area?
   (b) A regulation slowpitch ball has a diameter of 12.9 cm. Calculate its cross-sectional area.

23 The football used in both the C.F.L. and the N.F.L. has a diameter of 17 cm at its widest part.
   (a) What is the circumference of a regulation football?
   (b) Calculate cross-sectional area of its widest part.

3.8 Problem-Solving: Making The Problem Simpler

Some problems appear more difficult than they actually are because they involve large or awkward numbers. When this is the case, plan your solution by using smaller numbers to help you decide which operations to use. Once you have done this, then solve the original problem by using the large numbers you were given.

Example

A water pump can pump 8645 L of water in 1.8 h. How many kilolitres will it pump in 36.5 h? Express your answer to 1 decimal place.

To make the above example simpler, think of these steps:

Step 1 Think of a simpler problem.

A water pump can pump 10 L in 2 h.
How many kilolitres will it pump in 40 h?

Step 2 Think of the solution.

In 2 h, 10 L are pumped.

In 1 h, $\dfrac{10}{2}$ L or 5 L are pumped.

In 40 h, 40 × 5 or 200 L are pumped.

200 L is $\dfrac{200}{1000}$ L or 0.2 kL.

Now apply these steps to solve the original problem. Note, the similarity of the above steps to those in the following solution.

Solution

In 1.8 h, 8645 L are pumped.

In 1 h, $\dfrac{8645}{1.8 \text{ L}}$ or 4802.8 L are pumped.

In 36.5 h, 36.5 × 4802.8 L or 175 302 L are pumped.

175 302 L is $\dfrac{175\ 302}{1000}$ kL or 175.302 kL.

Thus, 175.3 kL are pumped, to 1 decimal place.

Another way of planning the solution to a problem is to use your rounding off skills for numbers. For example, you are asked to solve the following problem.

Example

To burn 1 L of fuel oil requires 19.63 L of air. An oil furnace used 138.4 L of oil. How many litres of air were needed?

Use your rounding off skills to *think of a simpler problem*.
To burn 1 L of fuel oil requires 20 L of air. An oil furnace used 140 L of oil. How many litres of air were needed?

Written Exercises

For each problem,
► first plan the solution to the problem by either using simpler numbers or rounding off the numbers.
► then, use the above plan, and solve the original problem.

1 (a) 51.7 L of gas have a mass of 59.3 kg. What is the mass of 34.2 L of gas?
  (b) A man jogs at a rate of 2.6 m/s. How many seconds will it take him to jog 493 m?

2 If 1 L of gasoline costs 34.9¢, how many litres of gasoline were purchased for $18.58?

3 Juan de Fuca Strait between Vancouver Island and the State of Washington is approximately rectangular in shape. It is about 159.8 km long and about 26.6 km wide. What is the approximate area of this body of water?

4 The Great Lakes in North America have a total surface area of about 151 536 km². Of this area, 53 912 km² are on Canadian territory. How much is not on Canadian territory?

5 Mount Logan in Canada is 6050.3 m high. If an elevator rises at a rate of 3.1 m/s, how long would it take the elevator to reach the top?

6 José is having a party and orders cold cuts for 68 people. He allows 0.25 kg of meat per person. Find the cost of the meat if 1 kg costs $5.98.

7 A company wants to paint a large gasoline storage tank on top and all around the tank. A litre of paint covers 8.8 m² and costs $6.95. How much will it cost to paint the container?

13.21 m
6.54 m

8 Fred has a spool of copper wire 100 m long. The following lengths are to be cut: 16.4 m, 28.5 m, 51.3 m.
  (a) What length of wire in all will be cut from the above spool?
  (b) How much wire will be left on the spool?

9 Linda has moved to a new home and wants to resod the backyard. Sod costs $1.30 for each square metre. Find the cost of sodding the yard if the yard has a circular flower bed, 5.56 m in diameter, which will not be sodded.

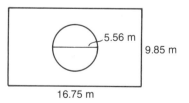
5.56 m
9.85 m
16.75 m

98

Skills To Practise: A Chapter Review

3.1 (a) Calculate the area of each triangle.

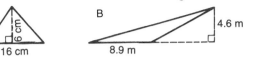

(b) Calculate the area of each parallelogram.

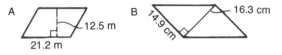

3.2 (a) Calculate the volume of a prism 10 cm high if it has a

    A triangular base   B square base
      area 12.8 m²   area 123.9 cm²

(b) Calculate the volume of each of the following prisms.

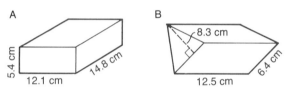

3.3 (a) Calculate the circumference of each circle.

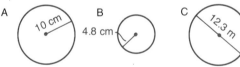

(b) Copy and complete the table.

	Radius	Diameter	Circumference
A	6.4 cm		
B		14.5 m	
C	23.0 cm		

3.4 (a) Calculate the area of each circle.

(b) Copy and complete the table.

	Radius	Diameter	Area
A	4.6 cm		
B		12.2 m	
C		29.3 cm	

3.5 (a) Calculate the volume of each cylinder.

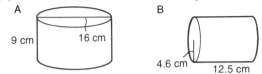

(b) Copy and complete the table.

	Diameter	Radius	Height	Volume of cylinder	Surface area of cylinder
A	16.8 cm		10.1 cm		
B		6.3 cm	6.2 cm		

3.6 Calculate the surface area of each of the following to 1 decimal place.

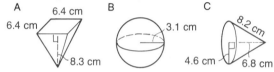

3.7 Calculate the volumes of shapes A, B, and C above.

3.8 (a) Round off the dimensions to 1 decimal place and use these rounded numbers to find the area of each figure.

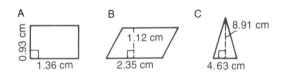

Use the given dimensions to calculate the area of each figure to 2 decimal places.

(b) Round off the dimensions to 1 decimal place and use these rounded numbers to find the volume of each solid.

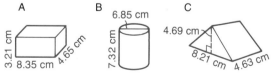

Use the given dimensions to calculate the volume of each solid to 2 decimal places.

Problems To Practise: A Chapter Review

3.1 Logos using triangles and parallelograms are shown. Make suitable measurements to calculate their areas.

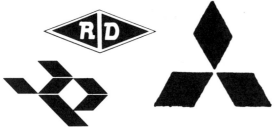

3.2 (a) The height of a prism is 12.5 m. The area of its base is 26.47 cm². Calculate the volume to 1 decimal place.

(b) A trench is dug as shown at right. Calculate the area of the triangular end. Calculate the amount of earth removed if the trench is 12.5 m in length.

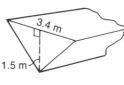

3.3 (a) The radius of the earth is about 6400 km. A satellite is 290 km above the earth's surface. Calculate the distance it travels in one of its circular orbits.

(b) Tina measured the diameter of the stationwagon wheel and found it to be 72.9 cm. Calculate the circumference. How far will the car go after 1800 turns of the wheel?

3.4 (a) The waste water treatment facility has a diameter of 17.8 m. Calculate the surface area of the treatment facility.

(b) The clockface on the city hall has a radius of 1.6 m. Calculate the surface area of the clock.

3.5 (a) Calculate the volume of the drum and the area of tin required to construct the drum (including 2 ends).

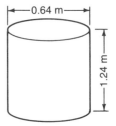

(b) Which holds more, cylinder A or cylinder B? Cylinder A: diameter 9.4 cm, height 8.2 cm. Cylinder B: radius 54 cm, height 7.9 cm.

3.6 (a) A basketball has a diameter of 28 cm. Calculate its surface area.

(b) A funnel is in the shape of a cone with radius 6.2 cm and slant height 18.3 cm. Calculate the surface area of the funnel.

3.7 (a) Calculate the approximate volume of the flask.

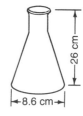

(b) A basketball has a radius of 12 cm. Find its volume to the nearest cubic centimetre.

3.8 Round off the numbers before solving each problem. Solve each problem and express your answers to 1 decimal place.

(a) A cylindrical hat box has a radius 18.25 cm and height 28.59 cm. Calculate the
   • volume of the box   • surface area of the box.

(b) A room has a floor with dimensions 3.6 m by 4.2 m and is 3.2 m high.
   • Calculate the cost of tiling the floor if tile costs $3.65/m².
   • Calculate the cost of wallpapering the room if 1 roll costs $8.69 and covers 6.7 m².

Chapter Checkup: A Practice Test

3.1 (a) Calculate the area of each shape.

A

12 cm

18 cm

B

6.3 cm

10.2 cm

(b) The base of a triangular garden is 16.2 m and the height is 12.2 m. Calculate its area.

(c) Make suitable measurements to calculate the area of the stamp.

3.2 (a) Calculate the volume of each of the following.

A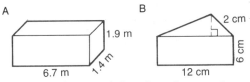

1.9 m

6.7 m

1.4 m

B

2 cm

6 cm

12 cm

(b) A rectangular trench is 1.6 m deep and 1.2 m wide. If the trench is 2.1 km long, calculate the amount of earth removed.

3.3 (a) Calculate the circumference of each circle.

A

60 cm

B

72 cm

How much further will B go than A if they are rolled for 800 turns?

(b) The blades of a helicopter form a twirling circle of radius 4.5 m. Calculate the distance a tip travels in 12 min if the blades turns at 300 r/min.

3.4 (a) Plastic tops for containers are shown. Calculate the area of each one.

small   3 cm   medium   4 cm   large   5 cm

(b) If the small top is placed on the large top, how much of the large top is seen?

3.5 (a) Calculate the volume and surface area of this cylinder.

12.5 m

1.2 m

(b) A concrete support for a bridge is cylindrical in shape. The diameter of the base is 0.64 m and the support is 6.2 m high. Calculate the amount of concrete needed to construct the support.

3.6 (a) Calculate the surface area of each of the following.

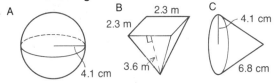

A

B   2.3 m

2.3 m

3.6 m

4.1 cm

C

4.1 cm

6.8 cm

(b) A sculpture in the shape of an inverted pyramid has a square top with sides 4.2 m by 4.2 m and slant height 3.5 m. What area of tin would be required to cover the whole sculpture?

3.7 (a) Calculate the volume of each of the following.

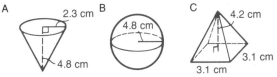

A   2.3 cm   B

4.8 cm

4.8 cm

C   4.2 cm

3.1 cm

3.1 cm

(b) Calculate the volume of gas in a balloon of radius 2.5 m.

3.8 Use rounded numbers to simplify each problem.

(a) The greatest price ever paid for a hat is 165 570 francs, (including tax). If 1 franc equals $0.245, calculate the price of the hat.

(b) The tallest totem pole is 48.8 m high. If it is cylindrical in shape and has a diameter of 1.2 m, calculate the amount of wood in the totem pole.

Consumer Tip: Working With Cheques

There is no need to carry around large amounts of money on your person. Nowadays, the smart consumer puts his or her money in a bank account and writes cheques.

Jennifer Jackson has her chequing account at this bank.

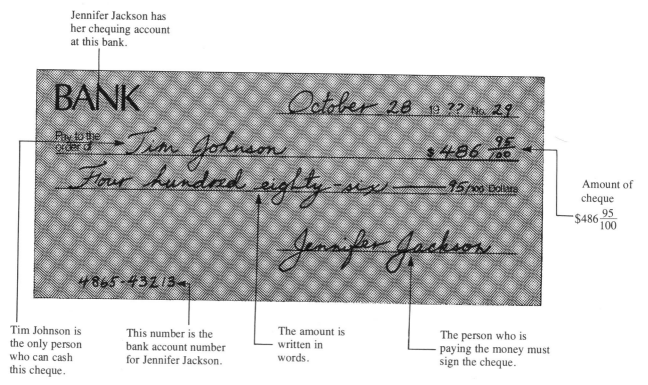

Amount of cheque
$486\frac{95}{100}$

Tim Johnson is the only person who can cash this cheque.

This number is the bank account number for Jennifer Jackson.

The amount is written in words.

The person who is paying the money must sign the cheque.

Whenever you write cheques, you must keep track of the balance of money you have in your chequing account.

Written Exercises

1 George has a balance of $486.25 in his account. He deposited $126.50 and wrote a cheque for $96.20 to buy a 10-speed bicycle. What is the balance in his account?

2 Lori has $168.20 in her account. She writes cheques for $29.60 for a tennis racket, and $16.28 for a radio. What is the balance in her account?

3 Jennifer has $965.35 in her account. She writes a cheque for $486.95 to buy a minibike. What is her balance?

4 Wyn's balance in her chequing account at the start of the month was $169.25. The balance at the end of the month was $36.48. What was the total value of the cheques she wrote that month?

4 Fractions to Use: Skills and Applications

factors and multiples, skills with common fractions, decimals for fractions, applications and problem-solving

Introduction

Fractions occur frequently in your everyday activities.

You often eat $\frac{1}{8}$ of a pizza.

Interest rates are often expressed as fractions.

Consumer sales frequently use fractions to tell you how much you are saving.

- To figure out what your share of the winnings is, you can use fractions.

How much does each person get?

4.1 Factors and Multiples

You need to learn the vocabulary of mathematics.

A factor of a number divides the given number evenly without a remainder.

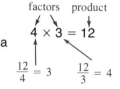

The **factors** of 12 are 1, 2, 3, 4, 6, and 12. You can say that 6 is a factor of 12 since $\frac{12}{6} = 2$, but 5 is not a factor of 12 since 12 can not be divided by 5 evenly.

A **multiple** of a given number is the product of the given number and another whole number. You can say that 12 is a multiple of 1, 2, 3, 4, 6, or 12. Since $12 = 4 \times 3$, then 12 is a multiple of 3. 12 is also a multiple of 4.

To write all the multiples of 3 you write

$\underset{3}{\underline{1 \times 3}} \quad \underset{6}{\underline{2 \times 3}} \quad \underset{9}{\underline{3 \times 3}} \quad \underset{12}{\underline{4 \times 3}}$ and so on.

Example 1
Write the factors of 18.

Solution
To find the factors of 18, think of which numbers divide 18 evenly.
$$\frac{18}{1} = 18 \quad \frac{18}{2} = 9 \quad \frac{18}{3} = 6 \quad \frac{18}{6} = 3 \quad \frac{18}{9} = 2 \quad \frac{18}{18} = 1$$
Thus 1, 2, 3, 6, 9, 18 are factors of 18.

Example 2
Which of the numbers 7, 3, and 4 are not factors of 56?

Solution
You can check by dividing each number into 56.

$\frac{56}{7} = 8, \quad \frac{56}{3}$ does not divide *evenly*, $\frac{56}{4} = 14$

Thus, 3 is not a factor of 56.   7 and 4 are factors!

Greatest Common Factor

The factors of 12 and 18 are shown.
Factors of 12   1, 2, 3, 4, 6, and 12
Factors of 18   1, 2, 3, 6, 9, and 18
The numbers 12 and 18 have the factors 1, 2, 3 and 6 in common. The greatest one of these factors is called the **greatest common factor**. Thus the greatest common factor (G.C.F.) of 12 and 18 is 6.

Least Common Multiple

Multiples of 2 are 2, 4, 6, 8, 10, 12, 14, 16, 18, . . .

Multiples of 3 are 3, 6, 9, 12, 15, 18, 21, . . .

The common multiples of 2 and 3 are 6, 12, 18, . . .

The least or lowest common multiple (L.C.M.) of 2 and 3 is 6.

1 What are the factors of each number?

   (a) 6   (b) 9   (c) 25

2 Which numbers are factors of 24?

   (a) 12   (b) 3   (c) 9   (d) 8

3 Which numbers are not factors of 48?

   (a) 24   (b) 3   (c) 9   (d) 8

4 What are the two greatest factors of each number?

   (a) 30   (b) 50   (c) 75   (d) 100

5 What are the missing factors?

   (a) $25 = 5 \times \square$ (b) $48 = \square \times 6$

   (c) $12 = 4 \times \square$ (d) $36 = 12 \times \square$

   (e) $75 = \square \times 25$ (f) $100 = 10 \times \square$

Written Exercises

A 1 Find the missing factors.

   (a) $16 = 2 \times \square$ (b) $16 = 16 \times \square$

   (c) $14 = \square \times 7$ (d) $14 = 1 \times \square$

   (e) $27 = 3 \times \square$ (f) $27 = 9 \times \square$

2 (a) What are the missing factors for 40?

   $1 \times \square = 40$ $4 \times \square = 40$

   $\square \times 20 = 40$ $\square \times 8 = 40$

   (b) Write all the factors for 40.

   (c) What is the greatest factor of 40?

3 Write all the factors of each number.

   (a) 9   (b) 16 (c) 24 (d) 49 (e) 45 (f) 56

4 Which numbers are factors of the first number?

   (a) 6   1, 2, 3, 4   (b) 8   1, 2, 3, 4

   (c) 15   1, 2, 3, 4, 5   (d) 20   2, 3, 5, 6, 15

5 Which of the following are not factors of 96?

   10, 6, 3, 5, 9, 12, 24, 8, 16, 48

6 Which of the following are factors of 100?

   10, 2, 25, 6, 8, 50

B 7 (a) Write the number 72 as a product of two factors in as many ways as you can.

   (b) Write all the factors of 72.

8 Which number has both 2 and 3 as a factor?

   (a) 6   (b) 10 (c) 15 (d) 24 (e) 36 (f) 75

9 Which number has both 6 and 5 as a factor?

   (a) 90   (b) 45   (c) 50   (d) 120

10 (a) What are the factors of 12? Of 18?

   (b) Which factors are common to 12 and 18?

11 (a) What are the factors of 24? Of 30?

   (b) Which factors are common to 24 and 30?

12 Find the *greatest common factor* for each of the following pairs of numbers.

   (a) 6, 8   (b) 8, 12   (c) 12, 15   (d) 9, 21

   (e) 10, 22 (f) 12, 20 (g) 16, 24   (h) 25, 30

13 Find the greatest common factor of each of the following.

   (a) 25, 30, 45 (b) 24, 36, 18 (c) 24, 48, 72

   (d) 42, 49, 56 (e) 27, 48, 36 (f) 18, 96, 64

14 Write the multiples

   (a) of 3. (b) of 4. (c) common to 3 and 4.

   (d) What is the least common multiple of 3 and 4?

C 15 Write the multiples

   (a) of 6. (b) of 8. (c) common to 6 and 8.

   (d) What is the least common multiple of 6 and 8?

16 Find the least common multiple of each pair of numbers.

   (a) 6, 10   (b) 8, 9   (c) 12, 16 (d) 18, 20

Problem-Solving Strategy: Another Way

There is usually more than one way of solving a problem. The more ways you know, the easier it is to solve the problem. For example, you have already seen one way of obtaining the greatest common factor and the least common multiple. Here is another method which uses your knowledge of prime factors.

▶ 2, 3, 5, 7, 11,... are **prime numbers**. A prime number has only two factors—1 and itself. $2 = 2 \times 1, 3 = 3 \times 1, 5 = 5 \times 1$

▶ 4, 6, 8, 9, 10,... are not prime numbers. They are called **composite numbers**, since they can be composed of factors in more than one way.

$4 = 2 \times 2$
$4 = 4 \times 1$

Find the Greatest Common Factor

To find the **greatest common factor** of 2 numbers, write the prime factors of each number. Then choose *common* prime factors as shown.

Greatest Common Factor $3 \times 5 = 15$

The greatest common factor of 30 and 45 is 15.

Find the Least Common Multiple

To find the **least common multiple** of 2 numbers, write the prime factors of each number.

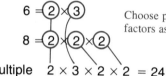

Least Common Multiple $2 \times 3 \times 2 \times 2 = 24$

Check whether 24 is the least common multiple of 6 and 8.

17 Which of the following are prime numbers?
(a) 4   (b) 5   (c) 9   (d) 15 (e) 17 (f) 23

18 Write each number as a product of prime factors. The first one has been done for you.
(a) 72

$72 =$ 8 $\times$ 9   Think of two factors, $72 = 8 \times 9$.
$= 2 \times 2 \times 2 \times 3 \times 3$ Then write each factor as a product of prime factors.

(b) 12 (c) 16 (d) 24 (e) 50 (f) 29 (g) 48
(h) Which of the above numbers is a prime number?

19 (a) Write 12 as a product of prime factors.
(b) Write 18 as a product of prime factors.
(c) Use the factors in (a) and (b) to find the least common multiple of 12 and 18.

20 (a) Write 24 as a product of prime factors.
(b) Write 36 as a product of prime factors.
(c) Use the factors in (a) and (b) to write the greatest common factor of 24 and 36.

21 Find the greatest common factor of each pair of numbers.
(a) 8, 12   (b) 6, 15   (c) 12, 20 (d) 30, 40

22 Find the least common multiple of each pair of numbers.
(a) 8, 9   (b) 6, 15   (c) 18, 24 (d) 6, 21
(e) 24, 36 (f) 12, 16 (g) 25, 30 (h) 32, 96

23 Find the least common multiple of each group of numbers.
(a) 6, 9, 12   (b) 8, 12, 16   (c) 10, 15, 18

Applications: Gears, Gears, Gears

Gears control many of the ways in which you move.

As gear A turns, it drives gear B.
    Gear A has 24 teeth.
    Gear B has 8 teeth.
When gear A turns once, gear B turns 3 times.

Gear C drives gear D. After how many turns will gear C and gear D return to the same position?

To find this out, list the following information.

	1 turn	2 turns	3 turns	4 turns	5 turns	6 turns
Gear C	12 teeth	24 teeth	⃝36 teeth	48 teeth	60 teeth	⃝72 teeth
Gear D	18 teeth	⃝36 teeth	54 teeth	⃝72 teeth	...	

The two gears will return to the same position when they turn through the same number of teeth.

    Gear C turns 3 times ($3 \times 12 = 36$ teeth)
    Gear D turns 2 times ($2 \times 18 = 36$ teeth)

Another way of finding the number of turns each gear makes before the gears return to the same position is to find the lowest common multiple of the numbers of teeth of the gears.
Write each number as a product of prime factors.

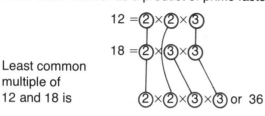

Least common multiple of 12 and 18 is   ②×②×③×③ or 36

24   The numbers of teeth for various gears are shown. Find how many turns it takes for both gears to return to the same position.

	Gear A Number of Teeth	Gear B Number of Teeth
(a)	12	20
(b)	60	90
(c)	40	42
(d)	30	84
(e)	60	36

25   There are two sets of sprockets on a bicycle, one on the rear wheel and one on the driving wheel.

Rear wheel sprocket   Driving wheel sprocket

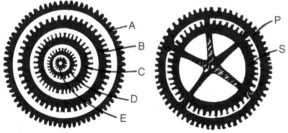

There are 10 combinations of sprockets that the chain of this bicycle can be on. Thus this bicycle is called a 10-speed bicycle.

List the different combinations that the chain can go on for the 10-speeds. For example, 2 combinations are shown.

S—A   P—C

Questions 26 to 30 refer to the bicycle illustrated in Question 25.

26   Sprocket A has 14 teeth. Sprocket P has 40 teeth. How many turns will occur before the 2 sprockets return to their original position?

27   Sprocket S has 52 teeth. Sprocket C has 20 teeth. How many turns will occur before the 2 sprockets return to their original position?

28   Sprocket P turns through 800 teeth.
     (a) How many turns will sprocket C make?
     (b) How many turns will the wheel make?
     (c) The diameter of the rear wheel is 68 cm. How far will the bicycle travel for the number of turns found in (b)?

29   Sprocket S turns through 546 teeth. If sprocket D has 24 teeth,
     (a) how many turns will sprocket D make?
     (b) how many turns will the wheel make?
     (c) The diameter of the rear wheel is 68 cm. How far will the bicycle travel for the number of turns found in (b)?

30   (a) Create a problem of your own based on the above information about the gears for bicycles.
     (b) Write a solution for your problem.

4.2 Working With Fractions

You have often seen numbers such as these in newspapers and in store windows.

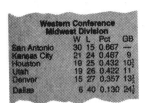

A fraction is used to show part of a whole.

$\frac{2}{3}$ means 2 out of 3 parts.

2 out of 3 parts are shaded.

The numbers 2 and 3 are called the **terms** of the fraction.

Called the numerator.
Tells how many equal ⟶ $\frac{2}{3}$ ⟵ Called the denominator.
parts are shaded.   Tells the number of equal parts.

Example 1
What fraction of each figure is shaded?

(a)

(b)

Solution
(a) The whole is in 8 equal parts.
The number of equal parts shaded is 5.
The fraction is $\frac{5}{8}$.

(b) The whole is in 6 equal parts.
The number of equal parts shaded is 5.
The fraction is $\frac{5}{6}$.

Example 2
From a poll of 25 car drivers, the data shown were recorded. What fraction of the drivers,

(a) wore seat belts?
(b) did not wear seat belts?
(c) had no comment?

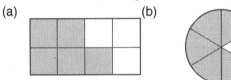

SAFETY POLL
Of the 25 drivers interviewed
17 wore seat belts
7 did not
1 no comment
It has been found that in most accidents the persons wearing seat belts were likely not be injured.

Solution
Total number of drivers is 25.
(a) Number of drivers that wore seat belts is 17.
The fraction is $\frac{17}{25}$.

(b) Number of drivers that did not wear seat belts is 7. The fraction is $\frac{7}{25}$.

(c) Number of drivers with no comment is 1.
The fraction is $\frac{1}{25}$.

Try These

1 What fraction of each figure is shaded?

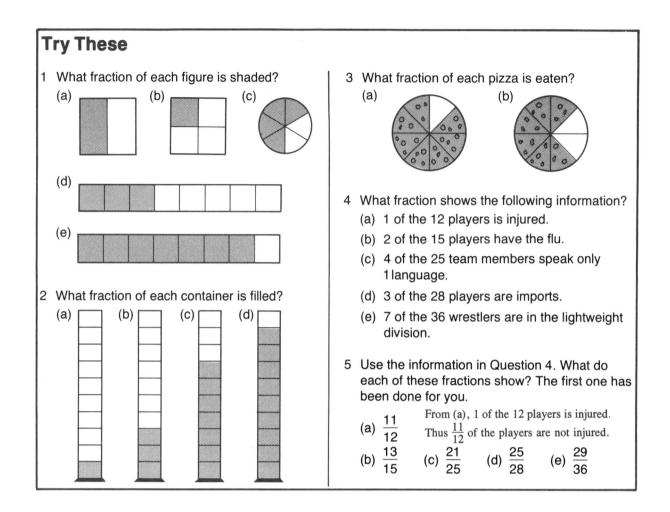

(a)   (b)   (c)

(d)

(e)

2 What fraction of each container is filled?

(a)   (b)   (c)   (d)

3 What fraction of each pizza is eaten?

(a)   (b)

4 What fraction shows the following information?
   (a) 1 of the 12 players is injured.
   (b) 2 of the 15 players have the flu.
   (c) 4 of the 25 team members speak only 1 language.
   (d) 3 of the 28 players are imports.
   (e) 7 of the 36 wrestlers are in the lightweight division.

5 Use the information in Question 4. What do each of these fractions show? The first one has been done for you.

(a) $\dfrac{11}{12}$ From (a), 1 of the 12 players is injured. Thus $\dfrac{11}{12}$ of the players are not injured.

(b) $\dfrac{13}{15}$ (c) $\dfrac{21}{25}$ (d) $\dfrac{25}{28}$ (e) $\dfrac{29}{36}$

Written Exercises

A 1 What fraction of each figure below is shaded?

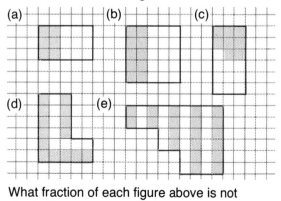

(a)   (b)   (c)

(d)   (e)

What fraction of each figure above is not shaded?

2 Write a fraction to show what part of each figure is shaded.

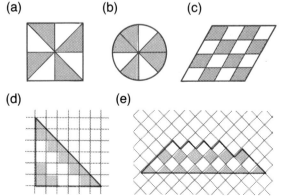

(a)   (b)   (c)

(d)   (e)

110

3 Draw a diagram to show each fraction.

(a) $\frac{1}{2}$ (b) $\frac{1}{4}$ (c) $\frac{1}{3}$ (d) $\frac{1}{5}$ (e) $\frac{2}{3}$ (f) $\frac{9}{10}$

4 What fraction of each of the following is shaded?

(a) (b)

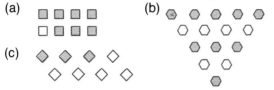

(c)

5 Each charity has collected the amount of money shown. Write a fraction to show what part has been collected.

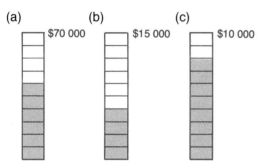

(a)   (b)   (c)

$70 000 $15 000 $10 000

6 Write a fraction to show how much jogging has been completed in each case.

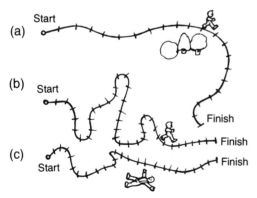

(a) Start

(b) Start

Finish

Finish

(c) Start

Finish

7 (a) What fraction of each tank is full?

(b) What fraction of each tank is empty?

B 8 Write a fraction to show each of the following.

(a) Four students share equally the expenses for a trip. What is each person's share?

(b) A pizza is shared equally among 6 people. How much does each person get?

9 What fraction is
(a) a minute of an hour?
(b) a second of a minute?
(c) a minute of a day?
(d) a day of a week?
(e) a month of a year?
(f) a day of your life to date?

10 Write a fraction to show how much of the recording tape is left.

	length of cassette tape	time used
(a)	30 min	5 min
(b)	60 min	40 min
(c)	90 min	45 min
(d)	120 min	90 min

11 For the survey,
(a) what fraction of drivers wear seat belts?
(b) what fraction of drivers do not wear seat belts?

SEAT BELT SURVEY
Of the 50 cars stopped the following results were obtained.

Number of drivers wearing seat belts   33
Number of drivers not wearing seat belts   17

C
12 Our alphabet has 26 letters with
• letters with line segments like A
• letters with curves like C
• letters with line segments and curves like B
What fraction of the letters are made
(a) entirely of line segments?
(b) entirely of curves?
(c) of line segments and curves?

Applications: Seating Capacities of Airplanes

The seating capacity of the Douglas DC-10 is large enough to hold the population of a small town.

Specifications:
Wing Span	50.4 m
Length	55.6 m
Width of Fuselage	6.0 m
Tail Height	17.7 m
Passenger Capacity	300

13 A Douglas DC-10 has 250 passengers on it.

(a) What fraction of the jet is filled?

(b) What fraction of the jet is not filled?

14 How many DC-10 plane loads would be needed to take all the residents of Caledonia (population 3540) on a Caribbean holiday?

15 A 3-story building is about 12.5 m high. How much higher is the tail of the Douglas DC-10?

16 Write a fraction to show what part of each plane is full.

(a) The DC-9 jet built in 1968 has a capacity of 125 passengers. For a trip from Winnipeg to Calgary the plane had 20 passengers.

(b) The DC-8 jet has 16 first-class seats. On a flight from Vancouver to Edmonton, there were 10 first-class passengers.

(c) The Viscount in 1955 had a seating capacity of 48 passengers. On a flight, 40 passengers flew from Halifax to St. John's.

17 The 747 jumbo jet has 32 first-class seats and 333 economy seats.

(a) What is the total seating capacity of the jumbo jet?

(b) On a flight from St. John's to Montreal, there were 24 first-class passengers. Write a fraction to show what part is filled?

(c) On a flight from Regina to Winnipeg there were 188 passengers. Approximately what fraction of the plane was full?

4.3 Needed Skills: Equivalent Fractions

The diagram shows two pizzas, each half eaten.

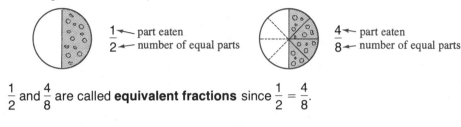

$\frac{1}{2}$ ← part eaten
— number of equal parts

$\frac{4}{8}$ ← part eaten
← number of equal parts

$\frac{1}{2}$ and $\frac{4}{8}$ are called **equivalent fractions** since $\frac{1}{2} = \frac{4}{8}$.

Often, equivalent fractions are used to simplify statements. Each statement tells you the same information.

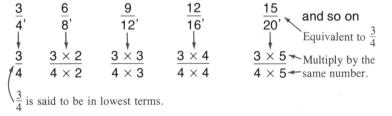

The fraction is $\frac{80}{100}$. ← ——— equivalent fractions ——— → The fraction is $\frac{4}{5}$.

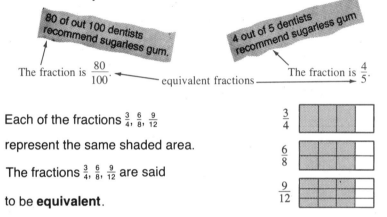

Each of the fractions $\frac{3}{4}, \frac{6}{8}, \frac{9}{12}$

represent the same shaded area.

The fractions $\frac{3}{4}, \frac{6}{8}, \frac{9}{12}$ are said

to be **equivalent**.

$\frac{3}{4}$

$\frac{6}{8}$

$\frac{9}{12}$

Equivalent fractions may be written for any fraction by multiplying the numerator and denominator by the same number, as follows.

$\frac{3}{4}, \quad \frac{6}{8}, \quad \frac{9}{12}, \quad \frac{12}{16}, \quad \frac{15}{20},$ and so on

Equivalent to $\frac{3}{4}$

$\frac{3}{4} \quad \frac{3 \times 2}{4 \times 2} \quad \frac{3 \times 3}{4 \times 3} \quad \frac{3 \times 4}{4 \times 4} \quad \frac{3 \times 5}{4 \times 5}$ ← Multiply by the same number.

$\frac{3}{4}$ is said to be in lowest terms.

Equivalent fractions are also obtained by dividing the numerator and the denominator by the same number, when a fraction in lowest terms is obtained.

To write a fraction in lowest terms, you use your skills with the greatest common factor (G.C.F.). (See Section 4.1).

$\frac{48}{60} = \frac{48 \div 12}{60 \div 12}$ Why do you divide by 12?

$= \frac{4}{5}$

$48 = 2 \times 2 \times 2 \times 2 \times 3$
$60 = 2 \times 2 \times 3 \times 5$
Greatest common factor $= 2 \times 2 \times 3 = 12$

Example 1

Find the missing term of $\frac{8}{10} = \frac{\square}{15}$.

Solution

To find the missing value, write the fraction in lowest terms.

$$\frac{8}{10} = \frac{8 \div 2}{10 \div 2}$$ — 2 is the G.C.F. of 8 and 10.

$$= \frac{4}{5}$$

Think! What do I multiply 5 by to obtain 15? $15 = 5 \times 3$

Thus, multiply the numerator of $\frac{4}{5}$ by 3.

Now find $\square$. $\frac{4}{5} = \frac{\square}{15}$

4×3

$$\frac{4}{5} = \frac{12}{15}$$

Check: $\frac{12}{15} = \frac{12 \div 3}{15 \div 3} = \frac{4}{5}$

Example 2

A bus holds 48 passengers. There are 6 empty seats. What fraction of the bus is filled? Express your fraction in lowest terms.

Solution

▶ Number of seats   48
Number of empty seats   6
Number of filled seats   42

▶ The fraction that shows what part of the bus is filled is

6 is the greatest common factor of 42 and 48.

$$\frac{42}{48} = \frac{42 \div 6}{48 \div 6} = \frac{7}{8}$$

Thus, $\frac{7}{8}$ of the seats are filled.

Try These

1 What two fractions may be used to show how much is shaded for each diagram?

(a)   (b)   (c)

(d)   (e)

2 What fraction of each of the following is not shaded? Express your fraction in lowest terms.

(a)   (b)   (c)

(d)   (e)   (f)

3 Which of the following fractions are equivalent to $\frac{1}{2}$?

(a) $\frac{2}{4}$ (b) $\frac{3}{12}$

(c) $\frac{4}{8}$ (d) $\frac{6}{15}$

4 Which of the following fractions are equivalent to $\frac{2}{3}$?

(a) $\frac{4}{12}$ (b) $\frac{4}{6}$ (c) $\frac{10}{15}$ (d) $\frac{12}{15}$

5 What is each fraction in lowest terms?

(a) $\frac{2}{4}$ (b) $\frac{2}{6}$ (c) $\frac{2}{8}$

(d) $\frac{6}{9}$ (e) $\frac{6}{12}$ (f) $\frac{6}{15}$

Written Exercises

Throughout the exercise, express the fractions in lowest terms.

A 1 What fraction of each figure is shaded?

(a) (b) (c)

(d) (e) (f)

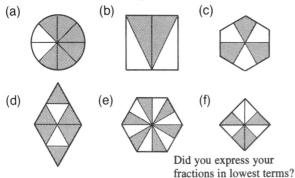

Did you express your
fractions in lowest terms?

2 For each diagram, a term of the fraction is
missing.
A What is the missing term?
B Write the fraction in lowest terms.

(a) (b)

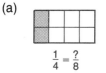

$\dfrac{1}{4} = \dfrac{?}{8}$

$\dfrac{1}{3} = \dfrac{?}{18}$

(c) (d)

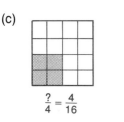

$\dfrac{?}{4} = \dfrac{4}{16}$

$\dfrac{?}{5} = \dfrac{4}{10}$

3 Write a fraction to show how much is shaded.

(a) (b) (c)

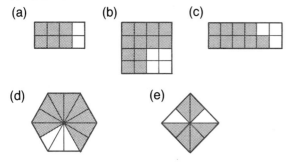

(d) (e)

(f) What do you notice about the answers
above?

4 Simplify each of the following.

(a) $\dfrac{6 \div 2}{8 \div 2}$ (b) $\dfrac{15 \div 5}{20 \div 5}$ (c) $\dfrac{12 \div 4}{16 \div 4}$

(d) $\dfrac{18 \div 6}{24 \div 6}$ (e) $\dfrac{9 \div 3}{12 \div 3}$ (f) $\dfrac{21 \div 7}{28 \div 7}$

(g) What do you notice about your answers?

5 Write each fraction in lowest terms.

(a) $\dfrac{12}{15}$ (b) $\dfrac{16}{20}$ (c) $\dfrac{15}{20}$ (d) $\dfrac{8}{10}$

(e) $\dfrac{18}{20}$ (f) $\dfrac{9}{24}$ (g) $\dfrac{20}{40}$ (h) $\dfrac{8}{12}$

6 Write two equivalent fractions for each of the
following.

(a) $\dfrac{3}{4}$ (b) $\dfrac{2}{3}$ (c) $\dfrac{3}{5}$ (d) $\dfrac{7}{10}$ (e) $\dfrac{4}{5}$ (f) $\dfrac{7}{8}$

7 Complete each of the following to obtain
equivalent fractions.

(a) $\dfrac{1}{4} = \dfrac{?}{8}$ (b) $\dfrac{2}{3} = \dfrac{8}{?}$ (c) $\dfrac{2}{5} = \dfrac{?}{10}$

(d) $\dfrac{3}{5} = \dfrac{?}{100}$ (e) $\dfrac{7}{10} = \dfrac{70}{?}$ (f) $\dfrac{2}{25} = \dfrac{?}{100}$

8 What fraction of a kilometre is each of the
following measures?

(a) 10 m   (b) 100 m   (c) 500 m
(d) 250 m   (e) 750 m   (f) 375 m

9 What fraction of a centimetre is each of the
following measures?

(a) 2 mm   (b) 5 mm   (c) 8 mm

10 Which of the following pairs of fractions are
equivalent?

(a) $\dfrac{1}{2}, \dfrac{4}{8}$ (b) $\dfrac{2}{3}, \dfrac{8}{10}$ (c) $\dfrac{3}{4}, \dfrac{12}{16}$ (d) $\dfrac{3}{5}, \dfrac{5}{10}$

11 For each of the following fractions, write an equivalent fraction with 100 as the denominator.

(a) $\dfrac{1}{2} = \dfrac{\square}{100}$ (b) $\dfrac{1}{4} = \dfrac{\square}{100}$ (c) $\dfrac{1}{10} = \dfrac{\square}{100}$

(d) $\dfrac{1}{5} = \dfrac{\square}{100}$ (e) $\dfrac{5}{10} = \text{e}\dfrac{\square}{100}$ (f) $\dfrac{2}{4} = \dfrac{\square}{100}$

12 For each of the following, replace ◉ with $<$, $>$ or $=$ to make each statement true.

(a) $\dfrac{1}{2}$ ◉ $\dfrac{1}{4}$ (b) $\dfrac{1}{2}$ ◉ $\dfrac{2}{4}$ (c) $\dfrac{1}{2}$ ◉ $\dfrac{1}{3}$

(d) $\dfrac{1}{2}$ ◉ $\dfrac{2}{3}$ (e) $\dfrac{3}{4}$ ◉ $\dfrac{1}{2}$ (f) $\dfrac{3}{4}$ ◉ $\dfrac{6}{8}$

B 13 Write a fraction for each of the following.

(a) Of 36 athletes, 6 want to go skiing.

(b) Of the 25 students, 10 want pizza.

(c) Of the 36 players, 24 are linemen.

14 (a) What fraction of each tank is full?

A   B

(b) What fraction of each tank is empty?

15 The chart below shows the various uses of energy for a particular city.

Energy Use	Part of Total
Homes	$\dfrac{16}{100}$
Business	$\dfrac{20}{100}$
Factories	$\dfrac{40}{100}$
Transportation	$\dfrac{24}{100}$

Write each of the fractions in lowest terms.

16 Each team has set an objective to obtain points. What fraction of the objective has each team reached?

	Team	Objective	Number of points obtained to date
(a)	Roughriders	20	9
(b)	Jets	42	29
(c)	Canucks	60	51
(d)	Blizzards	36	11

17 A disc jockey has the following types of records.

Folk   28   Easy-Listening 46
Rock   36   Country   20

What fraction of the records are
(a) folk?   (b) easy-listening? (c) rock?

18 After a survey of a parking lot, the following numbers were recorded for 100 cars.

	Last Year	This Year
Full Size Cars	52	42
Compact (domestic)	28	36
Compact (foreign)	20	22

What fraction of the total number of cars were

(a) full size, last year?

(b) compact (domestic), this year?

(c) full size, this year?

(d) compact (foreign), last year?

19 A football team consists of 30 players. Six were missing from a practice. What fraction of the team was absent?

20 The Student Council consists of 32 students. Eight were missing for a meeting. What fraction of the council was absent?

C 21 Each person has selected a book to read. Write a fraction to estimate what part of the book has been read? Use a simple fraction.

	Person	Pages in book	Pages read
(a)	Suzanne	464	117
(b)	Jack	680	512
(c)	Jennifer	720	430
(d)	Franko	520	345

4.4   Comparing Fractions

Each charity group set itself a goal for collecting money. Which group came closer to its goal?

To know which charity group did better, you need to be able to compare fractions.

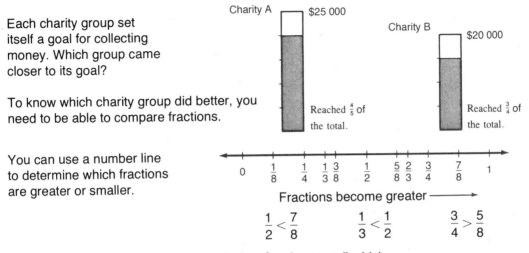

Charity A $25 000

Charity B $20 000

Reached $\frac{4}{5}$ of the total.

Reached $\frac{3}{4}$ of the total.

You can use a number line to determine which fractions are greater or smaller.

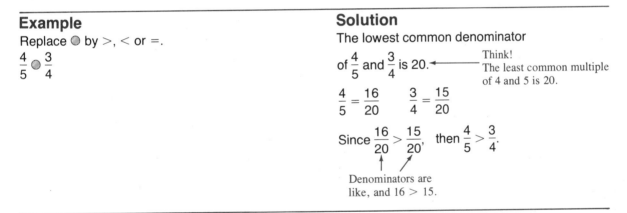

Fractions become greater ⟶

$$\frac{1}{2} < \frac{7}{8} \qquad \frac{1}{3} < \frac{1}{2} \qquad \frac{3}{4} > \frac{5}{8}$$

You may also use your skills with equivalent fractions to tell which is the greater of two fractions. You do this by first finding the lowest common denominator of the two fractions and then writing equivalent fractions with like denominators.

Example

Replace ● by >, < or =.

$$\frac{4}{5} \; ● \; \frac{3}{4}$$

Solution

The lowest common denominator

of $\frac{4}{5}$ and $\frac{3}{4}$ is 20.

Think! The least common multiple of 4 and 5 is 20.

$$\frac{4}{5} = \frac{16}{20} \qquad \frac{3}{4} = \frac{15}{20}$$

Since $\frac{16}{20} > \frac{15}{20}$, then $\frac{4}{5} > \frac{3}{4}$.

Denominators are like, and 16 > 15.

You may now answer the original question about Charity A and Charity B.

Charity A reached $\frac{4}{5}$ of its goal.

Charity B reached $\frac{3}{4}$ of its goal.

Since $\frac{4}{5} > \frac{3}{4}$, then Charity A has the better record.

But may not have received the greatest amount of money. Do you know why?

Fractions great than 1 may be recorded as follows.

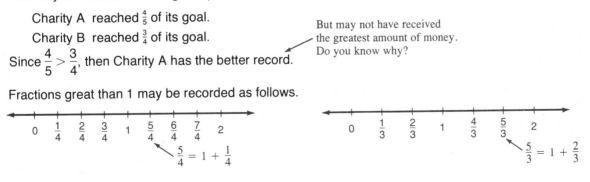

$$\frac{5}{4} = 1 + \frac{1}{4}$$

$$\frac{5}{3} = 1 + \frac{2}{3}$$

117

A fraction such as $\frac{5}{4}$ is called an **improper fraction**. For an improper fraction, the numerator is greater than the denominator.

From the number line $\frac{5}{4}$ represents 1 plus $\frac{1}{4}$.
You may write a mixed fraction as an improper fraction.

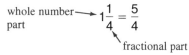

whole number part $\longrightarrow 1\frac{1}{4} = \frac{5}{4}$

fractional part

Try These

1 What is the missing numerator?

(a) $\frac{2}{3} = \frac{?}{6}$ (b) $\frac{1}{2} = \frac{?}{8}$ (c) $\frac{3}{4} = \frac{?}{12}$

(d) $\frac{1}{8} = \frac{?}{16}$ (e) $\frac{1}{3} = \frac{?}{9}$ (f) $\frac{2}{5} = \frac{?}{20}$

2 What is the missing denominator?

(a) $\frac{1}{4} = \frac{5}{?}$ (b) $\frac{3}{5} = \frac{12}{?}$ (c) $\frac{5}{8} = \frac{15}{?}$

(d) $\frac{3}{12} = \frac{1}{?}$ (e) $\frac{18}{36} = \frac{3}{?}$ (f) $\frac{5}{25} = \frac{1}{?}$

3 Which fraction of each pair is greater?

(a) $\frac{3}{5}, \frac{4}{5}$ (b) $\frac{7}{10}, \frac{9}{10}$ (c) $\frac{7}{8}, \frac{5}{8}$

(d) $\frac{4}{5}, \frac{4}{6}$ (e) $\frac{3}{5}, \frac{3}{4}$ (f) $\frac{6}{8}, \frac{6}{9}$

4 Which of $<, >$ or $=$ will make each of the following true?

(a) $\frac{7}{8} \circ \frac{6}{8}$ (b) $\frac{4}{9} \circ \frac{4}{8}$ (c) $\frac{5}{6} \circ \frac{10}{12}$

(d) $\frac{5}{6} \circ \frac{4}{6}$ (e) $\frac{3}{4} \circ \frac{12}{16}$ (f) $\frac{3}{8} \circ \frac{3}{7}$

5 Express each as a mixed fraction.

(a) $\frac{3}{2}$ (b) $\frac{4}{3}$ (c) $\frac{5}{4}$ (d) $\frac{7}{4}$

6 Express each as an improper fraction.

(a) $1\frac{1}{3}$ (b) $1\frac{1}{2}$ (c) $1\frac{1}{4}$ (d) $1\frac{2}{3}$

Written Exercises

A 1 Find the missing value.

(a) $\frac{2}{5} = \frac{2 \times ?}{2 \times 5}$ (b) $\frac{5}{6} = \frac{? \times 5}{2 \times 6}$

(c) $\frac{5 \times 5}{5 \times ?} = \frac{5}{6}$ (d) $\frac{7}{10} = \frac{? \times 3}{10 \times 3}$

(e) $\frac{7 \times 2}{? \times 2} = \frac{14}{16}$ (f) $\frac{5 \times ?}{8 \times 7} = \frac{5}{8}$

2 Complete each of the following.

(a) $\frac{1 \times 2}{4 \times 2} = \frac{?}{8}$ (b) $\frac{3 \times 3}{4 \times 3} = \frac{9}{?}$

(c) $\frac{3 \times 3}{5 \times 3} = \frac{?}{15}$ (d) $\frac{2 \times 4}{5 \times 4} = \frac{?}{20}$

3 What is the lowest common denominator for each pair of fractions?

(a) $\frac{1}{2}, \frac{1}{3}$ (b) $\frac{1}{4}, \frac{5}{8}$ (c) $\frac{3}{5}, \frac{3}{10}$

(d) $\frac{2}{3}, \frac{2}{5}$ (e) $\frac{1}{3}, \frac{5}{11}$ (f) $\frac{6}{7}, \frac{9}{10}$

4 For each pair, which fraction is greater?

(a) $\frac{1}{2}, \frac{6}{10}$ (b) $\frac{1}{2}, \frac{1}{3}$ (c) $\frac{3}{4}, \frac{4}{5}$ (d) $\frac{2}{3}, \frac{5}{6}$

(e) $\frac{1}{4}, \frac{3}{8}$ (f) $\frac{3}{10}, \frac{1}{5}$ (g) $1\frac{1}{3}, 1\frac{1}{2}$ (h) $1\frac{3}{4}, 1\frac{1}{2}$

5 Show which tank, A or B, has more fuel.

(a)

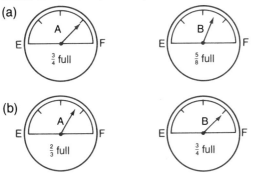

(b)

6 Write each improper fraction as a mixed fraction.

(a) $\frac{3}{2}$ (b) $\frac{5}{3}$ (c) $\frac{7}{3}$ (d) $\frac{9}{4}$

B 7 Use $<, >$ or $=$ to make each of the following true.

(a) $\frac{2}{3} \bullet \frac{3}{4}$ (b) $\frac{2}{5} \bullet \frac{3}{7}$ (c) $\frac{5}{6} \bullet \frac{7}{8}$

(d) $\frac{2}{3} \bullet \frac{4}{5}$ (e) $\frac{3}{8} \bullet \frac{1}{5}$ (f) $\frac{3}{5} \bullet \frac{3}{10}$

8 Which fraction of each pair is greater?

(a) $\frac{7}{8}, \frac{2}{3}$ (b) $\frac{4}{5}, \frac{2}{3}$ (c) $\frac{3}{8}, \frac{1}{4}$

9 Which of the following are True (T)? False (F)?

(a) $\frac{1}{2} < \frac{2}{3}$ (b) $\frac{1}{3} > \frac{3}{5}$ (c) $\frac{2}{3} > \frac{1}{3}$

10 Which fraction of each pair is greater?

(a) $3\frac{1}{2}, 3\frac{1}{4}$ (b) $2\frac{3}{4}, 2\frac{2}{3}$ (c) $8\frac{5}{6}, 8\frac{7}{8}$

11 (a) Find the lowest common denominator of each group of fractions.

A $\frac{3}{10}, \frac{2}{5}, \frac{1}{2}$ B $\frac{4}{5}, \frac{5}{4}, \frac{3}{2}$

(b) What fraction is greatest in A? in B?

12 Write each of the following sets of fractions in order from least to greatest.

(a) $\frac{3}{4}, \frac{2}{3}, \frac{1}{4}$ (b) $\frac{3}{5}, \frac{4}{5}, \frac{4}{7}$ (c) $\frac{3}{8}, \frac{1}{3}, \frac{1}{2}$

13 Marc finished $\frac{8}{9}$ of his goal for fund raising. Greg has finished $\frac{5}{6}$ of his goal for fund raising. Who completed more of his goal?

14 Matt and Phillip are in an egg eating contest. There are 50 eggs to each contestant. Matt has eaten $\frac{1}{10}$ of the eggs and Phillip has eaten $\frac{3}{15}$ of the eggs. Who is winning?

15 Christine practised scoring baskets. Out of 75 shots she scored 60 shots. She says her accuracy rating is $\frac{12}{15}$ while her coach says it's $\frac{4}{5}$. Who is correct?

16 Four hours after the car rally started, the up-to-the-hour results were posted.

Driver	Position
Maureen	At the $\frac{2}{3}$ mark
John	At the $\frac{4}{5}$ mark
Dennis	At the $\frac{3}{4}$ mark

Who was further ahead?

17 Tim and Tony both jog but set different goals to run per week.

	Total distance per week	Distance run by mid-week
Tim	32 km	24 km
Tony	36 km	26 km

By mid-week, who was nearer to his goal?

C 18 In a football game, the record at half-time for each quarterback was

Borgolio: $\dfrac{\text{Passes completed}}{\text{Passes thrown}} = \dfrac{5}{12}$

Zupata: $\dfrac{\text{Passes completed}}{\text{Passes thrown}} = \dfrac{8}{14}$

(a) Which fraction is larger?
(b) Which quarterback had the better record at half-time?

4.5 Decimals For Fractions

The basketball coach keeps a record of Janice's and Suzanne's shooting statistics.

Record of Free Throws

	Number attempted	Number made
Janice	24	18
Suzanne	30	24

It is easier to compare fractions if you write them as decimals.

For Janice

$$\frac{\text{Number of free throws made}}{\text{Number of free throws attempted}} = \frac{18}{24}$$

Calculation

$$= 0.75 \qquad \begin{array}{r} 0.75 \\ 24\overline{)18.00} \end{array}$$

$\frac{18}{24}$ means $18 \div 24$.   Thus, $\frac{18}{24} = 0.75$.

For Suzanne

$$\frac{\text{Number of free throws made}}{\text{Number of free throws attempted}} = \frac{24}{30}$$

$$= 0.8$$

Who has the better record?

Since $0.8 > 0.75$, then $\frac{24}{30} > \frac{18}{24}$. Thus Suzanne has the better record.

Some fractions have decimals that repeat.

Example 1
Write each fraction in decimal form.

(a) $\frac{1}{4}$ (b) $\frac{1}{3}$ (c) $\frac{7}{11}$

Solution

(a) $\frac{1}{4} = 0.25$

$$\begin{array}{r} 0.25 \\ 4\overline{)1.00} \\ \underline{8} \\ 20 \\ \underline{20} \\ 0 \end{array}$$

Since the remainder is 0, the decimal *ends*.

(b) $\frac{1}{3} = 0.3333\ldots$

$$= 0.\overline{3}$$

Placing a bar over the repeating digits is a compact way of writing the repeating decimal.

$$\begin{array}{r} 0.333 \\ 3\overline{)1.0000} \\ \underline{9} \\ 10 \\ \underline{9} \\ 10 \\ \underline{9} \\ 1 \end{array}$$

The remainder is not zero, and repeats. Thus the decimal repeats.

(c) $\frac{7}{11} = 0.6363\ldots$

$$= 0.\overline{63}$$

In this case, 63 repeats.

$$\begin{array}{r} 0.6363 \\ 11\overline{)7.00000} \\ \underline{6.6} \\ 40 \\ \underline{33} \\ 70 \\ \underline{66} \\ 40 \\ \underline{33} \\ 7 \end{array}$$

The pattern continues indefinitely.

Example 2

Which fraction is greater, $\dfrac{29}{33}$ or $\dfrac{15}{17}$?

Solution

$\dfrac{29}{33} = 0.878787\ldots$

Remember $\dfrac{29}{33}$ means $29 \div 33$.

```
    0.878...
33)29.000
   264
    260
    231
    290
    264
     26
```

$\dfrac{15}{17} = 0.8823\ldots$

Remember $\dfrac{15}{17}$ means $15 \div 17$.

```
     0.8823
17)15.0000
   136
    140
    136
      40
      34
      60
      51
       9
```

Since $0.8823\ldots > 0.8787\ldots$, then $\dfrac{15}{17} > \dfrac{29}{33}$.

To write a decimal as a fraction, you must remember what a decimal number represents.

$\quad$ 0.3 means 3 tenths or $\dfrac{3}{10}$.

$\quad$ 0.13 means 13 hundredths or $\dfrac{13}{100}$

$\quad$ 0.013 means 13 thousandths or $\dfrac{13}{1000}$ ⟵ fraction form

decimal form

Example 3

Write each decimal number as a fraction in lowest terms.

(a) 0.4 $\quad$ (b) 0.15

Solution

(a) 0.4 means $\dfrac{4}{10}$ $\qquad$ $\dfrac{4}{10} = \dfrac{4 \div 2}{10 \div 2}$

$\quad$ Thus $0.4 = \dfrac{2}{5}$. $\qquad\quad = \dfrac{2}{5}$

(b) 0.15 means $\dfrac{15}{100}$ $\qquad$ $\dfrac{15}{100} = \dfrac{15 \div 5}{100 \div 5}$

$\quad$ Thus $0.15 = \dfrac{3}{20}$. $\qquad\quad = \dfrac{3}{20}$

Try These

1 What is each fraction in decimal form?

$\quad$ (a) $\dfrac{3}{10}$ $\quad$ (b) $\dfrac{5}{10}$ $\quad$ (c) $\dfrac{7}{10}$ $\quad$ (d) $\dfrac{9}{10}$

$\quad$ (e) $\dfrac{45}{100}$ $\quad$ (f) $\dfrac{65}{100}$ $\quad$ (g) $\dfrac{8}{100}$ $\quad$ (h) $\dfrac{1}{100}$

2 What is a fraction for each decimal?

$\quad$ (a) 0.1 $\qquad$ (b) 0.3 $\qquad$ (c) 0.7

3 What is a fraction for each decimal?

$\quad$ (a) 0.01 $\qquad$ (b) 0.09 $\qquad$ (c) 0.11

$\quad$ (d) 0.13 $\qquad$ (e) 0.17 $\qquad$ (f) 0.99

4 What is a fraction for each decimal?

$\quad$ (a) 0.001 $\qquad$ (b) 0.013 $\qquad$ (c) 0.111

Written Exercises

A 1 Write each fraction in a decimal form.

(a) $\dfrac{1}{10}$ (b) $\dfrac{3}{10}$ (c) $\dfrac{7}{10}$ (d) $\dfrac{95}{100}$

(e) $\dfrac{3}{100}$ (f) $\dfrac{912}{1000}$ (g) $\dfrac{31}{100}$ (h) $\dfrac{2}{5}$

2 Write a decimal for each fraction.

(a) $\dfrac{1}{4}$ (b) $\dfrac{5}{4}$ (c) $\dfrac{7}{5}$ (d) $2\dfrac{1}{4}$

(e) $2\dfrac{1}{2}$ (f) $1\dfrac{4}{5}$ (g) $4\dfrac{3}{20}$ (h) $3\dfrac{1}{8}$

3 Write each of the following as a mixed fraction.

(a) $\dfrac{7}{2}$ (b) $\dfrac{7}{4}$ (c) $\dfrac{11}{4}$ (d) $\dfrac{25}{4}$ (e) $\dfrac{26}{4}$

(f) $\dfrac{27}{10}$ (g) $\dfrac{8}{8}$ (h) $\dfrac{41}{10}$ (i) $\dfrac{48}{12}$

4 Write a decimal numeral for each fraction in Question 3.

5 What is a fraction for each decimal?

(a) 0.1 (b) 0.01 (c) 0.001
(d) 0.3 (e) 0.33 (f) 0.333
(g) 0.033 (h) 0.003 (i) 0.030

6 Write each decimal as a fraction in lowest terms.

(a) 0.6 (b) 0.8 (c) 0.5
(d) 0.25 (e) 0.75 (f) 0.125
(g) 0.15 (h) 0.35 (i) 0.2

7 Write a fraction, in lowest terms for each decimal.

(a) 6.8 (b) 3.4 (c) 2.25
(d) 3.45 (e) 3.125 (f) 6.875

B 8 Write each decimal in a compact form.

(a) $\dfrac{3}{11} = 0.272727\ldots$

(b) $\dfrac{15}{99} = 0.151515\ldots$

(c) $\dfrac{1}{6} = 0.1666\ldots$

(d) $\dfrac{11}{15} = 0.7333\ldots$

(e) $\dfrac{7}{55} = 0.1272727\ldots$

9 Write a decimal for each fraction.

(a) $\dfrac{1}{3}$ (b) $\dfrac{2}{3}$ (c) $\dfrac{3}{13}$ (d) $\dfrac{1}{9}$

(e) $\dfrac{7}{15}$ (f) $\dfrac{5}{12}$ (g) $\dfrac{11}{24}$ (h) $\dfrac{1}{7}$

10 Find the decimal for each fraction. Determine which fraction is greater.

(a) $\dfrac{1}{4}, \dfrac{5}{8}$ (b) $\dfrac{3}{5}, \dfrac{3}{10}$ (c) $\dfrac{2}{3}, \dfrac{2}{5}$

(d) $\dfrac{5}{11}, \dfrac{1}{3}$ (e) $\dfrac{2}{3}, \dfrac{4}{5}$ (f) $\dfrac{5}{6}, \dfrac{7}{8}$

(g) $2\dfrac{3}{4}, 2\dfrac{2}{3}$ (h) $3\dfrac{1}{4}, 3\dfrac{1}{3}$ (i) $5\dfrac{1}{5}, 5\dfrac{2}{9}$

11 Which of the following fractions have repeating decimals?

(a) $\dfrac{4}{11}$ (b) $\dfrac{3}{4}$ (c) $\dfrac{5}{9}$ (d) $\dfrac{5}{8}$

(e) $\dfrac{8}{15}$ (f) $\dfrac{6}{12}$ (g) $\dfrac{7}{12}$ (h) $\dfrac{3}{20}$

12 Find the decimal for each fraction. For each group of fractions, determine which fraction is the greatest.

(a) $\dfrac{6}{7}, \dfrac{9}{10}, \dfrac{7}{8}$ (b) $\dfrac{3}{8}, \dfrac{1}{5}, \dfrac{1}{3}$

(c) $\dfrac{3}{5}, \dfrac{7}{10}, \dfrac{2}{3}$ (d) $1\dfrac{2}{3}, 1\dfrac{1}{4}, 1\dfrac{1}{5}$

(e) $2\dfrac{3}{8}, 2\dfrac{1}{3}, 2\dfrac{1}{2}$ (f) $5\dfrac{3}{4}, 5\dfrac{2}{3}, 5\dfrac{1}{4}$

13 Out of 75 shots, 48 hit the inside 2 rings of the target. In the next round, 52 out of 78 shots did so. Which was the better performance?

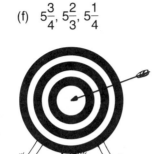

14 Out of 95 points, Jean received 69. Joseph got 65 out of 90 points. Who had the better performance?

15 Last year, at the end of the shipping season, $\frac{5}{12}$ of the ships were stuck in the ice. This year, $\frac{4}{11}$ of the ships were stuck. In which year was the record better?

16 During the gymnastic season, the records of Michael and Andrew were kept.

Michael	Gym Meet A	Gym Meet B	Gym Meet D
Points received	38	42	39
Total possible points	45	60	50

Andrew	Gym Meet A	Gym Meet C	Gym Meet E
Points received	41	47	36
Total possible points	45	65	55

Who has the better performance?

To compare the passing record for a quarterback, a fraction is used.

$$\text{Passing Record} = \frac{\text{number of completed passes}}{\text{number of passes thrown}}$$

17 Write a decimal for each of the following passing records.

(a) $\dfrac{10}{14}$ (b) $\dfrac{8}{16}$ (c) $\dfrac{7}{13}$

(d) $\dfrac{16}{21}$ (e) $\dfrac{15}{18}$ (f) $\dfrac{12}{22}$

18 Which player has the better passing record?

(a) Alfonso $\dfrac{5}{9}$, Jerome $\dfrac{6}{11}$

(b) Jackson $\dfrac{16}{22}$, Lorimer $\dfrac{13}{18}$

19 In a game, Lawson threw 23 passes and completed 12 of them. Harry threw 18 passes and completed 10 of them. Who has the better record?

C 20 The passing record of two quarterbacks for 3 games is shown. Who has the better passing record?

Clark	Game 1	Game 2	Game 3
Passes completed	6	9	8
Passes thrown	13	15	14

Marc	Game 1	Game 2	Game 3
Passes completed	8	7	12
Passes thrown	15	18	16

Calculators and Patterns

When obtaining decimals for fractions, you can often see patterns. For example, these decimals are computed on the calculator.

$$\frac{1}{11} = 0.090909\ldots = 0.\overline{09}$$

$$\frac{2}{11} = 0.181818\ldots = 0.\overline{18}$$

Based on the above pattern, you might predict the decimals for $\frac{3}{11}$, $\frac{4}{11}$, and so on, to be

$$\frac{3}{11} = 0.272727\ldots = 0.\overline{27}$$

$$\frac{4}{11} = 0.363636\ldots = 0.\overline{36}$$

You can check your predictions by computing the decimals.

21 (a) What is the decimal for $\frac{1}{4}$?
   (b) Use the decimal in (a) to predict the decimal for $\frac{3}{4}$.

22 (a) What is the decimal for $\frac{1}{8}$?
   (b) Use the decimal in (a) to predict the decimal for A $\frac{3}{8}$ B $\frac{5}{8}$ C $\frac{7}{8}$
   (c) Check your predictions by calculating the decimals for A, B, and C.

23 (a) Write a decimal for
   A $\frac{1}{27}$ B $\frac{2}{27}$ C $\frac{3}{27}$
   (b) Use your results in (a) to predict the decimal for
   D $\frac{4}{27}$ E $\frac{5}{27}$ F $\frac{6}{27}$
   (c) Check your predictions by calculating the decimals for D, E, and F.

24 (a) What is the decimal for $\frac{1}{3}$?
   (b) Use the answer in (a) to predict the decimal for $\frac{2}{3}$.

25 (a) Express each of the following as a decimal.
   A $\frac{1}{9}$ B $\frac{2}{9}$ C $\frac{3}{9}$
   (b) Use the pattern in (a) to predict the decimal for D $\frac{4}{9}$ E $\frac{5}{9}$ F $\frac{6}{9}$
   (c) Check your predictions by calculating the decimals for D, E, and F.

26 (a) Write a decimal for A $\frac{1}{99}$ B $\frac{4}{99}$ C $\frac{12}{99}$
   (b) Use the pattern in (a) to predict a decimal for D $\frac{15}{99}$ E $\frac{23}{99}$ F $\frac{98}{99}$
   (c) Check your predictions by calculating the decimals for D, E, and F.

27 (a) Write a decimal for
   A $\frac{1}{999}$ B $\frac{31}{999}$ C $\frac{126}{999}$
   (b) Use the pattern in (a) to write a decimal for
   D $\frac{369}{999}$ E $\frac{421}{999}$ F $\frac{998}{999}$

Applications: Patterns in Sports

On the previous page, you found patterns with fractions. Often patterns are useful in helping sports managers to make predictions that will help them win a game or determine which player is better.

For example, in a crucial face-off in a hockey game the coach is the one who decides who is to take the face-off.

The records of two players are shown.

	Federko	Goodenough
Number of face-offs tried	109	126
Number of face-offs won	53	62
Number of face-offs won / Number of face-offs tried	$\frac{53}{109}$	$\frac{62}{126}$

To find who has the better record, the decimal equivalent is calculated (to 3 decimal places).

$$\frac{53}{109} \doteq 0.486 \qquad \frac{62}{126} \doteq 0.492$$

Since 0.492 > 0.486, then Goodenough might be selected to try to win the face-off.

When comparing decimals express your answers to 3 decimal places when necessary.

28 Which of the two players would you use for an important face-off?

	Harris	Butler
Number of face-offs won	96	48
Number of face-offs tried	138	91

29 The ratio

$$\frac{\text{Shots on goal}}{\text{Number of games played}}$$

is used to calculate a player's record for shots on goal. Which of these two players has the better record for shots on goal?

	Davise	Bourne
Shots on goal	23	36
Number of games played	49	78

30 (a) Who has the best record for shots on goal?

	Williams	Schultz	Moxey
Shots on goal	32	48	59
Number of games played	42	58	69

(b) Which player would you, as coach, send into the final minutes of a game to try to win the game?

31 The ratio

$$\frac{\text{number of successful shots}}{\text{number of shots attempted}}$$

is used to calculate a player's record for completing shots. Which of these two players has the better record for completing shots from the foul line in basketball?

	Beverly	Diane
Number of successful shots	69	93
Number of shots attempted	123	143

32 (a) Who has the best record for completing shots from the foul line in basketball?

	Gillies	Browne	Edwards
Number of successful shots	23	31	42
Number of shots attempted	42	63	79

(b) The basketball game is tied. Which of the above three would probably have the best chance of winning the game?

33 The ratio $\dfrac{\text{number of hits}}{\text{number of times at bat}}$ is used to calculate a player's batting average. Who has the better batting average?

	Regson	Player
Number of hits	143	128
Number of times at bat	365	324

34 (a) Which of the following players has the best batting average?

	Gilbert	Wilson	Grant
Number of hits	32	40	24
Number of times at bat	69	83	54

(b) Which of the 3 batters, would you, as manager, send in as a replacement for a batter?

35 (a) From the newspaper clipping, who has the best record for

$$G \div GP?$$

Games Played   Goals

(b) Arrange the players in order of the best record to worst record for G ÷ GP.

(c) Which 2 players would you send into a game that have a good record for (G) ÷ (GP) and have the greatest number of points (PTS)?

Calculator Tip

The calculator is a useful tool for obtaining decimal equivalents of fractions.

Find the decimal for $\dfrac{7}{8}$.

Enter	Calculator Display
C	0
7	7
÷	7.0000000
8	8
=	0.8750000

$$\frac{7}{8} = 0.875$$

4.6 Adding Fractions

In each of the following situations, skill in the addition of fractions is needed. Can you see why?

You need your skills in equivalent fractions to add fractions. You may add **like fractions**.

$$\frac{3}{10} + \frac{1}{10}$$ ⎡The fractions are like fractions.

$$= \frac{4}{10}$$ ⎡Add the numerators 3 + 1 = 4.

Think about what each fraction shows.

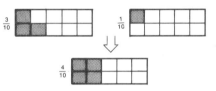

You need to obtain like fractions before you add the following fractions.

$$\frac{1}{2} + \frac{3}{10}$$ —— You cannot add unlike fractions.

$$= \frac{5}{10} + \frac{3}{10}$$ —— Now the fractions are like.

$$= \frac{8}{10}$$ —— Add the numerators. 5 + 3 = 8.

$$= \frac{4}{5}$$ —— ⎡Express your answer in lowest terms. $\frac{8}{10} = \frac{8 \div 2}{10 \div 2} = \frac{4}{5}$

You may think of these diagrams to see the addition of fractions.

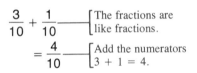

Example 1

Find each sum.

(a) $\frac{1}{2} + \frac{3}{4}$ (b) $\frac{2}{3} + \frac{1}{4}$ (c) $\frac{3}{8} + \frac{1}{6}$

Use your work with equivalent fractions to write like fractions.

Solution

Remember: find the lowest common denominator.

(a) $\frac{1}{2} + \frac{3}{4}$

$= \frac{2}{4} + \frac{3}{4}$

$= \frac{5}{4} = 1\frac{1}{4}$

(b) $\frac{2}{3} + \frac{1}{4}$

$= \frac{8}{12} + \frac{3}{12}$

$= \frac{11}{12}$

(c) $\frac{3}{8} + \frac{1}{6}$

$= \frac{9}{24} + \frac{4}{24}$

$= \frac{13}{24}$

The skills you learned for adding fractions must be extended when adding mixed fractions.

Example 2

Find the sum. $6\frac{3}{4} + 2\frac{1}{2}$

Solution

$$6\frac{3}{4} + 2\frac{1}{2} = 6\frac{3}{4} + 2\frac{2}{4}$$

Write like fractions by finding the lowest common denominator of the fractions.

$$= 8\frac{5}{4}$$

Remember: $\frac{5}{4} = 1\frac{1}{4}$

$$= 9\frac{1}{4}$$

$8\frac{5}{4} = 8 + \frac{5}{4} = 8 + 1\frac{1}{4} = 9\frac{1}{4}$

Example 3

To repair a minibike, the following hours of labour were needed.

Repair chain assembly $1\frac{1}{2}$ h

Tune up for the motor $1\frac{3}{4}$ h

Labour costs $12.80/h. What was the total labour cost?

Refer to your Steps For Solving Problems, page 04.

Solution

Total time for labour.

$$1\frac{1}{2} + 1\frac{3}{4} = 1\frac{2}{4} + 1\frac{3}{4}$$

Write improper fraction as a mixed fraction.

$$= 2\frac{5}{4}$$

$\frac{5}{4} = 1\frac{1}{4}$

$$= 3\frac{1}{4}$$

Cost for 1 h of labour $12.80
Cost for 3 h of labour $3 \times \$12.80 = \$38.40$
Cost for $\frac{1}{4}$ h of labour $\dfrac{\$12.80}{4} = \$\ 3.20$

Total Cost $41.60

Always be sure to make a final statement when answering the problem.

The total labour cost to repair the minibike was $41.60.

Try These

1 Match each diagram to find the sum.

(a) $\frac{1}{4} + \frac{1}{4}$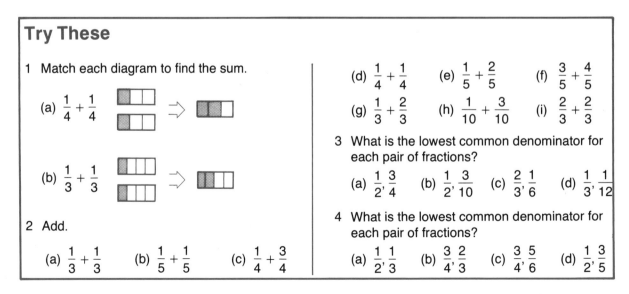

(b) $\frac{1}{3} + \frac{1}{3}$

2 Add.

(a) $\frac{1}{3} + \frac{1}{3}$ (b) $\frac{1}{5} + \frac{1}{5}$ (c) $\frac{1}{4} + \frac{3}{4}$

(d) $\frac{1}{4} + \frac{1}{4}$ (e) $\frac{1}{5} + \frac{2}{5}$ (f) $\frac{3}{5} + \frac{4}{5}$

(g) $\frac{1}{3} + \frac{2}{3}$ (h) $\frac{1}{10} + \frac{3}{10}$ (i) $\frac{2}{3} + \frac{2}{3}$

3 What is the lowest common denominator for each pair of fractions?

(a) $\frac{1}{2}, \frac{3}{4}$ (b) $\frac{1}{2}, \frac{3}{10}$ (c) $\frac{2}{3}, \frac{1}{6}$ (d) $\frac{1}{3}, \frac{1}{12}$

4 What is the lowest common denominator for each pair of fractions?

(a) $\frac{1}{2}, \frac{1}{3}$ (b) $\frac{3}{4}, \frac{2}{3}$ (c) $\frac{3}{4}, \frac{5}{6}$ (d) $\frac{1}{2}, \frac{3}{5}$

Written Exercises

Write the answers to the following questions in lowest terms.

A 1 Use each diagram to find the sum.

(a) $\frac{1}{2} + \frac{1}{4}$ (b) $\frac{1}{4} + \frac{3}{8}$

(c) $\frac{1}{2} + \frac{1}{3}$

2 Find each sum.

(a) $\frac{1}{10} + \frac{1}{10}$ (b) $\frac{1}{4} + \frac{3}{4}$ (c) $\frac{3}{5} + \frac{1}{5}$

(d) $\frac{3}{4} + \frac{3}{4}$ (e) $\frac{5}{10} + \frac{1}{10}$ (f) $\frac{3}{10} + \frac{2}{10}$

3 What is the lowest common denominator for each fraction? Find each sum.

(a) $\frac{1}{2} + \frac{1}{4}$ (b) $\frac{1}{3} + \frac{1}{6}$ (c) $\frac{1}{4} + \frac{3}{8}$

4 Find each sum.

(a) $\frac{3}{4} + \frac{1}{2}$ (b) $\frac{5}{6} + \frac{1}{3}$ (c) $\frac{3}{10} + \frac{2}{5}$

(d) $\frac{25}{100} + \frac{5}{10}$ (e) $\frac{3}{10} + \frac{26}{100}$ (f) $\frac{3}{100} + \frac{1}{10}$

5 Find the total time for each exercise.

(a) running $\frac{3}{4}$ min, $\frac{1}{2}$ min

(b) situps $\frac{1}{4}$ min, $\frac{1}{2}$ min

(c) chinups $\frac{3}{4}$ min, $\frac{3}{4}$ min

6 What is the lowest common denominator for each fraction? Find each sum.

(a) $\frac{1}{2} + \frac{1}{3}$ (b) $\frac{2}{3} + \frac{1}{4}$ (c) $\frac{3}{5} + \frac{1}{3}$

7 Find each sum.

(a) $\frac{3}{8} + \frac{1}{3}$ (b) $\frac{3}{4} + \frac{1}{6}$ (c) $\frac{2}{3} + \frac{1}{10}$

8 Find the total time taken for each event.

		Lap 1	Lap 2
(a)	Backstroke	$\frac{1}{3}$ min	$\frac{3}{4}$ min
(b)	Freestyle	$\frac{1}{3}$ min	$\frac{1}{2}$ min
(c)	Underwater	$\frac{2}{3}$ min	$\frac{3}{4}$ min

B 9 Find the sum of mixed fractions.

(a) $3\frac{1}{4} + 2\frac{1}{4}$ (b) $3\frac{1}{5} + 2\frac{3}{5}$ (c) $2\frac{1}{3} + 3\frac{2}{3}$

(d) $4\frac{3}{8} + 3\frac{7}{8}$ (e) $5\frac{9}{10} + 6\frac{3}{10}$ (f) $2\frac{3}{10} + 2\frac{7}{10}$

10 Find the sum.

(a) $1\frac{1}{2} + 3\frac{1}{4}$ (b) $2\frac{1}{3} + 2\frac{1}{6}$ (c) $3\frac{1}{4} + 1\frac{3}{8}$

11 Add mixed fractions.

(a) $3\frac{3}{10} + 5\frac{1}{10}$ (b) $4\frac{1}{5} + 6\frac{3}{5}$ (c) $5\frac{1}{2} + 2\frac{5}{8}$

12 Scuba divers are always aware of the time spent on a dive. Find the total time spent scuba diving.

searching for coral $15\frac{1}{2}$ min

collecting starfish $8\frac{3}{4}$ min

13 Find the total time exercised by each student.

		Running	Situps
(a)	Jerome	$5\frac{1}{4}$ min	$3\frac{1}{2}$ min
(b)	Jennifer	$3\frac{1}{2}$ min	$1\frac{1}{2}$ min
(c)	Joseph	$2\frac{1}{2}$ min	$\frac{3}{4}$ min

Applications: Fractions and Everyday Problems

You often need to add fractions.

The situations in which you may need to add fractions might differ, but the steps for solving the problems are always the same.

To solve each of the following problems, you need to add fractions. Review the following *Steps For Solving Problems*.

Step A Understand the problem.
"What information am I given?"
"What information am I asked to find?"
Step B Decide on the method.
Step C Find the answer.
Step D Check the answer.
Step E Make a final statement.

14 In constructing a well, $\frac{5}{8}$ of the depth is drilled on the first day. On the second day, $\frac{1}{4}$ of the depth is drilled. What fraction of the depth in all has been drilled at the end of the second day?

15 The Corner Store sold $2\frac{3}{4}$ cases of cola on Friday and $6\frac{1}{2}$ cases on Saturday. How many cases of cola were sold in all?

16 A machine gear is made from an alloy containing $\frac{3}{10}$ parts aluminum and $\frac{1}{100}$ part copper. What fraction of the alloy is aluminum and copper?

17 Joanne used a cassette tape to record songs.

Rock music $\frac{1}{4}$ of the tape
Ballads $\frac{1}{3}$ of the tape

What fraction of the tape has been used?

18 A gardener designs a garden so that $\frac{1}{5}$ of the area contains roses, $\frac{3}{10}$ contains marigolds and $\frac{1}{4}$ contains petunias. What fraction of the garden in all is made up of these flowers?

19 Sid performed the following exercises during a workout.

Situps $12\frac{1}{2}$ min   Running
Chinups $10\frac{1}{4}$ min   on the spot $5\frac{3}{4}$ min

How long did he exercise in all?

20 Maxine typed an assignment as shown.

Friday $3\frac{1}{2}$ h   Sunday $1\frac{1}{3}$ h
Saturday $2\frac{3}{4}$ h

What was the total time for typing?

21 In one month, Dan went to 4 parties. The amounts of time he spent at the parties are as follows:

Party 1 $5\frac{1}{2}$ h   Party 3 $2\frac{1}{2}$ h
Party 2 $4\frac{3}{4}$ h   Party 4 $4\frac{1}{3}$ h

For how many hours in all did Dan party that month?

22 The school band practised the following amounts of time during a 2-week period.

Week 1 $2\frac{1}{2}$ h, $1\frac{2}{3}$ h   Week 2 $3\frac{1}{2}$ h, $2\frac{3}{4}$ h

(a) For how long in all did the band practise during week 1? week 2?

(b) For how long in all did the band practise during the 2-week period?

4.7 Subtracting Fractions

Steps similar to those used in adding fractions are used in subtracting fractions.

$$\frac{3}{8} - \frac{1}{8} = \frac{3-1}{8}$$ ← The fractions are like. Thus subtract numerators.

$$= \frac{2}{8} = \frac{1}{4}$$ ← Write the fraction in lowest terms.

To subtract unlike fractions (different denominators), find the lowest common denominator of the fractions.

$$\frac{1}{2} - \frac{3}{8}$$

$$= \frac{4}{8} - \frac{3}{8}$$ ← The fractions are like. Subtract the numerators. $4 - 3 = 1$

$$= \frac{1}{8}$$

You may think of these diagrams to help you subtract fractions.

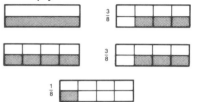

Example 1

Calculate.

(a) $\frac{3}{10} - \frac{1}{10}$ (b) $\frac{1}{2} - \frac{3}{10}$ (c) $\frac{3}{4} - \frac{1}{6}$

Solution

(a) $\frac{3}{10} - \frac{1}{10}$

$$= \frac{3-1}{10}$$

$$= \frac{2}{10} = \frac{1}{5}$$

(b) $\frac{1}{2} - \frac{3}{10}$

$$= \frac{5}{10} - \frac{3}{10}$$

$$= \frac{2}{10} = \frac{1}{5}$$

(c) $\frac{3}{4} - \frac{1}{6}$

$$= \frac{9}{12} - \frac{2}{12}$$

$$= \frac{7}{12}$$

Some steps may eventually be done mentally.

To subtract mixed fractions, you need to use your previous skills.
Compare the following.

$$6\frac{3}{4} - 2\frac{1}{2} = 6\frac{3}{4} - 2\frac{2}{4}$$

Subtract whole numbers. $6 - 2$

$$= 4\frac{1}{4}$$

Subtract fractions. $\frac{3}{4} - \frac{2}{4} = \frac{1}{4}$

$$6\frac{1}{2} - 2\frac{3}{4} = 6\frac{2}{4} - 2\frac{3}{4}$$

$$= 5\frac{6}{4} - 2\frac{3}{4}$$ ← Why is $6\frac{2}{4} = 5\frac{6}{4}$?

$$= 3\frac{3}{4}$$

Example 2

An air tank for scuba diving contains $12\frac{1}{2}$ min of air. Mary uses $6\frac{3}{4}$ min for a quick dive. How much air is left?

Solution

Amount of air in tank $12\frac{1}{2}$ min

Amount Mary uses $6\frac{3}{4}$ min

Subtract to find how much air is left.

$$12\frac{1}{2} - 6\frac{3}{4} = 12\frac{2}{4} - 6\frac{3}{4}$$

$$= 11\frac{6}{4} - 6\frac{3}{4}$$

$$= 5\frac{3}{4}$$

Thus, $5\frac{3}{4}$ min of air are left.

Try These

1 Match each diagram to find the difference.

(a) $\dfrac{3}{4} - \dfrac{1}{4}$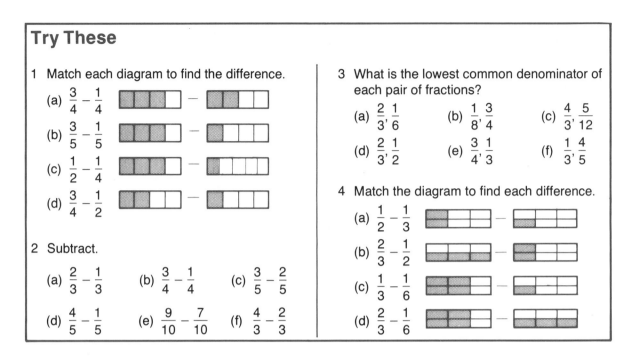

(b) $\dfrac{3}{5} - \dfrac{1}{5}$

(c) $\dfrac{1}{2} - \dfrac{1}{4}$

(d) $\dfrac{3}{4} - \dfrac{1}{2}$

2 Subtract.

(a) $\dfrac{2}{3} - \dfrac{1}{3}$ (b) $\dfrac{3}{4} - \dfrac{1}{4}$ (c) $\dfrac{3}{5} - \dfrac{2}{5}$

(d) $\dfrac{4}{5} - \dfrac{1}{5}$ (e) $\dfrac{9}{10} - \dfrac{7}{10}$ (f) $\dfrac{4}{3} - \dfrac{2}{3}$

3 What is the lowest common denominator of each pair of fractions?

(a) $\dfrac{2}{3}, \dfrac{1}{6}$ (b) $\dfrac{1}{8}, \dfrac{3}{4}$ (c) $\dfrac{4}{3}, \dfrac{5}{12}$

(d) $\dfrac{2}{3}, \dfrac{1}{2}$ (e) $\dfrac{3}{4}, \dfrac{1}{3}$ (f) $\dfrac{1}{3}, \dfrac{4}{5}$

4 Match the diagram to find each difference.

(a) $\dfrac{1}{2} - \dfrac{1}{3}$

(b) $\dfrac{2}{3} - \dfrac{1}{2}$

(c) $\dfrac{1}{3} - \dfrac{1}{6}$

(d) $\dfrac{2}{3} - \dfrac{1}{6}$

Written Exercises

A 1 Find the difference shown by each diagram.

(a) $\dfrac{3}{4} - \dfrac{1}{2}$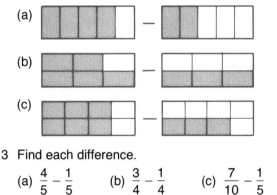

(b) $\dfrac{2}{3} - \dfrac{1}{6}$

2 What difference is shown by each diagram? Find the difference.

(a)

(b)

(c)

3 Find each difference.

(a) $\dfrac{4}{5} - \dfrac{1}{5}$ (b) $\dfrac{3}{4} - \dfrac{1}{4}$ (c) $\dfrac{7}{10} - \dfrac{1}{5}$

(d) $\dfrac{3}{4} - \dfrac{1}{2}$ (e) $5\dfrac{4}{5} - \dfrac{1}{10}$ (f) $\dfrac{5}{6} - \dfrac{1}{3}$

4 Find how much longer Lap 1 is than Lap 2.

	Lap 1	Lap 2
(a)	$\dfrac{3}{4}$ min	$\dfrac{1}{2}$ min
(b)	$\dfrac{1}{2}$ min	$\dfrac{1}{4}$ min
(c)	$\dfrac{1}{2}$ min	$\dfrac{1}{3}$ min

5 What difference is shown by each diagram? Find the difference?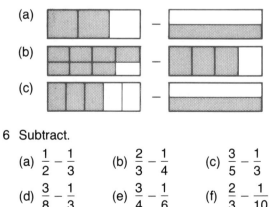

(a)

(b)

(c)

6 Subtract.

(a) $\dfrac{1}{2} - \dfrac{1}{3}$ (b) $\dfrac{2}{3} - \dfrac{1}{4}$ (c) $\dfrac{3}{5} - \dfrac{1}{3}$

(d) $\dfrac{3}{8} - \dfrac{1}{3}$ (e) $\dfrac{3}{4} - \dfrac{1}{6}$ (f) $\dfrac{2}{3} - \dfrac{1}{10}$

132

7 A part of each of the following pizzas is eaten. Calculate how much of each pizza is left.

(a)   (b)

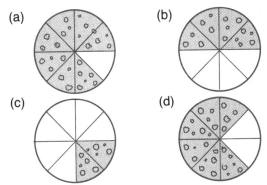

(c)   (d)

8 Find the difference.

(a) $3\frac{1}{4} - 2\frac{1}{4}$ (b) $3\frac{3}{5} - 2\frac{1}{5}$ (c) $4\frac{2}{3} - 2\frac{1}{3}$

(d) $3\frac{1}{2} - 2\frac{1}{4}$ (e) $4\frac{3}{6} - 3\frac{1}{3}$ (f) $3\frac{7}{8} - 2\frac{1}{4}$

9 (a) What is the lowest common denominator of the fractions $3\frac{1}{3}$ and $2\frac{1}{4}$?

(b) Find $3\frac{1}{3} - 2\frac{1}{4}$?

10 Subtract.

(a) $3\frac{2}{3} - 1\frac{1}{2}$ (b) $6\frac{5}{6} - 3\frac{1}{4}$ (c) $8\frac{1}{3} - 2\frac{1}{5}$

(d) $5\frac{1}{2} - 3\frac{3}{5}$ (e) $6\frac{2}{5} - 2\frac{3}{4}$ (f) $5\frac{1}{4} - 3\frac{2}{3}$

11 (a) What is the lowest common denominator of the fractions $\frac{3}{4}$, $\frac{1}{2}$, and $\frac{1}{8}$?

(b) Find $\frac{3}{4} + \frac{1}{2} - \frac{1}{8}$.

12 Calculate.

(a) $\frac{3}{8} + \frac{1}{2} - \frac{1}{4}$ (b) $\frac{5}{8} - \frac{3}{8} + \frac{1}{4}$

(c) $\frac{1}{4} + \frac{1}{2} - \frac{1}{8}$ (d) $\frac{5}{6} - \frac{1}{4} + \frac{1}{3}$

13 Calculate.

(a) $2\frac{1}{4} + 3\frac{1}{2} - 1\frac{5}{8}$ (b) $3\frac{1}{8} + 2\frac{1}{2} - 3\frac{1}{4}$

(c) $3\frac{3}{8} - 2\frac{1}{2} + 3\frac{1}{4}$ (d) $3\frac{1}{3} - 2\frac{1}{6} + 3\frac{1}{2}$

14 Before the trip, the tank is $\frac{3}{4}$ full. During a trip $\frac{2}{3}$ of a tank is used. How much is in the tank now?

15 After the party, $\frac{3}{4}$ of a cake is left. If Michael eats $\frac{1}{2}$ of the cake for breakfast, how much cake is now left?

16 Robin used a cassette tape to record songs.
Dance music $\frac{1}{3}$ of the tape.
Ballads $\frac{3}{8}$ of the tape.
What fraction of the tape is still left?

17 A scuba tank has $15\frac{3}{4}$ min of air left. If $5\frac{1}{2}$ min are used, how much air is left?

18 Landing the glider took $6\frac{1}{2}$ min. The take-off took $2\frac{3}{4}$ min. How much more time did the landing take?

19 A bearing contains $\frac{1}{4}$ part aluminum and $\frac{2}{3}$ part copper. The remainder is iron. What fraction of the bearing is iron?

20 A student spends $\frac{1}{3}$ of the time sleeping, $\frac{1}{4}$ of the time on school work and $\frac{1}{8}$ of the time watching T.V. What fraction of the day is left for other activities?

21 A photographer develops $\frac{1}{4}$ of pictures in the first hour and $\frac{1}{3}$ of the pictures in the second hour. The remainder is developed in the third hour. What fraction is developed in the third hour?

Applications: Fractions And Music

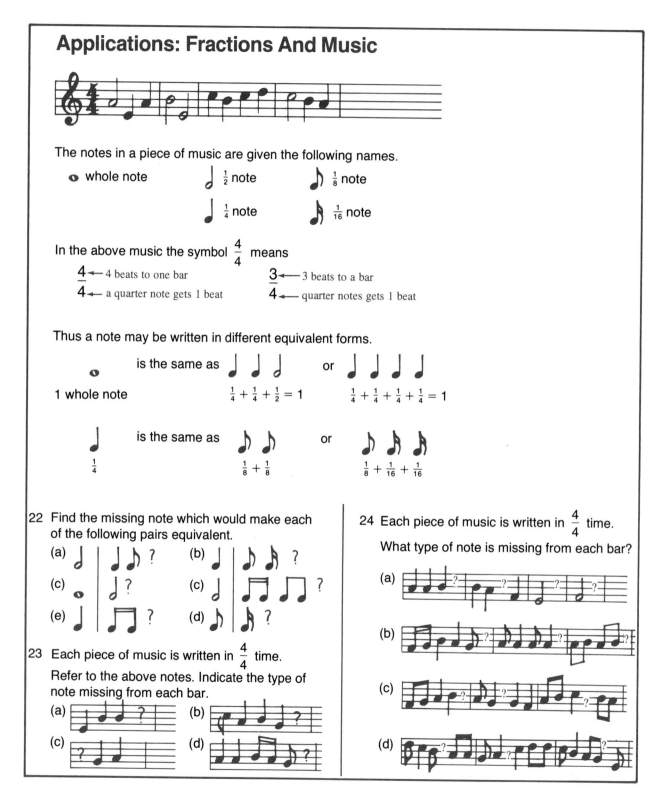

The notes in a piece of music are given the following names.

𝅝 whole note   𝅗𝅥 $\frac{1}{2}$ note   ♪ $\frac{1}{8}$ note

𝅘𝅥 $\frac{1}{4}$ note   𝅘𝅥𝅯 $\frac{1}{16}$ note

In the above music the symbol $\frac{4}{4}$ means

$\frac{4}{4}$ — 4 beats to one bar $\frac{3}{4}$ — 3 beats to a bar
— a quarter note gets 1 beat   — quarter notes gets 1 beat

Thus a note may be written in different equivalent forms.

𝅝   is the same as   𝅘𝅥 𝅘𝅥 𝅗𝅥   or   𝅘𝅥 𝅘𝅥 𝅘𝅥 𝅘𝅥

1 whole note $\frac{1}{4} + \frac{1}{4} + \frac{1}{2} = 1$ $\frac{1}{4} + \frac{1}{4} + \frac{1}{4} + \frac{1}{4} = 1$

𝅘𝅥   is the same as   ♪ ♪   or   ♪ 𝅘𝅥𝅯 𝅘𝅥𝅯

$\frac{1}{4}$ $\frac{1}{8} + \frac{1}{8}$ $\frac{1}{8} + \frac{1}{16} + \frac{1}{16}$

22 Find the missing note which would make each of the following pairs equivalent.

(a) 𝅘𝅥 | 𝅘𝅥 ♪ ?   (b) 𝅘𝅥 | 𝅘𝅥 ♪ 𝅘𝅥𝅯 ?

(c) 𝅝 | 𝅗𝅥 ?   (c) 𝅗𝅥 | ♫ ♫ ?

(e) 𝅘𝅥 | ♫ ?   (d) ♪ | 𝅘𝅥𝅯 ?

23 Each piece of music is written in $\frac{4}{4}$ time. Refer to the above notes. Indicate the type of note missing from each bar.

(a)   (b)

(c)   (d)

24 Each piece of music is written in $\frac{4}{4}$ time.

What type of note is missing from each bar?

(a)

(b)

(c)

(d)

4.8 Multiplying Fractions

You may use the addition of fractions to obtain an answer for the product of fractions.

$$\frac{1}{4} + \frac{1}{4} + \frac{1}{4} = \frac{3}{4} \qquad\qquad 3 \times \frac{1}{4} = \frac{3}{4}$$

The same result may be obtained by multiplying.

$$3 \times \frac{1}{4} = \frac{3}{1} \times \frac{1}{4} = \frac{3 \times 1}{1 \times 4} \text{\small — Multiply numerators.}$$
$$\text{\small — Multiply denominators.}$$
$$= \frac{3}{4}$$

Thus to multiply fractions, you may multiply as shown.

$$\frac{1}{2} \times \frac{3}{5} = \frac{1 \times 3}{2 \times 5} \text{\small — Multiply numerators.}$$
$$\text{\small — Multiply denominators.}$$
$$= \frac{3}{10}$$

To find $\frac{1}{2}$ of $\frac{3}{5}$, you may think of the following.

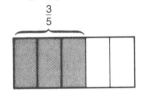

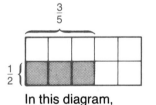

In this diagram,
3 equally shaded parts represent $\frac{3}{5}$.

In this diagram,
3 equally shaded parts represent $\frac{3}{10}$.

Thus, $\frac{1}{2}$ of $\frac{3}{5} = \frac{3}{10}$.

But $\frac{1}{2} \times \frac{3}{5} = \frac{1 \times 3}{2 \times 5} = \frac{3}{10}$ \qquad Thus $\frac{1}{2}$ of $\frac{3}{5} = \frac{1}{2} \times \frac{3}{5} = \frac{3}{10}$.

Thus you may replace "of" with $\times$ when multiplying fractions.

Example 1

Calculate.

(a) $\frac{2}{3} \times \frac{4}{5}$ \qquad (b) $\frac{2}{3} \times \frac{1}{4}$

Solution

(a) $\frac{2}{3} \times \frac{4}{5} = \frac{2 \times 4}{3 \times 5}$
$$= \frac{8}{15}$$

(b) $\frac{2}{3} \times \frac{1}{4} = \frac{\overset{1}{2}}{3} \times \frac{1}{\underset{2}{4}}$
$$= \frac{1 \times 1}{3 \times 2}$$
$$= \frac{1}{6}$$

Remember
• multiply numerators.
• multiply denominators.

To multiply mixed fractions, write each mixed fraction as an improper fraction.

Example 2
Find each product.

(a) $8 \times 3\frac{1}{4}$ (b) $1\frac{1}{3} \times 3\frac{3}{10}$

Solution

(a) $8 \times 3\frac{1}{4}$

$= \frac{8}{1} \times \frac{13}{4}$

$= \frac{\overset{2}{\cancel{8}}}{1} \times \frac{13}{\underset{1}{\cancel{4}}}$

$= \frac{2 \times 13}{1 \times 1}$

$= 26$

(b) $1\frac{1}{3} \times 3\frac{3}{10}$

$= \frac{\overset{2}{\cancel{4}}}{\underset{1}{\cancel{3}}} \times \frac{\overset{11}{\cancel{33}}}{\underset{5}{\cancel{10}}}$

$= \frac{2 \times 11}{1 \times 5}$

$= \frac{22}{5}$

$= 4\frac{2}{5}$

Example 3
There were 864 spectators at the basketball game. If $\frac{3}{4}$ of them were students, how many students were there?

Solution

$\frac{3}{4}$ of $864 = \frac{3}{4} \times 864$

$= \frac{3}{\underset{1}{\cancel{4}}} \times \overset{216}{\cancel{864}}$

$= 3 \times 216 = 648$

There were 648 students.

Try These

1 Which product may be matched with which diagram?

(a) $\frac{1}{4} \times \frac{1}{3}$

(b) $\frac{1}{2} \times \frac{1}{3}$

(c) $\frac{1}{4} \times \frac{2}{3}$

(d) $\frac{2}{3} \times \frac{1}{2}$

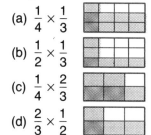

2 What product may be calculated using each diagram?

(a)   (b)

(c)

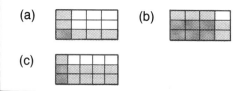

3 Find each product.

(a) $\frac{1}{2} \times \frac{1}{3}$ (b) $\frac{1}{2} \times \frac{1}{4}$ (c) $\frac{1}{2} \times \frac{1}{5}$

(d) $\frac{1}{3} \times \frac{2}{3}$ (e) $\frac{2}{3} \times \frac{1}{5}$ (f) $\frac{3}{8} \times \frac{1}{2}$

4 Calculate.

(a) $\frac{1}{2}$ of 10   (b) $\frac{1}{3}$ of 15   (c) $\frac{2}{3}$ of 30

(d) $\frac{1}{4}$ of 40   (e) $\frac{2}{4}$ of 40   (f) $\frac{3}{4}$ of 40

5 What is each mixed fraction as an improper fraction?

(a) $1\frac{1}{2}$ (b) $1\frac{1}{3}$ (c) $1\frac{3}{5}$ (d) $1\frac{3}{8}$

(e) $2\frac{3}{4}$ (f) $2\frac{7}{8}$ (g) $2\frac{3}{4}$ (h) $2\frac{5}{6}$

Written Exercises

In each of the following questions, give your answers in lowest terms.

A 1 Calculate.

(a) $\frac{1}{2}$ of 24   (b) $\frac{1}{3}$ of 27   (c) $\frac{2}{3}$ of 27

(d) $\frac{3}{4}$ of 16   (e) $\frac{3}{8}$ of 24   (f) $\frac{3}{10}$ of 25

2 Find each of the following.

(a) $\frac{2}{3}$ of 48¢   (b) $\frac{3}{5}$ of 60 m

(c) $\frac{4}{5}$ of 100 kg   (d) $\frac{2}{3}$ of 99 km

(e) $\frac{3}{4}$ of 3 dozen   (f) $\frac{3}{5}$ of 2500 L

3 Multiply.

(a) $3 \times \frac{3}{4}$ (b) $5 \times \frac{1}{8}$ (c) $6 \times \frac{3}{5}$

(d) $8 \times \frac{3}{4}$ (e) $6 \times \frac{2}{3}$ (f) $\frac{2}{3} \times 9$

(g) $\frac{3}{4} \times 8$ (h) $16 \times \frac{3}{8}$ (i) $24 \times \frac{5}{6}$

4 Match each product with the diagram. Find the answers.

(a) $\frac{1}{2} \times \frac{3}{4}$

(b) $\frac{2}{3} \times \frac{1}{4}$

(c) $\frac{3}{5} \times \frac{1}{2}$

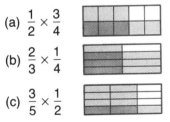

5 Find each product.

(a) $\frac{3}{4} \times \frac{1}{5}$ (b) $\frac{2}{3} \times \frac{4}{5}$

(c) $\frac{1}{4} \times \frac{3}{8}$ (d) $\frac{2}{5} \times \frac{2}{3}$

(e) $\frac{3}{8} \times \frac{1}{5}$ (f) $\frac{3}{5} \times \frac{1}{2}$

6 (a) There are 7 pizzas on a table as shown. How many whole pizzas are there in all?

(b) There are 6 pizzas, each with a piece missing as shown. How many whole pizzas are there in all?

7 Find each product.

(a) $3 \times \frac{1}{3}$ (b) $8 \times \frac{1}{8}$ (c) $\frac{3}{4} \times \frac{4}{3}$

(d) $\frac{5}{4} \times \frac{4}{5}$ (e) $\frac{3}{8} \times \frac{8}{3}$ (f) $\frac{9}{5} \times \frac{5}{9}$

What do you notice about each of the above answers?

8 A product may be written as shown.
$$\frac{2}{3} \times \frac{4}{5} = \left(\frac{2}{3}\right)\left(\frac{4}{5}\right).$$
Find each product.

(a) $\left(\frac{2}{3}\right)\left(\frac{1}{4}\right)$ (b) $\left(\frac{1}{6}\right)\left(\frac{3}{4}\right)$ (c) $\left(\frac{10}{3}\right)\left(\frac{3}{4}\right)$

(d) $\left(\frac{3}{4}\right)\left(\frac{4}{5}\right)$ (e) $\left(\frac{7}{8}\right)\left(\frac{4}{5}\right)$ (f) $\left(\frac{3}{10}\right)\left(\frac{5}{6}\right)$

9 Calculate.

(a) $\frac{1}{2} \times 12.4$ (b) $\frac{1}{3} \times 16.5$ (c) $\frac{2}{3} \times 3.6$

(d) $\frac{3}{4} \times 10.4$ (e) $\frac{4}{5} \times 10.5$ (f) $\frac{2}{3} \times 16.8$

(g) $\frac{3}{8} \times 48.8$ (h) $\frac{7}{8} \times 36.8$ (i) $\frac{3}{10} \times 12.5$

10 Calculate. The first one has been done for you.

(a) $\dfrac{2}{3} \times \dfrac{3}{5} \times \dfrac{1}{2}$ Simplify the steps before multiplying.

$$\dfrac{2}{3} \times \dfrac{3}{5} \times \dfrac{1}{2}$$
$$= \dfrac{\overset{1}{\cancel{2}}}{\underset{1}{\cancel{3}}} \times \dfrac{\overset{1}{\cancel{3}}}{5} \times \dfrac{1}{\underset{1}{\cancel{2}}}$$
$$= \dfrac{1 \times 1 \times 1}{1 \times 5 \times 1} = \dfrac{1}{5}$$

(b) $\dfrac{3}{4} \times \dfrac{1}{3} \times \dfrac{7}{8}$

(c) $\dfrac{1}{3} \times \dfrac{2}{3} \times \dfrac{6}{5}$

(d) $\dfrac{3}{4} \times \dfrac{1}{3} \times \dfrac{8}{3}$

(e) $\dfrac{4}{5} \times \dfrac{10}{3} \times \dfrac{1}{8}$

(f) $\dfrac{3}{8} \times \dfrac{4}{3} \times \dfrac{1}{10}$

(g) $\dfrac{3}{10} \times \dfrac{5}{6} \times \dfrac{1}{2}$

B 11 Calculate.

(a) $4 \times \dfrac{2}{3}$

(b) $4 \times 1\dfrac{2}{3}$

(c) $\dfrac{1}{4} \times 1\dfrac{2}{3}$

(d) $8 \times \dfrac{3}{4}$

(e) $8 \times 3\dfrac{3}{4}$

(f) $\dfrac{1}{8} \times 3\dfrac{3}{4}$

(g) $10 \times \dfrac{1}{5}$

(h) $10 \times 2\dfrac{1}{5}$

(i) $\dfrac{1}{10} \times 2\dfrac{1}{5}$

12 Multiply.

(a) $\dfrac{2}{3} \times 2\dfrac{1}{3}$

(b) $\dfrac{1}{4} \times 3\dfrac{1}{8}$

(c) $\dfrac{3}{5} \times 1\dfrac{2}{3}$

(d) $\dfrac{2}{3} \times 3\dfrac{1}{4}$

(e) $3\dfrac{1}{2} \times \dfrac{4}{5}$

(f) $3\dfrac{1}{8} \times \dfrac{4}{3}$

13 Calculate.

(a) $1\dfrac{1}{8} \times \dfrac{8}{9}$

(b) $\dfrac{3}{4} \times 1\dfrac{1}{3}$

(c) $\dfrac{2}{5} \times 2\dfrac{1}{2}$

(d) $1\dfrac{1}{5} \times \dfrac{5}{6}$

(e) $\dfrac{3}{8} \times 2\dfrac{2}{3}$

(f) $\dfrac{4}{5} \times 1\dfrac{1}{4}$

What do you notice about each of the above answers?

14 Find each product.

(a) $2\dfrac{1}{4} \times 1\dfrac{3}{5}$

(b) $3\dfrac{3}{4} \times 3\dfrac{1}{8}$

(c) $2\dfrac{3}{4} \times 1\dfrac{1}{2}$

(d) $1\dfrac{3}{4} \times 6\dfrac{1}{.4}$

(e) $4\dfrac{1}{5} \times 2\dfrac{1}{4}$

(f) $2\dfrac{3}{10} \times 3\dfrac{1}{2}$

15 A ride on a roller coaster takes $2\dfrac{1}{2}$ min. Tom paid for 7 rides. How long was he on the roller coaster?

16 Heather works 4 d a week and $2\dfrac{3}{4}$ h/d at the hamburger stand. How many hours per week does she work?

17 Fred can sink 12 layups in 1 min. How many layups can he sink in $10\dfrac{1}{4}$ min?

18 Blue Hill Ski Resort is making artificial snow at the rate of $3\dfrac{1}{4}$ cm/d. What will be the depth of the snow in 25 d? (Assume no snow melted.)

19 Gail worked $\dfrac{3}{4}$ h yesterday and worked $\dfrac{1}{3}$ of that today. How long did she work today?

20 A weeping fig tree grew $1\dfrac{1}{5}$ cm last month. At this rate, what will be its height in 20 months?

21 4936 people attended a football game. If $\dfrac{3}{4}$ of these people were students, how many students were there?

22 The cost of a car insurance policy for 6 months is $\dfrac{3}{5}$ of the annual premium. Find the cost for 6 months if the annual premium is $250.

23 Greg earns $8/h. If he is paid $1\dfrac{1}{2}$ times his regular hourly rate for overtime, what is his hourly overtime rate?

C

24 Normally it takes John 20.4 s to run from first base to home plate. During the championship game, he was clocked at a speed $\dfrac{2}{3}$ of his usual time. How long did it take John to run the distance?

Applications: Problems For the Consumer

Stores have special sales to reduce the amount of merchandise they have in stock or to stimulate consumer buying.

Regular Price	$9.49
Discount $\frac{1}{4}$ off	$2.37
Sale Price	$7.12

The sale price of the record is $7.12.

To check whether your answer is reasonable, use your rounding skills.

$9.49 is rounded to $10.00
$\frac{1}{4}$ of $10

$$\begin{array}{r} 2.50 \\ \hline \$7.50 \end{array}$$

Thus the sale price is reasonable.

25 The regular price of each item is shown in each advertisement. Calculate the sale price.

(a) Bicycle $\frac{1}{4}$ off $96.

(b) Tennis set $\frac{1}{3}$ off $28.80

(c) Radio $\frac{1}{2}$ off $39.50

(d) Ski-Doo Motor Oil $\frac{2}{3}$ off $6.90

26 A "Rolling Stones" L.P. that regularly sells for $15.50 has been reduced by $\frac{1}{3}$. Calculate
(a) the amount of the reduction.
(b) the sale price of the album.

27 Copy and complete the table.

Item	Regular Price	Discount	Savings	Sale Price
Transistor radio	$8.90	$\frac{1}{2}$ off	?	?
Calculator	$39.50	$\frac{2}{3}$ off	?	?
L.P.	$7.64	$\frac{1}{4}$ off	?	?
Chess Set	$19.50	$\frac{1}{4}$ off	?	?
3-D Tic Tac Toe	$15.00	$\frac{1}{3}$ off	?	?

28 Calculate the total sale price, to the nearest cent, if you buy all of these items.

	Regular Price	Save
Skirt	$22.50	$\frac{1}{3}$ off
Blouse	$13.75	$\frac{1}{4}$ off
Jeans	$24.00	$\frac{1}{2}$ off

At the annual Sammy's Sale, the store displayed these advertisements.

Clothes $\frac{1}{3}$ off	Accessories $\frac{1}{2}$ off	Shoes $\frac{1}{4}$ off

29 Calculate the sale price of each purchase. Regular prices are shown.
(a) 1 pair of jeans $24.75; 1 belt $8.59.
(b) 1 sweater $16.50; 1 tie $9.50.
(c) 1 shirt $22.95; 1 purse $32.50.
(d) 1 pair of shoes $29.90; 3 pairs of socks at $3.95 each (pair).

30 Jean purchased 2 blouses at $16.50 each and 3 pairs of sneakers at $21.50 each. What is the total sale price of her purchases?

4.9 Dividing Fractions

To solve certain problems, you need to divide by a fraction.

> It takes 6 h in all to apply several coats of varnish to a cabinet. If it takes $\frac{3}{4}$ h to apply each coat (including drying time), how many coats are applied?

In order to solve this problem you must be able to answer these questions:

I What information am I given?

II What information am I asked to find?

You need to know how many $\frac{3}{4}$ h there are in 6 h.

Thus, to solve the problem, you need to find the answer to $6 \div \frac{3}{4}$.

You may find the answer by thinking of the following diagram.

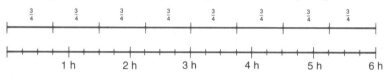

Thus, based on the above diagram, 8 coats are applied.

Using a diagram each time to find an answer is time consuming. You can use your skills with multiplication to develop a method of dividing fractions.

To calculate $\frac{3}{4} \div \frac{2}{3}$ think of the form $\dfrac{\frac{3}{4}}{\frac{2}{3}}$.

Then $\dfrac{3}{4} \div \dfrac{2}{3} = \dfrac{\frac{3}{4}}{\frac{2}{3}} = \dfrac{\frac{3}{4} \times \frac{3}{2}}{\frac{2}{3} \times \frac{3}{2}}$

To obtain 1 as the denominator, multiply by $\frac{3}{2}$ since $\frac{2}{3} \times \frac{3}{2} = 1$. The numerator *and* the denominator are both multiplied by the same number $\frac{3}{2}$.

$= \dfrac{\frac{3}{4} \times \frac{3}{2}}{1}$

$= \dfrac{3}{4} \times \dfrac{3}{2}$

From the above steps, the original division is now rewritten in terms of multiplication.

$$\frac{3}{4} \div \frac{2}{3} = \frac{3}{4} \times \frac{3}{2} = 1\frac{1}{8}$$

To divide by a fraction, invert and multiply by the fraction.

$$\frac{3}{4} \div \frac{2}{3} = \frac{3}{4} \times \frac{3}{2} = \frac{9}{8}$$

How are these related?

How are the operations related?

Example

Divide.

(a) $\frac{3}{8} \div \frac{1}{4}$ (b) $2\frac{1}{4} \div \frac{3}{4}$ (c) $4\frac{1}{2} \div 1\frac{1}{2}$

Solution

(a) $\frac{3}{8} \div \frac{1}{4}$

$= \frac{3}{8} \times \frac{4}{1}$

$= \frac{3}{8} \times \frac{4}{1}$

$= \frac{3}{2}$

$= 1\frac{1}{2}$

The reciprocal of $\frac{1}{4}$ is $\frac{4}{1}$

(b) $2\frac{1}{4} \div \frac{3}{4}$

$= \frac{9}{4} \div \frac{3}{4}$

$= \frac{9}{4} \times \frac{4}{3}$

$= \frac{9}{4} \times \frac{4}{3}$

$= 3$

(c) $4\frac{1}{2} \div 1\frac{1}{2}$

$= \frac{9}{2} \div \frac{3}{2}$

$= \frac{9}{2} \times \frac{2}{3}$

$= \frac{9}{2} \times \frac{2}{3}$

$= 3$

Try These

1 What is the reciprocal of each fraction?

(a) $\frac{1}{2}$ (b) $\frac{2}{3}$ (c) $\frac{3}{4}$ (d) $\frac{5}{2}$

(e) $\frac{3}{2}$ (f) $\frac{4}{3}$ (g) 3   (h) 8

2 What is the reciprocal of the fraction shown?

(a) $\square \div \frac{1}{4}$ (b) $\square \div \frac{5}{2}$ (c) $\square \div \frac{3}{2}$

(d) $\square \div \frac{2}{5}$ (e) $\square \div \frac{5}{3}$ (f) $\square \div \frac{3}{4}$

3 Express each division in terms of multiplication.

(a) $\frac{3}{8} \div 4$ (b) $\frac{4}{5} \div 5$ (c) $\frac{5}{8} \div \frac{1}{3}$

(d) $\frac{4}{10} \div 5$ (e) $\frac{1}{4} \div 8$ (f) $\frac{7}{8} \div 9$

4 Match each division question with its corresponding multiplication.

(a) $\frac{3}{4} \div \frac{2}{3}$ A $\frac{3}{4} \times \frac{5}{4}$

(b) $\frac{4}{3} \div \frac{3}{2}$ B $\frac{3}{4} \times \frac{3}{2}$

(c) $\frac{3}{4} \div \frac{4}{5}$ C $\frac{4}{3} \times \frac{4}{5}$

(d) $\frac{4}{3} \div \frac{5}{4}$ D $\frac{4}{3} \times \frac{2}{3}$

5 What is each division written in terms of multiplication? The first one is done for you.

(a) $\frac{1}{2} \div \frac{2}{3}$ $\frac{1}{2} \div \frac{2}{3} = \frac{1}{2} \times \frac{3}{2}$ $\frac{3}{2}$ is the reciprocal of $\frac{2}{3}$

(b) $\frac{1}{2} \div \frac{1}{3}$ (c) $\frac{2}{3} \div \frac{1}{2}$ (d) $\frac{3}{4} \div \frac{2}{3}$

Written Exercises

A 1 (a) What is the reciprocal of $\frac{3}{2}$?

(b) Calculate $\frac{3}{4} \div \frac{3}{2}$.

2 (a) What is the reciprocal of $\frac{4}{3}$?

(b) Calculate $\frac{5}{8} \div \frac{4}{3}$.

3 Calculate.

(a) $\frac{3}{4} \div \frac{1}{4}$ (b) $\frac{3}{5} \div \frac{1}{5}$ (c) $\frac{5}{9} \div \frac{1}{3}$

4 Simplify.

(a) $\frac{3}{8} \div \frac{1}{2}$ (b) $\frac{5}{6} \div \frac{2}{3}$ (c) $\frac{4}{9} \div \frac{3}{4}$

(d) $\frac{3}{8} \div \frac{3}{4}$ (e) $\frac{8}{9} \div \frac{8}{12}$ (f) $\frac{4}{7} \div \frac{7}{8}$

5 Simplify.

(a) $\frac{5}{6} \div 5$ (b) $\frac{3}{4} \div 9$ (c) $\frac{7}{9} \div 7$

(d) $\frac{9}{10} \div 6$ (e) $3 \div \frac{3}{5}$ (f) $9 \div \frac{3}{4}$

6 Simplify each of the following. Be sure you read carefully which operation to use.

(a) $14 \div \frac{7}{10}$ (b) $9 \times \frac{4}{3}$ (c) $12 \div \frac{2}{3}$

(d) $24 \div \frac{3}{4}$ (e) $56 \times \frac{8}{7}$ (f) $15 \div \frac{3}{2}$

(g) $36 \times \frac{1}{4}$ (h) $48 \div \frac{8}{5}$ (i) $32 \div \frac{1}{4}$

B 7 What is the reciprocal of each of the following?

(a) $1\frac{1}{2}$ (b) $3\frac{1}{3}$ (c) $4\frac{1}{2}$ (d) $4\frac{3}{4}$

8 Simplify.

(a) $5\frac{1}{2} \div 18$ (b) $3 \div 1\frac{1}{2}$ (c) $6\frac{2}{3} \div \frac{4}{5}$

(d) $63 \div 1\frac{1}{8}$ (e) $9\frac{1}{3} \div 2\frac{1}{3}$ (f) $7\frac{3}{5} \div 3\frac{4}{5}$

9 Calculate each of the following. Read carefully!

(a) $64 \div \frac{1}{2}$ (b) $\frac{6}{5} \times \frac{3}{2}$ (c) $12 \div \frac{15}{16}$

(d) $\frac{2}{3} \div \frac{1}{3}$ (e) $\frac{3}{9} \div \frac{3}{5}$ (f) $1\frac{2}{3} \times 1\frac{1}{5}$

(g) $1\frac{1}{4} \div \frac{5}{6}$ (h) $\frac{3}{4} \times 1\frac{1}{9}$ (i) $11\frac{2}{3} \div 4\frac{2}{3}$

10 It takes 15 h to finish the table. Each coat requires $\frac{3}{4}$ h to dry. How many coats are applied?

11 Sophie is having a pizza party on Saturday night. She ordered 8 pizzas. If the average person eats $\frac{1}{3}$ of a pizza, how many persons will 8 pizzas serve?

12 There are 8 large bags of pretzels for the party. Nancy uses bowls which hold $\frac{2}{3}$ of a bag. How many bowls are needed?

13 It takes 14 h to seal the special floor with varnish. If each coat requires $1\frac{3}{4}$ h to dry, how many coats are applied?

14 An archery program requires 6 h of instruction time. Each class lasts $\frac{1}{2}$ h. How many classes make up the program?

15 A novel has 210 pages. If Roma takes about $1\frac{3}{4}$ min to read each page, how long will it take her to read the book?

16 A driver education course requires 36 h of classroom instruction. How many lessons will be required if each lesson lasts

(a) $\frac{3}{4}$ h?   (b) $\frac{1}{2}$ h?   (c) $1\frac{1}{3}$ h?

17 (a) Lisa can shape an apple pie shell in $\frac{3}{4}$ min. How many could she shape in 3 h?

(b) Lesley needs $1\frac{2}{3}$ min to shape a pizza shell. How many could she shape in 3 h?

(c) Refer to (a) and (b). How much longer would it take Lesley to shape 100 shells than Lisa?

C

18 (a) Lori can type a statement in $\frac{1}{2}$ min. How many statements could she type in $2\frac{1}{2}$ min?

(b) Irene needs $\frac{2}{3}$ min to type a statement. How many statements could she type in 12 min?

(c) Which girl would type more statements in $\frac{1}{2}$ h? How many more?

142

Applications: Music For Fraction Lovers

The skills of addition and subtraction are helpful in understanding music. (See *Applications: Fractions and Music*, page 134.)
To find equivalent values of musical notes, you may use your multiplication skills with fractions.

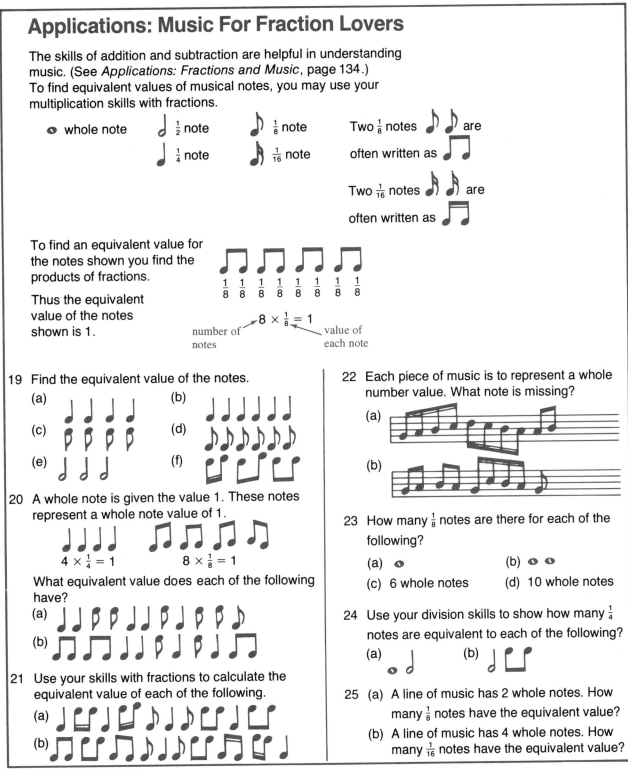

○ whole note $\frac{1}{2}$ note $\frac{1}{8}$ note   Two $\frac{1}{8}$ notes are often written as

$\frac{1}{4}$ note $\frac{1}{16}$ note

Two $\frac{1}{16}$ notes are often written as

To find an equivalent value for the notes shown you find the products of fractions.

Thus the equivalent value of the notes shown is 1.

$\frac{1}{8}$ $\frac{1}{8}$ $\frac{1}{8}$ $\frac{1}{8}$ $\frac{1}{8}$ $\frac{1}{8}$ $\frac{1}{8}$ $\frac{1}{8}$

number of notes → $8 \times \frac{1}{8} = 1$ ← value of each note

19 Find the equivalent value of the notes.
(a)
(b)
(c)
(d)
(e)
(f)

20 A whole note is given the value 1. These notes represent a whole note value of 1.

$4 \times \frac{1}{4} = 1$ $8 \times \frac{1}{8} = 1$

What equivalent value does each of the following have?
(a)
(b)

21 Use your skills with fractions to calculate the equivalent value of each of the following.
(a)
(b)

22 Each piece of music is to represent a whole number value. What note is missing?
(a)

(b)

23 How many $\frac{1}{8}$ notes are there for each of the following?
(a) ○   (b) ○ ○
(c) 6 whole notes   (d) 10 whole notes

24 Use your division skills to show how many $\frac{1}{4}$ notes are equivalent to each of the following?
(a)   (b)

25 (a) A line of music has 2 whole notes. How many $\frac{1}{8}$ notes have the equivalent value?
    (b) A line of music has 4 whole notes. How many $\frac{1}{16}$ notes have the equivalent value?

143

4.10 Problem Solving: Knowing Vocabulary

Before you can solve any problem you must be able to understand the words in the problem, and also be able to follow the instructions given. In other words, if you don't understand what you are being asked to do, you will not be able to solve the problem. The following exercises give you practice in
▶ translating words into mathematics.
▶ following instructions.

Written Exercises

1 Find the square of the sum $\frac{1}{2} + \frac{2}{3}$.

2 Add the product $\left(\frac{2}{3}\right)\left(\frac{3}{5}\right)$ to the difference $\frac{3}{4} - \frac{1}{4}$.

3 From the sum $\frac{3}{8} + \frac{1}{4} + \frac{1}{3}$ subtract the product $\left(\frac{2}{3}\right)\left(\frac{3}{4}\right)\left(\frac{4}{5}\right)$.

4 Find the square of the difference $\frac{3}{8} - \frac{1}{4}$.

5 From the difference $4\frac{2}{3} - 1\frac{1}{4}$ subtract the product $\left(1\frac{2}{3}\right)\left(1\frac{1}{8}\right)$.

6 Subtract the square of $\frac{2}{3} - \frac{1}{3}$ from the product $\left(\frac{4}{5}\right)\left(\frac{5}{3}\right)$.

7 From the product $\left(\frac{4}{3}\right)\left(1\frac{4}{5}\right)$ subtract the quotient $2\frac{2}{3} \div 1\frac{1}{7}$.

8 Increase the square of $1\frac{2}{3} - \frac{4}{5}$ by the sum $1\frac{1}{8} + 2\frac{2}{3}$.

9 Decrease the sum $1\frac{3}{4} + 3\frac{5}{8}$ by the product $\left(1\frac{2}{3}\right)\left(1\frac{1}{8}\right)$.

10 Divide the greater of the following answers by $\frac{1}{3}$.

A $\frac{2}{3} - \frac{1}{6}$ B $1\frac{1}{3} - \frac{5}{6}$

11 Subtract the difference $1\frac{1}{4} - \frac{3}{8}$ from the greater of the following.

A $1\frac{2}{3} + 2\frac{1}{2}$ B $2\frac{2}{3} - \frac{5}{8}$

12 Follow these instructions.

A To the sum $\frac{1}{2} + \frac{1}{3}$ add the product $\left(\frac{3}{4}\right)\left(\frac{1}{6}\right)$.

B To your answer in A, add the difference $\frac{1}{2} - \frac{1}{3}$.

C Subtract the square of $\frac{1}{3} - \frac{1}{6}$ from your answer in B.

D Take $\frac{1}{2}$ of your answer in C.
What is your final answer?

13 Follow these instructions.

A Increase the sum $\frac{1}{3} + \frac{1}{4}$ by the product $\left(1\frac{1}{8}\right)\left(\frac{2}{3}\right)$.

B Decrease your answer in A by $\frac{1}{4} \div \frac{1}{8}$.

C Find the square of your answer in B.

D Divide your answer in C by the result $\frac{1}{3} - \frac{1}{4}$.
What is your final answer?

Skills to Practise: A Chapter Review

4.1 (a) Write the factors of 36.

(b) Find the greatest common factor of each of the following.

    A 6, 8   B 27, 45   C 8, 12, 18

(c) Find the least common multiple of each of the following groups of numbers.

    A 16, 24   B 4, 6, 18

4.2 (a) What fraction of each diagram is shaded?

A    B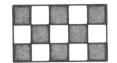

(b) What fraction is
A a metre of a kilometre?
B a centimetre of a metre?
C a millimetre of a centimetre?

4.3 (a) Find each missing term.

    A $\dfrac{2}{3} = \dfrac{?}{12}$ B $\dfrac{6}{8} = \dfrac{15}{?}$

(b) Which symbol, $>$ or $<$, can be used to make each of the following statements true?

    A $\dfrac{1}{2} \bullet \dfrac{3}{4}$ B $\dfrac{4}{5} \bullet \dfrac{3}{4}$

(c) Each person decided to jog the amount of time each week shown in the chart. Write a fraction to show the amount of time each person actually jogged.

	Person	Objective	Actual Amount
A	Benson	30 min	12 min
B	Ean	40 min	25 min
C	Eleanor	60 min	40 min

4.4 (a) Which of the following are true?

    A $\dfrac{1 \times 3}{2 \times 3} = \dfrac{3}{6}$ B $\dfrac{2 \times 4}{5 \times 4} > \dfrac{8}{20}$

(b) Write the fractions from smallest to greatest.
$\dfrac{3}{4}, \dfrac{3}{5}, \dfrac{6}{9}$

(c) Find the missing value.

    A $\dfrac{2}{3} = \dfrac{?}{15}$ B $\dfrac{7}{10} = \dfrac{14}{?}$

4.5 (a) Find the decimal numeral for each fraction.

    A $\dfrac{1}{8}$ B $\dfrac{3}{7}$ C $1\dfrac{1}{2}$ D $\dfrac{1}{6}$ E $\dfrac{5}{12}$ F $\dfrac{3}{11}$

(b) Write a decimal for $\frac{4}{15}$ and $\frac{5}{12}$ and decide which fraction is greater.

4.6 (a) Find each sum.

    A $\dfrac{5}{6} + \dfrac{1}{3}$ B $\dfrac{2}{3} + \dfrac{3}{4}$ C $3\dfrac{1}{4} + 2\dfrac{1}{8}$

(b) Find the sum of $1\frac{3}{4}$, $2\frac{1}{2}$, and $3\frac{1}{8}$.

(c) Which sum is greater, A or B?

    A $\dfrac{1}{2} + \dfrac{1}{5}$ B $\dfrac{1}{4} + \dfrac{1}{3}$

4.7 (a) Calculate. Express your answer in lowest terms.

    A $\dfrac{3}{2} - \dfrac{1}{2}$ B $\dfrac{3}{4} - \dfrac{1}{4}$ C $\dfrac{5}{6} - \dfrac{1}{6}$

    D $\dfrac{7}{9} - \dfrac{4}{9}$ E $\dfrac{8}{10} - \dfrac{3}{10}$ F $1\dfrac{2}{3} - 1\dfrac{1}{3}$

(b) Calculate.

    A $\dfrac{7}{10} + \dfrac{1}{5} - \dfrac{4}{5}$ B $\dfrac{3}{10} + \dfrac{4}{5} - \dfrac{1}{2}$

4.8 (a) What is the missing number in each of the following?

    A $3 \times \square = 1$ B $\dfrac{2}{3} \times \square = 1$ C $\dfrac{5}{4} \times \square = 1$

(b) Find each product.

    A $\dfrac{1}{3} \times \dfrac{3}{5}$ B $\dfrac{1}{2} \times 4$ C $\dfrac{2}{5} \times \dfrac{5}{8}$

    D $\dfrac{3}{4} \times \dfrac{16}{9}$ E $3\dfrac{1}{2} \times 8$ F $2\dfrac{3}{4} \times 1\dfrac{1}{2}$

4.9 (a) What is the reciprocal of each fraction?

    A $\dfrac{2}{3}$ B $\dfrac{5}{4}$ C $2\dfrac{2}{3}$

(b) Calculate.

    A $\dfrac{3}{8} \div \dfrac{1}{2}$ B $12 \div \dfrac{2}{3}$ C $9\dfrac{1}{3} \div 4\dfrac{2}{3}$

4.10 Calculate.

    A $2\left(\dfrac{1}{2} + \dfrac{1}{3}\right)$ B $\left(\dfrac{3}{4} + \dfrac{1}{2}\right) \div \dfrac{1}{2}$ C $\dfrac{3}{4} \times \dfrac{1}{2} \div \dfrac{7}{8}$

Problems to Practise: A Chapter Review

4.1 (a) Which of the following have both 3 and 5 as a factor?

　　A 40　　B 30　　C 24　　D 45

　(b) Which of the following numbers can be described as follows?
- It has 5 prime factors.
- Its greatest common factor with 64 is 8.

　　　A 40　　　B 72　　　C 56

4.2 (a) Twelve players are needed for a football team on the field. Near the end of the game the coach made 8 substitutions. What fraction of the team was changed?

　(b) The *roster* of a team is the number of players the team has. What fraction of each team is healthy?

	Sport	Roster	Number of Injuries
A	Football	28	4
B	Basketball	16	3
C	Hockey	18	2
D	Water polo	15	3
E	Wrestling	20	4

4.3 (a) Marlene and her twin Melanie jog 27 km each week. By mid-week of one week they had jogged 12 km. What fraction of the distance did they still need to jog?

　(b) Morris bought a case of 144 cans of dog food for his golden retriever. If 60 cans have been eaten, what fraction is left?

4.4 (a) In the first few innings of a baseball league game, Fred pitched 16 fastballs out of 64 pitches. In another game, Fred pitched 12 fastballs out of 50 pitches. In which game was the fraction of fastballs more?

　(b) In an archery competition Jerome was given 80 arrows. Sixty of his arrows hit the target. The contest manager said his accuracy was $\frac{6}{8}$. The president said his accuracy was $\frac{12}{15}$. Which person was correct?

4.5 (a) For the football game, who has the better record?

	Passes thrown	Passes completed
Johnson	28	22
Swenson	19	16

　(b) Last month out of 26 icebergs sighted 15 of them were considered a shipping hazard. In the next month 35 icebergs were sighted and 23 were hazardous. Which month had the greater fraction of hazardous icebergs?

4.6 During the month of December, it snowed for $\frac{3}{4}$ h one day, $6\frac{1}{2}$ h another day, and $5\frac{3}{4}$ h the last day of the month. How many hours did it snow for the month?

4.7 (a) Calculate.

　　A $\frac{7}{8} - \frac{5}{8}$　　B $\frac{7}{8} - \frac{1}{4}$　　C $\frac{2}{3} - \frac{1}{8}$

　　D $9\frac{2}{3} - 6\frac{1}{2}$　　E $12 - 3\frac{1}{3}$　　F $2\frac{1}{2} - 1\frac{3}{4}$

　(b) A baseball pitcher estimates that $\frac{1}{2}$ of the balls he throws are fastballs, $\frac{1}{6}$ are sliders and the remainder are curveballs. What fraction of the pitches he throws are curveballs?

4.8 Johnson jogs $\frac{2}{3}$ h/d. How many hours of jogging does he do in

　　A 1 week?　　B a 30-d month?　　C May?

4.9 The math course requires 110 h of instructions in order to obtain a credit. How many lessons are required if each lesson lasts

　　A $\frac{1}{2}$ h?　　　B 50 min?　　　C 70 min?

4.10 Translate each of the following into symbols, then calculate.

　(a) Subtract $\frac{1}{2}$ from the sum of $\frac{3}{4}$ and $\frac{7}{8}$.

　(b) Increase the product of $1\frac{1}{2}$ and $\frac{1}{4}$ by $\frac{3}{4}$.

　(c) Decrease the sum of $2\frac{1}{3}$ and $3\frac{1}{2}$ by $1\frac{1}{4}$.

　(d) Find the sum of the quotients $\frac{3}{4} \div \frac{3}{2}$ and $1\frac{2}{3} \div \frac{4}{3}$.

Chapter Checkup: A Practice Test

4.1 (a) Write all the factors of 50.
   (b) Find the greatest common factor of
      A 25, 30   B 3, 8, 12

4.2 (a) Write a fraction to show what part is shaded.

   (b) For a spaghetti eating contest, 100 kg of
   spaghetti was prepared. Louise ate 10 kg
   of spaghetti. What fraction did Louise eat?

4.3 (a) Which pair of fractions are equivalent?
      A $\dfrac{6}{8}, \dfrac{12}{16}$ B $\dfrac{10}{12}, \dfrac{15}{20}$
   (b) The group made 8 dozen muffins for
   breakfast during the ski trip. Four of them
   became soggy. What fraction were usable?

4.4 (a) Find the missing values.
      A $\dfrac{4}{5} = \dfrac{?}{25}$ B $\dfrac{14}{?} = \dfrac{7}{8}$
   (b) Max shot 88 baskets in basketball and got
   77 of them in. Ken shot 25 baskets and 20
   got in. Who had the better shooting ability?

4.5 (a) Find the decimal for each fraction.
      A $\dfrac{1}{4}$ B $\dfrac{5}{8}$ C $\dfrac{1}{20}$ D $\dfrac{4}{15}$
   (b) At the dart contest, of 60 shots, Harry
   scored with 53. In the same contest out of
   55 shots, (5 were disqualifed) 48 were
   scored. Who had the better scoring record?

4.6 (a) The following hours are the amounts of
   time Carol spent delivering handbills last
   week.

Wednesday	$2\frac{2}{3}$ h	Friday	$1\frac{1}{2}$ h
Thursday	$3\frac{1}{4}$ h	Saturday	$6\frac{3}{4}$ h

   A How many hours in all were handbills
   delivered?

B Carol earns $4.20/h to deliver handbills.
   How much did she earn?
   (b) Find each sum.
      A $\dfrac{3}{4} + \dfrac{3}{8}$ B $2\dfrac{4}{5} + 3\dfrac{3}{4}$ C $2\dfrac{2}{3} + 1\dfrac{1}{2} + 5\dfrac{1}{6}$

4.7 (a) Doug, Hugh and Andy bought a motorbike
   that they can all share on the weekend.
   Doug has $\frac{7}{15}$ interest, while Hugh has $\frac{1}{3}$
   interest. What interest does Andy have in
   the bike?
   (b) Harry spends $8\frac{1}{2}$ h/d at his job. He has $\frac{3}{4}$ h
   for lunch and two breaks for coffee of $\frac{1}{3}$ h
   each. How many hours is actually spent
   working?

4.8 (a) Find each product.
      A $8 \times \dfrac{1}{8}$ B $\dfrac{2}{7} \times \dfrac{3}{4}$ C $\dfrac{3}{10} \times \dfrac{5}{6}$ D $\dfrac{2}{3} \times 2\dfrac{1}{3}$
   (b) Last spring Ginger collected sap from the
   maple trees and discovered that
   the 8 pails that she used were only
   $\dfrac{3}{4}$ full. If she poured the sap into clean pails,
   how many pails did she fill completely?

4.9 (a) Calculate.
      A $6 \div 1\dfrac{1}{2}$ B $\dfrac{6}{5} \div \dfrac{2}{3}$ C $\dfrac{3}{4} \div \dfrac{9}{10}$ D $5\dfrac{2}{5} \div 1\dfrac{1}{10}$
   (b) Jean spent 75 h this summer training
   in the pool. Each swim session lasted
   $\frac{3}{4}$ h. How many sessions did she swim?

4.10 (a) Calculate each of the following.
      A $3\left(\dfrac{3}{4} - \dfrac{1}{2}\right)$ B $\left(\dfrac{3}{4} + \dfrac{1}{2}\right) \div \dfrac{2}{3}$
      C $\left(3\dfrac{3}{4} \div 1\dfrac{1}{2}\right) \div 2$ D $1\dfrac{1}{2} \times \dfrac{3}{4} \div 1\dfrac{1}{8}$
   (b) Translate each of the following. Then
   calculate.
   A Divide the difference $1\dfrac{3}{4} - 1\dfrac{1}{3}$ by $\dfrac{3}{4}$.
   B Find the sum of $\dfrac{3}{4} \times \dfrac{2}{3}$ and $1\dfrac{1}{4} \times 1\dfrac{2}{3}$.

 **Integers and Applications**

operations with integers, skills with substitution, applications and problem-solving

Introduction

Mathematics is often used to express an idea in a general way. Numerals written with the symbols + and − are called **signed numbers** and frequently occur in your everyday activities. For example:

Temperatures (°C)		
	Low overnight	High yesterday
Whitehorse	−7	5
Prince George	0	8
Prince Rupert	−2	11
Vancouver	2	11
Victoria	5	9
Jasper	−1	5
Edmonton	−2	0
Calgary	−2	4
Lethbridge	−2	4
Yellowknife	−11	−6
Prince Albert	−2	3
Saskatoon	−3	1
Regina	−1	1
Winnipeg	−3	5
Timmins	−12	7
North Bay	−7	7
Sudbury	−7	7
Muskoka	−7	9
Windsor	−1	6
London	−5	4
Trenton	−4	7
Kingston	−3	5
Petawawa	−7	10
Ottawa	−4	9
Montreal	−4	9
Quebec City	−5	6
Fredericton	1	4
Moncton	0	1

You will study how integers are used to express ideas about opposites.

5.1 Working With Another Number: Integers

Ideas about opposites often occur in your everyday language. Each of the following shows opposite ideas.

- He walked *up* the stairs.
- Go 20 paces *West*.
- The temperature of Death Valley is 50°C *above* zero.

He walked *down* the stairs.
Go 20 paces *East*.
The temperature of Mount Everest is 79°C *below* zero.

To show a gain of 5 you use the plus symbol +
   +5 means a gain of 5

To show a loss of 5 you use the minus symbol −
   −5 means a loss of 5

The set of integers is shown as follows.
$$I = \{ \ldots, -3, -2, -1, 0, +1, +2, +3, \ldots \}$$
A number line is used to draw the graph of integers.

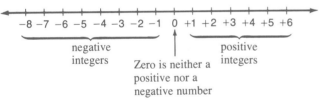

Example 1
Use the number line. Draw the graph of $\{-3, -2, -1, 0, +1, +2\}$.

Solution
Draw the number line. Use a dot to show each integer in the given set.

On the number line, opposites are the same distance from zero, but in opposite directions.

  Thus, the opposite of −2 is +2.
           the opposite of +2 is −2.

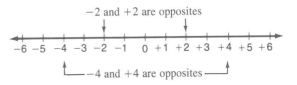

The number line shows the order of integers. For example in the above graph

$-3 < 0$ -3 is less than 0 since -3 is to the left of 0.

$+2 > -1$ $+2$ is greater than -1, since $+2$ is to the right of -1.

Example 2

Use the symbols $>$ or $<$ to make the following true.

(a) -4 ◉ $+3$ (b) $+3$ ◉ $+2$ (c) -3 ◉ -4

Solution

Think of the number line

(a) $-4 < +3$

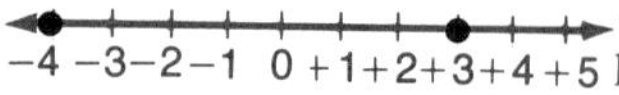

-4 is to the left of $+3$

(b) $+3 > +2$

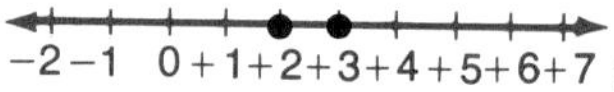

$+3$ is to the right of $+2$

(c) $-3 > -4$

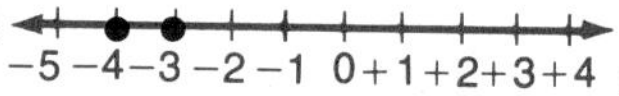

-3 is to the right of -4.

Try These

1 What is the opposite of each integer?
(a) $+2$ (b) -3 (c) $+5$
(d) -8 (e) -12 (f) $+15$

2 Which integer does ▨ represent?
(a) ▨ is the opposite of -2.
(b) $+6$ is the opposite of ▨.
(c) -13 is the opposite of ▨.

3 (a) $+6$ represents 6 up. What does -6 represent?

(b) -25 represents a loss of 25. What does $+25$ represent?
(c) -8 represents 8 south. What does $+8$ represent?
(d) $+17$ represents 17 forward. What does -17 represent?

4 An number line is shown. 0 is marked.

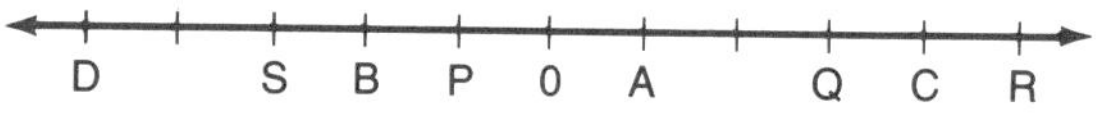

D   S   B   P   0   A   Q   C   R

What integer should be placed at each of the following letters?
(a) A (b) P (c) D (d) Q (e) S (f) B (g) R (h) C

Written Exercises

A 1 Integers may be used to show opposites. Write an integer to show each of the following.
(a) 750 m above sea level (b) a loss of $7
(c) a loss of 4 points   (d) 5 steps forward
(e) an increase of 15 m   (f) 8 steps down
(g) 10 steps to the right (h) a gain of 2 m
(i) an increase of 12 kg   (j) a decrease of 7 m²
(k) a decrease of 12 mL   (l) a profit of $10
(m) a drop of 9 points   (n) 3 under par
(o) 3 m below sea level   (p) 5 floors up

2 Five paces to the right is shown by $+5$. Five paces to the left is shown by -5. What does each of the following integers show?
(a) $+7$ (b) -7 (c) -9 (d) $+12$
(e) 0   (f) -15 (g) $+15$ (h) $+24$

3 The integer $+8$ m represents 8 m above sea level. What does each of the following integers represent?
(a) $+5$ m (b) -4 m (c) $+9$ m (d) -10 m
(e) -9 m (f) 0 m (g) $+13$ m (h) -13 m

4 The integer −4 represents a loss of 4 points. What does each of the following integers represent?

(a) −3   (b) +5   (c) −7   (d) +10
(e) −12   (f) 0   (g) +18   (h) −18

5 Which integer is greater?

(a) +4, +3   (b) −4, +2   (c) −4, −3
(d) −5, 0   (e) +4, −3   (f) 0, +5

B 6 Write an integer to show each of the following.

(a) The lowest point on the earth's surface is 10 859 m below sea level.
(b) In the Bay of Fundy, Nova Scotia, the tide may fall 16 m.
(c) Little Bear, a mountain peak in Colorado, is 4278 m above sea level.
(d) The average depth of the Pacific Ocean is 4188 m.
(e) Lake Eyre in Australia is 12 m below sea level.

7 Write the next two integers for each of the following.

(a) less than +4   (b) greater than +2
(c) less than −1   (d) greater than −1

8 For each of the following, describe the integers shown. The first one is done for you.

(a)

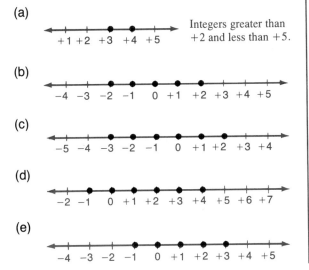

Integers greater than +2 and less than +5.

9 Write the integers that are described as follows.

(a) less than +6 and greater than +1.
(b) less than +4 and greater than −1.
(c) greater than −3 and less than +2.
(d) greater than −5 and less than 0.

10 Use the number line. Draw the graph for each of the following integers.

(a) −3, −1, 0, +1, +3   (b) −8, −6, −4, −2, 0
(b) The integers less than +2
(c) The integers greater than −3.
(d) The integers greater than −4 and less than +3.
(e) The integers between −5 and +1

11 The symbol for "greater than" is >. +3 > −3.
The symbol for "less than" is <. −3 < +3.
Which of the following are true (T)? false (F)?

(a) +11 < −15   (b) +6 > −6
(c) −25 < +2   (d) +40 < −40
(e) −15 < −15   (f) 0 < −1

12 Write > or < for ◉ to make each of the following true.

(a) +5 ◉ +9   (b) −4 ◉ −2
(c) +1 ◉ −1   (d) 0 ◉ −2
(e) −30 ◉ 0   (f) −52 ◉ −68

13 Write the integers in order from least to greatest.

(a) −3, +3, +6   (b) −9, +4, −3
(c) +8, −3, −9   (d) +6, −6, 0

C 14 You may use symbols to compare integers in a shorter way. For example, −3 < −2 and −2 < +5 is written as −3 < −2 < +5.
Use the symbols < and > to compare the following integers.

(a) −7, +1, +8   (b) +10, 0, −5
(c) 0, +11, −4   (d) −6, −9, −14
(e) −7, +6, −4   (f) 0, −1, +5

Applications: Temperatures and Integers.

You may use integers to show temperatures.

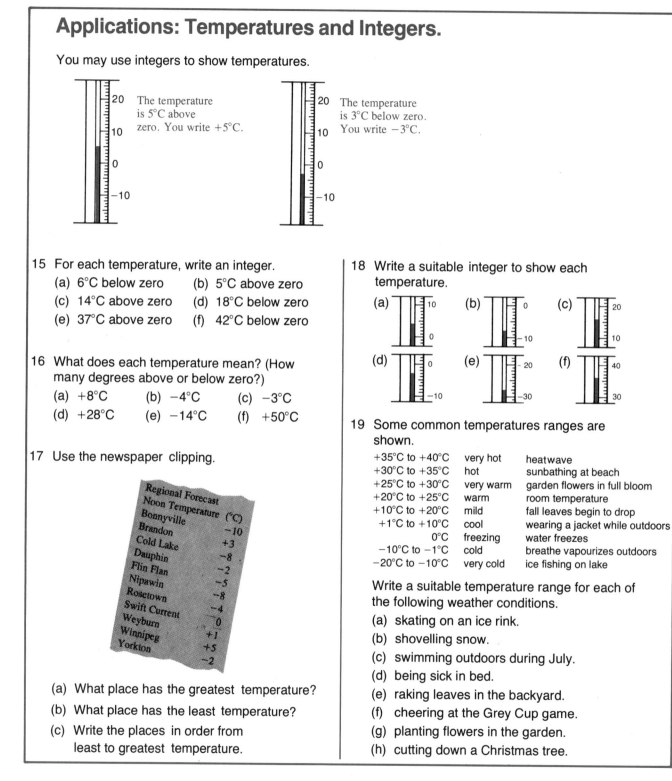

The temperature is 5°C above zero. You write +5°C.

The temperature is 3°C below zero. You write −3°C.

15 For each temperature, write an integer.
   (a) 6°C below zero   (b) 5°C above zero
   (c) 14°C above zero   (d) 18°C below zero
   (e) 37°C above zero   (f) 42°C below zero

16 What does each temperature mean? (How many degrees above or below zero?)
   (a) +8°C   (b) −4°C   (c) −3°C
   (d) +28°C   (e) −14°C   (f) +50°C

17 Use the newspaper clipping.

Regional Forecast
Noon Temperature (°C)
Bonnyville	−10
Brandon	+3
Cold Lake	−8
Dauphin	−2
Flin Flan	−5
Nipawin	−8
Rosetown	−4
Swift Current	0
Weyburn	+1
Winnipeg	+5
Yorkton	−2

   (a) What place has the greatest temperature?
   (b) What place has the least temperature?
   (c) Write the places in order from least to greatest temperature.

18 Write a suitable integer to show each temperature.
   (a)   (b)   (c)
   (d)   (e)   (f)

19 Some common temperatures ranges are shown.

+35°C to +40°C	very hot	heatwave
+30°C to +35°C	hot	sunbathing at beach
+25°C to +30°C	very warm	garden flowers in full bloom
+20°C to +25°C	warm	room temperature
+10°C to +20°C	mild	fall leaves begin to drop
+1°C to +10°C	cool	wearing a jacket while outdoors
0°C	freezing	water freezes
−10°C to −1°C	cold	breathe vapourizes outdoors
−20°C to −10°C	very cold	ice fishing on lake

Write a suitable temperature range for each of the following weather conditions.
   (a) skating on an ice rink.
   (b) shovelling snow.
   (c) swimming outdoors during July.
   (d) being sick in bed.
   (e) raking leaves in the backyard.
   (f) cheering at the Grey Cup game.
   (g) planting flowers in the garden.
   (h) cutting down a Christmas tree.

5.2 Adding Integers

If you have a bank account you may use integers to show your deposits and withdrawals.

+$50, a deposit of 50 dollars.
−$30, a withdrawal of 30 dollars.

Date	Deposits Canadian Bank Account No.6945-306			
	Deposit		Withdrawal	Balance
June 25				$45
July 2	$45			$67
July 9	$22			$51
July 16			$16	$28
July 23	$35		$23	$63
July 30	$12			$75

When you are thinking about addition, you can think about adding points in a game.

Addition of integers   *Meaning*

A $(+5) + (+2) = +7$

a gain of 5 points.   a gain of 2 points.   results in a gain of 7 points.

B $(-3) + (-5) = -8$ ◄——— Think (a loss of 3 points) followed by (a loss of 5 points).

C $(-3) + (+5) = +2$ ◄——— Think (a loss of 3 points) followed by (a gain of 5 points).

D $(-5) + (+3) = -2$ ◄——— Think (a loss of 5 points) followed by (a gain of 3 points).

You may also use a number line to show the above addition of integers.

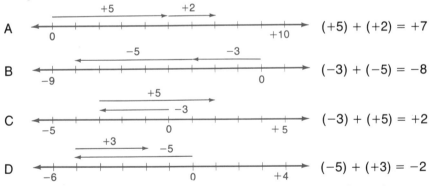

A $(+5) + (+2) = +7$

B $(-3) + (-5) = -8$

C $(-3) + (+5) = +2$

D $(-5) + (+3) = -2$

You may use integers when translating word problems, as shown in Example 1.

Example 1

A camper travelled due north for 10 km. After turning around, the camper travelled 3 km south. What was the camper's final position?

Solution

Due north 10 km	+ 10 km
Due south 3 km	− 3 km
Total	+ 7 km

The camper's final position is 7 km due north.

Example 2

Find the following sums.

(a) $(+6) + (-2)$ (b) $(-3) + (+5)$

Solution

(a) $(+6) + (-2) = +4$

If you need to, you may think of the sum as

a gain of 6 followed by a loss of 2 is a gain of 4

$\underbrace{(+6)}$ $+$ $\underbrace{(-2)}$ $=$ $\underbrace{(+4)}$

(b) $(-3) + (+5) = +2$

If you need to, you may think of a number line to help you find the sum.

If you wish, you may write positive integers such as +5 and +3 as 5 and 3. However negative integers such as −6 and −2 must *always* be written with the negative sign.

To find a sum of more than two integers you add as follows.

Example 3

Find this sum. $8 + (-2) + (-3)$

Solution

Write	Think
$8 + (-2) + (-3)$	Add the first 2 integers.
$= 6 + (-3)$	
$= 3$	Now add these 2 integers.

Try These

1 What is the sum of each of these?
   (a) a gain of 3 and a gain of 5.
   (b) a gain of 8 and a gain of 12.
   (c) a loss of 2 and a loss of 7.
   (d) a loss of 9 and a loss of 4.

2 What is the sum of each of the following?
   (a) a gain of 8, a loss of 4
   (b) a loss of 6, a gain of 3
   (c) a loss of 4, a gain of 6
   (d) a gain of 6, a loss of 8
   (e) a loss of 12, a gain of 12

3 Find the sum of each of the following.

   (a) $+4$ gain of 4   (b) $+4$ gain of 4
       $+2$ gain of 2 -2 loss of 2

   (c) $+3$ gain of 3   (d) -5 loss of 5
       -4 loss of 4 $+6$ gain of 6

4 Find the final result for each of the following.
   (a) up 5 floors, down 3 floors.
   (b) down 4 floors, up 3 floors.
   (c) up 3 floors, up 6 floors.
   (d) down 4 floors, down 8 floors.

Written Exercises

A 1 What is the sum of the integers shown on the number line?

(a)

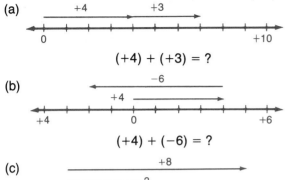

$(+4) + (+3) = ?$

(b)

$(+4) + (-6) = ?$

(c)

$(-3) + (+8) = ?$

(d)

$(-3) + (-5) = ?$

2 Find each sum.

(a)

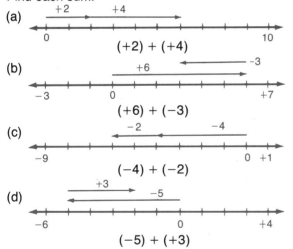

$(+2) + (+4)$

(b)

$(+6) + (-3)$

(c)

$(-4) + (-2)$

(d)

$(-5) + (+3)$

3 Find the following sums. Use a number line to help you.

(a) $(+6) + (+3)$ (b) $(+4) + (-3)$
(c) $(-7) + (-2)$ (d) $(+4) + (+2)$
(e) $(-6) + (+3)$ (f) $(-6) + (+5)$
(g) $(-6) + (+6)$ (h) $(-4) + (-4)$

4 Add each of the following. Think of $+$ as "followed by".

(a) $(+5) + (+4)$ (b) $(-5) + (-4)$
(c) $(-6) + (-2)$ (d) $(+6) + (-2)$
(e) $(+5) + (-4)$ (f) $(-5) + (+4)$

5 Use an integer to show the final position of each of the following.

(a) Lowering a diver 10 m and then raising him 8 m.

(b) Raising a flag 16 m and then lowering it 2 m.

(c) Diving up 2 m and then going down 5 m.

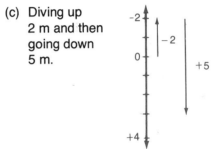

(d) A kite rising 52 m, dropping 16 m, rising 12 m, and then falling 17 m.

(e) A weather balloon rising 8 m, dropping 6 m, rising 3 m, and then falling 5 m.

B 6 Find the sum of the integers.
(a) 3, −2   (b) −3, 2   (c) −3, −2 (d) 5, −4
(e) −5, 4   (f) −5, −4 (g) 6, −9   (h) −6, 9

7 Find the sum of the integers.
(a) 3, 2   (b) 5, 4   (c) −6, 3   (d) 8, −9
(e) −7, 8   (f) −12, 5 (g) −5, 16 (h) −8, 3

8 Find each sum.
(a) $2 + 6$ (b) $-8 + 4$ (c) $8 + (-2)$
(d) $-7 + (-7)$ Remember $-7 + (-7)$ means $(-7) + (-7)$.

(e) $10 + 5$ (f) $-9 + (-7)$ (g) $0 + 8$
(h) $1 + (-4)$ (i) $-9 + 4$ (j) $-11 + 5$
(k) $19 + (-19)$ (l) $20 + (-40)$ (m) $-30 + (-20)$

155

9 Evaluate. *Means find each sum.*
   (a) 3 + (−2)   (b) −3 + 2   (c) −3 + (−2)
   (d) −8 + 9   (e) 8 + (−9)   (f) −8 + (−9)
   (g) 7 + (−3)   (h) −7 + (−3)   (i) −7 + 3

10 Evaluate
   (a) −5 + 7   (b) 3 + (−4)   (c) −2 + (−1)
   (d) −8 + 8   (e) 0 + (−8)   (f) −9 + (−6)
   (g) 4 − 1   (h) 6 + (−8)   (i) −3 + (−2)

11 Find the sums.
   (a) 3 + (−2) + 5   (b) −4 + (−6) + 1
   (c) −2 + 8 + (−5)   (d) −3 + (−6) + (−1)
   (e) −4 + 8 + (−2) + (−1) + 3
   (f) 19 + (−3) + (−2) + (−1) + 6 + (−5)

12 Last Monday Jessica had $264 in her account. On Tuesday she wrote cheques for $69 and $92. On Thursday she deposited $21.

   (a) Use integers to show how you obtain the balance of her account.

   (b) What is the balance at the end of the week?

C13 Morley has $365 in his account. The following was done.

Monday	Withdrawal $22	Deposit $36
Tuesday	Withdrawal $113	Deposit $28
Wednesday	Deposit $46	
Thursday	Deposit $65	
Friday	Withdrawal $39	Deposit $18

   (a) Use integers to show how to obtain the balance of the account.

   (b) What is the balance at the end of the week?

Integers and Golf

You have probably seen integers used on TV to show golf scores.

   +5 means 5 above par
   −3 means 3 below par

14 In a recent golf tournament, Sandra Post had the following scores for 4 holes: −2, +1, −1, −2. What was her total score for the 4 holes above?

15 Find the total score for each player for 5 holes.
   (a) Jennifer   −3, +2, −1, −2, +1
   (b) Stephen   −3, +2, +1, 0, −2
   (c) Wendy   −2, −1, 0, +1, +2

16 To qualify for a golf tournament, a player's total score must be less than +5. Which player(s) did not qualify?
   A Wendel +1, −2, +4, −3, +2, 0, +1, −2, −2
   B Story   −1, −2, +3, +2, 0, −1, −3, +1, +2
   C Vince   −2, +1, 0, +3, +2, +1, −1, +2, 0
   D Como   −3, +1, −1, −2, +3, +4, −1, +1, +3

Calculator Tip

The calculator can be used to find the balance of a chequing account. What is the final balance?

Previous balance $26.92   Deposit $25.00
Withdrawal $12.16   Withdrawal $19.38

Enter	Calculator Display
C	0
26.92	26.92
−	26.920000
12.16	12.16
+	14.760000
25.00	25.00
−	39.760000
19.38	19.38
=	20.380000

The balance is $20.38.

Applications: Plus-Minus Standings in Hockey

One of the ways to evaluate a hockey player's performance is by using a Plus-Minus system.

- If a player is on the ice and a goal is scored by the player's team, the player receives a +1.

- If the player is on the ice and the opposing team scores a goal, the player receives a −1.

After a game, a player's plus-minus standing can be calculated.

Salming +1, −1, +1, +1   Plus-minus standing is +2.
$(+1) + (−1) + (+1) + (+1) = 2$

17 For a hockey game, the plus minus results are shown. Find the plus-minus standing for each player.
   (a) Taylor   +1, −1, +1, +1, −1
   (b) Dionne   +1, −1, −1, −1, +1, −1
   (c) Williams −1, −1, +1, −1, −1, −1

18 Place the plus-minus standings of the following players in order from least to greatest.
   (a) Affleck   −1, −1, +1, +1, −1, +1
   (b) Sittler   +1, −1, +1, +1, −1, −1, +1
   (c) Gibbs   +1, −1, −1, −1, +1, +1, −1

19 Which of the following players has the best plus-minus standing?
   (a) Plett   −1, +1, −1, −1, +1, −1
   (b) Bennett   −1, +1, +1, +1, −1, −1, +1
   (c) Bourbonnais +1, +1, −1, +1, +1, +1

20 The plus-minus scores for 4 games are shown for the players. Find each player's final plus-minus standing.
   (a) DeBlois   −2, +3, −1, +2

   (b) Duguay   −3, +2, −1, +3
   (c) Gardner   −2, −1, +3, −1

21 The plus-minus standings for the players, before a game, are shown.
      Gardner −3   Boldirev   −2
      Schmautz +2   Middleton   0
   After playing a game in Vancouver, the plus-minus results of the game are added. What is the final plus-minus standing of each player?
      Gardner   −1, +1, +1, −1, +1
      Boldirev   −1, −1, −1, +1, +1
      Schmautz   +1, +1, +1, +1, −1
      Middleton   −1, +1, −1, −1

22 For each player, calculate the total plus-minus standing.

	Scored	Scored Against
Bob Gainey	28	32
Danny Gare	36	26
Bobby Clarke	42	23
Lanny MacDonald	28	36
Gordie Howe	16	23
Doug Jarvis	12	24
Don Luce	13	13
Dickie Moore	19	20

5.3 Subtracting Integers

Wildlife in Canada's High Arctic has adapted to extremes in climate. The Arctic hare endures winter temperatures of −47°C and summer temperatures as high as 24°C.

To subtract integers you first need to *understand* how the subtraction of integers works. For example, you can think of a subtraction in terms of related addition.

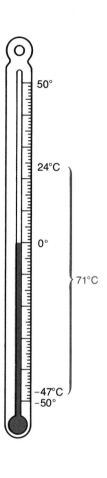

Subtraction	Related addition
10 − 6 = 4	10 + (−6) = 4

You can also think of the subtraction of integers in terms of related addition.

Subtraction	Related addition
−8 − 6 = ▯	−8 + (−6) = −14

> Since you know −8 + (−6) = −14,
> you use this result to obtain the value of ▯.
> ▯ = −14

Thus to subtract 6, you add its opposite, −6. Study the chart.

Subtraction	Related addition
6 − 4 = ▯	6 + (−4) = 2
−6 − 4 = ▯	−6 + (−4) = −10
−6 − (−4) = ▯	−6 + (+4) = −2

> To subtract an integer, you add its opposite.

Example 1

Find the following differences.

(a) −6 − 8

(b) −6 − (−8)

Solution

(a) $-6 - 8 = -6 + (-8)$
$= -14$

+8 and −8 are opposites. To subtract an integer add its opposite.

(b) $-6 - (-8) = -6 + (+8)$
$= +2$

The opposite of −8 is +8. Thus add the opposite.

You may also use a pattern to find a difference.

Example 2	Solution

Example 2

Complete the pattern by doing the following subtractions.

(a) 4 4 4   4   4   (b) −3 −3 −3 −3
   2 1 0 −1 −2   2   1   0 −1
   ? ? ?   ?   ?   ?   ?   ?   ?

Solution

(a) Subtract

  4 4 4   4   4
  2 1 0 −1 −2
  2 3 4   5   6

(b) Subtract

  −3 −3 −3 −3
    2   1   0 −1
  −5 −4 −3 −2

Example 2 illustrates:

> To subtract an integer, add its opposite.

To calculate the range of temperatures the Arctic hare is exposed to, you subtract.

summer temperature   24°C
winter temperature   −47°C

Subtract to find the range of temperatures.
$24 − (−47) = 24 + 47$
$= 71$

The range of temperatures is 71°C.

Try These

1 What is the opposite of each integer?

(a) +3   (b) −2   (c) +1   (d) −4
(e) −3   (f) +5   (g) +2   (h) −1

2 Think of each of the following subtractions in terms of related additions. Then find the difference.

(a) 6 − 2   (b) 9 − 2
(c) 7 − 2   (d) 12 − 8
(e) 10 − 8   (f) 9 − 8
(g) 15 − 10   (h) 4 − 3
(i) 20 − 14

3 What are the missing values?

	Subtraction	Related Addition
(a)	4 − (+3)	4 + (?)
(b)	8 − (−2)	8 + (?)
(c)	−8 − (−2)	−8 + (?)

How are these related?

4 State the related addition for each of the following. The first one has been done for you.

                  related addition
(a) (+2) − (+4)   (+2) + (−4)
(b) (+6) − (+3)   (c) (−6) − (+4)
(d) (−8) − (+5)   (e) (+5) − (−2)
(f) (+9) − (−3)   (g) (−2) − (−3)

Written Exercises

A In Questions 1 to 4, the integer +5 is used so that you can see patterns to help you learn how to subtract integers.

For Questions 5 and 6 look for a pattern to help you subtract.

1 For each subtraction the related addition is shown. Find the value of ▨.

Subtraction	Related Addition
(a) $(+11) - (+3) = $ ▨	$(+11) + (-3) = $ ▨
(b) $(+7) - (+10) = $ ▨	$(+7) + (-10) = $ ▨
(c) $(+12) - (+18) = $ ▨	$(+12) + (-18) = $ ▨
(d) $(+9) - (+16) = $ ▨	$(+9) + (-16) = $ ▨

2 Copy and complete the chart.

Subtraction	Related Addition
(a) $(+6) - (+3) = ?$	$(+6) + (-3) = ?$
(b) $(-5) - (+2) = ?$	$(-5) + (-2) = ?$
(c) $(-4) - (-3) = ?$	$(-4) + (+3) = ?$
(d) $(+3) - (+3) = ?$	$(+3) + (-3) = ?$
(e) $(-8) - (-8) = ?$	$(-8) + (+8) = ?$

3 For each subtraction, write the related addition to help you find the difference.

(a) $(+7) - (+9)$ (b) $(+10) - (+9)$
(c) $(+10) - (+12)$ (d) $(-7) - (-5)$
(e) $(+7) - (-9)$ (f) $(+6) - (-3)$
(g) $(-5) - (-7)$ (h) $(-8) - (-4)$

4 Evaluate. *In this question, to evaluate means to find the difference.*

(a) $(+7) - (-5) = $ ▨   (b) $(-8) - (-7) = $ ▨
(c) $(3) - (-1) = $ ▨   (d) $(+9) - (-7) = $ ▨
(e) $(-14) - (+3) = $ ▨   (f) $(-10) - (-6) = $ ▨
(g) $(+17) - (+10) = $ ▨ (h) $0 - (-5) = $ ▨
(i) $(+9) - 0 = $ ▨   (j) $(+7) - (-7) = $ ▨
(k) $(-4) - (-4) = $ ▨   (l) $(-8) - (+8) = $ ▨

5 What are the values of ▨?

A	B
$6 - 3 = $ ▨	$4 - 2 = $ ▨
$6 - 2 = $ ▨	$4 - 1 = $ ▨
$6 - 1 = $ ▨	$4 - 0 = $ ▨
$6 - 0 = $ ▨	$4 - (-1) = $ ▨
$6 - (-1) = $ ▨	$4 - (-2) = $ ▨
$6 - (-2) = $ ▨	$4 - (-3) = $ ▨
$6 - (-3) = $ ▨	$4 - (-4) = $ ▨

6 Complete each of the following.

(a)
$$\begin{array}{cccc} 4 & 4 & 4 & 4 \\ \underline{1} & \underline{0} & \underline{-1} & \underline{-2} \\ 3 & 4 & ▨ & ▨ \end{array}$$

(b)
$$\begin{array}{cccc} -2 & -2 & -2 & -2 \\ \underline{2} & \underline{1} & \underline{0} & \underline{-1} \\ -4 & -3 & ▨ & ▨ \end{array}$$

(c)
$$\begin{array}{cccc} -1 & -1 & -1 & -1 \\ \underline{2} & \underline{3} & \underline{4} & \underline{5} \\ -3 & -4 & ▨ & ▨ \end{array}$$

(d)
$$\begin{array}{cccc} 3 & 3 & 3 & 3 \\ \underline{-6} & \underline{-5} & \underline{-4} & \underline{-3} \\ 9 & 8 & ▨ & ▨ \end{array}$$

To subtract integers, think of adding the opposite.

$$-4 - (-3) = ? \qquad -4 + (+3) = -1$$

+3 is the opposite of −3

B 7 Find each difference.

(a) $6 - 3$ (b) $-2 - 1$ (c) $-5 - 4$
(d) $2 - 6$ (e) $3 - 5$ (f) $-4 - 8$
(g) $-2 - 2$ (h) $3 - 3$ (i) $+8 - 8$

160

8 Subtract each of the following.

(a) 10 (b) −7 (c) 4 (d) 15
    −6   −10   −2   −6
    ▯   ▯   ▯   ▯

(e) 8   (f) −10 (g) −17 (h) −22
    −3   −3   −11   3
    ▯   ▯   ▯   ▯

(i) −17 (j) 12 (k) −8 (l) −4
    14   −3   −9   −6
    ▯   ▯   ▯   ▯

9 Simplify.

(a) 10 − (−5)   (b) −8 − (−10)
(c) 40 − (−24)   (d) −16 − (−6)
(e) +9 − (−1)   (f) −10 − 13
(g) 17 − 21   (h) −12 − (−3)
(i) −16 − 13   (j) 22 − (−3)
(k) −19 − (−12)   (l) −21 − 23

10 Subtract.

(a) 5 from 12   (b) 8 from −3   (c) −1 from 2
(d) 6 from −13 (e) −8 from −7 (f) 14 from −2
(g) −5 from 0   (h) 0 from −5   (i) −5 from 10
(j) 10 from −5

11 Evaluate.

(a) 13 − (−3)   (b) 11 − (−8)
(c) −12 − (+6)   (d) −12 − (−3)
(e) 14 − (−2)   (f) −16 − (+3)
(g) −18 − (−3)   (h) −8 − (−12)
(i) 19 − 30

For Questions 12 to 14 you are asked to add or subtract. Read the *symbols carefully*.

12 Evaluate.

(a) 5 − 8   (b) 5 + 8   (c) 8 − 13
(d) 8 + 13   (e) −9 − 12   (f) −9 + 12
(g) 24 − 16   (h) 24 − (−16)
(i) 36 − (−3)   (j) 36 + (−3)

13 Simplify.

(a) 15 − (−25)   (b) −15 − (−25)
(c) −20 + 32   (d) 7 − (−43)
(e) −7 + 43   (f) 92 − (−21)
(g) 63 − (−4)   (h) −27 + 43
(i) 56 − (−8)   (j) −65 − (−103)
(k) 225 − (−410) − 36 (l) −6 − (−92) + 57

14 The following expressions involve more than two integers. The first one is done for you.

(a) 6 − (−2) + 3 $6 - (-2) + 3$
                        $= 6 + (+2) + 3$
                        $= \quad 8 \quad + 3$
                        $= 11$

(b) 7 − (−1) + (−3)
(c) (−10) − (−5) + 6
(d) (−7) − (−5) − (−3)
(e) (−12) − (−4) − (−4) − 5 − (−3) + 6
(f) 16 − 4 − (−2) + 10 − (−4) − (−1) + 8
(g) −15 − (−1) + 8 − 2 − (−3) − 9 + 4
(h) 0 − 4 + 6 − (−2) − 1 − (−3) + 7 − 5

C 15 Which has the greater value, the subtraction in Column A, or the subtraction in Column B?

	Column A	Column B
(a)	−3 − (−2)	−8 − (−5)
(b)	6 − (−12)	10 − (−3)
(c)	−14 − (−5)	14 − (−5)

16 Write the next integer for each pattern.

(a) −6 − (−5), −9 − (−7), 8 − 11
(b) −8 − (−6), 10 − 14,   −13 − (−7)

17 Find the missing integer.

(a) +7 − ▯ = 2   (b) −4 − ▯ = 5
(c) ▯ − (−3) = −8   (d) ▯ − (+7) = −10
(e) −9 − ▯ = 0   (f) ▯ − (+2) = 14
(g) 30 − ▯ = −40   (h) 12 − ▯ = −7
(i) 0 − ▯ = 3   (j) −6 − ▯ = −13

161

Applications: Temperature Change

The temperatures for Halifax are given in the chart.

morning temperature	afternoon temperature
−6°C	2°C

To calculate the increase in temperature from morning to afternoon, you subtract.

$2 - (-6) = 8$ ◀── In other words the temperature rose 8°C.

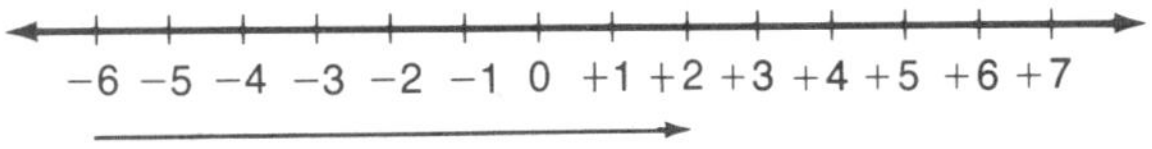

−6 −5 −4 −3 −2 −1 0 +1 +2 +3 +4 +5 +6 +7

Friday's Temperatures

	Morning temperature	Afternoon temperature
Charlottetown	−10	−2
Calgary	−19	−7
Edmonton	−8	5
Fredericton	−12	4
Halifax	−6	2
Jasper	−9	0
Moncton	−13	1
Montreal	−5	5
Ottawa	6	3
Prince Albert	−22	−10
Vancouver	3	7
Victoria	1	6
Winnipeg	−24	−7

18 Calculate the increase in temperature (from morning to afternoon) for each of the following places.

(a) Edmonton   (b) Jasper
(c) Moncton   (d) Ottawa
(e) Victoria   (f) Winnipeg
(g) Vancouver   (h) Calgary

19 Which place had the greater temperature increase, the place in Column A or the place in Column B?

	Column A	Column B
(a)	Prince Albert	Vancouver
(b)	Fredericton	Calgary
(c)	Charlottetown	Edmonton
(d)	Montreal	Victoria
(e)	Calgary	Moncton
(f)	Winnipeg	Fredericton

20 Which place in the given chart had,
(a) the greatest temperature increase?
(b) the least temperature increase?

21 Which places in the chart had the same temperature increase?

5.4 Substitution Skills and Integers

The skills you learn in mathematics which apply to one set of numbers may be used again when you learn about other sets of numbers, such as integers.

Example 1

Evaluate $a + b - c$ if $a = -3$, $b = -4$ and $c = -2$.

Solution

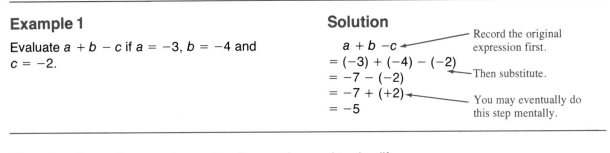

$a + b - c$ ← Record the original expression first.

$= (-3) + (-4) - (-2)$ ← Then substitute.

$= -7 - (-2)$

$= -7 + (+2)$ ← You may eventually do this step mentally.

$= -5$

The order of operations you learned earlier may be used to simplify the following example.

Example 2

Simplify $[-3 - 2] - [5 - 8]$.

Solution

$[-3 - 2] - [5 - 8]$ — Record the original expression first.

$= (-5) - (-3)$

$= -5 + (+3)$ — Then simplify each expression in each set of brackets.

$= -2$

Try These

1 Use $a = -1$ and $b = 0$. What is the value of each of the following?

   (a) $a + 5$ (b) $b + 3$ (c) $a - 3$

   (d) $b - 5$ (e) $8 - a$ (f) $6 - b$

2 Use $p = 1$, $q = -1$. What is the value of each of the following?

   (a) $p + 2$ (b) $p - 2$ (c) $2 - p$

   (d) $q - 3$ (e) $q + 3$ (f) $3 - q$

   (g) $p + q$ (h) $p - q$ (i) $q - p$

3 Use $m = -1$ and $n = +1$. What is the value of each of the following?

   (a) $m + 2$ (b) $n + 3$ (c) $2 - m$

   (d) $m - 2$ (e) $n - 2$ (f) $3 - n$

   (g) $m + n$ (h) $m - n$ (i) $n - m$

4 Use $m = +1$ and $n = -1$. What is the value of each of the following?

   (a) $m + n$ (b) $m - n$ (c) $n - m$

   (d) $m + m + n$ (e) $m + n + n$

   (f) $m - n + n$ (g) $m - m + n$

Written Exercises

A 1 Find the value of each expression. Use $a = -3$, $b = -2$.

    (a) $a + 6$ (b) $b - 3$ (c) $a - 6$

    (d) $b - 8$ (e) $9 - a$ (f) $6 + b$

2 Use $p = -4$, $q = 3$. Find the value of each expression.

    (a) $p + q$ (b) $p - q$ (c) $q - p$

    (d) $p + q - 3$ (e) $3 - p - q$

3 Use $s = -3$, $t = -2$, $u = 0$. Find the value of each expression.

    (a) $s + u$ (b) $s - u$ (c) $s + t$

    (d) $t - s$ (e) $t - u$ (f) $u - s$

    (g) $s + t + u$ (h) $s + t - u$

    (i) $s - t + u$ (j) $t - s - u$

4 Simplify each expression.

    (a) $8 + (6 - 3)$ (b) $8 - (6 - 3)$

    (c) Why do your answers differ in (a) and (b)?

5 Find the value of each expression.

    (a) $6 + (3 - 2)$ (b) $8 - (3 + 2)$

    (c) $-5 + [3 - (-2)]$ (d) $8 - [8 - (-3)]$

B 6 Use $a = -2$, $b = -1$, $c = 0$. Which expression has the greater value?

    (a) $a + b - c$ (b) $a - b - c$

7 If $p = 3$, $q = -2$, and $r = 5$, which expression has the greater value?

    (a) $p + q - r$ (b) $p - q - r$

8 Evaluate each expression. Use $a = 3$, $b = -2$, $c = -1$.

    (a) $a - b + c$ (b) $a - (b - c)$

    (c) What do you notice about your answers?

9 Evaluate each expression. Use $p = 3$, $q = -2$, $r = -1$.

    (a) $q - (p - r)$ (b) $q - p + r$

    (c) What do you notice about your answers?

10 Evaluate the expression $p - q + r$ for the following values.

    (a) $p = -3$, $q = 2$, $r = 0$

    (b) $p = 0$, $q = -3$, $r = 2$

    (c) $p = -3$, $q = 0$, $r = -4$

    (d) $p = -4$, $q = 3$, $r = 4$

11 Find the sweater number of each player. Use $p = -3$, $q = 4$, $r = -2$.

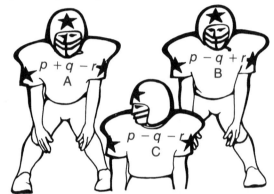

12 The captain of the team is the one whose sweater has the greatest integer. Who is the captain? Use $a = 5$, $b = -3$, $c = 2$.

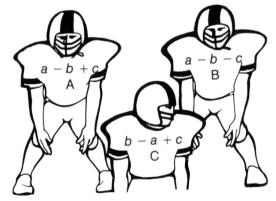

C 13 Simplify each of the following.

    (a) $-3 + (-3 - 2) + 5$

    (b) $2 - (-4 - 5) - (6 - 3)$

    (c) $3 - [-2 - (-2)] - (3 - 5)$

    (d) $[6 - (-3)] - [2 - (-3)]$

    (e) $[-8 - (-2)] + [-3 - (-4)]$

164

5.5 Solving Problems: Integers

The first step in solving a problem is to be sure that you understand the meanings of the words and thus be able to follow instructions accurately. In some problems, there are words that are translated into certain operations.

Example 1

By how much does $23 + (-3) + (-6)$ exceed $6 - (-3)$?

The word "exceed" suggests the operation of subtraction.

Solution

Sum: $23 + (-3) + (-6) = 14$
Difference: $6 - (-3) = \underline{9}$
Subtract 5

Thus $23 + (-3) + (-6)$ exceeds $6 - (-3)$ by 5.

> Steps For Solving Problems
> Step A To understand the problem you are to solve ask yourself:
>   (i) What information am I given?
>   (ii) What information am I asked to find?
> Step B Decide on a method. Translate the problem into mathematics.
> Step C Find the answer.
> Step D Check your answer in the *original* problem.
> Step E Write a final statement to answer the problem.

How are each of the above steps related to the solution of the following problem?

Example 2

North America's record high temperature is 57°C. The record low temperature is 120°C lower than this record high temperature. What is the record low temperature?

Solution

Record high temperature is 57°C.
Record low temperature is 120°C lower.

$$57 - 120 = -63$$

check: high temp 57°C
low temp $\underline{-63°C}$
difference 120°C

check

Thus the record low temperature is $-63°C$.

When you solve any mathematical problem, your solution must be planned in an organized way.

Written Exercises

A 1 Find the sum of $-3 + 2$, $-4 + 6$, and $-3 - 7$.

2 How much greater is $-3 + 8$ than $-3 - 8$?

3 By how much does $8 + (-3) + (-6)$ exceed $-9 + (-3) - (-3)$?

4 What is the total of $-4 - 3$, $-3 + (-3)$, $-2 - (-2)$?

5 By how much does $(-3) - (-6)$ exceed $2 + (-3) + (-6)$?

6 By how much does $(-3) + (-2) + (-6)$ exceed $-16 - (-3)$?

B 7 During a blizzard, the temperature was $-8°C$. The next day the temperature rose by $12°C$. What was the temperature reading the next day?

8 One day in Kamloops, the temperature was $9°C$. Over a 24-h period, the temperature dropped $21°C$. What was the temperature reading after 24 h?

9 The highest recorded temperature in Africa was at Aziziyah, Libya at $58°C$. The lowest recorded temperature in Africa was in Morocco and was $82°C$ lower. What is the lowest recorded temperature in Africa?

10 The common toad has been found at a depth of -340 m in a coal mine. The plant with the deepest root ever found is a fig tree, whose roots were discovered to a depth 118 m higher than where the toad was found. At what depth were the roots of the tree?

11 The lowest recorded temperature in the U.S.S.R. is $-59°C$. Europe's record high temperature is $109°C$ greater than the U.S.S.R.'s record low temperature. What is Europe's record high temperature?

12 The highest temperature ever recorded in Antarctica is $15°C$. The lowest recorded temperature is $-88°C$. How much greater is the record high temperature than the record low temperature?

13 On December 18 the temperature was $8°C$. From then until December 30th the temperature fell $2°C/d$.
    (a) What was the temperature on December 22nd?
    (b) What was the temperature on Christmas Day?
    (c) What was the first day on which water froze? (Water freezes at $0°C$.)
    (d) What was the temperature on December 30th?

C 14 The price of silver on September 1 was $16. The weekly changes in price are given as follows:

September 8	+2$
September 15	−3$
September 22	−1$
September 29	−2$

What was the price of silver on September 29th?

15 During the Arctic summer, a bird called the common red poll withstands temperatures as high as $27°C$. In the winter it endures temperatures that are $66°C$ lower. What is this lower Arctic winter temperature?

Applications: Record Depths

The deepest ocean "dives" ever recorded are shown on the scale at the right. Questions 16 to 24 are based on the chart.

16 The Benthoscope was 4267 m higher than the sponge. At what depth is the Benthoscope?

17 A fish was recorded at a depth, 2552 m deeper than the sponge. At what depth is the fish?

18 A sperm whale was recorded to be 7053 m higher than the fish. At what depth is the sperm whale?

19 The deepest breath-held dive is 1041 m higher than the record depth of the sperm whale. What was the depth of the breath-held dive?

20 The record depth of a seal is 515 m deeper than for a breath-held dive. How deep is the seal?

21 Just 318 m below the seal the greatest depth reached by a Bathysphere was recorded. What is the depth of the Bathysphere?

22 An amphiopod was recorded at a depth 1467 m deeper than the fish. What is the depth of the amphiopod?

23 The record depth reached by the Bathysphere was 777 m deeper than the depth of the dive using air by Gruener and Watson. What was their depth?

24 The depth reached by the Benthoscope was 9395 m higher than the the depth reached by the Bathyscaphe. What was the depth reached by the Bathyscaphe?

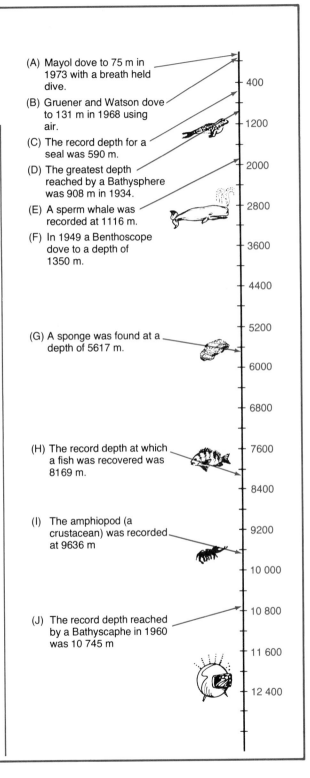

(A) Mayol dove to 75 m in 1973 with a breath held dive.

(B) Gruener and Watson dove to 131 m in 1968 using air.

(C) The record depth for a seal was 590 m.

(D) The greatest depth reached by a Bathysphere was 908 m in 1934.

(E) A sperm whale was recorded at 1116 m.

(F) In 1949 a Benthoscope dove to a depth of 1350 m.

(G) A sponge was found at a depth of 5617 m.

(H) The record depth at which a fish was recovered was 8169 m.

(I) The amphiopod (a crustacean) was recorded at 9636 m

(J) The record depth reached by a Bathyscaphe in 1960 was 10 745 m

5.6 Multiplying Integers

For each of 3 hockey games, Harriet
had the following plus-minus score.

Game 1	Game 2	Game 3
-2	-2	-2

Her total plus-minus score may be written

as a sum   *as a product*
$(-2) + (-2) + (-2)$ $3 \times (-2)$

From the above example it seems $3 \times (-2) = -6$. To find the value
of $3 \times (-2)$ examine the pattern below.

$3 \times 2 = 6$ Each product decreases by 3.
$3 \times 1 = 3$
$3 \times 0 = 0$ Based on the pattern
$3 \times (-1) = ?$ $3 \times (-1) = -3$
$3 \times (-2) = ?$ $3 \times (-2) = -6$

> I The product of a *positive* integer and a *negative* integer is a
> *negative* integer.

You may look at other patterns and obtain a similar result.

$2 \times 2 = 4$	$6 \times 2 = 12$
$2 \times 1 = 2$	$6 \times 1 = 6$
$2 \times 0 = 0$	$6 \times 0 = 0$
$2 \times (-1) = -2$	$6 \times (-1) = -6$
$2 \times (-2) = -4$	$6 \times (-2) = -12$

Example 1

Find each product.

(a) $2(-6)$

(b) $3(-8)$

(c) $(-5)(4)$

Solution

(a) $2(-6)$
  $= -12$
  You may think of
  $2 \times 6 = 12$.
  Then think of
  positive $\times$ negative $\rightarrow$ negative

(b) $3(-8)$
  $= -24$

(c) $(-5)(4)$
  $= -20$
  The order in which you multiply
  numbers does not affect
  the answer.
  $(-5)(4) = (4)(-5)$

You may use result I to find the product of 2 negative integers.

$(-3)(+2) = -6$
$(-3)(+1) = -3$
$(-3)(0) = 0$
$(-3)(-1) = ?$
$(-3)(-2) = ?$

The products
increase by 3. |

Thus, you may
complete the pattern.
$(-3)(-1) = +3$
$(-3)(-2) = +6$

$(+2)(-4) = -8$
$(+1)(-4) = -4$
$(0)(-4) = 0$
$(-1)(-4) = ?$
$(-2)(-4) = ?$

The products increase by 4. |

Thus you may
complete the
pattern.
$(-1)(-4) = +4$
$(-2)(-4) = +8$

The above patterns suggest

> II The product of a *negative* integer and a *negative* integer is a
> *positive* integer.

Example 2

Find each product.

(a) $(-2)(-5)$ (b) $(-6)(-2)$ (c) $-4(-3)$
↑ ↑ ↑
Remember which operation is understood here.

Solution

(a) $(-2)(-5)$
   $= +10$

You may think of $2 \times 5 = 10$.
Then remember
negative × negative → positive

(b) $(-6)(-2)$
   $= +12$

(c) $-4(-3)$
   $= +12$

Write $-4(-3)$
to mean $(-4)(-3)$.

Example 3

Calculate.

(a) $(-3)(-2)(-1)$ (b) $-3(-1)(-5)$

Solution

(a) $(-3)(-2)(-1)$
   $= (+6)(-1)$
   $= -6$

(b) $-3(-1)(-5)$
   $= (+3)(-5)$
   $= -15$

For the following exercise, use this summary for multiplying
integers.

I   The product of two integers with like signs is positive.

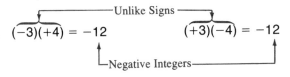

II   The product of two integers with unlike signs is negative.

169

Try These

1 Express each sum as a multiplication.
   (a) $3 + 3 + 3$ (b) $8 + 8 + 8 + 8$
   (c) $(-5) + (-5)$ (d) $(-9) + (-9)$
   (e) $(-2) + (-2) + (-2)$
   (f) $(-3) + (-3) + (-3) + (-3)$

2 Complete each pattern.
   (a) $3 \times (+2) = +6$ (b) $4 \times (+1) = +4$
        $3 \times (+1) = +3$ $4 \times (0) = 0$
        $3 \times (0) = 0$ $4 \times (-1) = ?$
        $3 \times (-1) = ?$ $4 \times (-2) = ?$

   (c) $(+2)(+2) = +4$ (d) $(+1)(+6) = +6$
        $(+1)(+2) = +2$ $(0)(+6) = 0$
        $(0)(+2) = 0$ $(-1)(+6) = ?$
        $(-1)(+2) = ?$ $(-2)(+6) = ?$
        $(-2)(+2) = ?$ $(-3)(+6) = ?$

3 Complete each pattern.
   (a) $(+2)(-1) = -2$ (b) $(-2)(+2) = -4$
        $(+1)(-1) = -1$ $(-2)(+1) = -2$
        $(0)(-1) = 0$ $(-2)(0) = 0$
        $(-1)(-1) = ?$ $(-2)(-1) = ?$

   (c) $(-6)(+2) = -12$ (d) $(+2)(-4) = -8$
        $(-6)(+1) = -6$ $(+1)(-4) = -4$
        $(-6)(0) = 0$ $(0)(-4) = 0$
        $(-6)(-1) = ?$ $(-1)(-4) = ?$

4 What is the value of each product?
   (a) $(0)(+5)$ (b) $(+8)(0)$ (c) $(0)(-6)$
   (d) $(-3)(0)$ (e) $(-4)(0)$ (f) $(0)(-12)$

Written Exercises

A 1 Copy and complete each pattern. Find each product.
   (a) $(+3)(+2) = ?$ (b) $(+2)(+5) = ?$
        $(+3)(+1) = ?$ $(+1)(+5) = ?$
        $(+3)(0) = ?$ $(0)(+5) = ?$
        $(+3)(-1) = ?$ $(-1)(+5) = ?$
        $(+3)(-2) = ?$ $(-2)(+5) = ?$

   (c) $(+2)(-3) = ?$ (d) $(-2)(+2) = ?$
        $(+1)(-3) = ?$ $(-2)(+1) = ?$
        $(0)(-3) = ?$ $(-2)(0) = ?$
        $(-1)(-3) = ?$ $(-2)(-1) = ?$
        $(-2)(-3) = ?$ $(-2)(-2) = ?$

2 Multiply.
   (a) $(+4)(-2)$ (b) $(+2)(-2)$ (c) $(0)(-2)$
   (d) $(-3)(+2)$ (e) $(-3)(+3)$ (f) $(-3)(+4)$
   (g) $(+3)(-1)$ (h) $(+3)(-2)$ (i) $(+3)(-3)$
   (j) $(-3)(+5)$ (k) $(-2)(+5)$ (l) $(-1)(+5)$

3 Find each product.
   (a) $(+4)(-4)$ (b) $(+3)(-1)$ (c) $(-5)(-3)$
   (d) $(+5)(0)$ (e) $(-2)(+2)$ (f) $(-4)(-3)$
   (g) $(-2)(+6)$ (h) $(-1)(-6)$ (i) $(0)(+1)$

4 Which of the following products have the same value?
   (a) $(+3)(-2)$ (b) $(-5)(0)$ (c) $(-4)(+3)$
   (d) $(-1)(-6)$ (e) $(-3)(+2)$ (f) $(+4)(0)$
   (g) $(-5)(0)$ (h) $(+3)(-6)$ (i) $(+5)(-4)$

You may write some products in a different form.
   $(+3)(-3)$ as $3(-3)$
   $(-4)(-3)$ as $-4(-3)$

B 5 Find each product.
   (a) $3(-2)$ (b) $4(-3)$ (c) $5(-5)$
   (d) $-2(+1)$ (e) $-3(+3)$ (f) $-4(+2)$
   (g) $-3(-1)$ (h) $-2(-3)$ (i) $-4(-4)$
   (j) $-6(-6)$ (k) $-4(+3)$ (l) $-6(-3)$

170

6 Complete each sentence by using the word positive or negative.

(a) The product of a positive integer and a positive integer is ▩.

(b) The product of a negative integer and a negative integer is ▩.

(c) The product of a positive integer and a negative integer is ▩.

(d) The product of a negative integer and a positive integer is ▩.

(e) The product of a ▩ integer and a negative integer is a negative integer.

(f) The product of a positive integer and a ▩ integer is a positive integer.

(g) The product of a ▩ integer and a negative integer is a positive integer.

(h) The product of a positive integer and a ▩ integer is a negative integer.

7 Calculate.

(a) $(-1)(+1)$ (b) $(+2)(-3)$ (c) $(-3)(+1)$

(d) $(-2)(0)$ (e) $(-1)(-2)$ (f) $(+6)(+5)$

(g) $(-8)(+5)$ (h) $(+5)(-4)$ (i) $(+6)(-3)$

8 Find each product.

(a) $(+1)(-1)$ (b) $(+1)(0)$ (c) $(-5)(+2)$

(d) $(-5)(-6)$ (e) $(-2)(+4)$ (f) $(+6)(-3)$

(g) $(-4)(+3)$ (h) $(0)(-4)$ (i) $(-2)(-3)$

(j) Which of the above products has the greatest value?

9 Multiply.

(a) $(-1)(+2)$ (b) $(+1)(-6)$ (c) $(0)(-4)$

(d) $(-1)(-3)$ (e) $(-2)(0)$ (f) $(-5)(-13)$

(g) $(+4)(-5)$ (h) $(-6)(-2)$ (i) $(-3)(+5)$

(j) Which of the above products has the least value?

10 Find each product.

(a) $-3(-5)$ (b) $-4(-2)$ (c) $5(-4)$

(d) $4(-5)$ (e) $(-3)(-2)$ (f) $-3(-2)$

(g) $-5(7)$ (h) $6(-8)$ (i) $-9(-3)$

11 To find the product of 3 integers, find the product of two of them first. The first one has been done for you.

(a) $(+6)(-3)(+1)$
$$(+6)(-3)(+1)$$
$$= (-18)(+1)$$
$$= -18$$

(b) $(+2)(-4)(-3)$ (c) $(-5)(+7)(-2)$

(d) $(-5)(-2)(-10)$ (e) $(+6)(-2)(-1)$

(f) $(-9)(+2)(-4)$ (g) $(0)(-10)(-7)$

(h) $(-15)(-2)(+3)$ (i) $(-6)(+6)(-10)$

12 The pool temperature at night without a pool cover drops 2°C/h.

(a) Use integers to show how to obtain the temperature drop in 5 h.

(b) The temperature is 25°C. What is the final temperature after 5 h?

13 The average temperature of Lake Tamagog drops 1°C/d during September.

(a) Use integers to show the temperature drop in 2 weeks.

(b) The temperature of Lake Tamagog is 23°C on September 1st. What is the temperature on September 15th?

14 The temperature on Mars drops 15°C/h during the Martian night.

(a) Use integers to show the temperature drop in 5 h.

(b) What is the temperature drop in 12 h?

C15 Find the integer represented by ▩ in each of the following.

(a) $-6 \times ▩ = -30$ (b) $-15 \times ▩ = 75$

(c) $▩ \times (-13) = -52$ (d) $9 \times ▩ = -81$

(e) $-24 \times ▩ = 144$ (f) $5 \times ▩ = -60$

5.7 Substitution With Integers

You can apply your skills in multiplying integers to calculate expressions.

Example

Find the value of $2p + 3q$ if $p = -1$, $q = -2$.

Solution

$2p + 3q$ ⟵ Record the original expression.

$= 2(-1) + 3(-2)$ ⟵ Use brackets to show the substitution.

$= -2 + (-6)$

$= -2 - 6$

$= -8$ ⟵ Use your earlier skills to calculate $2(-1)$ and $3(-2)$.

Written Exercises

A 1 Find the value of pq if,

   (a) $p = 1$, $q = -4$.   (b) $p = -2$, $q = 5$.

   (c) $p = -3$, $q = -7$.   (d) $p = -8$, $q = -7$.

   (e) $p = 10$, $q = -6$.   (f) $p = -12$, $q = 3$.

2 (a) Find the value of $6 + 2p$ for $p = -5$.

   (b) Find the value of $6 - 2p$ for $p = -5$.

   (c) Find the value of $2a + 3b$ for $a = -4$ and $b = -2$.

3 Evaluate each of these expressions for $a = -3$.

   (a) $3a + 1$ (b) $3a - 1$ (c) $2a + 6$

   (d) $4a - 3$ (e) $6 + 3a$ (f) $-4 - 2a$

B 4 Find the value of each expression. $x = -2$, $y = 3$.

   (a) $x + y$ (b) $x - y$ (c) $-x - y$

   (d) $2x + y$ (e) $2x - 3y$ (f) $3xy$

5 Which expression has the greater value? Use $t = -3$, $u = -2$.

   (a) $2t + 3u$ (b) $2t - 3u$

6 Evaluate each expression if $a = 3$, $b = -1$.

   (a) $-3(a + b)$ (b) $-3a - 3b$

   (c) What do you notice about your answers in (a) and (b)?

7 Evaluate each expression if $p = -2$, $q = 3$.

   (a) $4(p - q)$ (b) $4p - 4q$

   (c) What do you notice about your answers in (a) and (b)?

Use the following values for A, B, C, and so on. You may calculate the "integer product" for a name.

$$TED = (+7)(-8)(-9)$$
$$= (-56)(-9)$$
$$= +504$$

A	−12	N	+1
B	−11	O	+2
C	−10	P	+3
D	−9	Q	+4
E	−8	R	+5
F	−7	S	+6
G	−6	T	+7
H	−5	U	+8
I	−4	V	+9
J	−3	W	+10
K	−2	X	+11
L	−1	Y	+12
M	0	Z	+13

8 Calculate the integer product for each name.

   (a) KAY   (b) BOB   (c) IVY

   (d) LEO   (e) PEG   (f) NED

9 Calculate the integer product for each name.

   (a) TOM   (b) UNA   (c) KIT

   (d) Which person has the greatest value?

   (e) What is the integer product of your own christian name?

10 Find the integer product of each place.

   (a) EMO (b) OBA (c) AYR (d) LYN

11 Find the integer product of each place.

   (a) DUFF   (b) KYLE   (c) HYAS

   (d) LANG   (e) TOGO   (f) WEBB

5.8 Dividing Integers

The skills you learn in one sport are often helpful in another sport.

Similarly, the skills you learn in one topic of mathematics are often useful in other topics of mathematics.

Examples can be used to show what happens when integers are divided.

You already know that

$(+2)(+5) = +10.$ Therefore $\dfrac{+10}{+5} = +2$ or $\dfrac{+10}{+2} = +5.$

$(-2)(+5) = -10.$ Therefore $\dfrac{-10}{-2} = +5$ or $\dfrac{-10}{+5} = -2.$

$(+5)(-2) = -10.$ Therefore $\dfrac{-10}{+5} = -2$ or $\dfrac{-10}{-2} = +5.$

$(-5)(-2) = +10.$ Therefore $\dfrac{+10}{-5} = -2$ or $\dfrac{+10}{-2} = -5.$

The above examples illustrate:

I When integers with *like* signs are divided, the answer is positive.

II When integers with *unlike* signs are divided, the answer is negative.

Example 1

Calculate.

You may also write $\frac{-10}{2}$.

(a) $\frac{-10}{+2}$ (b) $\frac{+25}{-5}$ (c) $\frac{-15}{-5}$

Solution

(a) $\frac{-10}{+2}$
$= -5$

Think!
Unlike → Negative
Signs

(b) $\frac{+25}{-5}$
$= -5$

Think!
Unlike → Negative
Signs

(c) $\frac{-15}{-5}$
$= +3$

Think!
Like → Positive
Signs

Example 2

Find the value of ▨.

(a) $(-15) \div ▨ = 3$ (b) $(-30) \div ▨ = -6$

Solution

(a) Since $(-15) \div (-5) = 3$
then ▨ $= -5$.

(b) Since $(-30) \div 5 = -6$
then ▨ $= 5$.

You may check your answer by finding $(-5)(3) = -15$.

Check:
$(5)(-6) = -30$

Try These

1 Complete each of the following.

Multiplication	Division	
(a) $(+3)(+6) = +18$	$\frac{+18}{+6} = ?$	$\frac{+18}{+3} = ?$
(b) $(-3)(+6) = -18$	$\frac{-18}{+6} = ?$	$\frac{-18}{-3} = ?$
(c) $(+3)(-6) = -18$	$\frac{-18}{-6} = ?$	$\frac{-18}{+3} = ?$
(d) $(-3)(-6) = +18$	$\frac{+18}{-6} = ?$	$\frac{+18}{-3} = ?$

2 Complete each of the following.

Multiplication	Division	
(a) $(+4)(+6) = +24$	$\frac{+24}{+6} = ?$	$\frac{+24}{+4} = ?$
(b) $(-4)(+6) = -24$	$\frac{-24}{+6} = ?$	$\frac{-24}{-4} = ?$
(c) $(+4)(-6) = -24$	$\frac{-24}{+4} = ?$	$\frac{-24}{-6} = ?$
(d) $(-4)(-6) = +24$	$\frac{+24}{-6} = ?$	$\frac{+24}{-4} = ?$

3 Complete each of the following.

Multiplication	Division	
(a) $(+5)(+8) = +40$	$\frac{+40}{+5} = ?$	$\frac{+40}{+8} = ?$
(b) $(+5)(-8) = -40$	$\frac{-40}{+5} = ?$	$\frac{-40}{-8} = ?$
(c) $(-5)(+8) = -40$	$\frac{-40}{-5} = ?$	$\frac{-40}{+8} = ?$
(d) $(-5)(-8) = +40$	$\frac{+40}{-5} = ?$	$\frac{+40}{-8} = ?$

4 For each of the following, what sign will the answer be, positive or negative?

(a) $\frac{+6}{+3}$ (b) $\frac{+8}{-2}$ (c) $\frac{-12}{+2}$ (d) $\frac{-24}{-6}$

(e) $\frac{+16}{-4}$ (f) $\frac{-12}{+6}$ (g) $\frac{-40}{-8}$ (h) $\frac{+20}{+5}$

(i) $\frac{-25}{-5}$ (j) $\frac{+30}{-6}$ (k) $\frac{-28}{+7}$ (l) $\frac{-35}{+5}$

Written Exercises

A 1 Copy and complete.

(a) $(-4)(-7) = +28$ $\quad \dfrac{+28}{-4} = ?$ $\quad \dfrac{+28}{-7} = ?$

(b) $(+3)(-4) = -12$ $\quad \dfrac{-12}{+3} = ?$ $\quad \dfrac{-12}{-4} = ?$

(c) $(-4)(+4) = -16$ $\quad \dfrac{-16}{-4} = ?$ $\quad \dfrac{-16}{+4} = ?$

(d) $(-4)(-6) = +24$ $\quad \dfrac{+24}{-4} = ?$ $\quad \dfrac{+24}{-6} = ?$

2 For each of the following, $+5$ is written as 5. Copy and complete.

(a) $5(-5) = -25$ $\quad \dfrac{-25}{5} = ?$ $\quad \dfrac{-25}{-5} = ?$

(b) $(-4)(-9) = 36$ $\quad \dfrac{36}{-4} = ?$ $\quad \dfrac{36}{-9} = ?$

(c) $(-7)(7) = -49$ $\quad \dfrac{-49}{-7} = ?$ $\quad \dfrac{-49}{7} = ?$

(d) $-6(-8) = 48$ $\quad \dfrac{48}{-8} = ?$ $\quad \dfrac{48}{-6} = ?$

B 3 For each of the following questions
• decide whether the sign of the answer is positive or negative.
• then calculate.

(a) $\dfrac{-25}{+5}$ (b) $\dfrac{+30}{-6}$ (c) $\dfrac{-40}{-10}$ (d) $\dfrac{+49}{-7}$

(e) $\dfrac{-50}{+5}$ (f) $\dfrac{-50}{-5}$ (g) $\dfrac{55}{-11}$ (h) $\dfrac{-48}{-8}$

(i) $\dfrac{-72}{+9}$ (j) $\dfrac{-72}{-8}$ (k) $\dfrac{-100}{-10}$ (l) $\dfrac{+100}{-10}$

4 Calculate.

(a) $\dfrac{20}{-4}$ (b) $\dfrac{20}{-5}$ (c) $\dfrac{-20}{4}$ (d) $\dfrac{-20}{-4}$

(e) $\dfrac{16}{-8}$ (f) $\dfrac{-16}{-2}$ (g) $\dfrac{-16}{8}$ (h) $\dfrac{-16}{-8}$

(i) $\dfrac{36}{-6}$ (j) $\dfrac{-36}{-4}$ (k) $\dfrac{-36}{9}$ (l) $\dfrac{36}{-9}$

5 Find each quotient. ← This means to divide.

(a) $\dfrac{12}{-4}$ (b) $\dfrac{-12}{3}$ (c) $\dfrac{-12}{-4}$ (d) $\dfrac{12}{-6}$

(e) $\dfrac{24}{-8}$ (f) $\dfrac{-24}{-3}$ (g) $\dfrac{24}{-3}$ (h) $\dfrac{-24}{-6}$

(i) $\dfrac{-18}{6}$ (j) $\dfrac{18}{-3}$ (k) $\dfrac{-18}{-3}$ (l) $\dfrac{18}{-6}$

6 Evaluate. ← This means to divide.

(a) $48 \div (-6)$ (b) $(-48) \div (-8)$
(c) $(-48) \div 6$ (d) $(-72) \div 9$
(e) $72 \div (-8)$ (f) $(-72) \div (-9)$
(g) $64 \div (-8)$ (h) $(-64) \div 8$
(i) $(-64) \div (-8)$ (j) $(-81) \div 9$
(k) $(-81) \div (-9)$ (l) $81 \div (-9)$

7 Complete each sentence by using the words *positive* or *negative*.

(a) The quotient of a positive integer and a positive integer is ▓▓▓▓.

(b) The quotient of a negative integer and a negative integer is ▓▓▓▓.

(c) The quotient of a positive integer and a negative integer is ▓▓▓▓.

(d) The quotient of a negative integer and a positive integer is ▓▓▓▓.

(e) The quotient of a ▓▓▓▓ integer and a negative integer is a negative integer.

(f) The quotient of a positive integer and a ▓▓▓▓ integer is a positive integer.

(g) The quotient of a ▓▓▓▓ integer and a negative integer is a positive integer.

(h) The quotient of a positive integer and a ▓▓▓▓ integer is a negative integer.

In Questions 8 and 9, all positive and negative signs have been included.
- Decide whether the sign of the answer is positive or negative.
- Then divide.

8 Find each quotient.
  (a) $(-15) \div (+5)$ (b) $(+15) \div (-5)$
  (c) $(-20) \div (+4)$ (d) $+72 \div (-9)$
  (e) $\dfrac{+20}{-4}$ (f) $\dfrac{-25}{+5}$ (g) $\dfrac{-25}{-5}$ (h) $\dfrac{-18}{+3}$

9 Simplify.
  (a) $\dfrac{+35}{-5}$ (b) $\dfrac{-35}{+7}$ (c) $\dfrac{+48}{-6}$
  (d) $\dfrac{+49}{+7}$ (e) $\dfrac{-40}{-10}$ (f) $\dfrac{-66}{+66}$
  (g) $(+100) \div (-10)$ (h) $(-72) \div (-8)$

  (i) $(+36) \div (-6)$ (j) $(-42) \div (+3)$

10 Calculate.
  (a) $(+8) \div (-2)$ (b) $(-12) \div (+4)$
  (c) $(-24) \div (-12)$ (d) $0 \div (+6)$
  (e) $(+60) \div (-6)$ (f) $0 \div (-100)$
  (g) $(+39) \div (-13)$ (h) $(-50) \div (-50)$
  (i) $0 \div (100)$ (j) $(-150) \div (-15)$

11 Divide.
  (a) $50 \div (-50)$
  (b) $(-35) \div (-7)$
  (c) $90 \div (-9)$
  (d) $(-99) \div (-3)$
  (e) $(-121) \div (-11)$
  (f) $150 \div (-50)$
  (g) Which of the above has the greatest value?

12 There are $\div$ and $\times$ in the following. Read carefully. Find ▮.
  (a) $(-16) \div ▮ = 8$
  (b) $▮ \times (-3) = -36$

(c) $(-40) \div (-8) = ▮$
(d) $(-9) \times ▮ = +54$
(e) $▮ \times (-7) = +84$
(f) $(-10) \times ▮ = 90$
(g) $(-80) \div ▮ = -4$
(h) $▮ \div (-6) = -12$

13 Find the value of ▮ in each of the following.
  (a) $▮ \div (-3) = 6$
  (b) $(-22) \div ▮ = 11$
  (c) $(-30) \div (-5) = ▮$
  (d) $45 \div ▮ = -9$
  (e) $(-18) \div (-6) = ▮$
  (f) $(-34) \div ▮ = 2$
  (g) $▮ \div (-4) = 15$
  (h) $(-35) \div (-7) = ▮$

14 Find the value of each variable.
  (a) $(+24) \div a = -6$
  (b) $(-25) \div p = +5$
  (c) $m \div (-4) = +4$
  (d) $k \times (-2) = +20$
  (e) $(+30) \div w = -10$
  (f) $r \times (-8) = -48$
  (g) $(-12) \div (-4) = m$
  (h) $(-40) \div v = +8$
  (i) $y \times (-5) = -30$
  (j) $(+52) \div f = -13$

15 (a) Find the value of $20 \div m$ if $m = -10$.
   (b) Find the value of $p \div (-5)$ if $p = -25$.
   (c) Find the value of $-4w$ if $w = -7$.

C 16 Copy and complete the following chart.

a	-8	-15		-35	-50		-72		-100
b	-4		$+7$			-8		-16	
$a \div b$		-5	-3	-5	$+2$	-7	$+4$	-4	$+25$

Calculate $(-8) \div (-4)$ and then record the answer.

176

5.9   Integers and Averages

To calculate the average of whole numbers you add and then divide as shown below.

$$\frac{6 + 9 + 10 + 15}{4} = \frac{40}{4} = 10$$

The average of 6, 9, 10, and 15 is 10.

To calculate the average of integers, the same procedure is followed.

Example

Find the average of −6, −9, 10 and −15.

Solution

$$\frac{(-6) + (-9) + 10 + (-15)}{4} = \frac{-20}{4}$$

$$= -5$$

Divide by 4, since you are finding the average of 4 numbers.

Written Exercises

A 1 Find the average for each of the following.
   (a) −12, −8, 5   (b) −18, 16, −14, −13, 9
   (c) −9, −7, 15, 16, 12, −15, 14, −2
   (d) 11, 7, −8, 5, −7, −16, −3, −2, 4, 9

The temperatures of 4 Eastern Canada locations are recorded.

Summerville, P.E.I. −9°C   Bayfield, N.B. −6°C
New Glasgow, N.S. −12°C   Torbay, Nfld. −5°C

2 What is the average temperature?

3 How much more is the average temperature than the temperature at New Glasgow?

4 How much less is the average temperature than the temperature at Torbay?

The temperatures of 5 cities are recorded below.

Winnipeg	−20°C	Saskatoon	−27°C
Brandon	−25°C	North Battleford	−28°C
Regina	−22°C		

B 5 Find the average temperature.

6 How much more is the average temperature than the temperature at North Battleford?

7 How much less is the average temperature than the temperature at Winnipeg?

8 Find the average of the following temperatures.

Daytime temperature on Mars	30°C
Mercury freezes	−39°C
Carbon dioxide becomes a solid	−78°C
The coldest temperature ever recorded on earth.	−89°C

C 9 The average yearly temperatures of 5 desert regions are as follows:

Mojave	16°C	Mongolian	−3°C
Sahara	23°C	Australian	21°C
Antarctica	−17°C		

Calculate the average of these temperatures.

10 The minimum temperatures recorded in the deserts are as follows.

Mojave	−14°C	Australian	−7°C
Sahara	1°C	Antarctica	−29°C
Mongolian	−26°C		

Calculate the average of these temperatures.

Applications: Mining and Integers

Because there is such a great worldwide demand for valuable metals, prospectors are always trying to find new deposits. One of the newer methods of prospecting for deposits in the earth is the use of airplane or spacecraft photography.

Once it has been established that an area contains mineral or metal deposits, core samples are taken from the earth to determine how much of the various metals there are and at what depths they will be found.

Airplanes with sophisticated equipment can establish whether certain metals can be found in the earth.

11 At the Selkirk Mine core samples indicated gold at various levels.

September 23	−274 m
October 1	−284 m
October 15	−301 m
October 31	−325 m

What is the average depth of the gold?

12 From samples of cores taken from a mine site, copper was found at the following levels.

July 1	−147 m	July 7	−161 m
July 3	−154 m	July 8	−162 m
July 5	−157 m	July 10	−167 m

What is the average depth of the copper?

13 The depth of deepest penetration into the earth's crust is −9583 m. The depth of the deepest recorded drilling into the sea bed is 3340 m higher. What is the depth of the deepest recorded drilling into the sea bed?

14 The world's deepest open pit is in South Africa. Its depth is −370 m. The diameter of the pit is about 460 m. Calculate the open surface area of the mine.

15 The world's deepest mine is also in South Africa. The mine is 3470 m deeper than the world's deepest open pit in Question 14. What is the depth of the world's deepest mine?

5.10 Exponents and Integers

The nature of mathematics is such that a skill you learn in one topic may be used when dealing with another topic. For example, steps or procedures established for one type of number often extend to the study of other types of numbers.

In working with operations involving whole numbers and decimals, a certain order was used to do the calculations.

Order of Operations

▶ All calculations in brackets () are considered first.
▶ Do calculations involving exponents.
▶ Multiply or divide in the order they appear, (left to right).
▶ Add or subtract in the order they appear, (left to right).

Example 1
Simplify.

(a) $(-40) \div (-5) + 4$

(b) $[(-3)(-4) + (-5)(-2)] \div 2$

Solution
(a) $(-40) \div (-5) + 4$
$= 8 + 4 = 12$

(b) $[(-3)(-4) + (-5)(-2)] \div 2$
$= [12 + 10] \div 2$
$= 22 \div 2 = 11$

Example 2
Exponents are often used with integers.
  $(-3)^2$ means $(-3)(-3) = +9$
  -3^2 means $-3 \times 3 = -9$
Calculate.

(a) $(-2)^2 + (-3)^2 - (-4)^2$ (b) $\dfrac{2[(-4)^2 + (-3)^2]}{(-5)^2}$

Solution
(a) $(-2)^2 + (-3)^2 - (-4)^2$ (b) $\dfrac{2[(-4)^2 + (-3)^2]}{(-5)^2}$
$= 4 + 9 - 16$
$= 13 - 16$ $= \dfrac{2[16 + 9]}{25}$
$= -3$
                     $= \dfrac{2[25]}{25} = 2$

The order of operations is also needed to calculate the value of expressions when integers are the substitution values.

Example 3
For $m = -3$, $n = -2$, evaluate

(a) $m - n^2$ (b) $\dfrac{m^2 - n^2}{m + n}$

Be sure to record the original expression.

Solution
Use $m = -3$, $n = -2$
(a) $m - n^2 = -3 - (-2)^2$
$= -3 - 4 = -7$

(b) $\dfrac{m^2 - n^2}{m + n} = \dfrac{(-3)^2 - (-2)^2}{(-3) + (-2)} = \dfrac{9 - 4}{-5}$
$= \dfrac{5}{-5}$
$= -1$

Written Exercises

A 1 Evaluate.
(a) $(-8) + 10 \div (-5)$ (b) $[(-8) + 10] \div (-2)$
(c) $(-10) \times (-6) + 4$ (d) $(-6) \times [(-7) + 4]$

2 Calculate each of the following. The first one is
done for you. $(-3)^2 = (-3)(-3) = 9$
(a) $(-3)^2$
(b) $(-4)^2$ (c) $(+4)^2$ (d) $(+5)^2$
(e) $(+2)^3$ (f) $(-2)^3$ (g) $(+1)^3$

3 Simplify each of the following.
(a) $3(-3)^3$ (b) $(-3)^3 \div (-3)^2$
(c) $5(-5)^2$ (d) $(-5)^3 \div (-5)^2$

4 Calculate each of the following.
(a) $(-3)^2$ (b) -3^2 (c) $(-3)^2 - 3^2$
(d) $(-4)^2$ (e) -4^2 (f) $-4^2 - (-4)^2$

5 Simplify.
(a) $(+3)^3(-1)$ (b) $(-3)^3(-2)$ (c) $(-2)(-4)^2$
(d) $(-3)(-2)^2$ (e) $(-2)^2(-4)^2$ (f) $(-1)^2(-2)^3$

6 Calculate.
(a) $(-7) \times 2 - (4)^2$ (b) $(-12) - 2 \times (-10)^2$
(c) $(-12) \times (-4)^2 \div 8$ (d) $(-9) + (-8)^2 \div (-4)$

7 Simplify.
(a) $\dfrac{-6 - 30}{-4}$ (b) $\dfrac{-12 - 24}{-6}$ (c) $\dfrac{-42 + 18}{(-4)(3)}$

8 Find the square of each of the following
integers.
(a) -2 (b) 4   (c) -5 (d) 6
(e) $+14$ (f) -16 (g) 60   (h) 81

B 9 Calculate.
(a) $16 - 3^2$ (b) $20 - (-2)^2$
(c) $(-9)^2 + 9$ (d) $(-4)^2 - (-6)^2$
(e) $6^2 - 5^2$ (f) $5^2 - 3^2 - 2^2$

10 Simplify.
(a) $\dfrac{(-12) + (-4)(+6)}{(-6) \times (+3) \div (-2)}$

(b) $\dfrac{12 - (-20) \div 5}{(-36) \div 9}$

11 Calculate each of the following.
(a) $4 \times (-7) \div 4 + 12$
(b) $(-14) \div (-7) + (-9) \div (-3)$
(c) $90 - 3[2(-3 + 4) + 6]$
(d) $(-3)^2 - 8 + 5^2 - (-2)^2$
(e) $[(-60) - (-10)] \div 2$

12 Calculate each of the following. Use $a = -3$.
(a) $-2a^2$ (b) $(-2a)^2$ (c) $-(2a^2)$ (d) $-(2a)^2$

13 (a) Find a value for $4p^2$ when $p = 3$.
(b) Find a value for $4p^2$ when $p = -3$.
(c) Compare the answers in (a) and (b).

14 (a) Find a value for $-4p^2$ when $p = 3$.
(b) Find a value for $(-4p)^2$ when $p = -3$.

15 (a) Find a value for $(-4p^2)$ when $p = -3$.
(b) Find a value for $-(4p)^2$ when $p = -3$.
(c) Find a value for $(-4p)^2$ when $p = -3$.

16 Use $a = -3$. Evaluate.
(a) a^2 (b) $2a^2$ (c) $-2a^2$
(d) $3a - a^2$ (e) $5a - 2a^2$

17 Find the value of each number expression. The
value of the variable is given.
(a) $4m^2$, $m = -6$ (b) $16 + p^2$, $p = -1$
(c) $p^2 - 16$, $p = 1$ (d) $a^2 - 10$, $a = -3$

C
18 Use $x = -1$, $y = -2$. Evaluate.
(a) $x^2 + y^2$ (b) $3y^2 - x^2$
(c) $x^2 - 3y^2$ (d) $-4x^2 - y^2$

5.11 Problem-Solving: Using Patterns

You can solve some problems by looking for patterns. For example, to find A and B, look for a pattern for the given numbers.

3,   7,   11,   A,   B

$7 - 3 = 4$ $-11 - 7 = 4$

Thus A = 15, B = 19.

Sometimes you may need to look at the factors of the numbers in order to find a pattern. What are C and D?

6,   12,   24,   C,   D

2×3 $2 \times 2 \times 3$ $2 \times 2 \times 2 \times 3$ $C = 2 \times 2 \times 2 \times 2 \times 3$ $D = 2 \times 2 \times 2 \times 2 \times 2 \times 3$
$= 48$ $= 96$

Thus C = 48, D = 96.

In order to find the answer for each of the following, try to find a pattern.

Written Exercises

A 1 Complete the pattern by finding differences.

(a) 5, 12, 19, ?, ?   (b) 25, 31, 37, ?, ?

(c) $-96, 88, -80, ?, ?$

2 Complete the pattern by finding factors.

(a) 6, 18, 54, ?, ? (b) $-6, 36, -216, ?, ?$

(c) 1, 4, 9, 16, ?, ?

3 Find the missing numbers.

(a) 5, 9, 13, ?, ?, 25 (b) $-1, 3, -9, ?, ?, 243$

(c) $1, \frac{1}{2}, ?, \frac{1}{8}, ?, \frac{1}{32}$

(d) $-1, 3, -6, 10, -15, ?, ?$

4 (a) Do each calculation.
$1 \times 9 = ?$ $11 \times 9 = ?$ $111 \times 9?$

(b) Use your answers in (a) to predict the answers for 1111×9 and $11\,111 \times 9$.

B 5 (a) Calculate each of the following.
$10 - 1 = ?$
$100 - 11 = ?$
$1000 - 111 = ?$

(b) Use your answers in (a) to predict the result for $10\,000 - 1111$.

(c) Check your prediction in (b) by calculating the answer.

6 (a) Calculate each of the following.
$1 + 11 = ?$
$1 + 11 + 111 = ?$
$1 + 11 + 111 + 1111 = ?$

(b) Use your answers in (a) to predict the answer for
$1 + 11 + 111 + 1111 + 11\,111 = ?$
Check your prediction by calculating an answer.

C 7 Find the missing numbers.
$1 + 3 = ?$
$1 + 3 + 5 = ?$
$1 + 3 + 5 + 7 = ?$
$1 + 3 + 5 + 7 + 9 = ?$
(a) Predict an answer for
$1 + 3 + 5 + 7 + 9 + 11 = ?$
(b) Check your prediction by adding.

Skills To Practise: A Chapter Review

5.1 (a) What integer is 2 more than +2; 2 more than −2?

(b) What integer is 2 less than +2; 2 less than −2?

(c) Write the integers for each of the following.
  A greater than −3 and less than 3.
  B less than +2, but greater than −5.
  C between 4 and −1.

5.2 (a) Evaluate.
  A 7 + (−3)   B −5 + (−2)   C 10 + 7
  D −4 + 2 + (−1) + (−6) + 3 + (−1)

(b) Find the sum of each set of numbers.
  A −3, 4, −2, 6, −3, 8, −9
  B −10, −12, 13, −3, 14, 5

5.3 (a) Evaluate.
  A 3 − (−2)   B 8 − (−9)
  C 16 − 12   D −18 + 6

(b) Simplify.
  A 7 − (−1) + 3
  B −2 −(−1) + (−3) − (−2) + (−6)

5.4 (a) If $m = -3$, $q = -2$, evaluate each of the following.

  A 10 + m   B 10 − m   C q − 3
  D q + 8   E m + q   F m − q

(b) Simplify each expression.
  A −12 − 3 − 2   B −18 − (−8) − (−3)

5.5 (a) What is the total of −4 − 3, −6 + 3, 8 − 9?

(b) By how much does −3 − 8 exceed (−4) + (−8) + (−9)?

5.6 (a) Find each product.
  A (−3)(+4)   B (+6)(−3)   C (−3)(−4)

(b) Calculate.
  A (−3)(−2)(+6)   B (−4)(−2)(−3)

5.7 (a) Evaluate.

  A 5m −4 , when $m = -8$

  B 5m − 5, when $m = -5$

(b) Find the value of each expression if $g = -3$, $h = -2$.
  A 2g + h   B 3g − 2h

5.8 (a) Calculate.
  A (−4) ÷ (+2)   B (−8) ÷ (−4)
  C (+12) ÷ (−3)   D (−12) ÷ (−4)

(b) Evaluate each of the following.
  A $\dfrac{-25}{5}$ B $\dfrac{16}{-4}$ C $\dfrac{-27}{-3}$

5.9 Find the average of each of the following.
  (a) −11, 5, 19, −23, 15
  (b) 7, 16, 42, −3, −45, −35

5.10 Simplify.
  (a) $[(-20) + 5] \div (-5)$
  (b) $(-16) \div [(-4) - 4]$
  (c) $2(-5)^2 - 3(-2)^2$
  (d) $[(-7) - 4 + 5 - 3] \times 0$

5.11 Find the missing numbers for each pattern.
  (a) 2, −4, 6, −8, 10, _?_, _?_
  (b) 20, −18, 16, −14, 12, _?_, _?_
  (c) 1, −4, 7, −10, _?_
  (d) 1, −2, 4, −7, 11, −16, _?_, _?_

Problems To Practise: A Chapter Review

5.1 The data shown were gathered during the third week of January.

City	Temperature
Vancouver	18°C
Regina	6°C
Edmonton	−2°C
Winnipeg	−9°C
Kingston	2°C
Toronto	3°C
St. John's	6°C
Hamilton	2°C
Ottawa	−1°C
Whitehorse	−21°C
Calgary	−2°C
Montreal	4°C

(a) Which city was the warmest?

(b) Which city was the coldest?

(c) Write the temperatures from greatest to least.

5.2 (a) What is the result of an airplane climbing 800 m and then descending 120 m?

(b) Which sum is greater, A or B?

	A	B
(i)	−6 + (−3)	−2 + (−5)
(ii)	−9 + 5	−5 + 9
(iii)	−3 + 3	−8 + 5

5.3 The following chart appeared in a newspaper.

Canadian Temperatures (°C)	Low Overnight	High Yesterday
Dawson	−38	−32
Vancouver	7	15
Victoria	8	12
Edmonton	−12	0
Regina	−20	−7
Churchill	−24	−18
Winnipeg	−15	−13
Sudbury	−21	−16
Kingston	−17	−15
Ottawa	−19	−16
Fredericton	−24	−19
Halifax	−16	−8
St. John's	−22	−11

(a) Which city had the lowest overnight temperature?

(b) Which city had recorded the highest temperature yesterday?

(c) Which city had recorded the greatest increase in temperature?

(d) Which city recorded the least increase in temperature?

5.4 Which expression has the greatest value if $a = -3, b = -2$?

A $18 + a$ B $20 - b$
C $a + b + 25$ D $25 - a - b$

5.5 The record low temperature in the Mongolian Desert is −26°C. Its record high temperature is 42°C more. What is the record high temperature?

5.6 For each of the following numbers, find two integers which are factors of the given number. The first one is done for you.

(a) A −12 One pair of integers is −2, +6.
$$(-2)(+6) = -12.$$

(b) B −16   (c) +36   (d) +100   (e) −75

5.7 Find the value of each expression is $s = -1$ and $t = -3$.

(a) $2s + 3t$ (b) $3st$ (c) $-3s - 3t$

5.8 (a) Find ▨ in each of the following.

A $(-96) \div ▨ = -6$ B $▨ \times (-12) = 84$
C $▨ \div (-7) = -21$ D $-60 \div ▨ = -4$

5.9 The number of kilojoules per hour used by a female for the following activities are:

sleeping	230	walking	750
sitting	300	walking uphill	1500
standing	420	running	1760

What is the average number of kilojoules per hour for these activities?

5.10 Use $p = -4$. Evaluate

(a) $3p^2$ (b) $-5p^3$ (c) $2p - p^2$

(d) $\frac{1}{2}p^4$ (e) $\left(\frac{1}{2}p\right)^4$ (f) $9 - 2p^3$

5.11 Find each product.

A 1×1 B 11×11
C 111×111 D 1111×1111
E Use the pattern in A to D to predict your answer for 11 111 × 11 111. Check your prediction by calculating 11 111 × 11 111.

Chapter Checkup: A Practice Test

5.1 (a) Write the next two integers for
   A greater than −10   B greater than +9
   (b) Write the integers in order from least to greatest.
   −3, 4, 114, −24, −2, 1, −14, −1, 0
   (c) Write an integer to show each of the following.
   A The highest volcano in North America in Citlatepeti, Mexico, is 5700 m above sea level.
   B The record depth achieved for a breath-held dive is 86 m.

5.2 (a) Find each sum.
   A −3 + 8   B −6 − 3
   C 8 + (−3)   D 9 + (−6) + (−3)
   (b) Evaluate −4 + (−3) + 6 + (−2) + (−8).
   (c) Which player has the better total score for 5 holes of golf?
   A Palmer −2, +1, +2, −3, +1,
   B Angstrom −1, +1, −2, −1, +1

5.3 (a) Calculate.
   A 8 − (−3)   B −3 − (−2)
   C 23 − (−2) + (−3)
   (b) The points scored by Lesley are −23. The points scored by Gregg are −18. Who has the better score? By how many points?

5.4 (a) Calculate each expression if s = −3, t = 1.
   A s + t   B s − t
   C 10 − s + t   D 10 − (s + t)
   (b) Which expression has the least value if a = 0, b = −1, c = 1?
   A a + b + c   B a − b + c
   C a + b − c   D a − b − c

5.5 (a) How much greater is −8 − (−12) than (−8) + (−12)?
   (b) Australia's highest recorded temperature is 53°C. Its lowest recorded temperature is 75°C less. What is Australia's lowest recorded temperature?

5.6 (a) Calculate.
   A (−2)(+3)   B (−3)(−4)   C (+5)(−2)
   (b) Evaluate.
   A (−2)(+1)(−3)   B (−3)(−2)(−6)
   (c) The temperature change in the mixture was −2°C every 30 min. If the starting temperature was 4°C, what was the final temperature after 4 h?

5.7 Evaluate each expression if a = −3, b = −2.
   A 2a + b   B 3b − 2a

5.8 Simplify.
   A (−4)(−6) ÷ 24   B [(−6) − 3] + 15

5.9 The depths to which the tree roots extend are
   −8 m, −12 m, −9 m, −16 m, −5 m
   What is the average depth of the tree roots?

5.10 (a) Simplify each of the following.
   A (−16) ÷ (+4)   B (−30) ÷ (−6)
   (b) Which is greater, A or B?
   A (−16) + 4 − 15 ÷ 3 + 2 × (−4)
   B $\dfrac{(−5)(+6) − (+7)(−3)}{(+7)(−3) − (−3)(6)}$

5.11 (a) For each pattern, find the missing number.
   A 3, −6, 9, −12, 15, _?_, _?_
   B −25, 20, −15, 10, −5, _?_, _?_
   C 0, −2, 6, −12, 20, _?_, _?_
   (b) Find each product.
   A 6 × 7   B 66 × 67   C 666 × 667
   D Use your pattern in A to C to predict the answer for 6666 × 6667.
   E Check your prediction in D. Calculate 6666 × 6667.

Consumer Tip: Communication Codes

Whenever you make a phone call or post a letter, you use codes.

If you wish to make a long distance telephone call, you need to know the area code of the place you are calling.

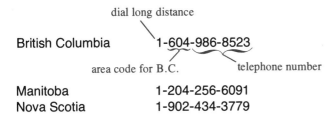

dial long distance

British Columbia   1-604-986-8523

area code for B.C.   telephone number

Manitoba   1-204-256-6091
Nova Scotia   1-902-434-3779

If you write the Canadian Postal Code as part of the address on a letter, you will obtain much quicker delivery service. Each postal code has 6 parts.

S 7 J   3 H 6

large area   Part of the large   smaller part of the area
on map   area on the map.   (such as side of street)

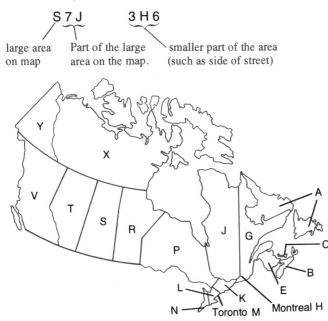

Written Exercises

1. Use the telephone book. If you dialed a long distance number using each of the following area codes, which province would you be calling?

   (a) 204   (b) 604   (c) 902

   (d) 506   (e) 519   (f) 403

2. The postal codes of different addresses are given. What place does each code represent?

   (a) B3A 4E1   (b) H1K 2H8   (c) A2A 2K2

   (d) S4V 4R7   (e) N5K 2V4   (f) M1T 2Y2

   (g) R3V 1N6   (h) T5R 3H3   (i) V3B 3N2

6 Ratios and Applications

skills with ratio, proportion, working with scale diagrams, maps, applications and problem-solving

Introduction

In many everyday situations you frequently compare one number with another. How many of these have you seen?

VANCOUVER WINS
3 out of 4 road games

FOOTBALL FLASH
Edmonton wins
against Ottawa
16 to 7

SHAPE UP
FOR
SUMMER
2 for the price of 1

Scale: 1 cm represents 25 cm

How many small pictures
compared to 1 large one?

6.1 Skills With Ratio

In sports, ratios are often used to compare the performances of teams, as well as players. These ratios can often affect a player's salary!

The chart below shows the records of two high school soccer teams.

	Stanley Park	Viscount
Games Won	3	7
Games Played	10	12

A comparison of one number with another is called a **ratio**. The ratio for Stanley Park compares *the number of games won* to *the numbers of games played*. This is often shortened to read *games won* to *games played*.

number of games won ⟶ 3 : 10 ⟵ number of games played

The symbol : means "is compared to".
Often "3 is compared to 10" is read just as "3 to 10".

The numbers 3 and 10 are called the **terms** of the ratio 3 : 10. The order of the terms of a ratio is very important. Thus, the ratio 3 : 10 is not the same as the ratio 10 : 3.

You may write a ratio in another form.

Colon form   3 : 10   Fraction form $\frac{3}{10}$

Example 1

The chart shows types of part-time jobs. Write a ratio to compare the number of students in part-time jobs.

Part-Time Job Survey	
Number of Students	Job
6	pizza deliverer
3	waiter
7	car wash attendant
11	clerk

(a) *pizza deliverers* to *car wash attendants*
(b) *clerks* to *waiters*

Solution

(a) Number of pizza deliverers is 6.
Number of car wash attendants is 7.
Ratio is 6 : 7   The fraction form

pizza   car wash   would be $\frac{6}{7}$.
deliverers   attendants

(b) Number of clerks is 11.
Number of waiters is 3.
Ratio is 11 : 3
clerks   waiters

When comparing measurements, the measurements must be
expressed in the *same units*, as shown in Example 2.

Example 2

The distances travelled in
1 min are shown. What is the
ratio of the distances
travelled by
(a) the ant and the turtle?
(b) the person and the car?

ant	2 m
turtle	9 m
person	53 m
car	2 km
train	1 km
plane	10 km

Solution

(a) Distance travelled by ant is 2 m.
   Distance travelled by turtle is 9 m.
   Ratio of *distance travelled by ant* to
   distance travelled by turtle is 2:9.

(b) Distance travelled by person is 53 m.
   Distance travelled by car is 2 km or
   2000 m.
   Ratio of *distance travelled by person* to
   distance travelled by car is 53:2000.

Try These

1 What are the terms of each of the following
  ratios?

   (a) 4:7   (b) 9:2   (c) 100:1
   (d) $\frac{3}{2}$ (e) $\frac{6}{11}$ (f) $\frac{1}{7}$

2 Use the diagram.

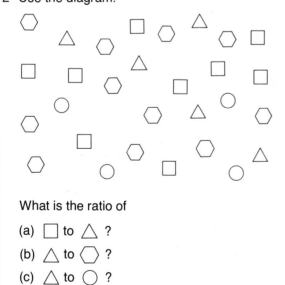

   What is the ratio of

   (a) ☐ to △ ?
   (b) △ to ⬡ ?
   (c) △ to ◯ ?

3 Use a ratio to compare each length.

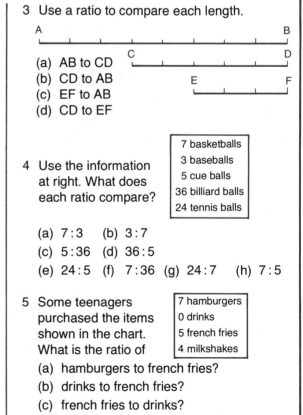

   (a) AB to CD
   (b) CD to AB
   (c) EF to AB
   (d) CD to EF

4 Use the information
  at right. What does
  each ratio compare?

| 7 basketballs |
| 3 baseballs |
| 5 cue balls |
| 36 billiard balls |
| 24 tennis balls |

   (a) 7:3   (b) 3:7
   (c) 5:36   (d) 36:5
   (e) 24:5   (f) 7:36   (g) 24:7   (h) 7:5

5 Some teenagers
  purchased the items
  shown in the chart.
  What is the ratio of

| 7 hamburgers |
| 0 drinks |
| 5 french fries |
| 4 milkshakes |

   (a) hamburgers to french fries?
   (b) drinks to french fries?
   (c) french fries to drinks?

188

Written Exercises

A 1 A number of stamps are shown. What is the ratio of

(a) 17¢ stamps to 14¢ stamps?

(b) 14¢ stamps to 17¢ stamps?

2 Write a ratio to compare the numbers of

(a) stars to hexagons.　(b) hexagons to stars.

(c) stars to pyramids.

3 Use the figure at the right. Write each ratio.

(a) red triangles to all triangles

(b) grey triangles to all triangles

(c) white triangles to red triangles

(d) grey triangles to white triangles

(e) all triangles to red triangles

4 For each figure, write the ratio of base to height.

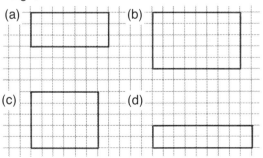

(a)　　　(b)

(c)　　　(d)

5 Use the road signs.

Write a ratio to compare

(a) signs with an arrow to signs without an arrow.

(b) signs using words to signs not using words.

6 For each rectangle find the ratio AB : AD.

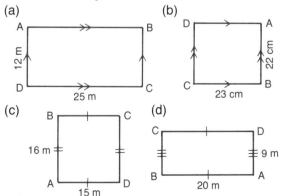

189

7 For each pair of rectangles, write the ratio *the perimeter of rectangle A* to *the perimeter of rectangle B*.

(a)

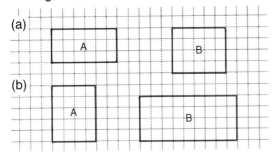

(b)

8 For each pair of rectangles, write a ratio comparing the smaller perimeter to the larger perimeter.

(a)

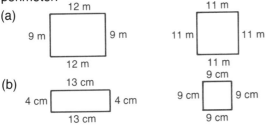

(b)

B 9 Write a ratio to compare the value of each of the following.
(a) a penny to a nickel (b) a dime to a penny
(c) a dime to a nickel (d) a quarter to a dime
(e) a dollar to a dime (f) a nickel to a quarter

10 Write the ratio *smaller* to *greater* to compare each of the following quantities.
(a) 4 cm, 3 cm (b) 8 km, 9 km
(c) 19 cm, 20 mm (d) 250 m, 5 km
(e) 25 m, 40 cm (f) 400 g, 2 kg
(g) 35 kg, 500 g (h) 2 t, 250 kg

11 For the given rectangle, write a ratio to compare
(a) length to width.
(b) width to length.
(c) length to perimeter.
(d) width to perimeter.

12 In a class, students had the following part-time jobs.

    A Service Station Attendant 6
    B Pizza Deliverer 5
    C Dishwasher 3
    D Handbills Distributor 3

Write a ratio to compare the following jobs.
(a) A to D (b) C to B
(c) D to C (d) B to D

13 A nut mixture is made of the following:

    cashews   40 g   peanuts   180 g
    filberts   10 g   Brazil nuts 40 g

Write a ratio to compare
(a) cashews to Brazil nuts.
(b) peanuts to filberts.
(c) filberts to cashews.
(d) Brazil nuts to peanuts.

14 Use the recipe for white bread. Write the ratio for each of the following.
(a) warm water to cold water
(b) milk to flour
(c) shortening to sugar
(d) sugar to milk

White Bread
25 mL sugar
125 mL warm water
125 mL cold water
1 package dry yeast
625 mL flour
125 mL milk
10 mL shortening

C 15 There is a village on the island of Anglesey in Wales called Llanfairpwllgwyngyllgogerychwyrndrobwyll-llantysiliogogogoch.
Write the ratios.
(a) a's to w's. (b) y's to o's.
(c) h's to d's. (d) y's to l's.
(e) i's to w's. (f) n's to l's.
(g) l's to all letters. (h) d's to all letters.

Applications: Ratios for Games

When playing card games you can use ratios to make comparisons that may help you win.

Questions 16 to 18 are based on the following information.

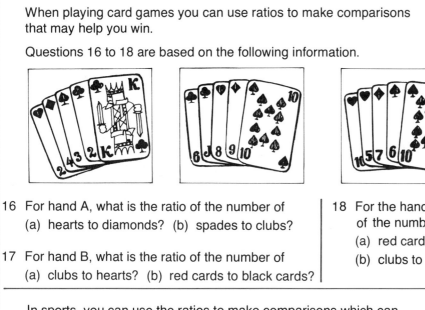

16 For hand A, what is the ratio of the number of
   (a) hearts to diamonds? (b) spades to clubs?

17 For hand B, what is the ratio of the number of
   (a) clubs to hearts? (b) red cards to black cards?

18 For the hands of cards shown, write the ratio of the number of
   (a) red cards to black cards.
   (b) clubs to diamonds. (c) spades to hearts.

In sports, you can use the ratios to make comparisons which can be used to make decisions such as:
• which starting players to use for a game.
• how much to pay a player.

Questions 19 to 22 are based on the following information.

The data for the NHL scoring and penalty records are shown in the table.

PLAYER	GP	G	A	PIM
Boldirev	80	24	38	40
Jensen	78	22	23	62
LaFleur	80	56	80	20
MacAdam	80	22	41	68
McKechnie	80	25	34	50
Monaham	76	18	26	48
Sargent	80	14	40	65
Trottier	76	30	42	34

Games Played — GP
Goals Scored — G
Assists — A
Penalties in Minutes — PIM

19 Write a ratio to compare *goals scored* to *games played* for each player.
   (a) Boldirev   (b) MacAdam
   (c) Sargent   (d) Trottier

20 Write a ratio to compare *games played* to *penalties in minutes* for each player.
   (a) LaFleur   (b) Monaham
   (c) Jensen   (d) McKechnie

21 Write a ratio to compare *goals scored* to *assists* for each player.
   (a) Trottier   (b) LaFleur
   (c) Boldirev   (d) MacAdam

22 The table shows the number of shots on goal and the goals scored by the Highville hockey team during the start of the hockey season.

Game	Shots on Goal	Goals Scored
1	23	3
2	17	2
3	29	4
4	19	1
5	11	1
6	25	3

   (a) Write a ratio for each game to compare *shots on goal* to *goals scored*.
   (b) Write a ratio to compare *total number of shots on goal* to *total number of goals scored*.

6.2 Ratios With 3 Terms

Sometimes you have to write a ratio comparing 3 numbers.

The ratio of tickets
adults to students to children
15 : 12 : 7

The amounts of chemicals in fertilizers are given by a 3-term ratio.

18 : 3 : 6

amount
of
nitrogen

amount
of
potassium

amount
of
phosphorus

In each of the examples above, three numbers are compared. Each number is again called a **term** of the ratio.

To compare the attendance on Monday, Tuesday, and Wednesday for the final Championship Hockey Games at St. John's Centennial Arena, you write the ratio

413 : 452 : 511

Number of
students that
attended on
Monday

Number of
students that
attended
on Tuesday.

Number of
students that
attended on
Wednesday

St. John's Centennial Arena	
Day	Attendance
Monday	413
Tuesday	452
Wednesday	511

A 3-term ratio is also a compact way of writing some 2-term ratios. For example, from the above 3-term ratio you may write these 2-term ratios.
• Ratio of Monday's attendance to Tuesday's attendance is 413 : 452.
• Ratio of Tuesday's attendance to Wednesday's attendance is 452 : 511.
• Ratio of Monday's attendance to Wednesday's attendance is 413 : 511.

Example 1

For a home game, the numbers of tickets sold are as follows.

  A 943 season tickets
  B 161 tickets bought at the door
  C   7 tickets bought on the street

Based on the information, write

(a) a 3-term ratio.   (b) a 2-term ratio.

Solution

(a) One 3-term ratio is

943 : 161 : 7

season
tickets

tickets
at the door

tickets
on the street.

What would the ratio
161 : 7 : 943
mean?

(b) A 2-term ratio is

161 : 7

tickets
at the door.

tickets
on the street

192

A diagram may provide information needed to write a ratio, as shown in Example 2.

Example 2

Write a ratio to compare the number of A's to the number of B's to the number of C's.

Solution

The number of A's is 7.
The number of B's is 8.
The number of C's is 10.
The ratio of *the number of A's* to *the number of B's* to *the number of C's* is $7:8:10$.

Try These

1 Information is given in the chart. What does each ratio mean?

Games Played
4 wins
5 ties
10 losses

(a) $4:5:10$ (b) $5:4:10$

(c) $5:10:4$ (d) $10:5:4$

2 A 3-term ratio can provide certain information.

Ratio of size of Pizzas ordered

$$43 : 28 : 10$$

large   medium   small

What is the ratio for

(a) large : small?   (b) small : large?

(c) medium : small? (d) medium : large?

3 Write the ratio *number of circles* to *number of triangles* to *number of squares*.

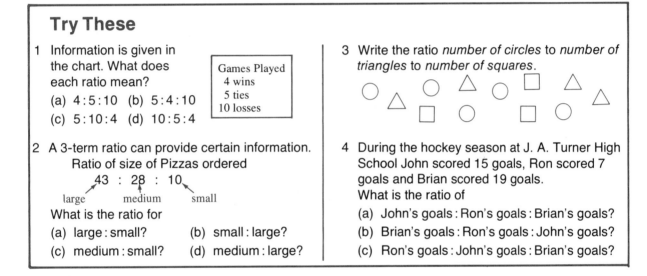

4 During the hockey season at J. A. Turner High School John scored 15 goals, Ron scored 7 goals and Brian scored 19 goals.

What is the ratio of

(a) John's goals : Ron's goals : Brian's goals?

(b) Brian's goals : Ron's goals : John's goals?

(c) Ron's goals : John's goals : Brian's goals?

Written Exercises

A 1 Write a ratio to compare each of the following.

(a) ◯ to △

(b) △ to ▢

(c) ▢ to ⬡

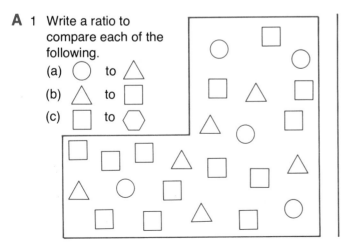

2 The equipment needed to field a baseball team is listed.

36 bats
20 gloves
5 face masks
18 caps
50 shoes (25 pairs)

Write a ratio to compare

(a) bats to caps.

(b) face masks to bats.

(c) gloves to shoes.

(d) bats to caps to gloves.

(e) shoes to face masks to gloves.

3 Use the signs that are shown.

(a) How many signs for speed limits are there?

(b) How many parking signs are there?

(c) How many signs show vehicle caution?

(d) How many signs are based on weather conditions?

(e) How many signs are there altogether?

(f) Write these ratios.

parking signs : speed signs : vehicle caution signs

weather condition signs : parking signs : total number of signs

B Questions 4 and 5 are based on the following information.

As a science project, the insects found in a 10-m² plot of backyard were recorded with the results as shown.

aphids	41
beetles	8
grasshoppers	13
ladybugs	23
mites	36
spiders	12

4 (a) What is the total number of insects?

(b) How many more grasshoppers than beetles?

(c) How many more spiders than beetles?

(d) What is the ratio of *grasshoppers* to *beetles* to *spiders*?

5 Write a ratio to compare each of the following.

(a) beetles to ladybugs (b) aphids to ladybugs

(c) beetles to ladybugs to mites

(d) aphids to ladybugs to mites

6 A bricklayer mixes mortar with three ingredients. He uses 5 parts cement, 14 parts sand and 3 parts lime. What is the ratio *sand* to *lime* to *cement*?

7 Viscount High offers a wide choice of subjects and options as shown in the table. Write the ratio of:

Subject	Number of Courses offered in the subject
Art	5
Business Ed.	12
Computer Science	6
English	17
French	6
Geography	9
History	11
Mathematics	19
Science	15
Technical Subjects	12

(a) *art to geography to science.*

(b) *computer science to history to technical*

(c) *mathematics to total number of courses to French.*

(d) *French to total number of courses to mathematics.*

Are the ratios in (c) and (d) the same? Why?

8 For the bag of fertilizer shown,

write the ratio

(a) *nitrogen* to *phosphorus*.

(b) *phosphorus* to *potassium*.

(c) *potassium* to *nitrogen*.

9 Refer to Question 8. What does each ratio
mean?

(a) 15:10:20   (b) 15:20

(c) 15:10   (d) 10:20:15

Questions 10 to 12 are based on the chart.
A chart can contain a great deal of information.

G: goals
A: assists
P: points

NHL leaders

	G	A	P
Simmer, LA	14	15	29
Dionne, LA	10	16	26
Taylor, LA	8	15	23
Gretzky, Edm	7	13	20
Barber, Pha	10	9	19
Salming, Tor	4	15	19
Nilsson, Cal	7	11	18
Bossy, NYI	10	7	17
Lukowich, Wpg	9	8	17
Federko, StL	5	12	17
Clarke, Pha	3	14	17

10 Write a ratio showing G : A : P for each player.

(a) Taylor   (b) Bossy   (c) Clarke

11 For Simmer of Los Angeles, what does each of
the ratios mean?

(a) 14:15   (b) 15:14

(c) 14:29   (d) 14:15:29

12 Interpret each ratio for Lukowich of Winnipeg.

(a) 9:8   (b) 8:9   (c) 9:17   (d) 9:8:17

Questions 13 to 16 are based on the standings
for the CFL (Canadian Football League).

W wins
L losses
T ties
F points
   scored
   by team
A points
   scored
   against
   the team

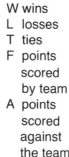

| CANADIAN LEAGUE (Final standings) | | | | | |
| Eastern Conference | | | | | |
	W	L	T	F	A	P
Hamilton	8	7	1	332	377	17
Montreal	8	8	0	356	375	16
Ottawa	7	9	0	353	393	14
Toronto	6	10	0	334	358	12
Western Conference						
Edmonton	13	3	0	505	281	26
Winnipeg	10	6	0	394	387	20
Calgary	9	7	0	407	355	18
B.C.	8	7	1	381	351	17
Saskatchewan	2	14	0	284	469	4
Future games						

13 What is the meaning of each ratio?

(a) W:L:T   (b) W:F:A

(c) L:F:T   (d) L:T:W

14 For each team, write the ratio W:L:T.

(a) Hamilton   (b) Edmonton   (c) Calgary

15 Interpret each ratio for Calgary.

(a) 7:9:0   (b) 9:7:0

(c) 9:7   (d) 7:0

C

16 For each ratio, choose the related team and
interpret the ratio.

(a) 2:14:0   (b) 8:7:381   (c) 8:7:332

6.3 Equivalent Ratios

There are bright stars and faint stars in the photograph. What is your estimate of the ratio of *bright stars* to *faint stars*?
From the picture
> the number of bright stars is 16.
> the number of faint stars is 32.

To make the comparison of bright stars to faint stars, you would write

Bright stars →16 : 32 ← Faint stars

This means for every bright star there are 2 faint stars. You may then write the ratio as

bright stars →1 : 2 ← faint stars

The ratios 16 : 32 and 1 : 2 are equivalent. 16 : 32 = 1 : 2

To write a ratio equivalent to a given ratio, multiply each term of the given ratio by the *same* number. The following ratios are equivalent.

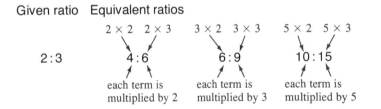

Given ratio   Equivalent ratios

The ratio 2 : 3 is said to be in **lowest terms** or in **simplest form** since

- all its terms are whole numbers and
- there is no common factor of all the terms.

Example 1

Find a ratio equivalent to 3 : 7.

Solution

Multiply each term of the ratio by the same number.
$$2 \times 3 = 6$$
$$2 \times 7 = 14$$
Thus, 6 : 14 is equivalent to 3 : 7.

To reduce a ratio to its lowest terms, you find the greatest common factor (G.C.F.) of the terms of the ratio and divide each term by this factor.

Example 2

Find an equivalent ratio in simplest form for 12:30.

Solution

Think of 12:30 as $\dfrac{12}{30}$.

Then $\dfrac{12}{30} = \dfrac{12 \div 6}{30 \div 6}$

$\quad\quad\ = \dfrac{2}{5}$

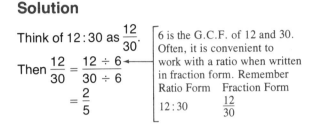

6 is the G.C.F. of 12 and 30. Often, it is convenient to work with a ratio when written in fraction form. Remember

Ratio Form	Fraction Form
12:30	$\dfrac{12}{30}$

The simplest form of 12:30 is 2:5.

To write a 3-term ratio such as 5:10:15 in lowest terms, each term of the ratio is divided by the same factor.

$$5:10:15 = 1 : 2 : 3$$
$$5 \div 5 \quad 10 \div 5 \quad 15 \div 5$$

To write an equivalent ratio for 1:2:3, each term is multiplied by the same number. The following ratios are equivalent.

$$1:2:3 \quad\quad 2:4:6 \quad\quad 3:6:9$$

Each term is multiplied by 2. Each term is multiplied by 3.

Try These

1 Which ratios are in lowest terms?

(a) 1:2 (b) 2:4 (c) $\dfrac{2}{6}$ (d) $\dfrac{3}{7}$

(e) 2:3:5 (f) 4:6:8 (g) 9:3:12

2 Which of the following ratios are equivalent to 1:2?

(a) 2:4 (b) 4:12 (c) $\dfrac{4}{8}$ (d) $\dfrac{3}{6}$

3 Which of the following ratios are equivalent to 2:3:4?

(a) 6:9:12 (b) 4:9:8

(c) 10:15:25 (d) 12:18:24

4 Which of the following ratios is not equivalent to the others?

(a) $\dfrac{4}{5}$ (b) $\dfrac{8}{10}$ (c) $\dfrac{45}{50}$ (d) $\dfrac{12}{15}$

5 In each of the following pairs of ratios, what number are the terms of the first ratio multiplied by to give the equivalent second ratio?

(a) 1:2, 4:8 (b) 2:3, 6:9 (c) $\dfrac{9}{10}, \dfrac{90}{100}$

6 Write one ratio equivalent to each of the following.

(a) 1:4 (b) 3:2 (c) 5:10 (d) 3:8

(e) 1:2:3 (f) 2:5:1 (g) 10:3:5

Written Exercises

A 1 Write two equivalent ratios for each of the following.

(a) 3:4   (b) 5:2   (c) 6:1   (d) 5:10

(e) 3:5:6   (f) 7:14:28   (g) 40:80:60

2 Each of the following ratios is equivalent to 1:2. Find the missing term.

(a) ▯:8   (b) 3:▯   (c) ▯:10

3 Write each ratio in lowest terms.

(a) 5:10   (b) 6:12   (c) 4:8   (d) 10:100

(e) 3:6:9   (f) 10:8:6   (g) 8:6:4

4 Write each ratio in simplest form.

(a) 3:9   (b) $\frac{6}{8}$

(c) $\frac{8}{20}$ (d) 10:4

(e) $\frac{100}{1000}$ (f) 1000:10

(g) 20:32   (h) 300:6

(i) 30:18:6   (j) 56:24:16

(k) 81:54:36

5 In each of the following pairs of ratios, by what number were the terms of the first ratio multiplied, to get the second equivalent ratio?

(a) 4:5, 20:25   (b) 3:2, 12:8

(c) 1:5:2, 3:15:6   (d) 3:2:6, 12:8:24

6 Sandra is 15 a old. Her sister Stephanie is 10 a old. Their father is 40 a old. Write a ratio to compare

(a) Sandra's age to Stephanie's age.

(b) Stephanie's age to Sandra's age.

(c) Father's age to Sandra's age.

(d) Father's age to Stephanie's age.

(e) Stephanie's age to Father's age.

7 The number of medals won on the first day of the Olympics is shown. Write a ratio in lowest terms to compare the number of medals won.

(a) Canada to U.S.S.R.

(b) Finland to U.S.A.

(c) France to Finland

(d) Canada to U.S.A.

(e) Canada to U.S.A. to U.S.S.R.

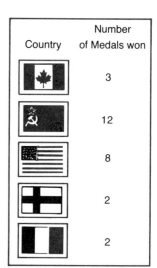

Country	Number of Medals won
	3
	12
	8
	2
	2

B 8 Each of the following ratios is equivalent to 2:3. Find each missing term.

(a) ▯:6   (b) 6:▯   (c) ▯:12   (d) 10:▯

9 Which of the following are true?

(a) $\frac{4}{8} \overset{?}{=} \frac{1}{2}$ (b) $\frac{6}{9} \overset{?}{=} \frac{12}{18}$ (c) $3:5 \overset{?}{=} 9:15$

(d) $2:3:5 \overset{?}{=} 8:12:20$ (e) $3:9:4 \overset{?}{=} 1:3:2$

10 Find each missing term.

(a) 3 is to 6 as 5 is to ▯.

(b) 6 is to 18 as 7 is to ▯.

(c) 15 is to 45 as ▯ is to 24.

(d) 27 is to 9 as ▯ is to 5.

11 For each of the following, replace ▯ by = or ≠.

(a) $1:2 \,▯\, 7:14$ (b) $\frac{4}{8} \,▯\, \frac{16}{20}$ (c) $\frac{18}{24} \,▯\, \frac{9}{15}$

(e) $3:5:1 \,▯\, 6:10:2$ (e) $18:10:6 \,▯\, 6:3:2$

C12 Write a ratio in lowest terms.

(a) There are 5 red marbles for every 10 blue marbles.

(b) 12 out of 20 students prefer reading the newspaper to comic books.

(c) 10 out of 24 persons interviewed prefer hockey over football.

Investigating Ratios

13 (a) Estimate a ratio for the number of

A ☆ to ⊘ .
B ⊘ to ☆ to △ .

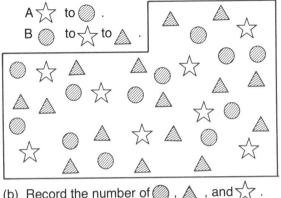

(b) Record the number of ⊘ , △ , and ☆ .
Write the ratios

A ☆ to ⊘ .

B ⊘ to ☆ to △ .

How accurate were
your estimates in (a),
compared to your
answers in (b)?

14 (a) Use the picture of the crowd.

Estimate a ratio for the number of
A men to women.   B children to men.

(b) Record the number of men, women, and
children in the picture. Write the ratio for

A men to women.   B children to men.

15 (a) Estimate a ratio
for the number of
Canadian stamps
to foreign
stamps.

(b) How many
Canadian stamps
and foreign
stamps are
there? Write
these numbers
as a ratio.

How accurate was your
estimate in (a) compared
to your answer in (b)?

16 Edie made chocolate
chip cookies from
these ingredients.

250 mL chopped nuts
500 mL chocolate chips
350 mL brown sugar
350 mL white sugar
450 mL creamy butter
400 mL homogenized milk

Write, in lowest terms, the ratio of

(a) chopped nuts to white sugar

(b) chocolate chips to homogenized milk

(c) brown sugar to creamy butter

(d) chocolate chips to white sugar to
chopped nuts

(e) chopped nuts to white sugar to
chocolate chips

17 Choose two ingredients from each recipe
provided and write a suitable ratio.

Flowerpot Bread	Chili Con Carne
175 g strong white flour	225 g red kidney beans
225 g whole meal flour	1 large onion
15 g lard	1 garlic clove
15 g fresh yeast	50 g butter
250 mL water	450 g raw minced beef
2 mL salt	15 mL chili powder
2 mL sugar	25 g tomato puree

Applications: Ratios and Newspaper Articles

Information in newspaper articles is often given as a ratio. How are ratios used in each of the following headings?

By Law Bye-Bye
Council Votes
9 opposed to the by-law
2 for the by-law

ELECTION RESULTS
5 in every 24 persons interviewed are happy about the recent election.

THEY DO IT AGAIN!
Jets beat Flames
No fire left
2 to 1

The final medal standings at the last Pan American Games are recorded in the newspaper article. Answer the following questions.

PAN AMERICAN GAMES RECORD TIMES

San Juan, Puerto Rico (AP):
When it was all over, the final medal standings for the top 10 teams were records for many of the competing countries.

Country	Gold	Silver	Bronze
United States	127	92	45
Cuba	65	49	32
Canada	24	44	67
Mexico	3	6	28
Argentina	12	7	17
Brazil	9	13	14
Puerto Rico	2	9	11
Venezuela	1	4	7
Dominican Republic	0	5	7
Chile	1	4	6

18 For Canada, write the ratio
gold medals won to *silver medals won*.

19 For Mexico, write the ratio
silver medals won to *bronze medals won*.

20 Write a ratio to compare the gold medals won by

(a) Mexico and Canada.

(b) Brazil and Argentina.

(c) Puerto Rico and Canada.

21 Write a ratio to compare the silver medals won by

(a) Mexico and Venezuela.

(b) Chile and Venezuela.

(c) Venezuela and Canada.

22 Write a ratio to compare the bronze medals won by

(a) Brazil and Mexico.

(b) Dominican Republic and Mexico.

(c) Cuba and Mexico.

23 Refer to the newspaper article. Write the information in the headline as a ratio. Is it in simplest terms?

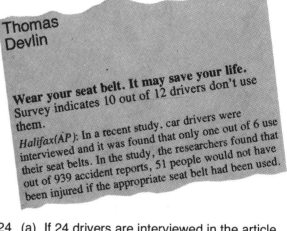

Thomas Devlin

Wear your seat belt. It may save your life.
Survey indicates 10 out of 12 drivers don't use them.

Halifax(AP): In a recent study, car drivers were interviewed and it was found that only one out of 6 use their seat belts. In the study, the researchers found that out of 939 accident reports, 51 people would not have been injured if the appropriate seat belt had been used.

24 (a) If 24 drivers are interviewed in the article how many would you expect
• to be wearing seat belts?
• not to be wearing seat belts?

(b) If 60 cars were stopped at random, how many drivers would you expect to be wearing seat belts?

25 One afternoon, during the survey, 25 drivers were found to be wearing seat belts. How many cars were stopped for the interview?

6.4 Solving Proportions

A proportion is an equation that shows that two ratios are equal. For example, the following are called **proportions**.

$$2:3 = 4:6 \qquad 2:3:5 = 4:6:10$$

From a proportion comparing two 3-term ratios such as $2:3:5 = 4:6:10$, you can write the following proportions involving 2-term ratios.

$$2:3 = 4:6, \, 3:5 = 6:10, \, 2:4 = 3:6, \text{ and so on.}$$

For a record collection, the ratio of *the number of singles* to *the number of LP's* is $3:5$.

Use s to represent the number of singles. There are 25 LP's. To find the number of singles, you need to solve the proportion:

$s:25 = 3:5$. You may write $\dfrac{s}{25} = \dfrac{3}{5}$.

Example 1

Find the missing term in $s:25 = 3:5$.

Solution

Write an equivalent ratio for $\dfrac{3}{5}$.

$$\frac{3}{5} = \frac{3 \times 5}{5 \times 5} \qquad \text{compare} \longrightarrow \frac{15}{25} = \frac{3}{5}$$

$$= \frac{15}{25} \qquad\qquad \text{with} \longrightarrow \frac{s}{25} = \frac{3}{5}.$$

$$\text{Thus} \qquad\qquad s = 15.$$

The missing term is 15.

The solution of the proportion $\dfrac{s}{25} = \dfrac{3}{5}$ gives the answer to the question "How many single records are there?" Thus there are 15 singles.

But the solution to some problems often requires the use of a different strategy. To solve the proportion in Example 2, you first need to write one of the ratios in lowest terms.

Example 2

Solve the proportion $\dfrac{10}{m} = \dfrac{35}{21}$.

Solution

Write $\dfrac{35}{21} = \dfrac{35 \div 7}{21 \div 7} = \dfrac{5}{3}$

Thus solve the proportion $\dfrac{10}{m} = \dfrac{5}{3}$.

Compare the proportions.

$$\frac{10}{m} = \frac{5}{3} \qquad \frac{10}{6} = \frac{5}{3}$$

Thus $m = 6$.

To solve the proportion $m:3:5 = 6:9:y$ you must remember that the proportion can be written as follows:

$$m:3 = 6:9 \quad \text{and also} \quad 3:5 = 9:y$$

Example 3
Solve for m and y if $m:3:5 = 6:9:y$.

Solution
To solve the proportion $m:3:5 = 6:9:y$, solve the following proportions.

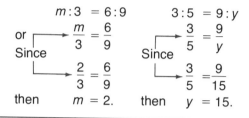

$$m:3 = 6:9 \qquad 3:5 = 9:y$$

or $\dfrac{m}{3} = \dfrac{6}{9}$ $\qquad$ $\dfrac{3}{5} = \dfrac{9}{y}$

Since $\dfrac{2}{3} = \dfrac{6}{9}$ $\qquad$ Since $\dfrac{3}{5} = \dfrac{9}{15}$

then $m = 2$. $\qquad$ then $y = 15$.

Try These

1 For each of the following write 2 equivalent ratios.

(a) $1:2$ (b) $2:3$ (c) $3:5$

(d) $5:2$ (e) $4:1$ (f) $7:3$

(g) $2:3:1$ (h) $4:5:3$ (i) $5:2:5$

2 What is the missing value?

(a) $2:3 = 4:\square$ (b) $4:8 = \square:4$ (c) $\square:8 = 3:4$

(d) $\dfrac{2}{7} = \dfrac{\square}{21}$ (e) $\dfrac{15}{\square} = \dfrac{3}{5}$ (f) $\dfrac{8}{5} = \dfrac{24}{\square}$

3 Which are true (T)? Which are false (F)?

(a) $\dfrac{1}{3} \overset{?}{=} \dfrac{4}{12}$ (b) $\dfrac{1}{2} \overset{?}{=} \dfrac{5}{10}$ (c) $\dfrac{6}{5} \overset{?}{=} \dfrac{12}{10}$

(d) $\dfrac{5}{6} \overset{?}{=} \dfrac{15}{18}$ (e) $\dfrac{3}{200} \overset{?}{=} \dfrac{2}{300}$ (f) $\dfrac{11}{14} \overset{?}{=} \dfrac{3}{2}$

4 What is the missing value?

(a) $2:3:1 = \square:6:2$ (b) $4:1:2 = 8:\square:4$

(c) $3:1:2 = 9:3:\square$ (d) $2:3:4 = 6:\square:12$

Written Exercises

A 1 By what number was each term of the ratio $4:5$ multiplied to give each of the following equivalent ratios?

(a) $8:10$ (b) $24:30$ (c) $12:15$

(d) $28:35$ (e) $16:20$ (f) $20:25$

2 Each of the following is equivalent to $\frac{8}{3}$. How was each of the following obtained?

(a) $\dfrac{24}{9}$ (b) $\dfrac{40}{15}$ (c) $\dfrac{16}{6}$ (d) $\dfrac{32}{12}$

3 By what number was each term of the ratio $3:2:5$ multiplied to give each of the following equivalent ratios?

(a) $9:6:15$ (b) $15:10:25$ (c) $12:8:20$

(d) $21:14:35$ (e) $18:12:30$ (f) $6:4:10$

4 Replace $\square$ by either $=$ or $\ne$.

(a) $2:3 \square 10:15$ (b) $15:20 \square 4:5$

(c) $\dfrac{3}{7} \square \dfrac{12}{28}$ (d) $\dfrac{40}{20} \square \dfrac{8}{5}$ (e) $\dfrac{30}{100} \square \dfrac{3}{10}$

5 Find the value of ▢.

(a) $\dfrac{3}{5} = \dfrac{▢}{10}$ 　(b) $\dfrac{4}{7} = \dfrac{▢}{7}$ 　(c) $\dfrac{5}{6} = \dfrac{40}{▢}$

(d) $\dfrac{16}{▢} = \dfrac{12}{15}$ 　(e) $\dfrac{▢}{20} = \dfrac{28}{8}$ 　(f) $\dfrac{150}{25} = \dfrac{54}{▢}$

6 Find each missing term.

(a) $\dfrac{x}{8} = \dfrac{30}{12}$ 　(b) $\dfrac{16}{8} = \dfrac{6}{p}$ 　(c) $\dfrac{12}{m} = \dfrac{36}{15}$

(d) $y:30 = 1:3$ 　　(e) $m:12 = 7:24$

(f) $\dfrac{25}{30} = \dfrac{15}{r}$ 　　(g) $\dfrac{u}{18} = \dfrac{5}{30}$

7 Find the missing value in each of the following.

(a) $\dfrac{1}{4} = \dfrac{x}{4}$ 　(b) $\dfrac{2}{5} = \dfrac{x}{10}$ 　(c) $\dfrac{a}{3} = \dfrac{4}{6}$

(d) $\dfrac{t}{7} = \dfrac{4}{14}$ 　(e) $\dfrac{x}{100} = \dfrac{2}{50}$ 　(f) $\dfrac{w}{6} = \dfrac{8}{3}$

8 In the diagram, the ratio of stars to triangles is 3:2. The number of triangles is 8.

　　Let n be the number of stars.

(a) Solve the proportion to find the value of n.
　　$n:8 = 3:2$.

(b) Use the diagram to check your answer in (a).

　　Remember, to solve some proportions, it may be
　　necessary *first* to write a ratio in lowest terms.

B 9 Find each missing term.

(a) $4:2 = x:6$ 　(b) $x:75 = 12:36$

(c) $\dfrac{3}{15} = \dfrac{6}{m}$ 　(d) $25:x = 5:3$

(e) $x:10 = 2:5$ 　(f) $\dfrac{9}{4} = \dfrac{36}{x}$

10 Solve each proportion.

(a) $\dfrac{9}{▢} = \dfrac{12}{36}$ 　(b) $\dfrac{2}{3} = \dfrac{20}{▢}$ 　(c) $\dfrac{10}{15} = \dfrac{8}{▢}$

(d) $\dfrac{▢}{16} = \dfrac{3}{8}$ 　(e) $\dfrac{▢}{15} = \dfrac{60}{24}$ 　(f) $\dfrac{40}{65} = \dfrac{15}{▢}$

11 Equivalent pairs of ratios are given below. Use a proportion to find each missing term.

(a) $3:2,\ 30:x$ 　　(b) $12:15,\ 8:y$

(c) $\dfrac{2}{6},\ \dfrac{24}{q}$ 　　(d) $p:16,\ 16:12$

12 Find the value of m if the ratios $3:21$ and $14:m$ are equivalent.

13 What is the value of x if $24:56$ and $\dfrac{14}{6}:x$ are equivalent?

14 Replace ▢ by either $=$ or $\neq$.

(a) $2:3:5\ ▢\ 8:12:20$

(b) $20:40:10\ ▢\ 4:8:3$

(c) $18:3:6\ ▢\ 6:1:2$

(d) $4:6:7\ ▢\ 20:30:40$

15 From the proportion $x:8:m = 3:2:5$, other proportions can be written. Which of the following proportions cannot be used to find m or x?

(a) $x:8 = 3:2$ 　　(b) $8:m = 2:5$

(c) $x:3 = 8:2$ 　　(d) $x:m = 3:5$

(e) $8:2 = m:5$ 　　(f) $m:8 = 5:2$

16 For each of the following, write proportions that involve 2-term ratios.

(a) $1:2:3 = 3:6:9$

(b) $12:18:9 = 4:6:3$

(c) $2:3:4 = 10:15:20$

(d) $4:8:6 = 12:24:18$

C

17 Find the missing value in each proportion.

(a) $12:7:20 = 3:▢:5$

(b) $1:▢:2 = 3:9:6$

(c) $4:10:6 = ▢:20:12$

(d) $12:4:8 = 6:2:▢$

(e) $2:1:▢ = 4:2:10$

(f) $12:6:3 = 4:▢:1$

6.5 Solving Problems With Proportions

In order to become better in a particular skill, an athlete will practise that single skill over and over.

You have learned some essential steps for solving problems. These steps may be applied *over and over again*, even if the mathematical skills needed to solve the problem are different. Review these steps.

Step A To understand the problem you are to solve ask yourself
    (i) What information am I given?
    (ii) What information am I asked to find?
Step B Decide on a method. Translate the problem into mathematics.
Step C Find the answer.
Step D Check your answer in the *original* problem.
Step E Write a final statement to answer the problem.

Identify Steps A, B, C, D, and E in the following examples.

Example 1

Out of every 100 telephone calls dialed, 15 of them are wrong numbers. How many wrong numbers are there out of 240 calls dialed?

Step A: I What information am I given?
           II What information am I asked to find?

Solution

You are given:
Wrong numbers dialed: telephone calls dialed
$= 15:100$
Use W to represent the number of wrong calls.
$$W:240 = 15:100 \quad \text{Step B: Decide on the method.}$$
$$\text{or } \frac{W}{240} = \frac{15}{100} \quad \text{Simplify the ratio.}$$
$$\frac{15}{100} = \frac{15 \div 5}{100 \div 5} = \frac{3}{20}$$
$$\frac{W}{240} = \frac{3}{20}$$
$$\frac{36}{240} = \frac{3}{20} \quad \text{Step C: Find the answer.}$$
Thus, $W = 36$.

        Step D: Check your answer
               $15:100 = 3:20$
               $36:240 = 3:20$ checks

Thus, when 240 calls are dialed, the number of wrong numbers dialed is 36.

              Step E: Make a final statement.

In Example 1, the word *ratio* did not occur, yet you used your skills with ratios and proportions to solve the problem. Often you must *carefully* interpret the information given in a problem in order to choose an appropriate method to solve it.

Example 2

John and Shirley combined their money in the ratio 7:3 to buy a lottery ticket.
They won $10 000!
How should the winnings be divided?

In this example, a clue word occurs in the problem that may help you choose an appropriate method.

Clue word is "ratio" in this case. The clue word is just the starting point.

Solution

The winnings are to be divided in the ratio 7:3.
The winnings are split into 10 parts.
The value of one part is
$10 000 ÷ 10 = $1000.

$$7:3 \\ 7 + 3 = 10$$

Thus, John receives $7000. ←— 7 parts.
Shirley receives $3000. ←— 3 parts.

Be sure to check the answer you find in the original problem.

Written Exercises

A 1 In each table, the ratio of the numbers in A is equal to the ratio of the numbers in B. Find the missing terms. The first one has been done for you.

(a)

A	15	42
B	m	504

$$\frac{15}{42} = \frac{m}{504} \qquad 12 \times 15 = 180$$

since $\frac{15}{42} = \frac{180}{504}$ ←— $12 \times 42 = 504$

then $m = 180$.

(b)

A	r	26
B	63	39

(c)

A	48	116
B	p	145

(d)

A	48	63
B	64	s

(e)

A	54	q
B	90	125

2 For each chart, the ratios shown are equal. Find the missing terms.

(a)

	Mickey	Brady
A: goals scored	63	s
B: shots on goal	168	288

(b)

	Sorenson	Lysiak
A: goals scored	p	210
B: shots on goal	312	336

(c)

	Nat	Bo
A: points scored	r	742
B: games played	686	848

3 Before a Grey Cup game a quarterback's ratio of passes completed to passes thrown is 6:14. During the game, 21 passes were thrown. How many were completed if the pre-game ratio was maintained?

4 At a camp it took 3 L of shampoo to wash 36 heads. How many litres would be needed to wash 64 heads?

5 Out of every 30 students, 24 bring their lunch to school. How many students out of every 100 bring their lunch to school?

6 At the International Dock, 12 hovercraft arrive for every 30 boats that leave. How many hovercraft arrived in a day, if 120 boats left?

7 In baseball the following ratio is used to compare performances of players.
    Number of hits to *number of times at bat*.
These two players have the same performance. What is the missing value?

	Number of hits	Number of times at bat
Dodgson	24	36
Canuck	?	39

8 Jean and Marg agree to share the profit from a garage sale in the ratio 5:2. The profit is $1260. How much does each person get?

9 In a survey, it was found that 15 out of 42 passengers have only carry-on luggage.
   (a) Out of 504 passengers, how many would you expect to have only carry-on luggage?
   (b) During the day it was found that 195 passengers had only carry-on luggage. How many passengers flew that day?

10 For a commercial cake dough, flour, milk and butter are mixed in the ratio 12:5:1. For one batch, 30 L of milk is used.
   (a) How much butter is needed for that batch?
   (b) How much flour is needed for that batch?

B 11 A cook at a barbeque used 4 kg of beef to make 20 hamburgers. If 5 kg more had been brought, how many hamburgers in all could have been made?

12 An athlete made 342 successful jumps in the course of a week. If her rate of success to her rate of failure was 2:1, how many jumps did she fail?

13 The Camera Club and Wrestling Club bought 100 lottery tickets. The money spent was in the ratio,
   Camera Club : Wrestling Club = 12:13.
   One of the tickets won $5000. How much will each club receive?

14 Using a pulley arrangement, a person can lift 225 kg with a pull of 10 kg.
   (a) How many kilograms can be lifted with a pull of 1 kg?
   (b) If 270 kg were lifted, how much was the pull?

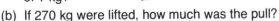

15 The cost of a boat and the cost of a trailer is in the ratio 5:2. The total cost of the boat and the trailer is $2100.
   (a) What is the cost of the boat?
   (b) What is the cost of the trailer?

16 At a party, each person used 6 ice cubes. If each bag contained 72 ice cubes, and 8 bags were used, how many people were at the party?

Some vehicles have drive shafts that turn the rear wheels.

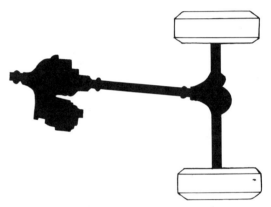

An axle ratio for a vehicle expresses the number of revolutions of the drive shaft for every turn of the rear wheels. That is, an axle ratio of 5:1 means that the drive shaft turns 5 times for each complete turn of the rear wheels.

17 A vehicle has an axle ratio of 5:1. Find the number of times the drive shaft turns if the rear wheels turn 200 times.

18 In a particular vehicle, the drive shaft turns 400 times. How many times do the rear wheels turn?

C
19 For 1000 turns of the drive shaft, how many times do the rear wheels turn for each axle ratio?
   (a) 10:3   (b) 2.5:1

Applications: Glaciers and Icebergs

Would you believe that about $\frac{1}{10}$ of the earth's land surface has permanent glaciers on it? When pieces at the edge of the glacier break off, they float away and become icebergs.

The part of the iceberg that you see above the water is really the smaller part. The ratio of the mass of the part above the water to the mass of the part below the water is

    Above : Below = 1 : 9.

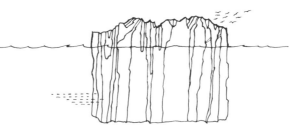

20 A chunk from a glacier breaks off and floats away. The mass of the part of the iceberg above the surface of the water is 1113 kg. What is the mass of the part below the surface?

21 The mass of the part of an iceberg showing above the water was 20 t. What mass was below the water?

22 The mass of an iceberg is 560 t. What mass of the iceberg is above the surface of the water?

23 The mass of a good-sized iceberg is 240 000 t.
    (a) What mass of the iceberg is under water?
    (b) What mass of the iceberg is above water?

24 An ice cube in a drink measures 2.5 cm by 2.5 cm by 2.5 cm. If 1 cm³ of water has a mass of 1 g, what mass of the ice cube is
    (a) below the surface?
    (b) above the surface?

25 The Arctic ice is about 60 m thick. The average shoulder height of a person is 1.6 m. How many persons would have to stand, shoulder upon shoulder, to reach the top of the ice?

26 The tallest iceberg ever sighted reached a height of 167.5 m above the Atlantic Ocean. The height of the great pyramid of Cheops in Egypt is 146.6 m. How much higher is the iceberg?

6.6 Ratio and Scale Diagrams

A scale diagram is a drawing representing a real object. Maps, photographs, and blueprints are representations of real objects.

A scale diagram of a guitar is drawn. The real guitar is 100 cm or 1 m in length. The length of the scale diagram is 5 cm. Then 5 cm represent 100 cm.

The ratio 5 : 100 is the **scale** of the diagram.

The first term corresponds to the measure on the scale diagram.   The second term corresponds to the measure on the actual object.

To write a ratio comparing the measures on the diagram with the measures on the actual object, the measures *must* be in the same units.
Since 5 : 100 = 1 : 20, then the scale of the diagram, in simplest terms, is 1 : 20 or
1 cm represents 20 cm. ◄─ This means 1 cm on the diagram represents 20 cm on the real guitar.

Example 1
Calculate the width of the widest part of the guitar.

Solution
From the diagram, the width of the widest part of the guitar is 1.9 cm.   Use the scale on the diagram.

1 cm represents 20 cm
1.9 cm represent 1.9 × 20 cm
or 38 cm.
Thus, the widest part of the guitar is 38 cm.

In Example 1, the scale diagram is smaller than the actual object. A scale diagram may be used not only as a representation of a large object but also of a small object.

Example 2

A scale diagram of a termite is shown, with a scale of

20 cm represent 1 cm.

length on diagram   length on actual object

What is the actual length of the termite to 1 decimal place?

Solution

The length of the termite in the diagram is 3.4 cm.

20 cm represent 1 cm

1 cm represents $\frac{1}{20}$ cm

3.4 cm represent $3.4 \times \frac{1}{20}$ cm or 0.17 cm

The length of the termite is 0.2 cm.

To write a ratio for a scale given in different units, you need to write both measures in the same units as shown in Example 3.

Example 3

Write a ratio for the scale

1 cm represents 10 m.

Solution

1 cm represents 10 m.   1 cm = 100 cm

1 cm represents 1000 cm.   10 m = 1000 cm

Thus the ratio to show the scale is 1 : 1000.

Try These

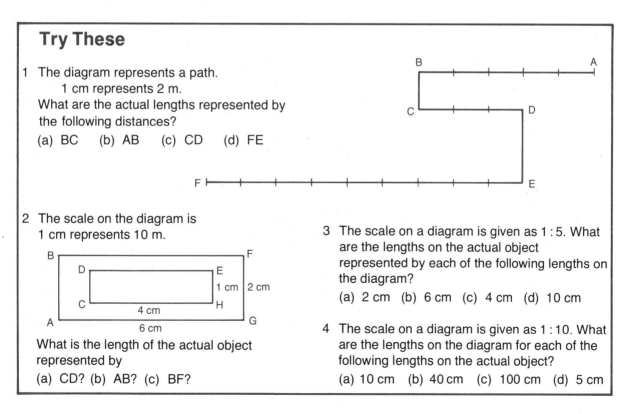

1 The diagram represents a path.

    1 cm represents 2 m.

What are the actual lengths represented by the following distances?

(a) BC   (b) AB   (c) CD   (d) FE

2 The scale on the diagram is

    1 cm represents 10 m.

What is the length of the actual object represented by

(a) CD? (b) AB? (c) BF?

3 The scale on a diagram is given as 1 : 5. What are the lengths on the actual object represented by each of the following lengths on the diagram?

(a) 2 cm (b) 6 cm (c) 4 cm (d) 10 cm

4 The scale on a diagram is given as 1 : 10. What are the lengths on the diagram for each of the following lengths on the actual object?

(a) 10 cm (b) 40 cm (c) 100 cm (d) 5 cm

Written Exercises

A 1 What does each of these scales on a diagram mean?

   (a) 1:8   (b) 1:20   (c) 20:1

   (d) 1:100   (e) 100:1   (f) 7:30

2 A measurement of 2 cm is made on a diagram. Calculate the corresponding measure on the actual object for each of the following scales.

   (a) 1:4   (b) 1:5

   (c) 1:10   (d) 1:25

   (e) 1:50   (f) 1:100

   (g) 1:1000   (h) 1:10 000

3 An insect is drawn to the scale
    20 cm represent 1 cm.
What is the length on the actual insect of each of the following?

   (a) 10 cm   (b) 1 cm   (c) 0.5 cm

4 A diagram of a cruiser is drawn to the scale 1:25. What is the length on the diagram of each of these actual measurements?

   (a) 100 cm   (b) 4 m   (c) 2.5 m

5 These scales have not been expressed in lowest terms. How would you rewrite them?

   (a) 3:12   (b) 5:25   (c) 10:40

   (d) 4 cm represent 60 m

   (e) 15 m represent 3 cm

   (f) 7 cm represent 63 km

   (g) 60 m represent 3 cm

6 The scale on a diagram is 1 cm represents 4 m. Calculate the actual length represented by each of the following measures on the scale diagram.

   (a) 2 cm   (b) 8 cm   (c) 12 cm

   (d) 12.5 cm   (e) 1.45 cm   (f) 0.4 cm

   (g) 18.25 cm (h) 50.5 cm

7 The scale of the diagram of a tennis court is 1 cm represents 5 m. Find the measures of the length and width of the actual tennis court.

8 The scale of the photograph is
       1 cm represents 1 m

Calculate the actual

   (a) length of the car.   (b) height of the car.

   (c) width of a tire.   (d) height of the man.

9 The Calgary Tower is shown. Calculate the measures on the actual tower represented by each of the following.

   Scale
   1 cm represents 75 m

   (a) AB

   (b) CD

   (c) EF

   (d) GH

10 The floor plan of a cottage is shown.

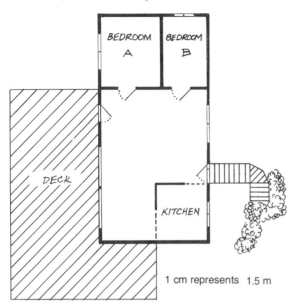

1 cm represents 1.5 m

Use the scale to calculate the actual
(a) length of the cottage.
(b) width of bedroom A.
(c) perimeter of the kitchen.
(d) width of the outside deck.

B 11 A movie company makes a large model of a domino to a scale of 1 m represents 2.5 mm. The width of the actual domino is 15 mm. How wide is the model domino?

12 Mount Everest is the highest mountain peak in the world. It measures 8850 m. How high would a drawing be if the scale used were 1 cm represents 1 km?

13 A model of a submarine is constructed to the scale of 1 : 50. The length of the model is 32 cm. Calculate the length of the actual submarine.

14 In order to make a drawing of a housefly, a scale of 50 : 1 is used. If the length of the fly on the scale drawing is 1.25 cm, find the length of the actual fly.

15 The scale shown for the house fly is 5 : 1.

What is the actual
(a) width of the fly's head?
(b) length of the wing?

16 A pet supplies company makes a statue of a diver for aquariums. They used an actual height of 2.8 m to make the model. If the scale of the statue is 1 cm represents 0.8 m, how tall is the statue ?

17 The wing span of a jet is 15 m. The scale for a model is
    1 cm represents 75 cm.
Calculate the wing span on the model.

18 The model of a sewer pipe is made to the scale 2 cm represents 1 m. If the width of the model pipe is 6 cm, how wide is the actual pipe?

19 The Channel 8 Sports Team constructs a model of a golf course using the scale 1 cm represents 10 m. The model is 75 cm wide. How wide is the actual golf course?

C20 A miniature railway is constructed to a scale of 1 : 20. If the model caboose is 15 cm long, what is the actual length, in metres, of the real caboose?

21 A television image of the height of a horse is 21 cm and that of its jockey is 19 cm. If the actual height of the horse is 164 cm, find the height of the jockey.

Applications: Playing Fields

A diagram of a basketball court is drawn to the scale
    1 cm represents 2 m.
To find the width of the actual court, measure the width of the court in the diagram.
    Width is 7 cm.
    1 cm represents 2 m
    7 cm represent 14 m
The players on each team are shown by A, B, C, D, E, and A′, B′, C′, D′, E′.

Questions 22 to 29 are based on the above scale diagram.

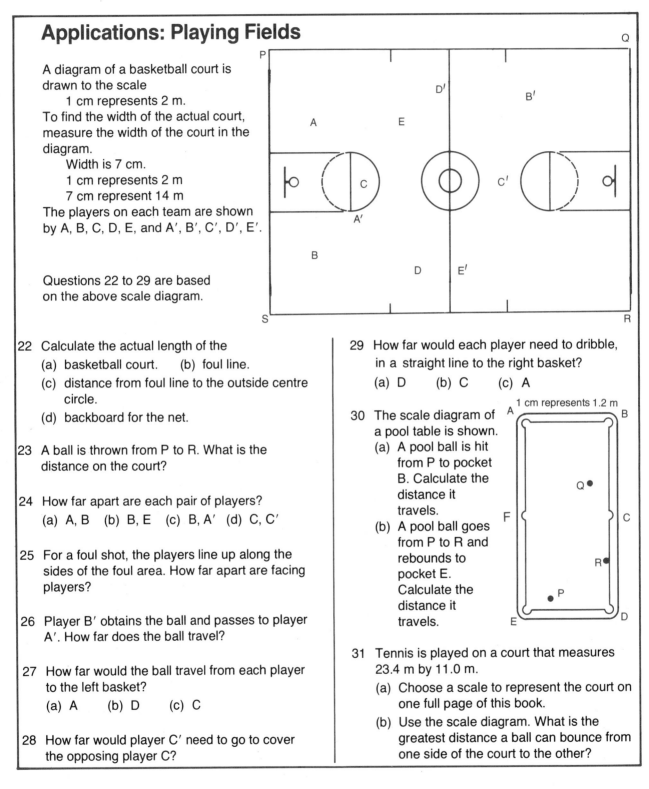

22 Calculate the actual length of the
  (a) basketball court.   (b) foul line.
  (c) distance from foul line to the outside centre circle.
  (d) backboard for the net.

23 A ball is thrown from P to R. What is the distance on the court?

24 How far apart are each pair of players?
  (a) A, B (b) B, E (c) B, A′ (d) C, C′

25 For a foul shot, the players line up along the sides of the foul area. How far apart are facing players?

26 Player B′ obtains the ball and passes to player A′. How far does the ball travel?

27 How far would the ball travel from each player to the left basket?
  (a) A   (b) D   (c) C

28 How far would player C′ need to go to cover the opposing player C?

29 How far would each player need to dribble, in a straight line to the right basket?
  (a) D   (b) C   (c) A

30 The scale diagram of a pool table is shown.
  (a) A pool ball is hit from P to pocket B. Calculate the distance it travels.
  (b) A pool ball goes from P to R and rebounds to pocket E. Calculate the distance it travels.

31 Tennis is played on a court that measures 23.4 m by 11.0 m.
  (a) Choose a scale to represent the court on one full page of this book.
  (b) Use the scale diagram. What is the greatest distance a ball can bounce from one side of the court to the other?

212

Investigations: Scale Diagrams

32 For each of the following, a scale is given. Calculate the length
of the actual object represented by the lengths shown.

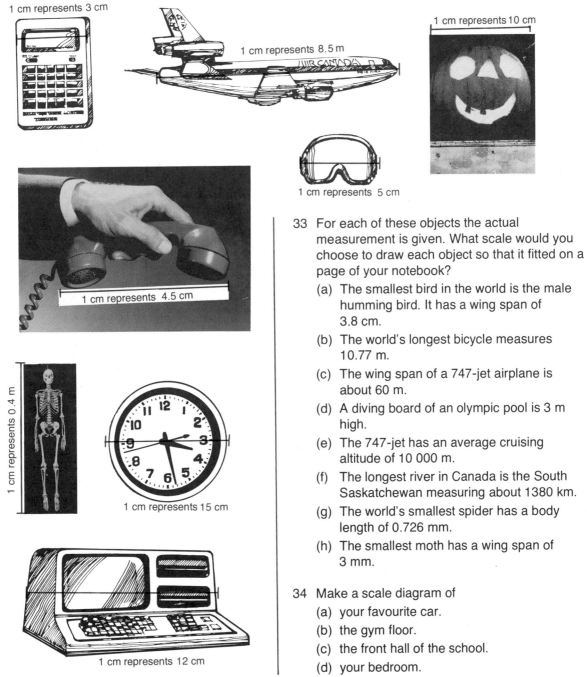

1 cm represents 3 cm

1 cm represents 8.5 m

1 cm represents 10 cm

1 cm represents 5 cm

1 cm represents 4.5 cm

1 cm represents 0.4 m

1 cm represents 15 cm

1 cm represents 12 cm

33 For each of these objects the actual
measurement is given. What scale would you
choose to draw each object so that it fitted on a
page of your notebook?

(a) The smallest bird in the world is the male
humming bird. It has a wing span of
3.8 cm.

(b) The world's longest bicycle measures
10.77 m.

(c) The wing span of a 747-jet airplane is
about 60 m.

(d) A diving board of an olympic pool is 3 m
high.

(e) The 747-jet has an average cruising
altitude of 10 000 m.

(f) The longest river in Canada is the South
Saskatchewan measuring about 1380 km.

(g) The world's smallest spider has a body
length of 0.726 mm.

(h) The smallest moth has a wing span of
3 mm.

34 Make a scale diagram of
(a) your favourite car.
(b) the gym floor.
(c) the front hall of the school.
(d) your bedroom.

6.7 Maps As Scale Diagrams

A map is an example of a scale diagram. It represents a part of the earth's surface. The scale on the map of Alberta and British Columbia is

1 cm represents 130 km.

↖ distance on   ↖ distance on the
the map   earth's surface

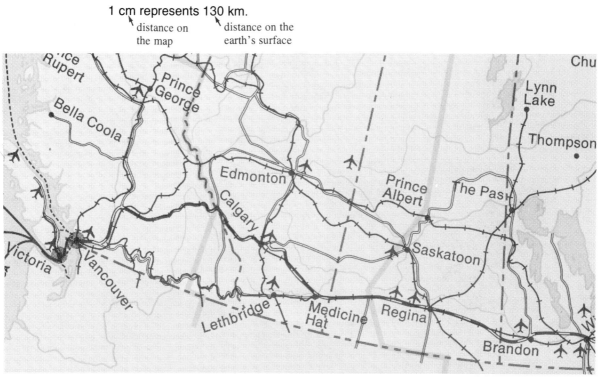

Example 1

Find the "straight line distance" from Edmonton to Vancouver.

This distance is shorter than the actual distance you would drive by car, since by car you would travel along curved highways, etc.

Solution

From the map, the straight line distance measures 6.3 cm.

1 cm represents 130 km
6.3 cm represent 6.3 × 130 km
or 819 km

Thus, the straight line distance from Edmonton to Vancouver is 819 km.

To write a ratio for the scale 1 cm represents 130 km, each distance must be in the same units.

130 km = 130 000 m
= 13 000 000 cm

The scale of the map would then be written as the ratio

distance on →1 : 13 000 000 ↖ corresponding distance
map   on the earth's surface

Example 2

The scale of a wall map of Prince Edward Island is 1 : 20 000. The actual distance on a line from Seacrow Pond to East Point is 169 km. What is the distance on the map?

Solution

Scale 1 : 20 000 means
20 000 cm
= 200 m
= 0.2 km

1 cm represents 20 000 cm
or 1 cm represents 0.2 km.
Thus use
0.2 km is represented by 1 cm
1 km is represented by 5 cm ◄—— $1 \div 0.2 = 5$
169 km is represented by 169×5 cm
or 845 cm.
845 cm = 8.45 m ◄—— Remember 1 m = 100 cm.
The distance on the map is 8.45 m. ◄—— (A big wall!)

Try These

1 On a map, a distance of 30 km is shown by 1 cm. What is the scale?

2 The scale on a map is 1 cm represents 3 km. What is the actual distance for each distance on the map?
(a) 4 cm   (b) 6 cm   (c) 10 cm

3 The scale on a map is 1 cm represents 10 km. What is the distance on the map for each of these actual distances?
(a) 10 km   (b) 100 km   (c) 125 km

4 The scale on the map of a park is 1 : 100. What is the actual distance for each of the following?
(a) 1 cm   (b) 10 cm   (c) 100 cm

5 For each map, find the missing distances.

	Scale	Distance on Map	Actual Distance
(a)	1 cm represents 10 km	10 cm	?
(b)	1 cm represents 100 km	?	1000 km
(c)	1 cm represents 250 km	?	500 km
(d)	1 cm represents 1000 km	4 cm	?

Written Exercises

A 1 On a map, the scale is 1 cm represents 12.5 km. Find the actual distance to 1 decimal place for each of the following distances on the map.
(a) 2 cm   (b) 2.1 cm   (c) 10 cm
(d) 10.5 cm   (e) 5.8 cm   (f) 12.3 cm

2 The scale on a map is 1 cm represents 125 km. Find the distance on the map to 1 decimal place for each actual distance.
(a) 250 km   (b) 1000 km   (c) 60 km
(d) 100 km   (e) 280 km   (f) 550 km

3 The actual distance driven and the distance on the map are shown. Write the scale in the form 1 cm represents ▊ km.

	Actual Distance	Distance on Map
(a)	8 km	1 cm
(b)	8 km	6 cm
(c)	50 km	5 cm
(d)	50 km	8 cm
(e)	100 km	2.5 cm

4 Write each ratio in the form 1 cm represents ▊ km.
(a) 1 : 100 000   (b) 1 : 1 000 000   (c) 1 : 1 250 000

5 The scale on a map of the logging camp is 1 : 1000. What is the distance on the map for each actual distance at the logging camp?
   (a) 100 m   (b) 1 km   (c) 3.5 km

Questions 6 to 10 are based on the following diagram.

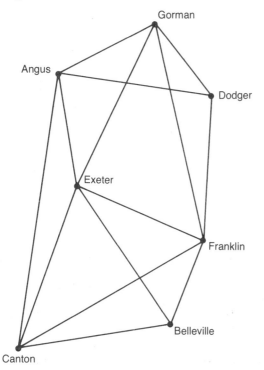

Gorman

Angus

Dodger

Exeter

Franklin

Belleville

Canton

6 The scale of the map is
      1 : 10 000 000.
   Write the above ratio in the form
      1 cm represents ▨ km

7 Measure and record the distance in centimetres between each place. What is the distance on the map between
   (a) Angus and Dodger?
   (b) Franklin and Canton?
   (c) Belleville and Exeter?
   (d) Gorman and Franklin?

8 What is the total distance of a round trip from Angus through Dodger, Franklin, and Canton?

9 Which trip is further? By how much?
   (a) Exeter to Belleville to Franklin
   (b) Exeter to Angus to Canton

10 How much further is it to go from Dodger to Angus via Gorman, than to go there directly?

B 11 The scale on a map is given as
         1 cm represents 80 km.
      The actual distance from Vancouver, B.C. to Edmonton, Alberta, is 800 km. What would be the distance on the map between these two cities?

12 The scale on a map is 1 cm represents 400 km. How far is Calgary from Ottawa to the nearest kilometre if the distance on the map is 7.5 cm?

13 In an atlas, the scale used is 1 cm for every 650 km. How far is it actually from New York to London if it is 8.5 cm away on the map?

14 If you travel from the very tip of England in the south to the northern most tip in Scotland, you would cover a distance of approximately 1000 km. The scale on a map is 1 cm represents 650 km. How many centimetres on a map would represent this distance?

15 Liechtenstein is one of the smallest countries in Europe. On a map, the scale is 1 cm represents 3.2 km. On that map, the country measures 7 cm from north to south, and 3 cm from east to west.
   (a) How far is it from the northern border to the southern border?
   (b) How far is it from the east to the west?

16 On a map, the distance from London to Paris is 350 km. If the distance on the map is 3.5 cm, what is the scale on the map?

Questions 17 to 25 are based on the map shown for Regina, Saskatchewan. Round off all your answers to 1 decimal place.

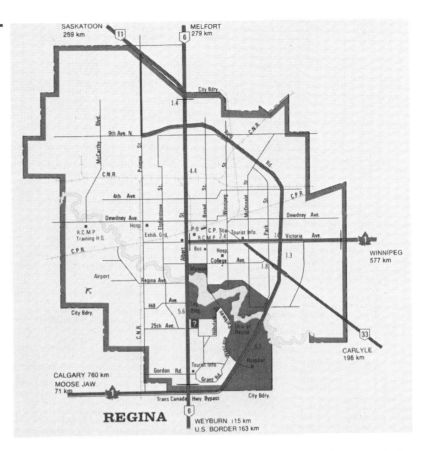

17 (a) The scale of the map is 1 : 100 000. What does this scale mean?

  (b) Write the scale in (a) in the form 1 cm represents ▯ km.

18 Find the actual distance that corresponds to each of these measures on the map.

  (a) 4 cm   (b) 5.5 cm   (c) 0.8 cm

19 These actual distances were measured in Regina. Calculate the distances (in centimetres) on the map.

  (a) 5 km   (b) 10 km   (c) 8.5 km
  (d) 9.6 km   (e) 7.9 km   (f) 12.5 km

20 A distance of 6.2 cm is measured on the map. How far would the actual distance be measured in Regina?

21 Jeannette drove 3.8 km in Regina. What distance does this represent on the map?

22 Jay measured a distance from his school to the Legislative Buildings as 4.5 cm. How far is the actual distance?

23 During a tour of Regina, a distance of 18.5 km was travelled. What is the distance in centimetres on the map?

24 Use the map to find each actual distance.

  (a) Victoria Avenue

  (b) Albert Street

25 (a) How far did you travel along Pasqua Street from the intersection of Pasqua Street and 25th Avenue, to the intersection of Pasqua Street and 9th Avenue N?

  (b) Use the names on the map. Describe a short trip in Regina.

  (c) Find the actual distance travelled for the trip in (b).

217

6.8   Problem-Solving: Information From A Diagram

Often a diagram provides some of the information required to solve
the problem. For example, in baseball the distance a pitcher stands
from the batter is represented by this length.

Scale: 1 cm represents 2 m.

In soccer the distance a player is from the goal mouth when he is
taking a penalty shot is represented by this length.

Scale: 1 cm represents 4 m.

You need to interpret the given information on the diagram
accurately in order to decide which is the longer distance.

Written Exercises

1 (a) Use the above scale diagram to calculate
the distance the pitcher is from the batter.
 (b) Use the above scale diagram to
calculate the distance the player is
from the goal mouth.
 (c) Which of the above distances is longer?

Questions 2 to 5 are based on the
following information.
The scale drawing shown at the bottom
of the page compares the heights that
an average person can jump on the
various planets.

2 How much higher can you jump on the
moon than on the earth ?

3 The Olympic record for the men's standing
high jump on earth is 1.63 m. What would
you expect the record to be on Mars?

4 The men's world running high jump on
earth is 2.4 m. What would you expect the
record to be on the moon?

5 The women's world running
high jump is 2.1 m. What
would you expect the record
to be on Jupiter?

Jupiter Earth Mars Moon

Questions 6 to 9 are based
on the diagram about the
earth's atmosphere drawn
to scale at the side
of the page.

6 Returning from a space
mission, you enter the
thermosphere. How far
will you travel towards
the earth before you
reach the mesophere?

7 A weather balloon
reaches the top of the
stratosphere. How high is it?

8 A jet is flying at the
boundary of the
troposphere and
stratosphere. What is its
altitude?

9 (a) By how much is the
stratosphere thicker
than the troposhere?
 (b) By how much is the
thermosphere thicker
than the
mesosphere ?

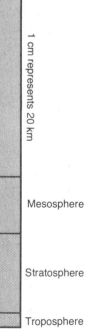

Thermosphere

1 cm represents 20 km

Mesosphere

Stratosphere

Troposphere

Skills To Practise: A Chapter Review

6.1 (a) Write a ratio of width to height for each of the following.

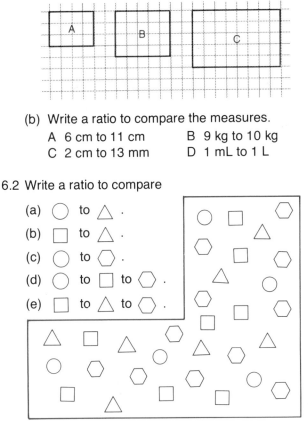

(b) Write a ratio to compare the measures.
   A 6 cm to 11 cm   B 9 kg to 10 kg
   C 2 cm to 13 mm   D 1 mL to 1 L

6.2 Write a ratio to compare

(a) ◯ to △ .

(b) ▢ to △ .

(c) ◯ to ⬡ .

(d) ◯ to ▢ to ⬡ .

(e) ▢ to △ to ⬡ .

6.3 (a) Which ratio is not equivalent to the others?
   A 4:6   B 5:10   C 6:9
(b) Write each ratio in simplest form.
   A 6:8   B 16:10   C 12:24
(c) Each ratio is equivalent to 3:4. Find the missing term.
   A $p:12$ B $9:q$ C $r:20$

6.4 (a) Find the missing value.
   A $m:8 = 30:12$ B $\dfrac{2}{5} = \dfrac{n}{10}$
(b) The ratios in each pair below are equal. Find the missing term.
   A $3:15, 6:m$ B $s:18, 12:27$

(c) Find the missing value in the proportion
   $2:m:4 = 6:18:12$.

6.5 For each table, the ratios of G to H are equal. Find the missing value.

(a)

| | G Trucks | m | 72 |
| | H Cars | 63 | 108 |

(b)

| | G Sweaters | 123 | 117 |
| | H Shoes | 164 | k |

6.6 (a) A measurement of 5 cm is made on a diagram. Calculate the corresponding measure on the actual object for each scale.

   A 1:5   B 5:1   C 10:1   D 1:10

(b) A hovercraft is drawn to the scale 1:20. What is the length on the diagram of each of the following measures?
   A 10 m   B 2 m   C 3.2 m

6.7 (a) The scale on a map is 1 cm represents 8.5 km. What is the actual distance for these measures on the map?
   A 10 cm   B 12.5 cm   C 0.8 cm

(b) The scale of a park for endangered species is 1 cm represents 2.8 km. What is the distance on the map for each of the following actual distances?
   A 12 km   B 8.0 km   C 46.5 km

6.8 Find the actual lengths the following line segments represent if each line segment is drawn to the scale shown
(a) ——————
   1 cm represents 10 m
(b) ———————————
   1 cm represents 2 km
(c) ————————————————
   1 cm represents 0.5 m

Problems To Practise: A Chapter Review

6.1 The seating capacity of four aircrafts is shown in the table. Write a ratio to compare the number of seats for

Aircraft	Number of Passengers
D.C.8	137
747	365
Vanguard	108
Viscount	51

(a) D.C.8 to 747. (b) Vanguard to 747.

(c) 747 to Viscount. (d) Viscount to D.C.8.

6.2 This 3-term ratio is used to show the quantities of material in a mixture used to pave a driveway.

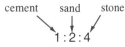

cement sand stone

1 : 2 : 4

Write a ratio to show

(a) cement to sand. (b) stone to cement.

6.3 (a) Write each ratio in lowest terms.
   A There are 2 CB'ers for every 20 people.
   B Out of every 12 trips, 3 go to Hawaii.
   C 4 out of every 16 bales are used for home insulation.

(b) The following amounts of fish were caught.

Write a ratio to show
A cod to haddock.
B haddock to salmon.
C herring to salmon.
D cod to haddock to salmon.

Cod	2 t
Haddock	4 t
Herring	5 t
Salmon	8 t

6.4 (a) What is the value of x if the ratios 12:3 and x:30 are equivalent?

(b) The number of bales of hay needed is given by finding the missing term for the equivalent ratios m : 16 and 3 : 8.

(c) The 3-term ratios 6:2:m and 12:4:8 are equivalent. Find the value of m.

6.5 (a) During the year, a school required 15 kg of chalk for 26 classrooms. Portables have been added and the number of classrooms has increased to 34. How much chalk is needed now?

(b) At Edmonton International Airport the ratio of international flights to domestic flights is 3:25.
   A How many international flights are there for 125 domestic flights?
   B How many domestic flights would there be for 27 international flights?

6.6 The photograph is taken with the scale shown.

1 cm represents 4 m

Calculate, to 1 decimal place
A the actual length of the jet engine.
B the actual height of the tail above the tarmac.

6.7 (a) The actual distance of the Trans Canada highway is 7871 km. What is this distance, to the nearest tenth of a centimetre, on a map with scale 1 cm represents 60 km?

(b) The largest inland navigation system in North America is the St. Lawrence Seaway. On a map on the wall of the Seaway Headquarters, the St. Lawrence Seaway measures 13.46 m. If the scale of the map is 1 cm represents 0.28 km, find the actual length of the St. Lawrence Seaway.

6.8 (a) The height of Angel Falls in Venezuela is represented by the line segment below. How tall is Angel Falls?

Scale 1 cm represents 130 m

(b) If the height of Tugela Falls in South Africa is 948 m, which falls is higher, Angel or Tugela Falls? By how much?

Chapter Checkup: A Practice Test

6.1 (a) Write a ratio to compare

A 3 cm to 8 cm.   B 4 g to 9 g.

C 1 g to 1 kg.   D 1 cm to 1 m.

(b) Use the newspaper clipping. Write a ratio to compare the numbers of medals won by

A Britain and Bulgaria.

B Switzerland and Denmark.

C Greece and Canada.

Country	Number of Medals Won
Bulgaria	40
Canada	20
Britain	21
Yugoslavia	9
Denmark	5
Switzerland	2
Greece	3
Venezuela	1

6.2 (a) Write a ratio to compare

A ⬡ to △ .

B ⬜ to ◯ .

C △ to △

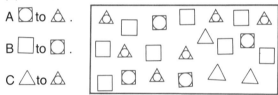

(b) After 3 rounds of golf the following scores are shown.

	Round 1	Round 2	Round 3
Tewell	67	73	64
Renner	65	68	71

Interpret each of the following ratios.

A 67 : 73   B 65 : 68   C 67 : 64 : 73

6.3 (a) Which ratios are equivalent to 4 : 5?

A 12 : 15   B 16 : 25   C 20 : 25

(b) Use the information in the chart. Write a ratio to show the value of

A corn to potatoes.

B nursery stock to fruit.

Value of Crops	
Corn	$ 3 million
Potatoes	21 million
Fruit	24 million
Nursery Stock	12 million

6.4 (a) Find the missing value in each proportion.

A $16 : 4 = m : 10$ B $4 : m : 1 = 24 : 12 : 6$

(b) The number of basketballs needed is given by the value of b in the equivalent ratios 6 : 12 : 24 and 2 : b : 8. What is the value of b?

6.5 (a) For each table, the ratios are equal. Find the missing value.

Shots on Goal

42	p
60	80

Floor Exercise

Games Played

384	412
s	515

Water Exercise

(b) At the Hamilton Airport out of every 8 planes that take off 3 are primarily cargo planes. How many planes landed in a week if 42 cargo planes landed in the week?

6.6 A Boeing 727 aircraft is drawn using the scale 1 cm represents 5.9 m.

(a) What is the length of the actual wing span if it measures 5.6 cm in the diagram?

(b) What is the length of the plane on the diagram if the actual length is 46.6 m?

6.7 (a) Find the missing data for each map.

Scale	Distance on map	Actual distance
A 1 cm represents 10 km	43 cm	?
B 1 : 1000	43.8 cm	?

(b) The scale on a map is 1 cm to 100 km. The actual distance from Golden, B.C. to Salmon Arm, B.C. is 225 km. What is the distance on the map between these two places?

6.8 (a) In 1973, Mayol recorded the deepest breath-held dive shown by the line segment A. How deep was Mayol's dive to the nearest metre?

(b) The record Scuba dive is shown by the segment B. How deep was the dive to the nearest metre?

SCUBA means *Self-Contained Underwater Breathing Apparatus*

(c) Which was deeper, A or B and by how many metres?

A — 1 cm represents 20 m

B — 1 cm represents 25 m

7 Applying Skills With Rate

development of skills with rate, consumer skills, unit cost, flow charts, applications and problem-solving

Introduction

Knowing about rates will be very helpful in understanding many items which you will meet when reading newspapers, magazines, etc.

The fastest speed on water reached is 556 km/h in May 1939.

MINI BIKE RENTAL
$5.00/h

Pizza Helper	$4.50/h
Car Washer	$3.75/h
Movie Usher	$4.25/h

7.1 Working With Rate

When learning about ratios you compared quantities expressed in the *same* units, such as

Ratio
4 m to 12 m

same unit

Ratio
33 cases to 28 cases

same unit

A **rate** is a special type of ratio which compares quantities expressed in *different* units.

Rate
$5.90 paid for each hour worked.

dollar   time

└── different units ──┘

You write this rate as $5.90/h.

You may write rates in simplest terms. For example, flower seeds are spread at a nursery at the following rate.

    400 g of seed for 100 m² of soil
or   4 g of seed for 1 m² of soil

Thus the rate is 4 g/m².

The G.C.F. of 400 and 100 is 100.
Thus $\frac{400}{100} = \frac{4}{1}$

Example 1

Write a ratio for each of the following rates. What does each rate mean in simplest terms?

(a) scoring points
    24 points scored in 30 games

(b) typing words
    500 words typed in 10 min

(c) buying things
    12 items for 98¢

Solution

(a) $\frac{24}{30} = \frac{24 \div 6}{30 \div 6} = \frac{4}{5}$

Thus 24 points scored in 30 games is equivalent to 4 points scored in 5 games.

(b) $\frac{500}{10} = \frac{500 \div 10}{10 \div 10} = \frac{50}{1}$

Thus, 500 words typed in 10 min is equivalent to 50 words typed in 1 min.

(c) $\frac{12}{98} = \frac{12 \div 2}{98 \div 2} = \frac{6}{49}$

Thus, 12 items for 98¢ is equivalent to 6 items for 49¢.

Example 2

A 747-jet can travel a distance of 1395 km in 3 h. What distance would the jet travel in 7 h (flying at the same rate)?

Solution

Let the distance covered be x km.

Write the proportion.

$$\frac{x}{7} = \frac{1395}{3}$$

Distance travelled in kilometres.

Time taken in hours.

Solve the proportion.

$$\frac{3x}{7} = 1395$$

$$3x = 1395 \times 7$$

$$\frac{3x}{3} = \frac{1395 \times 7}{3}$$

$$x = 3255$$

Make a final statement.

The distance covered is 3255 km.

Try These

1 What is the rate in simplest terms for each of the following?
   (a) 8 pictures for 4 people
   (b) 12 tickets for 12 people
   (c) 10 goals in 5 games
   (d) $36 for 6 h work
   (e) 10 seats empty for every 5 people
   (f)   12 penalty minutes for 2 games
   (g) 12 hot dogs for 4 people
   (h) 6 points in 3 games

2 What is a ratio in simplest terms for each of the following rates?
   (a) Penny scored 8 points in 2 games.
   (b) Barry jogs at a rate of 9 m in 3 s.
   (c) Gasoline flows at the rate of 10 L in 10 min.
   (d) $6.80 was paid for 2 h work.
   (e) The candle burns 2 cm in 2 h.
   (f)   10 words were typed in 4 s.
   (g) 30 pizzas are eaten in 10 min.

3 Find the missing value in each chart.

   (a) Jogging Speed

Time	1 s	2 s	3 s	4 s
Distance	2 m	?	?	?

   (b) Submarine Sandwiches

Number of subs	1	2	3	4
Cost	$2	?	?	?

Written Exercises

Express each of the following rates in simplest terms.

A 1 Write each rate.
   (a) Margaret walks 20 m in 10 s.
   (b) The water tower empties at the rate of 100 L in 2 s.
   (c) The printer produces 1200 sheets in 30 s.
   (d) Mike picked 5 baskets of cherries in 45 min.
   (e) Sam typed a 2000-word story in 50 min.
   (f) On 100 m² of lawn, 5 kg of Kentucky grass seed are used.
   (g) The cost of the tree is $1.00 for 20 cm.

2 At the annual Fun Run at Brandon, the following tallies were kept of the participants. Write each rate in laps per minute.

	Runner	Number of laps around the track	Time taken in minutes
(a)	Brenda	28	28
(b)	Nancy	30	25
(c)	Bernice	20	16
(d)	Triada	24	20
(e)	Juinita	27	21
(f)	Ashley	30	26
(g)	Melanie	29	24

3 A minibike travelled at 40 km/h.
   (a) How far will it travel in 1 h?
   (b) How far will it travel in 2 h 15 min?
   (c) How long will it take to go 800 km?

4 The water fountain uses water at the rate of 20 L/min.
   (a) How many litres are used in 1 min?
   (b) How many litres are used in 1 h?
   (c) How many litres are used in 1 h 30 min?
   (d) The bathtub holds 180 L. How long will it take to fill it?

5 Use the ad. How much will you be paid to work
   (a) for 1 h?
   (b) an 8-h day?
   How long will it take you to earn
   (c) $42.75?   (d) $21.38?

WANTED
Gardener's Helper
$4.75/h

6 The jet climbed 12 m/s. How far will it climb in 1 min?

7 The cost of constructing the tower was $45/m. Calculate the total cost if the tower is 10 m high.

8 Larry earns $5.25/h washing cars. How much will he make in an 8-h day?

9 A skydiver falls at the rate of 50 m/s.

How long will it take to fall
   (a) 500 m?   (b) 1 km?

B 10 Maureen scored 34 points in 2 basketball games.
   (a) How many points did she score per game?
   (b) How many points would you expect her to score in 10 games?

11 Jose jogged around 60 fence posts in 10 min.
   (a) How many fence posts did Jose jog around per minute?
   (b) At this rate, how many fence posts could Jose jog around in 2 h?

12 Your heart beats 75 times in a minute. How many beats does your heart beat in a day?

13 At the post-office 480 letters are sorted each minute. How many letters per second are sorted?

14 A short story of 15 000 words was typed in 10 h. What was the rate of typing?

15 A section of land, 400 m² in area, is used for trees and costs $20 000. Calculate the cost per square metre.

16 At the range, 20 golf balls are hit every 10 s. If the golf range is open 9 h on Saturday, how many balls are hit?

17 Jerome's compact car consumed 200 L to travel 2500 km. Calculate the rate of fuel consumption in
   (a) kilometres per litre. (b) litres per kilometre.

18 Use the ads. Will you make more for working 10 h at the bowling alley or 12 h at the pizza hut?

ACE BOWLING ALLEY
General help required in central area. $4.75/h.
No experience needed.
Phone 827-4859.

DRIVERS
2 people required for pizza deliveries. Car supplied.
$4.25/h.
EL GRECO PIZZA
241-9319

19 Jason types 234 words in 6 min.
   (a) How long would it take him to type 3145 words?
   (b) About how long will it take him to type the words in the article shown below?

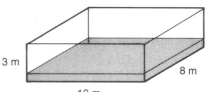

Device Uses Tiny TV Cameras to Help The Blind "See" Pictures on Their Skin

San Francisco (AP)—Two researchers have developed an electronic system which projects television images into the skin of blind persons to help them discern objects, measure distances and even detect normal print.

A person using the portable system wears a pair of eyeglass frames on which is mounted a tiny television camera made up of hundreds of transistors.

The camera is connected through a vest-worn battery network to a shield of electrodes taped to the subject's stomach. The entire unit has a mass of about 2 kg.

When the transistors scan objects in front of them, they send the exact pattern to the corresponding electrodes, which then trace the image on the stomach in a series of electrical impulses.

"Thus if we held up the shape of a square in front of a person wearing the camera, he would feel the electrodes literally drawing a square on his stomach," explained Dr. Collins.

The electrical stimulation is safe and painless, Dr. Collins said. He described it as feeling "like a light vibration, or a fly crawling across the skin."

He said the stomach was chosen because "it offers a large area of sensitive skin".

A blind person using the system can learn to "read" the alphabet in a few dozen hours, Dr. Collins said.

"At first a person is conscious that the image is projected on his stomach, but after a while he begins to get the physical impression of a 3-dimensional object located in front of him in space," Dr. Collins said.

At its present level, the 3-mm square television camera uses only 1024 transistors attached to the same number of electrodes and renders fairly crude images. As the number of transistors increase, the resolution of the picture improves and it becomes clearer.

C 20 Water flows from a garden hose at the rate of 20 L/min. How long would it take to fill the following tank?

3 m

8 m

10 m

7.2 Applications of Rate: Unit Cost

You often see two different advertisements for the same product. In order to determine which is the better buy you calculate the **unit cost**.

2 kg cost $4.30

1 kg costs $\dfrac{\$4.30}{2}$ or $2.15

The unit cost is $2.15/kg.

Example 1

Which is the better buy?

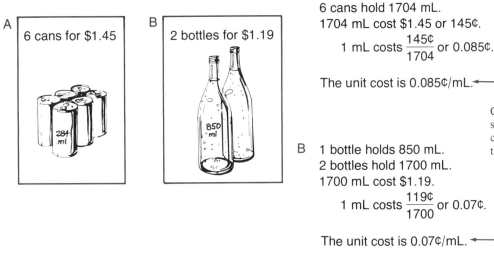

A — 6 cans for $1.45

B — 2 bottles for $1.19

284 ml

850 ml

Solution

A 1 can holds 284 mL.
6 cans hold 1704 mL.
1704 mL cost $1.45 or 145¢.

    1 mL costs $\dfrac{145¢}{1704}$ or 0.085¢.

The unit cost is 0.085¢/mL.

> Calculate the answer so that you may compare the unit costs.

B 1 bottle holds 850 mL.
2 bottles hold 1700 mL.
1700 mL cost $1.19.

    1 mL costs $\dfrac{119¢}{1700}$ or 0.07¢.

The unit cost is 0.07¢/mL.

Thus, the better buy is the 2 bottles for $1.19.

Example 2

If 5 kg of rhubarb cost $2.35, how much would you pay for 12 kg?

Solution

Calculate the unit cost.

    5 kg cost $2.35

    1 kg costs $\dfrac{\$2.35}{5}$ or 47¢

Calculate the cost of 12 kg.
    1 kg costs $0.47
    12 kg cost 12 × $0.47 or $5.64.

The unit cost is 47¢/kg.

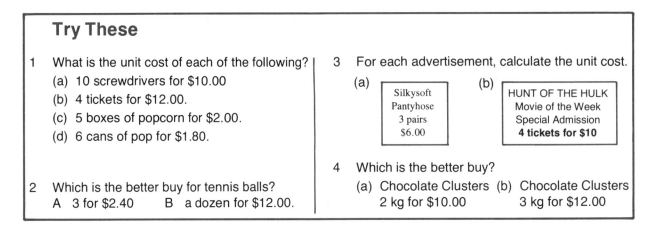

Try These

1 What is the unit cost of each of the following?
   (a) 10 screwdrivers for $10.00
   (b) 4 tickets for $12.00.
   (c) 5 boxes of popcorn for $2.00.
   (d) 6 cans of pop for $1.80.

2 Which is the better buy for tennis balls?
   A 3 for $2.40   B a dozen for $12.00.

3 For each advertisement, calculate the unit cost.
   (a)
   | Silkysoft |
   | Pantyhose |
   | 3 pairs |
   | $6.00 |

   (b)
   | HUNT OF THE HULK |
   | Movie of the Week |
   | Special Admission |
   | **4 tickets for $10** |

4 Which is the better buy?
   (a) Chocolate Clusters   (b) Chocolate Clusters
       2 kg for $10.00   3 kg for $12.00

Written Exercises

Throughout the exercise, express your answers to the nearest cent.

A 1 For each of the following, calculate the cost of one item (the unit cost).
   (a) 4 tins of chocolate pudding for $2.38.
   (b) 5 packages of pre-mixed pizzas for $3.69.
   (c) A case of 8 1-L cans of oil for $9.95.
   (d) 4-roll package of toilet paper for $1.69.
   (e) A 24-can case of soft drinks for $5.95.

2 For each advertisement find the unit cost.

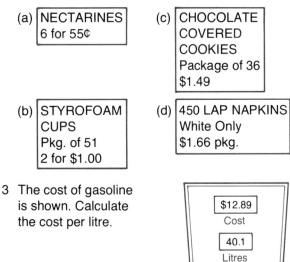

(a) | NECTARINES |
    | 6 for 55¢ |

(b) | STYROFOAM |
    | CUPS |
    | Pkg. of 51 |
    | 2 for $1.00 |

(c) | CHOCOLATE |
    | COVERED |
    | COOKIES |
    | Package of 36 |
    | $1.49 |

(d) | 450 LAP NAPKINS |
    | White Only |
    | $1.66 pkg. |

3 The cost of gasoline is shown. Calculate the cost per litre.

| $12.89 |
| Cost |

| 40.1 |
| Litres |

B 4 (a) The cost of 6 grapefruit is 89¢. Find the cost of 10 grapefruit.
   (b) How much would 12 glasses cost if 5 glasses cost $4.00?
   (c) How much would a 24-can case of pop cost if the cans sell at 5 for 95¢?

5 Marty can pick 4 baskets of delicious apples in 30 min. At this rate, how many baskets can Marty pick in 5 h?

6 The rock group travelled 1980 km in 4 d. At this rate, how far would they travel in 9 d?

7 If 48 L of gasoline cost $13.50, how many litres of gasoline could you buy for $9?

8 Gasoline sells for 28.9¢/L. What is
   (a) the cost of 10.5 L?   (b) the cost of 30.8 L?
   (c) Harriett paid $11.97 for gas. How many litres of gas were bought?

Applications: The Better Buy

Often, the unit price is the best aid when calculating the better buy. However, there are several things you must take into consideration before making a decision.

▶ One item might be less expensive than another. However, if you have to drive 15 km to buy the cheaper item and only travel 2 km to buy the other, then the money you save might be consumed by spending it on gas.

▶ Pop in a large bottle is often a better price than pop in a smaller can. However, if you were to go camping or on a canoe trip, a large bottle would be cumbersome.

Which is the better buy for a camping trip?

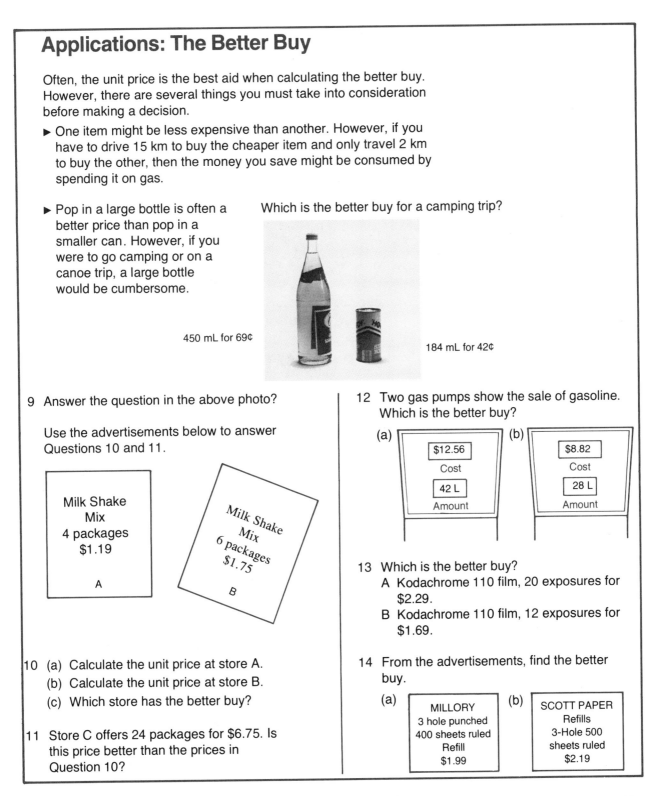

450 mL for 69¢

184 mL for 42¢

9 Answer the question in the above photo?

Use the advertisements below to answer Questions 10 and 11.

Milk Shake
Mix
4 packages
$1.19

A

Milk Shake
Mix
6 packages
$1.75

B

10 (a) Calculate the unit price at store A.
(b) Calculate the unit price at store B.
(c) Which store has the better buy?

11 Store C offers 24 packages for $6.75. Is this price better than the prices in Question 10?

12 Two gas pumps show the sale of gasoline. Which is the better buy?

(a)

| $12.56 |
| Cost |
| 42 L |
| Amount |

(b)

| $8.82 |
| Cost |
| 28 L |
| Amount |

13 Which is the better buy?
A Kodachrome 110 film, 20 exposures for $2.29.
B Kodachrome 110 film, 12 exposures for $1.69.

14 From the advertisements, find the better buy.

(a)

MILLORY
3 hole punched
400 sheets ruled
Refill
$1.99

(b)

SCOTT PAPER
Refills
3-Hole 500
sheets ruled
$2.19

7.3 Comparing Rates of Speed

If you travel along the Trans Canada Highway at 60 km/h, this means that in 1 h you travel 60 km. If you walk along the highway at 7 km/h, then you travel 7 km in 1 h.

- To calculate the distance travelled, use

$$\text{distance travelled} = \text{speed} \times \text{time}$$

- To calculate the speed, use

$$\text{speed} = \frac{\text{distance travelled}}{\text{time taken}}$$

- To calculate the time taken, use

$$\text{time taken} = \frac{\text{distance travelled}}{\text{speed}}$$

Example 1

The distance from Mexico City to Paris is 9183 km. The time taken by jet is 16.5 h. Calculate the speed of the jet to 1 decimal place.

Solution

$$\begin{aligned}
\text{Speed} &= \frac{\text{distance travelled}}{\text{time taken}} \\
&= \frac{9183}{16.5} \text{ (km/h)} \\
&= 556.5 \text{ (km/h)}
\end{aligned}$$

Thus, the speed of the jet is 556.5 km/h.

If you wish to compare rates of speed, you must calculate both rates in the *same units*.

Example 2

The speed of an elephant is calculated to be 50 km/h. A rabbit can run a distance of 58 m in 4 s.

(a) Find the speed of each animal.
(b) Which animal can travel faster?

Solution

Express both speeds in metres per second (m/s).

Elephant
In 1 h, the elephant can travel 50 km.
In 3600 s, the elephant can travel 50 000 m.
In 1 s, the elephant can travel $\frac{50\ 000}{3600}$ or 13.9 m/s.

Rabbit
In 4 s, the rabbit can travel 58 m.
In 1 s, the rabbit can travel $\frac{58}{4}$ or 14.5 m/s.

Thus, the rabbit can travel faster than the elephant,

Try These

1 Fill in the missing part.

  (a) speed = $\dfrac{\text{distance}}{?}$ (b) distance = ? × time

  (c) time = $\dfrac{?}{\text{speed}}$ (d) ? = speed × time

2 Complete the chart if the rate of speed is 10 km/h.

	(a)	(b)	(c)	(d)
distance travelled (km)	20	?	40	?
time taken (h)	?	3	?	6

3 Peter jogs at the rate of 8 km/h. How far will he travel in

  (a) 1 h?   (b) 2 h?   (c) 10 h?

4 Suzanne walks at the rate of 5 km/h. How long will it take her to travel

  (a) 5 km?   (b) 10 km? (c) 50 km?

Written Exercises

A 1 Jason travelled 400 m in 20 s on the minibike. Find the speed in metres per second (m/s).

2 A jet travelled 1600 km in 4 h. Calculate its speed in kilometres per hour (km/h).

3 Michael took 20 min to walk 800 m uphill. Find his speed in metres per minute (m/min).

4 A car is travelling at 90 km/h. How long will it take it to travel 540 km?

5 An airplane can fly at 800 km/h. How far will it travel in 3 h?

6 A train is travelling at 120 km/h. How many hours does the train take in order to travel

  (a) 360 km?   (b) 920 km?

7 Jeanne drove her car at a speed of 80 km/h.

  (a) How far would she drive in 1 h? 4 h?

  (b) How long would it take her to drive 400 km?

B 8 Lydia cycled at a speed of 12 km/h. If she went riding for 3 h, how far did she travel?

9 Mme. Paris jogs at a speed of 3 m/s.

  (a) How far will she jog in 1 min?

  (b) How long will it take her to jog 99 m?

10 Calculate the speed for the following cases. Round off your answer to 1 decimal place.

	Distance Travelled	Time Taken	Average Speed
(a)	240 km	6 h	?
(b)	115 m	65 s	?
(c)	69.8 km	1.4 h	?

11 Find your average speed in metres per second if you ran 1200 m in 60 s.

12 Carlo ran a distance of 5.5 km in 90 min. Calculate his speed in kilometres per minute.

13 Joanne ran 400 m in 90 s. Calculate her speed to 1 decimal place.

14 Joanne walked 6.8 km in 2 h. Find her speed

  (a) in kilometres per hour.

  (b) in metres per minute.

C 15 During his NHL career, Bobby Hull's slapshot was timed at 170 km/h. In a play-off game he shot at the net from a distance of 10 m. How much time did the goalie have in order to stop the shot?

Applications: Maps and Rates of Speed

You may use a map to calculate the time taken to travel on a highway. The sketch shows the distances between cities.

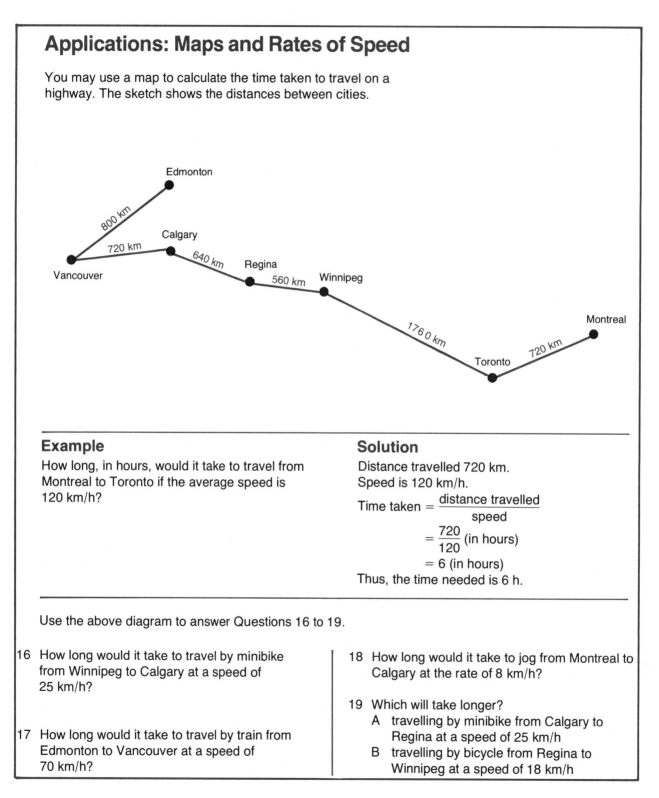

Example

How long, in hours, would it take to travel from Montreal to Toronto if the average speed is 120 km/h?

Solution

Distance travelled 720 km.
Speed is 120 km/h.

$$\text{Time taken} = \frac{\text{distance travelled}}{\text{speed}}$$

$$= \frac{720}{120} \text{ (in hours)}$$

$$= 6 \text{ (in hours)}$$

Thus, the time needed is 6 h.

Use the above diagram to answer Questions 16 to 19.

16 How long would it take to travel by minibike from Winnipeg to Calgary at a speed of 25 km/h?

17 How long would it take to travel by train from Edmonton to Vancouver at a speed of 70 km/h?

18 How long would it take to jog from Montreal to Calgary at the rate of 8 km/h?

19 Which will take longer?
   A travelling by minibike from Calgary to Regina at a speed of 25 km/h
   B travelling by bicycle from Regina to Winnipeg at a speed of 18 km/h

For Questions 20 to 23 use the scale map below of Halifax.

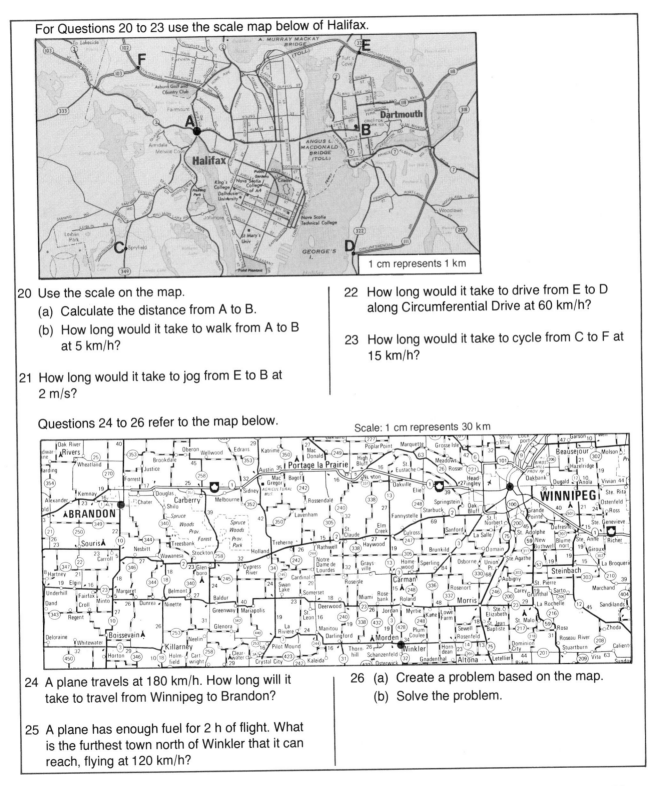

1 cm represents 1 km

20 Use the scale on the map.
   (a) Calculate the distance from A to B.
   (b) How long would it take to walk from A to B at 5 km/h?

21 How long would it take to jog from E to B at 2 m/s?

22 How long would it take to drive from E to D along Circumferential Drive at 60 km/h?

23 How long would it take to cycle from C to F at 15 km/h?

Questions 24 to 26 refer to the map below.

Scale: 1 cm represents 30 km

24 A plane travels at 180 km/h. How long will it take to travel from Winnipeg to Brandon?

25 A plane has enough fuel for 2 h of flight. What is the furthest town north of Winkler that it can reach, flying at 120 km/h?

26 (a) Create a problem based on the map.
   (b) Solve the problem.

7.4 Applications: Rates and Humans

As you work or exercise your heartbeat rate changes. Normally, your heart beats about 70 times per minute. When you play volleyball your heart beats 130 times per minute. Normally you breathe about 10 times per minute. If you play volleyball this rate will double to 20 times per minute.

Example

Shovelling heavy snow, or digging, causes the heart to beat about 150 times per minute. For 15 min of shovelling, how many more times will your heart beat than during a normal activity period.

Solution

Normal Activity
   Number of heartbeats in 1 min is 70.
   Number of heartbeats in 15 min is 1050.

Shovelling
   Number of heartbeats in 1 min is 150.
   Number of heartbeats in 15 min is 2250.

Difference 2250
$$\underline{1050}$$
       1200

Your heart beats 1200 times more during 15 min of shovelling snow.

The kilojoule (kJ) is the food unit of energy. The more kilojoules you take in when you eat, the more exercise you need. In the following problems you will see that some types of exercise consume more kilojoules than others.

Try These

1   Under normal conditions you breathe 10 times in a minute. How many times would you breathe in an hour?

2   When shovelling snow, you breathe 40 times per minute. How many more breaths would you take in 1 h than the breaths you would take in Question 1?

3   About 25 kJ (of energy) are used up during 1 min of walking. How long would you need to walk to use up 1000 kJ?

4   A hamburger is equivalent to 1500 kJ. How long would you need to walk to use up the energy in a hamburger?

Written Exercises

Throughout the exercises, round off your answers to 1 decimal place unless otherwise indicated.

A 1 In a year the average Canadian eats 36 kg of beef. How much is eaten in a week?

2 Each year the average Canadian eats 18 kg of poultry. How much is eaten in a week? Round off to 2 decimal places.

3 The average person at rest has a heartbeat rate of 70 times per minute and takes 10 breaths per minute. How many heartbeats would there be for each breath?

4 Playing tennis will cause your heart to beat about 140 times per minute. How many heartbeats during 6 games, each game lasting 45 min?

5 When you are shopping your heartbeat is about 100 beats in a minute and you take 14 breaths in a minute. For a shopping trip lasting 50 min, how many
   (a) heartbeats?   (b) breaths?

6 Bill Rodgers of the U.S. set the record for the 25 000-m run in 1 h 14 min.
   (a) How far did he run in 5 min?
   (b) How far did he run in 10 min?
   (c) How long would it take him to run 100 km?

7 If it takes 1 min of jogging to use up 84 kJ, how many minutes of jogging would it require to use up 1004 kJ?

B 8 It takes 1 min of walking to use up 25 kJ.
   (a) How many minutes of walking would you require to use up the 1130 kJ in a candy bar?
   (b) How many minutes of walking would you require to use up the 1732 kJ in a piece of fruit pie?

9 Swimming uses up 50 kJ for every minute. How many minutes of swimming would it require to use up the 1500 kJ of a hamburger?

In competitive swimming, you use up about 80 kJ/min.

10 After 1 min of bicycling you have used up 34 kJ.
   (a) How many minutes of bicycling would you require to use up 665 kJ?
   (b) How many minutes of bicycling would you require to use up the 1740 kJ of a helping of spareribs?

11 While playing volleyball your heart beats 130 times per minute. Which of the activities below will produce the greater number of heartbeats?
   A 3 games of volleyball, 12 min each game?
   B a 45-min volleyball game?

12 When you carry your clubs in golf you breathe 18 times per minute. How many breaths would you take while carrying your clubs in a golf game that lasted 6 h, if you carried your clubs two-thirds of the time?

C
13 A person is clocked at a speed of 32.2 km/h. A cheetah is clocked at a speed of 104.7 km/h. How much longer would it take the person to run 1000 km than a cheetah?

7.5 Applications: Rates and Nature

Did you know that certain types of birds have been clocked at speeds in excess of 250 km/h?

There are many more amazing facts from the world of nature which involve the study of rate. The exercise that follows introduces you to a few of them.

Written Exercises

1 The greatest amount of rainfall that fell in 1 min occurred in Maryland on July 4, 1955, at which time 31 mm fell. If the rain had continued to fall at this rate how much would have fallen in
   (a) 5 min?   (b) 1 h?

2 Panama recorded the greatest amount of rainfall that fell in 5 min (in 1911). During that time 63 mm fell. How much would the water level have risen in a pool if it rained at this rate for 1 h? Express your answer to the nearest tenth of a metre.

3 The greatest rainfall ever recorded in one year was 22 990 mm in India in 1861.
   (a) How many metres is this?
   (b) What was the average monthly rainfall in 1861?

4 Diamonds and pearls are measured in carats. The carat is a unit of mass equal to 0.2 g.
   (a) What is the mass of a 3-carat diamond?
   (b) Find the mass of a 5.5-carat diamond.

5 A cat's heartbeat was recorded as 35 beats in 15 s.
   (a) How many heartbeats per minute?
   (b) A dog has a heartbeat rate of 70 beats in 40 s. Which has the faster heartbeat, a dog or a cat?

Animals can run at varying speeds. In Questions 6 to 8 you will explore the various speeds.

Animal	Approximate speed (km/h)
Cat	50
Cheetah	110
Elk	70
Elephant	40
Lion	50
Pig	15
Rabbit	55
Squirrel	20

6 Calculate the speeds of the animals in metres per second.

7 In 4 h, how much further will a lion run than an elephant?

8 In 5 h, how much farther will a squirrel run than a pig?

9 A cheetah is known to be one of the fastest animals, with a speed of 110 km/h.
   (a) How long does the cheetah take to go 100 m?
   (b) How far can it go in 10 s?

10 A bat has been recorded flying at a speed of 29 km/h. A humming bird has been clocked at 97 km/h. How much longer will it take a bat to fly 10 km than a humming bird?

7.6 Working With Flow Charts

You have probably learned different ways of arranging
▶ steps for organizing your work.
▶ steps for solving a problem.

A flow chart can also be used to help you organize your work.
Certain shapes are used as visual aids to organize instructions.

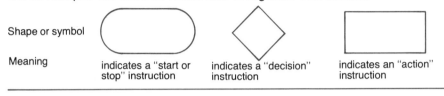

Shape or symbol

Meaning | indicates a "start or stop" instruction | indicates a "decision" instruction | indicates an "action" instruction

Example 1

Write in a flow chart the instructions you would give to a person to change the flat on a car.

Solution

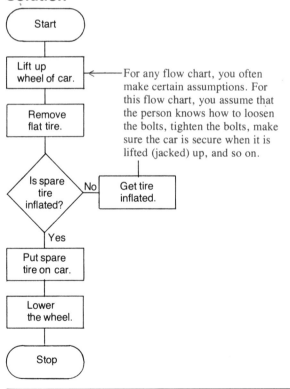

For any flow chart, you often make certain assumptions. For this flow chart, you assume that the person knows how to loosen the bolts, tighten the bolts, make sure the car is secure when it is lifted (jacked) up, and so on.

Example 2

Write in a flow chart the instructions to obtain the value of the expression

$$\frac{x^2 + 1}{2} + 5, \text{ for values of } x.$$

Solution

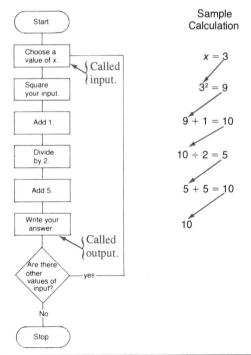

Flow charts can also be used to organize instructions for doing calculations, such as in the following example.

Written Exercises

A 1 The input is 5. What is the output for each of the following instructions?

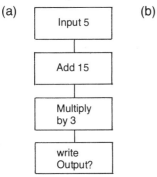

(a)
| Input 5 |

| Add 15 |

| Multiply by 3 |

| write Output? |

(b)
| Input 5 |

| Divide by 3 |

| Multiply by 9 |

| write Output? |

2 Use each of the following numbers as input values in the flow chart at right.

(a) 4   (b) 6

(c) 123   (d) −5

(e) −3   (f) 0

(g) $\dfrac{1}{2}$ (h) $\dfrac{3}{4}$

(i) 0.5   (j) 1.75

(What do you notice about your answers each time?)

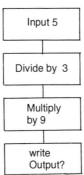

Start

Write a number (input).

Add the number to itself.

Add 8.

Divide by 2.

Subtract your input number.

Write the final answer (output).

Stop

B 3 (a) Follow these instructions.

Step 1   Start
Step 2   Write the number 2.
Step 3   Multiply this number by 5.
Step 4   Subtract 4 from your result.
Step 5   Divide your answer by 3.
Step 6   Add 10.
Step 7   Write your answer.
Step 8   Stop

(b) Write the above instructions as a flow chart.

4 Construct flow charts to find the output for each of the following then use the given input to check whether the instructions are correct.

(a) $6n - 4$; 2   (b) $3(n - 1)$; 5

(c) $2n^2 + 2$; 3   (d) $\dfrac{3n - 4}{2}$; 4

(e) $(n + 1)^2$; −2   (f) $\dfrac{2(n - 5)^2}{3}$; 11

Investigating Flow Charts

For each of the following, use a flow chart to organize the steps or instructions.

5 A flow chart is shown for making a telephone call.
  ▶ Choose a telephone number. Follow the instructions to make the call.
  ▶ Are there any other instructions you would include in this list of instructions?

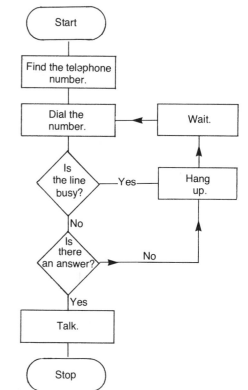

6 Write a list of instructions to open a door that is locked. Use a flow chart.

7 Construct a flow chart to describe the route you take to get to school each morning.

8 Construct a flow chart for taking a bus to a football game after school.

9 You are in the lunchroom. Write the instructions needed to leave your place and get more food.

7.7 Problem Solving: Assumptions

When you solve problems, you often make assumptions.

Example 1

When playing basketball, David scores at least every 5 min. How many points would you expect David to score in a game lasting 1.5 h?

Solution

To solve the problem you assume that indeed a point will be scored every 5 min by David.

1.5 h = 90 min

In 5 min David scores 1 point.

In 90 min David scores $\frac{90}{5}$ points or 18 points.

Written Exercises

A For Questions 1 to 5
- ▶ solve the problem.
- ▶ list any assumptions that you make to find your answer.

1 An 18-story apartment building requires 42 doors for all of its rooms on each floor. How many doors are required for the whole building?

2 In a survey, 24 out of 32 students had cavities. Out of 160 students, how many would have cavities?

3 Six football teams each consist of 30 players. During a game, each player needs about 1.5 m of tape. How much tape is needed in all for 3 games?

4 A builder must supply 16 concrete slabs for the sidewalk in front of a house. How many slabs need to be ordered for a street with 28 houses?

5 On the average, 6 letters are placed on the conveyor belt every second. How many letters does the conveyor belt carry in 8 h?

B 6 At a temperature of 28°C a cricket chirps about 44 times per minute.
- (a) Calculate the number of chirps in 1 h.
- (b) Calculate the number of chirps in 1 week.
- (c) What assumptions do you make in finding your answers in (a) and (b)?

7 A lighthouse operator can see about 24 km from the lighthouse.
- (a) Calculate the area that can be observed by the lighthouse operator.
- (b) What assumption do you make in finding your answer in (a)?

8 On the average, 4 chocolate bars are wrapped by a machine every second.
- (a) How many chocolate bars can be wrapped in 8 h?
- (b) How many chocolate bars can be wrapped in 1 a?

9 A helicopter can have a cruising speed of about 195 km/h.
- (a) How far would you expect the helicopter to fly in 5.2 h?
- (b) How long would it take to fly 850 km?

Skills to Practise: A Chapter Review

Express your answers to 1 decimal place.

7.1 Write the ratio for each rate in simplest terms.
   (a) Crude oil flows at the rate of 20 L in 15 min.
   (b) 45 hot dogs are eaten in 25 min.

7.2 What is the unit cost for each of the following?
   (a) 8 tickets for $24.00.
   (b) 24 soft drinks for $6.99.

7.3 Use the following information to find the speed .

distance covered	150 km	48 km
time taken	3 h	3.5 h
speed	?	?

What are the units?

7.4 Running causes the heart to beat 110 times per minute. Calculate the number of beats for each amount of time.
   (a) 3.5 min
   (b) half an hour

7.5 Calculate the distance each animal travelled in 1.5 h.
   (a) elephant at 42 km/h
   (b) lion at 56 km/h

7.6 Copy the following flow chart symbols and insert words to illustrate what each symbol means.

7.7 Each statement occurs on a package of consumable goods. List any assumptions you can for each statement.
   (a) contents 150 nails
   (b) mass 2.5 kg
   (c) contents 1.5 L
   (d) makes 4 servings
   (e) mix 1 can of water with contents

Problems to Practise: A Chapter Review

Express your answers to 1 decimal place.

7.1 Denise earned $3.75/h working at the Hamburger Deluxe.
   (a) How much can Denise earn if she works an 8 h shift on a Saturday?
   (b) If Denise worked every Saturday last year, how much money did she make?

7.2 During the trip Herb's group travelled 350 km in 8 h. How far did they go in 6.5 h?

7.3 At the track meet, the average speed for 1 lap of the track was 10.5 km/h. Calculate the time for 1 lap if the length of the lap is 400 m.

7.4 The average Canadian watches 1200 h of television in a year. How many hours would the average Canadian watch
   (a) in a week?   (b) in a day?

7.5 The largest pearl discovered has a mass of 6.37 kg.
   (a) How many carats is this?
   (b) If it is presently valued at $6 000 000, what is its value per carat?

7.6 Construct a flow chart to show the steps in preparing a bowl of soup for lunch. List any assumptions you make in constructing your flow chart.

7.7 The canine "high jump" record is held by an Alsatian named "Crumstone Danko", owned by the DeBeers Mining Co., who scaled a 3.43 m high wall, without a springboard, in Pretoria, South Africa, in May, 1942.
   (a) How many jumps would this canine have to make in order to reach a total of 1 km?
   (b) What assumptions do you make in obtaining your answer in (a)?

240

Chapter Checkup: A Practice Test

Express your answers as needed to 1 decimal place.

7.1 (a) Express each rate in simplest terms.
- Jennifer jogs 15 m in 16 s.
- 36 pizzas were ordered in 8 h.

(b) The heart beats about 90 times in a minute for fast walking. How many times would your heart beat during 1 h of walking? during a day of walking?

7.2 (a) For each advertisement, calculate the unit cost.

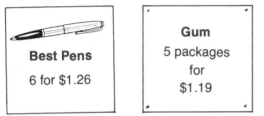

Best Pens

6 for $1.26

Gum

5 packages
for
$1.19

(b) Mark paid 38.9¢/L for gasoline during a trip. If he paid $18.25 how many litres of gasoline did he buy?

7.3 (a) Complete the chart. Michael jogs at the rate of 12 km/h.

distance travelled	36	?	?	42
time taken	?	3	4.5	?

(b) An elephant ran 145 km in 14 h. Calculate its speed in kilometres per hour; metres per minute.

7.4 The farthest distance walked in exactly 2 h was 28 165 m, done by Jose Marin of Spain.
(a) What was his rate of speed?
(b) How far would he walk in 10 min at this speed?
(c) How long would it take him to walk 150 km at this speed?

7.5 (a) Calculate each speed in metres per minute.
▶ squirrel 18 km/h ▶ cougar 39 km/h

(b) The world's strongest currents are the Nakwakto Rapids, Slingsky Channel, British Columbia, where the flow rate can reach 29.6 km/h. At this rate, how long would it take you to the nearest second to travel 1 km.

7.6 (a) For a flow chart, what do these mean?

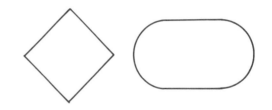

(b) Use a flow chart to list the instructions in order for filling the gas tank of a car.

7.7 (a) What assumption is made for each statement?
A The machine produces 128 packages gum each minute.
B Julie rode her mini bike at a speed of 28.5 km/h (her top speed).

(b) The Lawson family skied a distance of 130 m/min. They started their trip at noon and finished at 18:00.
A Calculate how many metres they skied.
B What assumption do you make in finding your answer?

A Cumulative Review: Problems (Chapters 1-7)

An important skill in problem solving is being able to decide which skill you need to use to solve a problem. For this reason, these problems are not given in any special order. Look for the clues in each problem to help you decide which skill you need.

1 Morris bought a case containing 144 cans of dog food for his golden retriever. If 60 cans have been eaten, what fraction is left?

2 Raoul Gonzales set the record for the 50 000 m walk. His time was 3 h 42 min.
   (a) What was his rate of speed in kilometres per hour, to 1 decimal place?
   (b) How far would he go in 15 min at this rate?

3 A pizza costs $13.25 and has a diameter of 50 cm.
   (a) Calculate the cost of the pizza per square centimetre.
   (b) What is your share if you eat 2 pieces of an 8 piece pizza?

4 Brett breaks his hockey sticks and as a result had to buy 6 sticks in one season. The prices of the sticks were $8.97, $6.89, $9.99, $7.52, $8.49 and $8.42. If he had bought 6 sticks at the beginning of the season for $5.97 each, how much could he have saved?

5 Calculate the area of each stamp.
   (a)   (b)

6 The aquarium is 36.9 cm in length and 20.5 cm wide.
   (a) Calculate the amount of water the aquarium can hold if the sides are 26.8 cm high.

   (b) The water is lowered 4.5 cm. How much water is left?

7 The moon orbits the earth once every 29.5 d. This represents the time interval between one full moon and the next. How many full moons do we see in 1 a?

8 During the Fund Raising Drive the following amounts were raised.

George	$30	Barb	$35
Mary	$17	Cy	$34
Frank	$25	Elaine	$68

   Write a ratio to compare the amounts raised by
   (a) George and Barb.   (b) Cy and Elaine.
   (c) Mary and Frank.   (d) Frank and Barb.
   (e) Mary, Elaine, and Barb.
   (f) George, Cy, and Frank.

9 A farmer planted 160 rows of cabbages, each row containing 240 heads of cabbage.
   (a) If the farmer can pack 24 cabbages in one crate, how many crates are needed to ship all the heads of cabbages when harvested?
   (b) What assumptions do you make in finding your answer in (a)?

10 The dimensions of the playing fields for a variety of sports are given. Determine a suitable scale so that each playing field could be drawn on one page of this book.

(a)	Basketball	26 m	14 m
(b)	Soccer	100 m	73 m
(c)	Karate	8 m	8 m
(d)	Boxing	6.1 m	6.1 m
(e)	Table Tennis	2.7 m	1.5 m

8 Working With Per Cent

skills with per cent, the basic problems, consumer skills, per cent and business, applications and problem-solving

Introduction

It is difficult to read the newspaper, watch T.V., or browse through magazines, without being exposed to the concept of per cent.

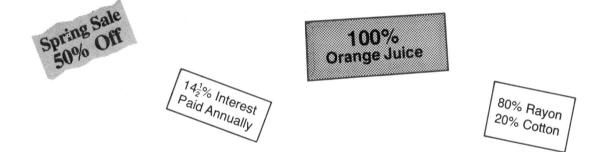

Spring Sale 50% Off

$14\frac{1}{2}\%$ Interest Paid Annually

100% Orange Juice

80% Rayon 20% Cotton

Per cent affects decisions in business, in health, in travel, in fact, in almost anything.

Only 6% of the small fish placed in a stream survive.

Despite an increase of 8% in the cost of air fares, there was an increase of 6% in the number of air passengers.

8.1 Working With Per Cent

Each day, you see ideas involving per cent.

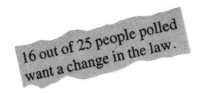

10% take their holidays in the Caribbean

Per cent means "per hundred" and the symbol % is used to show "parts of one hundred".

1 part out of 100 equal parts or 1%

10 equal parts out of 100 equal parts or 10%

25 equal parts out of 100 equal parts or 25%

You can show a ratio.

1 : 100   10 : 100   25 : 100

equal parts shaded ⟋   ⟍ total number of equal parts

For example, in the diagram 25 squares of equal area out of 100 squares of equal area are shaded. You can write this information in the following forms:

fraction form   decimal form   per cent form
$\frac{25}{100}$ 0.25   25%

Thus $\frac{25}{100}$ = 0.25 = 25%. ⟵ As a ratio you interpret this as 25 equal parts out of 100 equal parts or 25 : 100

The skills you learn in one topic of mathematics are used to develop skills in another topic of mathematics. To express a fraction as a per cent, you write an equivalent fraction with denominator 100.

244

Example 1

Write each as a per cent.

(a) 0.35   (b) $\frac{5}{8}$

Solution

(a) 0.35 means $\frac{35}{100}$.   Thus $\frac{35}{100} = 35\%$.

(b) To write a per cent, a decimal equivalent may be written first.

$$\frac{5}{8} = 0.625 \qquad 0.625 = \frac{62.5}{100}$$

Thus $\frac{62.5}{100} = 62.5\%$.

Example 2

Write a fraction for each of the following.

(a) 50%   (b) $37\frac{1}{2}\%$

Solution

(a) 50% means $\frac{50}{100}$. ← 50 equal parts in a 100 equal parts

But $\frac{50}{100} = \frac{1}{2}$. ← Express the fraction in lowest terms.

Thus $50\% = \frac{1}{2}$.

(b) $37\frac{1}{2}\%$ means $\dfrac{37\frac{1}{2}}{100}$ $37\frac{1}{2} = \frac{75}{2}$

Thus $37\frac{1}{2}\% = \dfrac{\frac{75}{2}}{100}$

$$= \frac{75}{2} \div 100 = \frac{75}{2} \times \frac{1}{100}$$

$$= \frac{\overset{3}{\cancel{75}}}{2} \times \frac{1}{\underset{4}{\cancel{100}}}$$

Thus $37\frac{1}{2}\% = \frac{3}{8}$. $= \frac{3}{8}$

Example 3

Out of every 75 cars sold, 32 are compact cars. What per cent is this? Express your answer to 1 decimal place.

Be sure to make a final statement to answer the problem.

Solution

$\dfrac{\text{number of compact cars}}{\text{total number of cars}} = \dfrac{32}{75}$ ← Find the decimal equivalent for $\frac{32}{75}$.

$$\frac{32}{75} = 0.42\overline{6}$$

$$= 0.427 \text{ (to 3 decimal places)}$$

Thus $\frac{32}{75} = 42.7\%$

The percentage of compact cars sold is 42.7%.

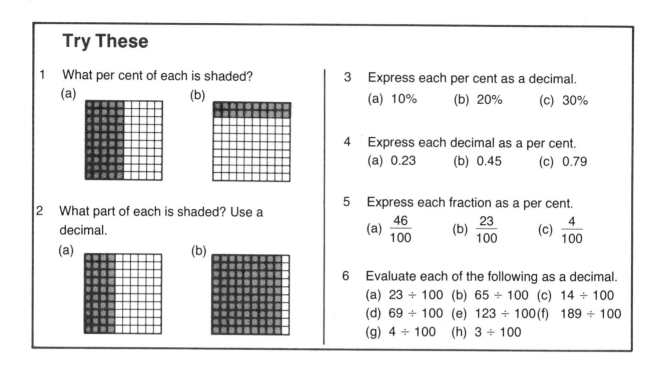

Try These

1 What per cent of each is shaded?
   (a)   (b)

2 What part of each is shaded? Use a
   decimal.
   (a)   (b)

3 Express each per cent as a decimal.
   (a) 10%   (b) 20%   (c) 30%

4 Express each decimal as a per cent.
   (a) 0.23   (b) 0.45   (c) 0.79

5 Express each fraction as a per cent.
   (a) $\frac{46}{100}$ (b) $\frac{23}{100}$ (c) $\frac{4}{100}$

6 Evaluate each of the following as a decimal.
   (a) 23 ÷ 100 (b) 65 ÷ 100 (c) 14 ÷ 100
   (d) 69 ÷ 100 (e) 123 ÷ 100 (f) 189 ÷ 100
   (g) 4 ÷ 100   (h) 3 ÷ 100

Written Exercises

In the following questions, round off your answers where
necessary to 1 decimal place.

A 1 Write a per cent to show how much of each
   (a) is shaded   (b) is not shaded.

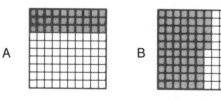

A   B

2 Write a per cent and a decimal to show how
   much of each of the following is shaded.
   (a)   (b)   (c)

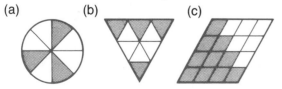

3 What do each of the following mean as a ratio?
   (a) 2%   (b) 12%   (c) 25%   (d) 75%
   (e) 2.5%   (f) 12.1%   (g) $13\frac{1}{2}$%   (h) $33\frac{1}{3}$%

4 Write each per cent as a decimal.
   (a) 25%   (b) 37%   (c) 8%   (d) 63.5%

5 Write each decimal as a per cent.
   (a) 0.39   (b) 0.75   (c) 0.47   (d) 0.8
   (e) 0.31   (f) 0.01   (g) 0.963 (h) 0.108

6 Write each of the following as a per cent.
   (a) $\frac{7}{10}$ (b) $\frac{29}{100}$ (c) $\frac{4}{5}$ (d) $\frac{6}{25}$
   (e) $\frac{24}{100}$ (f) $\frac{1}{5}$ (g) $\frac{2}{3}$ (h) $\frac{3}{4}$

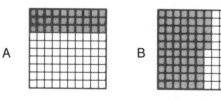

246

7 Express each of the following per cents as a fraction.

(a) 25%   (b) 50%   (c) 30%   (d) 60%

(e) 2%   (f) $37\frac{1}{2}$% (g) $12\frac{1}{2}$% (h) 87.5%

8 Write the per cent in each advertisement as a decimal.

(a)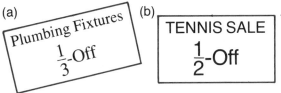

Plumbing Fixtures
$\frac{1}{3}$-Off

(b)
TENNIS SALE
$\frac{1}{2}$-Off

9 Find the missing values.

(a) $\frac{\square}{100} = 7\%$ (b) $\frac{2}{5} = \square\%$ (c) $\frac{3}{5} = \frac{\square}{100}$

(d) $48\% = \frac{\square}{100}$ (e) $\square\% = \frac{1}{5}$ (f) $\frac{\square}{100} = 0.52$

B 10 Write a per cent for each of the following.

(a) 4 out of 10 students take French

(b) 3 out of 5 T.V. sets are colour T.V.'s

(c) Out of every 50 schools, 40 offer an auto mechanics course

11 What per cent is each of the following?

(a) one centimetre of one metre

(b) one milligram of one gram

(c) one gram of one kilogram

(d) one centilitre of one litre

12 (a) Out of 139 ethnic publications there are 7 Portuguese publications. What percentage is this?

(b) Susan Nattross shot 190 out of 200 clay birds to win the fifth successive women's world trap shooting championship. What per cent did she shoot?

(c) Out of 49 runners that started the world's most northerly marathon 34 completed the run. What per cent is this?

13 For a trip, 36 km was by canoe and 2 km was by portage. What per cent was

(a) by canoe?   (b) by portage?

14 In the pulp and paper industry it has been determined that 100 L of water is used to produce 1 kg of paper. What percentage of 500 L of water is used to produce 1 kg of paper?

15 Nickel production is given as follows.

Country	Per cent
U.S.S.R.	21.9%
Cuba	7.3%
Canada	?
Other	30.8%
Total	100%

What per cent does Canada mine?

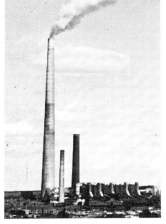

The tallest chimney in the world is the chimney of the International Nickel Company of Canada.

16 Out of every $25,

$6 is spent on entertainment.
$8 is spent on clothes.
$2 is spent on travel.
the remainder is spent on food.

What percentage of the money is spent on

(a) clothes?   (b) entertainment   (c) travel?

(d) What per cent is spent on food?

C 17 For a camping trip,

25 people arrived by train.
36 people arrived by bus.
6 people arrived by plane.
120 people arrived by car.

(a) What per cent came by train?

(b) What per cent came by car?

(c) What per cent did not come by bus?

(d) Use the information in (a), (b), and (c) to calculate what per cent came by plane.

247

8.2 Comparing Per Cents: Applications

The performance of players can be compared by using percentages. The chart below shows the records of three high school quarterbacks.

Quarterback	Passes Attempted	Passes Completed
Boudreau	42	27
Piggoso	39	24
Albertson	46	32

To compare the above records, the percentages of passes completed of passes attempted are calculated to 1 decimal place.

Boudreau $\quad \dfrac{27}{42} = 0.643$ or 64.3%

Piggoso $\quad \dfrac{24}{39} = 0.615$ or 61.5%

Albertson $\quad \dfrac{32}{46} = 0.696$ or 69.6%

From the above results, Albertson has the best record.

Example 1

Express your answer to 1 decimal place.
(a) What per cent is 23 out of 60?
(b) 9 out of 35 is what per cent?

Solution

(a) 23 out of 60 is given by $\dfrac{23}{60}$.

$\dfrac{23}{60} = 0.38\overline{3}$ 　　Think or calculate.
$\qquad\qquad\qquad\quad 0.383 \times 100\%$
$\qquad\qquad\qquad\quad = 38.3\%$ to 1 decimal place

$\dfrac{23}{60} = 38.3\%$ to 1 decimal place

(b) 9 out of 35 is given by $\dfrac{9}{35}$.

$\dfrac{9}{35} = 0.2571$ 　　Express your answer to a sufficient number of decimal places so that you may round off correctly.

$\dfrac{9}{35} = 25.7\%$ to 1 decimal place

Example 2

The fisheries collected samples of fish at the hatchery in order to check their growth.

	Number of fish over 5 cm	Number of fish obtained
Sample A	29	42
Sample B	42	66

Which sample had the greater percentage of fish over 5 cm? Calculate your answers to 1 decimal place.

Solution

Sample A

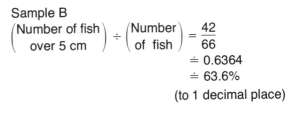

$$\left(\begin{array}{c} \text{Number of fish} \\ \text{over 5 cm} \end{array}\right) \div \left(\begin{array}{c} \text{Number} \\ \text{of fish} \end{array}\right) = \frac{29}{42}$$

$$\doteq 0.6905$$

$$\doteq 69.1\%$$

(to 1 decimal place)

Sample B

$$\left(\begin{array}{c} \text{Number of fish} \\ \text{over 5 cm} \end{array}\right) \div \left(\begin{array}{c} \text{Number} \\ \text{of fish} \end{array}\right) = \frac{42}{66}$$

$$\doteq 0.6364$$

$$\doteq 63.6\%$$

(to 1 decimal place)

Thus, Sample A had the greater percentage of fish over 5 cm.

Try These

1   What per cent does each fraction represent?

(a) $\dfrac{20}{100}$ (b) $\dfrac{50}{100}$ (c) $\dfrac{65}{100}$ (d) $\dfrac{39}{100}$

2   Express each of the following as a per cent?

(a) $\dfrac{7}{10}$ (b) $\dfrac{3}{10}$ (c) $\dfrac{1}{2}$ (d) $\dfrac{1}{4}$

3   Use per cents to show which fraction of each of the following pairs of fractions is greater.

(a) $\dfrac{65}{100}, \dfrac{7}{10}$ (b) $\dfrac{9}{10}, \dfrac{92}{100}$

(c) $\dfrac{52}{100}, \dfrac{1}{2}$ (d) $\dfrac{70}{100}, \dfrac{3}{4}$

4   Express each of the following as a per cent.

(a) 60 out of 100 people went to the beach on Saturday.

(b) 35 out of 100 people interviewed preferred Hawaii.

(c) 78 out of 100 people go for a regular check-up.

5   On the weekend the information was collected.

Saturday: 7 out of 10 people interviewed skied.

Sunday: 69 out of 100 people interviewed skied.

During which day did the greater percentage of people ski?

Written Exercises

In the following questions, round off your answer, where necessary, to 1 decimal place.

A 1 Write a per cent for each of the following.

(a) $\dfrac{70}{100}$ (b) $\dfrac{6}{10}$ (c) $\dfrac{3}{4}$ (d) $\dfrac{4}{5}$

2 Write a per cent for each of the following. Which per cent in each pair is greater?

(a) $\dfrac{4}{5}, \dfrac{3}{4}$ (b) $\dfrac{7}{10}, \dfrac{3}{4}$ (c) $\dfrac{4}{5}, \dfrac{79}{100}$ (d) $\dfrac{3}{10}, \dfrac{1}{4}$

3 Write a per cent for each of the following.

(a) $\dfrac{1}{3}$ (b) $\dfrac{1}{9}$ (c) $\dfrac{2}{3}$ (d) $\dfrac{2}{15}$ (e) $\dfrac{24}{49}$

4 Write a per cent for each of the following. Which per cent in each pair is greater?

(a) $\dfrac{4}{5}, \dfrac{5}{6}$ (b) $\dfrac{5}{6}, \dfrac{8}{12}$ (c) $\dfrac{17}{39}, \dfrac{18}{42}$ (d) $\dfrac{27}{52}, \dfrac{28}{53}$

5 What per cent is
(a) 35 of 70? (b) 6 of 30?
(c) 12 of 40? (d) 21 of 63?

6 Write a per cent for each of the following.
(a) 22 out of 30 people interviewed wash their cars on Saturday.
(b) 3 out of 80 bolts were defective.

B 7 Michelle earned $120 last year working part-time after school. During the year she spent $80. What percentage of her money did she spend?

8 Diane earned $16 last week but spent $9. Frances earned $27 and spent $18. Who spent the greater percentage of her salary?

9 Out of a total income of $24 000, a family saves $1500. What percentage of the total income is
(a) saved? (b) spent?

10 Which machine has the lowest percentage of worn parts?

Machine	Worn parts	Total number of parts
A	12	39
B	17	65
C	22	80
D	39	57
E	46	110

11 Melanie works in a self-serve gas station and submits a record of the day's receipts.

Type of Receipts	Amount of Sales
Regular Lead-free gas	$240
Super Lead-free gas	$190
Regular gas	$350
Super gas	$260
Oil and Transmission Fluid	$108
Maintenance Supplies, bolts, windshield fluid	$ 86
Miscellaneous (soda pop)	$ 52

(a) What are the total receipts of the day?
(b) What percentage of the total sales is
(i) regular lead-free gas (ii) regular gas
(c) What percentage of the total sales is oil and transmission fluid?

C 12 Refer to the chart in Question 11.
(a) The sales of regular gas doubled the next day. The other sales remained the same. What percentage of total sales the next day was regular gas?
(b) The sales of oil and transmission fluid decreased by $42 on Wednesday. The other sales remained the same. What percentage of the total sales on Wednesday was for oil and transmission fluid?

Applications: Sports and Standings

A team's standings in its league indicate whether or not that team will make the playoffs.

In the National Hockey League (NHL) the top 16 teams *only* are in the playoffs.

13 The Westown Wildcats have won 15 of their 22 games. Eastern Royals have won 17 of their 25 games.
   (a) Write each team's record as a per cent.
   (b) Which team has the better record?

14 The standings of the Vancouver League basketball teams are shown below.

Team	Games Won	Games Played
Rovers	46	65
Wildcats	37	64
Redmen	44	68
Bulldogs	41	66
Warriors	35	69

   (a) For each team, write the following record as a per cent.
   $$\left(\begin{array}{c}\text{Number of}\\\text{games won}\end{array}\right) \div \left(\begin{array}{c}\text{Number of}\\\text{games played}\end{array}\right)$$
   (b) Arrange the team standings from first place to last place.

15 For each pitcher, the records compiled over one year are shown.

Player	Innings Played	Innings Won
Rudolph May	175	143
James Clancy	251	103
Scott McGregor	252	196

   Who won the greatest percentage of innings?

16 The Central Conference passing records were printed in the newspaper.

Player	Number of completed passes	Number of passes thrown
Vase	16	40
Boddicher	10	24
Campbell	25	38
Ketchabau	9	22
Forster	6	15
DeCarlo	12	20
McWhirter	8	12

   (a) For each player, write the record
   $$\left(\begin{array}{c}\text{Number of passes}\\\text{completed}\end{array}\right) \div \left(\begin{array}{c}\text{Number of passes}\\\text{thrown}\end{array}\right)$$
   as a per cent to show each player's passing record.
   (b) Which player had the best record?
   (c) Which player had the worst record?

17 A hockey team has the following players on the ice for each period (with no penalties).
   2 forwards   1 centre
   2 defencemen 1 goalie
   What percentage of the team is made up of
   (a) defencemen?   (b) forwards?
   (c) centres?   (d) goalies?

8.3 Percentage of a Number and Its Applications

There are many times that you need to know about percentages.

What percentage of the tires are defective?

20% Off

How much will I save?

In the above photo, 1% of the tires are defective. If 1000 tires are made each day, how many are defective?

1% of 1000 means $\frac{1}{100}$ of 1000 $= \frac{1}{100} \times 1000$

$= 10$

Thus 10 tires are defective.

Thus, if you know what 1% of the tires are you can calculate *any* per cent.

12% of 1000 $= 12 \times 10$

$= 120$

1% of the tires is 10. If you know what 1% of the tires is, you can calculate 12% of the tires.

The above approach is often referred to as **the 1% method**.

However, to calculate with per cent, it is best to write the per cent as a decimal.

1% of 1000 $= 0.01 \times 1000$ 12% of 1000 $= 0.12 \times 1000$

$= 10$ $= 120$

Example 1

Find the percentage of each number.

(a) 3% of 160

(b) 50% of 173

(c) 15.2% of 37

(d) $9\frac{1}{2}$% of 236

Solution

(a) 3% of 160
$= 0.03 \times 160$
$= 4.8$

(b) 50% of 173
$= 0.50 \times 173$
$= 86.5$

(c) 15.2% of 37
$= 0.152 \times 37$
$= 5.624$

(d) $9\frac{1}{2}$% of 236
$= 9.5$% of 236
$= 0.095 \times 236$
$= 22.42$

Example 2

About 110 000 people arrived at Winnipeg Airport one year. Of these, 7.08% came from Chicago. How many people flew in from Chicago?

Solution

Total number of people is 110 000.
Number of people from Chicago
    7.08% of 110 000
  $= 0.0708 \times 110\ 000$
  $= 7788$
Thus 7788 people flew in from Chicago that year.

Example 3

In Canada, 45% of Canadian homes have colour televisions.
(a) At Muskoken High School, the students represent 475 homes. How many homes have colour television?
(b) How many homes do not have colour television?

Solution

(a) Total number of homes is 475.
    Number with colour T.V. is 45% of 475
                    $= 0.45 \times 475$
                    $= 213.75$
    About 214 homes
    have colour television.

(b) Total number of homes is   475.
    Number with colour T.V.   214
    Number without colour T.V. 261
    Thus, about 261 homes are without colour television.

> Check: 45% of homes have colour T.V.
>   Thus 55% of homes have no colour T.V.
>   55% of 475 $= 0.55 \times 475$
> $= 261.25$
> Thus 261 homes have no colour T.V.
>   Checks.

Try These

1 Calculate.
  (a) 10% of 100   (b) 20% of 200
  (c) 10% of 250   (d) 20% of 400

2 Calculate.
  (a) 1% of 40   (b) 1% of 400
  (c) 1% of 480   (d) 1% of 4800

3 (a) Estimate which you think is greater.
     A 10% of 100   B 1% of 2000
  (b) Which is greater, A or B?

4 (a) Estimate which you think is more money.
     A 10% of $200   B 50% of $100
  (b) Which is greater, A or B?

5 What is 10% less than each of the following?
  (a) $100   (b) $1000   (c) $10 000

6 What is 10% more than each of the following?
  (a) $100   (b) $1000   (c) $10 000

Written Exercises

In the following questions, round off your answers, when necessary to 1 decimal place unless otherwise indicated.

A 1 Find the percentage of each number. Round off your answer to the nearest whole number.
(a) 4% of 160   (b) 5% of 60   (c) 9% of 60

2 Find the percentage of each number.
(a) 69% of 1850 (b) 33% of 562 (c) 7% of 10

3 (a) Estimate which you think is more, A or B.
  A 15% of 465   B 23% of 296
(b) Calculate A and B above.

4 Find the percentage of each number. Round off your answers to the nearest whole number.
(a) 4.2% of 20   (b) 9.8% of 84
(c) 24.6% of 512   (d) 48.7% of 320

5 (a) Estimate which you think is more, A or B.
  A 29.2% of 125   B 43.5% of 62
(b) Calculate A and B above.

6 Find the percentage of each number.
(a) $3\frac{1}{2}$% of 400   (b) $15\frac{3}{4}$% of 17 500

7 (a) Estimate which you think is more, A or B.
  A $14\frac{3}{4}$% of 2000   B $28\frac{1}{2}$% of 2500
(b) Calculate A and B above.

8 Calculate. Express answers to the nearest cent.
(a) 8% of $486.00   (b) 12% of $396.50
(c) $10\frac{1}{2}$% of $950   (d) $13\frac{3}{4}$% of $12 500

9 Find each of the following. Round off your answer to the nearest whole number.
(a) 6% of $200   (b) 35% of 40 games
(c) 32% of 86 boys   (d) 12% of 340 cm

B 10 If 2% of milk is butterfat, how much butterfat is there in 60 L of milk?

11 Rhonda bought a bicycle for $119.50. She sold it after one year at a loss of 15%. By how much money did the bicycle depreciate?

12 One year Canadians spent $250 million going to the movies. If at least 80% of that was spent on U.S. feature movies, how much money was spent on seeing U.S. features?

13 One year 31.6 million U.S. visitors came to Canada. If 64.2% of those visitors stayed a day, how many visitors stayed a day?

14 A digital watch as shown costs $39.95. If 15% off is given, what is the sale price of the watch?

15 The total length of the Trans-Canada Highway is 7871 km.
(a) If 5.77% of the highway is in Alberta, how many kilometres are in Alberta?
(b) If 8.3% of the highway is in Saskatchewan, how many kilometres are in Saskatchewan?

C 16 Do you know why ice floats? When water freezes its volume increases by about 12%. Find the volume of ice when these amounts of water freeze.
(a) 100 mL   (b) 150 mL   (c) 600 mL
(d) 10.2 L   (e) 49.2 L   (f) 5.8 L

254

Applications: The Average Canadian

How does it feel to be average? Did you know that in Canada an average of 57% of the total population has telephones. But comparing these results to other countries, are we really average?

Soviet Union: 7% of its population have telephones.
England: 38% of its population have telephones.
Cuba: 3% of its population have telephones.
Pakistan: 0.3% of its population have telephones.

17 In Canada 57% of the total population have telephones. If Canada's population is 23.5 million, how many people have telephones?

18 7% of the people of the Soviet Union possess a telephone. The population of the Soviet Union is 261.5 million. How many of this population have telephones?

19 In England 38% of the people own telephones, but in Cuba only 3% of the people have telephones. If Cuba's population is 10 million and there are a total of 55.8 million people in the United Kingdom, how many more telephones are there in the United Kingdom than in Cuba?

20 The average Canadian reads for 30 min each day. 30% of the people buy the book they are reading. In Niagara Falls, which has 70 500 people, how many people would buy their book?

21 20% of Canadians borrow the book which they are reading from a friend. If Alberta has a population of 1 900 000 people, how many Albertans borrow their reading material from a friend?

22 Only 15% of Canadians borrow books from the library. If the population of Vancouver is 1 172 200, how many Vancouverites would borrow their books from the library?

23 70% of Canadian adults own at least one credit card. Ottawa has a population of 300 000. How many people own a credit card?

24 The muscle mass of the average Canadian is 43% of the body mass. If Gregg's body mass is 70 kg, what is his muscle mass?

25 The skin mass of the average Canadian is 26% of the body mass. If Jennifer has a body mass of 69.2 kg, what is her skin mass?

26 Are Canadians bony? The bone mass of the average Canadian is 17.5% of the body mass. What is the bone mass for each person with the following body masses?

Tiger Filliams   96.3 kg
Daryl Sitling   87.6 kg
Bobby Kertola   72.3 kg

27 Only 2.2% of the average Canadian's body mass is brains. If Mark has a body mass of 72.3 kg, what is his brain mass?

8.4 Solving Problems About Per Cent: Making Decisions

To solve a problem about per cent, you need to clearly identify,

   I what information you are given.
   II what information you are asked to find.

Once you have identified the above information you can decide on the method to use. There are 3 basic problems involving per cent, illustrated by the following.

Type	*Problem*
A Finding the per cent of a number.	Find 15% of 320.
B Finding the per cent.	What per cent of 5000 is 4200?
C Finding the number.	If 25% of a number is 20, find the number.

To solve a word problem involving per cents, you need to identify clearly which of the above types you are working with.

Example

An inspector decided that 4200 out of 5000 cartons of eggs were Grade A large. What percentage of the cartons were Grade A large?

Solution

Number of Grade A large cartons is 4200.
Total number of cartons is 5000.
Percentage of Grade A large cartons is given by

$$\frac{4200}{5000} \times 100\% = 0.84 \times 100\%$$
$$= 84\%$$

Thus, 84% of the cartons were Grade A large.

Try These

1   (a) 1% of a number is 48. What is 10% of the number?

    (b) 1% of a number is 6.5. What is 10% of the number?

2   (a) What is 1% of 2400?

    (b) What is 10% of 2400?

3   10% of a number is 360. What is 1% of the number?

4   1% of a number is 48. What is
    (a) 10% of the number?
    (b) 100% of the number?

5   (a) 1% of a number is 6.2. What is 100% of the number?

    (b) 1% of a number is 5.36. What is 100% of the number?

6   What per cent of
    (a) 100 is 10?   (b) 100 is 65?   (c) 200 is 50?

Written Exercises

For each of the following, round off your answer to 1 decimal place, where required.

A 1 Find the value of ▨.
  (a) 10% of a number is 72.
     1% of the number is ▨.
     100% of the number is ▨.

  (b) 20% of a number is 35.
     1% of the number is ▨.
     100% of the number is ▨.

2 (a) Find 12% of 240.
  (b) What is 30% of 45?

3 What per cent is
  (a) 50 of 100? (b) 50 of 200? (c) 25 of 75?

4 Find the value of ▨.
  (a) 40% of 12 is ▨.   (b) 200 is ▨% of 1000.
  (c) 10% of ▨ is 22.   (d) 12% of 250 is ▨.
  (e) 36 is ▨% of 144.   (f) 25% of ▨ is 24.

B
5 (a) What per cent is 30 of 60?
  (b) What per cent is 42 of 294?

6 A banana is about 76% water. If the amount of water in a banana was 114 g, what was the total mass of the banana?

7 Tony won 5 events in a track meet last year. This year he won 20% more than he did last year. How many events did he win this year?

8 In a light bulb factory about 7% of all light bulbs manufactured are defective. How many light bulbs of 8652 manufactured are defective?

9 Out of a total of 48 points, Debra scored 21 points. What per cent did she score?

10 In one season, a goaltender stopped 320 out of 436 shots on goal. What per cent of the shots on goal resulted in goals?

11 Homogenized milk contains 4% butterfat. Calculate the amount of butterfat in 12.4 L of homogenized milk.

12 A peach consists of 89.1% water. For a peach that is 125 g, how much is water?

13 The label on a box of cereal indicates the contents per serving. For a serving, what per cent is
  (a) protein?
  (b) carbohydrates?

SERVING SIZE

28 g = 1 serving

TYPICAL NUTRIENT
VALUE PER SERVING:
Protein   1.5 g
Fat   0.2 g
Total Carbohydrates   25.8 g
Other   0.5 g

14 A soft-drink dealer determined that 55% of the soft drinks sold were colas. If 33 cases of cola were sold, how many cases of soft drinks were sold in all?

15 In basketball a free throw is awarded when another player commits a foul. At a tournament, Sheila was successful on 18 of her 25 free throws. What per cent were successful?

C16 For a human being, 43% of the body mass is muscle.
  (a) The mass of muscle John has is 25.8 kg. What is his body mass?
  (b) The mass of muscle that Sandra has is 21.5 kg. What is her body mass?

8.5 Per Cents Greater Than 100%

You have probably seen many examples of per cents greater than 100%.

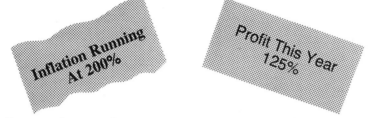

Inflation Running At 200%

Profit This Year 125%

Stamp collectors often deal with per cents greater than 100%.

In 1971 the catalogue value of the stamp shown at right was $28.

Ten years later the catalogue value of the stamp was shown as $375. By what per cent had the stamp increased in price?

$$\frac{\text{Increase in price}}{\text{Price in 1971}} \times 100\%$$

$$= \frac{375 - 28}{28} \times 100\%$$

$$= \frac{347}{28} \times 100\%$$

$$= 12.39 \times 100\% \qquad \text{Which is a great deal more than 100\%.}$$

$$= 1239\%$$

The stamp had increased 1239% in price.

Example 1

(a) Calculate 120% of 1360 people.
(b) Calculate 1340% of $28 (to the nearest dollar).

Solution

Remember
$$120\% = \frac{120}{100} = 1.2$$

(a) 120% of 1360 = 1.20 × 1360
= 1632
Thus 120% of 1360 people is 1632 people.

(b) 1340% of $28 = 13.40 × $28
= 375.2
Thus 1340% of $28 is $375 to the nearest dollar.

Example 2

Refer to the newspaper advertisement that occurred in the 1920's.

OUR IMPERIAL PARLOUR LAMP **$6.39**

ROSE PINK COLOUR. WILD GEESE DECORATION. GENUINE GOLD-PLATED SOLID BRASS TRIMMED THE VERY NEWEST

SUPERB DECORATION

The decoration on this lamp consists of flying wild geese on ivory white with feet, head and wings tinted in their natural colours.

No. 3K1025

Price **$6.39**

(a) The price of the lamp after 10 a was 145% of the original price. What was the price 10 a later?

(b) Today you would pay about $450.00 for a replica of the lamp. By what per cent of the original value has the value of the lamp increased?

Solution

(a) Original price of Imperial Parlour Lamp is $6.39.

$$145\% \text{ of } \$6.39 = 1.45 \times \$6.39$$
$$= \$9.27$$

Thus you would pay $9.27 for the lamp.

(b) Calculate the per cent increase.

$$\frac{\text{price increase}}{\text{original price}} \times 100\%$$

$$= \frac{443.61}{6.39} \times 100\%$$

Increase in price
$450 - \$6.39$
$= \$443.61$

$$= 69.42 \times 100\%$$
$$= 6942\%$$

Thus the value of the lamp has increased 6942%.

Try These

1 What is
   (a) 1% of 50?   (b) 100% of 50?
   (c) 200% of 50?   (d) 500% of 50?

2 What is
   (a) 1% of 300?   (b) 100% of 300?
   (c) 200% of 300? (d) 400% of 300?

3 Calculate.
   (a) 50% of 100 kg   (b) 100% of 100 kg
   (c) 125% of 100 kg   (d) 150% of 100 kg

4 Calculate.
   (a) 125% of 100 L   (b) 150% of 100 cm
   (c) 175% of 100 m   (d) 200% of 100 mg

5 Calculate.
   (a) 200% of 100 cm   (b) 300% of 200 L
   (c) 150% of 100 kg   (d) 175% of 1000 cm
   (e) 225% of $100   (f) 325% of $1000

Written Exercises

Express answers to 1 decimal place or to the nearest cent.

A 1 Calculate.
   (a) 50% of 625
   (b) 75% of 625
   (c) 100% of 625
   (d) 125% of 625

2 Calculate.
   (a) 120% of 450
   (b) 140% of 122
   (c) 110% of 236
   (d) 109% of 480

3 Find each of the following.
   (a) 115% of $270
   (b) 109% of 465 m
   (c) 175% of 390 kg
   (d) 225% of 450 mg

4 Find each of the following.
   (a) 125% of 225 kg
   (b) $125\frac{1}{2}$% of 360 kg
   (c) 125.5% of 460 kg
   (d) $125\frac{3}{4}$% of 550 kg

5 (a) Estimate which is greater.
      A 165% of 265 kg   B 120% of 600 kg
   (b) Calculate which is greater.

6 Which is greater, A or B?

	A	B
(a)	100% of 200	200% of 100
(b)	300% of 200	200% of 300

B 7 When a balloon was blown up some more, it expanded to 130% of its original volume. If the original volume was 120 L, calculate the new volume.

8 The Beaver Stamp was worth $225 10 a ago. It has increased 490% in value. What is its value today?

9 The original height of a fir tree was 12.3 m. If the tree grew to 123% of its original height, calculate how high it is now.

10 A 1948 silver dollar was worth $260 10 a ago. Today it has appreciated 330% in price. What is its value today?

11 The traffic in downtown Vancouver during the Christmas holidays is 170% of the regular traffic. If there are 68 000 cars on the road during the regular traffic, how many cars are there on the road during the holidays?

12 The antique car shown in the photograph was bought for $38 000 3 a ago. The price today is 250% of that price. What is its value today?

13 Jennifer managed a business and received $19 800 last year. This year her salary is 112% of last year's. What is her salary this year?

14 Twenty years ago the average family of four spent approximately $18.60 a week on groceries. The groceries today are 315% of what they were 20 a ago. How much is an average family of four spending on groceries today?

C 15 Refer to Question 14. If the price of groceries is to increase by about 13% each year, how much will the groceries cost after
   (a) 2 a ?   (b) 3 a?   (c) 4 a?

8.6   Per Cent and Purchases

The original or regular price of the record album
is $7.88. Since the store is having a sale, a
discount of 25% is given.

Original or regular price	$7.88
Discount 25%	$1.97
Sale Price	$5.91

Calculate the discount.
25% of $7.88 = 0.25 × $7.88
= $1.97

Advertisements often tell what percentage of the price is subtracted
or discounted during a sale. If a sign indicates 25% off, then you
save 25% on every dollar of the regular price. The "per cent off" is
called the **discount rate**.

In the above example, the rate of discount is 25%. The amount that
is "marked off" is the **amount of discount**. For example, the $1.97
in the above problem is the amount of discount. Remember:

▶ Sale Price = Regular Price − Discount
▶ Discount = Regular Price − Sale Price

Example 1

The Record Shoppe had a sale in which it offered
records at a discount of 35%. What did Melanie
pay for an album originally priced at $8.95?

Solution

Step 1 Find the discount.
35% of $8.95 = 0.35 × $8.95
= $3.13 (to the
nearest cent)

Step 2 Find the sale price.
Sale Price = Regular Price − Discount
= $8.95 − $3.13
= $5.82

Thus, Melanie paid $5.82 for the album.

Example 2

June bought an overnight case in a sale for $22.95. The regular price was $38.80.

(a) How much was the discount?

(b) What was the discount rate to the nearest per cent?

Solution

(a) Find the discount.

Discount = Regular Price − Sale Price
= $38.80 − $22.95
= $15.85

(b) Find the discount rate.

Think! You need to answer:
$15.85 is what per cent of $38.80?

amount of discount → $\dfrac{15.85}{38.80} \times 100\% = 0.409 \times 100\%$
regular price →

$= 40.9\%$

Thus the rate of discount is 41%.

In Example 3, if you know the sale price and the discount you can work backwards and determine the selling price (or regular price). For example, if the discount is 20% then

Sale Price = 80% of Selling Price

Example 3

The sale price of a 10-speed bicycle is $100. If the discount is 20%, calculate the selling price.

Solution

Rate of discount = 20%
Sale Price = $100
Thus 80% of selling price = $100.

80% of a number is 100

1% of a number is $\dfrac{100}{80}$

100% of a number is $100 \times \dfrac{100}{80} = \overset{5}{\cancel{100}} \times \dfrac{100}{\underset{4}{\cancel{80}}}$

$= \dfrac{500}{4}$

$= 125$

Thus, the selling price is $125.

Try These

1 The rate of discount for each item is 10%. What is the amount of discount?
   (a) Film $3.00   (b) Hawaii Trip $870.00
   (c) All Weather Blazer $43.00

2 The rate of discount is 10%. Calculate the sale price.
   (a) Protein Shampoo $2.00
   (b) Fashion Denims $20.00

3 Calculate the sale price.
   (a) Protein Supreme $6.00, 20% off
   (b) Anniversary Footwear $30.00, 30% off
   (c) Vacation Package $460, 50% off

4 Calculate the amount of discount for each of the following.
   (a) Swedish Steel Set $36.00
   (b) Humidifier $80.00
   (c) Firelog 2 boxes $11.00

   Home Needs $\frac{1}{2}$-off Sale

Written Exercises

A 1 What is the amount of discount for each item if the rate of discount is 20%?

Item	Regular Price
(a) Aquarium Tank	$16.80
(b) Scuba Set	$23.96
(c) Car Air Filter	$ 6.25

2 Calculate the sale price for each item if the rate of discount is 25%.

Item	Regular Price
(a) Sneakers	$39.40
(b) Tennis Raquet	$16.25

3 For each item, calculate the
 • amount of discount. • sale price.

Item	Selling Price	Discount
(a) Headphones	$ 23.75	20% off
(b) Speaker	$ 36.90	35% off
(c) Turntable	$189.65	40% off

4 Calculate the sale price of each item.

(a)
```
Franklin Stove
Regularly $349.98
Save 14%
```

(b)
```
Save 43%
Phasar multi-function
alarm chronograph
Reg. $59.99
```

5 Calculate the rate of discount for each item.

Item	Selling Price	Sale Price
(a) 12 Rolls of film	$ 33.48	$ 25.11
(b) Gadget bag	$ 46.90	$ 32.83
(c) Camera	$189.60	$161.15

6 Calculate the rate of discount for each item. The regular price has been marked down and the sale price is shown.

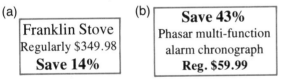

(a)
```
All-quilted
Throw Style
Bedspreads
Were $44.98
Now $29.98
```

(b)
```
Router/sabre
saw table
Reduced from 89.98
Now 69.98
```

7 Copy and complete the following table.

	Selling price	Rate of discount	Sale price
(a)	$38.60	15%	?
(b)	$35.89	25%	?
(c)	?	33%	$19.50
(d)	$65.00	?	$60.00

B 8 An $85 coat is on sale. It is marked "$33\frac{1}{3}$% off".
 (a) What is the amount of discount?
 (b) What is the sale price of the coat?

9 Lori bought a bicycle at a 35%-off sale. If the regular price was $129.95, calculate the sale price.

10 The selling price of a typewriter is $165. If a discount of $29.70 is given for paying by cash, what percentage of the selling price is the discount?

11 The regular price of a fountain pen is $7.95. What is the sale price if the pen is sold at a discount of 20%?

12 Helen is selling her fibreglass skis for $60. The skis originally cost $110. At what rate of discount is Helen selling her skis?

13 During a special sale, a guitar was marked 20%-off, and sold for $85. A banjo was marked 25%-off and sold for $72.
 (a) What was the regular price of the guitar?
 (b) What was the regular price of the banjo?
 (c) Which instrument had the greater discount?

C 14 A customer received a 25% discount on a suit during a sale. He also received a 5% discount on the sale price for paying cash. If he paid $120.50 in cash for the suit, what was the regular price of the suit?

Applications: Suggested List Price

The manufacturer of stereo components might sell a stereo to a retail store for $215.50. This is called the **cost price**. The manufacturer will also give the retail store a **suggested list price** for the stereo. The store then calculates a discount on the suggested list price to determine the **selling price** in the store.

Suggested List Price	$350	15% of $350
Discount 15%	52.50	$= 0.15 \times \$350$
Selling Price	$297.50	$= \$52.50$

The selling price is often referred to as the **regular** (or original price). At certain times of the year, the store may offer yet a further discount to stimulate consumer spending. This is called the **sale price**.

Selling price	$297.50	20% of 297.50
After holiday discount 20%	59.50	$= 0.20 \times 297.50$
Sale Price	$238.00	$= \$59.50$

And of course, any store would not survive if there was no profit.

Selling or Regular Price	$297.50	or	Sale Price	$238.00
Cost Price	$215.50		Cost Price	$215.50
Profit	$ 82.00			$ 22.50

There is more profit when the stereo is sold at the regular price than at the sale price.

15 Calculate the selling price for each item.

	Item	Suggested List Price	Rate of Discount
(a)	Batteries	$ 86.50	15%
(b)	Tires	$ 52.40	12%
(c)	Radio	$129.80	20%
(d)	Tape Deck	$169.30	23%

16 Calculate the rate of discount for each of the following.

	Item	Suggested List Price	Selling Price
(a)	Portable Radio	$ 69.50	$ 51.75
(b)	Ear Phones	$ 35.40	$ 28.95
(c)	Record Player	$129.65	$103.95

17 The suggested list price of a portable typewriter is $230. The cost price to the retailer is $165.
   (a) A store obtains the selling price after a discount of 15%. What is the selling price?
   (b) What is the profit to the retailer in (a)?

18 The suggested list price of a tennis set is $119.80.
   (a) Calculate the discount rate if the amount of discount is $29.95.
   (b) What is the selling price?
   (c) The cost price is 60% of the suggested list price. What is the profit?
   (d) Calculate the sale price if an after-inventory sale offers a further 18% discount.
   (e) Calculate the store's profit in (d).

8.7 Sales Tax and Applications

In most provinces you must pay sales tax on some of the items you purchase. Each province sets its own rate. The retailer collects the sales tax for the province from the customer when the item is purchased.

Rate of sales tax	Province
11%	Newfoundland
9%	Prince Edward Island
8%	New Brunswick Quebec Nova Scotia
7%	Ontario
6%	British Columbia
5%	Manitoba Saskatchewan
No Tax	Alberta

Selling price $12.70
Sales tax $ 0.89 ← 7% of 12.70
Amount you pay $13.59 $= 0.07 \times 12.70$
                               $= 0.889$

Example

(a) Calculate the sales tax at 5% if you buy the following:

Aquarium	$18.25
Light	$9.65
Thermometer	$2.69
Pump	$16.25

(b) What change will you receive from $50?

Solution

(a) Total purchases   Sales Tax
    $18.25   5% of 46.84
    $ 9.65 $= 0.05 \times 46.84$
    $ 2.69 $= 2.342$
    $16.25   The sales tax is $2.34.
    $46.84

(b) Total selling price $46.84
    Sales tax $ 2.34
    Total cost $49.18
    Amount of money given $50.00
    Total cost $49.18
    Change $ 0.82
    Thus the change received from $50.00 is 82¢.

Try These

1. What is the rate of sales tax in each of the following provinces?
   (a) Prince Edward Island (b) Nova Scotia
   (c) Manitoba   (d) Newfoundland
   (e) Ontario   (f) Alberta

2. Estimate which amount, A or B, is the correct amount of sales tax on each item purchased in Saskatchewan.

			A	B
(a)	Cassette tape	$ 1.89	9¢	90¢
(b)	Disc washer	$19.90	10¢	95¢
(c)	Ski jacket	$69.00	$3.45	$0.35
(d)	Tire	$83.00	$41.50	$4.15

3. *About* how much sales tax will you pay in Quebec for each item?
   (a) L.P. record $10.00
   (b) All weather
       sweater $29.00
   (c) Stereo set $500.00

4. For each pair of provinces, in which province will you pay more sales tax?
   (a) Manitoba   Nova Scotia
   (b) Saskatchewan   Alberta
   (c) New Brunswick   Ontario
   (d) Quebec   British Columbia

Written Exercises

Round off all answers where necessary to the nearest cent.

A 1 Find each of the following.
  (a) 5% of $6.50
  (b) 9% of $13.20
  (c) 8% of $14.36
  (d) 6% of $76.35

2 Calculate the sales tax in Manitoba for each item.
  (a) Camping stove $36.00
  (b) Sleeping bag $29.50

3 Calculate the sales tax in Ontario for each item.
  (a) Headphones $18.96
  (b) Cassette auto tape player $69.25
  (c) Desk top computer $999.99

4 In which province will you pay more sales tax? How much more?
  (a) Sweat suit $23.65
       Ontario, Prince Edward Island
  (b) Jogging shoes $28.75
       Newfoundland, British Columbia
  (c) Early morning jacket $39.40
       Manitoba, Alberta

5 Copy and complete the chart.

	Item	Province	Selling price	Total price
(a)	Helmet	British Columbia	$ 34.60	?
(b)	Snowmobile drive track	Nova Scotia	$ 93.50	?
(c)	Insulated boots	Quebec	$ 49.65	?

6 Which total cost is correct, A or B?

	Selling price	Province	A	B
(a)	Alpine skis $129.65	Manitoba	$136.13	$138.73
(b)	Ski boots $63.59	New Brunswick	$ 66.77	$ 68.68
(c)	Ski bindings $73.25	Alberta	$ 73.25	$ 79.11
(d)	Skiing outfit $133.76	Newfoundland	$135.04	$148.47

B 7 Calculate the sales tax at 5% on a record which costs $1.69.

8 The price of a pair of cords is $16.95. If the rate of sales tax is 8%, calculate the total price.

9 (a) How much sales tax at 5% would you pay if a record player costs $89.50?
   (b) How much change will you get from $100?

10 A blouse costs $27 in British Columbia. Calculate the total cost.

11 On a trip to New Brunswick, Joanne bought a lobster trap for $29.35. What did she pay in all?

12 Calculate the amount of sales tax you would pay, in the province that you are living in, on each of these items. What is the total purchase price?

(a)
```
        Ski Wear
Nylon shell, nylon lining
   Originally $69.98
 Now reduced by 22%
```

(b)
```
Supple leather
    coats

 Reg. $199
 Now $179
```

13 (a) Calculate the cost of a colour T.V. for $495.98 in British Columbia including sales tax.
   (b) How much more will you pay in Ontario for the same purchase?

C 14 During a recent trip Betty bought souvenirs.

Flag	$ 3.69	Postcard set	$ 6.25
Slides	$16.25	Wood carvings	$36.95

If she paid $63.14 in all, what province did she visit?

266

8.8 Per Cent and Business

Everywhere in business you will find per cents being used. Have you seen any of these?

SOUNDSONAR 50%
NEW OFF MSL
SLIM LINE
AM/FM
STEREO
with cassette $119 cash 'n' carry
AC/DC Stereo

Earn $13\frac{1}{4}\%$ interest

Growing Money

When you deposit money in a bank account, as a payment for the privilege of using your money, the bank pays you interest at a certain rate. The amount of money that you have in your bank account is called the **principal**.

Lesley opened a bank account and deposited $100.00. The bank pays her 13%/a simple interest.

Principal	$100
Amount of interest at 13%/a	13
Total amount at the end of 1 a	$113

13% of $100
= 0.13 × $100
= $13

Example 1

Alan deposited $239 in a bank account on August 31 after working for the summer. The bank pays $13\frac{1}{2}\%$/a simple interest. Calculate the amount in his account after 2 a.

Solution

Principal	$239.00
Amount of interest	
at $13\frac{1}{2}\%$/a	$ 32.27
Total Amount	$271.27

$13\frac{1}{2}\%$ of $239
= 0.135 × 239
= 32.265

Thus, the amount in the account after 1 a is $271.27.

The next year Alan does not deposit any more money in his account. The amount of $271.27 will still earn interest.

New principal	$271.27
Amount of interest at $13\frac{1}{2}\%$/a	$ 36.62
Total amount at the end of 2 a	$307.89

Thus the amount in his account after 2 a is $307.89.

Borrowing Money

The money you deposit in a bank account is then loaned by the bank to other people who want to borrow money. The bank charges the person who is borrowing the money a certain amount of interest.

Suppose a person borrows $460 from the bank. The bank charges 16%/a to lend money. $460 is called the principal.

Principal	$460	
Amount of interest charged at 16%/a	$ 73.60	$\begin{aligned} &16\% \text{ of } 460 \\ &= 0.16 \times 460 \\ &= 73.60 \end{aligned}$
Amount the borrower pays back to the bank.	$533.60	

How does the bank make money? It pays the depositer $13\frac{1}{2}$%/a for the use of his or her money. The bank then uses this money to lend to someone else and charges this borrower 16%/a. The difference in the amount of interest charged to the borrower and the amount of interest paid to the depositor is the amount the bank makes.

Example 2

Kim borrowed $125 for a vacation trip at 15% and agreed to pay back the bank in 1 a. Calculate the interest she was charged and the amount she paid back in all (in 1 a).

Solution

Rate of interest charged 15%

Principal	$125.00	$\begin{aligned} &15\% \text{ of } \$125 \\ &= 0.15 \times 125 \\ &= 18.75 \end{aligned}$
Amount of interest	$ 18.75	
Amount paid back	$143.75	

Thus Kim was charged $18.75 in interest and paid back $143.75 in all.

There are many other cases in business in which the calculations of per cents are required. For example, if you work at selling a product, you may often be paid a commission, at a certain rate, as shown in Example 3.

Example 3

For selling subscriptions, Joey is paid 5% of sales. If each subscription is $26.89 and in 1 week Joey sells 43 subscriptions, calculate the commission paid.

Solution

Step 1   *Calculate total sales*

Cost of 1 subscription	$26.89
Cost of 43 subscriptions	43 × $26.89
	= $1156.27

Step 2   *Calculate commission*

Total sales	$1156.27
Commission of 5% paid	$ 57.81

Thus, the commission paid to Joey is $57.81.

Try These

1. What is the interest paid on each amount after 1 a if the rate of interest is 10%/a?

   (a) $100   (b) $200   (c) $125

2. You borrow money and agree to pay 10%/a interest. How much interest will you owe for each loan after a year?

   (a) $400   (b) $650   (c) $950
   (d) $126   (e) $728.50   (f) $635.25

3. Leah is paid a 10% commission for sales she makes on the telephone. Calculate the amount she is paid each week.

   (a) Week 1 $623   (b) Week 2 $465
   (c) Week 3 $923   (d) Week 4 $690

4. Jill is paid 1% for each policy she sells. Calculate the amount of commission she gets for each policy.

   (a) Whole Life Policy $20 000
   (b) Annuity Policy $35 000

Written Exercises

Express answers to the nearest cent.

A 1 Calculate the interest earned for each deposit for 1 a at the interest rate given.

(a) $600 at 13%/a   (b) $212 at 15%/a

2 Find the amount of interest paid on each of these deposits after 1 a.

	Amount	Rate of Interest
(a)	$40.00	10%/a
(b)	$55.00	12%/a
(c)	$84.60	9%/a
(d)	$468.10	$8\frac{1}{2}$%/a

3 You may often receive interest even though you do not keep the money in the bank for 1 a. Calculate the interest for each deposit. The first one is done for you.

(a) $500 at 12%/a for 6 months.

   Interest for 1 a = 12% of $500 = $60
   Interest for 6 months or half a year = $60 ÷ 2 = $30

(b) $800 at 14%/a for 6 months.

(c) $960 at 12%/a for 3 months.

(d) $365 at $10\frac{1}{2}$%/a for 1 month.

4 Calculate the amount of money you would pay back to the bank at the end of a year.

	Amount borrowed	Rate of interest
(a)	$915.90	16%/a
(b)	$17.88	$15\frac{1}{2}$%/a
(c)	$889.55	$16\frac{3}{4}$%/a

5 Calculate the total amount owed to the bank at the end of each time period.

(a) $710 at 15%/a for 6 months.

(b) $710 at 16%/a for 3 months.

(c) $710 at $13\frac{1}{2}$%/a for 9 months.

6 Calculate the commission received for each of the following sales.

	Amount of sales	Rate of commission
(a)	$465	3%
(b)	$690.25	5%
(c)	$30 600	6%
(d)	$123 600	$2\frac{1}{2}$%
(e)	$4650	3.9%

Working With Interest

B 7 The rate of interest paid on a bank account is 13%/a. Find the interest paid after a year if the amount in the account is $630.50.

8 When you purchase a Canada Savings Bond, it pays interest as if you had deposited the money in a bank. How much would a $200 bond pay in one year at $9\frac{3}{4}$%/a?

9 Jay borrowed $400 from a bank in order to buy a motorcycle and agreed to pay at the rate of interest of 16%/a. At the end of a year, how much money would Jay pay back to the bank?

10 Who pays the greater amount of interest on a loan?
   (a) Mr. Bacon borrowed $950 for a year. He paid 13%/a interest.
   (b) Mr. Wong borrowed $1050 for a year. He paid $12\frac{1}{2}$%/a interest.

11 The rate of interest paid by a bank is 12%/a. Find the interest paid on a deposit of $800
   (a) after a year.   (b) after 6 months.
   (c) after 3 months.

12 The rate of interest at a bank is 10%/a. The bank also states that interest is calculated monthly.
   (a) Calculate the interest earned on a deposit of $520 after 1 month.
   (b) What is the total amount in the bank account at the end of the month?
   (c) Calculate the total interest earned in the second month.

13 Find the missing values in the following table.

	Amount deposited	Rate of interest	Interest paid	Length of time
(a)	$200	14%/a	?	1 month
(b)	$350	13%/a	?	2 months
(c)	$450	12%/a	?	2 months

Working With Commissions

14 Telly receives 4% commission on all lottery tickets he sells. Calculate his commission if last month he sold $895 worth of tickets.

15 Pat's mother sells homes. Her rate of commission is 3%. Calculate her commission on a house which sold for $85 000.

16 For selling cosmetics Laura receives a rate of commission of 15%. If her total sales amounted to $225.00, how much commission did she earn?

17 The total sales were $420. The commission paid was $30. Find the rate of commission.

18 Shirley receives a base salary of $135 a week and a commission of 2% of sales. What did she earn altogether in a week when she sold $1850 worth of cosmetics?

19 Rose Mary receives commissions at the rate of 12% for the first $15 000 of sales and 30% for sales in excess of $15 000. What is her commission on $27 000 of sales?

20 Jackson sells two cars. Each car is priced at $6245.80. If his rate of commission is $2\frac{1}{2}$% how much commission does he receive?

21 Robin sells cars on commission. She receives 5% for new cars and 4% for used cars. How much commission does she earn if she sold two used cars totalling $7120 and one new car selling for $6895?

Skills to Practise: A Chapter Review

3.1 Find the missing value.

(a) $\dfrac{\square}{100} = 12\%$ (b) $\dfrac{4}{5} = \square\%$ (c) $\dfrac{\square}{100} = 0.52$

3.2 Write a per cent for each of the following. Which is greater?

(a) $\dfrac{3}{10}, \dfrac{2}{5}$ (b) $\dfrac{1}{4}, \dfrac{2}{5}$

3.3 Find the value of $\square$.

(a) 40% of 350 is $\square$.

(b) 400 is $\square$% of 2000.

3.4 Calculate each of the following.

(a) What per cent of 800 is 200?

(b) What is 30% of 12?

(c) 6% of a number is 60. What is the number?

3.5 Which is heavier?

A 175% of 1250 kg   B 225% of 850 kg

3.6 Calculate the sale price of each item.

(a)   (b)

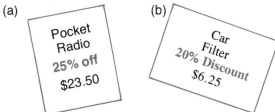

3.7 Copy and complete.

	Selling price	Rate of sales tax	Amount of sales tax	Total cost
(a)	$49.50	8%	?	?
(b)	$123.50	7%	?	?

3.8 Calculate the amount of money you have after a year.

	Amount	Rate of interest
(a)	$450	16%
(b)	$290	14.5%

Problems To Practise: A Chapter Review

8.1 Out of 195 pothead whales, that were heading for the beaches (and almost certain death), 60 were diverted to deep water. What percentage (a) lived?   (b) died?

8.2 Of the 38 forest fires started last year, 25 were caused by carelessness. Of the 52 house fires started over the same period, 37 were caused by carelessness. Write each record as a per cent.

8.3 During the soccer season, Jay scored with 12% of his shots on goal.

(a) If he made 62 shots on goal during the season, how many goals did he score?

(b) If he improved his record by 10% the next year, how many goals did he get?

8.4 Darlene Benson earns $2.50/h working at Hamburger Delight. If she receives a 10% increase, how much will she make per hour now?

8.5 When a gas was heated it expanded to 135% of its original volume. If the original volume was 25 L, calculate the new volume.

8.6 The regular price of a badminton set is $14.75. The rate of discount is 20%.

(a) Calculate the amount of the discount.

(b) What is the sale price?

8.7 In Manitoba, a football costs Marnie $15.90. Calculate the total cost, including sales tax.

8.8 (a) The rate of interest paid is 13%/a. Find the interest paid after 1 a if the amount in the account is $630.50.

(b) What amount of commission is received for selling $465 of merchandise if the rate of commission is 3%?

Chapter Checkup: A Practice Test

8.1 (a) Write

　　　A $\dfrac{3}{4}$ as a per cent.

　　　B 70% as a fraction.
　　　C 49% as a decimal.

　　(b) South Africa mines 67.4% of all the gold in
　　　　the world. The U.S.S.R. mines 13.5% and
　　　　the rest of the world, except for Canada,
　　　　mines 13.9%. What percentage of gold
　　　　does Canada mine?

8.2 Write a per cent for each of the following.
　　A 12 out of 16 fast-food outlets had clean
　　　washroom facilities.
　　B 14 out of 25 service stations had clean
　　　washroom facilities.
　　Which had the better record?

8.3 (a) What per cent is 45 of 90?
　　(b) What is 40% of 480?
　　(c) Out of 180 school days last year, Margaret
　　　　was absent for 6% of them. How many
　　　　days was she absent?

8.4 (a) What is 70% of 220?
　　(b) 72 is 15% of what number?

　　(c) Beaconsfield High School won 75% of its 16
　　　　games. How many games did it win?

8.5 (a) Calculate.
　　　A 110% of $290
　　　B 165% of 250 kg

　　(b) A company's earnings for this month
　　　　increased 16.5% over last month. If the
　　　　earnings were $980 000 for last month,
　　　　find this month's earnings.

8.6 (a) Copy and complete the chart.

	Regular Price	Rate of Discount	Sale Price
A	$15.95	2%	?
B	?	25%	$150.00
C	$90.00	?	$50.00

　　(b) The regular price for a pair of ice skates is
　　　　$44.50. Calculate the sale price if a
　　　　discount if 15% is given.

8.7 (a) What is the total cost for each item
　　　　including 7% sales tax?

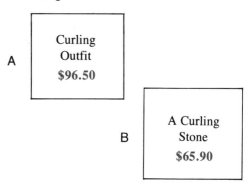

A Curling Outfit $96.50

B A Curling Stone $65.90

　　(b) Jacques bought a new 10-speed bicycle.
　　　　The regular price was $135, but there was
　　　　a tag on the bike indicating "20% off". If
　　　　the bicycle was bought in Newfoundland,
　　　　what was the total cost of the bicycle?

Consumer Tip: Per Cent And Tipping

You have probably been in a restaurant and left a tip with your payment. The term tip probably means "To Improve Performance".

If you are happy with the service you leave a tip, which is usually a percentage of the bill.

If you are not happy with the service, you may or may not leave a tip.

> Your food bill is $9.00
> You wish to leave 10% tip
> Amount of tip = 10% of $9.00
> $\qquad = 0.10 \times \$9.00$
> $\qquad = 90¢$

Written Exercises

1 Find 10% of each amount.
  (a) $1.50   (b) $2.00   (c) $4.50
  (d) $9.50   (e) $3.25   (f) $7.85

2 For each of the following, you include a 10% tip with your bill. What amount will you pay?
  (a) $6.50   (b) $9.85   (c) $14.25

3 Include a 15% tip to pay for each of the following amounts.
  (a) $1.75   (b) $3.60   (c) $8.25

4 The bill for Jean and her friends is $16.25.
  (a) Calculate a 15% tip.
  (b) If Jean pays tips, how much is the total bill, rounded to the nearest half dollar?

5 The staff of the General M Store had its Christmas party at the restaurant. The restaurant adds on a 15% gratuity (tip) to the amount spent. What is the total amount of the bill if $485.25 was spent?

For Questions 6 to 8, use the menu.

6 Betty orders an egg, English muffin and milk. She leaves a 10% tip. What will her breakfast cost in all?

7 For a snack, Michella ordered snapper soup, a B-L-T sandwich and a milk. If she leaves a 15% tip, how much will she pay in all to the nearest half dollar?

8 The basketball team ordered the following.
>   4 turkey open clubs
>   3 Reuben Grill
>   2 Tenderloin steak sandwiches
>   4 soup de jour
>   2 chef salads
>   8 side orders of French fried potatoes
>   12 milk

  (a) Calculate the total cost of the meal.
  (b) What is the amount of gratuity at 15% rounded to the nearest dollar?
  (c) If there are 11 persons, what is the average cost?

One Egg, Any Style	1.60
Buttermilk Pancakes	2.15
French Toast	2.40
Starters	
Snapper Soup	1.95
Soup de Jour	1.25
Sandwich Board	
Tenderloin Steak Sandwich	5.95
B-L-T Sandwich	3.25
Turkey Open Club	3.95
Reuben Grill	4.35
Chef's Salad	4.25
Side Orders	
French Fried Potatoes	80¢
Cottage Cheese	80¢
English Muffin	65¢
Beverages	
Tea, Milk, Coffee	75¢

Applications and Skills With Geometry

properties and skills, constructions, designs, circles, right triangles, applications and problem-solving

Introduction

The need to know about geometry is everywhere. You have already developed skills in finding the perimeter, area, and volume of various geometric figures. Where does the geometry occur in the photo ?

Geometry builds.

- • a point
- • → a ray
- ←→ a line
- • a line segment
- a triangle

a square   a rectangle   a quadrilateral
                                          a polygon of 4 sides

a pentagon   a hexagon   and so on .
a polygon of 5 sides   a polygon of 6 sides

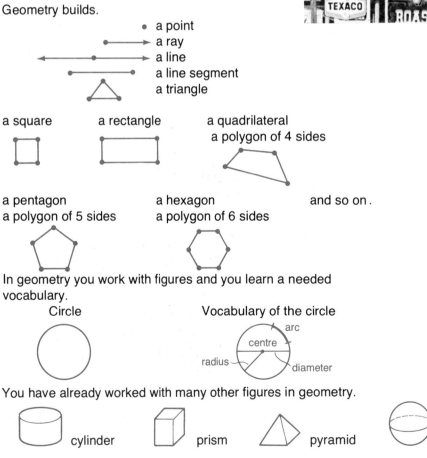

In geometry you work with figures and you learn a needed vocabulary.

Circle   Vocabulary of the circle

                                         arc
                                  centre
                     radius   diameter

You have already worked with many other figures in geometry.

cylinder   prism   pyramid   sphere

9.1 Working With Geometry

Angles play an important role in your everyday activities.

Knowing the angle at which to bank the ball off the side of a pool table is important for a good shot.

Step ladders are built to open at a certain angle for safety.

In the radar room of an airport, angles can be seen on a radar screen. One arm of the angle turns and the other arm is stationary.

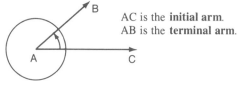

AC is the **initial arm**.
AB is the **terminal arm**.

Letters are used to label angles. The vertex letter is placed in the middle.

∠BAC or ∠CAB

└─ vertex ─┘

The standard unit of measure for angles is called the **degree**.

There are 360 degrees (360°) in a complete turn.

360°

There are 180 degrees (180°) in a half turn.

180°

There are 90° in a quarter turn.

This symbol is used to indicate the angle.

You use a **protractor** to measure angles.

There are 2 scales on the protractor, each measuring 0° to 180°.

0 line or start of the scale   centre of the protractor

Example
Measure ∠PQR.

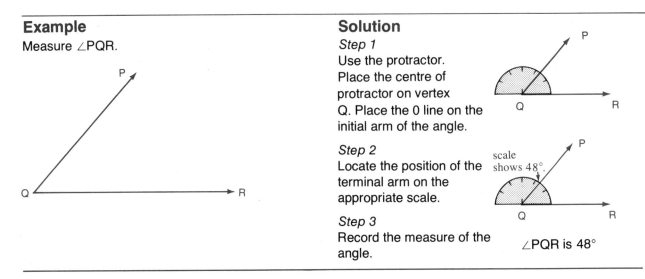

Solution

Step 1
Use the protractor. Place the centre of protractor on vertex Q. Place the 0 line on the initial arm of the angle.

Step 2
Locate the position of the terminal arm on the appropriate scale.

scale shows 48°.

Step 3
Record the measure of the angle.

∠PQR is 48°

The protractor can also be used to construct angles.

Angles are given special names depending on their size.

Name of angle	Measure of angle
Acute	between 0° and 90°
Right	90°
Obtuse	between 90° and 180°
Straight	180°
Reflex	between 180° and 360°

In the exercise that follows you will see many other ways in which angles occur as part of your everyday activities.

Try These

1 What is the name of each angle?

2 What type of angle is each of the following: acute, right, obtuse, straight or reflex?
(a)　　(b)　　　　(c)　　(d)

(e)　　　　　　　(f)

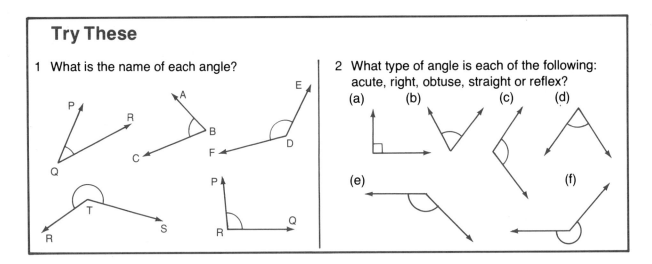

Written Exercises

A 1 Measure each length to the nearest
 • centimetre • tenth of a centimetre.

(a) ─────────

(b) ──────────────────

(c) ────────────────

(d) ──────────────────────

2 Find each of the following measures, to the nearest tenth of a centimetre.

(a) The width of this book.

(b) The thickness of this book.

(c) The length of your pen or pencil.

(d) The width of your thumb.

(e) The width of your hand span.

(f) The length of your longest finger.

3 What is the measure of each angle?

(a)   (b)

(c)   (d)

4 Estimate the size of each angle.
 Then measure each angle.

(a)   (b)

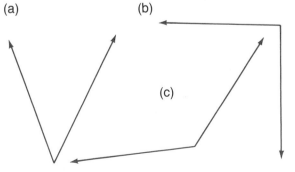

(c)

5 Use a protractor. Construct each of the following angles in your notebook.

(a) ∠ABC = 13°   (b) ∠PQR = 39°

(c) ∠PET = 89°   (d) ∠JKL = 90°

(e) ∠STU = 160°   (f) ∠EFG = 180°

What type are each of the above angles?

6 Use a protractor. Construct an angle equal in size to each of the following in your notebook.

(a)   (b)

(c)

B 7 For each of the following angles,
 ► estimate the size. ► classify the angle.
 ► measure the angle.

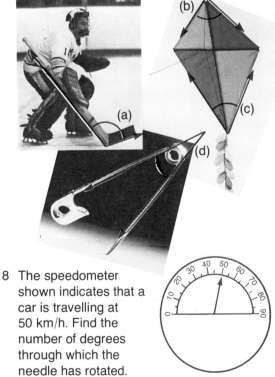

8 The speedometer shown indicates that a car is travelling at 50 km/h. Find the number of degrees through which the needle has rotated.

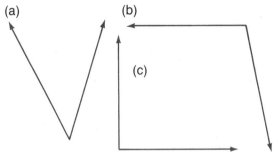

277

9 (a) The speedometer of a car registers 90 km/h. What angle is shown by the needle?

(b) What angle is shown by each speed?
- 30 km/h
- 50 km/h

10 Measure the angle of the bank for each ball.

(a)

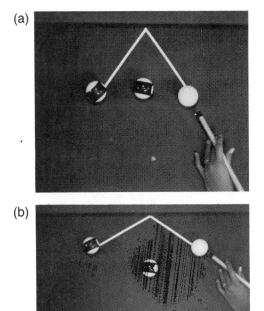

(b)

11 Measure the angle of each ski slope.

(a)

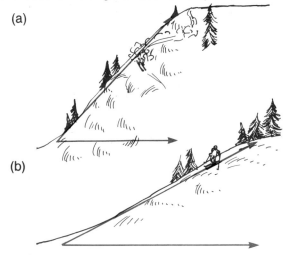

(b)

(c) Which slope probably requires a more experienced skier?

12 Use the diagram. Copy and complete the chart.

	Name of angle	Estimate	Measure
(a)	∠PTS	?	?
(b)	∠PTQ	?	?
(c)	∠QTR	?	?
(d)	∠RTS	?	?
(e)	sum of angles above	?	?

13 In the diagram ∠PQR and ∠OQS are a pair of **vertically opposite angles**.

(a) Measure ∠OQS and ∠PQR. What do you notice about their measures?

(b) Measure ∠PQO and ∠RQS. What do you notice about their measures?

14 (a) Draw any two intersecting lines.

(b) Measure the pairs of vertically opposite angles.

(c) What do you notice about the above measures?

15 (a) Repeat the steps in Question 14.

(b) What do you notice about the measures of vertically opposite angles?

16 Use your results in Questions 13 to 15. What general conclusion can you make about your results?

Applications: Navigation And Bearings

An airplane approaching an airport is given a **bearing** and a distance. The bearing of an airplane is expressed as an angle in degrees measured from the North in a clockwise direction.

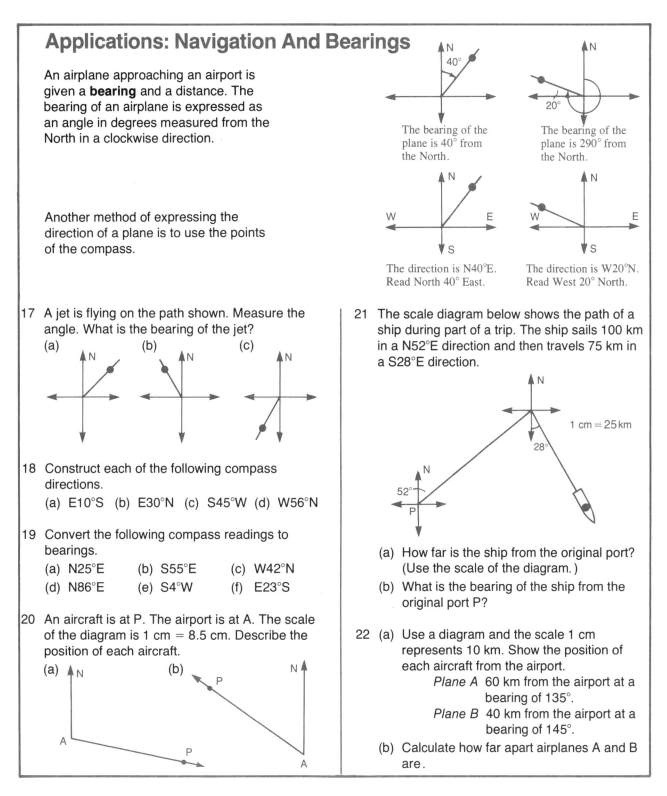

The bearing of the plane is 40° from the North.

The bearing of the plane is 290° from the North.

Another method of expressing the direction of a plane is to use the points of the compass.

The direction is N40°E. Read North 40° East.

The direction is W20°N. Read West 20° North.

17 A jet is flying on the path shown. Measure the angle. What is the bearing of the jet?
(a)   (b)   (c)

18 Construct each of the following compass directions.
(a) E10°S (b) E30°N (c) S45°W (d) W56°N

19 Convert the following compass readings to bearings.
(a) N25°E   (b) S55°E   (c) W42°N
(d) N86°E   (e) S4°W   (f) E23°S

20 An aircraft is at P. The airport is at A. The scale of the diagram is 1 cm = 8.5 cm. Describe the position of each aircraft.
(a)   (b)

21 The scale diagram below shows the path of a ship during part of a trip. The ship sails 100 km in a N52°E direction and then travels 75 km in a S28°E direction.

1 cm = 25 km

(a) How far is the ship from the original port? (Use the scale of the diagram.)

(b) What is the bearing of the ship from the original port P?

22 (a) Use a diagram and the scale 1 cm represents 10 km. Show the position of each aircraft from the airport.
  Plane A 60 km from the airport at a bearing of 135°.
  Plane B 40 km from the airport at a bearing of 145°.

(b) Calculate how far apart airplanes A and B are.

9.2   Triangles Around Us

Triangles are an important part in the construction of towers and buildings.

Triangles are used to support the top of the roof.

Triangles are given special names depending on the lengths of their sides.

Scalene Triangle: A scalene triangle has sides of all different lengths.

Isosceles Triangle: An isosceles triangle has two sides equal in length.

Equilateral Triangle: An equilateral triangle has three sides equal in length.

To do constructions in geometry, it is often helpful to first draw a sketch of the work you intend to do as shown in Example 1.

Example 1
Construct an equilateral triangle with sides 4 cm.

Solution
Step 1
Draw a rough sketch of the figure.

Step 2
Draw a line. Mark a point A. Use a ruler to mark point B such that AB is 4 cm.

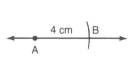

Step 3
Use centre A. Draw an arc with radius 4 cm.

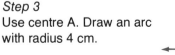

Step 4
Use centre B. Draw an arc with radius 4 cm. Name the intersection point C.

Step 5
Draw the sides of the triangle.

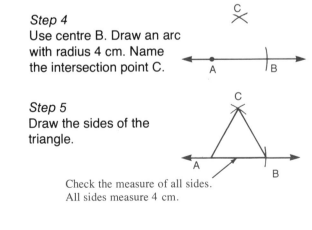

Check the measure of all sides.
All sides measure 4 cm.

Triangles are also given special names depending on the measures of their angles.

This symbol is used to show a right angle.

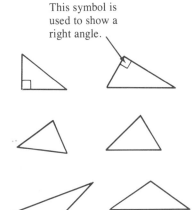

Right Triangle: A right triangle has an angle that measures 90°.

Acute Triangle: An acute triangle is a triangle with all angles less than 90°.

Obtuse Triangle: An obtuse triangle is a triangle with one angle greater than 90°.

A protractor is used to construct some triangles.

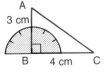

Try These

1 Name each triangle as scalene, isosceles, or equilateral.

  (a)   (b)   (c)

  (d)   (e)   (f)

2 Name each triangle as acute, obtuse, or right.

  (a)   (b)   (c)   (d)

Written Exercises

A 1 (a) Measure the sides of △ABC.

    (b) What type of triangle is it?

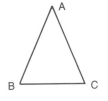

2 (a) Measure the angles of △DEF.

    (b) What type of triangle is it?

3 ► Measure the sides and angles of each triangle.
   ► Name the type of triangle in terms of its angles.

    (a)   (b)

                 (c)

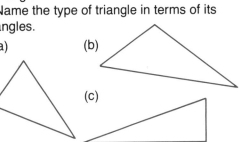

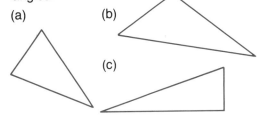

281

B 4 Roof trusses are shown in the photo. Make suitable measurements to construct a copy.

5 A roof truss is shown. Make suitable measurements to construct a copy of the truss.

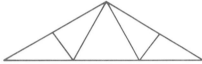

6 (a) Use the sketch. Construct the triangle.
  (b) Measure ∠A. What do you notice?

7 (a) Use the sketch. Construct the triangle.
  (b) Measure each angle. Which angle has the smallest measure?

8 (a) Construct an equilateral triangle with sides measuring 6.5 cm.
  (b) Write a flow chart to organize the instructions to show how to construct an equilateral triangle.

9 △ABC has the following measures.
  ▶ Construct each triangle.
  ▶ Name the type of triangle it is.
  (a) AC = 8 cm, BC = 6 cm, ∠C = 49°
  (b) AB = 6 cm, ∠B = 90°, BC = 8 cm
  (c) BC = 5.5 cm, ∠B = 26°, ∠C = 105°
  (d) AC = 5 cm, BC = 6 cm, AB = 7 cm

Investigating Properties: Triangles

10 (a) Construct the triangle shown.
   (b) What type of triangle is it?
   (c) Measure the remaining angles. What do you notice about the measures?

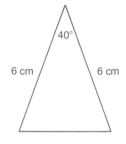

11 (a) Construct any isosceles triangle.
   (b) Measure the angles. What do you notice about the measures?

12 Based on your results about the angles in Questions 10 and 11, what do you think is a property of an isosceles triangle?

13 (a) Construct an equilateral triangle with sides 4.5 cm.
   (b) Measure the angles. What do you notice about their measures?

14 (a) Construct any equilateral triangle.
   (b) Measure the angles. What do you notice about their measures?

15 Based on your results in Questions 13 and 14, what do you think is a property of an equilateral triangle?

16 (a) Construct a triangle with sides measuring 4.5 cm, 6.8 cm, 7.5 cm.
   (b) Measure the angles in the triangle.
   (c) Find the sum of the angles.
   (d) Round your sum in (c) to the nearest 10. degrees.

17 (a) Construct any triangle.
   (b) Measure the angles in your triangle.
   (c) Find the sum of the angles.
   (d) Round your sum in (c) to the nearest 10. degrees. What do you notice?

9.3 Bisecting Angles

To **bisect** a figure means to divide it into two equal parts. You often need to know how to bisect.

To divide the piece of pizza into 2 equal parts, you need to bisect an angle.

To find the centre of the plate, you need to bisect angles.

For the diagram,
∠BAD = ∠DAC
Thus, AD is the **bisector** of
∠BAC.

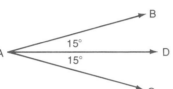

In this section you will bisect angles using a straightedge (ruler) and compasses.

Example

Find the bisector of ∠ABC.

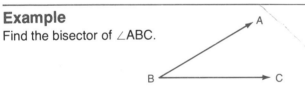

Solution

The arcs of circles are shown.

Step 1
Draw the arc with centre B. Name the intersection points P and Q.

Step 2
Use centre P. Draw an arc.

Step 3
Use centre Q and the same radius as in Step 2. Draw an arc to intersect the arc shown at T.

Step 4
Join BT. BT is the bisector of ∠ABC.

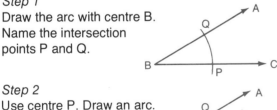

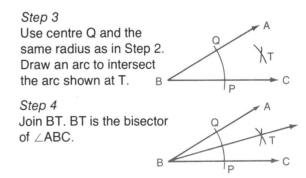

Try These

1 The diagram shows all the steps for bisecting the obtuse angle BAP. Describe the steps in order.

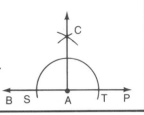

2 The diagram shows all the steps for bisecting the straight angle BAP. Describe the steps in order.

Written Exercises

A 1 (a) Draw an angle of 70°.

(b) Draw the bisector of the angle.

(c) What is the measure of each part? Check by measuring.

2 (a) Draw an angle of 154°.

(b) Draw the bisector of the angle.

(c) What is the measure of each part? Check by measuring.

3 In each photo, an angle is shown.
▶ Copy the angle on a separate piece of paper.
▶ Find the bisector of the angle. Use only a straightedge and compasses.

4 (a) Draw an acute angle and construct its bisector.

(b) Check your accuracy. Measure the angles.

B 5 A bolt is to be drilled at the centre of the square.

(a) Copy the square onto a piece of paper.

(b) Bisect the angles. The intersection of the bisectors is the location of the hole.

6 Bolts are to be placed at these locations on a face plate.

(a) Copy the diagram onto a separate piece of paper.

(b) Bisect each angle to find the location of the bolts.

7 Copy the diagram. Find the path the ship is required to take to pass through the opening.

8 (a) Draw a straight angle.

(b) Divide the angle in (a) into 2 equal parts. What is the measure of each part?

(c) Use steps (a) and (b) to construct an angle that measures 90°.

9 Refer to Question 8.

(a) Construct an angle that measures 90°.

(b) Bisect the angle in (a). What is the measure of each part?

(c) Use steps (a) and (b) to construct an angle that measures 45°.

10 (a) Draw an obtuse angle.

(b) Divide the angle in (a) into 4 equal parts.

C

11 Write a flow chart to organize the instructions to construct the bisector of ∠ABC.

Applications: Designs And Logos

Many companies use logos to advertise. A logo is a symbol designed by a company so that people can immediately identify the company by the logo. Many logos are based on a design that uses the bisector of angles.

Using bisectors of angles, you can make up your own original designs and logos.

12 (a) Construct a copy of this design.

(b) Use your own shading to complete the design.

13 For the design, ∠BAC is bisected. Construct a copy of the design.

14 To construct the design, a line is drawn through the centre of the circle. The straight angle is then bisected, and so on.

15 Make a copy of this design.

16 Examine how this diagram is constructed. Then make a similar diagram.

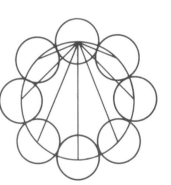

17 For each logo,
   ► examine how the bisector of an angle is used.
   ► then construct a copy of the logo.

18 Construct a design or logo of your own using bisectors of angles.

9.4 Right Bisectors

You often need to know how to bisect line segments.

To draw the white line on
the highway you need to
find the middle of the road.

The line drawn through the midpoint of SR and
at right angles to SR is called the **right
bisector**.

PQ bisects the line SR at O.
(PQ is the right bisector of
SR since $\angle SOP = 90°$.)

The steps needed to construct the right bisector of a line segment
are given in Example 1.

Example 1
Find the right bisector of the line segment AB.

Solution

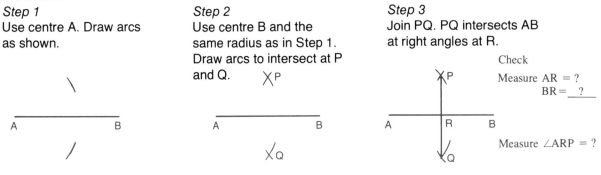

Step 1
Use centre A. Draw arcs
as shown.

Step 2
Use centre B and the
same radius as in Step 1.
Draw arcs to intersect at P
and Q.

Step 3
Join PQ. PQ intersects AB
at right angles at R.

Check
Measure AR = ?
BR = ___?___

Measure $\angle ARP$ = ?

When two lines meet at right angles, they are said to be
perpendicular to each other.

The need to find the right bisector of line segments occurs
frequently in your study of geometry.

Example 2
A bolt is to be placed half
way along the brace AB.
Use a straightedge and
compasses to find the
location of the bolt.

Solution
Construct the right bisector
of AB.
The position of the bolt is
at Q.

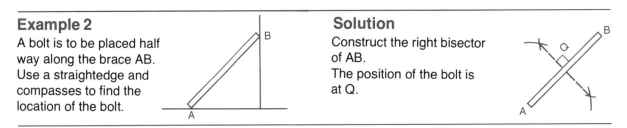

Each of the following words may suggest a clue for you to use the skill of finding the right bisector.
- ► Find the midpoint.
- ► Find the middle.
- ► Where will the plank balance?
  and so on.

Make a list of other clue words that occur in the following exercises.

Try These

1 The diagram shows the steps for bisecting the line segment AB. Describe the steps in order.

2 The diagram shows the steps for bisecting the line segment CD. Describe the steps in order.

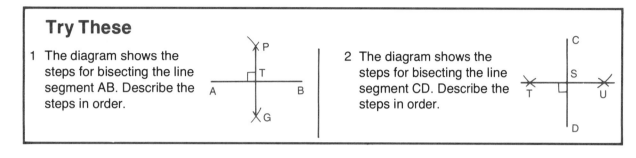

Written Exercises

A 1 (a) Draw a line segment 8 cm in length.
   (b) Construct the right bisector of the line segment.
   (c) What is the measure of each part? Check by measuring.

2 Draw line segments in each position. Then construct the right bisector of each of them.

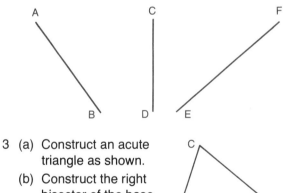

3 (a) Construct an acute triangle as shown.
   (b) Construct the right bisector of the base, BA.

4 (a) Construct an obtuse triangle as shown.
   (b) Construct the right bisector of the base, CD.

5 (a) Construct an equilateral triangle.
   (b) Construct the right bisector of one of its sides.

6 A line segment is drawn on a piece of paper. How can you find the right bisector by folding the paper?

7 (a) Draw a line segment AB on a piece of paper.
   (b) Fold the paper to find the right bisector of AB.
   (c) Measure each part of the line segment.

B 8 In each photo, line segments are marked.
   ► Copy the line segments onto a separate piece of paper.
   ► Find the right bisector of the line segments. Use only a straightedge and compasses.

287

9 (a) Draw a line segment AB 4 cm in length.
  (b) Divide AB into 4 equal parts.

10 A support is to be placed under the wood at its centre. Copy the diagram and locate the position of the support.

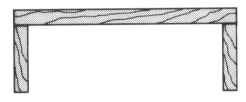

11 A crane is to lift the piece of steel.

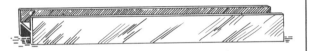

Copy the diagram. Find the position where the steel should be lifted.

Refer to the map below to answer Questions 12 and 13.

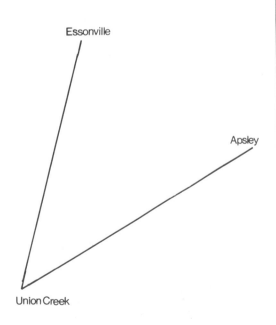

12 A plane leaves Union Creek and is to fly on a path that takes it half-way between Apsley and Essonville.
  (a) Copy the places on a separate piece of paper.
  (b) Construct the flight path of the plane.

13 The scale of the map is 1 cm represents 11.4 km. During its flight how close does the plane approach Essonville?

14 A brace is to be placed halfway along the support CD. Copy the diagram and find the point at which the brace is placed.

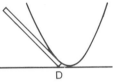

15 Right bisectors of line segments have been used to construct this design. Make a copy of the design.

16 Make a copy of each design.
  (a)   (b)

17 To construct each logo, you need to use the skill of bisecting line segments.
  ▶ Identify how the right bisector is used.
  ▶ Construct a copy of the logo.

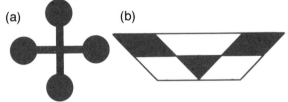

C

18 Write a flow chart to organize the instructions to construct the right bisector of a line segment AB.

Investigating Constructions

bisecting angles

19 (a) Draw an acute triangle (all angles less than 90°).
   (b) Bisect each angle.
   (c) What do you notice about the bisectors of the angles?

20 (a) Construct an equilateral triangle.
   (b) Bisect each angle.
   (c) What do you notice about the bisectors of the angles?

21 (a) Draw any triangle.
   (b) Bisect each angle.
   (c) What do you notice about the bisectors of the angles?

22 (a) Use the diagram shown below. Draw it in your notebook and bisect each of the four angles formed.

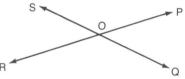

   (b) What appears to be true about the bisectors?

23 (a) Draw any two intersecting lines as shown.
   (b) Construct the bisectors of the four angles.
   (c) What do you notice about the bisectors of the angles?
   (d) Repeat the above steps for another pair of intersecting lines. What do you notice about the bisectors of the angles?

bisecting sides

24 (a) Draw an acute triangle.
   (b) Bisect each side.
   (c) What do you notice about the bisectors of the sides?

25 (a) Construct an isosceles triangle.
   (b) Bisect each side.
   (c) What do you notice about the bisectors of the sides?

26 (a) Draw any triangle.
   (b) Bisect each side.
   (c) What do you notice about the bisectors of the sides?
   (d) Repeat the above steps for other triangles.

27 (a) Construct an equilateral triangle.
   (b) Construct the bisectors of all sides.
   (c) Construct the bisectors of all angles.
   (d) What do you notice about the bisectors in (b) and (c)?

28 (a) Repeat the steps in Question 27 for other equilateral triangles.
   (b) What do you notice about the bisectors of the angles and sides that are constructed?

9.5 Constructing Perpendiculars

Lines that are perpendicular occur frequently in your everyday work. Where do they occur in the following situations?

To calculate the area of the triangle, you need to find the measure of its height (or altitude).

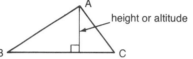

To do so, you need to learn to draw a perpendicular from the point A to the side BC as shown in Example 1.

Example 1

Construct a perpendicular from A to BC.

• A

B ————————— C

Solution

Step 1
Use centre A. Draw arcs as shown to intersect BC at E and F.

Step 2
Use centre E. Draw an arc below BC.

Step 3
Use centre F and same radius as in Step 2. Draw an arc to cut the first arc at D. Join AD.

Check
∠AGE = 90°.
Thus AD ⊥ BC

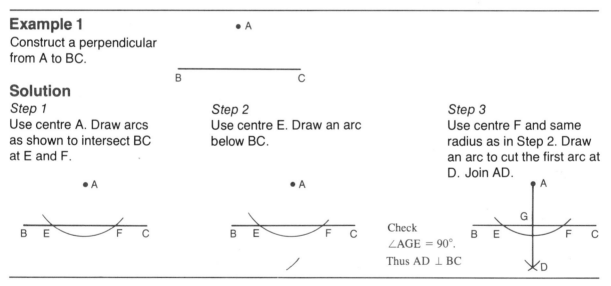

If a point is *on the line*, a perpendicular can be constructed as shown.

Choose a point .   Bisect the straight angle.

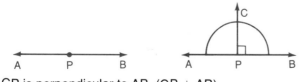

CP is perpendicular to AB. (CP ⊥ AB)

Example 2

(a) Construct the altitude of the stamp from F to DC.

(b) What is the area of the stamp?

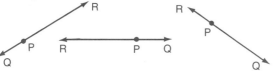

Solution

(a) Construct the altitude.

(b) Measure DC = 4.6 cm.
Measure FH = 3.3 cm.

$$A = \frac{1}{2} \times b \times h$$
$$= \frac{1}{2} \times 4.6 \times 3.3$$
$$= 7.6$$

The area of the stamp is 7.6 cm².

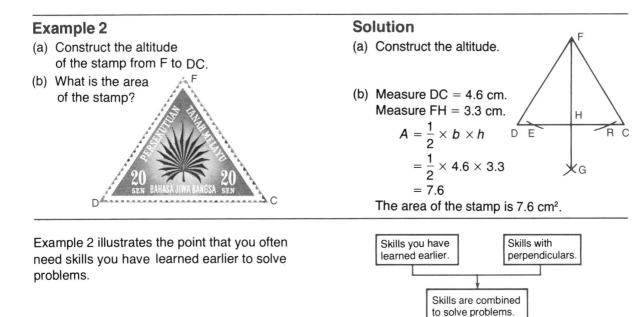

Example 2 illustrates the point that you often need skills you have learned earlier to solve problems.

Skills you have learned earlier.

Skills with perpendiculars.

Skills are combined to solve problems.

Try These

1 A diagram to construct the perpendicular to the line BC at P is shown. What are the steps of the construction?

2 A diagram to construct the perpendicular from P to the line BC is shown. What are the steps of the construction?

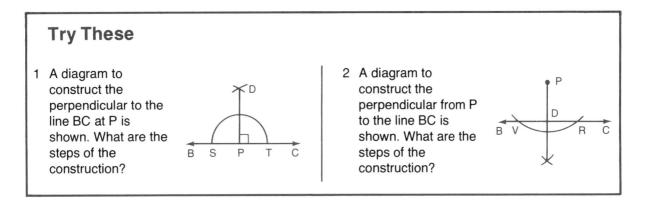

Written Exercises

A 1 Draw line segments in the same position as shown below. Construct a line perpendicular to RQ at point P in the line.

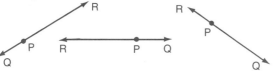

2 (a) Draw any line AB.

(b) Choose any point C on the line.

(c) Draw a perpendicular to the line AB at C.

3 Draw line segments similar in position to those which are shown below. Construct a line perpendicular to MN from a point P.

(a)　　　　　　　(b)

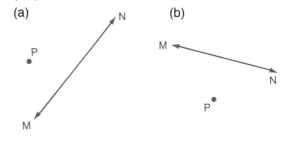

291

4 An altitude of triangle LMN is shown.

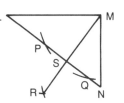

(a) How are the points P and Q located?

(b) How is the point R located?

(c) Which line segment is the altitude of the triangle?

(d) How many altitudes can be constructed for any triangle?

5 Make a copy of each triangle. Construct the altitude of the triangle from P to RS.

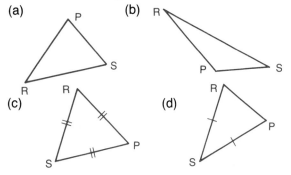

(a)

(b)

(c)

(d)

6 A perpendicular support is to be placed from P to AB.

(a) Copy the diagram.

(b) Construct the support.

B 7 A bridge is built as shown. A perpendicular support is placed on the rock, R, in the river.

(a) Copy the diagram.

(b) Construct the support.

8 To calculate the distance from the boat to the shore a perpendicular is drawn.

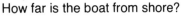

1 cm represents 1 km

How far is the boat from shore?

Questions 9 to 11 are based on the map.

To complete these questions, locate the places on the map and make a diagram showing the places.

9 A plane flies from Mooseland to Ogden. On the map how far is Bridgeville from the path of the plane?

10 A plane flies from Liscomb to Loganville. On the map, how far is Addington from the flight path?

11 The south shore of Nova Scotia is marked by AB. How far in centimetres is Addington from AB?

12 (a) Construct an equilateral triangle with sides 8 cm.

(b) Construct the altitudes.

(c) Measure each altitude. What do you notice about the measures?

C 13 Write a flow chart to organize the instructions for each construction.

(a) Construct a perpendicular from a point P to a line AB.

(b) Construct a perpendicular to a point P in the line AB.

292

Applications: Concurrent Lines And Centre Of Gravity

Earlier, you investigated these properties of triangles. (See *Investigating Constructions*.)

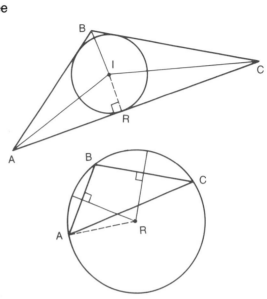

Angle bisectors of a triangle

The bisectors of the angles of any triangle are **concurrent** (meet in a point I). The point I is called the **incentre**.
To construct the **incircle** of △ABC, construct a perpendicular from I to a side AC. The incircle has radius IR.

Right bisectors of a triangle

The right bisectors of the sides of any triangle are concurrent. They meet in a point R, called the **circumcentre**.
To construct the circumcircle of △ABC, use centre R and radius RA.

14 For each triangle, construct its incircle and circumcircle.
(a) isosceles   (b) right   (c) obtuse

For Questions 15 to 17 use stiff cardboard to construct the triangle.

15 For each type of triangle
▶ construct the incentre, I .
▶ can you balance the triangle at I?
(a) acute (b) obtuse (c) right (d) equilateral

16 (a) Construct any triangle.
(b) Locate the incentre I. Can you balance the triangle at I?

17 (a) Construct any triangle.
(b) Locate a point so that if suspended it will balance as shown.

18 The **centre of gravity** of a triangle is the point at which the triangle can be balanced. Describe a procedure for locating the centre of gravity of a triangular piece of cardboard, tin, and so on.

19 For each triangle, construct its altitudes and extend them.
(a) acute   (b) obtuse
(c) right   (d) equilateral
What do you notice about your results above?
The **orthocentre** of a triangle is the point at which the altitudes meet.

20 Construct the incentre, orthocentre and circumcentre for each type of triangle.
(a) acute   (b) obtuse
(c) right   (d) equilateral

21 Use your results in Question 20 . For which triangles do some of the points
(a) lie outside of the triangle?
(b) lie on a side of the triangle?
(c) coincide (occur at the same place)?

9.6 Problem Solving: A Type of Thinking

Once you have learned the properties of figures, you can apply
these properties to the solution of problems or to computations.

The measure of a straight
angle is 180°.

180°

The measure of a right
angle is 90°.

90°

Example 1

Find the missing measures.

(a)

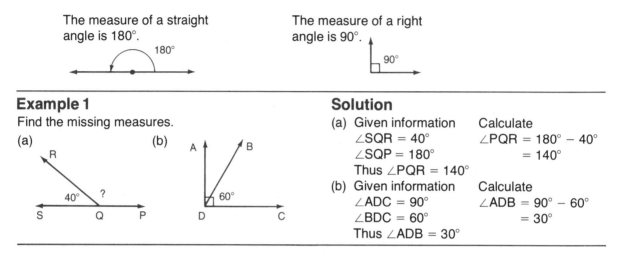

R

40°   ?

S   Q   P

(b)

A   B

60°

D   C

Solution

(a) Given information   Calculate
    $\angle SQR = 40°$ $\angle PQR = 180° - 40°$
    $\angle SQP = 180°$ $= 140°$
    Thus $\angle PQR = 140°$
(b) Given information   Calculate
    $\angle ADC = 90°$ $\angle ADB = 90° - 60°$
    $\angle BDC = 60°$ $= 30°$
    Thus $\angle ADB = 30°$

While you were investigating the properties of triangles these
statements seemed to be true.

I	II	III
For any triangle, the sum of the measures of the angles is 180°.	In an isosceles triangle, the angles opposite the equal sides are equal.	In an equilateral triangle, all angles are equal.

A

B   C

$\angle A + \angle B + \angle C = 180°$

A

B   C
AB = AC
$\angle B = \angle C$

A

B   C
AB = AC = BC
$\angle A = \angle B = \angle C$

Example 2

What is the missing measure in the triangle?

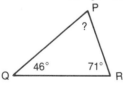

P

?

Q   46°   71°   R

Solution

Step 1   Find the sum of the angles given.

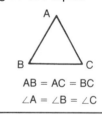

$\angle Q = \ \ 46°$
$\angle R = \ \ 71°$
$117°$

Step 2   Subtract to find the missing angle.

$180°$
$- 117°$
$63°$

Thus $\angle P = 63°$.

Thus, by using the above properties of triangles you can find the
missing measures of the angles *without using a protractor*.

294

The diagram below shows a sketch of this type of thinking.

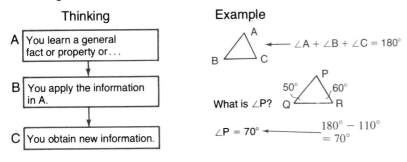

Thinking

A | You learn a general fact or property or...

B | You apply the information in A.

C | You obtain new information.

Example

$\angle A + \angle B + \angle C = 180°$

What is $\angle P$?

$\angle P = 70°$ ← $180° - 110° = 70°$

You use this type of thinking not only in mathematics, but also in many other subjects.

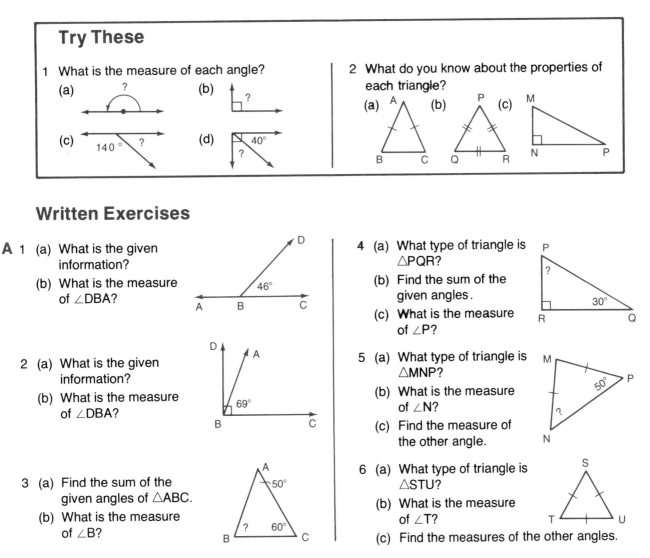

Try These

1 What is the measure of each angle?

(a) ?

(b) ?

(c) 140° ?

(d) 40° ?

2 What do you know about the properties of each triangle?

(a) A B C

(b) P Q R

(c) M N P

Written Exercises

A 1 (a) What is the given information?

(b) What is the measure of $\angle DBA$?

46°

A   B   C

D

2 (a) What is the given information?

(b) What is the measure of $\angle DBA$?

69°

D   A   B   C

3 (a) Find the sum of the given angles of $\triangle ABC$.

(b) What is the measure of $\angle B$?

A 50°

? 60°

B C

4 (a) What type of triangle is $\triangle PQR$?

(b) Find the sum of the given angles.

(c) What is the measure of $\angle P$?

P ? 30°

R   Q

5 (a) What type of triangle is $\triangle MNP$?

(b) What is the measure of $\angle N$?

(c) Find the measure of the other angle.

M 50° P

N ?

6 (a) What type of triangle is $\triangle STU$?

(b) What is the measure of $\angle T$?

(c) Find the measures of the other angles.

S

T   U

B 7 Find the missing measure.

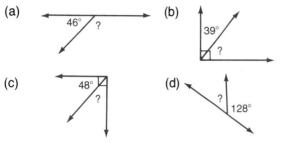

(a) 46° ?

(b) 39° ?

(c) 48° ?

(d) ? 128°

8 Find the measure of the missing angle in each of the following.

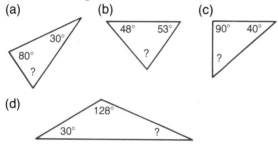

(a) 30° 80° ?

(b) 48° 53° ?

(c) 90° 40° ?

(d) 128° 30° ?

9 Find the measure of the missing angle in each triangle.

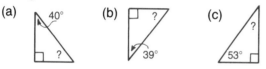

(a) 40° ?

(b) ? 39°

(c) ? 53°

10 (a) What type of triangle is △PQR?

(b) What is the measure of ∠R?

(c) What do you know about ∠P and ∠Q?

(d) Find the measures of ∠P and ∠Q.

R 80° P Q

11 (a) What type of triangle is △PQR?

(b) What is the measure of ∠R?

(c) What do you know about ∠P and ∠Q?

(d) Find the measures of ∠P and ∠Q.

P R Q

12 For each triangle,
  I decide on what measures you are to find.
  II then use the information you are given to find I.

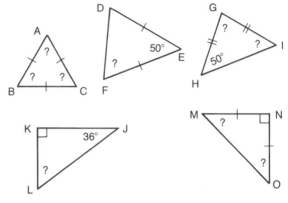

A ? B ? ? C

D 50° E ? F

G ? ? H 50° I

K 36° J L ?

M ? N ? O

13 Two angles of a triangle measure 40° and 70°.
  (a) What is the measure of the third angle?
  (b) What type of triangle is this?

14 A right triangle has one other angle measuring 41°. Find the measure of the third angle.

C

15 (a) Measure the angles of the polygon ABCD.

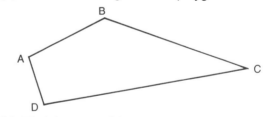

B A C D

  (b) Find the sum of the measures in (a).
  (c) Round off your sum in (b) to the nearest 10°.

16 (a) Draw any polygon with 4 sides.
  (b) Measure the angles and find the sum.
  (c) Round off your sum in (b) to the nearest 10°.
  (d) Repeat the above steps for other polygons of 4 sides.

17 Based on your results in Questions 15 and 16, what seems to be true about the sum of the angles of any polygon with 4 sides?

9.7 Geometry With Circles

The circle is used in many interesting ways. The following situations illustrate a few of these ways.

The baseball warm-up area uses a circle.

The circle is used in recreation and games. How many others do you know?

In order to investigate the properties of a circle you need to know the names of its parts.

Concentric circles have the same centre.

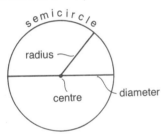

You also need to know the names of line segments and angles related to circles.

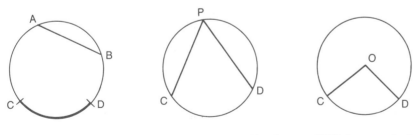

AB is a **chord**.
CD is an **arc.**

∠CPD is an **inscribed angle** on arc CD.

∠COD is a **central angle** on arc CD.

When you study mathematics or any other subject, you need to learn to follow instructions carefully. The exercises that follow provide practice not only in geometric skills, but also in following instructions.

1 From the diagram, name
   (a) a chord.
   (b) a radius.
   (c) a diameter.
   (d) an arc.
   (e) a semicircle.

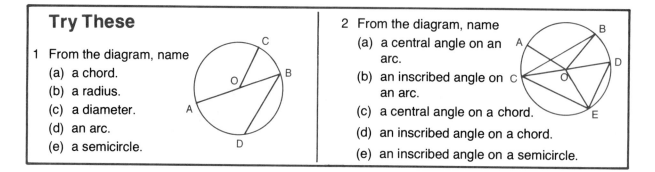

2 From the diagram, name
   (a) a central angle on an arc.
   (b) an inscribed angle on an arc.
   (c) a central angle on a chord.
   (d) an inscribed angle on a chord.
   (e) an inscribed angle on a semicircle.

Written Exercises

Skills With Circles

A 1 Construct a circle with
   (a) radius 5 cm.
   (b) diameter 8.4 cm.

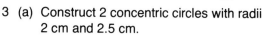

2 A sketch of concentric circles is shown. Construct a copy of the diagram.

3 (a) Construct 2 concentric circles with radii 2 cm and 2.5 cm.
   (b) Draw two diameters that are perpendicular to each other.

4 Use each of the following sketches. Construct a diagram for each one. O is the centre of each circle.

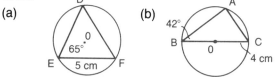

   (a)
   (b)

5 (a) Construct a circle with radius 4.5 cm.
   (b) Choose an arc of the circle. Draw an inscribed angle on the arc.
   (c) Measure the inscribed angle.

6 (a) Construct a circle with radius 2.8 cm.
   (b) Draw a chord 3 cm in length. Draw a central angle on the chord.
   (c) Measure the central angle.

Investigating Properties

B

> *Property I*: Questions 7 to 10 investigate a property of the chords of circles.

7 (a) Construct a circle with radius 4 cm. Mark the centre O.
   (b) Draw a chord, AB, of the circle, 6 cm in length.
   (c) Construct the right bisector of AB.
   (d) Through what point in the circle does the right bisector go?

8 (a) Construct any circle. Record the length of the radius. Mark the centre O.
   (b) Construct a chord of the circle.
   (c) Construct the right bisector of the chord.
   (d) Through what point in the circle does the right bisector go?

9 (a) Repeat the steps of Question 8 for circles with different radii and different chords.
   (b) Through what point in the circle does the right bisector go each time?

10 Use your results in Questions 7 to 9. Write a statement to record your observation.

Property II: Questions 11 to 14 investigate a property of angles drawn on the diameter of a circle.

11 (a) Construct a copy of the diagram. O is the centre.

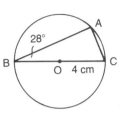

(b) Measure angle BAC. (∠BAC is drawn on the diameter of the circle.)

12 (a) Construct a circle with diameter 9 cm. Mark the centre O. Draw a diameter.

(b) Draw an angle on the diameter of the circle as in Question 11.

(c) Measure the angle in (b). What do you notice?

13 (a) Repeat the steps of Question 12 for circles with different radii and different angles drawn on the diameter.

(b) What is the measure of the angle drawn on the diameter?

14 Use your results in Questions 11 to 13. Write a statement to record your observation.

Property III: Questions 15 to 19 investigate a property of inscribed angles of a circle.

15 (a) A sketch is shown. Construct a copy of the diagram. The radius of the circle is 5 cm.

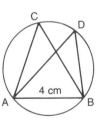

∠C and ∠D are inscribed angles on the chord AB.

(b) Measure ∠C, ∠D. What do you notice about the measures?

16 Repeat the steps in Question 15. Use a circle with diameter 8 cm.

17 (a) A sketch is shown. Construct a copy of the diagram. The radius of the circle is 6 cm.

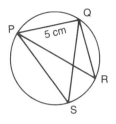

(b) Measure ∠S, ∠R. What do you notice about the measures?

18 Repeat the steps in Question 17. Use a circle with diameter 8.4 cm.

19 Use your results in Questions 15 to 18. Write a statement to record your observation.

Property IV: Questions 20 to 23 investigate a property of central and inscribed angles.

20 (a) A sketch is shown. The radius is 9 cm. Construct a copy of the diagram. Mark the centre O.

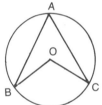

∠BAC is an inscribed angle

∠BOC is a central angle.

(b) Measure ∠BAC and ∠BOC.

21 (a) Construct a circle with radius 5 cm.

(b) Draw a central angle and an inscribed angle on the same arc as shown in Question 20.

(c) Measure the central angle and the inscribed angle. What do you notice about the measures?

22 Repeat the steps in Question 21 for a circle of your own.

23 Use your results in Questions 20 to 22. Write a statement to record your observation.

In the next section you will use the properties I, II, III, IV to do calculations about circles.

9.8 Using Properties Of Circles

An important aspect of your study of mathematics is your ability to use properties of figures and related skills to solve problems. You learned these properties of circles.

I The right bisector of any chord in a circle passes through the centre of the circle.

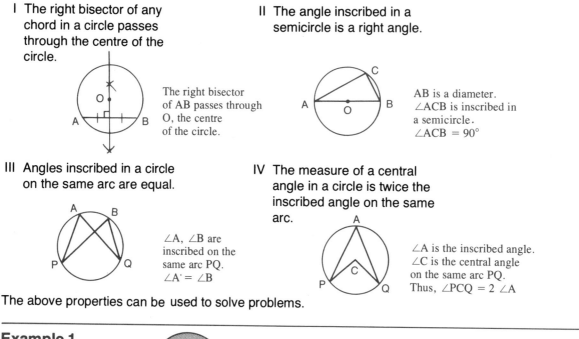

The right bisector of AB passes through O, the centre of the circle.

II The angle inscribed in a semicircle is a right angle.

AB is a diameter.
∠ACB is inscribed in a semicircle.
∠ACB = 90°

III Angles inscribed in a circle on the same arc are equal.

∠A, ∠B are inscribed on the same arc PQ.
∠A' = ∠B

IV The measure of a central angle in a circle is twice the inscribed angle on the same arc.

∠A is the inscribed angle.
∠C is the central angle on the same arc PQ.
Thus, ∠PCQ = 2 ∠A

The above properties can be used to solve problems.

Example 1
A circular disc is shown. Find the centre.

Solution

Step 1
Draw a chord AB. Construct the right bisector. (The right bisector passes through the centre of the circle.)

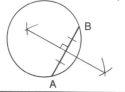

Step 2
Draw another chord PQ. Construct its right bisector. (The right bisector passes through the centre of the circle.)

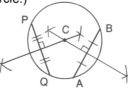

Step 3
Mark the intersection point C. The centre of the circle is C.

The above properties can also be used to solve numerical problems, as shown in Example 2.

Example 2

Find the missing values. Do not use a protractor.

(a)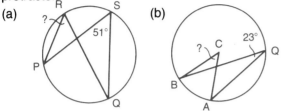

(b)

Solution

(a) ∠R and ∠S are inscribed angles on the same arc PQ.

$$∠R = ∠S$$

Since ∠S = 51°, then ∠R = 51°

(b) ∠Q is an inscribed angle. ∠C is a central angle on the same arc.

Then ∠C = 2 ∠Q. But ∠Q = 23°.

Thus ∠C = 2(23°)
= 46°

Try These

1 For each diagram, what property is shown for each circle?

2 The construction steps to find the centre of the circle are shown. What are the steps in order?

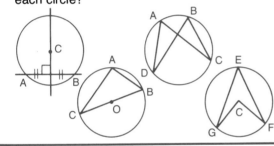

Written Exercises

A 1 (a) Which angles are equal?

(b) What is the value of ∠P?

2 (a) Which angle is the inscribed angle ? central angle ?

(b) What is the missing value of the angle ?

3 (a) Which angle is drawn on the diameter?

(b) What is the missing value ?

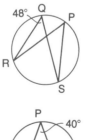

4 (a) Take a circular object. Trace it.

(b) Find its centre.

5 (a) Use a circular can. Trace its base.

(b) Find the centre of its base.

B 6 Find the missing measures. Do not use your protractor.

(a)   (b)   (c)

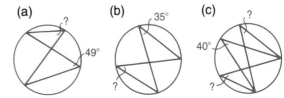

301

7 Find each missing measure.

(a)   (b)   (c)

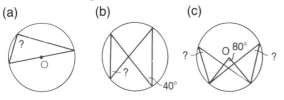

8 Find the missing measures.

(a)   (b)   (c)

9 The corner of a piece of paper is a 90° angle and is placed on a circle as shown.

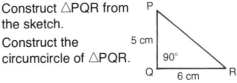

(a) Why is BC the diameter?

(b) How can the above corner be used to find the centre of the circle?

10 Three towns, Akron, Bellows, and Camden are shown.

A water reservoir is to be built the same distance from the three towns.

   A • Akron

   C • Camden

   B • Bellows

(a) Copy the diagram. Construct the right bisector of AB.

(b) Construct the right bisector of CB to intersect the other right bisector at R.

(c) Why is R the same distance from Akron, Bellows, and Camden?

11 (a) Draw any three points on a piece of paper A, B, C.

(b) Construct the right bisector of AB.

(c) Construct the right bisector of BC to intersect the right bisector of AB at O.

(d) Draw a circle with centre O through the points A, B, C.

12 The **circumcircle** of a triangle is the circle that passes through all the vertices of the triangle.

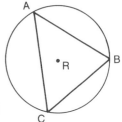

(a) Why is R on the right bisector of AB?

(b) Why is R on the right bisector of CB?

13 (a) Construct △PQR from the sketch.

(b) Construct the circumcircle of △PQR.

14 Draw any triangle PQR. Use the procedure in Question 11 to construct the circumcircle of △PQR.

Calculator Tip

In working with a calculator, you often need to use your common sense skills.
For example, to find each pattern, you need to decide *when to stop*.
Continue the pattern. Predict the answer.
Use your calculator to check.

A 1234 × 8 + 4 = ?
   12 345 × 8 + 5 = ?
   123 456 × 8 + 6 = ?

B 1 ÷ 99 = ?   2 ÷ 99 = ?
   3 ÷ 99 = ?   4 ÷ 99 = ?

C 9 × 321 − 1 = ?
   9 × 4321 − 1 = ?
   9 × 54 321 − 1 = ?

9.9 A Needed Skill: Square Roots For Geometry

In the study of mathematics, you often need to develop new skills in order to solve problems. Finding square roots is a skill that you will need to solve problems.

A square field has an area of 100 m². What is the measure of the sides?

```
┌──────────┐
│          │
│  100 m²  │
│          │
└──────────┘
```

Since $100 = (10)^2$, then 10 is a **square root** of 100. The length of the field is 10 m.

However, 100 can be written as a perfect square, as follows.
$100 = (10)^2$ ←——— 10 is the positive square root.
$100 = (-10)^2$ ←——— -10 is the negative square root.

In problems involving measurement, only positive square roots occur. The symbol $\sqrt{}$
is used to indicate the positive square root of a number.

$\sqrt{100} = 10$ ←——— Since 100 is a perfect square then the square root is quickly found.

There are several ways of finding the square root of a number that is not a perfect square. The easiest way is to use a calculator with a square root key.

When a calculator is not available you can use a table of square root values. These values are calculated by a computer, and give the square roots of numbers rounded off to 3 decimal places.
From the table,

$\sqrt{18} = 4.243$ (to 3 decimal places).
$\sqrt{60} = 7.746$ (to 3 decimal places).

— The number
— The square root of the number

1	1.000	26	5.099	51	7.141	76	8.718
2	1.414	27	5.196	52	7.211	77	8.775
3	1.732	28	5.292	53	7.280	78	8.832
4	2.000	29	5.385	54	7.348	79	8.888
5	2.236	30	5.477	55	7.416	80	8.944
6	2.449	31	5.568	56	7.483	81	9.000
7	2.646	32	5.657	57	7.550	82	9.055
8	2.828	33	5.745	58	7.616	83	9.110
9	3.000	34	5.831	59	7.681	84	9.165
10	3.162	35	5.916	60	7.746	85	9.220
11	3.317	36	6.000	61	7.810	86	9.274
12	3.464	37	6.083	62	7.874	87	9.327
13	3.606	38	6.164	63	7.937	88	9.381
14	3.742	39	6.245	64	8.000	89	9.434
15	3.873	40	6.325	65	8.062	90	9.487
16	4.000	41	6.403	66	8.124	91	9.539
17	4.123	42	6.481	67	8.185	92	9.592
18	4.243	43	6.557	68	8.246	93	9.644
19	4.359	44	6.633	69	8.307	94	9.695
20	4.472	45	6.708	70	8.367	95	9.747
21	4.583	46	6.782	71	8.426	96	9.798
22	4.690	47	6.856	72	8.485	97	9.849
23	4.796	48	6.928	73	8.544	98	9.899
24	4.899	49	7.000	74	8.602	99	9.950
25	5.000	50	7.071	75	8.660	100	10.000

Example
A square field is 88 m². What are its dimensions to 1 decimal place?

Solution
Think of a diagram.

From the table

$$\sqrt{88} = 9.381$$
$$= 9.4 \text{ to 1 decimal place}$$

Thus, the square field has dimensions 9.4 m by 9.4 m.

However, when neither a calculator nor a square root table is available, the square root of a number can be estimated as follows.

$$\sqrt{81} < \sqrt{88} < \sqrt{100}$$
$$9 < \sqrt{88} < 10$$

The square root, $\sqrt{88}$ is between 9 and 10. As an estimate of the square root use the average

$$\frac{9 + 10}{2} = 9.5$$ Check $(9.5)^2 = 90.25$

Since this is greater than 88, then 9.5 is too big.

The estimate of the square root is too big, so use another estimate. Use the average

$$\frac{9 + 9.5}{2} = 9.25$$ Check $(9.25)^2 = 85.56$

which is too small.

The estimate of the square root is too small, so another estimate can be used. Use the average

$$\frac{9.25 + 9.5}{2} = 9.38$$ Check $(9.38)^2 = 87.98$

Thus, $\sqrt{88} = 9.4$ to 1 decimal place.

approximately equal to 88

Try These

1 What is the square root of each number?
   (a) $(6)^2 = 36$ (b) $(7)^2 = 49$
   (c) $(2.1)^2 = 4.41$ (d) $(2.5)^2 = 6.25$

2 What are the missing whole numbers used to estimate each square root?
   (a) $? < \sqrt{20} < ?$
   (b) $? < \sqrt{30} < ?$
   (c) $? < \sqrt{50} < ?$
   (d) $? < \sqrt{70} < ?$

3 (a) The square root of a number is 5. What is the number?
   (b) The square root of a number is 8. What is the number?

304

Written Exercises

A 1 Write each number as a perfect square. Then write its positive square root.

   (a) 64   (b) 81   (c) 121

   (d) 196   (e) 256   (f) 625

2 Use the table. Find the square root of each number to 1 decimal place.

   (a) 12   (b) 40   (e) 84

   (d) 72   (e) 42   (f) 94

3 Use the table. Find the square root of each number to 2 decimal places.

   (a) 21   (b) 34   (c) 67

   (d) 91   (e) 82   (f) 95

4 Calculate. Express your answer to 1 decimal place.

   (a) $\sqrt{75}$ (b) $\sqrt{79}$ (c) $\sqrt{32}$

5 Estimate the square root of each of the following to 1 decimal place.

   (a) 6.9   (b) 15.8   (c) 75.6

   (d) 150   (e) 200   (f) 350

B Another method of finding square roots called **Newton's Method** is shown at the end of the section. You may wish to try the method before completing the following problems.

6 The area of a square is 81 cm². What are the measures of its sides?

7 The area of the stamp is 23 cm². Calculate its dimensions.

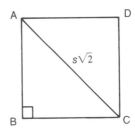

8 The distance AC in the square is given by $s\sqrt{2}$. Calculate AC for each value of s.

   (a) $s = 10.5$ (b) $s = 20.3$

9 The area of a square yard is 72 m². Find the perimeter of the yard to 1 decimal place.

10 A square lot has an area of 500 m².

   (a) Calculate the length of a side.

   (b) How much fencing is needed to enclose the lot?

The amount of time, t, in seconds, it takes an object to fall a distance, d, in metres, is given by the relationship

$$t = \sqrt{\frac{d}{4.9}}$$

11 An object fell 40 m. To find the time, use

$$\sqrt{\frac{40}{4.9}} = \sqrt{8.16}$$

   (a) Find the value of $\sqrt{8.16}$.

   (b) How long did it take the object to fall 40 m? Express your answer to 1 decimal place.

12 A rock is pushed over a cliff 75 m in height. How long will it take the rock to hit the water at the bottom of the cliff? Express your answer to 1 decimal place.

13 Use Newton's Method to find the square root of each number, to 1 decimal place.

   (a) 23   (b) 124   (c) 16.8

Newton's Method: Finding Square Roots

Another way of calculating square roots is the procedure known as
Newton's Method. The flow chart below demonstrates how
Newton's Method works.

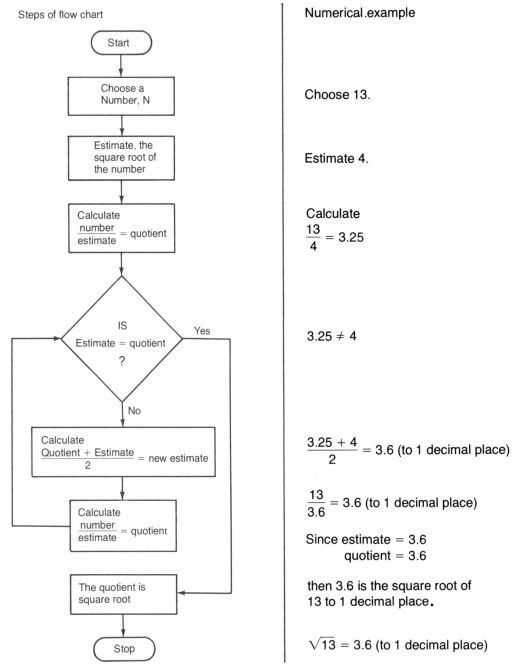

Steps of flow chart

Start

Choose a Number, N

Estimate, the square root of the number

Calculate
$$\frac{number}{estimate} = quotient$$

IS
Estimate = quotient
?

No

Calculate
$$\frac{Quotient + Estimate}{2} = new\ estimate$$

Calculate
$$\frac{number}{estimate} = quotient$$

The quotient is square root

Stop

Numerical example

Choose 13.

Estimate 4.

Calculate
$$\frac{13}{4} = 3.25$$

Yes

$3.25 \neq 4$

$$\frac{3.25 + 4}{2} = 3.6 \text{ (to 1 decimal place)}$$

$$\frac{13}{3.6} = 3.6 \text{ (to 1 decimal place)}$$

Since estimate = 3.6
        quotient = 3.6

then 3.6 is the square root of
13 to 1 decimal place.

$\sqrt{13} = 3.6$ (to 1 decimal place)

9.10 Property Of Right Triangles

Right triangles occur in many situations involving construction. Can you see the right triangles?

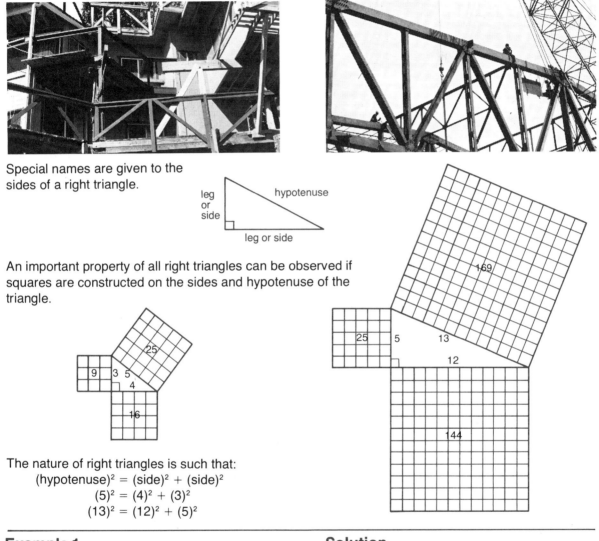

Special names are given to the sides of a right triangle.

An important property of all right triangles can be observed if squares are constructed on the sides and hypotenuse of the triangle.

The nature of right triangles is such that:

$$(\text{hypotenuse})^2 = (\text{side})^2 + (\text{side})^2$$
$$(5)^2 = (4)^2 + (3)^2$$
$$(13)^2 = (12)^2 + (5)^2$$

Example 1

What is the length AB, to 1 decimal place?

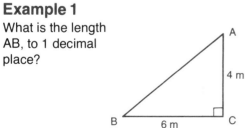

Solution

In △ABC, AB is the hypotenuse.

$$(\text{hypotenuse})^2 = (4)^2 + (6)^2$$
$$= 16 + 36$$
$$= 52$$

Thus hypotenuse $= \sqrt{52}$ (in metres)

From the table $\sqrt{52} = 7.2$ (to 1 decimal place)

Thus, AB = 7.2 m (to 1 decimal place).

The property of right triangles is the following.

> The square of the hypotenuse is equal to the sum of the squares on the other two sides.

The above property is often referred to as the **Pythagorean Theorem** or **Property**. It is named after the Greek mathematician, Pythagoras, who discovered the property.

The property of right triangles can be expressed as these relationships.

$$c^2 = a^2 + b^2$$
or $a^2 = c^2 - b^2$
or $b^2 = c^2 - a^2$

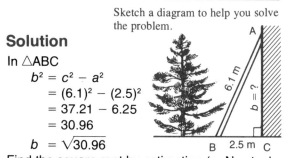

Example 2

A ladder, 6.1 m in length, is placed against a wall. If the base of the ladder is 2.5 m from the wall, how far up the wall does the ladder reach? Express your answer to 1 decimal place.

Solution

Sketch a diagram to help you solve the problem.

In △ABC

$$b^2 = c^2 - a^2$$
$$= (6.1)^2 - (2.5)^2$$
$$= 37.21 - 6.25$$
$$= 30.96$$
$$b = \sqrt{30.96}$$

Find the square root by estimation (or Newton's Method).

$$\sqrt{30.96} = 5.6 \text{ (to 1 decimal place)}$$

Thus, the ladder will reach 5.6 m up the wall.

Try These

1 Complete each of the following.

(a)
5, c, 3
$c^2 = (?)^2 + (?)^2$

(b)
h, 6, 3
$h^2 = (?)^2 + (?)^2$

(c)
h, 9, 5
$h^2 = (?)^2 + (?)^2$

(d)
12, 18, k
$k^2 = (?)^2 + (?)^2$

2 What is missing in each of the following?

(a) $c^2 = a^2 + ?$
(b) $a^2 = c^2 - ?$
(c) $b^2 = c^2 - ?$

A, b, c, C, a, B

3 What is missing in each of the following?

(a) $e^2 = f^2 + ?$
(b) $f^2 = e^2 - ?$
(c) $d^2 = e^2 - ?$

D, e, f, F, d, E

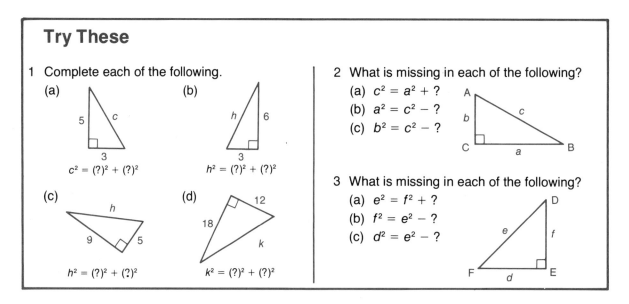

Written Exercises

A 1 Find the value of b to 1 decimal place if $b^2 = 53$.

2 Find the value of m to 1 decimal place if $m^2 = 90$.

3 Find the missing value in each of the following to 2 decimal places.
(a) $a^2 = 3^2 + 5^2$ (b) $c^2 = 6^2 + 7^2$
(c) $b^2 = 9^2 - 5^2$ (d) $b^2 = 10^2 - 8^2$

4 Find the missing values. Estimate the square roots to 1 decimal place.
(a) $a^2 = (1.8)^2 + (3.2)^2$
(b) $b^2 = (8.6)^2 - (5.3)^2$
(c) $c^2 = (7.3)^2 - (4.5)^2$
(d) $(5.8)^2 + (3.0)^2 = b^2$
(e) $c^2 = (9.8)^2 - (7.4)^2$

5 Calculate the length of the hypotenuse in each right triangle.

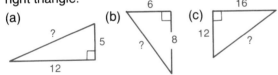

6 Find the missing measure for each triangle.

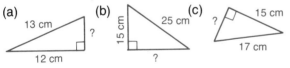

7 Find the missing value to 1 decimal place.

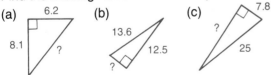

8 Find the length of each diagonal AC.

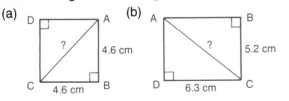

B 9 The span of a roof is the distance SP in the diagram. Calculate the span of the roof.

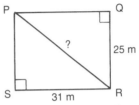

10 A corner lot is used as a short cut to school.

Calculate how much shorter the path PR is compared to walking along PQ and then QR.

11 Use the measures of this baseball diamond to calculate the length of the throw from home to second base.

12 A crane with a 19 m rotating lever drops a load of cement on the end of a 12-m cable so that the load is level with the base of the rotating arm as shown. How far is the load from the edge of the building?

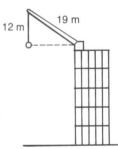

13 A ladder, 7 m long, is placed against a wall so that the foot of the ladder is 2.5 m from the wall. Calculate how high up the wall the ladder reaches.

C

14 (a) How long is each side of a square room that is 12.8 m between opposite corners?
(b) What is the area of the room?

309

Skills To Practise: A Chapter Review

9.1 Measure each angle. What type of angle is it?

(a) 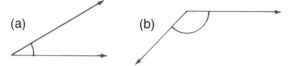   (b)

9.2 The measures of sides and angles are shown for triangles. What type of triangle is it?
(a) 5 cm, 8 cm, 5 cm   (b) 44°, 90°, 46°

9.3 Draw angles in these positions and bisect each of them.

(a)   (b)   (c)

9.5 Draw the line segments and P in the position shown. Construct the altitude from P to each line segment.

•P

9.6 What is the measure of the missing angle? Do not use a protractor.

20°

145°

9.7 (a) Construct circles that have radii measuring 2 cm, 3 cm, 4 cm, 5 cm, 6 cm.
(b) Use the circles in (a) to draw a design.

9.8 How are the angles A and B related in each diagram? O is the centre of the circle.

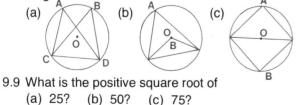

(a)   (b)   (c)

9.9 What is the positive square root of
(a) 25?   (b) 50?   (c) 75?

9.10 Find the missing values.
(a) $b^2 = 10^2 - 6^2$ (b) $m^2 = (1.2)^2 + (1.5)^2$

Problems To Practise: A Chapter Review

9.1 What is the angle between the hands for the clock for each time?
(a) 02:00 (2 am)
(b) 21:00 (9 pm)

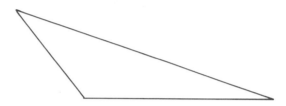

9.2 A triangle is shown. Make suitable measures. Construct a copy of the triangle.

9.4 Construct a design that uses bisectors of line segments and angles.

9.5 Take a piece of paper. Close your eyes. Mark a point P and a line segment AB. Construct a perpendicular from P to the line segment AB.

9.6 A right triangle ABC has an angle that measures 45°. What is the missing angle measure?

9.7 Use the sketch. Make a copy if ABCD is a square with AB = 4 cm.

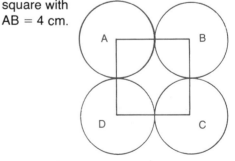

9.9 The area of a square gold medallion is 42 cm². What are its dimensions?

310

Chapter Checkup: A Practice Test

9.1 (a) Complete the chart for each angle.

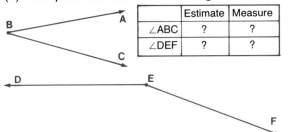

	Estimate	Measure
∠ABC	?	?
∠DEF	?	?

(b) Construct an angle which is equal to the sum of the angles above.

9.2 (a) Draw a sketch of the following triangle. Then construct it.
  △ABC has AB = 3 cm, BC = 4 cm and ∠B = 90°.

(b) Complete the following steps for at least two different triangles.
  A Construct any right triangle.
  B Measure the angles in the triangle.
  C Find the sum of the angles.
  D Round your sum in C to the nearest 10 degrees.

(c) What conclusion can you make based on your work in (b)?

9.3 (a) Draw an angle of 65°. Construct its bisector.

(b) For each piece of pizza,
  ▶ copy the angle.   ▶ find half of each piece.

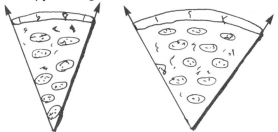

9.4 (a) Draw △ABC with these dimensions:
  AB = 6 cm, BC = 6 cm, ∠B = 90°.

(b) Construct the bisector of AC. Measure how far the midpoint of AC is from the vertex B.

9.5 (a) Construct an equilateral triangle with sides 6.5 cm in length.

(b) Find its incentre, orthocentre, and circumcentre.

(c) Draw the incircle and circumcircle for the triangle.

(d) Where is the centre of gravity of the triangle?

9.6 What is the missing measure of each triangle?

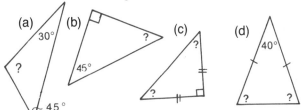

9.7 (a) Construct a diagram(s) to illustrate the meaning of each of the following.
  A central angle on a chord
  B inscribed angle on a chord
  C inscribed angle on a diameter

(b) How are the diagrams in A, B, C, the same? How are they different?

9.8 What is the value of each missing angle?

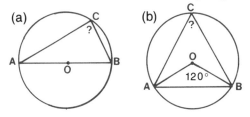

9.9 (a) What is the positive square root of 20? 85?

(b) A square patio is built using 36 square patio stones. What are the dimensions of the patio if each stone is 0.75 m² in area?

9.10 (a) Find the distance AC.

(b) How much shorter is AC than AB + BC?

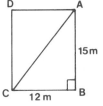

311

Extending Your Skills: Geometry

Cartesian co-ordinates, relations, slope and distance, reflections, translations, rotations, dilatations, applications and problem-solving

Introduction

Each point on the earth's surface can be identified by two numbers:

(60,120)

degrees of latitude   degrees of longitude

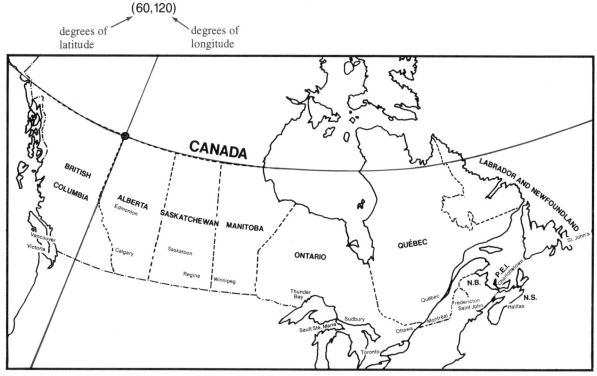

On a smaller part of the earth's surface and in mathematical studies a similar system is used. Ordered pairs of numbers, such as (4, 3) can be used to locate positions or describe a position. To relate positions on the earth's surface or on a plane involves the properties of transformations.

Transformations occur when you try to make a "flat" map of the earth's curved surface. The shape of North America, as it is seen on a map, is not really its true shape, but has been distorted.

10.1 Locating Position

If you are travelling and you want to locate a particular place you use a map. Many maps use a code system based on 2 pieces of information.

D—4

a letter   a number

The shaded region is shown by the code D4.
For example, try to find Leigh Street on the map without using a code. Then look in the region given by the code E6.

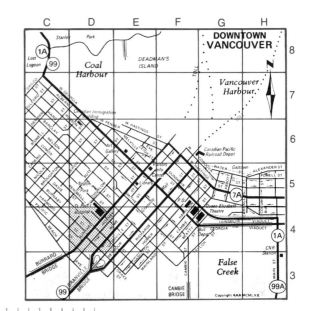

Two number lines drawn perpendicular to each other on a grid can also be used to locate positions. The point of intersection of the number lines is called the **origin**.

To locate a point you use the following components or **co-ordinates**.

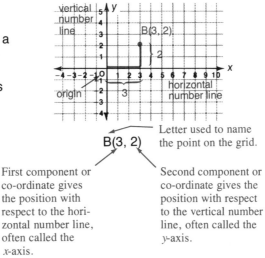

B(3, 2) ← Letter used to name the point on the grid.

First component or co-ordinate gives the position with respect to the horizontal number line, often called the x-axis.

Second component or co-ordinate gives the position with respect to the vertical number line, often called the y-axis.

To **plot** points, you use the given co-ordinates and locate the point on the grid. The grid is often called a **co-ordinate plane** or a **Cartesian plane** (in honour of the mathematician René Descartes).

Example

Plot the points.
A(3, 2)   B(2, 3)   C(−1, 4)   D(4, −1)

Solution

Draw a Cartesian plane.
Label the axes, then plot the points.

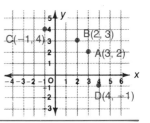

313

Example 1 illustrates that the co-ordinates (3, 2) and (2, 3) name different points. Thus, the *order* of the co-ordinates is important. For this reason, (3, 2) and (2, 3) are called **ordered pairs**.

Throughout your study of mathematics, skill in plotting points and working on the Cartesian plane will occur frequently.

Try These

For Questions 1 and 2, refer to the map.

1 Name a place in the location given by each of the following codes.
   (a) F3   (b) D4   (c) F5   (d) C6

2 (a) Choose a place on the map.
   (b) What is the code for this place?

   For Questions 3 to 5 refer to the diagram.

3 What are the co-ordinates of each point?
   (a) A   (b) B   (c) C   (d) D   (e) E   (f) F

4 Choose a point of your own. What are its co-ordinates?

5 Which points have the same
   (a) x co-ordinate?
   (b) y co-ordinate?

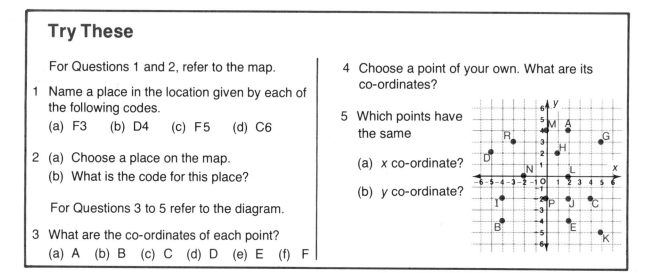

Written Exercises

A 1 Use the map. What is the code for each place?

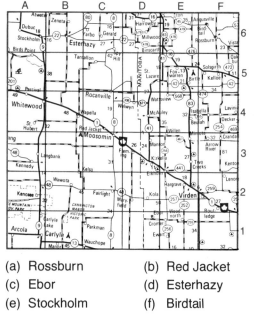

   (a) Rossburn   (b) Red Jacket
   (c) Ebor   (d) Esterhazy
   (e) Stockholm   (f) Birdtail

2 What are the co-ordinates of the points on the grid?

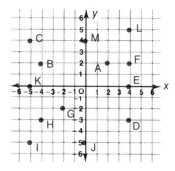

3 Which points in Question 2 have
   (a) the same x co-ordinate?
   (b) the same y co-ordinate?
   (c) equal co-ordinates?
   (d) a positive x co-ordinate?
   (e) a negative y co-ordinate?

4 Construct a Cartesian plane. Plot the following points.
(a) (3, 2)   (b) (−2, 5)   (c) (4, −1)
(d) (0, 4)   (e) (−7, 8)   (f) (−4, 0)
(g) (3, −11) (h) (−8, −4)   (i) (5, −10)

5 What are the co-ordinates of the vertices of each figure?

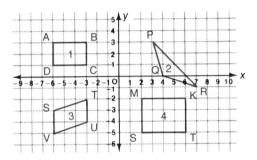

6 (a) A point is on the y-axis. What is its x co-ordinate?
(b) A point is on the x-axis. What is its y co-ordinate?

B 7 (a) Plot the points A(0, 8), B(4, −4), C(−4, 4).
(b) Join the three points in order. What figure do you think you have formed?

8 Plot each of the following sets of points. Join the points in order.
(a) A(0, 5), B(4, −3), C(−4, −3)
(b) D(−7, 1), E(−3, 1), F(−3, −3), G(−7, −3)
(c) P(4, 1), Q(−1, 6), R(−4, 3), S(1, −2)
(d) What type of figure do you think each of the above is?

9 (a) Plot the points P(2, 4), Q(−8, −4), R(−8, 4).
(b) Find the co-ordinates of a fourth point which will form a rectangle with P, Q, and R.

10 A square with co-ordinates A(0, 2), B(4, 6), C(8, 2) and D(?, ?) is plotted. What are the missing co-ordinates of D?

11 Plot the following points and join them.
    (1, 3)   (5, 7)   (−1, 1)   (0, 2)
Write 4 other points that fit the same pattern.

12 (a) Plot the following points.
    A(−7, −4)   B(−3, −2)   C(3, 1)
    D(−5, −3)   E(1, 0)   F(7, 4)
(b) Which point does not seem to belong here?
(c) Write the co-ordinates for two points that fit the above pattern.

13 The axes of the Cartesian plane divide it into four parts, or **quadrants**, which are named as shown. In which quadrant does each of these points occur?

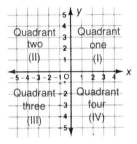

(a) (3, 1)   (b) (−4, 6)
(c) (−5, −2)
(d) (3, −8)   (e) (−2, 3)
(f) (1, −2)

14 Complete the following instructions.
(a) Join (−4, 4) to (4, 4)
(b) Join (4, 4) to (0, 0)
(c) Join (0, 0) to (−4, −4)
(d) Join (−4, −4) to (0, −4)
(e) Join (0, −4) to (4, −4)
Which letter of the alphabet have you made?

C

15 A letter is made from each set of instructions.
(a) Join (−6, −3) to (−4, 2) to (−2, − 3).
    Join $\left(-5\frac{1}{2}, -1\right)$ to $\left(-2\frac{1}{2}, -1\right)$.
(b) Join (−1, −3) to (−1, 2) to (3, −3) to (3, 2).
(c) Join (4, 2) to (6, 2) to (8, 2). Join (6, 2) to (6, −3).
What word have you made?

10.2 Introduction To Relations

A **table** or **chart** may be used to show how information is related.

The first number is two less than the second number.

First Number	Second Number
1	3
2	4
3	5
4	6

An **arrow diagram** may also be used to show how the numbers are related. The diagram at right shows the relation:

The first number is two less than the second number.

The arrow means "is two less than".

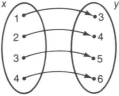

The above information can also be displayed by using ordered pairs.

    (1, 3)
    (2, 4)
    (3, 5)
    (4, 6)

The ordered pair (3, 5) shows that 3 is 2 less than 5.

A set of ordered pairs in mathematics is called a **relation**.

A graph of the ordered pairs can be drawn.

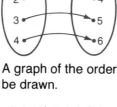

Other ordered pairs could be shown for the above relation if the components are integers.

←and so on (−1, 1), (1, 3), (2, 4), (3, 5), (4, 6), (5, 7) and so on→

   −1 is 2 less than 1

The graph of the relation is drawn.

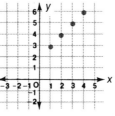

For the above relation, the components of the ordered pairs are related by a formula or equation.

(x, y)
   $y = x + 2$

If $x = 3$, then $y = x + 2$
                $= 3 + 2 = 5$
The ordered pair is (3, 5).

Different letters could also be used to show the above relation.

first component (t, d) second component

$d = t + 2$

For a relation, important words are used.

Domain All the first components of (x, y) are called the
domain of the relation.

Range All the second components of (x, y) are called the
range of the relation.

If the first component can be any real number, then you can find
many other ordered pairs that belong to the relation.

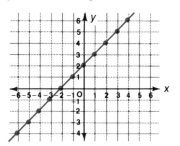
$\dfrac{1}{2}$ is 2 less than $\dfrac{5}{2}$

The graph of all the ordered
pairs is a straight line.

The equation or formula that
relates the co-ordinates is called
the **equation of the line**.

$y = x + 2$ is the equation of
the line, where x
represents any
number.

Since the graph of the relation is a straight line, it is referred to as a
linear relation.

Step 1
To draw the graph, make a table of values.

$y = 3x + 1$

x	y
0	1
1	4
2	7
−1	−2
−2	−5

$x = 1$
$y = 3x + 1$
$= 3(1) + 1$
$= 3 + 1$
$= 4$

Step 2
Plot the points,
(x, y)

Step 3
Draw a straight line
through the points.

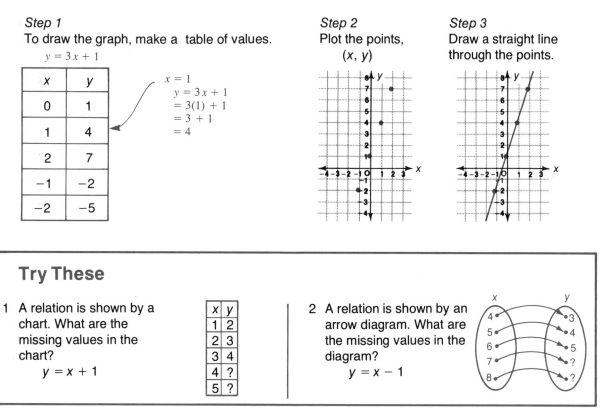

Try These

1 A relation is shown by a
chart. What are the
missing values in the
chart?

$y = x + 1$

x	y
1	2
2	3
3	4
4	?
5	?

2 A relation is shown by an
arrow diagram. What are
the missing values in the
diagram?

$y = x - 1$

Written Exercises

A 1 Various relations are shown by the tables (charts). Find the missing values.

(a)

x	y = x + 3
0	3
1	4
2	5
3	?
?	7

(b)

x	y = x − 1
2	1
3	2
4	3
?	4
6	?

(c)

x	y = 3x
1	3
2	6
3	9
4	?
?	15

2 Relations are shown by arrow diagrams. Find the missing values.

(a)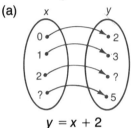

$y = x + 2$

(b)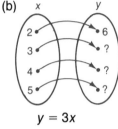

$y = 3x$

3 A relation is shown.
   (a) What is the domain?   (0, 0)   (1, 4)
   (b) What is the range?   (2, 8)   (3, 12)

4 A relation is shown. What are the ordered pairs of the relation?

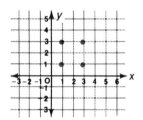

5 For each relation, write
   • the ordered pairs.
   • the domain.   • the range.

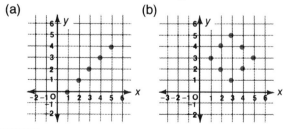

(a)   (b)

6 A relation is defined by
   (x, y)   y = x + 1

   (a) Draw a graph of the relation if x is any whole number.
   (b) Draw a graph of the relation if x is any integer.
   (c) Draw a graph of the relation for x any real number.
   (d) How are the graphs in (a), (b), and (c) alike? How do the graphs in (a), (b), and (c) differ?

7 A relation is shown by an arrow diagram.
   (a) Write the appropriate ordered pairs.
   (b) Draw a graph of the relation.

B 8 Draw a graph of each relation defined as follows.

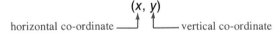
(x, y)
horizontal co-ordinate ⎯⏉ ⏉⎯ vertical co-ordinate

   (a) $y = 2x$, x is a whole number.
   (b) $y = 2x + 1$, x is an integer.
   (c) $y = 2x − 1$, x is any real number.

9 Draw a graph of each relation.

(t, d)
horizontal co-ordinate ⎯⏉ ⏉⎯ vertical co-ordinate

   (a) $d = 2t$,   t is a whole number
   (b) $d = t + 2$, t is any positive number

10 A relation is given by the ordered pairs.
   (t, d), t is a positive number.
   d = 2t

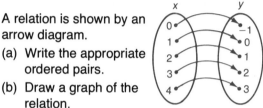

Find each missing value.
   (a) (1, ?)   (b) (?, 6)   (c) (2, ?)

318

11 A relation is given by
the ordered pairs.

(n, c), n is any
whole
number.
$c = 10n$

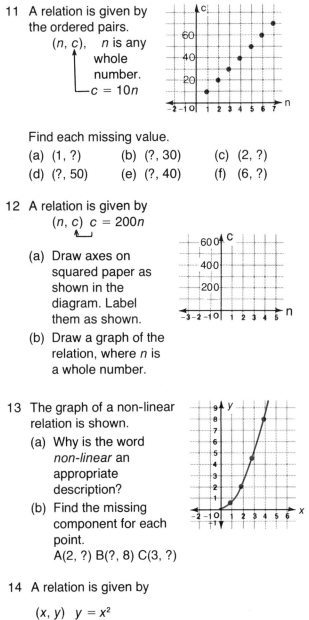

Find each missing value.

(a) $(1, ?)$ (b) $(?, 30)$ (c) $(2, ?)$

(d) $(?, 50)$ (e) $(?, 40)$ (f) $(6, ?)$

12 A relation is given by
(n, c) $c = 200n$

(a) Draw axes on
squared paper as
shown in the
diagram. Label
them as shown.

(b) Draw a graph of the
relation, where n is
a whole number.

13 The graph of a non-linear
relation is shown.

(a) Why is the word
non-linear an
appropriate
description?

(b) Find the missing
component for each
point.
A$(2, ?)$ B$(?, 8)$ C$(3, ?)$

14 A relation is given by

(x, y) $y = x^2$

(a) Copy and complete the
table of values.

(b) Use your answers in (a).
Plot the points shown by
(x, y).

(c) What word best describes
the graph, linear or
non-linear?

x	y
−3	?
−2	?
−1	?
0	?
1	?
2	?
3	?

15 For each relation, an equation is shown.
▶ Complete a table of values.
▶ Draw the graph of the relation. x represents
any number.

(a) $y = x^2 - 1$ (b) $y = \frac{1}{2}x^2$

16 A liquid is boiling and the amount of liquid left
after each hour is shown in the table.

Amount of liquid in litres	7	5	3.8	2.5	2	1.5	1.2
After time t, in hours	0	1	2	3	4	5	6

(a) Draw a graph of the relation (t, A)
shown by the ordered pairs.

(b) Join the points in (a) by a
smooth curve.

(c) Describe the graph of the relation.

C

17 Radioactive material, with a mass of 100 g, is
used in an experiment. The material decays
and data is recorded.

Amount of material left in grams.	65	42	27	18	11	7	5	3	2
After time, t, in hours	1	2	3	4	5	6	7	8	9

(a) Draw a graph of the relation shown by
(t, A)

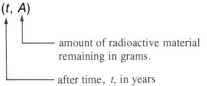

amount of radioactive material
remaining in grams.

after time, t, in years

(b) Join the points in (a) by a smooth curve.

(c) Why is the term "decay" an appropriate
word to describe the graph?

Applications: Linear Relations

Many relations occur in your everyday activities.
Tickets to the game cost $2
each. The formula that relates
the cost, C, and the number of
tickets, n, is

$\overset{\curvearrowleft}{C} = 2n$
$\underset{\text{cost}}{} \quad \overset{\nwarrow}{} \text{number of tickets}$

Cost of 1 ticket, $n = 1$.
$$C = 2n$$
$$= 2(1) = 2 \underset{\text{($2)}}{}$$

Cost of 2 tickets, $n = 2$.
$$C = 2n$$
$$= 2(2) = 4 \underset{\text{($4)}}{}$$

A table of values is used to
show the information.

number of tickets	cost (dollar)
0	0
1	2
2	4
3	6
4	8
and so on	

From the table of values the
ordered pairs are plotted. A
graph of the relation is shown.

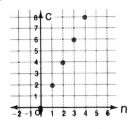

18 Ticket prices for students to the fairground is
$3. The formula that relates the cost, C, and
the number of tickets, n is given by $C = 3n$.

(a) Copy and complete a table of values for
the above relation.

(b) Use the table of values. Draw the graph of
the relation.

(c) For the relation, what are the missing
values?

A(6, ?)   B(?, 15)   C(?, 12)

19 At the car wash, 3 cars are washed every
minute. The total number of cars washed, T, is
given by
$T = 3t$ where t is the number of minutes.
For the relation, the ordered pairs are shown
by (t, T).

(a) Copy and complete the
table of values for the
relation.

t	T
0	?
1	?
2	?
3	?

(b) Use the table of values. Draw the graph of
the relation where t represents any real
number.

(c) For the relation, what are the missing values?
A(6, ?)   B(10, ?)   C(?, 21)

20 A car travels at a speed of 30 km/h. The
distance, d, in kilometres is given by
$d = 30t$, where t represents the time in
hours and is a positive number.
The relation is given by
$\overset{\curvearrowleft}{(t, d)} \overset{\nwarrow}{\longleftarrow} \text{distance travelled}$
$\underset{\text{time, in hours}}{} \quad \underset{\text{in kilometres}}{}$

(a) Label axes as
shown for the
Cartesian plane.

(b) Construct a graph
of the relation.

(c) Find the missing
values for each
ordered pair.
A(5, ?)   B(?, 90)   C(2.5, ?)

10.3 Working With Slope

In your everyday conversation you may have heard the terms,
"*slope* of the hill," "*pitch* of the roof, and so on. These terms are
described in mathematics.

Slope is defined as the ratio.

$$\text{slope} = \frac{\text{rise}}{\text{run}}$$

The ski slope in the valley
requires an expert.

for the ski hill
rise = 326 m
run = 621 m

$$\text{slope} = \frac{\text{rise}}{\text{run}}$$
$$= \frac{326}{621}$$

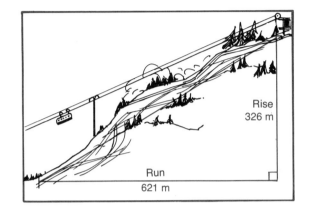

The pitch of this roof is designed
so that the snow will slide off.

for the roof
rise = 1.9 m
run = 4.1 m

$$\text{pitch} = \frac{\text{rise}}{\text{run}}$$
$$= \frac{1.9}{4.1}$$

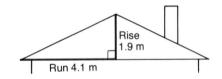

Example 1

A grid has been placed over the photo.
Calculate the slope of the supporting wire to 1
decimal place.

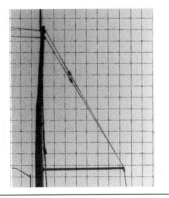

Solution

From the grid
rise = 12 units, run = 7.5 units

$$\text{slope} = \frac{12}{7.5}$$
$$= 1.6 \quad \text{(to 1 decimal place)}$$

The slopes of line segments and lines can also be calculated on the co-ordinate plane. The co-ordinates of points are required.

From the diagram

rise of AB = 5 − 1

run of AB = 6 − 3

$$\text{slope} = \frac{\text{rise}}{\text{run}}$$

$$= \frac{5 - 1}{6 - 3}$$

$$= \frac{4}{3}$$

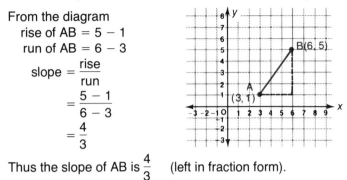

Thus the slope of AB is $\frac{4}{3}$ (left in fraction form).

From the co-ordinates, you can calculate the slope of the line segment.

$$\text{slope} = \frac{\text{difference in } y \text{ co-ordinates}}{\text{difference in } x \text{ co-ordinates}}$$

For segment CD the slope is negative.

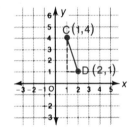

$$\text{slope} = \frac{\text{difference in } y \text{ co-ordinates}}{\text{difference in } x \text{ co-ordinates}}$$

$$= \frac{1 - 4}{2 - 1}$$

$$= \frac{-3}{1} \text{ or } -3$$

Negative slopes occur when you deal with the co-ordinates of points on the Cartesian plane.

Try These

For each of the following, leave the answer in fraction form.

1 The pitch of each roof is given by

$$\text{pitch} = \frac{\text{rise}}{\text{run}}$$

What is the pitch of each roof?

(a)   (b)

2 The slope of the hill is given by

$$\text{slope} = \frac{\text{rise}}{\text{run}}$$

What is the slope of each hill?

(a)   (b)   (c)

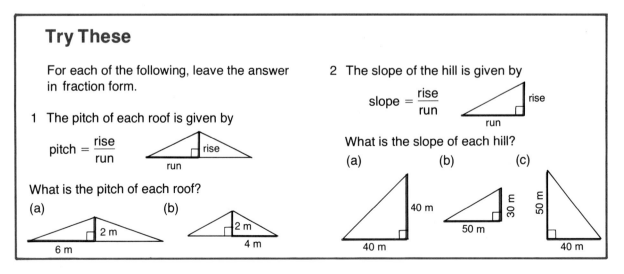

Written Exercises

A 1 Calculate the pitch of each roof to 1 decimal place.

(a)

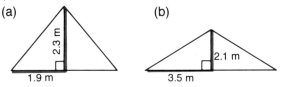

2.3 m

1.9 m

(b)

2.1 m

3.5 m

2 Calculate the slope of the path of the airplane.

20 m

100 m

3 Use the grid to calculate the slope of each of the following line segments.

(a)

(b)

B 4 For the line segment, calculate the
(a) rise. (b) run.
(c) slope.

5 For the line segment, calculate the
(a) rise. (b) run.
(c) slope.

6 For each line segment, calculate its rise, run, and slope.

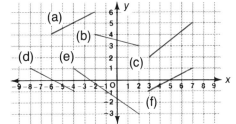

7 A line segment PQ has co-ordinates P(1, 4), Q(3, 1). Find the
(a) run of PQ. (b) rise of PQ. (c) slope of PQ.
(d) run of QP. (e) rise of QP. (f) slope of QP.
(g) What do you notice about the slopes?

8 Each pair of points are on the line. Find the slope.
(a) A(4, 5), B(3, 7) (b) C(1, 6), D(3, 9)
(c) E(−3, 4), F(−8, 1) (d) G(6, −5), H(9, −3)
(e) J(−5, −7), K(8, −2) (f) L(9, −1), M(0, 4)

9 Calculate the slope of each line segment.
(a) AB (b) BC
(c) CD (d) AD
(e) What do you notice about the above slopes?

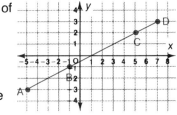

C 10 Construct each line.
(a) slope $\frac{2}{3}$, through (4, 5)

(b) slope $\frac{4}{5}$, through (−1, 3)

(c) slope $-\frac{1}{2}$, through (−3, −4)

(d) slope $-\frac{3}{2}$, through (4, −3)

323

Applications: Inclined Planes and Sliding

An inclined plane is placed as shown.
A protractor is used to measure the
angle.

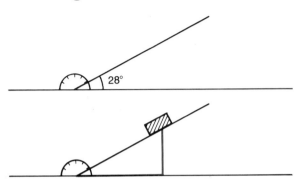

A block of material is placed on the
inclined plane. The slope of the
inclined plane can be calculated.

For Questions 11 to 13 use a smooth plank as
the inclined plane.

11 Use a block of wood on the inclined plane
   Step A Incline the plane until the block of
   wood begins to slide.
   Step B Record the angle of the plane at which
   the sliding begins
   Step C Record the slope of the inclined plane
   at which the sliding begins.

12 Repeat Steps A, B, and C of Question 11 a
   number of times. Record your data in a chart.

	Attempt 1	Attempt 2	Attempt 3
angle			
slope			

What do you notice about the values of the
angles and slopes?

13 Repeat Question 11 and 12 for different
   materials.
   (a) Use for the inclined plane, cardboard,
       steel, etc.
   (b) Use for the block of material, different
       types of wood, bricks, etc.

For Questions 14 and 15, use a smooth
plank as the inclined plane.

14 Use a block of wood. Incline the plane.
   Step A Push the block of wood gently.
   Continue this procedure until the block
   continues to slide on its own.

Step B Record the angle of the inclined plane
   at which the block continues to slide.
Step C Record the slope of the inclined plane
   at which the block continues to slide.

15 Repeat Steps A, B, C, of Question 14 a
   number of times. Record your data in a chart.

	Attempt 1	Attempt 2	Attempt 3
Angle at which the block continues to slide.			
Slope at which the block continues to slide.			

What do you notice about the values of the
angles and slopes?

16 Repeat Questions 14 and 15 for
   (a) inclined planes of different materials.
   (b) blocks of different materials.

17 Compare the results for each material.
   (a) Which of the following angles is greater?
       • The angle at which the block begins
         to slide (Questions 11 to 13).
       • The angle at which the pushed block
         continues to slide (Questions 14 to 16).
   (b) Which of the following slopes is greater?
       • The slope at which the block begins
         to slide (Questions 11 to 13).
       • The slope at which the pushed block
         continues to slide (Questions 14 to 16).

10.4 Calculating Distances

Skills you learn in one area of mathematics are often combined with new skills to solve problems. For example, you have already learned the Pythagorean property of right triangles. Now you can use this property to calculate distances on grids.

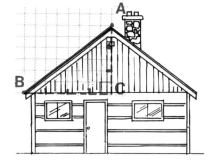

For example, the roof of a cottage is shown drawn to scale. What is the length of the sloped part AB?

Use the Pythagorean property.

$$AB^2 = AC^2 + BC^2 \quad AC = 6$$
$$= 6^2 + 8^2 \quad\quad BC = 8$$
$$= 36 + 64$$
$$= 100$$
$$AB = 10$$

Thus the length of the sloped part is 10 units.

The Pythagorean relationship can also be used to calculate the distance between two points on the Cartesian plane.

Example 1

Calculate the distance between the points P(−5, 1) and Q(3, 7).

Solution

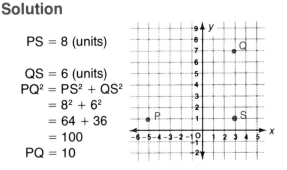

$$PS = 8 \text{ (units)}$$

$$QS = 6 \text{ (units)}$$
$$PQ^2 = PS^2 + QS^2$$
$$= 8^2 + 6^2$$
$$= 64 + 36$$
$$= 100$$
$$PQ = 10$$

Thus the distance between the points is 10 units.

Try These

Questions 1, 2 are based on the diagram.

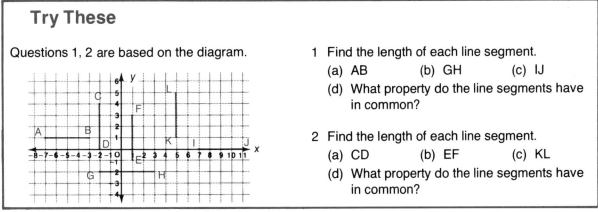

1 Find the length of each line segment.
   (a) AB   (b) GH   (c) IJ
   (d) What property do the line segments have in common?

2 Find the length of each line segment.
   (a) CD   (b) EF   (c) KL
   (d) What property do the line segments have in common?

325

Written Exercises

Calculate the length of line segments to 1 decimal place, unless otherwise indicated.

A 1 Use the diagram.
What is the length of
(a) CE? (b) DE?
(c) CD?

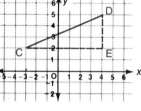

2 Use the diagram.
What is the length of
(a) PS? (b) ST?
(c) PT?

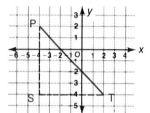

3 Calculate the length of each distance to the nearest whole number.

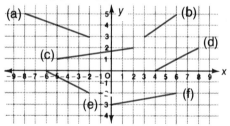

4 Calculate the length of the line segment joining each pair of points.
(a) P(2, 2), Q(4, 5)   (b) P(4, 1), Q(−1, 8)
(c) E(−1, −4), F(−8, 4) (d) R(3, 0), S(0, −7)

5 Which line segment is longer: AB or CD?
A(−3, 7), B(7, −3), C(−3, −3), D(5, 9)

B 6 Find the length
of each side
of the triangle.

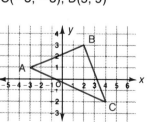

7 The co-ordinates of the vertices of a triangle are A(3, 4), B(9, 4), and C(9, 10).
(a) Find the length of each side.
(b) What type of triangle is it?

8 The co-ordinates of the vertices of a rectangle are P(5, −2), Q(−5, −5), R(−6, 1), and S(3, 4).
(a) Plot the rectangle.
(b) Find the lengths of its sides.

9 Find the perimeter of the triangle STV with co-ordinates S(−6, 2), T(−4, −5), U(3, −3).

10 Two jets have positions with co-ordinates (8, 2) and (−5, −3). How far apart are the planes?

11 A rescue ship, at (−4, 3), receives a distress signal from another ship at (7, −4). How far apart are the ships?

12 The path travelled
by Michael from
start to finish is
shown.

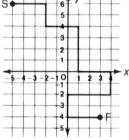

(a) What is the total distance travelled?
(b) What is the shortest distance from start to finish?

C 13 Points S(−7, −4) T(−3, −1) U(1, 2) are plotted. Calculate the following lengths.
(a) ST   (b) TU   (c) SU
(d) Find the sum of ST and TU. How does it compare with the length of SU?
(e) Based on the above results, what statement can you make about the points S, T, and U?

326

10.5 Reflections and Applications

When you think of reflections you probably think of the following.

When you look into the mirror you are looking at a **transformation** of yourself. Some types of reflections transform you to such an extent that you look very different from your real self.

When you look in a regular mirror, your image seems to be just as far back from the mirror as *you* yourself are in front of the mirror.

The reflection at right is in the line LE which is appropriately called the **reflection line**. A reflection in a line (such as LE) has the following properties.

- Points P and P′ are **equidistant** (equally distant) from the reflection line. (In other words, PS = P′S.)

- PP′ is perpendicular to the reflection line. (In other words, ∠PSE = 90°.)

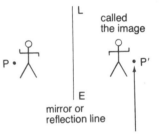

Use the symbol P′ to show the image of the point P.

Example 1

Find the image of
△ABC in the
reflection line ST.

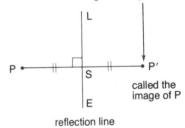

Solution

Step 1
To find the image of the triangle, use the properties of a reflection line above to reflect the vertices of the triangle through the reflection line ST.

Step 2
Join the vertices A′, B′, and C′ to obtain the image triangle.

The *x*- and *y*-axes can also be used as reflection lines for figures drawn on the Cartesian plane.

Example 2

A triangle with vertices P(−6, 4), Q(−5, −2), and R(−2, −4) is reflected in the *y*-axis. Find its image.

Solution

Step 1
Plot the triangle.

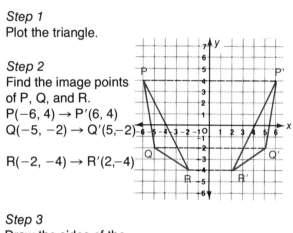

Step 2
Find the image points of P, Q, and R.
P(−6, 4) → P′(6, 4)
Q(−5, −2) → Q′(5,−2)
R(−2, −4) → R′(2,−4)

Step 3
Draw the sides of the image triangle.

How are the properties of a reflection used to find △P′Q′R′?

Points, and how they are related to one another, are important topics of study to scientists, architects, and so on. A **transformation** relates points and their images. A **reflection** is a transformation that relates points and their images in a certain way. You will study other types of transformations in the next few sections.

Try These

1 Use the diagram. Which points are reflections of each other in the reflection line?

2 A figure is reflected in a vertical line.

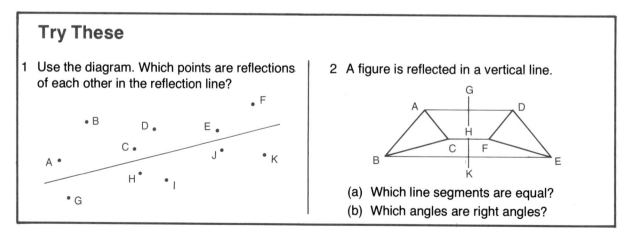

(a) Which line segments are equal?
(b) Which angles are right angles?

Written Exercises

A 1 The letter A is a reflection of itself in the reflection line RL. Which other letters have this property?

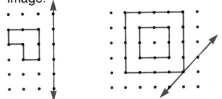

2 The letter H can be reflected in two ways as shown. Which other letters have this property?

3 Each message is what you obtain after it is reflected. Read the message. (You may need a mirror to help you.)

(a) Do you know any good books?

(b) Don't you look silly holding a mirror to read your book?

4 Make a copy of the points and the reflection line, ℓ. Construct the images of the points.

(a)   (b)   •   (c)

5 Make a copy of the figure and the reflection line. Use the properties of reflection to construct its image.

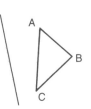

6 Make a copy of each figure and its corresponding reflection line. Use the properties of reflection to construct each image.

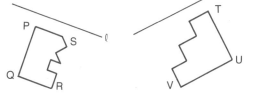

7 Make a copy of each figure and its corresponding reflection line. Use the properties of reflection to construct each image.

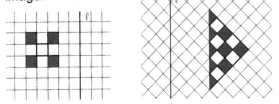

8 Use squared paper. Make a copy of each figure and its corresponding reflection line. Use the properties of reflection to construct each image.

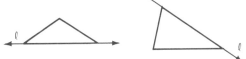

9 (a) Draw a triangle as shown. Reflect the triangle with respect to each of the reflection lines, ℓ.

(b) Draw a horizontal reflection line through each triangle. Find the image of the triangle in the reflection line.

(c) Draw a vertical reflection line through each triangle. Find the image of the triangle in the reflection line.

B 10 (a) Find the image of the rectangle through each of these reflection lines.

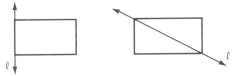

(b) Draw any reflection line through your rectangle. Construct the reflection of the rectangle.

329

11 Reflections have been used to make each design. How are reflections used for each design? Make a copy of each design.

(a)   (b)

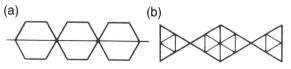

12 Make a copy of each design.

(a)   (b)

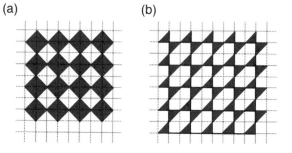

(c) Make a design of your own.

13 On graph paper draw the x- and y-axes. Plot each point. Find the image of each point for the reflection line.

(a) (4, 1); x-axis   (b) (−2, 5); x-axis

(c) (7, −2); y-axis   (d) (10, 5); y-axis

(e) (−8, −7); x-axis   (f) (5, 0); y-axis

14 Plot each figure on your own set of axes. Find the image of each figure by reflecting it
• first in the x-axis.
• then in the y-axis.

(a)   (b)

(c)   (d)

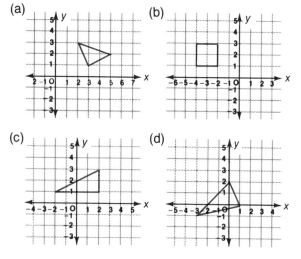

Questions 15 to 18 investigate certain properties of a reflection for a figure △XYZ.
    X(2, 2)   Y(4, 5)   Z(6, 3)

15 (a) Is the order of the vertices of △XYZ clockwise or counter-clockwise?

(b) Reflect △XYZ in the x-axis to find the image △X′Y′Z′. Is the order of the vertices clockwise or counter-clockwise?

16 (a) Calculate the distances XY, X′Y′; YZ, Y′Z′; XZ, X′Z′.

(b) What do you notice about your answers in (a)?

17 (a) Measure each pair of angles.
∠XYZ, ∠X′Y′Z′; ∠YZX, ∠Y′Z′X′; ∠YXZ, ∠Y′X′Z′

(b) What do you notice about your answers in (a)?

18 (a) Calculate the area of △XYZ and △X′Y′Z′.

(b) What do you notice about your answers in (a)?

19 Repeat the instructions of Questions 15 to 18 for each triangle.

(a) △XYZ   X(2, −2), Y(0, −3), Z(3, 2)

(b) △XYZ   X(1, 6), Y(2, −4), Z(−5, −2)

20 Rectangle PQRS has vertices
P(5, 3)   Q(7, −1)   R(3, −3)   S(1, 1)

(a) Apply the steps in Questions 15 to 18 to rectangle PQRS.

(b) Make a list of your observations.

21 (a) Choose a figure of your own and plot it on the Cartesian plane.

(b) Apply the steps in Questions 15 to 18 to your figure.

(c) Make a list of your observations.

22 Use your results in Questions 20 and 21. A figure is reflected in a line to obtain the image figure. For a reflection,

(a) what does not change?

(b) what does change?

Applications: Reflection In A Pool

Skills with reflections can be applied to the game of billiards. For example, to make the white cue ball hit the coloured ball you can deflect the ball as shown. Obtain the image of the coloured ball by using the edge of the billiard table as the reflection line.

The distance AB = AB′.

∠EAB = 90°

Then to make the shot, shoot at the image ball.

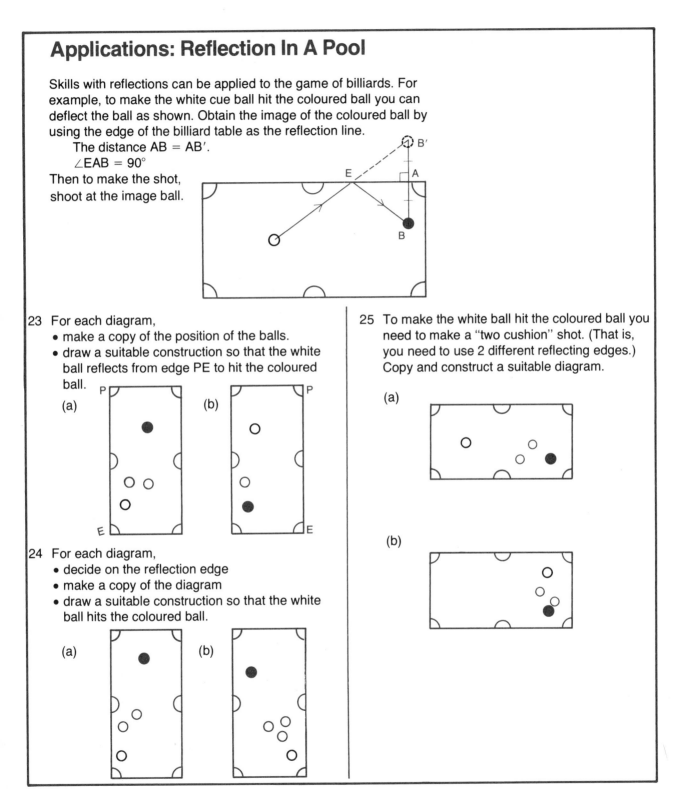

23 For each diagram,
   • make a copy of the position of the balls.
   • draw a suitable construction so that the white ball reflects from edge PE to hit the coloured ball.
   (a)   (b)

24 For each diagram,
   • decide on the reflection edge
   • make a copy of the diagram
   • draw a suitable construction so that the white ball hits the coloured ball.
   (a)   (b)

25 To make the white ball hit the coloured ball you need to make a "two cushion" shot. (That is, you need to use 2 different reflecting edges.) Copy and construct a suitable diagram.
   (a)

   (b)

10.6 Translating Figures

Many electronic games use a specific movement or series of movements. For example, each figure on the screen at the right moves in the same direction and the same distance at regular intervals.

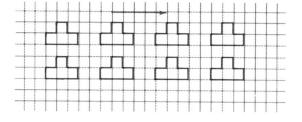

Each movement is a translation.

You may also call a translation a **slide**.

Two steps have been applied to the figure on the right.
- 4 units down
- 3 units to the left

The **translation arrow** shows
- the distance the figure is translated.
- the direction in which the figure is translated.

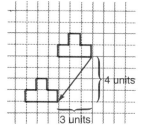

4 units

3 units

A translation is a transformation that relates points to their images in a certain way.

△ABC is translated. The result is the image figure △A′B′C′.
A translation, has the following properties:
- AA′ = BB′ = CC′
- AA′‖BB′‖CC′ — The line segments are parallel.

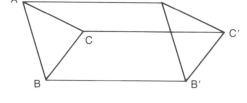

A translation arrow is used to find the image of a figure on the Cartesian plane.

Example

Use the translation arrow given at right to translate △ABC and thus find its image.

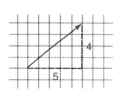

4

5

$A(-3, 3)$ $B(-5, -1)$ $C(-2, 0)$

How are the properties of a translation used to find △A′B′C′?

Solution

Sketch the triangle. First translate the figure 5 units to the right and then 4 units up.

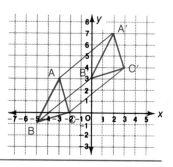

332

Translations are often used to create designs. How are translations used to create these designs?

Try These

1   Use the diagram. Which figures are translations of the figure □┐ ? Which are not? Give reasons for your choice.

2   A figure is translated.

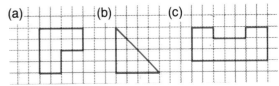

(a)   Which line segments are equal?
(b)   Which lines are parallel?

Written Exercises

Each square in Questions 3 and 4 represents 1 cm².

1   A figure is translated. Describe each translation.

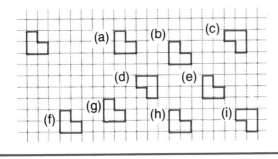

2   Each figure is translated. Describe the translation.

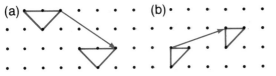

3   Translate each figure
   ▶ 5 cm to the right.
   ▶ 3 cm down.

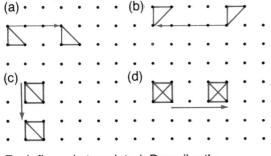

4   Translate each figure
   ▶ 6 cm to the left.
   ▶ 3 cm up.

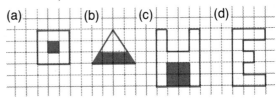

5 Make a copy of each figure. Use the translation arrow, and the properties of translation to draw the images.

(a) (b) (c)

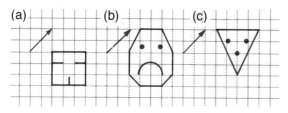

6 Make a copy of each figure and the corresponding translation arrow. Use the properties of translation to construct each image.

(a) (b) (c)

7 Make a copy of each figure and the corresponding translation arrow. Use the properties of translation to construct each image.

(a) (b) (c)

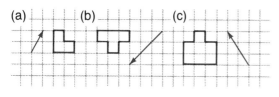

8 △ABC and its image △A'B'C' are shown. Why is △A'B'C' the translation image of △ABC?

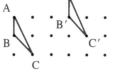

9 The image of each of the following original figures is shown. Copy each figure and its image. Find the direction and length of the translation arrow.

(a) (b) (c)

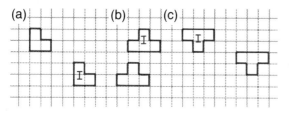

10 Draw a triangle as shown. Construct the image triangle with respect to each translation arrow.

(a) (b) (c) (d) (e) (f) (g)

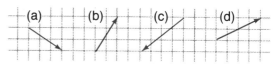

11 Draw a rectangle on squared paper. Construct the translation image for each translation arrow.

(a) (b) (c) (d)

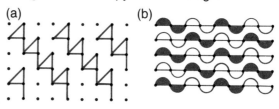

12 A translation has been used to make each design. How are translations used for each design? Make a copy of each design.

(a) (b)

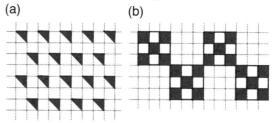

13 Make a copy of each design.

(a) (b)

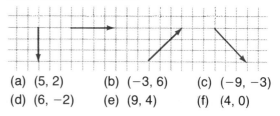

(c) Make a design of your own.

14 On squared paper draw the x- and y-axes. Plot each point. Find the image of each point for each translation arrow.

(a) (5, 2)   (b) (−3, 6)   (c) (−9, −3)
(d) (6, −2)   (e) (9, 4)   (f) (4, 0)

15 Translate each point for the following translation arrows.

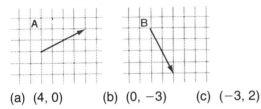

(a) (4, 0)   (b) (0, −3)   (c) (−3, 2)

16 ▶ Plot each figure on your own set of axes.
    ▶ Find the image of each figure for the translation arrow.

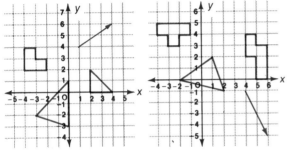

17 Describe the translations needed to move the box B out of the warehouse to position A.

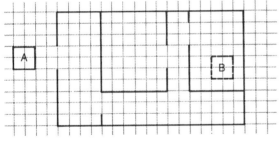

18 Describe the translations needed for ▣ to travel the corridor.

Questions 19 to 26 investigate certain properties of a translation for a figure △PQR.
    P(−3, 2)   Q(1, 4)   R(2, −1)

19 (a) Is the order of the vertices of △PQR clockwise or counter-clockwise?
    (b) Translate △PQR to find the image △P′Q′R′. Is the order of the vertices of △P′Q′R′ clockwise or counter-clockwise?

20 (a) Calculate the distances PQ, P′Q′; PR, P′R′; QR, Q′R′.
    (b) What do you notice about your answers in (a)?

21 (a) Measure each pair of angles.
        ∠PQR, ∠P′Q′R′; ∠QRP, ∠Q′R′P′; ∠RPQ, ∠R′P′Q′
    (b) What do you notice about your answers in (a)?

22 (a) Calculate the areas of △PQR and △P′Q′R′.
    (b) What do you notice about your answers in (a)?

23 Repeat the instructions of Questions 19 to 22 for each triangle.
    (a) △PQR   P(3, 0), Q(1, −1), R(4, 4)
    (b) △PQR   P(0, 7), Q(1, −3), R(−6, −1)

24 A rectangle ABCD is given by
    A(2, 1) B(4, −3) C(0, −5) D(−3, −1)
    (a) Apply the steps in Questions 19 to 22 to the rectangle ABCD.
    (b) Make a list of your observations.

25 (a) Choose a figure of your own and plot it on the Cartesian plane.
    (b) Apply the steps in Questions 19 to 22 to your figure.
    (c) Make a list of your observations.

26 Use your results in Questions 19 to 25. A figure is translated to obtain the image figure. For a translation what does
    (a) not change?   (b) change?

335

Applications: Sailing Trips

A wind pushes a boat from its original position A to position B. The boat is displaced from A to B. A translation arrow is used to show the **displacement**.

At B, the wind changes and pushes the boat as shown.

The diagram shows the ships original position A, and its final position C.

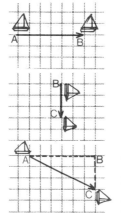

The translation arrow shows the displacement of the boat from A to C. The translation arrow represented by the arrow AC is called the **resultant displacement** of the arrow AB and arrow BC.

27 Make a copy of each diagram. Find the resultant displacement for each of the following.

(a) (b)

(c) (d)

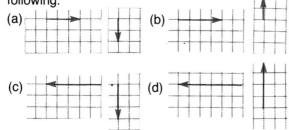

28 A sailboat begins at position A.
 ▶ Make a copy of the diagram. The translation arrows for each trip are shown. Name the co-ordinates of its final position.
 ▶ Construct the resultant displacement.
(a) A sailboat is at (0, 5).

First part of trip.   Second part of trip.

(b) A tanker is at (3, −2).

First part of trip.   Second part of trip.

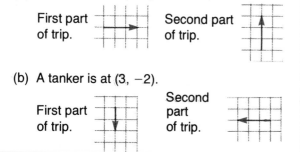

29 A cruise ship is at a port with co-ordinates (−3, −5). The translation arrows for 3 parts of the cruise are shown.
 (a) Find the co-ordinates of its final port.
 (b) Construct the resultant displacement for the cruise.

30 The co-ordinates of the home port of each cruise ship are shown. Each part of the trip is shown by an arrow.
 ▶ Find the co-ordinates of its final port.
 ▶ Construct the resultant displacement.

Home Port   Trips

(a) (2, 1)

(b) (−3, 1)

(c) (−4, −2)

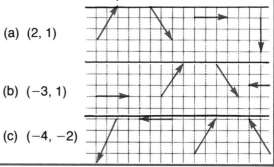

336

10.7 Rotations Around Us

The movement of the hands of a clock, the wheels of a bicycle, or the wipers on a car are just a few examples of a **rotation** about a point.

To show a rotation you must know the following information.
  I The point about which the figure is rotated (called the **centre of rotation** or **turn centre**).
 II The amount of turn (called the **angle of rotation**).
III The direction of rotation (**clockwise** or **counter-clockwise**).

counter-clockwise

positive

clockwise

negative rotation

A **turn arrow** shows the direction of the turn and the amount of turn.

$\frac{1}{4}$ turn (90°)
counter-clockwise

$\frac{1}{2}$ turn (180°)
clockwise

Example 1

Find the image by rotating the figure.
► The turn centre is point P.
► The angle and direction of the rotation is shown by the turn arrow.

180°

P

A   D

B   C

Solution

Step 1
Find the image of each point.

A ⟶ A'   C ⟶ C'
B ⟶ B'   D ⟶ D'

C'. . B'.

D'• . A'•

. P• .

A ⌐ D
B ⌐ C

Step 2
Join A', B', C', and D' to draw the image figure A'B'C'D'.

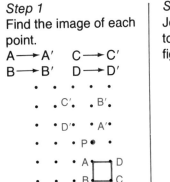

•C'⌐B'•

•D'⌐A'•

• P• •

A ⌐ D
B ⌐ C

Rotation images can be found on the Cartesian plane.

Example 2

Find the image of △PQR
P(3, 3)   Q(2, 1)   R(5, 1)
for a turn of 180° clockwise about the origin.

Solution

Step 1
Find the image of
each point.
P → P′
Q → Q′
R → R′

Sketch a diagram.

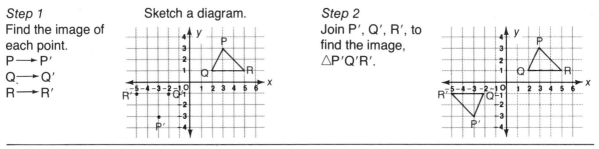

Step 2
Join P′, Q′, R′, to
find the image,
△P′Q′R′.

A rotation relates points in a special way. A rotation is thus a
transformation. Different designs can be created based on the
properties of rotation.

Try These

For each rotation a figure, AB, and its rotation
image about the turn centre T is shown. What is
▶ the angle of rotation?
▶ the direction of rotation?

(a)   (b)   (c)

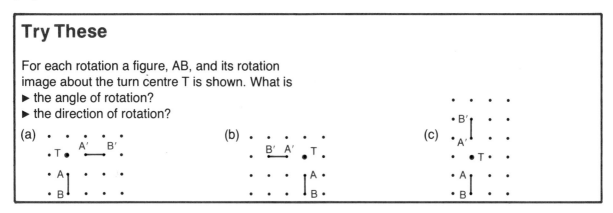

Written Exercises

A 1 (a) Each letter of the message has been
rotated either 90° or 180° clockwise. The
turn centres are indicated by a ●. What is
the message?

(b) Make a rotation message of your own.

2 A figure is rotated about a turn centre T.
Describe each rotation.

(a)   (b)

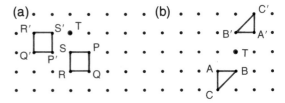

338

3 A turn arrow is shown. Copy each figure. Find the image. Use the turn centre T.

4 Make a copy of each figure. Use the turn arrow to find the image. Use the turn centre T.

(a)　　　(b)　　　(c)

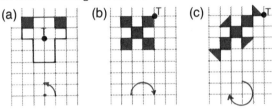

5 Find the image point under a $\frac{1}{4}$ turn (90°) about the origin of the following

(a)　　　　(b)　　　　(c)

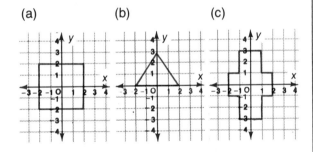

6 A rotation has been used to make the design.

(a) How is the design made?

(b) Make a copy of the design.

7 Make a copy of each design based on rotation.

(a)　　　　　　(b)

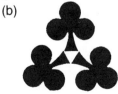

(c) Make a design of your own based on rotations.

Questions 8 to 12 investigate certain properties of rotation for a figure △MNP.

M(2, 0)　　N(5, 0)　　P(2, 4)

8 (a) Is the order of the vertices of △MNP clockwise or counter-clockwise?

(b) Rotate △MNP 90° clockwise to obtain the image △M′N′P′. Is the order of the vertices of the image clockwise or counter-clockwise?

9 (a) Calculate the distances MN and M′N′, MP and M′P′, NP and N′P′.

(b) What do you notice about your answers in (a)?

10 (a) Measure each pair of angles. ∠MNP and ∠M′N′P′, ∠NMP and ∠N′M′P′, ∠NPM and ∠N′P′M′.

(b) What do you notice about your answers in (a)?

11 (a) Calculate the areas of △MNP and △M′N′P′.

(b) What do you notice about your answer in (a)?

12 Repeat the instructions of Questions 8 to 11 for each triangle.

(a) △MNP　M(7, 2), N(7, −2) P(10, 0)

(b) △MNP　M(0, −2), N(0, −4), P(−3, −4)

13 A rectangle DEFG is given by D(3, −1) E(8, −1) F(8, 2), G(3, 2)

(a) Apply the steps in Questions 8 to 11 to the rectangle DEFG.

(b) Make a list of your observations.

14 (a) Choose a figure of your own and plot it on the Cartesian plane.

(b) Apply the steps in Questions 8 to 11 to your figure.

(c) Make a list of your observations.

15 Use your results in Questions 8 to 14. A figure is rotated to obtain the image figure. For a rotation,

(a) what does not change?

(b) what does change?

10.8   Working With Symmetry

Many appealing figures appear in the areas of advertising and nature. How many of these appeal to you?

Each of the above figures displays a property called **symmetry**.

Line Symmetry
The butterfly has line symmetry. One side can be reflected in the line, ℓ, to obtain the other side.

In other words, if the butterfly is folded along the line ℓ, the two sides will match. The line, ℓ, is called the **line of symmetry**.

2 lines of
symmetry

3 lines of
symmetry

4 lines of
symmetry

Rotational or turn symmetry
The figure at right cannot be folded along a line. However, the figure can be turned about the point T, and each image thus produced will fit on top of the given figure.

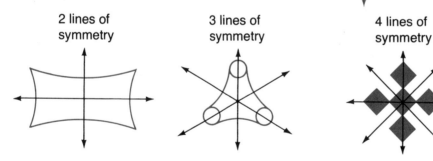

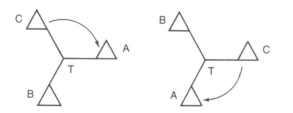

During a complete rotation about the point T, the figure fits onto itself three times. The figure is said to have **turn** or **rotational symmetry** of order 3. The **order of rotational symmetry** for a figure is the number of times the figure fits onto itself for a complete turn.

The order is 2, since the propellor fits onto itself twice for a complete turn.

The order is 3. Why?

The order is 4. Why?

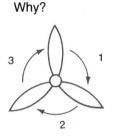

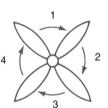

Each of the following figures fits onto itself after a half turn.

Each figure is thus said to have **point symmetry**.

Written Exercises

A 1 How many lines of symmetry do each of the following figures have?

(a)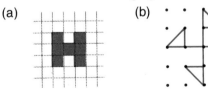

(b)

2 What is the order of rotational (turn) symmetry for each of the following figures?

(a)

(b)

3 Which of the figures in Questions 1 and 2 have point symmetry?

4 How many lines of symmetry does the logo have?

5 What is the order of turn symmetry for the logo?

6 What type of symmetry does each figure have?

(a)

(b)

7 What type of symmetry does each of the following have?

(a)

(b)

341

B 8 Construct each figure and draw its lines of symmetry.

(a) 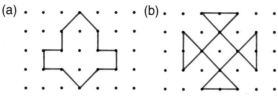 (b)

9 Construct each of the following types of figures. How many lines of symmetry are there?
(a) equilateral triangle   (b) square
(c) isosceles triangle   (d) rectangle

10 Squared paper is used to create designs that have symmetry.

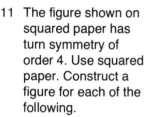

(a) How many lines of symmetry does each design have?
(b) Construct a design of your own. How many lines of symmetry does it have?

11 The figure shown on squared paper has turn symmetry of order 4. Use squared paper. Construct a figure for each of the following.

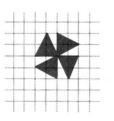

(a) A figure with turn symmetry of order 3.
(b) A figure with 2 lines of symmetry.
(c) A figure with point symmetry.

12 Figures are drawn with the following co-ordinates for its vertices.
▶ Draw each figure.
▶ What type of symmetry does each figure have? Indicate the order of turn symmetry. Draw the lines of symmetry.
(a) S(−6, 4), T(−5, 1), U(−7, 1)
(b) A(−4, 3), B(2, 3), C(2, −3), D(−4, −3)
(c) P(4, 3), Q(1, 0), R(−3, 4), S(0, 7)

13 ▶ Which logos have line symmetry? How many lines of symmetry are there?
▶ Which logos have turn symmetry? What is the order of the symmetry?
▶ Which logos have both line and turn symmetry?

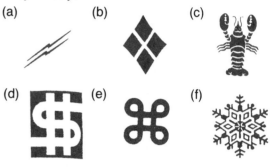

14 The letter A is said to have a vertical line of symmetry.
(a) Make a list of the other letters that have a vertical line of symmetry.
(b) A word is shown to have a vertical line of symmetry. Construct other words that have a vertical line of symmetry.
(c) Construct a sentence that has a vertical line of symmetry.

15 The letter B is said to have a horizontal line of symmetry.

(a) Make a list of the other letters that have a horizontal line of symmetry.
(b) The words below have a horizontal line of symmetry.

(c) Construct other words that have a horizontal line of symmetry.
(d) Construct a sentence that has a horizontal line of symmetry.

10.9 Enlargements And Reductions

You have already worked with some very important applications of enlargements, namely scale diagrams.

Enlargement 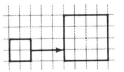 **Reduction**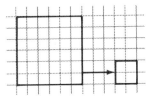

The properties of enlargements and reductions are important to solve many problems.

Because these figures have the same shape and size they are said to be **congruent**.

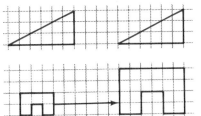

These figures have the same shape but not the same size. They are said to be **similar**.

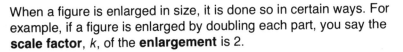

When a figure is enlarged in size, it is done so in certain ways. For example, if a figure is enlarged by doubling each part, you say the **scale factor**, k, of the **enlargement** is 2.

Similarly, when a figure is reduced in size, it is done so in a certain way. For example, when a figure is reduced by halving each part, you say the scale factor, k, of the **reduction** is $\frac{1}{2}$.

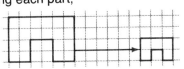

Example 1

Construct the image of each figure for the scale factor shown.

(a)   (b)

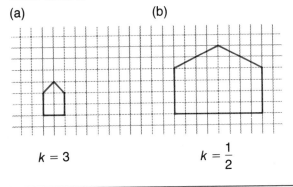

$k = 3$ $k = \frac{1}{2}$

Solution

(a) The scale factor is 3. Thus each length is tripled in size.

(b) The scale factor is $\frac{1}{2}$. Thus one half of each length is obtained.

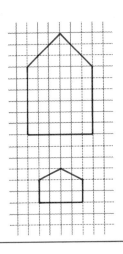

On the Cartesian plane, enlargements or reductions are made with respect to a point.
In the diagram △A′B′C′ is the enlargement image of △ABC with respect to the origin.

In the diagram, for an enlargement

$$\frac{OA}{OA'} = \frac{OB}{OB'} = \frac{OC}{OC'}$$

The scale factor is given by $\frac{OA}{OA'}$. Thus,

in the diagram,

the scale factor, $k = 2$ or $\frac{OA}{OA'} = 2$.

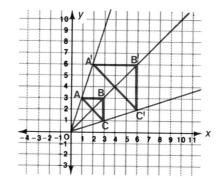

Example 2

A figure is given. Find its image under the reduction $k = \frac{1}{2}$.

Solution

$$k = \frac{1}{2}$$

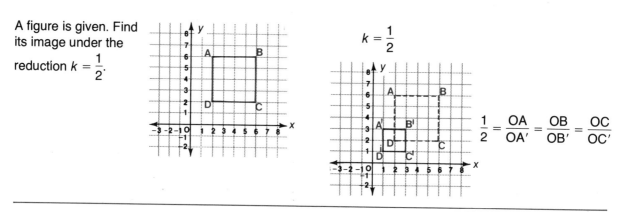

$$\frac{1}{2} = \frac{OA}{OA'} = \frac{OB}{OB'} = \frac{OC}{OC'}$$

Often an enlargement or a reduction is referred to as a **dilatation**.
You may then refer to the scale factor as the **dilatation factor**.

Try These

Each figure and its image are shown. What is the scale factor?

(a)　　　　　　(b)　　　　　　(c)　　　　　　(d)

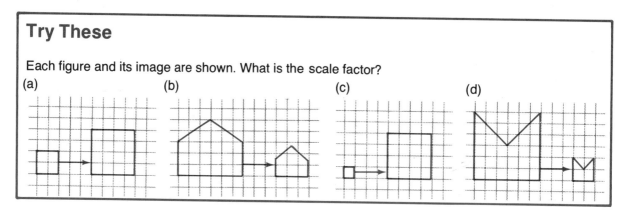

Written Exercises

A 1 Use squared paper. Construct the image of the given figure for each scale factor.

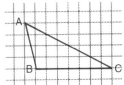

(a) $k = 4$ (b) $k = \dfrac{1}{2}$

(c) $k = 2.5$

2 A design is made based on a dilatation.

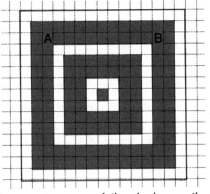

(a) Construct a copy of the design so that AB = 4 cm.

(b) Construct a design of your own that uses a dilatation.

3 Each logo uses a dilatation.
▶ Describe the dilatation.
▶ Construct a copy of the logo, twice as large.

B 4 Two similar triangles are shown.
(a) What is the scale factor?
(b) Calculate the ratios $\dfrac{AB}{DE}, \dfrac{BC}{EF}, \dfrac{AC}{DF}$.
What do you notice?
(c) Measure corresponding angles. What do you notice about the measures?
(d) Which line segments are parallel?,

5 Use your construction tools. Construct a triangle similar to △ABC for each scale factor.

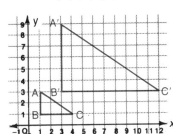

(a) $k = 2$ (b) $k = 0.5$

6 Two triangles are related as shown.
(a) What is the scale factor?
(b) How are the co-ordinates related?
(c) Measure corresponding angles. What do you notice about the measures?
(d) Measure corresponding sides. What do you notice about the measures?
(e) What is the ratio of corresponding sides?

7 A square ABCD is enlarged as shown.
(a) Which points correspond?
(b) Write a rule for the co-ordinates.
(c) Find the ratios of corresponding sides. What do you notice?
(d) Measure corresponding angles. What do you notice?

8 Based on your results in Questions 6 to 7 if two figures are similar, what
▶ does not change?   ▶ changes?

9 (a) Find the image of figure ABCD. Use the dilatation rule. Multiply both co-ordinates by 2.

(b) Mark all lines that are parallel.

345

Investigation: Areas And Scale Factors

10 Use the figure shown.

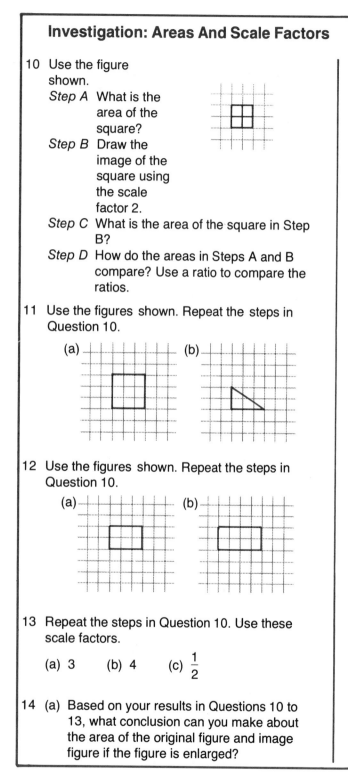

Step A What is the area of the square?

Step B Draw the image of the square using the scale factor 2.

Step C What is the area of the square in Step B?

Step D How do the areas in Steps A and B compare? Use a ratio to compare the ratios.

11 Use the figures shown. Repeat the steps in Question 10.

(a)

(b)

12 Use the figures shown. Repeat the steps in Question 10.

(a)

(b)

13 Repeat the steps in Question 10. Use these scale factors.

(a) 3   (b) 4   (c) $\frac{1}{2}$

14 (a) Based on your results in Questions 10 to 13, what conclusion can you make about the area of the original figure and image figure if the figure is enlarged?

(b) The image of a figure is found using scale factor k. Find the missing value.

$$\frac{\text{area of original figure}}{\text{area of image figure}} = ?$$

15 For each figure, a scale factor k is shown.
▶ Predict the area of the image.
▶ Verify your prediction. Draw the image.

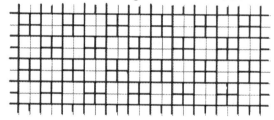

(a) $k = 2$ (b) $k = \frac{1}{2}$ (c) $k = 3$

You can use similar figures to tile a floor.

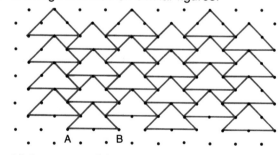

16 (a) Make a copy of each figure used in the above pattern.

(b) Why are the figures similar?

17 A design is based on similar figures.

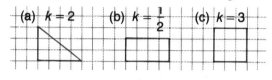

Make a copy of the design. Use AB = 4 cm.

18 Choose a figure of your own. Construct a design that uses similar figures.

10.10 Problem-Solving: Distorting Figures

The figure is similar to its image, as illustrated.

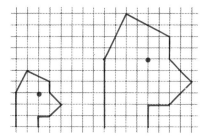

Each dimension is changed by the same scale factor. However, if different dimensions are changed by different scale factors, the figure is distorted.

Scale Factor 1, vertically, (stays the same).
Scale Factor 3, horizontally.

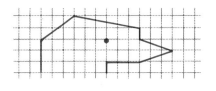

Scale Factor 2, vertically.
Scale Factor 1, horizontally, (stays the same).

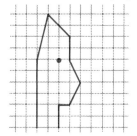

Written Exercises

1 The figure and its image are shown. What scale factors are used vertically and horizontally?

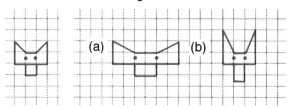

(a)　(b)

2 How is each distorted figure obtained?

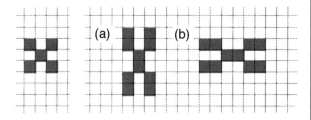

(a)　(b)

3 A figure is shown. Draw its distorted image.
- horizontal scale factor $k = 2$
- vertical scale factor $k = 4$

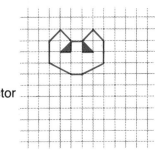

4 Plot the rectangle ABCD on the plane with the following co-ordinates.

A(4, 1)　B(10, 1)　C(10, 4)　D(4, 4)

Draw each distorted image. Multiply the
(a) x co-ordinate by 2, y co-ordinate by 3.

(b) x co-ordinate by $\frac{1}{2}$, y co-ordinate by 4.

Skills To Practise:
A Chapter Review

10.1 (a) What are the co-ordinates of each point shown?

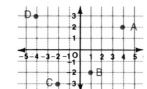

(b) Plot the points E(4, −3) and F(−8, −2).

10.2 (a) Draw a graph of the relation given by $y = 3x + 2$, where x is an integer.

(b) Draw the above graph again for x to represent any number.

10.3 Line segments are placed on a grid. Calculate the

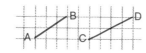

(a) rise. (b) run.
(c) slope.

10.4 Calculate the length of each line segment.

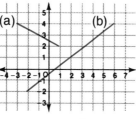

10.5 Construct the reflection image of △ABC. Use the reflection line shown.

10.6 Translate the given figure 3 units to the left and 4 units down.

10.7 Make a copy of each figure. Use your construction tools. Rotate each figure about the point A for the rotation angle shown.

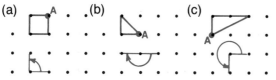

348

Problems To Practise:
A Chapter Review

10.1 Find the letter for each ordered pair and decode the message below.

(a) (3, 2), (−5, −1) (b) (3, −1), (−2, 6)
(c) (−6, 4), (2, 5), (7, 4), (−2, 2), (7, 0)
(d) Use a grid. Make up a message of your own.

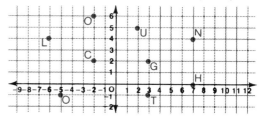

10.2 Which ordered pairs satisfy the relation given by $y = \frac{1}{2}x + 1$? Which do not satisfy the relation?

(a) (2, 2) (b) (3, 3) (c) (4, 3)

10.3 To find the slope of a line
• choose the co-ordinates of any two points.
• calculate the slope.
What is the slope of each line?

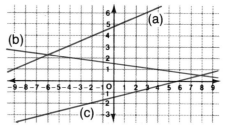

10.4 The co-ordinates of two places are given. Calculate the distance between them to 1 decimal place.

Sable Island (8, 1) Lina Island (−6, −7)

10.5 Use the reflection line to find the image of each figure.

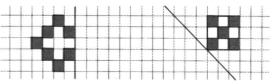

Chapter Checkup: A Practice Test

10.1 (a) Plot the points A(−3, 2), B(−3, −2), C(3, −2), D(3, 2). What type of figure is ABCD?

(b) Find the co-ordinates of a fourth point that gives a rectangle with these other vertices.
A(−1, 6)   B(−11, 6)   C(−11, −2)

10.2 (a) Find the missing value if each ordered pair satisfies the relation $y = 5x$.
A(3, ?)   B(−2, ?)   C(?, 15)

(b) Construct the graph of the relation $y = \frac{1}{2}x^2 + 1$.

10.3 (a) Calculate the slope of the line segment AB.

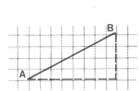

(b) The flight of a plane is shown in the diagram.

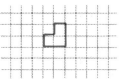

A If the run of the plane is 2 km, how high is the plane?

B If the airplane is 1500 m high, what distance along the ground has the plane travelled?

10.4 (a) Calculate the length of AB for A(4, 3) and B(−2, 1).

(b) Two snowmobiles are at co-ordinates (−4, 5) and (5, −4). How far apart are they?

10.5 (a) Draw any triangle and a line. Find the reflection of the triangle in the line you have drawn.

(b) Construct a design that uses a reflection of the figure shown.

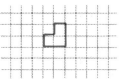

10.6 (a) Draw a triangle with vertices
A(4, 5)   B(2, −1)   C(−3, −4)
Find the translation image for the translation arrow.

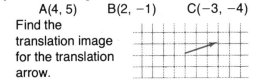

(b) What are the co-ordinates of each of these points for the above translation?
D(−4, 3)   E(−2, −1)   F(6, −3)

10.7 (a) Make a copy of each figure. Use the turn arrow to find the image. Use the turn centre T.

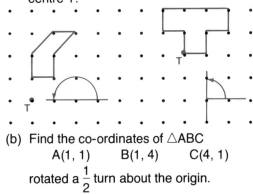

(b) Find the co-ordinates of △ABC
A(1, 1)   B(1, 4)   C(4, 1)
rotated a $\frac{1}{2}$ turn about the origin.

10.8 (a) Which of the figures have line symmetry? Rotational symmetry? Both symmetries?

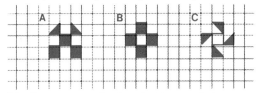

(b) Construct a design that has point symmetry.

10.9 For the figure shown, construct its image for
A scale factor 0.5.
B scale factor 1.5.

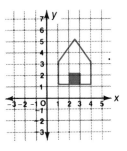

11 Working With Data: Graphs and Applications

samples and statistics, pictographs, bar, cirlce, line graphs, mean, median, mode, probability, applications and problem-solving

Introduction

Each day you are exposed to **data** or pieces of information presented to you in different forms.

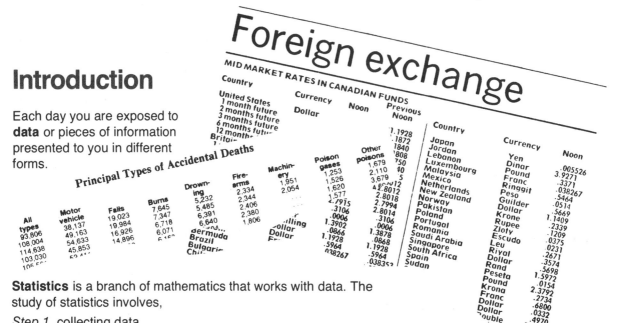

Statistics is a branch of mathematics that works with data. The study of statistics involves,

Step 1 collecting data.

Step 2 organizing the data in some way, (tables, charts, graphs, and so on.

Step 3 interpreting the data and using them in some useful way, to predict results or make business decisions and so on.

- How well do motorcycle tires stand up in racing?

- How well will the new line of pleasure boats sell?

- Who will win the next election?

- Where should the fast food outlet be built?

What are some effective ways of preventing accidents?

11.1 Working With Samples: Steps of Statistics

If you were an L.P. record manufacturer, you would be concerned with the quality of the records. A manufacturer might collect data and analyse them, using the following steps. The resulting statistics can be used to check the quality of the records.

Step A: Each record cannot be checked individually so a **sample** is chosen. The sample is a part of the complete shipment of records. The complete shipment of records is called the **population**. In order that the manufacturer can make a correct decision, the sample must be representative of all the records so the records must be selected at random. A **random sample** means that any record has an equal chance of being selected.

Step B: After the sample is obtained, the manufacturer will use this sample to conduct tests, collect data, and record the information. As you shall see, graphs of various types or tables are used to represent the data.

Step C: The information gathered in Steps A and B is then analyzed and the manufacturer can decide what percentage of the L.P. records is defective. If the percentage is too high for the sample, the manufacturer may decide to melt the complete batch of records.

Some methods used to collect information for a sample involving people are:

- The conducting of a **survey** or **poll** by telephone, on the street, in a supermarket, etc.
- The filling out of a **questionnaire** by people. This questionnaire may be handed out, mailed to, or delivered to the homes, etc., of the people of the sample.

Try These

1   Look at the three letters on the right.   B   I   Z

    (a) Which do you like the least?

    (b) Which do you think will be least liked by your class? How can you check your answer?

2   Look at the 3 numbers on the right.   **4**   **IV**

    (a) Which is your favourite? ▼▼▼

    (b) Which do you think might be the favourite of your class? How can you check your answer?

3   Look at these flags.

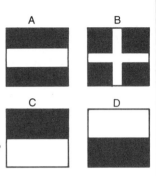

    (a) Which do you like the best?

    (b) Which one do you think might be the favourite flag of your class? How can you check your answer?

    (c) If you conducted a poll throughout your whole school, what might you expect your answer to be in (b)?

Written Exercises

1   You own a movie business, and you want to decide whether to obtain the rights to show a movie that has just been produced. How might you collect data to make your decision?

2   (a) Pick 3 comic strips from the newspaper.

    (b) Choose a method of collecting information to answer the question, "Which comic strip is not popular?"

3   (a) Construct a list of the various methods used by students to come to school.

    (b) Decide on a method of collecting information to answer the question, "Which is the most frequently used method of transportation to come to school?"

4   (a) Obtain a list of the 5 most frequently eaten fast foods.

    (b) Choose a method of collecting information to answer the question, "Which fast food is most popular?"

    (c) What percentage of the people chose the most popular fast food?

    (d) What percentage of the people chose the least popular fast food?

5   Refer to Question 4.

    (a) You are going to build a fast-food outlet near the school. Based on the data in Question 4, what fast foods should you sell?

    (b) Based on the success of your business in (a), you decide that you will open another fast-food outlet elsewhere. What might be your first step?

6 A part of the telephone book is shown.

```
MacNeil R W 34 Argyle Ave. . . . .  272-2840
MacNeil Rod 272 Bassett St. . . .   671-3951
MacNeill D 1140 Avenue Dr. . . . .  270-2953
MacNeill D 22 Don . . . . . . . . . .   822-9203
MacNeill Gil French Dr. . . . . . . .  826-3950
MacNeill J 1110 Haldon Rd. . . . . . 278-1839
MacNeill K 29 Kirkland . . . . . . . .  276-6391
MacNeill L A 889 Malvern . . . . . .  823-5290
MacNeill R J 2 Oyster . . . . . . . .  677-5500
MacNeill R T 557 Portugal . . . . .  677-3899
MacNeill T 1452 Portugal . . . . . .  275-3850
MacNeill Tex 34 Reid Ave. . . . . .  279-4644
MacNevin D 177 Glassco . . . . . .  278-0078
Macoomb B D 55 Beech . . . . . . . 823-3018
Macor J B 2201 Avenue Rd. . . . .  625-3759
Macor Ono 35 Lennox . . . . . . . .  822-4110
Macor R G 991 Lynar Cr. . . . . . .  678-3022
Macoretta G 563 Byng Ct. . . . . .  823-6689
MacPhail B 5 Courtney . . . . . . .  279-4859
MacPhail D 449 Sweeney Rd. . .  278-4424
MacPhail M 7 Passmore . . . . . . .  826-6999
MacPhail V 552 Reynolds . . . . . .  826-3232
MacPhaill A 114 Clubhouse . . . .  274-4787
MacPhaill A C 90 Peters . . . . . .  279-4545
MacPhaill D B 42 Rose Gdn. . . .  277-7041
MacPhaill E E 330 Thomas Ave.  270-6110
MacPhaill L 12 Victor . . . . . . . .  274-3411
MacPhee Art 550 Paisley . . . . . .  274-4888
MacPhee D G 8 Uxley . . . . . . . .  822-7028
MacPhee T 721 Varley Rd. . . . . .  822-6584
MacPhee Wm 52 Young Ave. . . .  826-7710
MacPherson A 386 Birdsey . . . .  828-4108
MacPherson A J 5 Calder Crt . . .  823-9931
MacPherson A R 74 Innis . . . . . .  826-1003
MacPherson D T 1120 Kepple . .  828-4209
MacPherson Ted 295 Montague   828-7750
MacPhie A L 420 Barcley Ave. . .  277-1010
MacPhie P 539 Crescent . . . . . .  823-2229
MacPhie Y 773 Parson Rd. . . . . .  823-6699
```

(a) Which combination of digits is most frequently used for the first 3 digits?

(b) Which digit is used most frequently for the fourth digit?

(c) Which digit is used most frequently for the last digit?

7 Use the newspaper clipping.

There are various scientific explanations about the origin of the oceans. One is that billions of years ago the new-born planet Earth may have been surrounded by heavy layers of clouds so thick that no sunlight could penetrate. The heavy clouds would have allowed the fiery earth to cool. This cooling would then have enabled the cloud cover to produce rain. Some scientists believe it may not have stopped raining on earth for thousands — maybe even millions — of years. This is supposed to have happened about two and a half *billion* years ago.

From the moment the rain began to fall, the land would begin to erode. Some of the rock would dissolve, and its minerals — including salt — would be carried into the expanding sea. Over millions of years, of course, this would make the waters salty.

Another theory suggests that the water for the oceans might have come from the new planet's molten core. The water might have been spewed out by volcanoes. As the volcanoes erupted they would have created great basins, or valleys, where the water would drain and collect into seas.

All the scientific versions of the origin of the oceans agree that every drop of water that existed on the earth or around it billions of years ago is still here. It may be in solid (ice), liquid, or gaseous form; it may be on the earth's surface or deep underground; it may be free or trapped in rock or within a living creature. But every drop is still here.

(a) Which letter of the alphabet occurs the most?

(b) Which letter occurs the least?

(c) Which word occurs the most?

8 The coats of arms of various provinces are shown.

(a) Which do you like the most?

(b) Conduct a poll to determine
   • the most liked.   • the least liked.

9 Four insects are magnified.

(a) Which do you like the least?

(b) Conduct a poll to determine which insect is liked the least.

Applications: Data Surveying

The data you collect for a sample represent the population. However, you may decide to obtain a sample that is more representative of the data.

Clustered Sampling

If you want to make a decision about the best type of car repair manual you would probably take a sample from car mechanics or persons who work at repairing cars. Taking a sample from a particular part of the population like this is called taking a **clustered sample**.

Stratified Sampling

To decide whether Canada should host the next Olympic Games, you would probably choose people from each province to fill in your questionnaire. The number of people that you choose from each province would be in the same proportion as the population of each province. Taking a random sample of a population in such a way that each subpopulation is represented proportionately is known as taking a **stratified sample**.

Destructive Sampling

To test whether a quantity of steaks is suitable, you might take a steak, cook it and taste it. However, it would be unlikely you could now sell this steak because you have eaten it. Thus the sample is destroyed. This is called destructive sampling.

---

10 To establish what is considered to be the most comfortable handle for a tennis racket, you might use a questionnaire and mail it to tennis players. What word best describes the sample?
A stratified   B clustered   C destructive

11 To test the quality of a cola, samples are taken from the production line. What word best describes this type of sampling?
A stratified   B clustered   C destructive

12 In order to collect ideas about how arena facilities might be improved, the various hockey organizations which use the arena complete questionnaires.

| Blackhawks | 60 members | Canucks | 100 members |
| Royal Nats | 80 members | Bandos | 50 members |

What type of sample would be obtained?
A stratified B clustered C destructive

13 To answer questions on each of the following topics what type of sample should be obtained?
(a) the quality of oranges
(b) the winner for an election
(c) where to put a fast-food outlet
(d) the type of film for a camera

14 To answer questions on the following subjects
• decide on a method of choosing the sample.
• obtain the sample. (Is it stratified, clustered, or destructive?)
(a) the effervescence of a ginger ale
(b) the most popular recording group
(c) where to put a hamburger stand in the school
(d) the most effective tire
(e) the quality of a running shoe

11.2 Gathering and Recording Data

The following information about the types of fish caught during a long weekend was gathered and recorded on a notepad. To show each fish, these letters were used.

P, pike, **B**, bass,
C, catfish, **S**, sunfish,
T, trout

```
P C B S C S P S S P
T S P C B P T C B S
B T C S P S C T S B
P S B S C T B S S P
```

The fish that were caught are a **sample** of the whole **population** of the fish in the lake.

How easily can you answer these questions using the above information or data?
A How many bass were caught?
B Which fish was caught the most?
C Which fish was caught the least?

To answer these questions, the information needs to be organized in a useful way. One way is to use a **tally chart**. A stroke is used to show each fish caught. The **frequency** is the number of fish caught.

Fish	Tally	Frequency
Perch	卌 |||	8
Bass	卌 ||	7
Catfish	卌 ||	7
Sunfish	卌 卌 |||	13
Trout	卌	5

Frequency ← Number of each type of fish caught.

Use the tally chart to answer the earlier questions.
A There were 7 bass caught.
B Sunfish were caught the most.
C Trout were caught the least.

Written Exercises

A Questions 1 to 5 are based on the following information.

The table below shows the answers of students to the question, "How many hours of homework did you do last week?"

Hours of homework in one week.

```
3  7  4  6  9  0  5  4  1  4  5  0  3  6  7
8  8  6  0  5  4  3  2  6  9  4  7  8  0  4
7  4  5  6  8  8  4  0  4  6  5  8  8  7  9
```

1 Construct a tally chart as shown.

Number of Hours	Tally	Frequency
0		
1		
2		

2 How many students were surveyed?

3 How many students did homework for
(a) 3 h?   (b) 4 h?   (c) 1 h?   (d) 8 h?

4 (a) What was the greatest amount of time spent on homework?
(b) How many students are there in (a)?

5 (a) What was the least amount of time spent on homework?
(b) How many students are there in (a)?

Questions 6 to 8 are based on the following information.

Students were asked the following question. "What is the distance to your favourite park?" The responses are shown as distances in kilometres.

Distance to favourite park (in kilometres)

```
0.5   4    6    12   21    6.8  10    5    3   10
3    15   14    5.6  13   11   10   10   20   19
8     7    7    14    7.3  1.2   8    6   24   23
```

6 Construct and complete a frequency table shown as the following.

Frequency Table

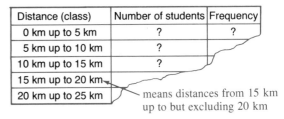

Distance (class)	Number of students	Frequency
0 km up to 5 km	?	?
5 km up to 10 km	?	
10 km up to 15 km	?	
15 km up to 20 km		
20 km up to 25 km		

means distances from 15 km up to but excluding 20 km

7 (a) How many students were interviewed?
(b) How many students said 15 km or more?
(c) How many students said less than 5 km?

8 Which statement is true?
A Most students go less than 10 km to their favourite park.
B Most students go further than 10 km to their favourite park.

B Questions 9 to 13 are based on the following information.

As a project, the students made a survey of the various sports that students play. Their findings were recorded in a tally chart. Each person survey named only 1 sport.

Tally Chart

	Sport	Tally	Frequency
A	Football	|||| |||| ||	?
B	Basketball	|||| |||| |||	?
C	Volleyball	?	9
D	Soccer	|||| ||||	?
E	Tennis	|||| ||||		?
F	Baseball	?	8
G	Archery	||||	?
H	Hockey	?	16
I	Swimming	|||| |||| |||| |||| ||||		?
J	Track & Field	|||| |||| |||| ||||	?

9 Copy and complete the tally chart.

10 Which sport was
(a) most popular?   (b) least popular?

11 How many students liked a sport that uses a ball?

12 (a) How many students were surveyed?
(b) What per cent chose swimming?
(c) What per cent chose basketball?

13 Arrange the sports from greatest participation to least participation.

___

Questions 14 to 17 are based on the following information.

For the fishing meet there were 25 teams entered. The number of legal size fish caught were recorded for each team.

```
 7 10 12  4  8  9  3 10  9 14  4  8  9
15  6 11 10  0  3  7  8 12 11 15 20
```

14 Construct a tally chart.

15 (a) How many fish did the winning team catch?
(b) What percentage of the teams did not win?

16 (a) What percentage of the teams caught 10 fish?
(b) What percentage of the teams caught less than 10 fish?

17 What was the average number of fish caught by each team? Express your answer to the nearest whole fish.

___

Questions 18 to 22 are based on the following information.

The number of pizzas made each day for one month

```
38  56  91  49  54  68  84  64  81  96
55  64  71  56  91  55  74  63  57  48
89  91  98 100  42  51  57  36  60  50
```

18 Construct a tally chart as follows for the above information.

Number of pizzas (class)	Frequency
0—10	?
10—20	?
20—30	?
and so on	

19 What was the record number of pizzas made?

20 How many pizzas in all were made?

21 On what percentage of the days were
(a) less than 50 pizzas made?
(b) more than 80 pizzas made?

22 What was the average number of pizzas made each day?

___

Questions 23 to 26 are based on the following information.

The time taken to run 50 m was recorded for the students (in seconds).

```
6.2  6.9  6.3  6.5  6.6  6.8  6.8  6.9  6.1
6.9  6.5  7.1  6.6  7.0  6.8  6.6  7.0  6.5
6.5  6.8  6.6  7.3  6.2  6.8  7.4  6.3  6.9
6.3  7.3  6.8  6.6  6.8  6.9  7.0  6.3  7.0
```

23 Construct a frequency table for the above information.

24 (a) What percentage of the students took 7.0 s to run 50 m?
(b) What percentage of the students took longer than 6.7 s to run the 50 m?

25 From fitness records, a student running the 50 m distance in less than 6.7 s is given an excellent rating. What percentage of the students were in the excellent rating?

26 From fitness records, students taking longer than 7.0 s are given a poor rating and are suggested for an overhaul. What percentage of the students were in the poor rating?

357

11.3 Graphs You Use: Pictographs

Newspapers often show information using pictures, as shown below. These graphs are called **pictographs** (picture graph).

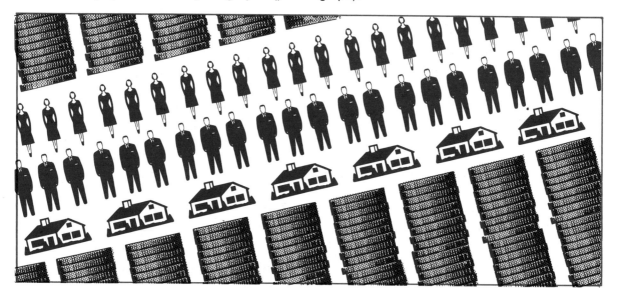

Presenting information in a pictograph allows comparisons to be made visually. The following pictograph shows the number of students doing various part-time jobs.

Part-Time Jobs

Small Store	♀ ♀ ♀ ♀ ♀
Supermarket	♀ ♀ ♀
Fast-Food Hamburger Outlet	♀ ♀ ♀ ♀ ♀
Newspapers	♀ ♀
Pizza Place	♀ ♀ ♀ ♀ ♀
Fish & Chips	♀ ♀ ♀
Babysitting	♀ ♀ ♀ ♀ ♀ ♀ ♀

Key ♀ = 5 students

To interpret the information accurately, the "key" or **legend** must be shown on the pictograph. From the pictograph you can easily see at a glance that

A the greatest number of students babysit as a part-time job.

B the least number of students deliver newspapers as a part-time job.

Try These

Questions 1 to 4 are based on the following information.

The number of students that walk and do not walk to school are shown by the following pictograph.

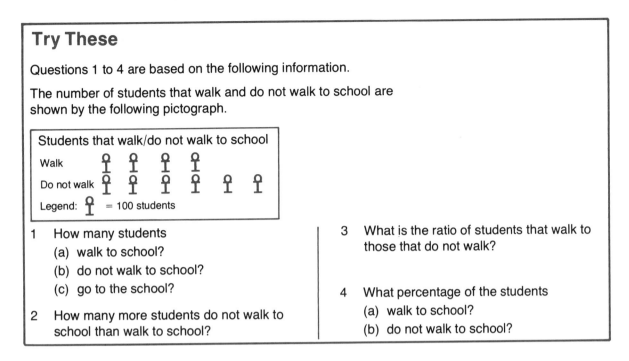

1   How many students
    (a) walk to school?
    (b) do not walk to school?
    (c) go to the school?

2   How many more students do not walk to school than walk to school?

3   What is the ratio of students that walk to those that do not walk?

4   What percentage of the students
    (a) walk to school?
    (b) do not walk to school?

Written Exercises

Questions 1 to 5 are based on the following pictograph.

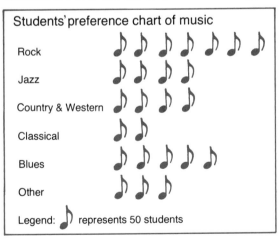

A 1 (a) Which type of music is most popular?
     (b) Which type of music is least popular?

  2 (a) How many students like country and western?
     (b) What percentage of the students like country and western?

3 What is the ratio of students that like rock to those that like classical?

4 (a) What percentage of the students like the Blues?
   (b) What percentage of the students do not like the Blues?

5 If the students were to buy 1000 records,
   (a) how many records would be jazz records?
   (b) how many records would be rock records?

Questions 6 to 9 are based on the following pictograph.

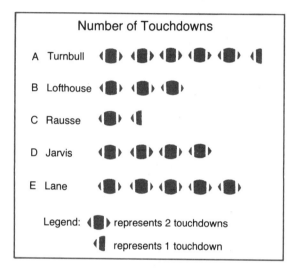

Number of Touchdowns

A Turnbull

B Lofthouse

C Rausse

D Jarvis

E Lane

Legend: represents 2 touchdowns
         represents 1 touchdown

6 Who scored
   (a) the greatest number of touchdowns?
   (b) the least number of touchdowns?

7 A touchdown is worth 6 points. How many points did each player score?

8 (a) What percentage of the touchdowns did Lofthouse score?
   (b) What percentage of the total points did Lofthouse score?
   (c) What do you notice about your answers in (a) and (b)?

9 In the next 3 games, some players scored more touchdowns.
      Lofthouse   2 touchdowns
      Turnbull   1 touchdown
      Lane   3 touchdowns
   What changes need to be made to the pictograph?

B Questions 10 to 14 are based on the following information.

Bobby Borety is the top scorer on the basketball team. His scores for the regular season games are shown in the chart below.

Game	1	2	3	4	5	6	7	8
Number of points	12	20	16	12	20	4	16	24

10 Construct a pictograph to show the information.

11 In which game were the
    (a) greatest number of points scored?
    (b) least number of points scored?

12 What is the ratio of points scored,
    (a) in the first game to the last game?
    (b) in the sixth game to the seventh game?

13 What percentage of the points were scored
    (a) in the first half of the season?
    (b) in the last half of the season?

14 What was the average number of points scored in a game during the season?

Questions 15 to 17 are based on the following information.

The number of points scored by players on a team are shown below.

Player	Kelly	Green	Tookey	Currie	Smith	Charron
Points	60	74	45	35	40	48

15 Use a hockey puck ⬤ to represent 10 points and ◖ to represent 5 points. Construct a pictograph to show the numbers of points scored.

16 What percentage of the total points
    (a) did Smith score?   (b) did Kelly score?

C 17 (a) Who scored the greatest percentage of points?
        (b) What was that percentage?

Applications: Pictographs For Fitness

Questions 18 to 22 are based on the following information.

To qualify for the fitness test for doing situps the following procedure is followed.

Rules for Situp
1. Lie on back. Feet apart. Hands, with fingers interlaced, behind neck.
2. Sit up and touch right elbow to left knee.
3. Return to starting position.
4. Sit up and touch left elbow to right knee. Return to starting position.
5. Continue Steps 1 to 4. Record the number completed.

The following pictograph was obtained for a group of students.

Legend: ᘯ = 25 students

0 to 35 situps (poor)	ᘯ ᘯ ᘯ ᘯ
35 to 45 situps (satisfactory)	ᘯ ᘯ ᘯ ᘯ ᘯ ᘯ
45 to 60 situps (good)	ᘯ ᘯ ᘯ ᘯ ᘯ ᘯ ᘯ
60 or more (excellent)	ᘯ ᘯ ᘯ

18 How many students are
   (a) excellent?   (b) satisfactory?

19 What percentage of the students are
   (a) excellent?   (b) satisfactory?

20 What percentage of the students do less than 35 situps?

21 Write a ratio to show
   (a) satisfactory students to poor students.
   (b) poor students to excellent students.

22 After the test was completed, 20 other students gave satisfactory results.
   (a) What change is needed to the pictograph?
   (b) How many students in all were tested now?
   (c) How many students were satisfactory in all?
   (d) What percentage of the students were satisfactory?

Questions 23 to 26 are based on the following information.

To qualify for the Shuttle Run the following procedure is followed.

Rules For Shuttle Run
1. Mark 2 lines as shown. Place 2 blocks of wood behind B.
2. Stand behind line A. Run and pick up 1 block. Return and place it behind line A.
3. Run and pick up the other block. Return and place it behind line A.
4. Record the time.

The following pictograph was obtained for a group of students.

Less than 10.0 s (excellent)	🏃 🏃 🏃
10.0 s up to 10.4 s (good)	🏃 🏃 🏃 🏃 🏃 🏃
10.4 s to 10.9 s (satisfactory)	🏃 🏃 🏃 🏃 🏃 🏃 🏃 🏃 🏃
10.9 s and up (poor)	🏃 🏃 🏃 🏃 🏃 🏃 🏃
Legend: 🏃 = 25 students	

Remember
10.0 s up to 10.4 s
Include 10.0 s, but
do not include 10.4 s.

23 How many students were
   (a) satisfactory?   (b) poor?

24 What percentage of the students were
   (a) satisfactory?   (b) poor?

25 What percentage of the students took
   (a) less than 10.4 s?   (b) 10.9 s and more?

26 After the test was completed, the results of 4 more students are shown for doing the Shuttle Run. 17.7 9.6 11 10
   (a) Redraw the pictograph.
   (b) How many students are poor now?
   (c) What percentage of the students are now satisfactory?

11.4 Interpreting Bar Graphs

In hockey, if a player breaks a rule, the player is assessed a penalty and asked to leave the game for a certain length of time,

A pictograph is used to show the penalty data given in the newspaper clipping.

P I M (penalties in minutes)
Bourne
Sutter   42
Aubry   69
Mondon   62
Redmond   38
Redmond   84

1 Hockey Puck 🏒 represents 10 min.

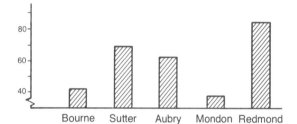

Bourne
Sutter
Aubry
Mondon
Redmond

Another graph that may be used to represent information is the **bar graph**. For a bar graph a scale is used to show the number of penalty minutes.

Summary
▶ For a pictograph, to find the number of penalty minutes, you need to know the **legend**. Namely, *what each symbol represents*. For example 🏒 represents 10 min.
▶ For a bar graph, to find the number of penalty minutes, you need to know the **scale** of the bar graph, namely, 1 unit represents 10 min.

Example
Construct a bar graph for the following information.

National Hockey League	
Team	Points
N.Y. Islanders	65
Detroit	44
Montreal	56
Toronto	31
Boston	47
Philadelphia	59
Rangers	53
Vancouver	26
Washington	14
Edmonton	14

Solution

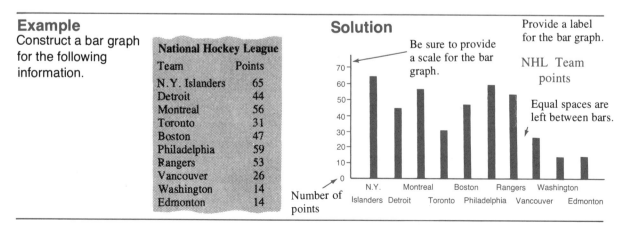

Be sure to provide a scale for the bar graph.

Provide a label for the bar graph.

NHL Team points

Equal spaces are left between bars.

Number of points

The above bar graph is referred to as a **vertical bar graph**. In the exercise that follows you will also work with horizontal bar graphs.

To construct a bar graph, you need to
▶ choose an appropriate scale and label it.
▶ place a title on your graph.
▶ label the appropriate columns.

Try These

Refer to the bar graph in the example on the previous page.

1 Which team had the largest number of points?

2 Which team had the lowest number of points?

3 Which team finished second in the season?

4 Which team finished fifth?

5 Which teams placed lower than Boston?

6 Which teams placed higher than Vancouver?

7 Which of the following teams had about the same number of points?
A Detroit   B Rangers
C Montreal   D Boston

Written Exercises

A Questions 1 to 6 are based on the information in the bar graph at right.

The bar graph gives the number of cassette tapes of a gold album sold.

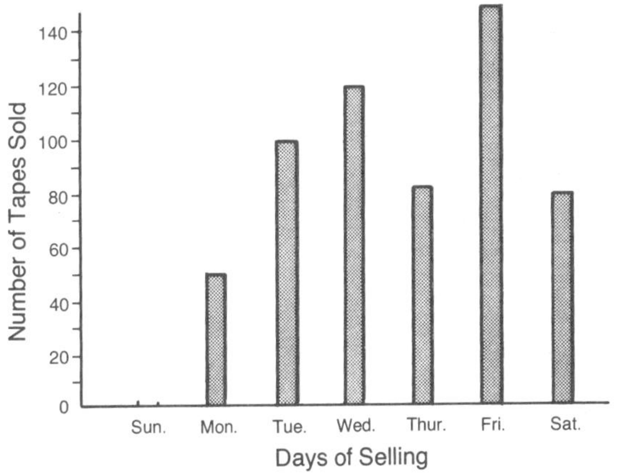

1 What is a suitable title for the bar graph?

2 On which day of the following pairs of days were more tapes sold?
(a) Mon., Wed.   (b) Thurs., Sun.
(c) Tues., Fri.   (d) Thurs., Sat.

3 On which day of the following pairs of days were fewer tapes sold?
(a) Tues., Wed.   (b) Thurs., Fri.
(c) Wed., Sat.   (d) Sat., Sun.

4 How many tapes were sold on
(a) Wed.?   (b) Fri.?   (c) Sat.?

5 On which days were more than
(a) 85 tapes sold?   (b) 60 tapes sold?

6 (a) How many more tapes were sold on Friday than Monday?
(b) How many tapes were sold in all for Monday and Tuesday?

B Questions 7 to 11 are based on the following information.

The bar graph below indicates the lengths of the 14 longest rivers in the world.

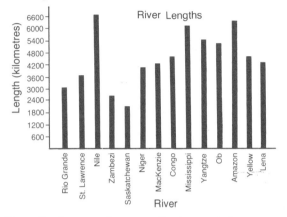

7 From the bar graph, name the longest river. How long is it?

8 How long is the shortest river? What is its name?

9 Compare the length of the following rivers. Which is longer?

(a) Nile, Congo (b) Rio Grande, St. Lawrence

10 Compare the lengths of the following rivers. Which is shorter?

(a) Yangtze, Amazon (b) Mississippi, Congo

11 What percentage of the rivers are

(a) more than 6000 km? (b) less than 3000 km?

Questions 12 to 14 are based on the following information.

The bar graph below shows the average daily food requirements of various age groups.

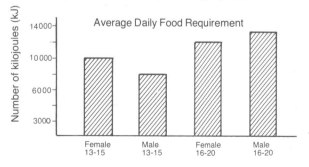

12 Which age group requires

(a) the highest number of kilojoules?

(b) the lowest number of kilojoules?

13 Carla is 14 a old and so far has consumed 6500 kJ.

(a) How many more kilojoules (kJ) does she require for that day?

(b) What percentage of her total for that day has she consumed?

14 Michael is 14 a old and consumed 3000 kJ at breakfast.

(a) How many more kilojoules are needed to obtain his average daily requirement?

(b) What percentage of his daily requirement of kilojoules did he consume at breakfast?

15 (a) Construct a horizontal bar graph for the following information.

Body of water	Average depth (metres)
Hudson Bay	90
Mediterranean Sea	1500
Arctic Ocean	1330
Atlantic Ocean	3740
Pacific Ocean	4190
Black Sea	1190

(b) The average depth of the Caribbean Sea is 2575 m. What percentage of the bodies of water in (a) are shallower?

(c) The average depth of the Red Sea is 540 m. What percentage of the bodies of water in (a) are deeper than the Red Sea?

(d) Create a question about the bar graph in (a). Answer the question.

11.5　Broken Line Graphs

A **broken line graph** may also be used to present data. One general feature of broken line graphs is that the information listed on the horizontal axis follows a fixed order or sequence. They may be used to show information recorded over a period of time and they show changes more clearly.

For example, because the information on the horizontal axis of the following bar graph follows a definite order, (Jan., Feb., Mar., etc...)

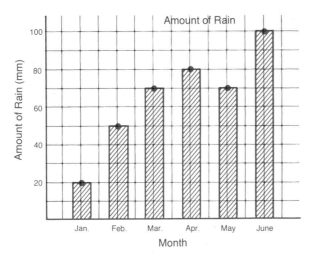

then the information in this bar graph can be recorded as a broken line graph as follows.

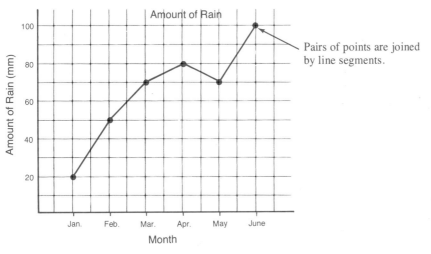

Choose an appropriate scale as shown.

The axes are labelled.

Written Exercises

A Questions 1 to 2 are based on the following table that shows the amount of gasoline used for a trip.

litres used	6	8	10	12	14	16	18	20
kilometres travelled	25.3	35.2	44.3	51.5	58.7	72.1	79.6	87.6

To show the above data, draw the following broken line graph.

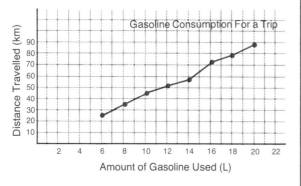

1 How much gasoline would you expect to use in order to travel
  (a) 40 km? (b) 60 km? (c) 85 km?

2 About how many kilometres would you have travelled if you had used each of these amounts of gasoline?
  (a) 7 L (b) 8.5 L (c) 18.5 L

3 This graph shows the records for the Women's Olympic Javelin.

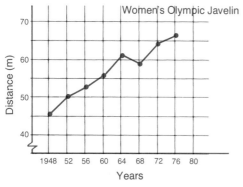

(a) What was the distance thrown in 1968?

(b) What was the distance thrown in 1952?

(c) Describe the graph from 1956 to 1960 as decreasing or increasing.

(d) Describe the graph from 1964 to 1968 as decreasing or increasing.

4 Use the graph to answer the question.

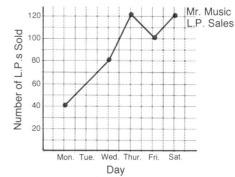

(a) How many L.P.'s were sold on Monday? Thursday? Saturday?

(b) On which days were there less than 110 L.P.'s sold?

(c) On which days were there more than 100 L.P.'s sold?

(d) On which days were there more than 130 L.P.'s sold?

B 5 The graph shows the number of calculators sold during one year by "CHIP Electronics Ltd."

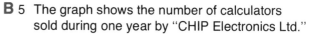
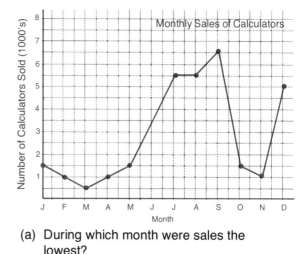

(a) During which month were sales the lowest?

(b) During which month were sales the highest?

(c) During which months were sales the same?

(d) How many calculators in all sold during the year?

(e) If each calculator sold for $39.95, how much money did the company make during the year?

Questions 6 to 8 are based on the following information and graph.

On Saturday a survey was made to determine how many people watched the Community T.V. Channel XKR. Programming begins at 07:00 and ends at midnight. The findings were plotted on a graph as shown below.

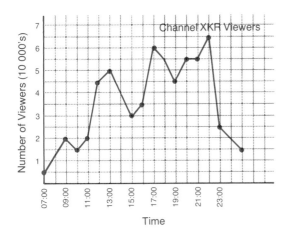

6 How many people watched Channel XKR at
(a) 09:00? (b) noon? (c) 15:00? (d) 22:30?

7 (a) What times of day are the popular viewing times?
(b) At what time of the day do the number of viewers peak?

8 At what time(s) were the following numbers of people watching the channel?
(a) 15 000   (b) 35 000

9 Draw a line graph to show the following data.
(a) Boy's Height/Mass Chart

Height (cm)	140	145	150	155	160	165	170	175	180	185
Average Mass (kg)	41	44	49	54	58	63	66	70	73	75

(b) Girl's Height/Mass Chart

Height (cm)	140	145	150	155	160	165	170	175	180	185
Average Mass (kg)	36	40	43	47	51	54	58	62	66	69

(c) How are the graphs in (a) and (b) alike?
(d) How are the graphs in (a) and (b) different?

10 Draw broken line graphs to show the following sets of data. The data are the average monthly temperatures.

(a) For Victoria, B.C., Canada

Month	J	F	M	A	M	J	J	A	S	O	N	D
Temp. (°C)	4	4	6	9	13	15	17	17	14	10	7	4

(b) For Miami, Florida, U.S.A.

Month	J	F	M	A	M	J
Temp.(°C)	22	23	24.5	26.5	27.5	28

Month	J	A	S	O	N	D
Temp.(°C)	29.5	30.5	29	27.5	23.5	22

(c) How are the graphs in (a) and (b) alike?
(d) How are the graphs in (a) and (b) different?

11 Gasoline consumption depends on a number of factors such as type of car, size of engine, speed, and so on. One car maker suggests the following gasoline consumptions at certain speeds for their new model.

Speed (km/h)	20	30	40	50	60	70	80	90	100
Gasoline (L/100 km)	8.4	9.6	9.9	10.4	10.6	10.8	11.3	11.9	12.4

(a) Draw a broken line graph for the above data.
(b) You drive at 40 km/h. How much gasoline will you use for a 500-km trip?
(c) You drive at 80 km/h. How much gasoline will you use for a 500-km trip?

11.6   Circle Graphs

Another way of representing data is to use a **circle graph** (also called a **pie graph**). Circle graphs are often used to show comparisons that involve per cents, as shown by the following information.

The following 5 students work at a local fast-food outlet. The hours worked one week are shown in the chart.

Student	Hours worked	Fraction of total	Per cent of total
Barbara	5	$\frac{5}{40}$	12.5%
Shirley	8	$\frac{8}{40}$	20%
RoseMary	12	$\frac{12}{40}$	30%
Elaine	5	$\frac{5}{40}$	12.5%
Valerie	10	$\frac{10}{40}$	25%
Total	40	Total	100%

To show the above information on a circle graph, the circle is marked into parts called **sectors**. The angle subtended by the arc of the sector at the centre of the circle is called the **central angle**.

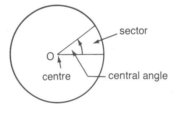

To determine what part of the circle graph should be used for each student, per cent calculations are performed as follows. The chart below shows us how the central angle for each student was found.

Student	Per cent	Calculation central angle
Barbara	12.5%	12.5% of 360° = 45°
Shirley	20%	20% of 360° = 72°
RoseMary	30%	30% of 360° = 108°
Elaine	12.5%	12.5% of 360° = 45°
Valerie	25%	25% of 360° = 90°
		Total = 360°

The above calculations are then used to construct the circle graph.

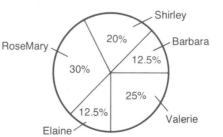

Try These

Questions 1 to 5 refer to this circle graph.

The time spent last summer by Derek at camp is shown by the circle graph.

sailing — swimming

fishing

1 (a) What fraction of the time was spent fishing?
   (b) What percentage of the time was spent fishing?
   (c) What is the measure of the central angle?

2 (a) What fraction of the time was spent swimming?
   (b) What percentage of the time was spent swimming?
   (c) What is the measure of the central angle?

3 (a) What fraction of the time was spent sailing and swimming?
   (b) What percentage of the time was spent sailing and swimming?

4   The total time spent in one week on the three activities is 20 h.
   (a) How many hours are spent fishing?
   (b) How many hours are spent sailing?

5 (a) What is the sum of all the central angles?
   (b) What is the sum of all the per cents for swimming, fishing, and sailing?

Written Exercises

A 1 (a) Estimate the percentage of each circle that is shaded.

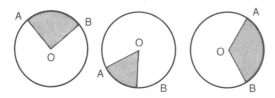

   (b) Find the measure of ∠AOB in each circle.
   (c) Calculate the percentage of the circle that is shaded.
   (d) Compare your answers to those in (a).
   (e) Calculate the percentage of the circle that is not shaded.

2   Construct a circle for each of the following to show
   (a) 25% shaded   (b) 50% shaded
   (c) 20% shaded   (d) 40% shaded
   (e) 45% shaded   (f) 83% shaded

Questions 3 to 5 are based on the following information.

In a survey, 350 persons indicated their favourite movie of the four shown. The results are shown in the circle graph.

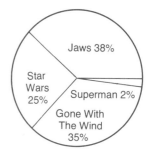

3 (a) Which show was preferred the most?
   (b) Which show was preferred the least?

4 (a) What percentage of the people preferred *Jaws*?
   (b) How many people was this?

5 (a) What percentage of the people preferred *Star Wars*?
   (b) How many people was this?

369

B Questions 6 to 8 are based on the following information.

The circle graph shows the number of hours spent by Henry during a 24-h day.

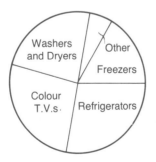

6 (a) Estimate the central angle for sleep. (Do not use a protractor.)
 (b) Use your answer in (a). About how many hours were spent sleeping?
 (c) Measure the central angle and calculate how much time was spent sleeping, to the nearest minute.

7 What percentage of the time was spent on
 (a) school? (b) chores and recreation?

8 How much time, to the nearest minute, was
 (a) spent on homework? (b) spent on meals?

Questions 9 to 12 are based on the following information.

The total sales for an appliance store in a month are shown in the circle graph.

9 The central angle for the washers and dryers is 85° What percentage of the total sales did the washers and dryers account for?

10 What percentage of the total sales did the colour T.V.s account for?

11 The total sales last month were $80 000. Calculate the amount of sales for
 (a) freezers. (b) colour T.V.s.

12 Which generated more sales, refrigerators or washers and dryers? How much more?

Questions 13 and 14 are based on the following information.

A recipe for Chili-Con-Carne contains the following ingredients.

Ingredient	Amount	Per Cent of total
Hamburger	520 g	?
Kidney Beans	280 g	?
Tomato Sauce	150 g	?
Tomato Paste	150 g	?
Chili Seasoning	60 g	?
Water	440 g	?

13 Find the percentage of each ingredient.

14 (a) Construct a circle graph to show the information for Chili-Con-Carne.
 (b) What is the measure of the central angle for hamburger? tomato sauce?

15 Construct a circle graph for each of the following sets of data.
 (a) Human Body (b) Causes of Air Pollution

Elements	Per cent
Carbon	19%
Oxygen	67%
Other	14%

Cause	Per cent
Industry	15%
Transportation	44%
People	9%
Fuel	20%
Other	12%

 (c) For each circle graph, write a problem about the information. Solve the problem.

C 16 (a) A concrete mix consists of 1.5 L of water, 3.8 L of sand, 1 L of cement, and 4.2 L of gravel. Construct a circle graph for the data.
 (b) For a similar concrete, how much cement is there if there are 40 L of concrete mix?

370

Applications: Food Content And Circle Graphs

Circle graphs can be used to show the nutritional content of various foods. The circle graph at right shows the food content of white bread.

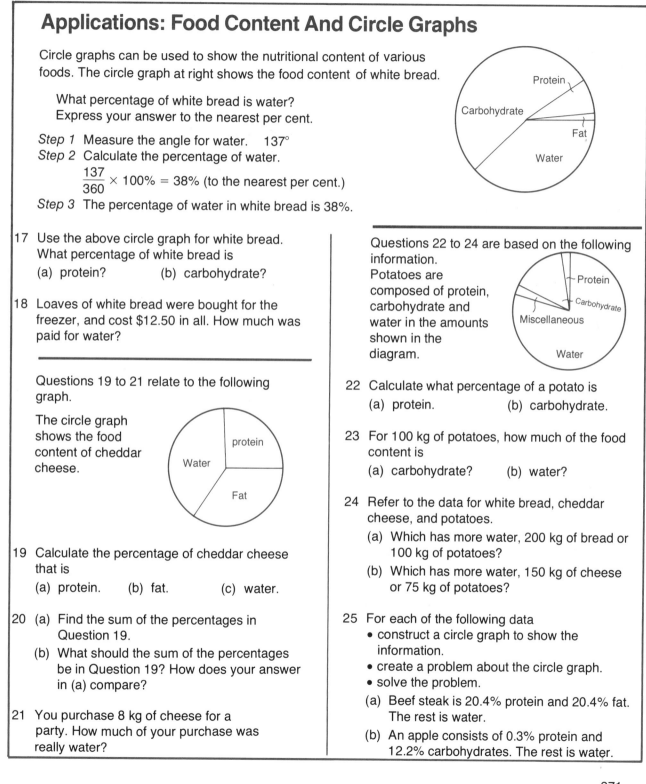

What percentage of white bread is water?
Express your answer to the nearest per cent.

Step 1 Measure the angle for water.   137°
Step 2 Calculate the percentage of water.

$$\frac{137}{360} \times 100\% = 38\% \text{ (to the nearest per cent.)}$$

Step 3 The percentage of water in white bread is 38%.

17 Use the above circle graph for white bread. What percentage of white bread is
   (a) protein?   (b) carbohydrate?

18 Loaves of white bread were bought for the freezer, and cost $12.50 in all. How much was paid for water?

Questions 19 to 21 relate to the following graph.

The circle graph shows the food content of cheddar cheese.

19 Calculate the percentage of cheddar cheese that is
   (a) protein.   (b) fat.   (c) water.

20 (a) Find the sum of the percentages in Question 19.
   (b) What should the sum of the percentages be in Question 19? How does your answer in (a) compare?

21 You purchase 8 kg of cheese for a party. How much of your purchase was really water?

Questions 22 to 24 are based on the following information.
Potatoes are composed of protein, carbohydrate and water in the amounts shown in the diagram.

22 Calculate what percentage of a potato is
   (a) protein.   (b) carbohydrate.

23 For 100 kg of potatoes, how much of the food content is
   (a) carbohydrate?   (b) water?

24 Refer to the data for white bread, cheddar cheese, and potatoes.
   (a) Which has more water, 200 kg of bread or 100 kg of potatoes?
   (b) Which has more water, 150 kg of cheese or 75 kg of potatoes?

25 For each of the following data
   • construct a circle graph to show the information.
   • create a problem about the circle graph.
   • solve the problem.
   (a) Beef steak is 20.4% protein and 20.4% fat. The rest is water.
   (b) An apple consists of 0.3% protein and 12.2% carbohydrates. The rest is water.

11.7 Calculations With Data: Mean, Median, Mode

To determine when a crop of cherries is ready to be picked a sample is taken from each tree. One hundred cherries are picked from each of 11 trees. The numbers of unripe cherries for each tree are:

15 3 17 23 12 18 24 15 8 15 28

Arithmetic Mean
The **arithmetic mean** is one representative of the data.
It is calculated by dividing the sum of the data by the number of data.

Example 1
(a) Calculate the arithmetic mean of the above data to the nearest whole number.

(b) Before a cherry crop will be picked, the mean must be less than 8. Will this crop be picked?

This means that each tree on the average has 16 cherries out of 100 that are not ripe.

Solution
(a) Calculate the mean.
  I Find the sum of the data.   178
  II Divide the sum by the number of items, namely 11. $\frac{178}{11} \doteq 16.2$
  Thus, the mean is 16.

(b) For a crop to be picked, the mean must be less than 8.
  The calculated mean is 16.
    Thus, this crop will not be picked!

Median
The **median** for the above set of data can also be found. To do so, the numbers are arranged from least to greatest.

3 8 12 15 15 15 17 18 23 24 28

least   middle number   greatest

The median for the set of data is 15, the middle number.

Finding the median of a set of numbers is not influenced by the least and greatest numbers. For example, the following set of data has the same median as the set of data above.

0 8 12 15 15 15 17 18 23 24 50

For an even number of results, the median is the average of the two middle numbers.

3 8 12 15 15 15 17 18 23 24 28 50

$$\frac{15 + 17}{2} = 16$$

The median is 16.

372

Mode

The **mode** is the result that occurs most often. For the data, 15 occurs 3 times.

3 8 12 <u>15 15 15</u> 17 18 23 24 28
mode

The mode of the data is 15.

The mode is not influenced by the least and greatest numbers.

Range

The range is another useful result to know. This is the difference between the least and greatest results. For example, the range for the following set of data is the difference between 3, the least number, and 28, the greatest number.

3 8 12 15 15 15 17 18 23 24 28

28 − 3 = 25

The range is 25.

The median, mode, mean and range enable you to analyze data and to determine how the data are clustered (bunched).

Example 2

For the following data, calculate the mean, median, mode, and range. Express your answer to 1 decimal place.

34 35 32 34 31 36 43 33 34

Solution

mean   I Find the sum.   312

II Divide by 9. $\dfrac{312}{9} = 34.\overline{6}$

The mean is 34.7.

median   Arrange the results in order from least to greatest.

31 32 33 34 34 34 35 36 43
↑
middle number

The median is 34.

mode   Use the results above. 34 occurs 3 times.
The mode is 34.

range   Find the difference between the smallest and greatest number.
43 − 31 = 12
The range is 12.

Try These

1 What is the mean for each of the following?

(a) 2 4 6   (b) 5 10 10 5

2 What is the median for each of the following?

(a) 1 3 5 7 9 13 15 18 21

(b) 3 6 9 10 12 13 13 15

3 What is the mode for each of the following?

(a) 9 3 6 5 4 3 1 9 8

(b) 3 16 18 12 13 16 14 16

4 What is the range for each of the following?

(a) 3 9 6 15 28 13 6 12

(b) 19 8 7 9 6 3 12 25

5 What is the mean, median, mode and range for each of the following?

(a) 3 15 4 5 3   (b) 2 8 6 4 12 4

Written Exercises

A 1 Find the mode for each of the following.

(a) 56 53 31 30 45 55 31

(b) 20 6 0 10 16 12 10 24 8

(c) 16 6 24 16 28 18 16 12 10

(d) 0 16 18 12 6 4 2 72 72 12

2 Find the arithmetic mean for each of the following sets of data. Round off your calculations when necessary to 1 decimal place.

(a) 43 49 56 61 45 52 74

(b) 46 48 50 50 52 53 49

(c) 6.6 5.9 6.8 9.6 5.2 6.9 9.9 8.8 9.6

(d) 30 30 45 28 31 31 45 30 40

3 Find the median and mode for each of the following.

(a) 96 160 97 100 97 98 97

(b) 7 12 9 8 7 11 5 7 3 2

(c) 19 18 28 60 18 21 14 17 18 16

4 (a) Find the mean and median for the following data.

14 18 22 11 38 21 19 15 16

(b) Do the data in (a) have a mode? Why?

5 (a) Find the mean, median, and mode for the following data.

7 14 14 8 9 11 8 10 7 6 8

(b) Which characteristic: the median, mode, or mean, is the easiest to find? Why?

6 (a) If the median of a set of numbers is 15, must 15 be one of the numbers of the data?

(b) Construct an example to illustrate your answer in (a).

7 (a) If the mode of a set of numbers is 15, must 15 be one of the numbers of the data?

(b) Construct an example to illustrate your answer in (a).

8 (a) If the mean of a set of numbers is 15, must 15 be one of the numbers of the data?

(b) Construct an example to illustrate your answer in (a).

B 9 For each of the following, find the

(a) mean.   (b) median.   (c) mode.   (d) range.

A 15 10 17 11 20 9 16 14 22

B 44 36 40 35 41 43 35

C 24 29 20 22 21 18 32 15 19 25

D 7.3 8.2 5.5 9.8 10.3 8.7 3.9 7.1 8.5

374

Questions 10 to 15 are based on the following.

A $\{4, 7, 9, 9, 11\}$

B $\{17, 29, 17, 12, 50, 17, 17, 25\}$

C $\{6, 7, 9, 19, 19, 35, 35, 67\}$

D $\{150, 123, 128, 149, 123, 19\}$

E $\{49, 40, 39, 58, 21, 56, 34, 7, 56\}$

F $\{1980, 24\}$

10 Find the mean and the median for each of the above sets.

11 (a) In which of the above sets is the mean greater than the median?
   (b) What do you know about the data when the mean is greater than the median?

12 (a) In which of the above is the median greater than the mean?
   (b) What do you know about the data when the median is greater than the mean?

13 What conclusion can you state when the mean and median are the same?

14 (a) Find the mode for each of the above sets.
   (b) What does the mode tell you about the data?

15 (a) Find the range for each of the above sets.
   (b) What does the range tell you about the data?

16 The numbers of cars that were sold for 10 consecutive months by Northstar Auto Sales were recorded as

   23 25 13 11 24 26 13 27 21 26

   (a) Find the mean.   (b) Find the mode.

17 In Victoria, B.C. the total rainfall in millimetres for each month during 1 a was as follows.

   66 84 132 147 171 195
   159 171 261 222 126 63

   (a) What is the mean?   (b) What is the median?

18 During a competition the judges awarded these points.

   7.0 7.0 9.6 9.4 10.0 8.8 9.2 9.8 9.0 8.5

   (a) Find the mean, median, and mode.
   (b) Which result in (a) do you think best describes the data?

19 For a Consumer Watch, the prices of different brands of peanut butter were recorded for the same size of jar.

   85¢ 79¢ 80¢ 77¢ 85¢ 93¢ 95¢ 99¢ 88¢

   (a) Find the mean of the prices.
   (b) Find the median of the prices.
   (c) Find the mode of the prices.
   (d) Which of the mean, median, or mode, best describes the price of peanut butter?

20 The number of accidents at an intersection for 12 consecutive months is shown below.

Month	J	F	M	A	M	J	J	A	S	O	N	D
Number of accidents	21	19	16	12	14	17	7	7	17	9	10	12

   (a) Find the mean, median, and mode.
   (b) Which of your answers in (a) best represents the data?
   (c) Based on the above data, what would you predict as the number of accidents for each of the next 3 months?

C 21 Lorimer High School's wrestling team has 6 wrestlers with a mean mass of 96 kg. If the masses of 5 of the wrestlers are 100 kg, 93 kg, 89 kg, 98 kg, and 95 kg, what is the mass of the sixth wrestler?

11.8 Working With Probability

You have probably heard statements such as the following:

▶ The chance of rain is 15%.
▶ The police department predicts that 25 accidents will occur during the weekend.
▶ Edmonton will probably win the Stanley Cup.

If you have attended any games such as soccer or football you will have probably seen the referee toss a coin at the start to decide which end a team will take. Each captain knows that the chances of winning the toss are equal. The coin, when tossed, will land either heads up or tails up. Thus each captain has a 1 out of 2 chance of winning. You write the probability as follows:

The probability of getting heads is $\frac{1}{2}$. $\frac{\text{number of favourable outcomes}}{\text{total number of possible outcomes}}$

Example

In a bag are 3 dimes, 6 nickels and a penny. What is the probability of choosing from the bag

(a) a dime? (b) a nickel?

(c) a quarter? (d) any coin?

In the example, a favourable outcome is choosing a coin you want. A possible outcome is choosing any coin, whether you want it or not. Thus, the number of possible outcomes is 10.

Solution

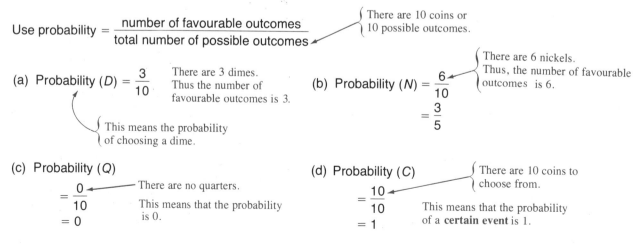

Use probability $= \dfrac{\text{number of favourable outcomes}}{\text{total number of possible outcomes}}$

{ There are 10 coins or 10 possible outcomes.

(a) Probability $(D) = \dfrac{3}{10}$

There are 3 dimes. Thus the number of favourable outcomes is 3.

{ This means the probability of choosing a dime.

(b) Probability $(N) = \dfrac{6}{10}$

$= \dfrac{3}{5}$

{ There are 6 nickels. Thus, the number of favourable outcomes is 6.

(c) Probability (Q)

$= \dfrac{0}{10}$

$= 0$

— There are no quarters.

This means that the probability is 0.

(d) Probability (C)

$= \dfrac{10}{10}$

$= 1$

{ There are 10 coins to choose from.

This means that the probability of a **certain event** is 1.

Written Exercises

A 1 Calculate the probability for each of the following.

	(a)	(b)	(c)	(d)
number of favourable outcomes	4	3	6	8
number of possible outcomes	9	10	12	20

2 In a bag are 12 cubes numbered 1 to 12. You choose one from the bag. After each question, you place the cube back in the bag. What is the probability that you will choose
   (a) a cube with 1?   (b) a cube with 12?
   (c) an even cube?   (d) an odd cube?
   (e) a cube with numbers less than 7?

B 3 A province of Canada is chosen at random.

   Alberta   British Columbia
   Manitoba   New Brunswick
   Newfoundland   Nova Scotia
   Ontario   Prince Edward Island
   Quebec   Saskatchewan

   What is the probability that the province
   (a) begins with the letter Q?
   (b) borders on the Pacific Ocean?
   (c) borders on the Atlantic Ocean?

4 A gum machine contains 40 white, 60 blue, 32 yellow and 18 orange pieces of gum. If the machine releases one piece at a time, find

   (a) P(blue).   Means the probability of getting a blue piece of gum.

   (b) P(orange). (c) P(yellow).   (d) P(white).

5 A deck of cards has 52 cards in all consisting of 13 diamonds, 13 clubs, 13 hearts, 13 spades. What is the probability of taking from a well-shuffled deck
   (a) an ace?   (b) a king?   (c) a 10 of clubs
   (d) a 5 of hearts?   (e) a black ace?
   (f) a red king?   (g) a face card?
   (h) an even-numbered card?

If you toss a coin 3 times in a row, what is the probability you will get 3 heads in a row? A **tree diagram** is used to make a list of all possible outcomes.

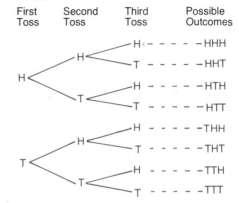

Use the tree diagram above for Questions 6 and 7.

6 (a) What is the total number of possible outcomes?
   (b) How many possible outcomes of HHH (three heads) are there?
   (c) What is the probability of tossing 3 heads in a row?

7 What is the probability of tossing
   (a) three tails in a row?
   (b) two heads and a tail (in any order)?
   (c) two tails and a head (in any order)?

8 (a) Draw a tree diagram for tossing a dime followed by a quarter.
   (b) How many possible outcomes are there?

9 Construct a tree diagram to show the possible outcomes of tossing 4 coins in a row.

10 Use the information in Question 9. What is the probability of tossing
   (a) 4 heads?
   (b) two tails and two heads (in any order)?
   (c) all coins alike?
   (d) three heads and a tail (in any order)?

Skills To Practise: A Chapter Review

The number of cars counted for 15 min at an intersection is shown.

Frequency Table

Car	Tally	Frequency
Toyota (compact)	THL THL III	?
Ford (full size)	THL II	?
Datsun (compact)	THL THL THL I	?
Chevrolet (full size)	THL THL	?
Chrysler (full size)	THL I	?

Use the tally chart to answer the following questions.

1 What was the frequency for
   (a) Toyotas? (b) Fords? (c) Datsuns?

2 Which type of car passed the intersection
   (a) the greatest (b) the least number of times?

3 What was the total number of
   (a) compact cars?   (b) full-size cars?

4 What was the total number of cars that passed in 15 min?

Questions 5 to 7 are based on the following graph.

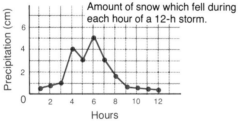

Amount of snow which fell during each hour of a 12-h storm.

5 (a) During which hour did the greatest amount of snow fall?
   (b) How much snow was this?

6 (a) During which hours did less than 1 cm of snow fall?
   (b) During which hours did more than 3 cm of snow fall?

7 During which hours did the snowfall
   (a) increase?   (b) decrease?

Problems to Practise: A Chapter Review

The faster a car goes, the greater the distance the car requires to come to a safe stop. The graph below shows the safe stopping distances at various speeds.

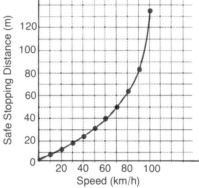

1 What is the safe stopping distance for each of the following speeds?
   (a) 30 km/h   (b) 40 km/h   (c) 50 km/h

2 What is the safe speed at which to drive if the safe stopping distance is
   (a) 20 m?   (b) 40 m?   (c) 60 m?

3 About how much greater is the safe stopping distance
   (a) at 40 km/h than at 20 km/h?
   (b) at 80 km/h than at 40 km/h?
   (c) at 100 km/h than at 50 km/h?

4 The chart below shows the population of the earth at different times.

Year	1650	1700	1750	1800	1850	1900	1950
Population in billions	0.60	0.62	0.80	0.95	1.20	1.70	12.55

   (a) Construct a broken line graph to show the data.
   (b) Use the graph. What do you estimate the population to be in the year 2000?

Chapter Checkup: A Practice Test

You deserve a rest!

Introduction to Algebra

operations with monomials, add and subtract polynomials, substitution skills, exponents, common factor, applications and problem-solving

Introduction

Regardless of what your future holds, you will need to be able to use mathematics. And, as you will learn in this chapter, an important part of mathematics is the study of algebra.

Skills in algebra are needed
▶ to calculate the exact path of the daredevil.
▶ to predict the profit of a store.

The study of algebra will help you to organize information to solve problems and also will enable you to use formulas to do calculations. Earlier, you noticed that skills in arithmetic were useful tools for solving problems. You will find that algebra is also a useful mathematical tool for solving problems.

Arithmetic problems deal with numbers which can be represented by numerals. For example,

The room measures 10 m by 10 m. What is the perimeter?

John is 15 a. Fareda is 13 a. How much older is John?

Algebra problems deal with numbers which vary or are unknown and thus must be represented by variable expressions. For example,

Salary = Wage/hour × number of hours

$E = mc^2$

The following chapters will enable you to answer the questions:
What is algebra? How is algebra used?

12.1 The Language of Algebra

The skills you learned with numbers in arithmetic are needed to learn similar skills in algebra. For example,

Expressions in arithmetic		Expressions in algebra
$2 + 2$		$x + x$
2^2	How are these	x^2
$3(4) - 7$	expressions the same?	$3x - 7$
$5(6) + 2(9)$	How are they different?	$5a + 2b$
$2(3)(5)$		pqr

Expressions such as $x + x$, x^2, $5a + 2b$ are referred to as **algebraic expressions**.

To work with algebra you need to learn its language.

Term

Algebraic expressions $\quad 2x + 3y \qquad 3y - 4x$

terms $\qquad\qquad$ terms

Terms of expressions are separated by plus or minus signs.

Monomial

A monomial has one term. For example, $3a$, $-7d$, $15x^2$, 10, x, xy are monomials.

Binomial

A binomial has two terms. For example, $3x + 4y$, $-a + b$, $5a + 6m$ are binomials.

Trinomial

A trinomial has three terms. For example, $5a - 3b + c$, $10a^2 + 3b^2 + 6c$, $m + 9n - 3$ are trinomials.

An algebraic expression is often called a **polynomial**.

Coefficient

The letter part is called the **literal coefficient** or the **variable coefficient**.

$$2b \qquad 5b \qquad -3b$$

The number part is called the **numerical coefficient**.

Like Terms

Terms that have the same literal coefficients are called **like terms**.

Like Terms $2mn \quad -3mn \quad 4mn$ — the same literal coefficient

Unlike $\quad 2a \quad 3b \quad -4c$ — different
Terms $\quad 2mn \quad 4mp \quad -3np$ — literal coefficients

Like terms may be added or subtracted as shown in Example 1.
Which of the following terms are like terms?

Example 1

Add (a) $14x, 3x, -5x, 6x$

(b) $3a, 4b, 2a, -2b$

Solution

(a) $14x + 3x - 5x + 6x$

    $= 17x - 5x + 6x$ With practice you may write the sum quickly.

    $= 12x + 6x$ $14x + 3x - 5x + 6x = 18x$

    $= 18x$ Think $(14 + 3 - 5 + 6 = 18)$

(b) $3a + 4b + 2a - 2b$

    $= 3a + 2a + 4b - 2b$ Collect like terms first.

    $= 5a + 2b$

Example 2

Simplify each of the following.

(a) $2x + 3x$

(b) $2a - 3b + 4a - 5b$

(c) $-6a - 3 + 10a$

Solution

(a) $2x + 3x$

    $= 5x$

(b) $2a - 3b + 4a - 5b$ Remember $-3b - 5b$

    $= 2a + 4a - 3b - 5b$ means $(-3b) + (-5b)$

    $= 6a \quad - 8b$ $= -8b$

(c) $-6a - 3 + 10a$

    $= -6a + 10a - 3$ This expression may not be simplified

    $= 4a - 3$ ◄———   further. Why?

Try These

1   What is the numerical coefficient of each of the following?

(a) $3x$ (b) $17y$ (c) $5xy$ (d) $\frac{1}{2}m^2n$

(e) $-5y$ (f) $-\frac{3}{2}x^2yz$ (g) xy^2 (h) $-x^2y$

(i)   What is the literal coefficient of each of the terms above?

2   Look at this list of terms.

    $-2x$ $-2xy^2$ $\frac{1}{2}x$ $-3b$ $3xy$

    $-2mn^2$ $5x$ $-5mn^2$ $6xy$ $-8x$

    $\frac{3}{2}b$ $12xy^2$ $2ab$ $\frac{1}{2}x^2y$ $9m^2n$

Which of them are like

(a) $3x$?   (b) $2b$?   (c) $-2xy^2$? (d) $3m^2n$?

Written Exercises

A   1   Which of the following pairs of terms are like terms?

(a) $3m, -2m$ (b) $4a, -5b$

(c) $3k, 2m$ (d) $4x, -6x$

(e) $4xy, -2xy$ (f) $3x^2y, -2xy^2$

2   Which of the following pairs of terms are unlike terms?

(a) $-2k, \frac{1}{2}k$ (b) $3p, 2pq$

(c) $3ab, -2ab$ (d) $3mn, -6np$

(e) $-8xy, 6xy$ (f) $8mn^2, -6m^2n$

3 Add each pair of terms.
   (a) $3x$, $2x$ (b) $-6y$, $-2y$
   (c) $8a$, $-6a$ (d) $6ab$, $-3ab$
   (e) $2xy$, $6xy$ (f) $-2x^2$, $4x^2$

4 Simplify each of the following.
   (a) $3a - 2a$ (b) $6b - 8b$
   (c) $6m - 2m$ (d) $-4p - 6p$
   (e) $4ab - 3ab$ (f) $-4x^2 - 2x^2$

5 Add the following terms.
   (a) $2x$, $3x$, $-4x$ (b) $-2m$, $3m$, $6m$
   (c) $3ab$, $2ab$, $-ab$ (d) $8mp$, $-2mp$, $6mp$

B 6 Simplify.
   (a) $2x + 5x - 3x$ (b) $4a - 2a + a$
   (c) $8n - 5n + n$ (d) $6pq + 3pq$
   (e) $9m^2n + 10m^2n$ (f) $7rq^2 - 4rq^2$

7 Simplify.
   (a) $2m + 3m + n$ (b) $2a + 3b + 4a$
   (c) $6x - 2y + 3x$ (d) $8k - 2m + k$
   (e) $2p - 3q + p$ (f) $-6g - 3f + 2g$

8 Add the following terms.
   (a) $4a$, $-3b$, $2a$ (b) $3m$, $-6p$, $2m$
   (c) pq, $-3pq$, $3pq$ (d) $2a$, $-3b$, $5b$
   (e) $2ab$, $-3ab$, $4a$ (f) $2r$, $-3r$, $5p$

9 Simplify each of the following by collecting like
   terms.
   (a) $3a + 2a + 3b - 2b$ (b) $4x + x - y + 3y$
   (c) $-x + 2x + 4 - 3y$ (d) $-6a - 4b + 7a - b$
   (e) $3y + 2x - y + x$ (f) $3m - m + m - 2m$

10 Which answers in Question 9 are
    (a) monomials? (b) binomials? (c) trinomials?

11 Simplify each of the following.
    (a) $3a + 7b - 2a + b$
    (b) $3x + 4y + 7x - y$
    (c) $3y^2 + 2y - 6y^2 + 2y$
    (d) $3x + 10 - 4x + 1$
    (e) $5a - 5 + 6a - 6$
    (f) $10x^2 - 5x + 5x - 9x^2$
    (g) $2xy + 3xy - x^2 + 3x^2$
    (h) $a^2 - 2a + 5 + 3a^2 - 2$

12 All the answers in Question 11 are
    polynomials. Which ones are
    (a) monomials? (b) binomials? (c) trinomials?

Calculator Tip

In your work in mathematics, you have seen
throughout this book the need to be organized.
Similarly, in working with a calculator you also
need to organize your work and plan your
calculations.
Use the following flow chart to help organize
your work.

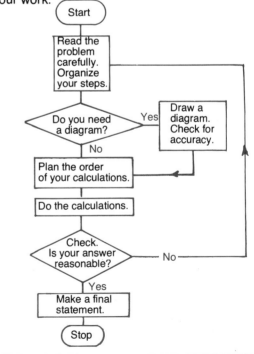

382

Applications: Developing Formula From Diagrams

Earlier you used various formulas to do calculations involving perimeter. With the skill of adding like terms you can develop many formulas. For example,

From the diagram, the perimeter, P, is given by

$P = l + w + l + w$

$P = 2l + 2w$

> You used this formula earlier to calculate perimeter.

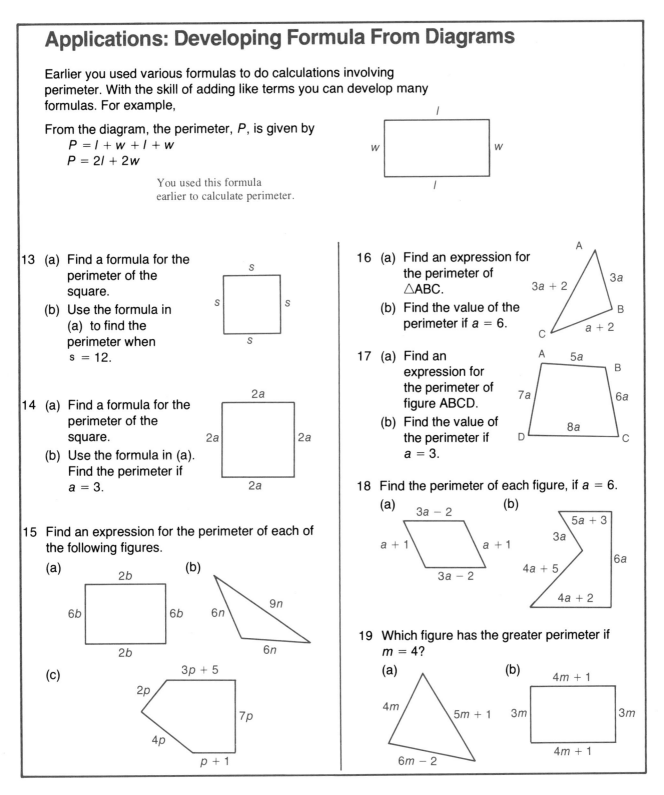

13 (a) Find a formula for the perimeter of the square.

(b) Use the formula in (a) to find the perimeter when $s = 12$.

14 (a) Find a formula for the perimeter of the square.

(b) Use the formula in (a). Find the perimeter if $a = 3$.

15 Find an expression for the perimeter of each of the following figures.

(a)

(b)

(c)

16 (a) Find an expression for the perimeter of $\triangle ABC$.

(b) Find the value of the perimeter if $a = 6$.

17 (a) Find an expression for the perimeter of figure ABCD.

(b) Find the value of the perimeter if $a = 3$.

18 Find the perimeter of each figure, if $a = 6$.

(a)

(b)

19 Which figure has the greater perimeter if $m = 4$?

(a)

(b)

12.2   Add And Subtract: Polynomials

Earlier you added like terms.

$4x + 3x$
$= 7x$

To subtract a term, you add its opposite.

$4x - (-2x)$
$= 4x + 2x$

The skill of adding terms can be applied to the addition and subtraction of polynomials. To add polynomials, often you need to simplify the polynomial by removing brackets.

Example 1

Simplify each of the following.

(a) $3m + (2m - 6n)$

(b) $(2a + 3b) + (4a - b)$

Solution

(a) $3m + (2m - 6n)$
    $= 3m + 2m - 6n$
    $= 5m - 6n$

(b) $(2a + 3b) + (4a - b)$
    $= 2a + 3b + 4a - b$
    $= 6a + 2b$ ◄——— $6a$ and $2b$ are unlike terms and thus cannot be simplified further.

To subtract an integer, you add its opposite.

$2 - (-3)$
$= 2 + (+3)$
$= 5$

These are opposite polynomials.

polynomial	opposite
$2x$	$-2x$
$-3y$	$3y$
$2x + y$	$-2x - y$

Just as with integers, to subtract a polynomial, you add its opposite.

Example 2

Simplify.

(a) $4x - (-3x + y)$

(b) $(2x + 4y) - (x - y)$

Solution

(a) $4x - (-3x + y)$ ◄——— The opposite of
    $= 4x + (3x - y)$ $-3x + y$ is $3x - y$.
    $= 4x + 3x - y$
    $= 7x - y$

(b) $(2x + 4y) - (x - y)$
    $= 2x + 4y + (-x + y)$
    $= 2x + 4y - x + y$
    $= x + 5y$

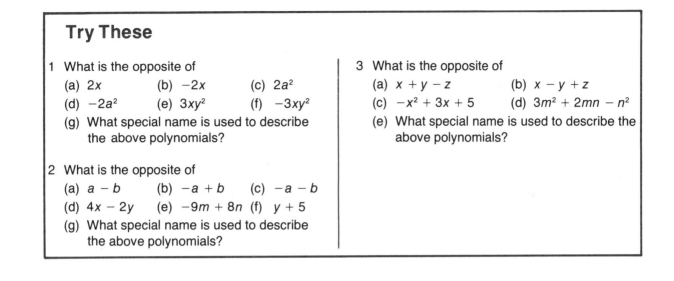

Try These

1 What is the opposite of
   (a) $2x$ (b) $-2x$ (c) $2a^2$
   (d) $-2a^2$ (e) $3xy^2$ (f) $-3xy^2$
   (g) What special name is used to describe
       the above polynomials?

2 What is the opposite of
   (a) $a - b$ (b) $-a + b$ (c) $-a - b$
   (d) $4x - 2y$ (e) $-9m + 8n$ (f) $y + 5$
   (g) What special name is used to describe
       the above polynomials?

3 What is the opposite of
   (a) $x + y - z$ (b) $x - y + z$
   (c) $-x^2 + 3x + 5$ (d) $3m^2 + 2mn - n^2$
   (e) What special name is used to describe the
       above polynomials?

Written Exercises

A 1 Write the opposite of each of the following.
   (a) $3x$ (b) $-3x$ (c) $4a^2$
   (d) $m - p$ (e) $-2m + p$ (f) $-2m - p$
   (g) $3a - b + c$ (h) $4a + b - c$
   (i) $-2a^2 - 3a + 5$ (j) $a^2 - 5a - 5$

2 Add.
   (a) $(2x + y) + 3x$ (b) $(y - 2x) + 2x$
   (c) $3k + (2k + m)$ (d) $5k + (2k - m)$
   (e) $(3m + p) + 3p$ (f) $(2r - s) + s$

3 Simplify.
   (a) $2a + (3a - 1)$ (b) $6x + (2x + 9)$
   (c) $9m + (9 - 2m)$ (d) $10p + (-3p - 4a)$
   (e) $(6r + 4) + 7r$ (f) $15w + (3m - 2w)$
   (g) $10a + (3a - 4b)$ (h) $4z + (x - 2z)$

4 Simplify.
   (a) $(3x + 2y) - (-2x)$ (b) $(5m - n) - (-n)$
   (c) $6x - (x + y)$ (d) $3m - (2m - m)$
   (e) $3k - (-2k + m)$ (f) $-4y - (-y - x)$

5 Follow instructions carefully. Add or subtract.
   (a) $(3m - p) + 3p$ (b) $(3m - p) - 3p$
   (c) $2k + (2k + s)$ (d) $2k - (2k + s)$
   (e) $(3ab - b) + 2ab$ (f) $(3ab - b) - 2ab$

6 Simplify.
   (a) $(3x + 8) + 4$ (b) $(3x + 8) - 4x$
   (c) $5 + (2a - 6)$ (d) $5 - (2a - 6)$
   (e) $3m + (2m - 2)$ (f) $3m - (2m - 2)$

7 Add.
   (a) $\begin{array}{r} 2x - 3y \\ 4x + 5y \\ \hline \end{array}$ (b) $\begin{array}{r} 2a - b \\ -a + 5b \\ \hline \end{array}$

   (c) $\begin{array}{r} 3m - 2n \\ 5m + 5n \\ \hline \end{array}$ (d) $\begin{array}{r} 3x - 2y + z \\ -2x + y - z \\ \hline \end{array}$

8 Subtract.

(a) $3m - 2p$
$\underline{2m + 2p}$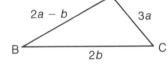

(b) $-4a + 5b$
$\underline{-a + 5b}$

(c) $-3k - 2s$
$\underline{3k - s}$

(d) $2a^2 - 3a + 5$
$\underline{a^2 - 2a - 4}$

B 9 Add.

(a) $4m + (5m + 9)$ (b) $6a + (10a - 4)$
(c) $(3p - 2) + 6p$ (d) $(-10r - 4) + 7r$
(e) $(2x^2 - 1) + (3x^2 + 7)$
(f) $(5a^2 + 3) + (-7a^2 - 4)$

10 Simplify.

(a) $8x + (6x - 3y)$
(b) $(8y - 15) + (y - 14)$
(c) $(10r^2 - 2r) + (10r^2 - 10r)$
(d) $(2x^2 - 3x + 5) + (4x^2 + 6x - 8)$

11 Find an expression for the perimeter of △ABC.

A, $2a - b$, $3a$, B, $2b$, C

12 Find an expression for the perimeter of figure ABCD.

$3x - 2y$, A, B, $3y$, $2x$, D, $4x + y$, C

13 Add the following.

(a) $10a - 3b$, $4a - b$ and $3a + 2b$
(b) $10a - 4b$, $-9c + 2a$ and $16a - 3c$
(c) $(2ab + 10ab^2)$ and $(4ab - 5ab^2)$

14 Complete each subtraction.

(a) $(7x - 5y) - (5x + 3y)$
(b) $(10 - 2x) - (7 - 2x)$
(c) $(2x - 4) - (x + 4)$
(d) $(3m - 1) - (-2m - 3)$

15 Simplify each of the following.

Simplify in this question may mean to add or to subtract. Read the symbols carefully!

(a) $(2x - 3y) + (x + y)$
(b) $(5a - 2b) - (3a + b)$
(c) $(8 + 7m) - (-8 - 7m)$
(d) $(8b - 4) + (-5b - 4)$
(e) $(12y^2 - 5z^2) - (12y^2 + 5z^2)$

16 Simplify.

(a) $(a^2 - 2a + 1) + (a^2 + 3a - 4)$
(b) $(3x^2 - 10x + 1) - (5x^2 + 2x - 6)$
(c) $(z^2 - 3z + 10) + (z^2 + 5z - 6)$

17 Simplify.

(a) $(a + b) + (a + b) + (a + b)$
(b) $(2x - 3y) + (7x + y) - x$
(c) $2x^2 + (4x + y^2) - x + (x^2 - y^2)$

C

18 Answer the skill-testing questions.

(a) To win a trip to Monte Carlo, answer the skill-testing question.

Which term in the simplified expression has the greater numerical coefficient?

$(3a - 2b) - (5a - 4b) - 3a$

(b) For a trip of your choice anywhere in Canada, answer the skill-testing question. Which term in the simplified expression has a numerical coefficient ending in zero?

$(4x^2 - 3x) - (5x^2 + 4x) - (3x + x^2)$

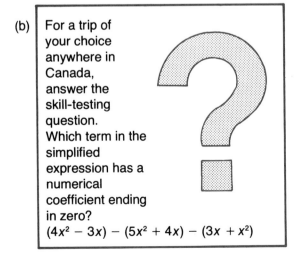

12.3 Following Instructions

You must understand the language of mathematics in order to follow instructions correctly.

In mathematics a symbol often represents different words with a similar meaning. For example,

Symbol	These words suggest the symbol.
+	plus, add, sum, increase, and so on.
−	minus, subtract, difference, exceeds and so on.

Example

From the sum of $2x$ and $3x - y$, subtract $3x - 4y$.

Solution

I Find the sum of $2x$ and $3x - y$.

$2x + (3x - y)$

$= 2x + 3x - y$

$= 5x - y$

II Subtract $3x - 4y$ from the sum.

$5x - y - (3x - 4y)$

$= 5x - y + (-3x + 4y)$

$= 5x - y - 3x + 4y$

$= 2x + 3y$

Written Exercises

1 Write 5 words that each of these symbols represent.

(a) +   (b) −

2 For each of the following, the symbol + is needed.

(a) Find the sum of $-3x + 1$ and $2x - 2$.

(b) Add $4a + 1$, $-5a$, and $7a + 6$.

(c) Find the total of $2x - 3y$, $4x$ and $-3x + 4y$.

(d) Find the result if $2a - 3b$ is increased by $-3a + b$.

3 For each of the following, the symbol − is needed.

(a) Subtract $4m - 3n$ from $-8m + 2n$.

(b) Find the difference if $3k - 2p$ is subtracted from $4k + 2p$.

(c) Find by how much $4k - s$ exceeds $k - 4s$.

(d) Find the result if $3p - 2q$ is decreased by $-p + q$.

For Questions 4 to 10, translate each of the following. Simplify your answers.

4 Find the sum of $3x^2 - 2x + 5$ and $4x^2 + 5x - 8$.

5 Subtract $4p^2 - 2pq + q^2$ from $-3p^2 + 2pq + q^2$.

6 Find the difference if $a^2 - 2ab + 5b^2$ is subtracted from $-a^2 + ab - 4b^2$.

7 From the sum of $x^2 + 3x$ and $3x - 5$ subtract $2x^2 - 5x + 5$.

8 From the sum of $2p + m$ and $3p - 3m$ subtract $-2p + m$.

9 By how much does $(3p - 2) + (2p - 6)$ exceed $(3p + 1) + (2p - 3)$?

10 Subtract $(3a + b) + (2a - b)$ from $(3a - 2b) + (-2b - 3a)$.

12.4 Substitution Skills In Algebra

An expression for the perimeter, P, of this figure can be written as follows:

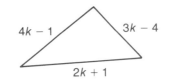

$P = (4k - 1) + (3k - 4) + (2k + 1)$

How would you write a simpler expression for the perimeter?

To calculate the perimeter, first simplify the expression.

$P = (4k - 1) + (3k - 4) + (2k + 1)$
$\quad = 4k - 1 + 3k - 4 + 2k + 1$
$\quad = 9k - 4$

If $k = 4$, calculate the value of P.

$P = 9k - 4$ ←— Record the expression,
$\quad = 9(4) - 4$ ←— then substitute $k = 4$.
$\quad = 36 - 4$ $\quad$ Replace k by 4 in the
$\quad = 32$ $\qquad$ expression.

Thus, the perimeter is 32 .

By applying algebraic skills you can simplify calculations when solving problems. For example:

Calculate the value of each expression using the values $a = 2$, $b = -3$.

A: $3a - 2b$
$\quad = 3(2) - 2(-3)$
$\quad = 6 + 6$
$\quad = 12$

B: $(2a - 2b) + a$
$\quad = [2(2) - 2(-3)] + (2)$
$\quad = 4 + 6 + 2$
$\quad = 12$

C: $(a - b) - (b - 2a)$
$\quad = [2 - (-3)] - [(-3) - 2(2)]$
$\quad = (2 + 3) - (-3 - 4)$
$\quad = 5 + 7$
$\quad = 12$

What do you notice about the answers found above? The expressions have the same value. This is no surprise because *the expressions are the same, but in a different form.*

A: $3a - 2b$

B: $(2a - 2b) + a$
$\quad = 2a - 2b + a$
$\quad = 3a - 2b$

C: $(a - b) - (b - 2a)$
$\quad = a - b - b + 2a$
$\quad = 3a - 2b$

Expressions A, B, and C are called **equivalent expressions** since for all values of the variables a and b, the expressions A, B, and C have the same value.

388

Try These

1 Find the value of the expression $3p - 2$ for each value of p.
  (a) $p = 1$ (b) $p = 2$ (c) $p = -1$

2 Find the value of the expression $b^2 + 1$ for each value of b.
  (a) $b = 1$ (b) $b = 0$ (c) $b = -1$

3 Find the value of the expression $3m + 2n$ for each pair of values.
  (a) $m = 1, n = 1$ (b) $m = 0, n = 1$
  (c) $m = 1, n = 0$

4 Find the value of each expression. Use $m = 1$, and $n = 1$.
  (a) $m + n$ (b) $m - n$ (c) $2m + n$
  (d) $2m - n$ (e) $3m + 2n$ (f) $3m - 2n$

Written Exercises

A 1 Use $x = 2$, $y = 4$, and find the value of
  (a) $2x - y$ (b) $-(y - 2x)$ (c) $-(-2x + y)$
  (d) What do you notice about the above answers?

2 Use $a = -2$, $b = 5$. Find the value of
  (a) $-4a + b$.   (b) $-(4a - b)$.
  (c) What do you notice about your answers?

3 If $a = 2$, find the value of
  (a) $3a - (2a - a)$.   (b) $2a$.
  (c) Why are the answers in (a) and (b) the same?

4 (a) Simplify $(5x - 2y) + (3x - 6y)$.
  (b) Simplify $(12x - 9y) - (4x - y)$.
  (c) Why are the expressions in (a) and (b) equivalent?

5 (a) Simplify $(7x - 4) + (5x + 1)$.
  (b) Use $x = 1$ to check your answer in (a).

6 (a) Simplify $(3a - 2b) + (a - b) - (3a + 5b)$.
  (b) Use $a = 1$, $b = 1$, to check your answer in (a).

7 (a) Simplify each expression.
    A $5a - (3a - 3b)$
    B $b + (2a + 2b)$
    C $4a - (2a - 3b)$
  (b) Which expressions in (a) are equivalent?

B 8 Simplify and then evaluate each expression if $x = 3$.
  (a) $(5x + 2x) + (3x + 4x)$
  (b) $(2x^2 - 5x) + (x^2 + 4x)$
  (c) $3x^2 + 4x - (3 + x) - (1 + x^2)$

9 Simplify each of the following. Check your answers.
  (a) $(2a + 4) + (3a - 2)$
  (b) $(10m + 3) - (7m - 3)$
  (c) $(6m^2 - 3m + 4) - (m^2 - m - 1)$
  (d) $(10ab - b\ ) - (ab - 2b\ )$

10 (a) Write an expression for the perimeter of this rectangle.
   (b) Simplify the expression in (a).
   (c) Find the perimeter of the rectangle if $x = 4$.

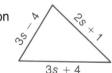

$8x - 2$

$5x - 1$

$8x - 2$

$5x - 1$

11 (a) Find an expression for the perimeter of the figure.
   (b) Find the value of the perimeter if $s = 4$.

$3s - 4$ $2s + 1$

$3s + 4$

C 12 (a) Subtract the total of $2x^2 - 5$ and $3x + 6$ from $3x^2 - 2x + 8$.
   (b) Use $x = 1$ to check your work in (a).

389

12.5 Multiplying Monomials

A diagram may be used as an aid in understanding how to multiply monomials.

I Each side of the rectangle is marked. The area of the rectangle in square units is given by

   Area $= 3m \times 2n$

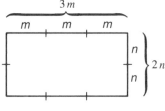

II The area can also be found by using the diagram as marked.

Area of each part is
$m \times n$ or mn

Area $= mn + mn + mn + mn + mn + mn$
     $= 6mn$

The areas in I and II are equal
Thus $3m \times 2n = 6mn$.
From results, such as the one above, a pattern for multiplying monomials can be seen.

$3m \times 2n = 6mn$ ———— Step A Multiply the numerical coefficients.

————— Step B Multiply the literal coefficients.

Example 1

Multiply each of the following.

(a) $(4a)(5b)$ (b) $-3k(2p)$ (c) $\left(-\dfrac{1}{2}m\right)(-4n)$

Solution

(a) $(4a)(5b) = 20ab$

Think
Step A multiply numerical coefficients

Step B multiply literal coefficients.

(b)
$-3k(2p) = -6kp$

Think
Step A $-3 \times 2 = -6$

Step B $k \times p = kp$

(c) $\left(-\dfrac{1}{2}m\right)(-4n) = 2mn$

Think
Step A $\quad = \left(-\dfrac{1}{2}\right)(-4) = 2$

Step B $m \times n = mn$

When you are multiplying monomials, remember: *the order in which you multiply does not affect the answer.*

$3m \times 2n$ means $3 \times m \times 2 \times n$

$$= 3 \times 2 \times m \times n$$

$$= 6mn$$

$$3m \times 2n = 6mn$$

Example 2

Jennifer drives her minibike at a speed of $2p$ km/h. How far will she go in

(a) 6 h?　　　　(b) $3t$ hours?

Solution

(a) Use distance = speed × time

　　distance $= (2p)(6)$ km 　　speed $= 2p$ km/h

　　　　　　$= 12p$ km 　　　time $= 6$ h

　Jennifer went $12p$ km in 6 h.

(b) Speed $2p$ km/h, time $3t$ hours

　distance = speed × time

　　　$= (2p)(3t)$ km

　　　$= 6pt$ km

　The distance travelled is $6pt$ km.

Try These

1　To find products of monomials, you need to multiply integers. Find each product.

(a) $(3)(-4)$　　　　(b) $(-2)(5)$

(c) $(-2)(-3)$　　　(d) $(-8)(2)$

(e) $3(-2)$　　　　 (f) $-2(-5)$

2　Find each product.

(a) $(3)(-4a)$　　　(b) $(-2)(5b)$

(c) $(-2)(-3m)$　　(d) $(-8)(2k)$

3　What is the numerical coefficient of each product?

(a) $(-2m)(5k)$　　(b) $(2m)(-5k)$

(c) $(2m)(5k)$　　 (d) $(-2m)(-5h)$

4　What is the literal coefficient of each product?

(a) $(3m)(6n)$　　 (b) $(4a)(-5b)$

(c) $(-3e)(-2f)$　 (d) $(8x)(-4y)$

Written Exercises

A 1　Find each product.

(a) $(2)(-3)$　　　(b) $(2a)(-3b)$

(c) $(-4)(-3)$　　 (d) $(-4m)(-3m)$

(e) $6(-2)$　　　　(f) $6k(-2m)$

2　Find each product.

(a) $(3a)(-4b)$　　(b) $(-2x)(5y)$

(c) $(-2k)(-3p)$　(d) $(-8m)(2n)$

(e) $3k(-2s)$　　　(f) $(-2r)(-5q)$

3　Which product has the greatest numerical coefficient?

A　$(2x)(3y)$　　　B　$(-3m)(4y)$

C　$(5k)(-2p)$　　 D　$(-3p)(-5q)$

4　Find each product.

(a) $2(3a)$　　　　(b) $3m(-4n)$

(c) $-4k(-5p)$　　(d) $-6a(3b)$

(e) $2s(-8p)$　　　(f) $6m(-5t)$

5 Look at the rectangle.
  (a) What is its height ?
  (b) What is its base?
  (c) Find its area.

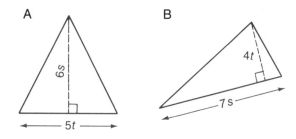

2m

3p

6 Look at the triangle.
  (a) What is its base?
  (b) What is its height?
  (c) What is its area?

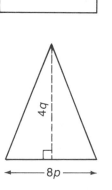

4q

8p

7 Find each product.
  (a) $(2a)(3.5b)$ (b) $(3m)(-4.2n)$
  (c) $(-3p)(-4.1q)$ (d) $(3.1s)(-2.5t)$
  (e) $(-3.6u)(2.5v)$ (f) $(-3.2x)(-4.5y)$

8 Simplify.
  (a) $(2a)(3b)(4c)$ (b) $-6s(2q)(-3r)$
  (c) $(2m)(-3n)(-5p)$ (d) $5m(-4p)(-2t)$

B   For Questions 9 to 13 the measures are in metres.

9 A rectangular field is $3k$ long and $4p$ wide. What is its area?

10 A rectangular pool is $5t$ long and $4s$ wide. What is its area?

11 A triangular garden has a base $3z$ long and height $6b$. What is its area?

12 Which rectangle has the greater area?

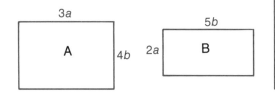

3a

A

4b

2a

5b

B

13 Which triangle has the greater area?

A   B

6s

5t

4t

7 s

14 A bus has 48 seats. How many seats do each of the following have?
  (a) 3 buses   (b) 4 buses   (c) d buses
  (d) k buses   (e) $3d$ buses   (f) $5k$ buses

15 An L.P. record costs $7.50. How much do each of the following cost?
  (a) 3 records   (b) 5 records
  (c) m records   (d) $6m$ records

16 A nickel has 5 cents. How many cents are there in
  (a) 4 nickels?   (b) 10 nickels?
  (c) n nickels?   (d) $4n$ nickels?

17 A peso is worth d cents. What is the value, in cents, of each of the following?

  (a) 4 pesos (b) 10 pesos
  (c) g pesos (d) $6\,g$ pesos

18 A 1948 Canadian Silver dollar is worth $\$h$. What is the value, in dollars, of each of the following?
  (a) 3 silver dollars   (b) 6 silver dollars
  (c) y silver dollars   (d) $8y$ silver dollars

C 19 Use $a = 3$ and $b = -5$. Which expression has the greatest value, A, B, C, or D?
    A $(3a)(2b)$ B $(-2a)(5b)$
    C $(-3a)(-4b)$ D $6a(-3b)$

12.6 Exponents And Multiplying Monomials

Earlier you found the product of exponents with numerical bases.

$2^4 = 2 \times 2 \times 2 \times 2$ and $2^3 = 2 \times 2 \times 2$

$2^4 \times 2^3 = (2 \times 2 \times 2 \times 2) \times (2 \times 2 \times 2)$

$\quad\quad = 2^7$

In the above example, note how the exponents are related.

$2^4 \times 2^3 = 2^7$

To find the following product in simplest terms, a similar procedure is used.

$a^4 = a \times a \times a \times a$ and $a^3 = a \times a \times a$

$a^4 \times a^3 = (a \times a \times a \times a) \times (a \times a \times a)$

$\quad\quad = a^7$

Again, note how the exponents are related.

$a^4 \times a^3 = a^7$

The above examples suggest a rule for multiplying monomials that involve exponents.

When you *multiply* like bases $\quad a^m \times a^n = a^{m+n} \quad$ you *add* the exponents.

Example 1

Simplify.

(a) $p^3 \times p^2$ (b) $k \times k^3$ (c) $(ab)(a^3b^4)$

Solution

(a) $p^3 \times p^2$ (b) $k \times k^3$ Remember: k means k^1

$\quad = p^{3+2}$ $= k^{1+3}$

$\quad = p^5$ $= k^4$

(c) $(ab)(a^3b^4) = a \times a^3 \times b \times b^4$ like bases

$\quad\quad\quad\quad\quad = a^{1+3} \times b^{1+4}$ With practice you can do this step mentally.

$\quad\quad\quad\quad\quad = a^4b^5$

Example 2

Simplify.

(a) $(2m^2)(3m^3)$ (b) $(-3k)(-2k^3)$

Solution

(a) $(2m^2)(3m^3) = 6m^5$

Think
Find the numerical coefficient. $\quad 2 \times 3 = 6$

Find the literal coefficient, $m^2 \times m^3 = m^{2+3} = m^5$

(b) $(-3k)(-2k^3) = 6k^4$

Think
Find the numerical coefficient $(-3)(-2) = +6$

Find the literal coefficient. $k + k^3 = k^{1+3} = k^4$

To evaluate an expression, simplify the expression first as shown in Example 3.

Example 3

Use $a = -1$, $b = 2$. Find the value of each of the following.

(a) $(-2a^2)(3a)$

(b) $(3ab)(-2ab^2)$

Solution

(a) $(-2a^2)(3a) = -6a^3$

Use $a = -1$, $-6a^3 = -6(-1)^3$

$\qquad\qquad\qquad = -6(-1)$

$\qquad\qquad\qquad = 6$

(b) $(3ab)(-2ab^2) = -6a^2b^3$

Use $a = -1$ $\qquad -6a^2b^3 = -6(-1)^2(2)^3$

$\quad b = 2$ $\qquad\qquad\qquad = -6(1)(8)$

$\qquad\qquad\qquad\qquad = -48$

Try These

1 What is the missing exponent?

(a) $m^2 \times m^2 = m^?$ (b) $m^3 \times m^3 = m^?$

(c) $m^3 \times m^5 = p^?$ (d) $p^2 \times p = p^?$

2 What is the missing exponent?

(a) $m^3 \times m^? = m^5$ (b) $s^? \times s^4 = s^6$

(c) $k^4 \times k^? = k^5$ (d) $p^2 \times p^? = p^3$

3 Find each product. Use a single base.

(a) $m^2 \times m^3$ (b) $p^2 \times p$

(c) $q \times q^5$ (d) $m^4 \times m^5$

4 Find each product. Use a single base.

(a) $3x^2 \times x^3$ (b) $-2y \times y^2$

(c) $m^2 \times 4m^2$ (d) $p^3 \times 5p$

Written Exercises

A 1 Write each as a power.

(a) $2^3 \times 2^4$ (b) $a^3 \times a^4$

(c) $3^2 \times 3^3$ (d) $m^2 \times m^3$

(e) 4×4^3 (f) $y \times y^4$

2 Simplify. Use a single base.

(a) $x^3 \times x^2$ (b) $2^5 \times 2$

(c) $m^3 \times m^2$ (d) $p \times p \times p \times p$

(e) $3^4 \times 3^3 \times 3$ (f) $p \times p^3$

3 What is the numerical coefficient for each product?

(a) $(-2a)(3a^2)$ (b) $(5b^3)(-2b)$

(c) $(4p^2)(-6p)$ (d) $(-3a^2)(-2a^3)$

4 What is the literal coefficient for each product?

(a) $(-3a^2)(2a^3)$ (b) $(-4m^3)(-2m)$

(c) $(5k)(-3k^2)$ (d) $(2p^3)(-3p)$

5 Look at the rectangle.

(a) What is its length?

(b) What is its width?

(c) What is its area?

6 Find the area of this rectangle.

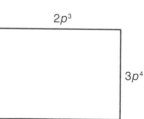

394

7 Find the area of this triangle.

2m²

6m³

B 8 Simplify.
  (a) $(a^2)(a^9)$ (b) $(2m^2)(m)$
  (c) $(a)(-a)$ (d) $(-3r)(5r^4)$
  (e) $(2p^8)(-p^3)$ (f) $(-3m^2)(7m^4)$
  (g) $(3n^8)(-2n)$ (h) $(-r^{10})(-3r^{20})$

9 Which of the following has the greatest numerical coefficient?
  (a) $(-2a^3)(a^3)$ (b) $(6a^4)(-2a^4)$
  (c) $(-2rs)(3rs)$ (d) $(-5mn)(-2mn)$
  (e) $(6xy)(-2xy)$ (f) $(-6xg)(2xg^3)$

10 Simplify.   Remember: $-2x(-6x)$ means $(-2x)(-6x)$
  (a) $-2x(-6x)$
  (b) $-3y(-3y)$ (c) $-4p(-p^2)$
  (d) $(7a)(0)$ (e) $-5a(2a)$
  (f) $-5x(-2x)$ (g) $4x(-2x)$
  (h) $8p(-4p)$ (i) $4w(-2w)$
  (j) $-4a^2(4a^2)$ (k) $-7p^3(3p)$

11 Which rectangle has the greater area, A or B?

4a²b

A   5ab²

B   7a²b²

3ab

12 Simplify.
  (a) $(2xy)(3xy^2)(4x^2y)$
  (b) $(3mn^2)(-2m^2n)(-3mn)$
  (c) $(-8a^2b)(-3ab)(-4b^3)$
  (d) $(3x^2y)(8xy^5)(6xy)$

13 Find the square of each of the following. The first one is done for you.
  (a) $2m$ Square of $2m$ is $(2m)^2 = (2m)(2m)$
  $= 4m^2$

  (b) $4a$ (c) $-2a$ (d) $-4a$
  (e) $2xy$ (f) $2a^2$ (g) $-3mn$

14 Simplify.
  (a) $(3a)^2$ (b) $(-2xy)^2$
  (c) $(4ab^2)^2$ (d) $(-3m^2n^3)^2$

15 Use $a = 2$ to find the value of each of the following.
  (a) $(a^2)(a^3)$ (b) $(2a^2)(5a)$
  (c) $(-a^2)(-2a)$ (d) $(3a)(-3a^2)$

16 Write each of the following with a single exponent.
  (a) $(2^5)^2$ (b) $(2^6)^3$ (c) $(3^2)^3$
  (d) $(4^3)^3$ (e) $(4^5)^2$ (f) $(2^3)^5$
  (g) $(5^3)^3$ (h) $(7^2)^3$ (i) $(8^2)^2$

17 Write each of the following with a single exponent.
  (a) $(x^3)^3$ (b) $(x^4)^6$ (c) $(w^2)^6$
  (d) $(p^2)^7$ (e) $(x^{10})^3$ (f) $(z^4)^4$
  (g) $(m^8)^3$ (h) $(n^4)^8$ (i) $(p^6)^9$

18 Use $m = 3$, $n = 2$. Find the area of each rectangle.

(a)   2mn

mn²

(b)   4m²n

5mn²

C 19 Use $m = 3$, $n = 2$. Which rectangle has the greater area, A or B?

8m²n

$\frac{1}{2}mn^2$ A

4m²n

B   2m²n

12.7 Dividing Monomials

It is often useful to think of your skills in arithmetic in order to learn skills in algebra.

arithmetic
$$\frac{2 \times 5}{5} = \frac{2 \times \cancel{5}}{\cancel{5}}$$
$$= 2$$

algebra
$$\frac{2a}{a} = \frac{2\cancel{a}}{\cancel{a}}$$
$$= 2$$

Just as in the multiplication of monomials, in order to divide monomials you need to obtain

A   the numerical coefficient.

B   the literal coefficient.

Example 1

Simplify each of the following.

(a) $\dfrac{-4mn}{2m}$ (b) $\dfrac{-8a^2}{-4a}$

Solution

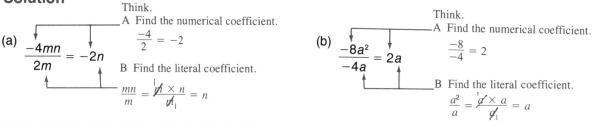

(a)
Think.
A Find the numerical coefficient.
$$\frac{-4}{2} = -2$$
$$\frac{-4mn}{2m} = -2n$$
B Find the literal coefficient.
$$\frac{mn}{m} = \frac{\cancel{m} \times n}{\cancel{m}_1} = n$$

(b)
Think.
A Find the numerical coefficient.
$$\frac{-8}{-4} = 2$$
$$\frac{-8a^2}{-4a} = 2a$$
B Find the literal coefficient.
$$\frac{a^2}{a} = \frac{\cancel{a} \times a}{\cancel{a}_1} = a$$

When you are evaluating expressions, it is best to simplify them first. This will reduce the number of calculations you need to do.

Try These

1 You need to know how to divide integers before you can divide monomials.
   Find each quotient.

(a) $\dfrac{8}{-2}$ (b) $\dfrac{-6}{3}$ (c) $\dfrac{-12}{-4}$

(d) $\dfrac{-10}{2}$ (e) $\dfrac{-16}{-8}$ (f) $\dfrac{-12}{6}$

2 Simplify.

(a) $\dfrac{8m}{-2}$ (b) $\dfrac{-6p}{3}$ (c) $\dfrac{-12k}{-4}$

(d) $\dfrac{-10p}{2}$ (e) $\dfrac{-16k}{-8}$ (f) $\dfrac{-12s}{6}$

3 What is the numerical coefficient of each quotient?

(a) $\dfrac{-16ab}{8b}$ (b) $\dfrac{-25pq}{-5p}$ (c) $\dfrac{36st}{-6s}$

4 What is the literal coefficient of each quotient?

(a) $\dfrac{-25pq}{5q}$ (b) $\dfrac{49su}{-7s}$ (c) $\dfrac{-28abc}{-4a}$

Written Exercises

A 1 Find each quotient.

(a) $\dfrac{20cd}{4d}$ (b) $\dfrac{20gh}{5g}$ (c) $\dfrac{20ru}{10u}$

(d) $\dfrac{-12ab}{2a}$ (e) $\dfrac{-12pq}{3q}$ (f) $\dfrac{-12st}{4t}$

(g) $\dfrac{-16mn}{-4n}$ (h) $\dfrac{-16uv}{-8v}$ (i) $\dfrac{-16de}{-2d}$

2 Find each quotient.

(a) $(8) \div (-2)$ (b) $(8ab) \div (-2a)$
(c) $(-16) \div (4)$ (d) $(-16pq) \div (4q)$
(e) $(-25) \div (-5)$ (f) $(-25sr) \div (-5sr)$

3 Find each quotient.

(a) $\dfrac{16ab}{4a}$ (b) $\dfrac{20pq}{-4q}$ (c) $\dfrac{-36mst}{-6ms}$

4 Simplify.

(a) $\dfrac{4a \times a \times b}{2a \times b}$ (b) $\dfrac{-8m \times m \times m}{-4m \times m}$

(c) $\dfrac{16p \times p \times p \times q}{-8p \times q}$ (d) $\dfrac{-25d \times f \times f \times f}{5f \times f}$

5 Which quotient has the greatest numerical coefficient?

(a) $\dfrac{25pq}{-5q}$ (b) $\dfrac{-20r\,s}{4r}$ (c) $\dfrac{-36ab}{6a}$

6 Find the value of each expression. Use $a = -2$.

(a) $\dfrac{8a}{2}$ (b) $\dfrac{-16a}{4}$ (c) $\dfrac{-24a}{-6}$

(d) $\dfrac{-25a^2}{2}$ (e) $\dfrac{-24a^2}{6}$ (f) $\dfrac{18a^2}{-9}$

7 Find the missing dimension for each rectangle.

(a) Area, $25pq$ (b) Area, $36abc$

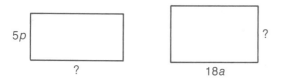

B 8 Simplify.

(a) $\dfrac{24mn}{6n}$ (b) $\dfrac{-24pq}{4q}$ (c) $\dfrac{36rs}{-6s}$

(d) $\dfrac{-25tu}{-5t}$ (e) $\dfrac{-20pq}{4q}$ (f) $\dfrac{28st}{-7t}$

9 Simplify.

(a) $\dfrac{2a^2}{a}$ (b) $\dfrac{-4a^3}{2a^2}$ (c) $\dfrac{8m^4}{4m^2}$

(d) $\dfrac{-6m^5}{3m^3}$ (e) $\dfrac{9p^4}{-3p}$ (f) $\dfrac{-10m^5}{-2m}$

10 Simplify.

(a) $(18ab) \div (-9a)$ (b) $(28ps) \div (-4s)$
(c) $(40tv) \div (-8v)$ (d) $(-45rq) \div (-9q)$

11 Use $a = -3$, $b = -2$. Find the value of each of the following. Remember to simplify first.

(a) $\dfrac{16a^2b}{-4a}$ (b) $\dfrac{-25ab^3}{-5b}$ (c) $\dfrac{-48a^3b^2}{6a}$

12 Which expression has the greater value if $x = -1$, $y = 2$?

A $\dfrac{30xy}{-6y}$ B $\dfrac{-30x^2y}{-5x}$

13 A rectangle has area $36ab$ square units. The width is $4b$ units. What is the length?

14 A rectangular pool has an area of $48pq$ square units. The length is $8q$ units. What is the width?

15 Kelly went $36pq$ km on her minibike. She travelled at the speed of $9q$ km/h. How many hours did her trip take?

16 The total cost of the racquets is $\$24ab$. If 1 costs $\$6a$, how many racquets are there?

C 17 Use $a = -1$, $b = -2$. Which expression has the greatest value?

A $(-16ab) \div (2a)$ B $(-25ab) \div (-5b)$
C $(36ab) \div (-18ab)$ D $(-30ab) \div (-6b)$

12.8 Exponents And Dividing Monomials

The rule for multiplying monomials that involve powers is shown by

$$2^3 \times 2^4 = 2^{3+4} \qquad a^m \times a^n = a^{m+n} \longleftarrow \text{add the exponents}$$

↑   ↑
like bases

To divide monomials that involve powers, you can develop a similar result.

$$\frac{2^5}{2^3} = \frac{2 \times 2 \times 2 \times 2 \times 2}{2 \times 2 \times 2}$$
$$= \frac{\cancel{2} \times \cancel{2} \times \cancel{2} \times 2 \times 2}{\cancel{2} \times \cancel{2} \times \cancel{2}}$$
$$= 2 \times 2 = 2^2$$

$$\frac{b^5}{b^3} = \frac{b \times b \times b \times b \times b}{b \times b \times b} \longleftarrow \text{5 factors of } b$$
$$\longleftarrow \text{3 factors of } b$$
$$= \frac{\cancel{b} \times \cancel{b} \times \cancel{b} \times b \times b}{\cancel{b} \times \cancel{b} \times \cancel{b}}$$
$$= b \times b = b^2$$

Thus

$$\frac{2^5}{2^3} = 2^3$$

How are the exponents related?

$$\frac{b^5}{b^3} = b^2.$$

The above examples suggest the following result.

To divide powers with like bases, subtract exponents.

$$\frac{a^m}{a^n} = a^{m-n} \qquad \text{Note } a \neq 0, \; m > n$$

Example 1

Simplify.

(a) $2^8 \div 2^4$ (b) $m^6 \div m^2$

Solution

(a) $\dfrac{2^8}{2^4} = 2^{8-4} \longleftarrow$ like bases, subtract exponents
$= 2^4$
$= 16$

(b) $\dfrac{m^6}{m^2} = m^{6-2}$
$= m^4$
m^4 cannot be simplified further.

To divide monomials involving powers,

Step A   find the numerical coefficient.(Use your skills with integers.)
Step B   find the literal coefficient.

$$\frac{a^m}{a^n} = a^{m-n} \quad \text{(Remember to subtract exponents.)}$$

To divide monomials that involve more than one base, remember to subtract exponents for *only* like bases.

Example 2

Simplify.

(a) $-16p^4 \div 4p^2$ (b) $\dfrac{-24a^3b^5}{3a^2b}$

Solution

Think!

(a) $\dfrac{-16p^4}{4p^2} = -4p^2$ A $\dfrac{-16}{4} = -4$

    B $\dfrac{p^4}{p^2} = p^{4-2} = p^2$

Think

(b) $\dfrac{-24a^3b^5}{3a^2b} = -8ab^4$ $\dfrac{-24}{3} = -8$

$\dfrac{a^3}{a^2} = a^{3-2} = a^1 \qquad \dfrac{b^5}{b} = b^{5-1} = b^4$

Try These

1 What is the missing exponent?

(a) $\dfrac{m^4}{m^2} = m^?$ (b) $\dfrac{y^5}{y^3} = y^?$ (c) $\dfrac{k^6}{k^3} = y^?$

2 What is the missing exponent?

(a) $\dfrac{x^6}{x^?} = x^{6-?}$
$= x^2$

(b) $\dfrac{p^?}{p^8} = p^{?-8}$
$= p^3$

3 What is the missing exponent?

(a) $\dfrac{d^8}{d^?} = d^5$ (b) $\dfrac{n^?}{n^3} = n^6$ (c) $\dfrac{t^4}{t^?} = t^3$

4 What is the numerical coefficient of each of the following?

(a) $\dfrac{-30x^3}{6x}$ (b) $\dfrac{25y^4}{-5y^2}$ (c) $\dfrac{-18m^6}{-9m^3}$

Written Exercises

A 1 Simplify each of the following.

(a) $\dfrac{2^4}{2^2}$ (b) $\dfrac{3^6}{3^5}$ (c) $\dfrac{5^4}{5^2}$

2 Simplify. Write each with a single base.

(a) $\dfrac{m^6}{m^4}$ (b) $\dfrac{n^4}{n^2}$ (c) $\dfrac{p^5}{p}$

3 Write each with a single base.

(a) $\dfrac{4p^4}{2p^3}$ (b) $\dfrac{-6q^4}{3q^2}$ (c) $\dfrac{8d^4}{4d}$

(d) $\dfrac{12f^8}{-2f^6}$ (e) $\dfrac{10m^7}{5m^5}$ (f) $\dfrac{-16n^5}{-4n}$

4 Simplify each of the following.

(a) $(4p) \div (2p)$ (b) $(-6a^3) \div (3a)$
(c) $(-8q^5) \div (-2q^3)$ (d) $(16r^4) \div (-4r)$
(e) $(12s^4) \div (-3s^3)$ (f) $(-25b^2) \div (-5b)$

B 5 Divide each monomial by the monomial in the middle of the circle.

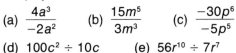

6 Simplify.

(a) $\dfrac{4a^3}{-2a^2}$ (b) $\dfrac{15m^5}{3m^3}$ (c) $\dfrac{-30p^6}{-5p^5}$

(d) $100c^2 \div 10c$ (e) $56r^{10} \div 7r^7$

7 Simplify.

(a) $\dfrac{m^4n^3}{m^2n^2}$ (b) $\dfrac{x^5y^4}{x^3y^2}$ (c) $\dfrac{p^6q^4}{pq}$

(d) $\dfrac{a^3b^2}{a^2}$ (e) $\dfrac{r^5s^4}{s^3}$ (f) $\dfrac{t^4u^3}{t^2}$

8 Simplify.

(a) $\dfrac{25x^4y^6}{5x^3y^5}$ (b) $\dfrac{-4x^6y^4}{2x^4y^3}$ (c) $\dfrac{-6m^6n^3}{m^4}$

9 Simplify. Remember $(2x)^2$ means $(2x)(2x)$.

(a) $\left(\dfrac{4x^6}{2x^4}\right)^2$ (b) $\left(\dfrac{6p^3}{-3p}\right)^2$

10 The area of the rectangle is $28x^3y^2$. Find the missing dimension.

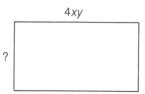

11 The area of the square is $25m^4n^6$. What is the missing dimension?

C 12 Use $a = -3$, $b = 2$. Find the value of each of the following.

(a) $\dfrac{16a^5b^4}{-4a^3b^2}$ (b) $\dfrac{-30a^3b^2}{-5a^2b}$

399

Applications: Scientific Notation

Writing very large numbers or very small numbers is often cumbersome. For example, the distance from the earth to the sun is 153 000 000 km. To write this number in a compact way, **scientific notation** or **standard notation** is used.

$$153\ 000\ 000 = 1.53 \times 10^8$$

— a power of 10

— a number between 1 to 10

13 To write numbers in scientific notation, you use 10^{-1} to mean $\dfrac{1}{10}$, 10^{-2} to mean $\dfrac{1}{10^2}$ and so on. What do each of the following mean?
(a) 10^2 (b) 10^{-3} (c) 10^{-4} (d) 10^4
(e) 10^{-5} (f) 10^5 (g) 10^{-6} (h) 10^6

14 Complete the chart.

	Number	Scientific notation
(a)	23 100.0	$2.31 \times 10^?$
(b)	2 310.0	$2.31 \times 10^?$
(c)	231.0	$2.31 \times 10^?$
(d)	23.1	$2.31 \times 10^?$
(e)	2.31	$2.31 \times 10^?$
(f)	0.231	$2.31 \times 10^?$
(g)	0.023 1	$2.31 \times 10^?$
(h)	0.002 31	$2.31 \times 10^?$

15 Each number is expressed in scientific notation. Write each of the following as a decimal.
(a) 4.63×10^2 (b) 9.62×10^5
(c) 3.21×10^4 (d) 2.91×10^3
(e) 9.76×10^6 (f) 6.91×10^{-1}
(g) 4.83×10^{-2} (h) 8.09×10^{-3}

16 Write each number in scientific notation.
(a) 692   (b) 6430   (c) 19.5
(d) 169 000 000   (e) 0.456   (f) 359 000
(g) 793   (h) 934 000
(i) 0.003 62   (j) 0.000 000 369

17 Express each number in scientific notation.
(a) The human body contains approximately 5340 mL of blood.
(b) The metric prefix "micro" means multiply by 0.000 001.
(c) Astronomers predict that the sun will survive as an energy source for another 7 500 000 000 a.
(d) The mass of a proton is approximately 0.000 000 000 000 000 000 000 001 68 g.

18 Express each of the following in scientific notation.
(a) The population of Canada is about 23 800 000.
(b) The amount of railway tracks in Canada is about 96 800 km.
(c) The area of Canada is about 10 000 000 km².
(d) The area of Alaska is 1 519 800 km².

19 The chart below lists the average wave lengths of certain types of radiation. Write each number in scientific notation.

	Type of radiation	Average wave length (metres)
(a)	Violet	0.000 000 392
(b)	Blue	0.000 000 457
(c)	Yellow	0.000 000 59
(d)	Red	0.000 000 658
(e)	X-rays	0.000 000 000 484
(f)	Gamma Rays	0.000 000 000 064

12.9 Product of a Monomial and a Polynomial

Very often, several of your mathematical skills are combined to develop yet another skill. Consider, for example, the multiplication of a polynomial by a monomial.

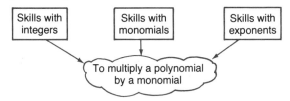

Thus to master any new skill, you must first have mastered several other skills.

The **distributive property** is used to simplify algebraic expressions.

In arithmetic the distributive property means	In algebra, the distributive property has a similar meaning.
$2(10 + 5)$ $= 2(10) + 2(5)$ $= 20 + 10 = 30$	$2(a + b)$ $= 2a + 2b$

The distributive property is also used to simplify the sum or difference of polynomials.

Example 1

Simplify each of the following.

(a) $5m(2m - 4n + 7p)$

(b) $2x(x - y) - 4x(x - y)$

Solution

(a) $\quad 5m(2m - 4n + 7p)$

$\quad = 5m(2m) + 5m(-4n) + 5m(7p)$

$\quad = 10m^2 - 20mn + 35mp$

(b) $\quad 2x(x - y) - 4x(x - y)$

$\quad = 2x(x) + 2x(-y) - 4x(x) - 4x(-y)$

$\quad = 2x^2 - 2xy - 4x^2 + 4xy$

$\quad = 2x^2 - 4x^2 - 2xy + 4xy \longleftarrow$ Collect like terms.

$\quad = -2x^2 + 2xy$

When you are evaluating an expression, if you do not simplify first, then you may have to do a greater number of calculations.

Try These

1 Express each of the following without parentheses.

(a) $2(x + 3)$ (b) $2(x - 3)$

(c) $3(y + 4)$ (d) $3(y - 4)$

(e) $2(2x + 1)$ (f) $2(2x - 1)$

2 Expand.

(a) $3(x - 3)$ (b) $-3(x - 3)$

(c) $4(2x + 1)$ (d) $-4(2x - 1)$

3 Expand.

(a) $3(x + y)$ (b) $-3(x + 2y)$

(c) $2(2x + 3y)$ (d) $-2(2x - 3y)$

Written Exercises

A 1 Express each of the following without brackets.
  (a) $2(x + 3)$ (b) $4(2x - 1)$
  (c) $-6(2m - 3)$ (d) $-4(-y + 2)$

2 Expand.
  (a) $-3(x + 2)$ (b) $7(-2r - 4w)$
  (c) $-7(-2m - 2)$ (d) $-9(-4d + e)$

3 Expand.
  (a) $2a(3a + 1)$ (b) $5b(b - 4)$
  (c) $-5m(6m - 2n)$ (d) $10w(-3w + 2z)$

4 Find the value of each of the following if $m = 1$.
  (a) $6m(-m + 2)$ (b) $-2m(3m - 6)$

5 Expand.
  (a) $2(a^2 + 5a - 1)$ (b) $-2m(m^2 - 3m - 4)$
  (c) $-8(-p^2 - 3p + 4)$ (d) $-3(f^2 - 2f - 8)$

6 (a) Multiply $(2x^2 - 4x + 3)$ by $2x$.
  (b) Multiply $(-p^2 - 2p - 5)$ by $-3p$.
  (c) Multiply $(-a^2 - 3a + 9)$ by $4a^2$.

7 Expand.
  (a) $p(p^2 - 3p - 2)$ (b) $-r(r^2 - 9r + 6)$
  (c) $a(4 - a - 5a^2)$ (d) $-w(4 + w - 7w^2)$

8 (a) Find an expression for the area of the rectangle.

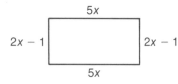

  (b) Find the area when $x = 4$.
  (c) Find the area when $x = 6$.

B 9 Simplify each of the following.
  (a) $4x + 2(x + 1)$ (b) $5x - 2(x - 3)$
  (c) $4(a - 3) - 3a$ (d) $-9(3m - 4) - 15$

10 Find the value of each expression if $a = 3$.
  (a) $6(2a + 4) - 3a$ (b) $15 + (-2)(a - 5)$
  (c) $-10a - 2(a + 7)$ (d) $-3(a - 8) - a$

11 Expand and simplify.
  (a) $5x + 4 - 2(x + 1)$
  (b) $3a - 4 + 2(a - 2)$
  (c) $-2p - 2(p - 3) + 6$

12 Find the value of each expression if $m = -3$.
  (a) $4(m - 1) + 3(m + 5)$
  (b) $5(m + 3) + 4(m + 4)$
  (c) $(m - 5) - 2(m - 5)$

13 If $e = 4$, find the value of the expression
  $5(e^2 + 2e - 1) - 4(e^2 - 6e - 8)$.

14 (a) Do not simplify. Evaluate
  $2(3a - b) - 3(a - 2b)$ for $a = 2$ and
  $b = 3$.
  (b) Simplify the expression in (a). Then
  evaluate the expression in (a) for $a = 2$
  and $b = 3$.
  (c) Which solution requires fewer
  computations, (a) or (b)?

15 Evaluate each of the following expressions for
  $a = -2$ and $b = -5$.
  (a) $4(2a - b) - 3(a + b)$
  (b) $-2(2a + b) - 3(5b - a)$
  (c) $4a(2b - a) - 3a(2b + a)$

16 (a) Find an expression, for the area of each of
  the following rectangles.

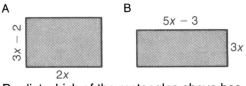

  (b) Predict which of the rectangles above has
  the greater area if $x = 6$.
  (c) Check your prediction in (b) by substituting
  $x = 6$.

12.10 Problem Solving: Saving Steps By Factoring

A formula can be used to find
the perimeter of a rectangle.

$P = 2l + 2w$

w

If you wish to use a calculator to calculate the above perimeter for
$l = 21.6$, $w = 16.5$, a factored form will save you some steps, as
shown in the following.

Calculations   Calculations

Expanded Form
$P = 2l + 2w$
$= 2(21.6) + 2(16.5)$ ✔✔
$= 43.2 + 33.0$ ✔
$= 76.2$

_____
3 calculations

Factored Form
$P = 2(l + w)$
$= 2(21.6 + 16.5)$ ✔
$= 2(38.1)$ ✔
$= 76.2$

_____
2 calculations

The reverse process of expanding is called **factoring**.

Expanding
$2m(m + 3) = 2m^2 + 6m$

Factoring
$2m^2 + 6m = 2m(m + 3)$ (Called a **common factor**.)

Example

What is the greatest common factor of the
expression $2mp + 4mk$?

Solution

The greatest common factor is $2m$.

$2mp + 4mk = 2m(? + ?)$
$= 2m(p + 2k)$

Think. $\frac{2mp}{2m} = p,$

$\frac{4mk}{2m} = 2k$

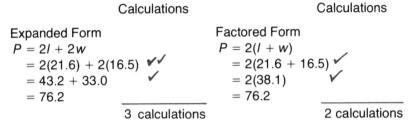

Try These

1 What are the factors of each of the
following?

   (a) $4ab$ (b) $8a^2b$

2 To find factors you need to know how to
divide.
Divide each of the following.

   (a) $\dfrac{36mn}{4m}$ (b) $64mn^2 \div (-16m)$

In finding common factors of expressions, the word
greatest is not written each time. Thus the instruction
   Find the common factor
means to find the greatest common factor (greatest is
understood).

403

Written Exercises

To find factors, you need to know your skills for dividing thoroughly

A 1 Simplify each of the following.

(a) $\dfrac{16}{-4}$ (b) $\dfrac{-25}{-5}$ (c) $\dfrac{-36}{6}$

(d) $-48 \div 3$ (e) $-24 \div 2$

2 Simplify.

(a) $4a \div 2$ (b) $\dfrac{4a}{4}$ (c) $\dfrac{-4a}{-a}$

(d) $\dfrac{-9ax}{3a}$ (e) $\dfrac{10ab}{-5a}$ (f) $\dfrac{-25pq}{-5q}$

3 Simplify.

(a) $\dfrac{18x^5}{-3x}$ (b) $\dfrac{-2a^2b}{ab}$ (c) $\dfrac{-10a^5}{-2a^3}$

(d) $\dfrac{9m^4}{3m}$ (e) $\dfrac{27k^2m}{-9km}$ (f) $\dfrac{-35m^8}{-5m}$

4 Divide.

(a) $\dfrac{-12ab}{-3b}$ (b) $-42a^2b \div 7ab$

5 Find the missing factor in each of the following.

(a) $10ab = (5a)(?)$ (b) $-21xy = (?)(-3x)$
(c) $8x^2 = (4x)(?)$ (d) $-4m^3 = (?)(-2m^2)$

6 $2m$ is a factor of each expression. What is the other factor?

(a) $12am$ (b) $-6m^2$ (c) $-8m^2p$

7 What is the greatest common factor for each pair?

(a) $6x, 3x$ (b) $4m^2, 5m$
(c) $-6m, -3p$ (d) $-3m^3, -8m^2$

8 What is the greatest common factor for each pair?

(a) $28n^2, -7n$ (b) $4xy, -2y^2$
(c) $12a^2, 18a^2b$ (d) $-5n^3, 15n^2$

B 9 • Find the common factor of each expression.
  • Write each expression in factored form.

(a) $4m + 4p$ (b) $8r - 4$
(c) $cm + cn$ (d) $pq - ps$

10 Find the factors of each expression. Check by multiplying the factors.

(a) $3x - 6$ (b) $4x - 12$
(c) $m^2 + mn$ (d) $m^2 - 4mn$
(e) $4y - 10y^2$ (f) $3k^2 - 9k$

11 Write the factors for each expression.

(a) $3x^3 - xy$ (b) $4p^3 + p^2d$
(c) $a^3x - 3a^2y$ (d) $20z^2 - 12z$
(e) $24d^4 - 8d^3$ (f) $6x^2 - 9x$

Did you check your work?

12 Factor the following expressions by first finding the common factor of each term.

(a) $3a + 3b + 3c$ (b) $2a - 4b - bc$
(c) $2x^2 - 4x + 2xy$ (d) $2p^3 - 4p^2 - 6p$

13 (a) Find the value of $3x^2y - 3xy^2$ for $x = 3$, $y = 2$.
  (b) Find the value of $3xy(x - y)$ for $x = 3$, $y = 2$.
  (c) Which calculation was easier, (a) or (b)?

14 • Find the factors of each expression.
  • Then evaluate each expression.

(a) $6m^2n - 3mn^2$, $m = 4$, $n = 7$
(b) $5p^2q - 5pq^2$, $p = 8$, $q = 7$
(c) $6p^3q + 6p^2q^2$, $p = 6$, $q = 4$

15 The perimeter of a rectangle is given by $P = 2l + 2w$ where l, length, and w, width. Calculate the perimeter for each rectangle.

(a) length 486 m, width 345 m
(b) length 9.6 m, width 4.5 m
(c) length 13.5 m, width 4.9 m

Skills To Practise: A Chapter Review

12.1 Simplify each of the following.
(a) $4m - 3m + 2m$ (b) $3x - 2y + 4x + y$

12.2 Simplify each of the following.
(a) $(3k - 2p) + (3p - 2k)$
(b) $(2m^2 + 3m) - (m^2 - m)$

12.3 Write $+$ or $-$ to represent each of the following words.
(a) sum (b) subtract (c) exceeds
(d) total (e) add (f) difference
(g) plus (h) less than

12.4 (a) Simplify each expression.
A $(2m + n) + (m + n)$
B $(5m + 5n) - (m + 3n)$
C $(4m + 3n) - (m + n)$
(b) Which expression in (a) is not equivalent to the others?

12.5 Find each product.
(a) $2x(3y)$ (b) $(-2m)(-p)$ (c) $-3(2k)$

12.6 Simplify.
(a) $3x(2x)$ (b) $4y(-y)$ (c) $3k(2k^2)$

12.7 Simplify.
(a) $\dfrac{12ab}{4a}$ (b) $\dfrac{-16pq}{-8p}$ (c) $-6a^3 \div (2a)$

12.8 Write each with a single base.
A $\dfrac{6p^3}{2p^2}$ B $\dfrac{-8m^5}{-4m^2}$ C $\dfrac{12t^2m}{-6tm}$

12.9 Find each product.
(a) $3(y - 2)$ (b) $-2(3 - k)$
(c) $2m(p + q)$ (d) $-3m(2m - 1)$

12.10 What is the common factor for each expression?
(a) $3mn + 6m$ (b) $2x^2 - 4x$

Problems To Practise: A Chapter Review

12.1 Find an expression for the perimeter of each figure. Which has the greater perimeter for $s = 3$?
(a) (b)

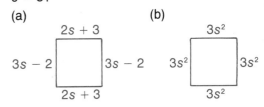

12.2 Which expression has the greater value if $m = 2$?
A $3m - 2n - (2m - 2n)$
B $5m + 3n - (2m + 3n)$

12.3 Find the sum of your answers for A and B.
A From the sum of $6xy$ and $4xy$, subtract $3xy$.
B Subtract $-12xy + 6xy$ from $24xy$.

12.4 (a) Simplify
$(3x^2 - 2x - 1) - (4x^2 - 5x + 1)$.
(b) Check your answer in (a).
(c) Which term in (a) has the smallest numerical coefficient?

12.5 A krona is worth m cents. What is the value of
(a) 6 krona? (b) $2k$ krona?

12.6 Use $a = -2$, $b = -1$. Find the value of
(a) $(2a)(3b)$ (b) $(3b)(-2b)$
(c) $(2a)(-3a^2)$ (d) $(-3b^2)(-2b)$
(e) Which has the greatest value?

12.7 A rectangular garden has an area of $24mn$ square units. The width is $3n$ units. What is the length?

12.8 The rectangle has a missing dimension. If the area is $16p^3q^5$, find the missing dimension.

12.10 (a) Express $3mn + 3n^2$ as a product.
(b) Use the expression in (a). Find its value for $m = 2.3$, $n = 4.6$.

Chapter Checkup: A Practice Test

12.1 (a) Simplify the expression
$2a^2 - 3a + 4 + 3a^2 - 2a - 6$.

(b) Find an expression for the perimeter of the figure. Find the value of the perimeter for $k = 6$.

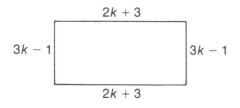

12.2 (a) Simplify each expression.
A $(2k - 3m) - (k - m)$
B $3m^2 - (2m^2 + m - 3) + 3m$

(b) To win a weekend holiday trip, answer the skill-testing question.
Which term has a 2-digit coefficient?
$(13x^2 + 9x - 8) - (4x^2 - 3) + 2x$

12.3 (a) Follow the instructions in each question. Then simplify the expressions.
A Find the sum of $2x$ and $5x$.
B Subtract $6mn$ from $8mn$.
C Find by how much $16m$ exceeds $8m$.

(b) Subtract the total of $3k - 2p$ and $4k - 5p$ from $2k - 3p$. Check your answer for $k = 1$, $p = 2$.

12.4 (a) Simplify the expressions.
A $(2x^2 - 2x - 3) + (x^2 - 2x - 2)$
B $(3x^2 + 4x - 5) - (2x^2 + 2x - 4)$
C $(5x^2 - 2x - 2) - (3x^2 + 2x + 3)$
D $(6x^2 - 5x + 1) - (3x^2 - x + 6)$

(b) Which expressions in (a) are equivalent?

(c) Which expression has the greatest value if $x = 1$: A, B, C, or D?

12.5 (a) Find each product.
A $(2m)(3k)$ B $(-4k)(-2p)$

(b) A "C" battery costs k cents. What is the cost of
A 4 batteries? B $3m$ batteries?

12.6 (a) Simplify.
A $(a^3)(a^5)$ B $(-2k^2)(k)$
C $(6m^4)(-3m^2)$ D $(-2w)(-3w^5)$

(b) Use $k = 3$, $p = 5$. What is the area of the rectangle?

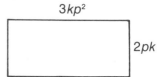

12.7 (a) Simplify each expression. Then, find the value of each if $m = -3$, $n = 2$.
A $\dfrac{-16mn}{2n}$ B $(-25m^3n) \div (-5m^2)$

(b) Susan went $48st$ km on her bike. She cycled at a rate of $6s$ km/h. How long did the trip take?

12.8 (a) Simplify each of the following.
A $\dfrac{12m^5}{6m}$ B $\dfrac{t^5m^3}{t^3m}$
C $16s^3 \div (-2s^2)$ D $(-25m^5) \div (-5m)$

(b) Which expression has the greater value if $m = 4$, $n = -3$?
A $\dfrac{25m^5n^4}{-5m^4n^3}$ B $\dfrac{-18m^3n^2}{-9mn}$

12.9 (a) Simplify.
A $3m + 2(m + 1)$
B $2(x - y) - 3(x + y)$

(b) The missing combination to the lock is given by the value of the expression if $m = 4$.
$3m^2 - 2m + m(m - 3) - 5m$

12.10 (a) Write each in factored form.
A $2ks + 4k^2$ B $3y^2 - 9y$

(b) To calculate values of the expression, write it in factored form.
$$A = \frac{1}{2}ah + \frac{1}{2}bh$$
Then find the value of A for $a = 14.8$, $b = 9.6$, $h = 2.5$.

13 Solving Equations and Problems

skills with equations, translating English to mathematics, strategies, and steps for solving problems, formulas, applications and problem-solving

13.1 Introduction To Equations: Systematic Trial

Which of the following sentences are true?

A   Wayne Gretzky plays hockey professionally.
B   The Governor-General of Canada plays hockey professionally.
C   ▨ plays hockey professionally.

Statement A is true.
Statement B is *not* true.
Statement C may be true or false depending on who ▨ stands for.

Which of the following mathematical sentences are true?

A $3 + 4 = 7$ true
B $2 + 4 = 7$ false
C $x + 4 = 12$ You don't know unless you know what number x stands for.

The **equation** $x + 4 = 12$ may be true or false depending on what the value of x is.
For example,

False
If $x = 5$, then
$\text{LS} = x + 4$ | $\text{RS} = 12$
$\quad = 5 + 4$
$\quad = 9$
$\qquad \text{LS} \neq \text{RS}$
Thus, $x + 4 = 12$
is not true if $x = 5$.

True
If $x = 8$, then
$\text{LS} = x + 4$ | $\text{RS} = 12$
$\quad = 8 + 4$
$\quad = 12$
$\qquad \text{LS} = \text{RS}$
Thus $x + 4 = 12$ is true
if $x = 8$.

Since 8 makes the equation $x + 4 = 12$ true, then 8 is said to **satisfy** the equation and is called a **root** of the equation.

When you are asked to **solve** an equation, you are being asked to find a root or value of the variable that satisfies the equation.

Example 1

Which of the values 5, 9, and 6, is a root of the equation $3x - 1 = 17$?

Solution

Try $x = 5$	Try $x = 9$	Try $x = 6$
LS $= 3x - 1$	LS $= 3x - 1$	LS $= 3x - 1$
$= 3(5) - 1$	$= 3(9) - 1$	$= 3(6) - 1$
$= 15 - 1$	$= 27 - 1$	$= 18 - 1$
$= 14$	$= 26$	$= 17$
RS $= 17$	RS $= 17$	RS $= 17$
LS $\neq$ RS	LS $\neq$ RS	LS $=$ RS
5 is not a root.	9 is not a root.	6 is the root.

One way to find a root of an equation, is by systematic trial. This is shown in Example 2.

Example 2

Solve $4y - 3 = 13$.

Solution

To solve the equation, a table of values is used.

Value of y	Value of $4y - 3$
1	1
2	5
3	9
4	13

Calculation
$4y - 3 = 4(1) - 3$
$= 4 - 3$
$= 1$

As you substitute you notice that the value of $4y - 3$ is increasing. Since the value you want is 13, you continue.
$4y - 3 = 4(4) - 3$
$= 16 - 3$
$= 13$

When $y = 4$, $4y - 13 = 13$.
The root of the equation is 4.

The **solution set** is the set of the roots of the equation. Thus the solution set for the equation in Example 2 is $\{4\}$.

When you solve an equation by systematic trial, use the values you calculate as clues to tell you that the pattern is leading you to the root.

Try These

1 For each equation, which value is the root?
   (a) $x + 8 = 9$ 2, 1
   (b) $4 + y = 8$ 4, 3
   (c) $m - 3 = 3$ 6, 7
   (d) $8 - p = 3$ 11, 5

2 Which of the values, 2, 3, and 4, is the root of $2m - 1 = 7$?

3 Which of the values, 4, 5, and 8, is the root of $5h = 25$?

4 Which of the values, 4, 8, and 12 is the root of $\dfrac{m}{4} = 3$?

Written Exercises

A 1 Match the root with the equation.

Equation	Root
(a) $x + 1 = 6$	3
(b) $y - 3 = 1$	5
(c) $2 + k = 5$	4

2 What is the root of each equation?

(a) $2m + 1 = 9$ (b) $2m - 1 = 3$

(c) $8 - y = 8$ (d) $8 + y = 11$

3 Solve. Verify your answer.

(a) $3m - 3 = 3$ (b) $9 - 2m = 11$

(c) $15 = 6y - 3$ (d) $6y + 3 = 33$

4 Find the solution set for each equation.

(a) $\dfrac{y}{3} = 6$ (b) $\dfrac{y}{3} + 1 = 7$

(c) $\dfrac{y}{3} - 1 = 3$ (d) $\dfrac{1}{3}m + 3 = 7$

5 For each equation, 2 values are given. Which one is the root?

(a) $y + 11 = 6$ 5, −5

(b) $5 + 2m = 3$ −1, 1

(c) $1 - 2m = 3$ −1, 1

(d) $2y + 8 = 2$ 3, −3

B 6 Match the root with its equation.

Equation	Root
(a) $3x - 1 = 8$	5
(b) $4y - 20 = 12$	3
(c) $6m = 30$	24
(d) $\dfrac{m}{3} = 8$	8

7 For each equation, 2 values are given. Which value is the root?

(a) $3m - 3 = -6$ −1, 2

(b) $8 - 2m = 14$ 3, −3

(c) $4x - 15 = -35$ −5, 5

8 Which of the values, 1, −1, and 0, is the root of the equation?

(a) $3(x + 2) = 3$ (b) $2(a + 1) + 3 = 5$

(c) $2y + 5 = y + 6$

9 Solve. Check your answer.

(a) $2a - 3 = 1$ (b) $3n = 12 - 3$

(c) $6 - 3y = 9$ (d) $2(x + 1) = 6$

(e) $2x + x = -6$ (f) $m \div 3 = 3$

10 What is the root of each equation?

(a) $4a - 6 = 6$ (b) $8 - 2y = 12$

(c) $5(a - 3) = 10$ (d) $2x - 5 = 3x$

11 Which equations have the same root?

(a) $4k = k + 9$ (b) $3(k - 2) = 3$

(c) $8 - 3k = -1$ (d) $\dfrac{k}{3} + 1 = 3$

12 Solve.

(a) $2m + 5 = 21$ (b) $3y - 4 = -19$

(c) $28 - 3r = -8$ (d) $\dfrac{p}{2} + 3 = 11$

(e) $-3p + 5 = 17$ (f) $\dfrac{2}{3}s = 16$

(g) $\dfrac{1}{4}t + 6 = 10$ (h) $8 - \dfrac{1}{2}g = 2$

C 13 Each equation involves decimals. Find the root.

(a) $3m + 3.5 = 9.5$ (b) $5y - 2.5 = 22.5$

(c) $4.5 + 2t = 2.5$ (d) $10.5 = 2.5t + 3$

13.2 Solving Equations: Using Algebra

Although the method of solving equations by systematic trial is straightforward, it can sometimes be very time-consuming.
For example,

What is the root of $4(a - 5) - 3a = 2a - 32$?

The development of a method of solving any equation is based on the following activity.

Here, the scale is balanced because the masses on each side are equal.	If you add the *same* quantity to *both* sides the scale will still be balanced.	If you subtract the *same* quantity from *both* sides, the scale will still be balanced.

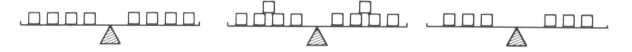

The above activity relates to the properties of equality.

> ### Properties of Equality

Addition
If $6 = (5 + 1)$ then $6 + 4 = (5 + 1) + 4$

Add the *same* values
to *both* sides.

Subtraction
If $6 = (5 + 1)$ then $6 - 4 = (5 + 1) - 4$

Subtract the *same* value
from *both* sides.

To solve an equation you need to *isolate* the variable. The properties of equality are used to solve the equation in Example 1.

Remember: to learn a procedure you first practise with straight-forward examples whose answers you know.

Example 1
Solve $x - 8 = 23$.

Solution
$$x - 8 = 23$$
$$x - 8 + 8 = 23 + 8$$
$$x = 31$$

In order to isolate the variable, add the *same* value to *both* sides.

In Example 1, think of solving an equation as the reverse procedure of building an equation.

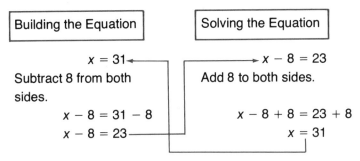

| Building the Equation | Solving the Equation |

$x = 31$

Subtract 8 from both sides.

$x - 8 = 31 - 8$
$x - 8 = 23$

$x - 8 = 23$

Add 8 to both sides.

$x - 8 + 8 = 23 + 8$
$x = 31$

Example 2

Solve and verify $3x = 2x + 15$.

Solution

$$3x = 2x + 15$$

$$3x - 2x = 2x + 15 - 2x$$
$$x = 15$$

Check or verify in the original equation.

$$\text{LS} = 3x \qquad\qquad \text{RS} = 2x + 15$$
$$= 3(15) \qquad\qquad\quad = 2(15) + 15$$
$$= 45 \qquad\qquad\qquad = 30 + 15$$
$$\qquad\qquad\qquad\qquad = 45$$

Thus, 15 is the root of the equation.

Try These

1 An important skill is to be able to simplify opposites.
  Simplify.
  (a) $-3 + 3$ (b) $8 - 8$
  (c) $-6 + 3 + 6$ (d) $-4 + 8 + 4$

2 Simplify each of the following.
  (a) $6y - 6y$ (b) $-3m + 3m$
  (c) $2k + 6k - 2k$ (d) $-4x + 3x + 4x$

3 Decide whether to add or subtract from each side.
  (a) $m + 8 = 12$ (b) $y - 3 = 6$
  (c) $12 + x = 2x$ (d) $3m = 2m - 8$

4 What is the missing step in each of the following?

  (a) $x + 6 = 12$
       $x + 6 - 6 = 12 - 6$
       ▭

  (b) $y - 4 = 16$
       $y - 4 + 4 = 16 + 4$
       ▭

  (c) $3m = 2m - 6$
       $3m - 2m = 2m - 6 - 2m$
       ▭

411

Written Exercises

A 1 For each equation
- ▶ decide which number to add to or subtract from both sides.
- ▶ then solve the equation.

(a) $y + 6 = 9$ 9, 6

(b) $9 + m = 15$ 15, 9

(c) $18 = p + 4$ 18, 4

2 For each equation
- ▶ decide which expression to add to or subtract from both sides.
- ▶ then solve the equation.

(a) $3y = 2y + 8$ 3y, 2y

(b) $9 + 2m = 3m$ 3m, 2m

(c) $2p + 3 = p$ 2p, p

3 First decide what ▨ represents. Then solve the equation.

(a) $p + 16 = 13$
$p + 16 - 16 = 13 + $ ▨

(b) $s - 18 = 25$
$s - 18 + $ ▨ $ = 25 + 18$

(c) $3s = 2s + 5$
$3s - 2s = 2s + 5 + $ ▨

4 Which equations have been built from $y = 3$?

(a) $y + 6 = 9$ (b) $y - 2 = 1$

(c) $y - 8 = 3$ (d) $18 = y + 15$

5 Which equations have been built from $m = -3$?

(a) $m + 6 = 3$ (b) $8 + m = 5$

(c) $6 + m = 9$ (d) $12 = m + 15$

B Show the complete steps of your solution of the equations in Questions 6 to 8.

6 Solve. Check your answers.

(a) $k - 8 = 12$ (b) $3 + m = 15$

(c) $20 + p = -5$ (d) $18 = 2 + s$

(e) $3m = 2m + 5$ (f) $8 + 3p = 4p$

7 Find the solution set.

(a) $8 + k = 3$ (b) $5 = 12 + p$

(c) $p - 3 = 13$ (d) $25 = m - 5$

(e) $5p = 4p - 8$ (f) $5p - 3 = 7p$

8 What is the root of each equation?

(a) $12 = m + 5$ (b) $18 = m - 6$

(c) $20 + 2s = 3s$ (d) $18p = 17p + 5$

9 Each equation involves decimals. Find the root.

(a) $p - 2.5 = 6.3$ (b) $6.5 + m = 4.5$

(c) $4k = 3k - 3.7$ (d) $3.5 + 2q = 3q$

10 A list of roots are shown. Match each root with an equation in the chart.

Equations
A $10 = 6 + 2m$
B $2m + 34 = 28$
C $3y = 2y + 3$
D $2 = 6 + 2m$

(a) -3 (b) 3

(c) 2   (d) -2

C 11 Which equations have the same solution set?

(a) $2 = 2m + 8$ (b) $3m = 2m - 3$

(c) $2m - 3 = 9$ (d) $8 + m = 3 + 2$

13.3 Solving Equations: Multiplication And Division

These two properties of equality have been used to solve equations.

Add equals to both sides. $\longrightarrow$

$$m = 6$$
$$m + 3 = 6 + 3$$

equals added

Subtract equals from both sides. $\longrightarrow$

$$m = 6$$
$$m - 3 = 6 - 3$$

equals subtracted

Two other properties of equality you can use to solve equations are shown.

Multiply both sides by equals. $\longrightarrow$

$$6 = 6$$
$$2 \times 6 = 2 \times 6$$

equals

Divide both sides by equals. $\longrightarrow$

$$6 = 6$$
$$\frac{6}{2} = \frac{6}{2}$$

equals

These properties can be applied either to the building of equations or to the solution of equations.

Build the equation

A
$$m = 6$$
$$2 \times m = 2 \times 6$$
$$2m = 12$$

How are the steps related? $\longrightarrow$

Solve the equation

$$2m = 12$$
$$\frac{2m}{2} = \frac{12}{2}$$
$$m = 6$$

Build the equation

B
$$m = 6$$
$$\frac{m}{2} = \frac{6}{2}$$
$$\frac{m}{2} = 3$$

How are the steps related? $\longrightarrow$

Solve the equation

$$\frac{m}{2} = 3$$
$$2 \times \frac{m}{2} = 2 \times 3$$
$$m = 6$$

Example 1

Solve

(a) $6y = 36$ (b) $\frac{m}{8} = 4$

Solution

(a) $6y = 36$

Ask: What operation can be used to isolate y?

$$\frac{6y}{6} = \frac{36}{6} \quad \text{Divide both sides by 6.}$$
$$\frac{6y}{6} = 6$$
$$y = 6$$

(b) $\frac{m}{8} = 4$

Ask: What operation can be used to isolate m?

$$8 \times \frac{m}{8} = 8 \times 4$$
$$8 \times \frac{m}{8} = 32$$
$$m = 32$$

413

The first step is solving an equation is to isolate the terms involving the variable.

Example 2

Solve $4m - 1 = -21$.

Solution

$$4m - 1 = -21$$
$$4m - 1 + 1 = -21 + 1$$
$$4m = -20$$
$$\frac{4m}{4} = \frac{-20}{4}$$
$$\frac{4m}{4} = -5$$
$$m = -5$$

Ask yourself: How do I isolate the terms containing the variables?

To solve the above equation by systematic trial would be time-consuming. The properties of equality below are important for solving equations.

Addition Property	Subtraction Property
$m + 2 = 12$ To solve, *subtract* 2.	$m - 2 = 12$ To solve, *add* 2.
↑ 2 *added*	↑ 2 *subtracted*

Multiplication Property	Division Property
$2m = 12$ To solve, *divide* by 2.	$\frac{m}{2} = 12$ To solve, *multiply* by 2.
└ *multiplied* by 2.	└ *divided* by 2.

Try These

1 An important skill in solving equations is to be able to simplify these expressions. Simplify.

(a) $\dfrac{3m}{3}$ (b) $\dfrac{6k}{6}$ (c) $\dfrac{4y}{4}$

(d) $\dfrac{-3x}{-3}$ (e) $\dfrac{-2p}{-2}$ (f) $\dfrac{-s}{-1}$

2 Simplify each expression.

(a) $3 \times \dfrac{p}{3}$ (b) $2 \times \dfrac{t}{2}$ (c) $6 \times \dfrac{y}{6}$

3 What needs to be done to isolate the variable?

(a) $3m = 6$ (b) $16 = 8y$

(c) $4 = -k$ (d) $25 = -5s$

(e) $\dfrac{m}{2} = 3$ (f) $\dfrac{p}{3} = 2$

4 What is the first step in solving each equation?

(a) $2m - 1 = 7$ (b) $2m + 1 = 7$

(c) $4 + 2m = 6$ (d) $4 - 2m = 6$

414

Written Exercises

A 1 For each equation
▶ decide which number to multiply or divide by.
▶ then solve the equation.

(a) $2m = 8$ (b) $4y = 12$ (c) $6p = -12$

(d) $\dfrac{k}{3} = 8$ (e) $\dfrac{a}{4} = -2$ (f) $\dfrac{s}{2} = 3$

(g) $-2t = 6$ (h) $\dfrac{w}{-2} = -4$ (i) $-5x = 25$

2 For each equation
▶ decide on your first step,
▶ then solve.

(a) $2m + 1 = 9$ (b) $3p - 3 = 6$

(c) $\dfrac{q}{2} + 1 = 8$ (d) $\dfrac{t}{3} - 2 = 6$

(e) $8 - x = 4$ (f) $8 - 2y = 4$

3 Decide what the missing value, ▨, is. Then solve.

(a) $4k = 12$ (b) $6x = -36$
$\dfrac{4k}{▨} = \dfrac{12}{▨}$ $\dfrac{6x}{▨} = \dfrac{-36}{▨}$

(c) $\dfrac{m}{2} = 6$ (d) $\dfrac{y}{6} = 3$

$▨ \times \dfrac{m}{2} = ▨ \times 6$ $▨ \times \dfrac{y}{6} = ▨ \times 3$

4 Which equation has *not* been built from $k = 12$?

(a) $2k = 24$ (b) $3k = -36$
(c) $3k = 36$ (d) $6 - k = -6$

(e) $\dfrac{k}{3} = 4$ (f) $\dfrac{k}{-4} = -3$

B 5 Solve each equation. Verify.

(a) $2k + 6 = 34$ (b) $3m - 4 = 23$

(c) $\dfrac{k}{3} + 1 = 4$ (d) $\dfrac{s}{2} - 3 = 11$

6 Find each solution set.

(a) $22 = 5p + 2$ (b) $11 = 2q - 3$

(c) $9 = \dfrac{p}{3} - 1$ (d) $9 = \dfrac{k}{2} + 3$

7 What is the root of each equation?

(a) $6m - 3 = 15$ (b) $3 + 4x = 23$
(c) $2 - 3y = 8$ (d) $14 - 2p = 8$

8 Solve.

(a) $4x = 2x - 16$ (b) $6y = 3y + 27$
(c) $12 + 2p = 6p$ (d) $18 - 6m = 12m$

9 Each equation involves decimals. Solve the equation.

(a) $2.5x + 6 = 13.5$ (b) $1.5y - 8 = 3$
(c) $3.5 = 2 + 1.5p$ (d) $13 = 6 - 3.5k$

10 Solve each equation.

(a) $-3m + 2 = 8$ (b) $-2q - 1 = 3$
(c) $20 = 8 - 2p$ (d) $13 = -2t + 3$

C
11 Which equations have the same solution set?

(a) $2m - 3 = -7$ (b) $3 + 2m = -1$
(c) $3 - 2m = 7$ (d) $-2m + 3 = 1$

Calculator Tip

To find the root of an equation, you can use a calculator. For example, to solve the equation,
$$4.5m + 3.6 = 14.4$$
you isolate the variable.
$$m = \dfrac{14.4 - 3.6}{4.5}$$
Then calculate.
$$m = 13.6$$
Solve. Round to 1 decimal place.

(a) $5.6p + 3.8 = 9.5$
(b) $6.2x - 9.2 = 5.8$
(c) $4.6 + 3.2y = 8.9$
(d) $8.2 - 3.4s = 6.2$

13.4 Solving Equations: Variables And Numbers On Both Sides

The principal step in solving equations is to isolate the terms containing the variable.

Example 1

Solve $4x - 5 = 2x + 15$.

Solution

Be sure you can justify each step of the solution.

$$4x - 5 = 2x + 15$$

$$4x - 5 + 5 = 2x + 15 + 5 \longleftarrow \text{Be sure to add}$$
$$4x = 2x + 20 \qquad \text{the } same \text{ number to } both \text{ sides.}$$

$$4x - 2x = 2x - 2x + 20$$
$$2x = 20$$
$$\frac{2x}{2} = \frac{20}{2} \qquad \text{Be sure to subtract the } same \text{ expression from } both \text{ sides.}$$
$$x = 10$$

Thus 10 is the root of the equation.

Remember, check your calculations by verifying in the *original* equation.

Example 2

Solve and verify $3k - 12 = 6k - 6$.

Solution

Decide on which side of the equation to isolate the variable.

$$3k - 12 = 6k - 6$$
$$3k - 12 + 6 = 6k - 6 + 6$$
$$3k - 6 = 6k$$
$$3k - 3k - 6 = 6k - 3k$$
$$-6 = 3k$$
$$\frac{-6}{3} = \frac{3k}{3}$$
$$-2 = k \qquad \text{Or you may write } k = -2$$

Thus, -2 is the root of the equation.

Check:

$$\begin{array}{l|l} \text{LS} = 3k - 12 & \text{RS} = 6k - 6 \\ = 3(-2) - 12 & = 6(-2) - 6 \\ = -6 - 12 & = -12 - 6 \\ = -18 & = -18 \end{array}$$

$$\text{LS} = \text{RS} \quad \text{checks}$$

Often in mathematics the same instruction may be expressed in different ways. Each of the following instructions ask you to solve the equation in Example 2 above.

Instruction
Find the root of the equation.
Find the solution set.

Final Statement
The root of the equation is -2.
The solution set is $\{-2\}$.

416

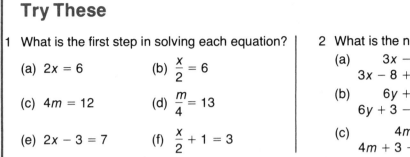

Try These

1 What is the first step in solving each equation?

(a) $2x = 6$ (b) $\dfrac{x}{2} = 6$

(c) $4m = 12$ (d) $\dfrac{m}{4} = 13$

(e) $2x - 3 = 7$ (f) $\dfrac{x}{2} + 1 = 3$

2 What is the next step?

(a) $\qquad 3x - 8 = 2x$
$\qquad 3x - 8 + 8 = 2x + 8$

(b) $\qquad 6y + 3 = 5y$
$\qquad 6y + 3 - 3 = 5y - 3$

(c) $\qquad 4m + 3 = 5m$
$\qquad 4m + 3 - 4m = 5m - 4m$

Written Exercises

A 1 For each solution, the next step is shown. Complete each solution.

(a) $\qquad 7y = 2y + 5$
$\qquad 7y - 2y = 2y + 5 - 2y$

(b) $\qquad 5k = 18 - 4k$
$\qquad 5k + 4k = 18 - 4k + 4k$

(c) $\qquad 20 - 3m = m$
$\qquad 20 - 3m + 3m = m + 3m$

2 To solve each equation

▸ decide what the first step is.
▸ solve the equation.

(a) $3y = 12 + y$ (b) $6y - 3 = 9$
(c) $9m = 4m - 10$ (d) $8y + 4 = 7y$
(e) $6k = 4k - 4$ (f) $6 - 3x = 3x$
(g) $4 - 3x = 6x$ (h) $25 - 2y = 3y$

3 Two values are given for each equation. Verify which value is the root.

Equation	A	B
(a) $7x = 2x + 10$	2	−2
(b) $3x = 5x - 8$	−4	4
(c) $7x - 9 = 5$	2	8
(d) $-2x = 6 - 3x$	3	6
(e) $3x + 7 = 2x - 19$	5	−26
(f) $8x - 2 = 6x - 28$	−13	15

4 Which value, A or B, is the root of the equation?

Equation	A	B
(a) $12x = 6x + 3$	$\dfrac{1}{2}$	$\dfrac{1}{3}$
(b) $9x - 1 = 6x$	$\dfrac{2}{3}$	$\dfrac{1}{3}$
(c) $4x + 3 = 2x + 4$	$\dfrac{1}{2}$	$\dfrac{3}{2}$

5 Which of the values shown is the root of the equation?

Equation	Values
(a) $2x + 8 = x - 12$	12, −20
(b) $18 + 3x - 5 = 65 - x$	13, −13
(c) $3 + 3x - 10 = 5x + 31$	9, −19

B 6 Solve and verify.

(a) $3x + 5 = 2x - 21$
(b) $7m + 1 = 4 + 4m$
(c) $3n + 11 = 3 - n$
(d) $4p + 8 = 3p - 22$
(e) $4k - 2 = 6k - 3$

7 Find the solution set.

(a) $2y + 3 = y - 37$
(b) $4 - 2a = 4a + 100$
(c) $3f - 2 = f - 60$
(d) $6a - 12 = 36 + 2a$

417

8 Find the root of each equation.
   (a) $5m - 2 = 2m + 4$
   (b) $6f + 10 = -12 - 5f$
   (c) $-7r - 1 = 2r + 26$
   (d) $6 - 8y = 2y - 44$

9 Solve.
   (a) $6y = 36 - 3y$ (b) $8y = 36 + 7y$
   (c) $2m = 6m - 20$ (d) $7p = 6 + 5p$
   (e) $2y + 1 = y + 4$ (f) $28 - y = 5y - 2$
   (g) $15 - 3p = 6p - 3$ (h) $9 + 6k = k + 34$
   (i) $d + 3 = 2d - 6$ (j) $3 + 7s = 9s - 5$

10 Which equation(s) have the same root?
   (a) $2y = 6y + 8$ (b) $8p + 14 = p$
   (c) $3 + 9m = 10m + 5$ (d) $2 + 7k = 20 - 2k$

11 Solve each equation. Verify your answers.
   (a) $4m - 3m = 5m - 28$
   (b) $3y + y - 7 = 2 - 2y$
   (c) $5k - 5 + 3k = 7k - 3$
   (d) $7p - 64 - 2p = 8 + 3p$

12 Use a flow chart to solve each of the following
    equations.
   (a) $5x - 2 = 10x - 3$
   (b) $4k - 2 = 6k - 3$
   (c) $30 - 4n = 6n + 15$

13 The missing combination for the lock is given
    by the root of the equation $3k - 16 = 2k + 12$.

14 The number of kilometres that Bev jogs each
    day is given by the root of the equation
    $3k - 2 = 5k - 14$.

15 The atmosphere of Venus is n times as heavy
    as that of the earth. Solve the equation to find
    n.
       $n + 27 = 2n - 3$

16 Decide what will be your first step. Then solve
    and verify each equation.
   (a) $3(m - 3) = 6$ (b) $2(3 - k) = 8$
   (c) $4k = 2(3 - k)$ (d) $14 = 7(a + 2)$

17 Solve each equation.
   (a) $2(m - 1) = 4$ (b) $4(3 - h) = 8$
   (c) $20p = 5(p - 3)$ (d) $8r = 4(2 - r)$

18 Find the solution set.
   (a) $3(s + 5) = 24$ (b) $2(5 - z) = 6$
   (c) $-12x = 4(2 - x)$ (d) $6t = 3(t + 3)$

19 Decide what will be your first step of the
    solution of each equation. Then solve each
    equation.
   (a) $6(x - 1) = 5(x + 3)$
   (b) $3(y - 6) = 4(y - 3)$
   (c) $5(2m - 4) = 9(m - 3)$

20 Solve and verify.
   (a) $3(2x - 1) = 5(x - 3)$
   (b) $2(1 - 3x) = 5(3 - x)$
   (c) $3(2 + 3x) = 8(x + 1)$

21 The height of a building is given by h, in
    metres. Solve the equation for h to find the
    height.
       $2(h + 3) = 3(h - 3)$

22 The width of a bridge is given by w, in
    metres. Find the width by solving the equation.
       $5(w - 1) = 4(w + 2)$

C 23 To win a trip on a jumbo jet, you need to add
    the roots of the equations A and B.
       A $4(2y + 6) = 48$
       B $7(m + 2) = 5(m + 4)$
    What is the sum required to win the trip?

418

Solving Inequations

In your earlier work with drawing graphs, you already solved simple inequations. The skills for solving equations can be extended to solving inequations as shown.

Solve

$$2x + 5 > 15, x \in I$$
$$2x + 5 - 5 > 15 - 5$$
$$2x > 10$$
$$\frac{2x}{2} > \frac{10}{2}$$
$$x > 5$$

Solution set is
$$\{6, 7, 8, \ldots\}$$

Solve

$$3(y - 1) < 2(y - 4), y \in I$$
$$3y - 3 < 2y - 8$$
$$3y - 2y < -8 + 3$$
$$y < -5$$

Solution set is
$$\{-6, -7, -8, \ldots\}$$

---

24 Solve $m \in I$.

(a) $10 + m < 15$ (b) $\frac{2}{3}m \leqq 5$

(c) $20 > 14 + m$ (d) $m + 32 \geqq 16$

25 Solve. Draw the graph of the solution set. The variable is an integer.

(a) $x + 2 > 7$ (b) $16 < m - 1$

(c) $-12 \leqq m + 5$ (d) $3k \geqq 12$

(e) $\frac{m}{3} < 2$ (f) $-7 \geqq \frac{p}{2}$

26 Complete the steps. Solve the inequations.

(a) $3(x - 2) \leqq 2x$ (b) $2(m - 3) > m - 5$
    $3x - 6 \leqq 2x$ $2m - 6 > m - 5$
    ▓▓▓▓▓▓▓   ▓▓▓▓▓▓▓

27 For the inequation, $3(8 + k) > 21$, which of the following are members of the solution set?

(a) 2   (b) 0   (c) −1 (d) 3   (e) −3 (f) −2

28 (a) What is the first step in solving the inequation

$$3x - 4 \leqq 2(x - 1), x \in I$$

(b) Solve the inequation in (a).

29 Find the solution set $x \in I$.

(a) $2(x - 1) > 18$

(b) $2(x + 2) \leqq 26$

(c) $2(x - 3) < -42$

(d) $3(x - 1) \geqq -27$

30 For the inequation $2(r + 4) \leqq 2(10 - 4)$, which of the following are members of the solution set?

(a) 4   (b) 2   (c) 3

(d) −3   (e) 0   (f) −100

31 (a) Solve $5(m + 2) \leqq 2(m + 11), m \in I$.
    (b) Draw a graph of the solution set in (a).

32 Find each solution set, $y \in I$.

(a) $2(y - 1) - 3 > 3(y - 2)$

(b) $3(y - 1) \leqq 4(y - 3) + 6$

33 Use a flow chart to show the steps for solving the inequation,
$$5(x + 3) \leqq 4(x + 1).$$

Applications: Breaking The Code

The young of various animals have been given special names.

kid

chick

CODE	
Code number	Name of young
−4	leveret
−3	foal
−2	calf
−1	gosling
0	parr
1	squab
2	piglet
3	cygnet
4	chick
5	lamb
6	duckling

In the table below, each name is given a code number.

To find the names of the young of various animals in the questions that follow, you need to solve the equations, then use the codes given in the table. For example,

What are young geese called?

Solve the equation, then use the code to find the name.

$$3(g - 1) = 2(g - 2)$$
$$3g - 3 = 2g - 4$$
$$3g - 3 + 3 = 2g - 4 + 3$$
$$3g = 2g - 1$$
$$3g - 2g = 2g - 1 - 2g$$
$$g = -1$$

From the table above, −1 is the code number of "gosling". Thus, the young of geese are called goslings.

Find the root of each equation in Questions 34 to 38. Then use the code to determine the name of the young of each animal given.

34 What are young donkeys called?
Solve the equation
$$7(d + 1) = 1 + 5d$$
and use the code.

35 What are young elephants called?
Solve the equation
$$2(e - 3) = 3(e - 5) + 11$$
and use the code.

36 What are young pigeons called?
Solve the equation
$$3(p + 4) = 15p$$
and use the code.

37 What are young swans called?
Solve the equation
$$5(s - 3) = 0$$
and use the code.

38 What are young turkeys called?
Solve the equation
$$4(t - 3) + 10 = 2(t + 3)$$
and use the code.

13.5 Skills For Translating Into Mathematics

The most important questions to ask yourself when you are solving any problem are:

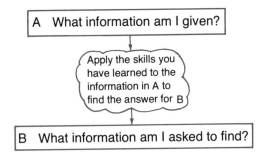

A   What information am I given?

Apply the skills you have learned to the information in A to find the answer for B

B   What information am I asked to find?

To apply the above process you need to be able to translate accurately the information in A into mathematics. For example, suppose someone poses this problem:

"I'm thinking of a number. If you double the number and subtract 5, the result is 23. What is the number?"

Use n to represent the number.

English	Symbols (Algebra)
I am thinking of a number.	n
Double the number.	$2n$
Subtract 5.	$2n - 5$
The result is 23.	$2n - 5 = 23$

The problem has been translated from English sentences into an equation that you can solve.

$$2n - 5 = 23$$
$$2n - 5 + 5 = 23 + 5$$
$$2n = 28$$
$$\frac{2n}{2} = \frac{28}{2}$$
$$n = 14$$
The number is 14.

Once you learn to translate accurately, you will be able to use this skill to solve problems.

Try These

1 *n* represents a number. What expression is used to show each of the following?

   (a) *n* increased by 12
   (b) *n* decreased by 4
   (c) the product of *n* and 6
   (d) 3 is subtracted from *n*
   (e) *n* is doubled
   (f) *n* is divided by 3
   (g) 8 is decreased by *n*

2 Match each English expression with the corresponding mathematical expression. *k* represents the number.

   (a) *k* is decreased by 6 $2k$
   (b) the sum of 15 and *k* $6 - k$
   (c) the product of 3 and *k* $k + 12$
   (d) *k* is doubled $k \div 3$
   (e) 6 decreased by *k* $3k$
   (f) *k* increased by 12 $k + 15$
   (g) *k* divided by 3 $k - 6$

Written Exercises

A 1 A variable is used to represent a number. Match the expression in Column I to the corresponding expression in Column II.

I *English Expression*	II *Translated Expression*
(a) a number decreased by 8	$5n$
(b) 7 decreased by a number	$p - 15$
(c) a number divided by 20	$y - 8$
(d) 8 divided by a number	$12 + m$
(e) the product of 5 and a number	$x - 16$
(f) 15 subtracted from a number	$\dfrac{8}{f}$
(g) the sum of 12 and a number	$\dfrac{w}{20}$
(h) a number diminished by 16	$7 - z$

2 What is an expression for each of the following?
   (a) a number *s*, decreased by 5
   (b) the sum of *y* and 3
   (c) the product of *p* and 18
   (d) the number 7 decreased by *k*
   (e) the number *n* increased by 25
   (f) 3 more than, 18 times a number *n*
   (g) one half of, a number *p* decreased by 9
   (h) 6 less than, 15 times a number *s*

3 Translate each of the following into symbols.
   (a) one-half of *q* is added to one-third of *q*
   (b) three times the sum of *n* and 5
   (c) one-third of the sum of *k* and 4
   (d) three times *w* is decreased by 10
   (e) *s* is doubled and increased by 5
   (f) *k* is tripled and decreased by 4
   (g) the product of 5 and *r* is increased by 26
   (h) one-quarter of *m* is decreased by 8

4 In each example, choose a variable for the number, then translate into mathematics. The first one has been done for you.
   (a) Seven is added to a number.

        Let *n* represent the number.
        The expression is $n + 7$.

   (b) Twelve is subtracted from a number.
   (c) A number is doubled and then decreased by 13.
   (d) A number is added to itself.
   (e) one-half of a number
   (f) One-half of a number is decreased by 16.
   (g) A number is multiplied by 5 and decreased by 9.
   (h) the product of a number and 30

B In Questions 5 to 11, find the expression that represents ▢.

5 The Spitfires won 8 more games than the Scouts.
   Let the number of games won by the Scouts be n.
   Then the number games won by the Spitfires is ▢.

6 The width of a rectangle is half of its length.
   Let the length, in metres, be represented by L.
   Then the width, in metres, is ▢.

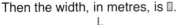

7 The height of a triangle is twice the base.
   Let the base, in centimetres, be represented by b.
   Then the height, in centimetres, is ▢.

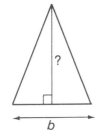

8 Jerome is 2 cm taller than Heather.
   Let Jerome's height, in centimetres, be represented by j.
   Then Heather's height, in centimetres, is ▢.

9 The height of a triangle is 4 cm more than the base.
   Let the base, in centimetres be represented by b.
   Then the height, in centimetres, is ▢.

10 Michael scored 5 more goals than Yuri.
   Let the number of goals scored by Michael be m.
   Then the number scored by Yuri is ▢.

11 George has $5 more than Morira.
   Let the amount, in dollars, George has be represented by g.
   Then the money Morira has, in dollars, is ▢.

12 For each of the following, use variables to translate the information. The first one has been done for you.
   (a) David has $4 less than Joya.

   Let the amount of money David has be represented by d.
   Then Joya has $(d + 4)$ dollars.

   (b) In Tennis, Hans won 8 more games than Lief.
   (c) Maria swam 28 cm more than Oona.
   (d) Bridget drives 12 km farther to work than Derrick.
   (e) Stacy took 15 min more than Helmut to cut the lawn.
   (f) Ron has jogged 2.5 km more than Monique.
   (g) In one week, Franco drinks twice the amount of milk that Elaine drinks.
   (h) Heinz received 48 more points than Carrie.

Consumer Tip

Line segments are used to construct the following symbol. Each consumer good is assigned a *universal product code* symbol and is found on the labels of packages. No two symbols are alike. An optical scanner reads the symbol, and the price is shown on the computerized checkout system.

These numbers and lines identify the manufacturer.

These numbers and lines identify the product; its name, size, colour, flavour, quality, grade and so on.

423

13.6 Steps For Solving Word Problems

To solve any problem you need to know,
   I What information you are asked to find.
  II What information you are given.

You also need to be able to translate accurately into mathematics.

The main steps for solving a problem are given.

> *Steps for Solving Problems*
> A Do you understand the problem? Ask yourself:
>   I What information am I asked to find?
>   II What information am I given?
> B Decide on a method.
> C Find the answer.
> D Check your answer. Is it reasonable?
> E Make a final statement to answer the original problem.

Example 1
Four times a number is added to 16 and the sum is 80. What is the number?

Solution
Let the number be represented by n.
Four times the number is added to 16. $4n + 16$
The sum is 80. $\qquad 4n + 16 = 80$
Now solve the equation.

$$4n + 16 = 80$$
$$4n + 16 - 16 = 80 - 16$$
$$4n = 64$$
$$\frac{4n}{4} = \frac{64}{4}$$
$$n = 16$$

The required number is 16.

Check:
4 times the number
$4 \times 16 \qquad 64$
add 16 $\qquad \underline{16}$
total is $\qquad 80$
          checks

Example 2
Twice as many adults as students watched the motor cavalcade. Admission was $4 for adults and $3 for students. If $1980 was collected, how many students went?

Solution
Let the number of students be $\qquad n$
Then the number of adults is $\qquad 2n$
Amount, in dollars collected for students is $\qquad n \times 3$ or $3n$
Amount collected for adults is $\qquad 2n \times 4$ or $8n$
Then, $\qquad 3n + 8n = 1980$
$$11n = 1980$$
$$\frac{11n}{11} = \frac{1980}{11}$$
$$n = 180$$

Thus, the number of students was 180.

Check:
students 180
adults 360

Amount Collected
$3 \times 180 = 540$
$4 \times 360 = \underline{1140}$
Checks   Total   1980

Try These

1 A number is represented by n. Write an expression for each of the following.
  (a) n increased by 8
  (b) one-third of n
  (c) 3 times n decreased by 15
  (d) 2 more than 5 times n
  (e) 6 less than a quarter of n
  (f) the product of 7 and n

2 A number is represented by n. What do each of the following mean?
  (a) $n + 8$ (b) $n - 8$ (c) $8n$
  (d) $2n$ (e) $2n + 3$ (f) $2n - 3$
  (g) $\frac{1}{2}n$ (h) $\frac{1}{2}n + 5$ (i) $\frac{1}{2}n - 5$
  (j) $3n - 1$ (k) $4n + 5$ (l) $5n - 3$

Written Exercises

A 1 Write an equation for each of the following using k as the variable. Then solve each equation for k.

(a) 6 less than, 8 times k is 18.

(b) One-half of, k increased by 4, is 36.

(c) 4 more than twice k is 80.

(d) One-fifth of k, decreased by 2, is 15.

(e) 3 less than, 8 times k is 45.

2 n represents a whole number. Write the expression for

(a) the next number.

(b) the next two consecutive numbers.

3 The number of coins in a jar is k. What is the value in cents if the coins are

(a) nickels?　　(b) dimes?

(c) quarters?　　(d) half dollars?

4 Shirley's age in years is represented by s. What is each age?

(a) Mark is 5 a younger.

(b) Stanley is twice as old.

(c) Eric is half as old.

(d) Gary is 5 a more than twice Shirley's age.

5 The cost of admission for adults is $8 and for students $4. There are twice as many adults as students. There are s students.

(a) How many adults are there?

(b) What is the total admission for students?

(c) What is the total admission for adults?

(d) What is the total admission collected?

6 Translate each of the following into symbols.

(a) A number decreased by 12 is 28.

(b) 10 divided by a number is 5.

(c) A number diminished by 24 is 16.

(d) A number increased by 53 is 76.

(e) A number subtracted from 100 is 72.

B 7 For each problem, decide

　I what information you are asked to find.

　II what information you are given.

Then, solve the problem.

(a) When 6 is added to a number, the sum is equal to 30. Find the number.

(b) Five is subtracted from twice a number and the result is 45. Find the number.

8 Solve each problem. (Be sure to verify your answer in the original problem.)

(a) A number is decreased by 17 and 47 is obtained. What is the number?

(b) A number is doubled and then increased by 18. The result is 66. Find the number.

(c) A number is doubled and then added to itself. If the sum is 108, find the number.

9 On a biking trip from Halifax to Sydney, Jennifer cycled 20 km more on the second day than on the first day. The total distance cycled was 104 km. How far did she cycle on the first day?

10 When 4 is added to one-quarter of a number, the result is 9. Find the number.

11 At the motor derby there were twice as many compact cars as full size cars. There were 384 cars. How many compact cars were there?

C 12 For her first parachute jump Elsie jumped 285 m farther than twice that jumped by Jeff. If the total distance jumped is 5913 m, find the distance each person jumped.

13.7 Using Diagrams To Solve Problems

Very often it is helpful to record the information given in a problem onto a diagram. This is especially true for geometry problems, where a diagram can help you see how to solve the problem.

Example 1

The length of a rectangular lot is twice as long as its width. If the perimeter is 90 m, find the dimensions of the lot.

Solution

Let the width, in metres, be represented by w. Then the length is $2w$.

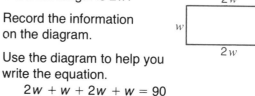

Record the information on the diagram.

Use the diagram to help you write the equation.

$$2w + w + 2w + w = 90$$
$$6w = 90$$
$$\frac{6w}{6} = \frac{90}{6}$$

$w = 15$ The width is 15 m.
The length is 30 m.

Check:
perimeter $= 15$ m $+ 30$ m $+ 15$ m $+ 30$ m
$= 90$ m   Checks

Because a value which you have just calculated is often used in the next step of your solution, it is important that you check your calculations at each step.

Example 2

The width of a rectangular parking lot is 22 m and the perimeter is 120 m.

(a) Find the measures of the sides.

(b) Find its area.

Solution

(a) Let the length in metres be represented by L. The expression for the perimeter of this rectangle is

$$L + 22 + L + 22 = 120$$
$$2L + 44 = 120$$
$$2L + 44 - 44 = 120 - 44$$
$$2L = 76$$
$$L = 38$$

Thus, the length is 38 m.

Check: Since the answer is needed to find the area, check for accuracy at this stage.
Perimeter $= 38$ m $+ 22$ m $+ 38$ m $+ 22$ m
$= 120$ m   checks.

(b) Area $=$ length $\times$ width   length $= 38$ m
$A = l \times w$ width $= 22$ m
$= 38 \times 22$
$= 836$

The area is 836 m².

Written Exercises

A 1 (a) Write an expression for the perimeter of each of the following figures.

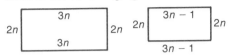

(b) Find the dimensions of each figure if $n = 4$.

2 The perimeter of each rectangle is shown. Find the dimensions of each rectangle.

(a)   (b)

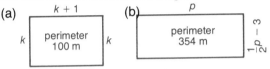

3 (a) Write an expression for the perimeter of the triangle.

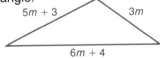

(b) Find the value of m in (a) if the perimeter is 133 cm.

(c) Find the length of each side.

(d) Check your answer in (c).

4 A diagram shows the distance in kilometres bicycled by two students.

The distance AC is 20 km in total.

(a) Find the distance each student rode.

(b) Check your answer in (a).

5 The distance from Buttonville to Chesapeake via Charleston is 224 km.

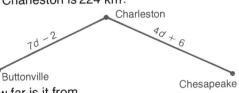

How far is it from

(a) Buttonville to Charleston?

(b) Charleston to Chesapeake?

(c) Check your answers in (a) and (b).

B 6 The sides of a triangle, in metres, are given by $3n - 4$, $3n + 9$, $4n + 5$.

(a) Draw a diagram to show the information.

(b) If the perimeter is 114 cm, find the length of each side.

7 Lori is 8 cm taller than Chris and Michael is 16 cm taller than Chris.

(a) Draw a diagram to show the information.

(b) If their total heights are 465 cm, find each of their heights.

8 The length and width, in metres, of a rectangular enclosure are given by the expression $8w + 5$ and $6w - 2$ respectively. If the perimeter is 972 m, calculate the dimensions.

9 The width of a rectangular field is 14 m and the perimeter is 86 m.

(a) Find the measure of the length.

(b) Find the area.

10 The world's largest swimming pool is the Orthlieb Pool in Casablanca, Morocco. Its length is 30 m more than 6 times its width.

(a) If its perimeter is 1110 m then find its dimensions.

(b) Find its area.

C 11 Use a flow chart to show the steps for solving the following problem. Then solve the problem.

The perimeter of a rectangle is 90 m.

(a) If the width is 15 m, find the measure of the length.

(b) Calculate its area.

13.8 Formulas And Solving Problems

Relationships are often expressed as an equation involving variables. For example,

distance = rate × time

$$d = r \times t$$

Example 1

The distance between Huron and Bantford is 105 km. How long would it take a gull to fly the distance non-stop at 15 km/h?

Solution

Use $d = r \times t$

$105 = 15t$ Substitute the values

$\dfrac{105}{15} = \dfrac{15t}{15}$ $r = 15$ (km/h)

             $t = ?$

$7 = t$ $d = 105$ (km)

Thus, the gull would take 7 h (non-stop).

Many relationships in industry or business are expressed as formulas. For example, the formula for calculating the simple interest, I, in dollars, on a principal amount of money in dollars, is given by

     $I = Prt$ where r is the interest rate per annum.
                       t is the length of time in years.

A bond you buy pays your interest each year.

Try These

1 The perimeter, P, of a rectangle is given by $P = 2(l + w)$ where l is the length and w is the width. What equation is needed to find the missing information? The first one is done for you.

(a) $l = 20$, $w = ?$, $P = 70$

     The equation is $70 = 2(20 + w)$

(b) $l = 12$, $w = ?$, $P = 36$

(c) $l = 25$, $w = ?$, $P = 90$

2 The volume, V, of a rectangular solid is given by $V = lwh$, where l = length, w = width, and h = height. What equation is needed to find the missing information?

(a) $V = 120$, $l = ?$, $w = 3$, $h = 5$

(b) $V = 80$, $l = 4$, $w = ?$, $h = 10$

(c) $V = 27.5$, $l = 2.5$, $w = 2$, $h = ?$

3 The formula for the density, D, of a substance with mass, M, and volume, V, is given by $D = \dfrac{M}{V}$. What equation do you need to solve to find the missing information?

(a) $D = 5$, $M = ?$, $V = 8$

(b) $D = 3$, $M = 36$, $V = ?$

Written Exercises

A Questions 1 to 3 are based on the formula.

> The distance travelled, d, is given by
> $d = rt$ where r is the rate of speed,
> t is the time taken.

1 For a mini-bike trip the time taken was 6 h. If the distance travelled was 87 km, what was the speed?

2 Monica jogged 10.8 km. If her speed was 7.2 km/h, calculate how long she jogged.

3 A hovercraft crossed the channel in 1.5 h. If the distance across the channel is 127.5 km, how fast was the hovercraft going?

Questions 4 to 6 are based on the following formula.

> The power of an electrical appliance is given by the formula
> $P = VI$ where P = power in watts (W)
> V = voltage in volts (V)
> I = current in amperes (A)

4 The voltage, V, of a refrigerator is 120 V. If power, P, is 1440 W, calculate the current, I.

5 The current, I, for a drill is 2.6 A. If its power, P, is 312 W, then calculate the voltage, V.

6 A battery charger draws a current of 1.8 A and has a power of 198 W. Calculate the voltage of the battery charger.

B 7 A plane's ground speed when flying with a tail wind is given by the following formula.
Ground speed = Air speed + Tail wind
$$G = A + T$$

(a) Find the ground speed when $A = 820$ km/h and $T = 30$ km/h.

(b) A jet has an air speed of 750 km/h. If the ground speed of the jet is 920 km/h, find the tail wind.

8 When a plane flies into a head wind its ground speed is given by the following formula.
Ground speed = Air speed − Head wind
$$G = A - H$$

(a) Find A when $H = 29$ km/h and $G = 738$ km/h.

(b) A Cessna plane has an air speed of 220 km/h. If its ground speed is 192 km/h, find the speed of the head wind.

Questions 9 to 11 are based on the following formula.

> The density of a substance, D, grams per cubic centimetre (g/cm³) is given by
> $D = \dfrac{M}{V}$ where M = mass, in grams
> V = volume, in cubic centimetres

9 A gold nugget has a volume of 0.9 cm³. If the density of gold is 19.3 g/cm³, what is the mass of the gold?

10 The largest nugget of gold ever found was 214.8 kg. If the density of gold is 19.3 g/cm³, calculate the volume of the gold nugget.

11 A cube of nickel has a mass of 18.1 g. The density of nickel is 8.9 g/cm³. Calculate the volume of the cube.

12 Refer to the formula for calculating interest.

(a) The interest earned on a bond invested for 2 a at 14%/a was $70. How much money did the bond cost?

(b) Sherry invested her summer earnings of $400 by buying a bond. The bond earned $192 in interest. For how many years did she keep the bond?

> Canada Savings Bond
> **Pays 16% interest**

429

Chapter Checkup: A Practice Test

13.1 (a) Find the root of the equation $4m - 8 = 32$.

(b) Write the solution set for $\frac{1}{3}k + 8 = 16$.

13.2 (a) Solve. Check your answers.

A $8 + 2p = 4p$ B $5m = 4m + 2$

(b) Find the solution set.

A $25 = y - 5$ B $20 - 3s = -2s$

(c) Which equations have been built from $p = -16$?

A $2p + 1 = -31$ B $2p - 3 = -35$

C $\frac{p}{4} - 1 = -3$ D $\frac{p}{2} - 1 = -7$

13.3 Values are shown for each equation. Which ones are not roots?

Equation

(a) $5y = 15 + 2y$ 5
(b) $4t - 5 = 7$ -3
(c) $-38 = 10m + 12$ 5
(d) $12x - 8 = 15x + 16$ -8
(e) $8k - 12 = k - 33$ -3

13.4 (a) The number of moons that Mars has is the root of the equation
$$8k - 3 = 10k - 7.$$

(b) Use a flow chart to solve the equation $4(4 - p) = 3(3 - p)$.

13.5 (a) Write an expression for each of the following.

A   3 times a number r, increased by 17
B   19 subtracted from 40 times a number k
C   8 less than, 5 times a number z

(b) Find the expression for ▯.

A   The number of girls at the concert is twice the number of boys. Let the number of boys be represented by b. Then the number of girls is ▯.
B   Peter is 6 a older than Jeanne. Let Jeanne's age in years be s. Then Peter's age is ▯.

13.6 Solve each problem.

(a) A number divided by 3 is equal to 60. Find the number.

(b) Nick is thinking of a whole number. If he multiples this number by 10 and then subtracts 5, the result is 125. Find the number.

(c) A building and a lot cost $120 000. The building costs $70 000 more than twice the cost of the lot. Find the cost of each.

13.7 (a) A path that spectators use to travel to and from the stadium is shown below. The path is 430 m long.

A Find the value of k.
B What is the length of each part of the path?

(b) The width of a rectangular field is 14 m and the perimeter is 86 m.
A Find the measure of the length.
B Find the area.

13.8 (a) A lead pipe has a mass of 48.3 g. The density of lead is 11.4 g/cm³. What is the volume of the lead pipe?

(b) The distance that an object falls is given by the formula,

$$d = \frac{1}{2}gt^2 \text{ where } d = \text{distance fallen in metres}$$

t = time in seconds

g is a constant

Jackie dropped a stone from a bridge 11 m high. It took 1.5 s for the stone to hit the water below. Calculate the value of g to 2 decimal places.

Selected Answers

Note: Answers for **Chapter Checkups** sections are provided in **Math Matters, Book 1, Teacher's Edition**.

CHAPTER 1

1.1 Written Exercises, page 4

1. a) 6631 b) 1769 c) 4902 d) 1262 e) 14 986 f) 5260
2. a) 3683 b) 5550 c) 27 152 d) 24 220 **3.** a) 4377 b) 6702 c) 1666 d) 6738 **4.** B **5.** a) C b) A c) B d) C e) C **6.** B
7. a) B b) C c) A d) B
8. a) 1008 b) 10 220 c) 10 656 d) 44 640 **9.** a) 41 b) 43 c) 59 d) 91 e) 0 **10.** a) 28 R 1 b) 36 R 2 c) 51 R 3 d) 99 R 4 e) 86 R 5 f) 96 R 6 **11.** 39 600
12. 68 700 **13.** 3000
14. a) chocolate milk b) cream c) 200 kJ, 600 kJ, 800 kJ, 380 kJ, 620 kJ, 740 kJ, 630 kJ, 330 kJ
15. a) Vancouver Sun b) Vancouver Sun and Montreal Gazette **16.** a) Saskatoon Star-Phoenix b) Saskatoon Star-Phoenix and Halifax Chronicle-Herald
17 a) 172 900 b) 141 900
18. a) 72 000 b) 145 000 c) 194 000 d) 250 000
19. a) elephant b) Arctic wolf
20. 1000 kg, 1100 kg, 29 500 kg, 17 300 kg, 8200 kg, 4100 kg, 4100 kg, 100 kg, 26 000 kg, 4100 kg, 4000 kg **21.** a) 60 kg b) 990 kg c) 1080 kg d) 3980 kg **22.** a) 29 000 kg b) 17 000 kg

1.2 Written Exercises, page 7

1. 6249 **3.** 63 a
4. 846 553 km **5.** 39 420 000
6. 38 321 **7.** 697 **8.** 73 d
9. 17 879 054 **10.** a) 6300 b) 2 299 500 **11.** 25 398
12. 410 km **13.** 40 cars
14. 249 895 km^2 **15.** 30
16. 37 min **17.** a) 964 h b) 954 h **18.** a) 2256 h b) 188 h c) September
19. a) 4770 km b) 10 337 km c) 2103 km d) 10 058 km
20. a) 4800 km b) 10 300 km c) 2100 km d) 10 100 km

21. a) 1098 km b) 8122 km c) 2119 km d) 18 546 km
22. a) 1000 km b) 8000 km c) 2000 km d) 19 000 km
23. A **24.** 5581 km
25. 3675 km **26.** 2279 km
27. A
29. 6785 km

1.3 Written Exercises, page 11

1. a) 22 b) 2 c) 4 d) 2 e) 3 f) 14 g) 13 h) 16 i) 24 j) 0
2. a) A 36, B 1 **3.** a) A 42, B 42
4. a) 5 b) 8 c) 65 d) 2 e) 3 f) 3 g) 2 h) 1 **5.** a) 55 b) 39 c) 22 d) 25 e) 20 **6.** a) 15 b) 84 c) 21 d) 27 **7.** 93
9. a) 738 b) 2648 c) 2520 d) 1692 **10.** Samuel **11.** 26
12. 96 **13.** a) ÷ b) × c) + d) ÷ e) ÷, + f) ÷, ÷ g) ×, –
14. a) $7 + 3 - 1 = 9$
b) $8 \times 3 \div 6 = 4$
c) $9 \times 6 - 4 = 50$
d) $12 \div 3 \div 4 = 1$
e) $10 \div (5 \div 5) = 10$
f) $12 \div 3 \times 4 = 16$
g) $28 \div 4 \times 7 = 49$
h) $6 \times 4 \div 3 \times 5 = 40$

1.4 Written Exercises, page 15

1. a) 6 b) 4 c) 2 d) 12 **2.** 54
3. a) 32 b) 28 **4.** a) 12 + 19 b) 31 **5.** a) 29 b) 21 **6.** a) 30 b) 8 c) 24 d) 56 **7.** a) 11 b) 19 c) 17 **8.** a) 27 b) 15 c) 39 d) 55 **9.** a) 19 b) 31 c) 38 d) 16 **10.** a) 17 b) 19 c) 21 d) 45 e) 30 f) 35
11. a) 24 b) 32 c) 116
12. a) 12 b) 18 c) 16 d) 64
13. a) 15 b) 0 c) 38 e) 12 f) 19 g) 24 h) 33 i) 17
14. a) 8, 18, 28 b) 8, 20, 32 c) 19, 35, 51 **15.** a) 11 b) 14
16. a) 9 b) 9 c) 12 d) 11
17. a) 7 b) 12 c) 18 d) 13 **18.** Falcons **19.** a) Reds b) Aeros

20. a) Blue Bombers 15, Alouettes 16, B.C. Lions 17, Argonauts 8, Tiger Cats 14 b) 3 c) 10
21. a) Capitals b) Oilers c) 4

1.5 Written Exercises, page 19

1. a) A b) A c) B d) B e) A f) A **2.** a) 4.7 b) 5.93 c) 0.137 d) 2.5 e) 3.9 f) 4.622 g) 9.92 h) 8.8 **3.** a) B b) B c) A d) A
4. a) Livio b) Ottis c) Irena d) Annelie **5.** a) 0.1, 1.0, 1.01, 1.011, 1.11, 11.0 b) 0.22, 0.232, 2.2, 2.22, 22.0, 22.2 c) 0.123, 1.123, 1.23, 12.3, 123.0, 123.1
6. a) 56.4, 45.6, 6.54, 5.064, 0.465 b) 12.96, 12.23, 12.2, 12.11, 12.1, 12.01 c) 0.150, 0.039, 0.015, 0.013, 0.0099, 0.0086 **7.** Mt. Peaks **8.** paint
9. Collins **11.** 2.1, 2.4, 1.7, 2.0, 2.2, 0.4, 2.2, 2.4 **12.** 185.0, 161.4, 161.6, 163.6, 205.3, 159.6 **13.** a) Day 2 b) Day 5 c) 8.72 h, 8.27 h, 4.96 h, 4.69 h, 3.16 h, 1.36 h **14.** a) Regina b) St. John's c) 18.3 mm, 18.5 mm, 22.6 mm, 53.3 mm, 57.2 mm, 59.2 mm, 90.7. mm, 110.7 mm, 137.2 mm, 145.0 mm

1.6 Written Exercises, page 22

1. a) 2.0 b) 16.4 c) 16.10 d) 43.88 e) 38.38 f) 3049.40
2. a) 2.8 b) 25.4 c) 2.7 d) 4.35 e) 89.72 f) 77.17
3. a) 269.31 b) 4377.917 c) 174.031 d) 806.586 e) 115.363 **4.** a) 61.961 b) 664.59 c) 948.1 d) 4003.1 e) 497.8 **5.** 8080.287
6. 12.286 **7.** 9571.93
8. 62.419 **9.** 11 799.8
10. a) $26.86 b) $345.89 c) $66.42 d) $158.99 e) $3.07 f) $9.86 **11.** a) $29.56, $31.12 b) $103.54 c) $1.76 d) $45.13, T $3.59 **12.** a) 362.1 km b) 118.9 km c) 888.4 km
13. a) 1152.2 km b) 1908.9 km c) 3018.9 km **14.** 4.15 m
15. 137 116.8 km **16.** 16 min
17. 2.886 L **18.** $106.10
19. a) 35, 35.4, 35.7 b) Aileen Riggin **20.** $1680

21. a) 1445.5 mm b) 1582.5 mm **22.** $25.80
23. $6.70 **24.** $40.06
25. $1.46 **26.** $18.90 **27.** 41¢
28. $1.60 **29.** $3.73 **30.** 95.70
31. a) $7.49 b) $1.50 c) $8.04

1.7 Written Exercises, page 27

1. a) 483 b) 496 c) 4196 d) 2963 e) 412.98 f) 696.1 g) 3 h) 345 **2.** a) 0.28 b) 0.222 **3.** a) B b) B c) B d) A **4.** a) 54.4 b) 28.8 c) 57.6 d) 16 e) 19.2 f) 20.7
5. a) 6.1 b) 18.3 c) 50.8 d) 8.5 **6.** a) 61.98 b) 2.86 c) 51.28 d) 7.73 **7.** a) 109 b) 128 c) 3.6 d) 4.8 e) 1.8
8. a) B b) A c) B d) A
9. a) 15.86 b) 0.77 c) 15.76 d) 0.12 e) 6.30 f) 2.54
10. a) 12.6 b) 6.1 c) 1 89.5 d) 2.1 e) 0.5 **11.** a) 7.92 b) 34.42 c) 90.72 d) 2.58 e) 87.38 **12.** a) 325.3 b) 59.49 c) 1.805 d) 228 119.5 e) 2849.24 f) 3.30
13. 0.06 mm **14.** $1.75
15. $98 40.55
16. A $4.19, B $4.75
17. 87.5 mg **18.** 87¢
19. a) $150.35 b) $341.00
20. 32.2¢/L **21.** a) $9.80 b) $10.35 c) $30.00
22. a) $26.45 b) $36.30
23. $32.04 **24.** a) 207.8 cm b) 41.56 cm c) Category C
25. a) $63.15 b) $107.50
26. a) $4.25 b) $5.75 c) $9.25
27. a) $1.58 b) $1.70 c) $1.31
28. b) $2.89
29. $2.25 **30.** a) $5.00 b) $5.25 c) (a) **31.** a) $6.25 b) $6.25 c) Equal value
32. a) $10.25 b) $9.95 c) (b)

1.8 Written Exercises, page 32

2. a) 3^3 b) 2^6 c) 6^4 d) 10^5
3. a) 8 b) 243 c) 256 d) 1 e) 1000 f) 125 g) 32 h) 100 000 **4.** a) 16 b) $\frac{1}{64}$ c) 225 d) 343 **5.** a) 4 b) $\frac{1}{5}$ c) 4 d) 9 e) 7 f) 5 g) 10 h) 4

6. a) 4 b) 16 c) $\frac{1}{27}$ d) 0.25
e) 36 f) 27 g) 81 h) 49 i) 1
j) $\frac{1}{25}$ k) 100 l) 1000
8. b) < c) < d) < e) > f) <
g) > h) < i) < j) < **9.** a) 18
b) 12 c) 18 d) 4 e) 26 f) 14
g) 52 h) 9 i) 898 j) 232
10. a) < b) < c) > d) >
e) = f) = **11.** (a) and F,
(b) and E, (c) and C, (d) and
D, (e) and B, (f) and A
12. a) 17 b) 9 c) 288 d) 8
13. a) 0.09, 0.0009
14. a) 0.008, 0.000 008 **15.** A
16. a) 0.01 b) 0.001 c) 0.0001
d) 0.04 e) 0.008 f) 0.0016
g) 0.25 h) 0.027 i) 0.000 01
j) 0.0001 k) 0.0004
17. a) 9 b) 0.09 c) 0.0009
d) 90 000 e) 1.69 f) 0.0169
g) 169 h) 16 900 i) 27
j) 0.000 027 k) 27 000
l) 27 000 000 **18.** a) 0.25
b) 0.0016 c) 0.000 01
19. a) 20 b) 4 c) 12 d) 64
20. a) 36 b) 144 c) 40
d) 1000 **21.** a) 11 b) 41 c) 4
d) 72 e) 162 f) 9 g) 3 h) 32
i) I **22.** a) 101 b) 9 c) 22 d) 3
e) 56 f) 13 g) 53 h) 7 i) 25
j) 79 k) 30 l) 9 **23.** a) A 9,
B 189 **24.** a) 10 b) 28 c) 2
d) 686 **25.** a) $3 \times (3 - 1)^2 = 12$
b) $(3 \times 2)^2 - 4 = 32$
c) $3 \times (2^2 - 4) = 0$
d) $(2 \times 5)^2 - 1 = 99$ **26.** a) 1
b) 1 c) 1 d) 1 e) 1 f) 1
27. A 18, B 8, C 10, D 6, E 2

1.9 Written Exercises, page 36

1. a) 14.4 b) 74.1 c) 291.2
d) 54.97 e) 4.14 f) 0.414
2. a) 22.63 b) 29.29 c) 4.65
d) 13.65 e) 7.81 f) 18.88
3. a) 6000 b) 10 000
c) 350 000 d) 320 **4.** a) 7
b) 10 c) 60 d) 5 **5.** a) A b) B
c) C d) C e) B f) A
6. a) 305.18 b) 19.32 c) 11.79
d) 717.91 e) 363.34 f) 29.62
g) 198.46 h) 388.21
i) 105 975.86 j) 424.96
7. a) \$37.20 b) \$27.37
c) \$97.51 d) \$1228.50
e) \$258.30 f) \$1520.28

8. a) \$23.88 b) \$30.80
c) \$126.75 d) \$593.81
9. a) \$93.75 b) \$105
d) \$120 **10.** a) \$6.36
b) \$14.64 c) \$13.40 d) \$16.75
e) \$18.72 **11.** 384 km
12. 112 g **13.** \$59.88
14. 26.6 h **15.** a) \$1150
b) \$1198.80

CHAPTER 2

2.1 Written Exercises, page 44

1. a) 141 m b) 14.4 m
c) 38.4 m d) 42.4 m **2.** C
3. a) 12 m b) 40 m c) 60 m
4. a) DE = 14 cm, EF = 6 cm,
Perimeter = 72 cm
b) UT = 14 cm, UV = 12 cm,
Perimeter = 124 cm
5. a) 13, 124 b) 11, 56 c) 6.9,
57 d) 4.6, 90.3 **6.** a) 26 m
b) \$163.54 **7.** a) 8.7 km
b) 1.74 h **8.** 36 m **9.** 67.2 m
10. a) 141.8 m b) \$381.44
11. 35.25 m **12.** 4.4 m
13. 4.88 m **14.** 17.1 m, 5.85 m,
5.85 m

2.2 Written Exercises, page 48

1. a) 360 cm² b) 576 cm²
c) 1280 cm² **2.** a) 4156 m²
b) 1142 m² c) 497 m²
3. a) 735 mm² b) 525 mm²
c) 336 mm² **4.** A 33.2 m²,
B 31.7 km², C 415.8 m²,
D 50 766.2 m² **5.** 24.4 m²
6. 72.3 m² **7.** a) 264.6 m²
b) \$2103.57 **8.** 7264 cm²
9. 809 m² **10.** 8337.5 m²
11. a) 26.58 cm² b) 100.44 cm²
c) 550.52 cm² d) 525.18 cm²
12. a) 296.66 m² b) \$2447.45
13. a) 2940 cm² b) 2310 cm²
c) 2040 cm² d) 2550 cm²
14. a) 2070 cm² b) 2460 cm²
c) 2790 cm² d) 2610 cm²
e) 2160 cm² **15.** 480 cm²
16. a) 360 cm²

2.3 Written Exercises

1. a) 36 cm³ b) 320 cm³
2. a) 936 cm³ b) 430.1 cm³

3. a) 42.8 m³ b) 124.2 m³
4. a) B b) B **5.** a) 2813.6 cm³
b) 2700 cm³ c) 1541.8 cm³
d) 538.6 cm³ **6.** a) 900 cm³
b) 960 cm³ c) 800 cm³
d) 7500 cm³ **7.** a) 124.4 m³
b) 219.3 m³ c) 825.4 m³
d) 328.7 m³ e) 558.7 m³
8. a) 94 860 cm³
b) 164 200 cm³ c) 3881.4 cm³
d) 33 334.2 cm³ **9.** 15.5
10. 71.6 m³ **11.** 4 m³
12. 1.7 m³ **13.** 2 trips
14. b) 1890 L
c) 1890 **15.** 1011.1 m³
16. 54 000 cm³ **17.** Box (b)
108.8 cm³ **18.** a) 3080 cm³
b) 5787.9 cm³ **19.** a) 12.7 L
b) 8.8 L **20.** a) 960 cm³
b) 384 cm³ c) 1344 cm³
21. a) 1404 cm³ b) 360 m³
22. a) 50.2 m³ b) 13568.3 m³
23. 31 440 cm³
24. 30 737.69 m³ **25.** 9.7 m³
26. 18.4 m³ **27.** a) 7267.7 cm³
b) 274.2 cm³ **28.** a) 67 L
b) 134 **29.** a) Top: 64260 cm³,
bottom: 91800 cm³ **30.** 8740 cm³

2.4 Written Exercises

1. a) 1340 cm² b) 43.6 m²
2. 5400 cm² **3.** a) 3.9 m²
b) 0.5 m³ **4.** 4842 cm²,
6616 cm³ **5.** a) 120 cm²
b) 1472 cm² **6.** 1) 1152 cm²
7. a) 864 cm² b) 864 cm²
c) 808 cm² **8.** a) 1065.4 cm²
b) 2257 cm² **9.** a) Left hand
(A) b) Left hand box (A)
10. a) 10 120 cm²
b) 68000 cm³
11. a) 960 cm²
b) 768 cm³ c) 128 cm²
12. b) A 1920 cm³, B 1600 cm³
c) A **13.** a) A, B, C 1728 cm³.
b) A 912 cm², B 984 cm²,
C = 864 cm² c) C

2.5 Written Exercises, page 62

1. \$6969.60 **2.** 120 m³ or
120 000 L **3.** b) 540 m
4. a) 541.5 m³ b) 59
6. a) 1800 cm³ b) twice
7. a) 378.6 cm³ **8.** \$1011.33

9. a) 17.4 m b) 14.98 m³
10. 11 136 cm³ **11.** 26040 m³
13. a) 4.2 m²
b) 46.3 m² **14.** 13.2 L **15.** 5
16. a) 83 cm × 28 cm × 64)cm
b) 18 856 cm² **17.** 2860 m²
18. \$2557.80 **19.** a) 140 m
b) \$1372.00 **20.** a) 114
b) 34 200 kg **21.** a) 764 400 mm²
b) 1 345 200 mm² c) 539 000 mm²

CHAPTER 3

3.1 Written Exercise

1. a) 900 cm²
c) 8.1 m² d) 1008 cm² **2.** a) 18
b) 24 c) 20 d) 56 **3.** a) 60
b) 140 c) 400 d) 500 e) 384
f) 2400 **4.** a) 450 cm²
b) 8.4 cm² **5.** a) 10 b) 15
c) 20 d) 10 e) 17.5 f) 16
6. a) 56 b) 100 c) 250 d) 168
e) 340 f) 625 **7.** a) 102 cm²
b) 100.8 cm² c) 5 m² d) 6.3 m²
e) 8.1 m² **8.** 468 cm²
9. 304 cm² **10.** 120.1 cm²
11. 455.0 cm² **12.** 103.76 m²
13. a) 190 cm² b) 190 cm²
14. a) 2.42 cm² b) 242 cm²
16. 32 m² **17.** 1.35 m²
18. a) 20.25 cm² b) 9.9 cm²
c) 30.15 cm² **19.** a) 123 cm²
b) 188 cm² **20.** a) 72 cm²
b) 12.5 cm² c) 31.2 cm²
22. a) 6.7 m² b) 125.6 m²
23. a) 14.3 cm² b) 78.2 cm²
24. 199.54 cm² **25.** a) 32 cm²
b) 688 cm² **26.** a) base and
height b) 5 cm² **27.** a) base and
height b) 7 cm² **28.** a) 2 cm²
b) 6 cm² **29.** a) 6.5 cm² b) 3.6 cm²
30. a) 18.4 cm² b) 25.8 m²

3.2 Written Exercises

1. a) A 48 cm² B 54 cm² b) A
720 cm³ B 648 cm³ **2.** a) 0.6 m³
b) 3.1 m³ c) 149.5 cm³
3. 2016 cm³ **4.** 305.9 m³
5. 826.6 cm³ **6.** a) 321.3 cm³
b) 271.5 cm³ **7.** a) 428 m³
b) 14.3 m³ **9.** 4.7 m² **11.** 4
12. 2539.2 cm³ **13.** a) 5.46 m²
b) 22.9 m² **14.** a) 815.6 cm²
b) 12070.3 cm³ **15.** 328.6 m³
16. 69.9 m³ **18.** 4.5 m³
19. a) 121.5 cm² b) 688 cm²
c) 33.1 m² **20** 5.2 L **21.** 10 cm²

. a) 75.4 cm b) 157 cm
c) 94.2 cm **2.** a) 78.5 cm
b) 113.04 cm c) 125.6 cm
d) 141.3 cm **3.** 110.5 cm
. 46.5 cm
. 74.1 cm **6.** 206 cm
7. a) 56.5 cm b) 17 cm
c) 39.3 cm **8.** a) 75.4 cm
b) 36.4 cm c) 76.6 cm
. a) 100 cm, 314 cm b) 360 cm,
130.4 cm c) 3.3 m, 20.7 m
d) 18.1 m, 113.7 m **10.** 18.8 m
1. 105.5 m **12.** 41 611.3 km
3. 22.3 m **14.** 25.4 m
5. 87.9 cm **16.** 238.6 m
7. 144.4 m **18.** a) 94.5 cm
b) 54.6 cm c) 78.8 cm
9. 5.7 m **20.** 45.8 m
1. a) 40 192 km b) 18 840 km
2. 452.4 turns **23.** a) 326.6 m
b) 301.4 m **24.** a) 125.8 m
b) 251.6 m c) 2516 m **25.** 170 m
6. a) 7.5 m b) 86 turns
7. a) 300.8 cm b) About
8 turns **28.** a) 8.2 m b) 2.5 m
c) Large: About 122 turns,
Small: 398 turns **29.** a) 11.9 m
b) 84 turns **30.** 5.4 **31.** 7.5 m

. a) 530.7 cm² b) 5.3 cm²
. a) 452.2 m² b) 4069.4 cm²
c) 301.6 cm² **3.** a) 201 m²
d) 706.5 cm² c) 66.4 cm²
. 388.6 cm² **5.** 538.9 cm²
7. 1.3 cm³
. 124.6 cm² **9.** 21.2 m²
0. 459.7 km² **13.** 3.5 m²
4. 530.7 cm² **15.** 55.4 m²
7. a) 5.3 m² b) 9.4 m²
c) 166.1 cm² **18.** a) 490.6 cm²
b) 1256 cm² **19.** 480.8 cm²
0. 264.9 cm² **21.** a) $3.90
b) 0.8¢/cm **22.** 0.6¢/cm
3. a) 0.73¢/cm² b) 0.62¢/cm²
c) 0.54¢/cm² d) (c)
4. 765.4 cm² **25.** a) 981.2 cm²
b) 1256 cm² c) (b) **26.** B
7. a) Square b) 0.42 cm²
8. a) 201 cm² b) 7.2 m²
c) 18.2 m² d) 36.2 cm²

1. a) 1092 cm³ b) 1400 cm³
2. a) 113.0 m³ b) 173.1 m³
c) 2703.0 cm³ **3.** a) 3 cm,
226.1 cm³ b) 9 cm, 5849.8 cm³
c) 13.8 cm, 627.9 cm³ d) 5 m,
94.2 m² **4.** 13272.2 cm³
5. 7234.6 cm³ **6.** 361 571 cm³
7. a) 265 m³ b) 31797.4 kg
8. a) 793.8 mL b) 327.8 mL
9. 2734.7 cm³ **10.** A
12. b) A 453.7 cm³, B 507.8 cm³,
C 393.9 cm³ **13.** a) 3014.4 cm³
b) 1100.3 L **15.** a) 432.6 cm²
b) 397.8 cm² c) 2002.6 cm²
d) 11.9 m² **16.** 196.9 cm²
17. 616.9 cm² **18.** 314 cm²
19. a) 2.826 m³ b) 7 L
21. 48.1 km³ **22.** 30711.1 km³
23. 55.2 km² **24.** Storm A
25. 7 km² **26.** 0.3 km²

1. a) 314 cm² b) 221.6 cm²
c) 366.2 cm² **2.** a) 803.8 cm²
b) 10563.0 cm² c) 289.4 cm²
3. a) 113.0 cm² b) 301.4 cm²
4. a) 266.9 cm² b) 678.2 cm²
c) 57.3 cm² **5.** a) 14.3 cm²
b) 17.6 cm² c) 74.8 cm²
6. a) 3060 cm² b) 62.7 m²
c) 10.8 m² d) 98.0 m²
7. 597.8 cm²
9. a) 514 457 600 km²
10. a) 459 727 400 km²
11. 181.4 cm² **12.** 23
13. 49.9 m² **14.** 813.9 cm²
15. B **16.** a) 2400 cm²
b) 1256 cm² c) Cube, by
1144 cm²

1. a) $\frac{4}{3}$ TTr³ b) 7234.6 cm³
2. a) 1766.3 cm³ b) 57.9 cm³
3. a) 2143.6 cm³ b) 65416.7 cm³
c) 1316.4 cm³ **4.** a) 3052.1 cm³
b) 407.5 m³ c) 1316.4 mm³
5. a) $\frac{1}{3}$ π r² h b) 21.0 cm³
6. a) $\frac{1}{3}$ 1wh b) 4.0 m³
7. a) 600 cm³
b) 320 cm³ c) 1071.8 cm³
d) 234.2 cm³ **8.** 18.3 m³
9. 71.4 m³ **10.** 195.3 m³
11. 5 181 000 mm³

12. 1402.4 g **13.** 4.8 m³
14. 2142.6 m³ **15.** 277.8 cm³
16. 29.1 m³ **17.** a) 70 cm
b) 390.4 cm² **18.** a) 68.5 cm
b) 373.1 cm² **19.** a) 76 cm
b) 141.3 cm c) 1129.9 cm²
20. a) 21.4 cm b) 23.2 cm
c) Hardball, by 6.7 cm²
21. 39 388.2 cm
22. a) 73.9 cm² b) 130.6 cm²
23. a) 53.4 cm b) 226.9 cm²

CHAPTER 4

1. a) 8 b) 1 c) 2 d) 14 e) 9
f) 3 **2.** a) 40, 10, 2, 5 b) 1, 2, 4,
5, 8, 10, 20, 40 c) 40 **3.** a) 1, 3,
9 b) 1, 2, 4, 8, 16 c) 1, 2, 3, 4, 6,
8, 12, 24 d) 1, 7, 49 e) 1, 3, 5, 9,
15, 45 f) 1, 2, 4, 7, 8, 14, 28, 56
4. a) 1, 2, 3 b) 1, 2, 4 c) 1, 3, 5
d) 2, 5 **5.** 10, 5, 9 **6.** 10, 2, 25,
50 **7.** a) 1 × 72, 2 × 36, 3 × 24,
4 × 18, 6 × 12, 8 × 9 b) 1, 2, 3,
4, 6, 8, 9, 12, 18, 24, 36, 72
8. (a), (d), (e) **9.** (a), (d)
10. a) 1, 2, 3, 4, 6, 12; 1, 2, 3, 6, 9,
18 b) 1, 2, 3, 6 **11.** a) 1, 2, 3, 4,
6, 8, 12, 24; 1, 2, 3, 5, 6, 10, 15,
30 b) 1, 2, 3, 6 **12.** a) 2 b) 4
c) 3 d) 3 e) 2 f) 4 g) 8 h) 5
13. a) 5 b) 6 c) 24 d) 7 e) 3
f) 2 **14.** a) 3, 6, 9, 12, 15, 18, 21,
24 b) 4, 8, 12, 16, 20, 24 c) 12,
24 d) 12 **15.** a) 6, 12, 18, 24,
30, 36, 42, 48, 54 b) 8, 16, 24,
32, 40, 48, 56, 64 c) 24, 48, . . .
d) 24 **16.** a) 30 b) 72 c) 48
d) 180 **17.** (b), (e), (f)
18. b) 2 × 2 × 3
c) 2 × 2 × 2 × 2
d) 2 × 2 × 2 × 3 e) 2 × 5 × 5
f) 29 g) 2 × 2 × 2 × 2 × 3
h) 29 **19.** a) 2 × 2 × 3
b) 2 × 3 × 3 c) 6
20. a) 2 × 2 × 2 × 3
b) 2 × 2 × 3 × 3 c) 12
21. a) 4 b) 3 c) 4 d) 10
22. a) 72 b) 30 c) 72 d) 42
e) 72 f) 48 g) 150 h) 96
23. a) 36 b) 48 c) 90
24. a) A 5 times, B 3 times
b) A 3 times, B 2 times
c) A 21 times, B 20 times

d) A 14 times, B 5 times
e) A 3 times, B 5 times **25.** S-B,
S-C, S-D, S-E, P-A, P-B, P-D,
P-E **26.** A 20 times, P 7 times
27. S 5 times, C 13 times
28. a) 40 b) 20 c) 42.7 m
29. a) 26 b) 12 c) 25.62 m

1.

	(a)	(b)	(c)	(d)	(e)
shaded	$\frac{6}{15}$	$\frac{10}{25}$	$\frac{8}{18}$	$\frac{14}{22}$	$\frac{20}{38}$
not shaded	$\frac{9}{15}$	$\frac{15}{25}$	$\frac{10}{18}$	$\frac{8}{22}$	$\frac{18}{38}$

2. a) $\frac{4}{8}$ b) $\frac{5}{8}$ c) $\frac{8}{16}$ d) $\frac{11}{18}$ e) $\frac{10}{21}$
4. a) $\frac{7}{8}$ b) $\frac{9}{15}$ c) $\frac{3}{8}$ **5.** a) $\frac{6}{10}$ b) $\frac{4}{10}$
c) $\frac{8}{10}$ **6.** a) $\frac{11}{21}$ b) $\frac{32}{40}$ c) $\frac{16}{25}$
7. a) $\frac{3}{8}$, $\frac{4}{6}$, $\frac{6}{9}$ b) $\frac{5}{8}$, $\frac{2}{6}$, $\frac{3}{9}$ **8.** a) $\frac{1}{4}$
b) $\frac{1}{6}$ **9.** a) $\frac{1}{60}$ b) $\frac{1}{60}$ c) $\frac{1}{1440}$
d) $\frac{1}{7}$ e) $\frac{1}{12}$ **10.** a) $\frac{25}{30}$ b) $\frac{20}{60}$ c) $\frac{45}{90}$
d) $\frac{30}{120}$ **11.** a) $\frac{33}{50}$ b) $\frac{17}{50}$ **12.** a) $\frac{15}{26}$
b) $\frac{3}{26}$ c) $\frac{8}{26}$ **13.** a) $\frac{250}{300}$ b) $\frac{50}{300}$
14. 12 **15.** 5.2 m **16.** a) $\frac{20}{125}$ b) $\frac{10}{16}$
c) $\frac{40}{48}$ **17.** a) 365 b) $\frac{24}{32}$ c) half-full

1. a) $\frac{3}{4}$ b) $\frac{1}{2}$ c) $\frac{1}{2}$ d) $\frac{3}{4}$ e) $\frac{1}{2}$ f) $\frac{1}{2}$
2. a) 2 b) 6 c) 1 d) 2 **3.** a) $\frac{3}{4}$
b) $\frac{3}{4}$ c) $\frac{3}{4}$ d) $\frac{3}{4}$ e) $\frac{3}{4}$ f) All
the same **4.** a) $\frac{3}{4}$ b) $\frac{3}{4}$ c) $\frac{3}{4}$ d) $\frac{3}{4}$
e) $\frac{3}{4}$ f) $\frac{3}{4}$ g) All the same **5.** a) $\frac{4}{5}$
b) $\frac{4}{5}$ c) $\frac{3}{4}$ d) $\frac{4}{5}$ e) $\frac{9}{10}$ f) $\frac{3}{8}$ g) $\frac{1}{2}$
h) $\frac{2}{3}$ **6.** a) $\frac{6}{8}$, $\frac{9}{12}$ b) $\frac{4}{6}$, $\frac{6}{9}$
c) $\frac{6}{10}$, $\frac{9}{15}$ d) $\frac{14}{20}$, $\frac{21}{30}$ e) $\frac{8}{10}$,
$\frac{12}{15}$ f) $\frac{14}{16}$, $\frac{21}{24}$ **7.** a) 2 b) 12 c) 4
d) 60 e) 100 f) 8 **8.** a) $\frac{1}{100}$
b) $\frac{1}{10}$ c) $\frac{1}{2}$ d) $\frac{1}{4}$ e) $\frac{3}{4}$ f) $\frac{3}{8}$ **9.** a) $\frac{1}{5}$
b) $\frac{1}{2}$ c) $\frac{4}{5}$ **10.** (a), (c) **11.** a) $\frac{50}{100}$
b) $\frac{25}{100}$ c) $\frac{10}{100}$ d) $\frac{20}{100}$ e) $\frac{50}{100}$ f) $\frac{50}{100}$
12. a) > b) = c) > d) <
e) > f) = **13.** a) $\frac{1}{6}$ b) $\frac{2}{5}$ c) $\frac{2}{3}$
15. $\frac{4}{25}$, $\frac{1}{5}$, $\frac{2}{5}$, $\frac{6}{25}$ **16.** a) $\frac{9}{20}$ b) $\frac{29}{42}$
c) $\frac{17}{20}$ d) $\frac{11}{36}$ **17.** a) $\frac{14}{65}$ b) $\frac{23}{65}$ c) $\frac{18}{65}$
18. a) $\frac{13}{25}$ b) $\frac{9}{25}$ c) $\frac{21}{50}$ d) $\frac{1}{5}$

19. $\frac{1}{5}$ 20. $\frac{1}{4}$ 21. a) $\frac{1}{4}$ b) $\frac{3}{4}$ c) $\frac{3}{5}$
d) $\frac{2}{3}$

4.4 Written Exercises, page 118
1. a) 2 b) 2 c) 6 d) 7 e) 8 f) 7
2. a) 2 b) 12 c) 9 d) 8 3. a) 6
b) 8 c) 10 d) 15 e) 33 f) 70
4. a) $\frac{6}{10}$ b) $\frac{1}{2}$ c) $\frac{4}{5}$ d) $\frac{5}{6}$ e) $\frac{3}{8}$
f) $\frac{3}{10}$ g) $1\frac{1}{2}$ h) $1\frac{3}{4}$ 5. a) A b) B
6. a) $1\frac{1}{2}$ b) $1\frac{2}{3}$ c) $2\frac{1}{3}$ d) $2\frac{1}{4}$
7. a) < b) > c) = d) < e) >
f) > 8. a) $\frac{7}{8}$ b) $\frac{4}{5}$ c) $\frac{3}{8}$ 9. a) T
b) F c) T 10. a) $3\frac{1}{2}$ b) $2\frac{1}{4}$ c) $8\frac{7}{8}$
11. a) A 10, B 20 b) A 2, B $\frac{3}{2}$
12. a) $\frac{1}{4}, \frac{2}{3}, \frac{3}{4}$ b) $\frac{4}{7}, \frac{3}{5}, \frac{4}{5}$ c) $\frac{1}{3}, \frac{3}{8}, \frac{1}{2}$
13. Marc 14. Phillip 15. Both
16. John 17. Tim 18. a) $\frac{8}{14}$
b) Zupata

4.5 Written Exercises, page 122
1. a) 0.1 b) 0.3 c) 0.7 d) 0.95
e) 0.03 f) 0.912 g) 0.31
h) 0.4 2. a) 0.25 b) 1.25
c) 1.4 d) 2.25 e) 2.5 f) 1.8
g) 4.15 h) 3.125 3. a) $3\frac{1}{2}$
b) $1\frac{3}{4}$ c) $2\frac{3}{4}$ d) $6\frac{1}{4}$ e) $6\frac{1}{2}$ f) $2\frac{7}{10}$
g) 1 h) $4\frac{1}{10}$ i) 4 4. a) 3.5
b) 1.75 c) 2.75 d) 6.25
e) 6.5 f) 2.7 g) 1.0 h) 4.1
i) 4.0 5. a) $\frac{1}{10}$ b) $\frac{1}{100}$ c) $\frac{1}{1000}$
d) $\frac{3}{10}$ e) $\frac{33}{100}$ f) $\frac{333}{1000}$ g) $\frac{33}{1000}$
h) $\frac{3}{1000}$ i) $\frac{3}{100}$ 6. a) $\frac{3}{5}$ b) $\frac{4}{5}$
c) $\frac{1}{2}$ d) $\frac{1}{4}$ e) $\frac{3}{4}$ f) $\frac{1}{8}$ g) $\frac{3}{20}$
h) $\frac{7}{20}$ i) $\frac{1}{5}$ 7. a) $6\frac{4}{5}$ b) $3\frac{2}{5}$
c) $2\frac{1}{4}$ d) $3\frac{9}{20}$ e) $3\frac{1}{8}$ f) $6\frac{7}{8}$
8. a) $0.\overline{27}$ b) $0.\overline{15}$ c) $0.1\overline{6}$
d) $0.7\overline{3}$ e) $0.\overline{384}\ \overline{615}$ 9. a) $0.\overline{3}$
b) $0.\overline{6}$ c) $0.\overline{230\ 769}$ d) $0.\overline{1}$
e) $0.4\overline{6}$ f) $0.41\overline{6}$ g) 0.4583
h) $0.\overline{142\ 857}$ 10. a) 0.25,
0.625, $\frac{5}{8}$ b) 0.6, 0.3, $\frac{3}{5}$
c) $0.\overline{6}$, 0.4, $\frac{2}{3}$ d) $0.\overline{45}$, $0.\overline{3}$, $\frac{5}{11}$
e) $0.\overline{6}$, 0.8, $\frac{4}{5}$ f) $0.8\overline{3}$, 0.875, $\frac{7}{8}$
g) 2.75, $2.\overline{6}$, $2\frac{3}{4}$ h) 3.25, $3.\overline{3}$, $3\frac{1}{3}$
i) 5.2, $5.\overline{2}$, $5\frac{2}{9}$

11. (a), (c), (e), (g),
12. a) $0.\overline{857\ 142}$, 0.9, 0.875, $\frac{9}{10}$
b) 0.375, 0.2, $0.\overline{3}$, $\frac{3}{8}$ c) 0.6, 0.7,
$0.\overline{6}$, $\frac{7}{10}$ d) $1.\overline{6}$, 1.25, 1.2, $1\frac{2}{3}$
e) 2.375, 2.3, 2.5, $2\frac{1}{2}$ f) 5.75, $5.\overline{6}$,
5.25, $5\frac{3}{4}$ 13. 52 out of 78
14. Jean 15. Last year
16. Michael 17. a) $0.\overline{714\ 285}$
b) 0.5 c) $0.\overline{538\ 461}$ d) $0.\overline{761\ 904}$
e) 0.83 f) $0.\overline{54}$ 18. a) Alfonso
b) Jackson 19. Harry 20. Marc
21. a) 0.25 b) 0.75 22. a) 0.25
c) A 0.375, B 0.625, C 0.875
23. a) A 0.037, B 0.074, C $0.\overline{1}$
c) D $0.\overline{148}$, E $0.\overline{185}$, F $0.\overline{2}$
24. a) $0.\overline{3}$ b) $0.\overline{6}$ 25. a) A $0.\overline{1}$,
B $0.\overline{2}$, C $0.\overline{3}$ c) D $0.\overline{4}$, E $0.\overline{5}$,
F $0.\overline{6}$ 26. a) A $0.\overline{01}$, B $0.\overline{04}$,
C $0.\overline{12}$ c) D $0.\overline{15}$, E $0.\overline{23}$,
F $0.\overline{98}$ 27. a) A $0.\overline{0001}$, B $0.\overline{031}$,
C $0.\overline{126}$ b) D $0.\overline{369}$, E $0.\overline{421}$,
F $0.\overline{998}$ 28. Harris 29. Davise
30. a) Moxey b) Moxey
31. Diane 32. a) Gillies
b) Gillies 33. Player
34. a) Wilson b) Wilson
35. a) Young b) Young, Jarvis,
Weir, Larose, Wilson, Pirus
Dupont, Irvine

4.6 Written Exercises, page 129
1. a) $\frac{3}{4}$ b) $\frac{5}{8}$ c) $\frac{5}{6}$ 2. a) $\frac{1}{5}$
b) 1 c) $\frac{4}{5}$ d) $1\frac{1}{2}$ e) $\frac{3}{5}$ f) $\frac{1}{2}$
3. a) $\frac{3}{4}$ b) $\frac{1}{2}$ c) $\frac{5}{8}$ 4. a) $1\frac{1}{4}$
b) $1\frac{1}{6}$ c) $\frac{7}{10}$ d) $\frac{3}{4}$ e) $\frac{14}{25}$
f) $\frac{13}{100}$ 5. a) $1\frac{1}{4}$ min b) $\frac{3}{4}$ min
c) $1\frac{1}{2}$ min 6. a) $6, \frac{5}{6}$ b) 12,
$\frac{11}{12}$ c) 15, $\frac{14}{15}$ 7. a) $\frac{17}{24}$ b) $\frac{11}{12}$
c) $\frac{23}{30}$ 8. a) $1\frac{1}{12}$ b) $\frac{5}{6}$ c) $1\frac{5}{12}$
9. a) $5\frac{1}{2}$ b) $5\frac{4}{5}$ c) 6 d) $8\frac{1}{4}$
e) $12\frac{1}{5}$ f) 5 10. a) $4\frac{3}{4}$ b) $4\frac{1}{2}$
c) $4\frac{5}{8}$ 11. a) $8\frac{2}{5}$ b) $10\frac{4}{5}$
c) $8\frac{1}{8}$ 12. $24\frac{1}{4}$ min 13. a) $8\frac{3}{4}$ min
b) 5 min c) $3\frac{1}{4}$ min 14. $\frac{7}{8}$
15. $9\frac{1}{4}$ 16. $\frac{31}{100}$ 17. $\frac{7}{12}$ 18. $\frac{3}{4}$
19. $28\frac{1}{2}$ min 20. $7\frac{7}{12}$ h
21. $17\frac{1}{12}$ h

22. a) $4\frac{1}{6}$ h, $6\frac{1}{4}$ h b) $10\frac{5}{12}$ h

4.7 Written Exercises, page 132
1. a) $\frac{1}{4}$ b) $\frac{1}{2}$ 2. a) $\frac{2}{5}$ b) $\frac{1}{3}$
c) $\frac{3}{8}$ 3. a) $\frac{3}{5}$ b) $\frac{1}{2}$ c) $\frac{1}{2}$ d) $\frac{1}{4}$
e) $\frac{7}{10}$ f) $\frac{1}{2}$ 4. a) $\frac{1}{4}$ min.
b) $\frac{1}{4}$ min c) $\frac{1}{6}$ min 5. a) $\frac{1}{6}$
b) $\frac{3}{4}$ c) $\frac{1}{10}$ 6. a) $\frac{1}{6}$ b) $\frac{5}{12}$
c) $\frac{4}{15}$ d) $\frac{1}{24}$ e) $\frac{7}{12}$ f) $\frac{17}{30}$
7. a) $\frac{7}{8}$ b) $\frac{1}{2}$ c) $\frac{1}{4}$ d) $\frac{3}{4}$
8. a) 1 b) $1\frac{2}{5}$ c) $2\frac{1}{3}$ d) $1\frac{1}{4}$
e) $1\frac{1}{6}$ f) $1\frac{5}{8}$ 9. a) 12 b) $1\frac{1}{12}$
10. a) $2\frac{1}{6}$ b) $3\frac{7}{12}$ c) $6\frac{1}{15}$
d) $1\frac{9}{10}$ e) $3\frac{13}{20}$ f) $1\frac{7}{12}$ 11. a) 8
b) $1\frac{1}{8}$ 12. a) $\frac{5}{8}$ b) $\frac{1}{2}$ c) $\frac{5}{8}$
d) $\frac{11}{12}$ 13. a) $4\frac{1}{8}$ b) $2\frac{3}{8}$ c) $4\frac{1}{8}$
d) $4\frac{2}{3}$ 14. $\frac{1}{12}$ 15. $\frac{1}{4}$ 16. $\frac{7}{24}$
17. $10\frac{1}{4}$ min 18. $3\frac{3}{4}$ min 19. $\frac{1}{12}$
20. $\frac{7}{24}$ 21. $\frac{5}{12}$ 22. a) $\frac{1}{8}$ b) $\frac{1}{16}$
c) $\frac{1}{2}$ d) $\frac{1}{8}$ e) $\frac{1}{8}$ f) $\frac{1}{16}$ 23. a) $\frac{1}{4}$
b) $\frac{1}{8}$ c) $\frac{1}{2}$ d) $\frac{1}{4}$ 24. a) $\frac{1}{4}, \frac{1}{4}, \frac{1}{2}, \frac{1}{2}$,
b) $\frac{1}{4}, \frac{1}{4}, \frac{1}{2}$ c) $\frac{1}{4}, \frac{1}{8}, \frac{1}{4}$ d) $\frac{1}{4}, \frac{1}{8}, \frac{1}{4}$

4.8 Written Exercises, page 137
1. a) 12 b) 9 c) 18 d) 12
e) 9 f) $7\frac{1}{2}$ 2. a) 32¢ b) 36 m
c) 80 kg d) 66 km e) 27
f) 1500 L 3. a) $2\frac{1}{4}$ b) $\frac{5}{8}$ c) $3\frac{3}{5}$
d) 6 e) 4 f) 6 g) 6 h) 6
i) 20 4. a) $\frac{3}{8}$ b) $\frac{1}{6}$ c) $\frac{3}{10}$
5. a) $\frac{3}{30}$ b) $\frac{8}{15}$ c) $\frac{3}{32}$ d) $\frac{4}{15}$
e) $\frac{3}{40}$ f) $\frac{7}{10}$ 7. a) 1 b) 1
c) 1 d) 1 e) 1 f) 1 All
equal to 1 8. a) $\frac{1}{6}$ b) $\frac{1}{8}$ c) $2\frac{1}{2}$
d) $\frac{3}{5}$ e) $\frac{7}{10}$ f) $\frac{1}{4}$ 9. a) 6.2
b) 5.3 c) 2.4 d) 7.8 e) 8.4
f) 11.2 g) 18.3 h) 32.2
i) 3.75 10. b) $\frac{7}{32}$ c) $\frac{4}{15}$ d) $\frac{2}{3}$
e) $\frac{1}{3}$ f) $\frac{1}{20}$ g) $\frac{1}{8}$ 11. a) $2\frac{2}{3}$
b) $6\frac{2}{3}$ c) $\frac{5}{12}$ d) 6 e) 30 f) $\frac{15}{132}$
g) 2 h) 22 i) $\frac{11}{50}$ 12. a) $1\frac{5}{9}$
b) $\frac{25}{32}$ c) 1 d) $2\frac{1}{6}$ e) $2\frac{4}{5}$ f) $4\frac{1}{6}$

13. a) 1 b) 1 c) 1 d) 1
e) 1 f) 1 All equal to 1
14. a) $3\frac{3}{5}$ b) $11\frac{23}{32}$ c) $4\frac{1}{8}$
d) $10\frac{15}{16}$ e) $9\frac{9}{20}$ f) $8\frac{1}{20}$
15. $17\frac{1}{2}$ min 16. 11 h 17. 133
18. $81\frac{1}{4}$ cm 19. $\frac{1}{4}$ h 20. 24 cm
21. 3702 22. $150 23. $12/h
24. 13.6 s 25. a) $72
b) $19.20 c) $19.75 d) $2.30
26. a) $5.17 b) $10.33
27. Radio $4.45, $4.45; Calcula
$26.33, $13.17; L.P. $1.91, $5.
Chess $4.88, $14.62; Tic Tac T
$5.00, $10.00 28. $37.31
29. a) $20.80 b) $15.75
c) $31.55 d) $30.33 30. $70.

4.9 Written Exercises, page 1
1. a) $\frac{2}{3}$ b) $\frac{1}{2}$ 2. a) $\frac{3}{4}$ b) $\frac{15}{32}$
3. a) 3 b) 3 c) 3 d) $1\frac{2}{3}$
4. a) $\frac{3}{4}$ b) $1\frac{1}{4}$ c) $\frac{16}{27}$ d) $\frac{1}{2}$
e) $1\frac{1}{3}$ f) $\frac{32}{49}$ 5. a) $\frac{1}{6}$ b) $\frac{1}{12}$
c) $\frac{1}{9}$ d) $\frac{3}{20}$ e) 5 f) 12
6. a) 20 b) 12 c) 18 d) 32
e) 64 f) 10 g) 9 h) 30
i) 128 7. a) $\frac{2}{3}$ b) $\frac{3}{10}$ c) $\frac{2}{9}$
d) $\frac{4}{19}$ 8. a) $\frac{11}{36}$ b) 2 c) $8\frac{1}{4}$
d) 56 e) 4 f) 2 9. a) 128
b) $1\frac{4}{5}$ c) $12\frac{4}{5}$ d) 2 e) $\frac{5}{9}$ f) 2
g) $1\frac{1}{2}$ h) $\frac{5}{6}$ i) $\frac{5}{2}$ 10. 20 11. 24
12. 12 13. 8 14. 12 15. 367
min 16. a) 48 b) 72 c) 27
17. a) 240 b) 108 c) $91\frac{2}{3}$ min
18. a) 5 b) 18 c) Lori, 15 mor
19. a) 1 b) $1\frac{1}{2}$ c) $\frac{1}{2}$ d) $\frac{3}{4}$
e) $1\frac{1}{2}$ f) $\frac{5}{8}$ 20. a) 2 b) 2
21. a) $1\frac{1}{2}$ b) $1\frac{7}{8}$ 22. a) $\frac{1}{4}$ b) $\frac{1}{8}$
23. a) 8 b) 16 c) 48 d) 80
24. a) 6 b) 3 25. a) 16 b) 64

4.10 Written Exercises, page
1. $1\frac{13}{36}$ 2. $\frac{9}{10}$ 3. $\frac{67}{120}$ 4. $\frac{1}{64}$
5. $1\frac{13}{24}$ 6. $1\frac{2}{9}$ 7. $\frac{1}{15}$ 8. $4\frac{977}{1800}$
9. $3\frac{1}{2}$ 10. $2\frac{1}{2}$ 11. $3\frac{7}{24}$
12. $\frac{79}{144}$ 13. $5\frac{1}{3}$

CHAPTER 5

5.1 Written Exercises, page 150

1. a) + 750 m b) − $7 c) − 4 points d) + 5 steps e) + 15 m f) − 8 steps g) + 10 steps h) + 2 m i) + 12 kg j) − 7 m² k) − 12 mL l) + $10 m) − 9 points n) − 3 o) − 3 m p) + 5 floors **2.** a) 7 paces right b) 7 paces left c) 9 paces left d) 12 paces right e) no movement f) 15 paces left g) 15 paces right h) 24 paces right
3. a) increase 5 m b) decrease 4 m c) increase 9 m d) decrease 10 m e) decrease 9 m f) no change g) increase 13 m h) decrease 13 m
4. a) loss of 3 b) gain of 5 c) loss of 7 d) gain of 10 e) loss of 12 f) no change g) gain of 18 h) loss of 18 **5.** a) + 4 b) + 2 c) − 3 d) 0 e) + 4 f) + 5 **6.** a) − 10859 m b) − 16 m c) + 4278 m d) − 4188 m e) − 12 m
7. a) + 2, + 3 b) + 3, + 4 c) − 3, − 2 d) 0, + 1 **9.** a) + 2, + 3, + 4, + 5 b) 0, + 1, + 2, + 3 c) − 2, − 1, 0, + 1 d) − 1, − 2, − 3, − 4 **11.** a) F b) T c) F d) T e) F f) F **12.** a) < b) < c) > d) > e) < f) >
13. a) − 3, + 3, + 6 b) − 9, − 3, + 4 c) − 9, − 3, + 8 d) − 6, 0, + 6
14. a) − 7 < 1 < 8 b) − 5 < 0 < 10 c) − 4 < 0 < 11 d) − 14 < − 9 < − 6 e) − 7 < − 4 < 6 f) − 1 < 0 < 5 **15.** a) − 6°C b) + 5°C c) + 14°C d) − 18°C e) + 37°C f) − 42°C **16.** a) 8°C above b) 4°C below c) 3°C below d) 28°C above e) 14°C below f) 50°C above
17. a) Winnipeg b) Bonnyville

5.2 Written Exercises, page 155

1. a) + 7 b) − 2 c) + 5 d) − 8 **2.** a) + 6 b) + 3 c) − 6 d) − 2 **3.** a) + 9 b) + 1 c) − 9 d) + 6 f) − 1 g) 0 h) − 8 **4.** a) + 9 b) − 9 c) − 8 d) + 4 e) + 1 f) − 1

5. a) − 2 m b) + 14 m c) − 3 m d) + 31 m e) 0
6. a) 1 b) − 1 c) − 5 d) 1 e) − 1 f) − 9 g) − 3 h) 3
7. a) 5 b) 9 c) − 3 d) − 1 e) 1 f) − 7 g) 11 h) − 5
8. a) 8 b) − 4 c) 6 d) − 14 e) 15 f) − 16 g) 8 h) − 3 i) − 5 k) 0 l) − 20 m) − 50 **9.** a) 1 b) − 1 c) − 5 d) 1 e) − 1 f) − 17 g) 4 h) − 10 i) − 4 **10.** a) 2 b) − 1 c) − 3 d) 0 e) − 8 f) − 15 g) 3 h) − 2 i) − 5 **11.** a) 6 b) − 9 c) 1 d) − 10 e) 4 f) 14
12. a) 264 + (− 69) + (− 92) + 21
13. b) $384.00
14. − 4 **15.** a) − 3 b) − 2 c) 0 **16.** Vince, Como
17. a) + 1 b) − 2 c) − 4
18. − 1, 0, 1 **19.** Bourbonnais
20. a) 2 b) 1 c) − 1
21. Gardner − 2, Boldirev − 3, Schmautz 5, Middleton − 2
22. Gainey − 4, Gore 10, Clarke 19, MacDonald − 8, Howe − 7, Jarvis − 12, Luce 0, Moore − 1

5.3 Written Exercises, page 160

1. a) +8, +8 b) −3, −3 c) −6, −6 d) −7, −7
2. a) +3, +3 b) −7, −7 c) −1, −1 d) 0, 0 e) 0, 0
3. a) − 2 b) 1 c) − 2 d) − 2 e) 16 f) 9 g) 2 h) − 4
4. a) 12 b) − 1 c) 4 d) 16 e) − 17 f) − 4 g) 7 h) 5 i) 9 j) 14 k) 0 l) − 16 **5.** A: 3, 4, 5, 6, 7, 8, 9 B: 2, 3, 4, 5, 6, 7, 8
6. a) 5, 6 b) − 2, − 1 c) − 5, − 6 d) 7, 6 **7.** a) 3 b) − 3 c) − 9 d) − 4 e) − 2 f) − 12 g) − 4 h) 0 i) 0 **8.** a) 16 b) 3 c) 6 d) 21 e) 11 f) − 7 g) − 6 h) − 25 i) − 31 j) 15 k) 1 l) 2 **9.** a) 15 b) 2 c) 64 d) − 10 e) 10 f) − 23 g) − 4 h) − 9 i) − 29 j) 25 k) − 7 l) − 44
10. a) 7 b) − 11 c) 3 d) − 19 e) 1 f) − 16 g) 5 h) − 5 i) 15 j) − 15 **11.** a) 16 b) 19 c) − 18 d) − 9 e) 16 f) − 19 g) − 15 h) 4 i) − 11 **12.** a) − 3 b) 13 c) − 5 d) 21 e) − 21 f) 3 g) 8 h) 40 i) 39 j) 33 **13.** a) 40 b) 10 c) 12 d) 50 e) 36

f) 113 g) 67 h) 16 i) 64 j) 38 k) 599 l) 143 **14.** b) 5 c) 1 d) 1 e) 0 f) 37 g) − 10 h) 8 **15.** a) A b) A c) B **16.** a) − 4 b) − 8 **17.** a) 5 b) − 9 c) − 11 d) − 3 e) − 9 f) 16 g) 70 h) 19 i) − 3 j) 7 **18.** a) + 13°C b) + 9°C c) + 14°C d) − 3°C e) + 5°C f) + 17°C g) + 4°C h) + 12°C **19.** a) A b) A c) B d) A e) B f) A
20. a) Winnipeg b) Vancouver
21. Charlottetown and Halifax; Calgary and Prince Albert

5.4 Written Exercises, page 164

1. a) 3 b) − 5 c) − 9 d) − 10 e) 12 f) 4 **2.** a) − 1 b) − 7 c) 7 d) − 4 e) 4 **3.** a) − 3 b) − 3 c) − 5 d) 1 e) − 2 f) 3 g) − 5 h) − 5 i) − 1 j) 1
4. a) 11 b) 5 **5.** a) 7 b) 3 c) 0 d) − 3 **6.** a − b − c
7. p − q − r **8.** a) 4 b) 4 c) Equal **9.** a) − 6 b) − 6 c) Equal **10.** a) − 5 b) 5 c) − 7 d) − 3 **11.** A: 3, B: − 9, C: − 5
12. A **13.** a) − 3 b) 8 c) 5 d) 4 e) − 5

5.5 Written Exercises, page 166

1. − 9 **2.** 18 **3.** 8 **4.** − 13
5. 10 **6.** 2 **7.** 4°C **8.** − 12°C
9. − 24°C **10.** − 222 m
11. 50°C **12.** 103°C **13.** a) 0°C b) − 6°C c) December 22nd d) − 16°C **14.** $12 **15.** − 39°C
16. 1350 m **17.** 8169 m
18. 1116 m **19.** 75 m
20. 590 m **21.** 908 m
22. 9636 m **23.** 131 m
24. 10 745 m

5.6 Written Exercises, page 170

1. a) 6, 3, 0, − 3, − 6 b) 10, 5, 0, − 5, − 10 c) − 6, − 3, 0, 3, 6 d) − 4, − 2, 0, 2, 4 **2.** a) − 8 b) − 4 c) 0 d) − 6 e) − 9 f) − 12 g) − 3 h) − 6 i) − 9 j) − 15 k) − 10 l) − 5
3. a) − 16 b) − 3 c) 15 d) 0 e) − 4 f) 12 g) − 12 h) 6 i) 0
4. a) − 6 b) 0 c) − 12 d) 6 e) − 6 f) 0 g) 0 h) − 18 i) − 20 **5.** a) − 6 b) − 12

c) − 25 d) − 2 e) − 9 f) − 8 g) 3 h) 6 i) 16 j) 36 k) − 12 l) 18 **6.** a) positive b) positive c) negative d) negative e) positive f) positive g) negative h) negative
7. a) − 1 b) − 6 c) − 3 d) 0 e) 2 f) 30 g) − 40 h) − 20 i) − 18 **8.** a) − 1 b) 0 c) − 10 d) 30 e) − 8 f) − 18 g) − 12 h) 0 i) 6 j) (d) **9.** a) − 2 b) − 6 c) 0 d) 3 e) 0 f) 65 g) − 20 h) 12 i) − 15 j) (g)
10. a) 15 b) 8 c) − 20 d) − 20 e) 6 f) 6 g) − 35 h) − 48 i) 27
11. b) 24 c) 70 d) − 100 e) 12 f) 72 g) 0 h) 90 i) 360
12. a) 5 × (− 2) b) 15°C
13. a) 14 × (− 1) b) 90°C
14. a) 5 × (− 15) b) 180°C
15. a) 5 b) − 5 c) 4 d) − 9 e) − 6 f) − 12

5.7 Written Exercises, page 172

1. a) − 4 b) − 10 c) 21 d) 56 e) − 60 f) − 36 **2.** a) − 4 b) 16 c) − 14 **3.** a) − 8 b) − 10 c) 0 d) − 15 e) − 3 f) 2 **4.** a) 1 b) − 5 c) − 1 d) − 1 e) − 13 f) − 18 **5.** a) − 12 b) 0
6. a) − 6 b) − 6 c) Equal
7. a) − 20 b) − 20 c) Equal
8. a) + 288 b) + 242 c) − 432 d) + 16 e) + 144 f) + 72
9. a) 0 b) − 96 c) + 56 d) KIT
10. a) 0 b) + 264 c) − 720 d) − 12 **11.** a) − 3528 b) − 192 c) + 4320 d) − 72 e) − 168 f) − 9680

5.8 Written Exercises, page 175

1. a) − 7, − 4 b) − 4, + 3 c) + 4, − 4 d) − 6, − 4
2. a) − 5, 5 b) − 9, − 4 c) 7, − 7 d) − 6, − 8 **3.** a) − 5 b) − 5 c) 4 d) − 7 e) − 10 f) 10 g) − 5 h) 6 i) − 8 j) 9 k) 10 l) − 10 **4.** a) − 5 b) − 4 c) − 5 d) 5 e) − 2 f) 8 g) − 2 h) 2 i) − 6 j) 9 k) − 4 l) − 4
5. a) − 3 b) − 4 c) 3 d) − 2 e) − 3 f) 8 g) − 8 h) 4 i) − 3 j) − 6 k) 6 l) − 3 **6.** a) − 8 b) 6 c) − 8 d) − 8 e) − 9 f) 8 g) − 8 h) − 8 i) 8 j) − 9 k) 9 l) − 9

7. a) positive b) positive
c) negative d) negative
e) positive f) positive
g) negative h) negative
8. a) −3 b) −3 c) −5 d) −8
e) −5 f) −5 g) 5 h) −6
9. a) −7 b) −5 c) −8 d) 7
e) 4 f) −1 g) −10 h) 9 i) −6
j) −14 **10.** a) −4 b) −3 c) 2
d) 0 e) −10 f) 0 g) −3 h) 1
i) 0 j) 10 **11.** a) −1 b) 5
c) −10 d) 33 e) 11 f) −3
g) (d) **12.** a) −2 b) 12 c) 5
d) −6 e) −12 f) −9 g) 20
h) 72 **13.** a) −18 b) −2 c) 6
d) −5 e) 3 f) −17 g) −60
h) 5 **14.** a) −4 b) −5 c) −16
d) −10 e) −3 f) 6 g) 3
h) −5 i) 6 j) −4 **15.** a) −2
b) 5 c) 28 **16.**

a	−8	15	−21	−35	−50
	56	−72	64	−100	
b	−4	3	7	7	−25
	−8	−18	−16	−4	
ab	2	−5	−3	−5	2
	−7	4	−4	25	

5.9 Written Exercises, page 177
1. a) −5 b) −4 c) 3 f) 0
2. −8°C **3.** 4°C **4.** 3°C
5. −24.4°C **6.** 3.6°C **7.** 4.4°C
8. −44°C **9.** 8°C **10.** −15°C
11. −296 m **12.** −158 m
13. −6243 m **14.** 166 106 m²
15. −3840 m

5.10 Written Exercises, page 180
1. a) −10 b) −1 c) 64 d) 18
2. b) 16 c) 16 d) 25 e) 8
f) −8 g) 1 **3.** a) −81 b) −3
c) 125 d) −5 **4.** a) 9 b) −9
c) 0 d) 16 e) −16 f) −32
5. a) −27 b) 54 c) −32
d) −12 e) 64 f) −8 **6.** a) −30
b) −212 c) −25 d) −24
7. a) 9 b) 6 c) 2 **8.** a) 4 b) 16
c) 25 d) 36 e) 196 f) 256
g) 3600 h) 6561 **9.** a) 7 b) 16
c) 90 d) −20 e) 11 f) 12
10. a) −4 b) −4 **11.** a) 5 b) 5
c) 66 d) 22 e) −25
12. a) −18 b) 36 c) −18
d) −36 **13.** a) 36 b) 36

14. a) −36 b) 144 **15.** a) −36
b) −144 c) 144 **16.** a) 9 b) 18
c) −18 d) −15 e) −33
17. a) 144 b) 17 c) −15
d) −1 **18.** a) 5 b) 11 c) −11
d) −8

5.11 Written Exercises, page 181
1. a) 26, 33 b) 43, 49 c) 72,
−64 **2.** a) 162, 486 b) 1296,
−7776 c) 25, 36 **3.** a) 17, 21
b) 27, −81 c) $\frac{1}{4}$, $\frac{1}{16}$ d) 21,
−28 **4.** a) 9, 99, 999 b) 9999,
99 999 **5.** a) 9, 89, 889
b) 8889 **6.** a) 12, 123, 1234
b) 12 345 **7.** a) 4, 9, 16, 25
b) 36

CHAPTER 6

6.1 Written Exercises, page 189
1. a) 5:4 b) 4:5 **2.** a) 13:10
b) 10:13 c) 13:0 **3.** a) 5:16
b) 3:16 c) 8:5 d) 3:8
e) 16:5 **4.** a) 7:3 b) 8:5
c) 6:5 d) 9:2 **5.** a) 12:3
b) 4:11 **6.** a) 25:12 b) 22:23
c) 16:15 d) 20:9 **7.** a) 1:1
b) 9:13 **8.** a) 21:22 b) 17:18
9. a) 1:5 b) 10:1 c) 2:1
d) 5:2 e) 10:1 f) 1:5
10. a) 3:4 b) 8:9 c) 2:19
d) 1:20 e) 4:250 f) 1:5
g) 1:70 h) 1:8 **11.** a) 3:2
b) 2:3 c) 3:10 d) 1:5
12. a) 2:1 b) 3:5 c) 1:1
d) 5:3 **13.** a) 1:1 b) 18:1
c) 1:4 d) 2:9 **14.** a) 1:1
b) 1:5 c) 2:5 d) 1:5
15. a) 3:4 b) 1:1 c) 2:1
d) 6:11 e) 3:4 f) 4:11
g) 11:59 h) 1:59 **16.** a) 1:1
b) 1:2 **17.** a) 2:1 b) 2:3
18. a) 1:1 b) 5:6 c) 1:1
19. a) 3:10 b) 11:40 c) 7:40
d) 15:38 **20.** a) 4:1 b) 19:12
c) 39:31 d) 8:5 **21.** a) 5:7
b) 7:10 c) 12:19 d) 22:41
22. a) 23:3, 17:2, 29:4, 19:1,
11:1, 25:3 b) 62:7

6.2 Written Exercises, page 193
1. a) 5:6 b) 6:13 c) 13:0

2. a) 2:1 b) 2:5 c) 5:36
d) 18:9:10 e) 10:1:40
3. a) 3 b) 1 c) 13 d) 3 e) 18
f) 1:3:13, 3:1:18 **6.** 14:3:5
7. a) 5:9:15 b) 6:11:12
c) 19:112:6 d) 6:112:19
8. a) 10:20 b) 20:15
c) 15:10 **10.** a) 8:15:23
b) 10:7:17 c) 3:14:17
d) 10:16:26
11. a) goals : assists
b) assists : goals
c) goals : points for
d) goals : assists : points for
13. a) wins : losses : ties
b) wins : points for : points against
c) losses : points for : ties
d) losses : ties : wins
14. a) 8:7:1 b) 13:3:0
c) 9:7:0
15. a) losses : wins : ties
b) wins : losses : ties
c) wins : losses d) losses : ties
16. a) Saskatchewan
wins : losses : ties
b) B.C. wins : losses : points for
c) Hamilton
wins : losses : points for

6.3 Written Exercises, page 198
1. a) 6:8, 9:12, etc. b) 10:4,
15:6, etc. c) 12:2, 18:3, etc.
d) 1:2, 2:4, etc. e) 6:10:12,
9:15:18, etc. f) 1:2:4, 2:4:8,
etc. g) 2:4:3, 4:8:6, etc.
2. a) 4 b) 6 c) 5 **3.** a) 1:2
b) 1:2 c) 1:2 d) 1:10
e) 1:2:3 f) 5:4:3 g) 4:3:2
4. a) 1:3 b) $\frac{3}{4}$ c) $\frac{2}{5}$ d) 5:2
e) $\frac{1}{10}$ f) 100:1 g) 5:8 h) 50:1
i) 5:3:1 j) 7:3:2 k) 9:6:4
5. a) 5 b) 4 c) 3 d) 4
6. a) 3:2 b) 2:3 c) 8:3
d) 4:1 e) 1:4 **7.** a) 1:4
b) 1:4 c) 1:1 d) 3:8
e) 3:8:12 **8.** a) 4 b) 9 c) 8
d) 15 **9.** a) T b) T c) T d) T
e) F **10.** a) 10 b) 21 c) 8
d) 15 **11.** a) = b) ≠ c) ≠
d) = e) ≠ **12.** a) 1:2 b) 3:5
c) 5:12 **13.** b) A 2:3, B 3:4:2
16. a) 5:7 b) 5:4 c) 7:9
d) 10:7:5 e) 5:7:10
18. 6:11 **19.** 3:14 **20.** a) 1:8
b) 3:4 c) 7:12 **21.** a) 3:2
b) 1:1 c) 1:11 **22.** a) 1:2

b) 1:4 c) 8:7 **23.** 10:12, No,
5:6 **24.** a) 20 yes, 4 no b) 50
25. 30

6.4 Written Exercises, page 202
1. a) 2 b) 6 c) 3 d) 7 e) 4
f) 5 **2.** a) × 3 b) × 5 c) × 2
d) × 4 **3.** a) 3 b) 5 c) 4 d) 7
e) 6 f) 2 **4.** a) = b) ≠ c) =
d) ≠ e) = **5.** a) 6 b) 4 c) 48
d) 20 e) 20 f) 90 **6.** a) 20
b) 3.5 c) 11.25 d) 10 e) 3.5
f) 18 g) 3 **7.** a) 1 b) 4 c) 2
d) 2 e) 4 f) 16 **8.** a) 12
9. a) 12 b) 25 c) 30 d) 15
e) 4 f) 120 **10.** a) 27 b) 30
c) 12
d) 6 e) 37.5 f) $24\frac{3}{8}$ **11.** a) 20
b) 10 c) 7.2 d) $21\frac{1}{3}$ **12.** 98
13. $5\frac{4}{9}$ **14.** a) = b) ≠ c) = d)
15. (d) **17.** a) $\frac{7}{4}$ b) 3 c) 8 d) 4
e) 5 f) 2

6.5 Written Exercises, page 20
1. b) 42 c) 60 d) 84 e) 75
2. a) 108 b) 195 c) 600.25
3. 9 **4.** $5\frac{1}{3}$ L **5.** 80 **6.** 48 **7.** 28
8. Jean $900, Marg $360
9. a) 180 b) 546 **10.** a) 6 L
b) 72 L **11.** 45 **12.** 171
13. Camera $2400,
Wrestling $2600 **14.** a) 22.5 kg
b) 12 kg **15.** a) $1500 b) $600
16. 96 **17.** 1000 **18.** 80
19. a) 300 b) 400
20. 10 0717 kg **21.** 180 t
22. 56 t **23.** a) 216 000 t
b) 24 000 t **24.** a) 14.1 g
b) 1.56 g **25.** 38 **26.** 20.9 m

6.6 Written Exercises
2. a) 8 cm b) 10 cm c) 20 cm
d) 50 cm e) 1 m f) 2 m
g) 20 m h) 200 m **3.** a) 0.5 cm
b) 0.5 mm c) 0.25 mm
4. a) 4 cm b) 16 cm c) 10 cm
5. a) 1:4 b) 1:5 c) 1:4
d) 1:1500 e) 500:1
f) 1:900 000 g) 2000:1
6. a) 8 m b) 32 m c) 48 m
d) 50 m e) 5.8 m f) 1.6 m
g) 73 m h) 202 m **11.** 6 m
12. 8.85 cm **13.** 16 m **14.** 0.25 m
15. a) 1 mm b) 3 mm **16.** 3.5 cm

17. 20 cm **18.** 3 m **19.** 750 m
20. 3 m **21.** 148.4 cm

6.7 Written Exercises

1. a) 25 km b) 26.25 km
c) 125 km d) 131.25 km
e) 72.5 km f) 153.75 km
2. a) 2 cm b) 8 cm c) 0.48 cm
d) 0.8 cm e) 2.24 cm f) 4.4 cm
3. a) 8 km b) 1.3 km c) 10 km
d) 6.25 km e) 40 km
4. a) 1 km b) 10 km
c) 12.5 km **5.** a) 10 cm
b) 100 cm c) 350 cm
6. 100 km **11.** 10 cm
12. 3000 km **13.** 5500 km
14. 1.5 cm **15.** a) 22.4 km
b) 9.6 km **16.** 1 cm represents
100 km **17.** b) 1 km
18. a) 4 km b) 5.5 km
c) 0.8 km **19.** a) 5 cm
b) 10 cm c) 8.5 cm d) 9.6 cm
e) 7.9 cm f) 12.5 cm
20. 6.2 km **21.** 3.8 cm
22. 4.5 km **23.** 18.5 cm
24. a) 4.4 km b) 6.4 km

6.8 Written Exercises, page 218

1. a) 11.4 m b) 18.4 m c) (d)
2. 6.7 times **3.** 4.5 m
4. 16.1 m **5.** 0.95 m **6.** 278 km
7. 50 km **8.** 8 km **9.** a) 34 km
b) 248 km

CHAPTER 7

7.1 Written Exercises, page 225

1. a) 2 m/s b) 50 L/S
c) 40 sheets/s d) $\frac{1}{9}$ basket/min
e) 40 words/min f) 20 m²/kg
g) 5 ¢/cm **2.** a) 1 b) $1\frac{1}{5}$ c) $1\frac{1}{4}$
d) $1\frac{1}{5}$ e) $1\frac{2}{7}$ f) $2\frac{4}{13}$ g) $1\frac{5}{24}$
3. a) 40 km b) 90 km c) 20 h
4. a) 20 L b) 1200 L c) 1800 L
d) 9 min **5.** a) $4.75 b) $38
c) 9 h d) 4.5 h **6.** 720 m
7. $450 **8.** $42 **9.** a) 10 S
b) 20 S **10.** a) 17 b) 170
11. a) 6 b) 720 **12.** 108 000
13. 8 **14.** 25 words/min
15. $50/m² **16.** 64 800 balls
17. a) 12.5 km/L b) 0.08 L/km
18. pizza place **19.** a) 80.6 min
b) 7.9 min **20.** 200 h

7.2 Written Exercises, page 228

1. a) 60¢ b) 74¢ c) $1.24
d) 42¢   25¢ **2.** a) 9¢ b) 1¢
c) 4¢ d) 0.4¢ **3.** 32.1¢/L
4. $1.48 b) $9.60 c) $4.56
5. 40 **6.** 4455 km **7.** 32 L
8. a) $3.03 b) $8.90 c) 41.4 L
9. can **10.** a) 29.8¢ b) 29.2¢
c) B **11.** Yes **12.** pump (a)
13. A **14.** Scott Paper

7.3 Written Exercises

1. 20 m/s **2.** 400 km/h
3. 40 m/min **4.** 6 h **5.** 2400 km
6. a) 3 h b) 7 h 40 min
7. a) 80 km, 320 km b) 5 h
8. 36 km **9.** a) 180 m b) 33s
10. a) 40 km/h b) 1.8 m/s
c) 49.9 km/h **11.** 20 m/s
12. 0.06 km/min **13.** 4.4 m/s
14. a) 3.4 km/h b) 56.7 m/min
15. 0.21 s **16.** 48 h **17.** 11.4 h
18. 460 h **19.** B

7.4 Written Exercises

1. 0.7 kg **2.** 0.35 kg **3.** 7
4. 37 800 **5.** a) 5000 b) 700
6. a) 16 89.2 m b) 3378.4 m
c) 4 h 56 min **7.** 12 min
8. a) 45.2 min b) 69.3 min
9. 30 min **10.** a) 19.6 min
b) 51.2 min **11.** B **12.** 4320
13. 21.5 h

7.5 Written Exercises, page 236

1. a) 155 mm b) 1860 mm
2. 0.8 m **3.** a) 23 m
b) 1915.8 mm **4.** a) 0.6 g
b) 1.1 g **5.** a) 140 b) cat
6. speeds in m/s: 13.9, 30.6, 19.4,
11.1, 13.9, 4.2, 15.3, 5.6
7. 40 km **8.** 25 km **9.** a) 3.3 s
b) 306 m **10.** 14.5 min

7.6 Written Exercises, page 238

1. a) 60 b) 15 **2.** all 4 **3.** a) 12

7.7 Written Exercises, page 239

1. 756 **2.** 120 **3.** 810 m **4.** 448
5. 172 800 **6.** a) 2640
b) 443 520 **7.** a) 1808.6 km²
8. a) 115 200 b) depends on
assumptions **9.** a) 1014 km
b) 4.4 h

CHAPTER 8

8.1 Written Exercises, page 246

1. a) A 30%, B 70% b) A 65%,
B 35% **2.** a) 37.5%, 0.375
b) 44.4%, 0.$\overline{4}$ c) 37.5%, 0.375
3. a) 1 : 50 b) 3 : 25 c) 1 : 4
d) 3 : 4 e) 1 : 40
f) 121 : 1000 g) 27 : 200 h) 1 : 13
4. a) 0.25 b) 0.37 c) 0.08
d) 0.635 **5.** a) 39% b) 75%
c) 47% d) 80% e) 31% f) 1%
g) 96.3% h) 10.8% **6.** a) 70%
b) 29% c) 80% d) 24% e) 24%
f) 20% g) 66.7% h) 75%
7. a) ¼ b) ½ c) $\frac{3}{10}$ d) $\frac{3}{5}$
e) $\frac{1}{50}$ f) $\frac{3}{8}$ g) $\frac{1}{8}$ h) $\frac{7}{8}$
8. a) 0.$\overline{3}$ b) 0.5 **9.** a) 7 b) 40
c) 60 d) 48 e) 20 f) 52
10. a) 40% b) 60% c) 80%
11. a) 1% b) 0.1% c) 0.1%
d) 1% **12.** a) 5.1% b) 95%
c) 69.4% **13.** a) 94.7%
b) 5.3% **14.** 20% **15.** 40%
16. a) 32% b) 24% c) 8%
d) 36% **17.** a) 13.4% b) 64.2%
c) 80.7% d) 3.2%

8.2 Written Exercises, page 250

1. a) 70% b) 60% c) 75%
d) 80% **2.** a) 80%, 75% b) 70%,
75% c) 80%, 79% d) 30%, 25%
3. a) $33\frac{1}{3}$% b) 11.1% c) 66.7%
d) 13.3% e) 49% **4.** a) 80%,
83.3% b) 83.3%, 66.7%
c) 43.6%, 42.9% d) 51.9%,
52.8% **5.** a) 50% b) 20%
c) 30% d) 33.3% **6.** a) 73.3%
b) 3.8% **7.** 66.7% **8.** Frances
9. a) 6.3% b) 93.8% **10.** D
11. a) $1286 b) (i) 18.7%
(ii) 27.2% c) 8.4%
12. a) 42.8% b) 5.3%
13. a) 68.2%, 68% b) Wildcats
14. a) 70.8%, 57.8%, 64.7%,
62.1%, 50.7% b) Rovers,
Redmen, Bulldogs, Wildcats,
Warriors **15.** Rudolph May
16. a) 40%, 41.7%, 65.8%, 40.9%,
40%, 60%, 66.7% b) McWhirter
c) Vase, Forster **17.** a) 33.3%
b) 33.3% c) 16.7% d) 16.7%

8.3 Written Exercises

1. a) 6 b) 3 c) 5 **2.** a) 1276.5

b) 185.5 c) 0.7 **3.** b) A 69.8,
B 68.1 **4.** a) 1 b) 8 c) 126
d) 156 **5.** b) A 36.5, B 27
6. a) 14 b) 2756.3 **7.** b) A 295,
B 712.5 **8.** a) $38.88
b) $47.58 c) $99.75
d) $1718.75 **9.** a) $12 b) 14
c) 28 d) 41 cm **10.** 1.2 L
11. $17.93 **12.** $200 million
13. 20.3 million **14.** $33.96
15. a) 454.2 km b) 653.3 km
16. a) 112 mL b) 168 mL
c) 672 mL d) 11.4 L e) 55.1 L
f) 6.5 L **17.** 13.4 million
18. 18.3 million **19.** 20.9 million
20. 21 150 **21.** 380 000
22. 175 830 **23.** 210 000
24. 30.1 kg **25.** 18 kg
26. Tiger 16.9 kg, Daryl 15.3 kg,
Bobby 12.7 kg **27.** 1.6 kg

8.4 Written Exercises, page 257

1. a) 7.2, 720 b) 1.75, 175
2. a) 28.8 b) 13.5 **3.** a) 50%
b) 25% c) 33.3% **4.** a) 4.8
b) 20 c) 220 d) 30 e) 25
f) 96 **5.** a) 50% b) 14.3%
6. 150 g **7.** 6 **8.** 606 **9.** 43.8%
10. 73.4% **11.** 0.5 L **12.** 111.4 g
13. a) 5.4% b) 92.1% **14.** 60
15. 72% **16.** a) 60 kg b) 50 kg

8.5 Written Exercise, page 260

1. a) 312.5 b) 468.8 c) 625
d) 781.3 **2.** a) 540 b) 170.8
c) 259.6 d) 523.2 **3.** a) $310.5
b) 506.9 m c) 682.5 kg
d) 1012.5 mg **4.** a) 281.3 kg
b) 451.8 kg c) 577.3 kg
d) 691.6 kg **5.** B **6.** a) A = B
b) A = B **7.** 156 L **8.** $1327.50
9. 15.1 m **10.** $1118
11. 115 600 **12.** $95 000
13. $22 176 **14.** $58.59
15. a) $74.81 b) $84.54
c) $95.52

8.6 Written Exercise, page 263

1. a) $3.36 b) $4.79 c) $1.25
2. a) $29.55 b) $12.19
3. a) $4.75, $19.00 b) $12.92,
$23.98 c) $75.86, $113.79
4. a) $300.98 b) $34.19
5. a) 25% b) 30% c) 15%
6. a) 33.3% b) 22.2%

7. a) \$32.81 b) \$26.92
c) \$29.10 d) 7.7% **8.** a) \$28.33
b) \$56.67 **9.** \$84.47 **10.** 18%
11. \$6.36 **12.** 45.5%
13. a) \$106.25 b) \$96 c) Banjo
14. \$169.12 **15.** a) \$73.53
b) \$46.11 c) \$103.84
d) \$130.36 **16.** a) 25.5%
b) 18.2% c) 19.8%
17. a) \$195.50 b) \$30.50
18. a) 25% b) \$89.85
c) \$17.97 d) \$73.68 e) \$1.80

8.7 Written Exercises, page 266

1. a) 33¢ b) \$1.19 c) \$1.15
d) \$4.58 **2.** a) \$1.80 b) \$1.48
3. a) \$1.33 b) \$4.85 c) \$70.00
4. a) P.E.I., 47¢ b) Nfld., \$1.44
c) Man., \$1.97 **5.** a) \$36.68
b) \$100.98 c) \$53.62 **6.** a) A
b) B c) A d) B **7.** 8¢
8. \$18.31 **9.** a) \$4.48 b) \$6.02
10. \$28.62 **11.** \$31.70
13. a) \$525.74 b) \$4.96
14. Alberta

8.8 Written Exercises, page 269

1. a) \$78 b) \$31.80 **2.** a) \$4.00
b) \$6.60 c) \$7.61 d) \$39.79
3. b) \$56 c) \$28.80 d) \$3.19
4. a) \$1062.44 b) \$20.65
c) \$1038.55 **5.** a) \$763.25
b) \$738.40 c) \$781.89
6. a) \$13.95 b) \$34.51
c) \$1836 d) \$3090 e) \$181.35
7. \$81.97 **8.** \$19.50 **9.** \$464
10. Mr. Wong **11.** a) \$96
b) \$48 c) \$24 **12.** a) \$4.33
b) \$524.33 c) \$4.37
13. a) \$2.33 b) \$7.58 c) \$9.00
14. \$35.80 **15.** \$2550
16. \$33.75 **17.** 7.1% **18.** \$172
19. \$5400 **20.** \$312.29
21. \$629.55

CHAPTER 9
9.1 Written Exercises, page 277

3. a) 45° b) 135° c) 39° d) 90°
4. a) 48° b) 92° c) 130°
7. a) obtuse b) acute c) acute
8. 100° **9.** a) 180° b) 60°
c) 100° **10.** a) 72° b) 119°

11. a) 45° b) 28° **12.** a) 112°
b) 68° c) 55° d) 125° e) 360°
13. a) equal b) equal

9.2 Written Exercises, page 281

1. b) isosceles **2.** b) scalene
3. a) scalene b) obtuse
c) right **6.** b) 90° **7.** b) ∠S
9. a) scalene or acute b) right
c) scalene or acute d) scalene or
acute **10.** b) isosceles c) equal
11. b) two angles equal
13. b) equal **14.** b) equal

9.3 Written Exercises, page 284

1. c) 35° **2.** c) 77° **8.** b) 90°
9. b) 45°

9.4 Written Exercises, page 287

1. c) 4 cm

9.5 Written Exercises, page 291

4. c) MS d) 3 **12.** c) equal

9.6 Written Exercises, page 295

1. b) 134° **2.** b) 21° **3.** b) 70°
4. a) right b) 120° c) 60°
5. a) isosceles b) 50° c) 80°
6. a) equilateral b) 60° c) 60°
7. a) 134° b) 51° c) 42° d) 52°
8. a) 70° b) 79° c) 50° d) 22°
9. a) 50° b) 51° c) 37°
10. a) isosceles b) 80°
c) equal d) 50°; 50°
11. a) isosceles b) 90°
c) equal d) 45°; 45°
12. ∠A = ∠B = ∠C = 60°
∠F = 65° ∠G = 80° ∠I = 50°
∠L = 54° ∠M = 45°
∠O = 45° **13.** a) 70°
b) isosceles **14.** 90°

9.7 Written Exercises, page 298

7. d) centre **8.** d) centre
9. b) centre **11.** b) 90°
12. c) 90° **13.** b) 90°
15. b) equal **17.** b) equal

9.8 Written Exercises, page 301

1. a) ∠Q = ∠P; ∠R = ∠S
b) 48° **2.** b) 80° **3.** a) ∠U
b) 90° **6.** a) 49° b) 35° c) 40°
7. a) 60° b) 72° c) 50°
8. a) 90° b) 40° c) 40°

9.9 Written Exercises, page 305

1. a) 8 b) 9 c) 11 d) 14 e) 16
f) 25 **2.** a) 3.5 b) 6.3 c) 9.2
d) 8.5 e) 6.5 f) 9.7 **3.** a) 4.58
b) 5.83 c) 8.19 d) 9.54
e) 9.06 f) 9.75 **4.** a) 8.7
b) 8.9 c) 5.7 **5.** a) 2.6 b) 4.0
c) 8.7 d) 12.2 e) 14.1 f) 18.7
6. 9 cm **7.** 4.8 cm **8.** a) 14.8
b) 28.7 **9.** 33.9 m
10. a) 22.4 m b) 89.6 m
11. a) 2.9 b) 2.9 s **12.** 2.2s
13. a) 4.8 b) 11.1 c) 4.1

9.10 Written Exercises, page 309

1. 7.3 **2.** 9.5 **3.** a) 5.83
b) 9.22 c) 7.48 d) 6.00
4. a) 3.7 b) 6.8 c) 5.7 d) 6.5
e) 6.4 **5.** a) 13 b) 10 c) 20
6. a) 5 cm b) 20 cm c) 8 cm
7. a) 10.2 b) 5.4 c) 23.8
8. a) 6.5 cm b) 8.2 **9.** 7.7 m
10. 16 m **11.** 39.6 **12.** 14.7 m
13. 6.5 m **14.** a) 9.1 m b) 83 m²

CHAPTER 10
10.1 Written Exercises, page 314

1. a) F6 c) C4 c) D1 d) B6
e) A6 f) F6 **3.** a) D, E, F, L; J, M;
B, H; C, I, K b) C, M;
A, B, E, F, K; D, N; I, J c) A, G, I
d) A, D, E, F, L, e) D, G, H, I, J
5. A(−6, 3), B(−3, 3), C(−3, 1),
D(−6, 1); S(−6, −3), T(−3, −2)
U(−3, −4) V(−6, −5) P(3, 3)
Q(4, 0) R(7, −1); M(2, −2)
K(6, −2) T(6, −5) S(2, −5)
6. a) 0 b) 0 **7.** b) right triangle
8. a) isosceles triangle
b) square c) rectangle
9. b) (2, −4) **10.** (4, −2)
12. b) (7, 4) 13 a) 1 b) 11
c) 111 d) IV e) II f) IV **14.** Z
15 ANT

10.2 Written Exercises, page 318

1. a) 6, 4 b) 5, 5 c) 12, 5
2. a) 4, 3 b) 9, 12, 15
3. a) {0, 1, 2, 3} b) {0, 4, 8, 12}

10. a) 2 b) 3 c) 4 **11.** a) 10
b) 3 c) 20 d) 5 e) 4 f) 60
13. b) 2, 4, 4.5 **14.** c) non-linear
18. c) 18, 5, 4 **19.** a) 0, 3, 6, 9
c) 18, 30, 7 **20.** c) 150, 3, 75

10.3 Written Exercises, page 3⫶

1. a) 1.2 b) 0.6 **2.** 0.2
3. a) $\frac{9}{10}$ b) $\frac{9}{5}$ **4.** a) 2 b) 5
c) $\frac{2}{5}$ **5.** a) −3 b) 6 c) $-\frac{1}{2}$
6. a) 2, 4, $\frac{1}{2}$ b) −1, 4, $-\frac{1}{4}$
c) 3, 4, $\frac{3}{4}$ d) −2, 4, $-\frac{1}{2}$
e) −4, 6, $-\frac{2}{3}$ f) 2, 4, $\frac{1}{2}$
7. a) 2 b) −3 c) $-\frac{3}{2}$ d) −2
e) 3 f) $-\frac{3}{2}$ **8.** a) −2 b) $\frac{3}{2}$
c) $\frac{3}{5}$ d) $\frac{2}{3}$ e) $\frac{5}{13}$ f) $-\frac{5}{9}$
9. a) $\frac{1}{2}$ b) $\frac{1}{2}$ c) $\frac{1}{2}$ d) $\frac{1}{2}$
e) equal

10.4 Written Exercises, page 3⫶

1. a) 7 b) 3 c) 7.6 **2.** a) 6
b) 6 c) 8.5 **3.** a) 6.3 b) 3.6
c) 7.1 d) 4.5 e) 4.5 f) 6.1
4. a) 3.6 b) 8.6 c) 10.6 d) 7.6
5. CD 6 AB = 5.4 AC = 7.6
BC = 5.4 **7.** a) AB = 6 BC = 6
AC = 8.5 b) isosceles **8.** b) 10
10.4, 6.3, 6.3 **9.** 24.9 **10.** 13.9
11. 13.0 **12.** a) 26 b) 12.8
13. a) 5 b) 5 c) 10 d) equal
c) collinear

10.5 Written Exercises, page 3⫶

1. H, I, M, O, T, V, W, X, Y
2. I, O, X **13.** a) (4, −1)
b) (−2, −5) c) (−7, −2)
d) (−10, 5) e) (−8. 7) f) (−5, 0⫶

10.6 Written Exercises, page 3⫶

1. a) 3R (right) b) 4L (left)
c) 3D (down) d) 3R
2. a) 3R, 2D b) 3R, 1U (up)
9. a) 4R, 3D b) 1R, 3U
c) 5L, 2U **28.** a) (3, 8) b) (0, 0)
29 a) (1, −8) **30.** a) (9, −2)
b) (2, 1) c) (−9, 0)

10.7 Written Exercises, page 338

1. a) HI THERE **2.** 90°CW, 180°CW or CCW

10.8 Written Exercises, page 341

1. a) 3 b) 4 **2.** a) 2 b) 4 **3.** 1b, 2a, 2b **4.** 4 **5.** 2 **6.** a) point b) line or turn **7.** a) line b) turn c) line **9.** a) 3 b) 4 c) 1 d) 2 **10.** a) 4,1 **12.** a) line b) line or turn c) line or turn **13.** line symmetry: b, c, e, f turn symmetry: a, b, d, e, f **14.** a) H, I, M, O, T, V, W, X, Y **15.** a) C, D, E, H, I, K, O, X

10.9 Written Exercises, page 345

4. a) 3 b) equal d) AB∥DE, AC∥DF, BC∥EF **6.** 3 c) equal e) 1:3 **7.** c) equal d) equal e) equal

10.10 Written Exercises, page 347

1. a) 2 vert, 1 hor b) 1 vert, 2 hor **2.** a) 1 vert, 2 hor b) 1.5 vert, 1 hor **4.** a) A′(8, 3) B′(20, 3), C′(20, 12) D′(8, 12) b) A′(2, 4) B′(5, 4), C′(5, 16) D′(2, 16)

CHAPTER II

11.1 Written Exercises, page 352

6. a) 823 and 826 b) 3 and 4 c) O **7.** a) e b) z c) the **10.** B **11.** C **12.** A and B **13.** a) Destructive b) Stratified c) Stratified d) Clustered

11.2 Written Exercises, page 356

1.
h	0 1 2 3 4 5 6 7 8 9
f	6 0 1 3 9 5 6 5 7 3

2. 45 **3.** a) 3 b) 9 c) 1 d) 7 **4.** a) 9 h b) 3 **5.** a) 0 b) 5
6.
students	5	10	9	2	4
frequency	5	10	9	2	4

7. a) 30 b) 6 c) 5 **8.** A **10.** a) Swimming b) Archery **11.** 63 **12.** a) 130 b) 20% c) 10% **13.** Swimming, Track and field, Hockey, Basketball, Football, Tennis, Volleyball, Soccer, Baseball, Archery.

15. a) 20 b) 96% **16.** a) 12% b) 56% **17.** 9 **19.** 100 **20.** 1989 **21.** a) 16.7% b) 30% **22.** 66 **24.** a) 11.1% b) 55.6% **25.** 44.4% **26.** 11.1%

11.3 Written Exercises, page 359

1. a) Rock b) Classical **2.** a) 200 b) 16% **3.** 7 : 2 **4.** a) 20% b) 80% **5.** a) 160 b) 280 **6.** a) Turnbull b) Rausse **7.** Turnbull 66, Lofthouse 36, Rausse 18, Jarvis 48, Lane 60 **8.** a) 13.2% b) 13.2% c) same **11.** a) 8 b) 6 **12.** a) 1 : 2 b) 1 : 4 **13.** a) 48.4% b) 51.6% **14.** 15.5 **16.** a) 13.2% b) 19.9% **17.** a) Green b) 24.5%

11.4 Written Exercises, page 363

2. a) Wed. b) Thur. c) Fri. d) Thur. **3.** a) Tue. b) Thur. c) Sat. d) Sun. **4.** a) 120 b) 150 c) 80 **5.** a) Tues., Wed., Fri. b) Tues., Wed., Thur., Fri., Sat. **6.** a) 100 b) 150 **7.** Nile, 6600 km **8.** Saskatchewan, 1900 km **9.** a) Nile b) St. Lawrence **10.** a) Yantze b) Congo **11.** a) 21.4% b) 14.3% **12.** a) Male 16-20 b) Male 13-15 **13.** a) 3500 kJ b) 65% **14.** a) 8500 kJ b) 26.1% **15.** b) 66.7% c) 83.3%

11.5 Written Exercises, page 366

1. a) 9 L b) 14.5 L c) 19 L **2.** a) 30 km b) 37 km c) 80 km **3.** a) 58 m b) 50 m c) increasing d) decreasing **4.** a) 40, 120, 120 b) Mon, Tues, Wed, Fri c) Thurs, Sat d) None **5.** a) Mar b) Sept c) Feb, Apr, Nov, Jan; May, Oct; July, Aug. d) 34 000 e) $1358 300 **6.** a) 20 000 b) 45 000 c) 30 000 d) 45 000 **7.** a) 13:00, 17:00, 22:00 b) 22:00 **8.** a) 10:00, 24:00, 01:00 b) 11:30, 14:30, 16:00, 22:45

11.6 Written Exercises, page 369

1. b) 90°, 60°, 120° c) 25%, 16.7%, 33.3% e) 75%, 83.3%, 66.7% **3.** a) Jaws b) Superman **4.** a) 38% b) 133 **5.** a) 25% c) 88 **6.** c) 8 h 20 min **7.** a) 19.4% b) 25% **8.** a) 1 h 48 min. b) 3 h 28 min. **9.** 23.6% **10.** 26.4% **11.** a) $13 333.33 b) $21 111.11 **12.** Refrigerators by $3 333.33 **13.** Hamburger 32.5%, Beans 17.5%, Sauce 9.4%, Paste 9.4%, Chili 3.8%, Water 27.5% **14.** a) 117°, 34° **16.** b) 3.8 L **17.** a) 8.1% b) 52.8% **18.** $4.76 **19.** a) 25.8% b) 34.2% c) 40% **20.** a) 100% b) 100% **21.** 3.2 kg **22.** a) 2.8% b) 15.3% **23.** a) 15.3 kg b) 79.2 kg **24.** a) potato b) cheese

11.7 Written Exercises, page 374

1. a) 31 b) 10 c) 16 d) 12, 72 **2.** a) 54.3 b) 49.7 c) 7.7 d) 34.4 **3.** a) median 97, mode 97 b) median 7, mode 7 c) median 18, mode 18 **4.** a) mean 19.3, median 18. b) No **5.** a) mean 9.3, median 8, mode 8. b) mode **6.** a) No **7.** a) Yes **8.** a) No **9.** A) 14.9, 15, None, 13 B) 39.1, 40, 35, 9 C) 22.5, 21.5, None, 17 D) 7.7, 8.2, None, 6.4 **10.** A 8, 9; B 23, 17; C 24.6, 19; D 115.3, 125.5; E 40, 40; F 1002, 1002 **11.** a) B,C **12.** a) A,D **14.** a) A:9; B:17; C:19,35; D:123; E:56; F:None **15.** a) A:7; B:38; C:61; D:131; E:51, F:1956 **16.** a) 20 9 b) 13 **17.** a) 149.8 b) 153 **18.** a) 8.8, 9.1 **19.** a) 86.8¢ b) 85¢ c) 85¢ **20.** a) 11.3, 11, 7 **21.** 101 kg

11.8 Written Exercises, page 377

1. a) $\frac{4}{9}$ b) $\frac{3}{10}$ c) $\frac{1}{2}$ d) $\frac{2}{5}$ **2.** a) $\frac{1}{12}$ b) $\frac{1}{12}$ c) $\frac{1}{2}$ c) $\frac{1}{2}$ e) $\frac{1}{2}$ **3.** a $\frac{1}{10}$ b) $\frac{1}{10}$ c) $\frac{2}{5}$ **4.** a) $\frac{2}{5}$ b) $\frac{3}{25}$ c) $\frac{16}{75}$ d) $\frac{4}{15}$

5. a) $\frac{1}{13}$ b) $\frac{1}{13}$ c) $\frac{1}{52}$ d) $\frac{1}{52}$ e) $\frac{1}{26}$ f) $\frac{1}{26}$ g) $\frac{4}{13}$ h) $\frac{5}{13}$ **6.** a) 8 b) 1 c) $\frac{1}{8}$ **7.** a) $\frac{1}{8}$ b) $\frac{3}{8}$ c) $\frac{3}{8}$ **8.** a) 4 **9.** a) $\frac{1}{16}$ b) $\frac{3}{8}$ c) $\frac{1}{8}$ d) $\frac{1}{4}$

CHAPTER 12

12.1 Written Exercises, page 381

1. like a, d, e unlike b, c, f **2.** b, d, f **3.** a) 5x b) −8y c) 2a d) 3ab e) 8xy f) 2x² **4.** a) a b) −2b c) 4m d) −10p e) ab f) −6x² **5.** a) x b) 7m c) 4ab d) 12mp **6.** a) 4x b) 3a c) 4n d) 9pq e) 19m²n f) 3rq² **7.** a) 5m + n b) 6a + 3b c) 9x − 2y d) 9k − 2m e) 3p − 3q f) −4g − 3f **8.** a) 6a − 3b b) 5m − 6p c) pq d) 2a + 2b e) 4a − ab f) 5p − r **9.** a) 5a + b b) 5x + 2y c) x − 3y + 4 d) a − 5b e) 2y + 3x f) m **10.** a) f b) a, b, d, e c) c **11.** a) a + 8b b) 10x + 3y c) 4y − 3y² d) 11 − x e) 11a − 11 f) x² g) 2x² + 5xy h) 4a² − 2a + 3 **12.** a) f b) a, b, c, d, e, g c) h **13.** a) P = 4s b) 48 **14.** a) P = 8a b) 24 **15.** a) 16b b) 21 n c) 17p + 6 **16.** a) 7a + 4 b) 46 **17.** a) 26a b) 78 **18.** a) 46 b) 142 **19.** A

12.2 Written Exercises, page 385

1. a) −3x b) 3x c) −4a² d) −m+p e) 2m − p f) 2m + p g) −3a + b − c h) −4a − b + c i) 2a² + 3a − 5 j) −a² + 5a + 5 **2.** a) 5x + y b) y c) 5k + m d) 7k − m e) 3m + 4p f) 2r **3.** a) 5a − 1 b) 8x + 9 c) 7m + 9 d) 7p − 4a e) 13r + 4 f) 13w + 3m g) 13a − 4b h) 2z + x **4.** a) 5x + 2y b) 5m c) 5x − y d) 2m e) 5k − m f) x − 3y **5.** a) 3m + 2p b) 3m − 4p c) 4k + s d) − s e) 5ab − b f) ab − b **6.** a) 3x + 12 b) 8 − x c) 2a − 1 d) 11 − 2a e) 5m − 2 f) m + 2 **7.** a) 6x + 2y b) a + 4b c) 8m + 3n d) x − y

8. a) $m - 4p$ b) $-3a$
c) $-6k - s$ d) $a^2 - a + 9$
9. a) $9m + 9$ b) $16a - 4$
c) $9p - 2$ d) $-3r - 4$
e) $5x^2 + 6$ f) $-2a^2 - 1$
10. a) $14x - 3y$ b) $9y - 29$
c) $20r^2 - 12r$ d) $6x^2 + 3x - 3$
11. $5a + b$ **12.** $9x + 2y$
13. a) $17a - 2b$
b) $28a - 4b - 12c$
c) $6ab + 5ab^2$ **14.** a) $2x - 8y$
b) 3 c) $x - 8$ d) $5m + 2$
15. a) $3x - 2y$ b) $2a - 3b$
c) $16 + 14m$ d) $3b - 8$ e) $-10z^2$
16. a) $2a^2 + a - 3$
b) $-2x^2 - 12x + 7$
c) $2z^2 + 2z + 4$ **17.** a) $3a + 3b$
b) $8x - 2y$ c) $3x^2 + 3x$
18. a) $2b$ b) $-10x$

12.3 Written Exercises, page 387
1. a) plus, add, and, more than, increase, etc. b) less, minus, subtract, difference, decrease, etc. **2.** a) $-x - 1$ b) $6a + 7$
c) $3x + y$ d) $-a - 2b$
3. a) $-12m + 5n$ b) $k + 4p$
c) $3k + 3s$ d) $4p - 3q$
4. $7x^2 + 3x - 3$ **5.** $-7p^2 + 4pq$
6. $-2a^2 + 3ab - 9b^2$
7. $-x^2 + 11x - 10$ **8.** $7p - 3m$
9. -6 **10.** $-4b - 5a$

12.4 Written Exercises, page 389
1. a) 0 b) 0 c) 0 d) Equal
2. a) 13 b) 13 c) Equal **3.** a) 4
b) 4 **4.** a) $8x - 8y$
b) $8x - 8y$ **5.** a) $12x - 3$
6. a) $a - 8b$ **7.** A, B, C
equivalent, $2a + 3b$ **8.** a) 42
b) 24 c) 23 **9.** a) $5a + 2$
b) $3m + 6$ c) $5m^2 - 2m + 5$
10. b) $26x - 6$ c) 98
11. a) $8s + 1$ b) 33
12. a) $x^2 - 5x + 7$

12.5 Written Exercises, page 391
1. a) -6 b) $-6ab$ c) 12
d) $12m^2$ e) -12 f) $-12km$
2. a) $-12ab$ b) $-10xy$ c) $6kp$
d) $-16mn$ e) $-6ks$ f) $10qr$
3. D **4.** a) $6a$ b) $-12mn$
c) $20kp$ d) $-18ab$ e) $-16ps$
f) $-30mt$ **5.** a) $3p$ b) $2m$
c) $6mp$ **6.** a) $8p$ b) $4q$ c) $16pq$

7. a) $7ab$ b) $-12.6mn$
c) $12.3pq$ d) $-7.75st$ e) $-9uv$
f) $14.4xy$ **8.** a) $24abc$ b) $36qrs$
c) $30mnp$ d) $40mpt$ **9.** $12kp$
10. $20st$ **11.** $9bz$ **12** A **13.** A
14. a) 144 b) 192 c) $48d$
d) $48k$ e) $144d$ f) $240k$
15. a) \$22.50 b) \$37.50
c) \$7.5 m d) \$45m **16.** a) 20
b) 50 c) $5n$ d) $20n$ **17.** a) $4d$ ¢
b) $10d$ ¢ c) gd ¢ d) $6gd$ ¢
18. a) \$3h b) \$6h c) \$hy
d) \$8hy **19.** D

12.6 Written Exercises, page 394
1. a) 2^7 b) a^7 c) 3^5 d) m^5
e) 4^4 f) y^4 **2.** a) x^5 b) 2^6 c) m^5
d) p^4 e) 3^8 f) p^4 **3.** a) -6
b) -10 c) -24 d) 6 **4.** a) a^5
b) m^4 c) k^3 d) p^4 **5.** a) $4p$
b) $2p$ c) $8p^2$ **6.** a) $6p^7$ **7.** $6m^5$
8. a) a b) $2m^3$ c) $-a^2$
d) $-15r^5$ e) $-2p$ f) $-21m^6$
g) $-6n^9$ h) $3r^{30}$ **10.** a) $12x^2$
b) $9y^2$ c) $4p^3$ d) 0 e) $-10a^2$
f) $10x^2$ g) $-8x^2$ h) $-32p^2$
i) $-8w^2$ j) $-16a^4$ k) $-21p^4$
11. B **12.** a) $24x^4y^4$ b) $18m^4n^4$
c) $-96a^3b^5$ d) $144x^4y^7$
13. b) $16a^2$ c) $4a^2$ d) $16a^2$
e) $4x^2y^2$ f) $4a^4$ g) $9m^2n^2$
14. a) $9a^2$ b) $4x^2y^2$ c) $16a^2b^4$
d) $9m^4n^6$ **15.** a) 32 b) 80 c) 16
d) -72 **16.** a) 2^{10} b) 2^{18} c) 3^6
d) 4^9 e) 4^{10} f) 2^{15} g) 5^9 h) 7^6
i) 8^4 **17.** a) x^9 b) x^{24} c) w^{12}
d) p^{14} e) x^{30} f) z^{16} g) m^{24} h) n^{32}
i) p^{54} **18.** a) 144 b) 4320 **19.** B

12.7 Written Exercise, page 397
1. a) $5c$ b) $4h$ c) $2r$ d) $-6b$
e) $-4p$ f) $-3s$ g) $4m$ h) $2u$
i) $8e$ **2.** a) -4 b) $-4b$ c) -4
d) $-4p$ e) 5 f) 5 **3.** a) $4b$
b) $-5p$ c) $6t$ **4.** a) $2a$ b) $2m$
c) $-2p^2$ d) $-5 df$ **5.** a, b
6. a) -8 b) 8 c) -8 d) -50
e) -16 f) -8 **7.** a) $5q$ b) $2 bc$
8. a) $4m$ b) $-6p$ c) $-6r$ d) $5u$
e) $-5p$ f) $-4s$ **9.** a) $2a$
b) $-2a$ c) $2 m^2$ d) $-2 m^2$
e) $-3 p^3$ f) $5 m^4$ **10.** a) $-2b$
b) $-7p$ c) $-5t$ d) $5r$
11. a) -24 b) -60 c) -288
12. A **13.** $9a$ **14.** $6 p$ **15.** $4p$
16. $4b$ **17.** A

12.8 Written Exercises, page 399
1. a) 4 b) 3 c) 25 **2.** a) m^2
b) n^2 c) p^4 **3.** a) $2p$ b) $-2q^2$
c) $2 d^3$ d) $-6 f^2$ e) $2 m^2$ f) $4n^4$
4. a) 2 b) $-2 a^2$ c) $4 q^2$
d) $-4 r^3$ e) $-4 s$ f) $5b$
5. a) $-8m^2$ b) $12 m^3$ c) $-18 m^4$
d) $12 m^2$ e) $4 m$ **6.** a) $-2 a$
b) $5 m^2$ c) $6 p$ d) $10 c$ e) $8 r^3$
7. a) m^2n b) x^2y^2 c) p^5q^3
d) ab^2 e) r^5s f) t^2u^3 **8.** a) $5xy$
b) $-2 x^2y$ c) $-6 m^2n^3$ **9.** a) $4x^4$
b) $4 p^4$ **10.** $7 x^2y$ **11.** $5 m^2n^3$
12. a) -144 b) 36

12.9 Written Exercises, page 402
1. a) $2x + 6$ b) $8x - 4$
c) $-12m + 18$ d) $4y - 8$
2. a) $-3x - 6$ b) $-14r - 28w$
c) $14m + 14$ d) $36d - 9e$
3. a) $6a^2 + 2a$ b) $5b^2 - 20b$
c) $-30m^2 + 10mn$
d) $-30w^2 + 20wz$ **4.** a) 6 b) 6
5. a) $2a^2 + 10a - 2$
b) $-2m^3 + 6m^2 + 8m$
c) $8p^2 + 24p - 32$
d) $-3f^2 + 6f + 24$
6. a) $4x^3 - 8x^2 + 6x$
b) $3p^3 + 6p^2 + 15p$
c) $-4a^4 - 12a^3 + 36a^2$
7. a) $p^3 - 3p^2 - 2p$
b) $-r^3 + 9r^2 - 6r$
c) $4a - a^2 - 5a^3$
d) $-4w - w^2 + 7w^3$
8. a) $10x^2 - 5x$ b) 140 c) 330
9. a) $6x + 2$ b) $3x + 6$
c) $a - 12$ d) $-27m + 21$
10. a) 51 b) 19 c) -50 d) 12
11. a) $3x + 2$ b) $5a - 8$
c) $-4p + 12$ **12.** a) -10 b) 4
c) 8 **13.** 179 **14.** a) 18 b) 18
c) b **15.** a) 25 b) 87 c) -8
16. A $6x^2 - 4x$ B $15x^2 - 9x$

12.10 Written Exercises, page 404
1. a) -4 b) 5 c) -6 d) -16
e) -12 **2.** a) $2a$ b) a c) 4
d) $-3x$ e) $-2b$ f) $5p$
3. a) $-6x^4$ b) $-2a$ c) $5a^2$
d) $3m^3$ e) $-3k$ f) $7m^7$ **4.** a) $4a$
b) $-6a$ **5.** a) $2b$ b) $7y$ c) $2x$
d) $2m$ **6.** a) $6a$ b) $-3m$
c) $-4mp$ **7.** a) $3x$ b) m c) -3
d) $-m^2$ **8.** a) $7n$ b) $2y$ c) $6a^2$
d) $5n^2$ **9.** a) $4(m + p)$

b) $4(2r - 1)$ c) $c(m + n)$
d) $p(q - s)$ **10.** a) $-3(x - 2)$
b) $4(x - 3)$ c) $m(m + n)$
d) $m(m - 4n)$ e) $2y(2 - 5y)$
f) $3k(k - 3)$ **11.** a) $x(3x^2 - y)$
b) $p^2(4p + d)$ c) $a^2(ax - 3y)$
d) $4z(5z - 3)$ e) $8d^3(3d - 1)$
f) $3x(2x - 3)$
12. a) $3(a + b + c)$
b) no common factor
c) $2x(x - 2 + y)$
d) $2p(p^2 - 2p - 3)$ **13.** a) 18
b) 18 c) b **14.** a) 84 b) 280
c) 8640 **15.** a) 1662 m
b) 28.2 m c) 36.8 m

CHAPTER 13
13.1 Written Exercises, page 409
1. a) 5 b) 4 c) 3 **2.** a) 4 b) 2
c) 0 d) 3 **3.** a) 2 b) -1 c) 3
d) 5 **4.** a) 18 b) 18 c) 12
d) 12 **5.** a) -5 b) -1 c) -1
d) -3 **6.** a) 3 b) 8 c) 5 d) 24
7. a) -1 b) -3 c) -5
8. a) -1 b) 0 c) 1 **9.** a) 2
b) 3 c) -1 d) 2 e) -2 f) 2
10. a) 3 b) -2 c) 5 d) -5
11. a, b, c **12.** a) 8 b) -5 c) 12
d) 16 e) -4 f) 24 g) 16 h) 12
13. a) 2 b) 5 c) -1 d) 3

13.2 Written Exercises, page 412
1. a) 3 b) 6 c) 14 **2.** a) 8 b) 9
c) -3 **3.** a) -3 b) 43 c) 5
4. a, b, d **5.** a, b, d **6.** a) 20
b) 12 c) -25 d) 16 e) 5 f) 8
7. a) -5 b) -7 c) 16 d) 30
e) -8 f) -3 **8.** a) 7 b) 24
c) 20 d) 5 **9.** a) 8.8 b) -2
c) -3.7 d) 3.5 **10.** a) B b) C
c) A d) D **11.** a, b, d.

13.3 Written Exercises, page 415
1. a) 4 b) 3 c) -2 d) 24
e) -8 f) 6 g) -3 h) 8 i) -5
2. a) 4 b) 3 c) 14 d) 24 e) 4
f) 2 **3.** a) 3 b) -6 c) 12 d) 18
4. b **5.** a) 14 b) 9 c) 9 d) 28
6. a) 4 b) 7 c) 30 d) 12
7. a) 3 b) 5 c) -2 d) 3
8. a) -8 b) 9 c) 3 d) 1
9. a) 3 b) $7\frac{1}{3}$ c) 1 d) -2
10. a) -2 b) -2 c) -6 d) -5
11. a, b, c

13.4 Written Exercises, page 417

1. a) 1 b) 2 c) 5 2. a) 6 b) 2
c) -2 d) -4 e) -2 f) 1 g) $\frac{4}{9}$
h) 5 3. a) 2 b) 4 c) 2 d) 6
e) -26 f) -13 4. a) $\frac{1}{2}$ b) $\frac{1}{3}$
c) $\frac{1}{2}$ 5. a) -20 b) 13 c) -19
6. a) -26 b) 1 c) -2 d) -30
e) $\frac{1}{2}$ 7. a) -40 b) -16 c) -29
d) 12 8. a) 2 b) -2 c) -3
d) 5 9. a) 4 b) 36 c) 5 d) 3
e) 3 f) 5 g) 2 h) 5 i) 9
j) 4 10. a, b, c 11. a) 7 b) $\frac{3}{2}$
c) 2 d) 36 12. a) $\frac{1}{5}$ b) $\frac{1}{2}$ c) $\frac{3}{2}$
13. 28 14. 6 km 15. 30 16. a) 5
b) -1 c) 1 d) 0 17. a) 3 b) 1
c) -1 d) $\frac{2}{3}$ 18. a) 3 b) 2
c) -1 d) 3 19. a) 21 b) -6
c) -7 20. a) -12 b) -13 c) 2
21. 15 m 22. 13 m 23. 6
24. a) $\{4, 3, 2, \dots\}$
b) $\{7, 6, 5, \dots\}$ c) $\{5, 4, 3, \dots\}$
d) $\}-16, -15, -14, \dots\}$
25. a) $\{6, 7, 8, \dots\}$
b) $\{18, 19, 20, \dots\}$
c) $\{-17, -16, -15, \dots\}$
d) $\{4, 5, 6, \dots\}$ e) $\{5, 4, 3, \dots\}$
f) $\{-14, -15, -16, \dots\}$
26. a) $\{6, 5, 4, \dots\}$ b) $\{2, 3, 4, \dots\}$
27. a, b, d 28. b) $\{2, 1, 0, \dots\}$
29. a) $\{11, 12, 13, \dots\}$
b) $\{11, 10, 9, \dots\}$
c) $\{-19, -20, -21, \dots\}$
d) $\{-8, -7, -6, \dots\}$ 30. b, d, e, f
31. a) $\{4, 3, 2, \dots\}$
32. a) $\{0, -1, -2, \dots\}$
b) $\{3, 4, 5, \dots\}$
33. $\{-11, -12, -13, \dots\}$
34. foal 35. calf 36. squab
37. cygnet 38. chick

13.5 Written Exercises, page 422

1. a) $y - 8$ b) $7 - z$ c) $\frac{W}{20}$ d) $\frac{8}{f}$
e) $5n$ f) $p - 15$ g) $12 + m$
h) $x - 16$. 2. a) $s - 5$ b) $y + 3$
c) $18p$ d) $7 - k$ e) $n + 25$
f) $18n + 3$ g) $\frac{p-9}{2}$ h) $15s - 6$
3. a) $\frac{9}{2} + \frac{6}{3}$ b) $3(n + 5)$ c) $\frac{k+4}{3}$
d) $3w - 10$ e) $2s + 5$ f) $3k - 4$
g) $5r + 26$ h) $\frac{m}{4} - 8$ 4. b) $n - 12$
c) $2n - 13$ d) $n + $ e) $\frac{n}{2}$ f) $\frac{n}{2} - 16$
g) $5n - 9$ h) $30n$ 5. $n + 8$ 6. $\frac{L}{2}$

7. $2b$ 8. $j - 2$ 9. $b + 4$ 10. $m - 5$
11. $g - 5$ 12. b) $g + 8$
c) $n + 28$ d) $d + 12$ e) $h + 15$
f) $m + 2.5$ g) $2e$ h) $c + 48$

13.6 Written Exercises, page 425

1. a) 3 b) 68 c) 38 d) 85
e) 6 2. a) $n + 1$ b) $n + 2$, $n + 3$
3. a) $5k$ b) $10k$
c) $25k$ d) $50k$ 4. a) $s - 5$ b) $2s$
c) $\frac{1}{2}s$ d) $2s + 5$ 5. a) $2s$
b) \$4s c) \$16s d) \$20s
6. a) $n - 12 = 28$ b) $\frac{10}{n} = 5$
c) $n - 24 = 16$ d) $n + 53 = 76$
e) $100 - n = 72$ 7. a) 24 b) 25
8. a) 64 b) 24 c) 36 9. 42 km
10. 20 11. 256 12. Jeff 1876 m,
Elsie 4037 m

13.7 Written Exercises, page 427

1. a) A $10n$, B $10n - 2$
b) A 8 x 12, B 8 x 11 2. a) 24.5,
25.5 b) 120, 57 3. a) $14 m + 7$
b) 9 c) 27,58,48
4. a) Sabrina 15.75 km,
Ian 4.25 km 5. a) 138 km
b) 86 km 6. b) 27.2 cm, 40.2 cm,
46.6 cm 7. b) Chris 147 cm,
Lori 155 cm, Michael 163 cm
8. 281 m, 205 m 9. a) 29 m
b) 406 m² 10. a) 75 m, 480 m
b) 36 000 m² 11. a) 30 m
b) 450 m²

13.8 Written Exercises, page 429

1. 14.5 km/h 2. 1.5 h
3. 85 km/h 4. 12 A 5. 120
6. 110 7. a) 850 km/h
b) 170 km/h 8. a) 767 km/h
b) 28 km/h 9. 17.37 g
10. 11.1 cm³ 11. 2 cm³
12. a) \$250 b) $3a$

CHAPTER 1

Skills to Practise: A Chapter Review, page 38

1.1 a) A 360, B 400, C 5400,
D 5000, E 29 690, F 29 700,
G 30 000 b) A ii, B ii, C iii, D i
1.2 a) 4661 b) 25 904
1.3 a) 11 b) 51 c) 3 d) 2
1.4 a) 27 b) 22 c) 30
1.5 a) A 3.7, B 14.94, C 9.879,
D 14.9, E 3.97 b) 0.5043,

0.543, 3.054, 3.45, 3.54
1.6 a) 215.1 b) 534.6
c) \$61.98 1.7 a) A 2.772,
B 83.49, C 6.3 b) A 17.6, B 7.5,
C 10.3 1.8 a) A 24, B 23, C 392,
D 486, E 0.0492, F 0.0342
b) A 28, B 88, C 97, D 17
1.9 a) A \$20.28, B \$67.50,
C \$97.75, D \$28.71, E \$179.64,
F \$255.44 b) A 354, B 646.6,
C 10.2, D 84.63, E 53.04,
F 53.28, G 4.416, H 26.82
c) A 11.9, B 13.7, C 12.4, D 4.4,
E 15.8, F 41.4, G 15.4, H 2.3

Problems to Practise: A Chapter Review, page 39

1.1 a) 4100 kg b) 4100 kg
c) 4000 kg d) 8200 kg
1.2 a) 2467 b) 4003 c) 20 142
1.3) A 90 B 33 1.4 a) 633
b) 19 563 1.5) 4.21, 4.43, 4.63
1.6 a) \$15.28 b) \$1.04
1.7 a) \$17.25 b) 8 1.8 a) 8
b) 20 c) A =, B > 1.9 a) \$59.00
b) \$44.50 c) \$32.00 d) \$21.50
(Answers will vary.)

CHAPTER 2

Skills to Practise: A Chapter Review, page 65

2.1) 108.7 cm 2.2) A 28.56 m²,
B 111.68 m² 2.3) 10 143.12 m³
2.4 a) 1900 cm² b) 6.3 m²
c) 973.52 cm² 2.5 a) A division,
B subtraction (or addition),
C division, D addition
b) A perimeter, B volume,
C area, D area

Problems to Practise: A Chapter Review, page 65

2.1 a) 40 cm b) 6.6 m
2.2 a) 360 cm² b) 255 cm²
2.3 a) 3 417 600 cm³ or 3.4 m³
b) \$169.93 2.4) 6859.35 cm²

CHAPTER 3

Skills to Practise: A Chapter Review, page 99

3.1 a) A 48 cm², B 20.5 m²
b) A 265 m², B 1732.9 cm²
3.2 a) A 1.28 m³, B 1239 cm³
b) A 967.0 cm³, B 332 cm³
3.3 a) A 62.8 cm, B 30.1 cm,
C 38.6 m b) A diameter =12.8 cm,
circumference = 40.2 cm,
B radius = 7.25 m,
circumference = 45.5 m,

C diameter = 46.0 cm,
circumference = 144.4 cm
3.4 a) A 452 cm², B 72.3 cm²,
C 59.4 m² b) A diameter = 9.2 cm,
area = 66.4 cm²,
B radius = 6.1 m, area = 116.8 m²,
C radius = 14.65 cm,
area = 673.9 cm²
3.5 a) A 1808 cm³, B 207.6 cm³
b) A radius 8.4 cm, volume
2237.7 cm³, surface area
965.9 cm²; B diameter 12.6 cm,
volume 772.7 cm³, surface area
245.3 cm² 3.6) A 147.2 cm²,
B 120.7 cm², C 184.9 cm²
3.7) A 113.3 cm³, B 124.7 cm³,
C 150.6 cm³ 3.8 a) A 1.26 cm²,
B 2.64 cm², C 20.47 cm²;
A 1.26 cm², B 2.63 cm²,
C 20.63 cm² b) A 126.34 cm³,
B 272.83 cm³, C 88.64 cm³;
A 124.64 cm³, B 269.63 cm³,
C 89.14 cm³

Problems to Practise: A Chapter Review, page 100

3.1) 1.6 cm², 2.97 cm²,
1.48 cm² 3.2 a) 330.9 cm³
b) 2.6 m², 31.9 m³
3.3 a) 42 013 km b) 228.9 cm,
412 031 cm or 4.12 km
3.4 a) 248.7 m² b) 8.0 m²
3.5 a) 0.40 m³, 3.14 m²
b) cylinder B 3.6 a) 2462 cm²
b) 239.5 cm² 3.7 a) 503.2 cm³
b) 7235 cm³ 3.8 a) 30 074.5 cm³,
5389.9 cm² b) \$58.40, \$69.52

CHAPTER 4

Skills to Practise: A Chapter Review, page 145

4.1 a) 1, 2, 3, 4, 6, 9, 12, 18, 36
b) A 2, B 9, C 2 c) A 48, B 108
4.2 a) A $\frac{4}{10}$, B $\frac{8}{15}$ b) A $\frac{1}{1000}$, B $\frac{1}{100}$,
C $\frac{1}{10}$ 4.3 a) A 8, B 20 b) A $\frac{1}{2} < \frac{3}{4}$,
B $\frac{4}{5} > \frac{3}{4}$ c) A $\frac{2}{5}$, B $\frac{5}{8}$, C $\frac{2}{3}$ 4.4 a) A
b) $\frac{3}{5}, \frac{6}{9}, \frac{3}{4}$ c) A 10, B 20
4.5 a) A 0.125, B $0.\overline{428\ 571}$,
C 1.5, D $0.1\overline{6}$, E $0.41\overline{6}$, F $0.\overline{27}$
b) $\frac{4}{15} = 0.2\overline{6}$, $\frac{5}{12} = 0.41\overline{6}$, $\frac{5}{12} > \frac{4}{15}$
4.6 a) A $1\frac{1}{6}$, B $1\frac{5}{12}$, C $5\frac{3}{8}$ b) $7\frac{3}{8}$
c) A 4.7 a) A 1, B $\frac{1}{2}$, C $\frac{2}{3}$, D $\frac{1}{3}$, E $\frac{1}{2}$,
F $\frac{1}{3}$ b) A $\frac{1}{10}$, B $\frac{3}{5}$ 4.8 a) A $\frac{1}{3}$, B $\frac{1}{2}$,
C $\frac{4}{5}$ b) A $\frac{1}{5}$, B 2, C $\frac{1}{4}$, D $\frac{4}{3}$, E 28,

F $4\frac{1}{8}$ **4.9** a) A $\frac{3}{2}$, B $\frac{4}{5}$, C $\frac{3}{8}$ b) A $\frac{3}{4}$, B 18, C 2 **4.10)** A $1\frac{1}{3}$, B $2\frac{1}{2}$, C $\frac{3}{7}$

Problems to Practise: A Chapter Review, page 146

4.1 a) B, D b) B **4.2** a) $\frac{2}{3}$ b) A $\frac{1}{7}$, B $\frac{3}{16}$, C $\frac{1}{9}$, D $\frac{1}{5}$, E $\frac{1}{5}$ **4.3** a) $\frac{5}{9}$ b) $\frac{7}{12}$
4.4 a) the second game b) the contest manager
4.5 a) Swenson b) the next month **4.6)** 13 h **4.7** a) A $\frac{1}{4}$, B $\frac{5}{8}$, C $\frac{13}{24}$, D $3\frac{1}{6}$, E $8\frac{1}{3}$, F $\frac{3}{4}$ b) $\frac{1}{3}$
4.8) A $4\frac{2}{3}$ h, B 20 h, C $15\frac{2}{3}$ h
4.9) A 220, B 132, C $94\frac{2}{7}$
4.10 a) $\left(\frac{3}{4} + \frac{7}{8}\right) - \frac{1}{2} = \frac{9}{8}$
b) $\left(1\frac{1}{2} \times \frac{1}{4}\right) + \frac{3}{4} = \frac{9}{8}$
c) $\left(2\frac{1}{3} + 3\frac{1}{2}\right) - 1\frac{1}{4} = 4\frac{7}{12}$
d) $\left(\frac{3}{4} \div \frac{3}{2}\right) + \left(1\frac{1}{3} \div \frac{4}{3}\right) = 1\frac{3}{4}$

CHAPTER 5

Skills to Practise: A Chapter Review, page 182

5.1 a) $+4, 0$ b) $0, -4$ c) A $-2, -1, 0, +1, +2$; B $-4, -3, -2, -1, 0, +1$; C $0, 1, 2, 3$
5.2 a) A 4, B -7, C 17, D -7 b) A 1, B 7 **5.3** a) A 5, B 17, C 4, D -12 b) A 11, B -8
5.4 a) A 7, B 13, C -5, D 6, E -5, F -1 b) A -17, B -7
5.5 a) -11 b) 10 **5.6** a) A -12, B -18, C 12 b) A 36, B -24
5.7 a) A -44, B -30 b) A -8, B -5 **5.8** a) A -2, B 2, C -4, D 3 b) A -5, B -4, C 9
5.9 a) 1 b) -3 **5.10** a) 3 b) 2 c) 38 d) 0 **5.11** a) $-12, 14$ b) $-10, 8$ c) 13 d) $22, -29$

Problems to Practise: A Chapter Review, page 183

5.1 a) Vancouver
b) Whitehorse c) $18°C, 6°C, 6°C, 4°C, 3°C, 2°C, 2°C, -1°C, -2°C, -2°C, -9°C, -21°C$
5.2 a) climbing 680 m b) (i) B (ii) B (iii) A **5.3** a) Dawson
b) Vancouver c) Regina d) Winnipeg and Kingston
5.4) D **5.5)** $16°C$
5.6 b) $(-8)(+2)$ c) $(-6)(-6)$ d) $(+10)(+10)$ e) $(-25)(+3)$ Answers will vary. **5.7** a) -9 b) 9 c) 12 **5.8)** A 16, B -7,

C 147, D 15 **5.9)** 826.6 kJ
5.10 a) 48 b) 320 c) -24 d) 128 e) 16 f) 137 **5.11)** A 1, B 121, C 12 321, D 1 234 321, E 123 454 321

CHAPTER 6

Skills to Practise: A Chapter Review, page 219

6.1 a) A $3:4$, B $4:5$, C $5:8$ b) A $6:11$, B $9:10$, C $20:13$, D $1:1000$ **6.2** a) $5:7$ b) $8:7$ c) $5:11$ d) $5:8:11$ e) $8:7:11$
6.3 a) B b) A $3:4$, B $8:5$, C $1:2$ c) A 9, B 12, C 15 **6.4** a) A 20, B 4 b) A 30, B 8 c) 6 **6.5** a) 42 b) 156 **6.6** a) A 25 cm, B 1 cm, C 0.5 cm, D 50 cm b) A 0.5 m, B 0.1 m, C 0.16 m
6.7 a) A 85 km, B 106.25 km, C 6.8 km b) A 4.3 cm, B 2.9 cm, C 16.6 cm **6.8** a) 30 m b) 10.6 km c) 3.35 m

Problems to Practise: A Chapter Review, page 220

6.1 a) $137:365$ b) $108:365$ c) $365:51$ d) $51:137$
6.2 a) $1:2$ b) $4:1$
6.3 a) A $1:10$, B $4:1$, C $1:4$ b) A $1:2$, B $1:2$, C $5:8$, D $1:2:4$ **6.4** a) 120 b) 6 c) 4
6.5 a) 19.62 kg b) A 15, B 225
6.6) A 6 m, B 9.2 m
6.7 a) 131.2 cm b) 376.88 km
6.8 a) 949 m b) Angel Falls, by 1 m

CHAPTER 7

Skills to Practise: A Chapter Review, page 240

7.1 a) $4:3$ b) $9:5$ **7.2** a) 1 ticket for $3.00 b) 1 soft drink for 29¢
7.3) 50 km/h, 13.7 km/h
7.4 a) 385 b) 3300
7.5 a) 63 km b) 84 km
7.6) Answers will vary.
7.7 Answers will vary.

Problems to Practise: A Chapter Review, page 240

7.1 a) $30.00 b) $1560.00
7.2) 284.4 km **7.3)** 2.3 min
7.4 a) 23.1 h b) 3.3 h
7.5 a) 1274 carats b) $4709.58
7.6) Answers will vary.
7.7 a) 291.5 b) Each jump is 3.43 m.

A Cumulative Review, page 242

1) $\frac{7}{12}$ **2** a) 13.5 km/h b) 3.4 km

3 a) 6.7 ¢/cm² b) $\frac{1}{4}$ **4)** $14.46
5 a) 7.29 cm² b) 8.32 cm²
6 a) 20.3 L b) 16.9 L **7)** 12.4
8 a) $6:7$ b) $1:2$ c) $17:25$ d) $5:7$ e) $17:68:35$ f) $30:34:25$ **9** a) 1600 b) Answers will vary.
10 a) 1 cm represents 1.5 m b) 1 cm represents 5 m c) 1 cm represents 0.5 m d) 1 cm represents 0.5 m e) 1 cm represents 0.2 m Answers will vary.

CHAPTER 8

Skills to Practise: A Chapter Review, page 271

8.1 a) 12 b) 80 c) 52
8.2 a) $30\% < 40\%$ b) $25\% < 40\%$ **8.3** a) 140 b) 20% **8.4** a) 25% b) 3.6 c) 1000 **8.5)** A **8.6** a) $17.63 b) $5.00 **8.7** a) $3.96, $53.46 b) $8.65, $132.15
8.8 a) $522.00 b) $332.05

Problems to Practise: A Chapter Review, page 271

8.1 a) 30.8% b) 69.2%
8.2) 65.8% of the forest fires, 71.2% of the house fires
8.3 a) 7 b) 13 **8.4)** $2.75
8.5) 33.75 L **8.6** a) $2.95 b) $11.80 **8.7)** $16.70
8.8 a) $81.97 b) $13.95

CHAPTER 9

Skills to Practise: A Chapter Review, page 310

9.1 a) $30°$, acute b) $140°$, obtuse **9.2** a) isosceles b) right **9.6)** $15°$
9.8 a) $\angle A = \angle B$ b) $2 \times \angle A = \angle B$ c) $\angle A + \angle B = 180°$ **9.9** a) 5 b) 7.071 c) 8.660 **9.10** a) 8 b) 2.265

Problems to Practise: A Chapter Review, page 310

9.1 a) $60°$ b) $90°$ **9.6)** $45°$
9.8) 6.481 cm by 6.481 cm

CHAPTER 10

Skills to Practise: A Chapter Review, page 348

10.1 a) A $(4, 2)$, B $(1, -2)$, C $(-2, -3)$, D $(-4, 3)$ **10.3** a) 2 b) 3 c) $\frac{2}{3}$ **10.4** a) 4.472 units b) 10 units

Problems to Practise: A Chapter Review, page 348

10.1 a) GO b) TO c) LUNCH
10.2 a) Satisfies. b) Does not satisfy. c) Satisfies. **10.3** a) $\frac{1}{2}$ b) $-\frac{1}{8}$ c) $\frac{1}{4}$ **10.4)** 16.1 units

CHAPTER 11

Skills to Practise: A Chapter Review, page 378

1 a) 13 b) 7 c) 16 **2** a) Datsun b) Chrysler (full size) **3** a) 29 b) 23 **4)** 52 **5** a) hour 6 b) 5 cm **6** a) hours 1, 2, 9, 10, 11, 12 b) hours 4, 5, 6, 7 **7** a) hours 1, 2, 3, 4, 6 b) hours 5, 7, 8, 9, 10, 11, 12

Problems to Practise: A Chapter Review, page 378

1 a) 18 m b) 21 m c) 30 m
2 a) 35 km/h b) 60 km/h c) 80 km/h **3** a) 11 m b) 40 m c) 100 m **4** b) Answers will vary.

CHAPTER 12

Skills to Practise: A Chapter Review, page 405

12.1 a) $3m$ b) $7x - y$
12.2 a) $k + p$ b) $m^2 + 4m$
12.3 a) $+$ b) $-$ c) $-$ d) $+$ e) $+$ f) $-$ g) $+$ h) $-$
12.4 a) A $3m + 2n$, B $4m + 2n$, C $3m + 2n$ b) B **12.5** a) $6xy$ b) $2mp$ c) $-6k$ **12.6** a) $6x^2$ b) $-4y^2$ c) $6k^3$ **12.7** a) $3b$ b) $2q$ c) $-3a^2$ **12.8)** A $3p$, B $2m^3$, C $-2t$ **12.9** a) $3y - 6$ b) $-6 + 2k$ c) $2mp + 2mq$ d) $-6m^2 + 3m$ **12.10** a) $3m$ b) $2x$

Problems to Practise: A Chapter Review, page 405

12.1 a) $10s + 2$ b) $12s^2$ (b) has the greater perimeter for $s = 3$ **12.2)** B **12.3)** $37xy$
12.4 a) $-x^2 + 3x - 2$ c) the constant term, -2
12.5 a) $6m$ cents b) $2km$ cents **12.6** a) 12 b) -6 c) 48 d) -6 e) (c) **12.7)** $8m$ units **12.8)** $4p^2q^4$
12.10 a) $3n(m + n)$ b) 95.22

Index